Len Evans'
Complete Book of
Australian
WINE

Len Evans'
Complete Book of
Australian
WINE

Facts On File
New York • Oxford • Sydney

Acknowledgements

The Publisher would like to thank Len Evans, John Hanley, Paul Lloyd and Ian Mackay for their advice on the maps used in this book. The maps were drawn by Christie & Eckermann Art and Design Studio.

Thanks are due to those wine companies which supplied labels and photographs for this edition.

The following are gratefully acknowledged as sources of the photographs in this book.

Botobolar Vineyard 100 D. & J. Bowen 339 Brokenwood Vineyard 56 Chateau Yaldara 284 Foster's Wines 432 Goonawarra Wines 171 Grant Burge Wines 268 Hainault Wines 415 C. A. Henschke & Co. 250 Houghton Winery 368–9 Jane Brook Estate 371 Jolimont Wines 124–5 Lake's Folly Vineyards 60 Moorilla Estate 418–9, 426, 428, 456 Mountadam Wine Co. 252 Oakvale Winery 70 Redbank Winery 164 Rothbury Estates 73 Ryecroft Vineyards 326 W. Salter & Son 284 The Silos Winery 122, 123 B. Stonier 208 Tarrawarra Vineyard Pty Ltd 227, 228 Weldon Trannies 6, 8, 11, 12, 14, 16, 27, 28, 30, 31, 38–9, 45, 50, 53, 58, 59, 63, 82, 86, 87, 91, 92, 102, 103, 129, 130, 135, 138, 139, 146, 150, 156, 158, 182, 183, 187, 188, 237, 238, 240, 256, 261, 262–3, 264, 266, 269, 273, 274, 285, 287, 288, 289, 302, 305, 312, 316, 318, 321, 325, 334, 335, 340, 342, 345, 347, 348, 350, 394, 424, 431, 436, 438, 448, 454, 462, 463, 468, 469, 470, 472, 474, 475, 476, 477, 481 J. L. & P. A. Wilson 296, 308 Wolf Blass Wines International 292

A Kevin Weldon Production
Published by Weldon Publishing
a division of Kevin Weldon and Associates Pty Limited
372 Eastern Valley Way, Willoughby, NSW 2068, Australia

First published in 1973 as *Australia and New Zealand Complete Book of Wine*
Reprinted 1974, 1975
Revised edition 1976, *Australian Complete Book of Wine*
Revised edition 1984, *Len Evans' Complete Book of Australian Wine*
Revised edition 1990

Designed by Christie & Eckermann Art and Design Studio

Jacket photograph by Andrew Warn

Typeset in Goudy Old Style by Savage Type Pty Ltd, Queensland
Printed in Australia by Griffin Press Limited, Adelaide

ISBN 0-8160-2631-9

10 9 8 7 6 5 4 3 2 1

CONTENTS

INTRODUCTION

Len Evans

There have already been three editions and many impressions of the various forms of this book, since it first appeared in 1973. During this time, more than 140 000 copies have been sold, the largest sale of any major reference wine book in the country.

The last edition of *Len Evans' Complete Book of Australian Wine* was published in 1984, and a lot has happened since then. Indeed, one of the features of all Australian wine books is a certain degree of desperation: as soon as any edition or impression 'goes to bed', another twenty vineyards, fifteen wineries and a couple of thousand wines are bound to appear. It is absolutely impossible to be completely up to date by the time any edition hits the bookshelves.

That is why we have taken a slightly different tack this time.

First, we have elected not to provide tasting notes. It used to be all very well to print the total list of Grange Hermitages and to comment knowledgeably about the quality of the '53, but that does not mean much today. And if one raves about a particular Coonawarra red of a certain year, fate often decrees that the next vintage is only half as good. André Simon made one of the wisest points ever about wine: 'There are no good wines — only good bottles.'

Recently Lucie Rie, England's greatest potter, who is regarded as a national living treasure, was asked, 'What are your favourite potters?'

'I have no favourite potters,' she replied, 'only favourite pots.'

As I get older, I become more and more aware of such profundities.

As a vigneron, I will state unequivocally that it is impossible to set out to make great wine and be sure of achieving it. You may put every effort, every skill, every financial resource into the task, and still fail. Even when every intention is there, if you do finally achieve greatness, or even a measure of it, the result will contain an element of luck. Great wine is a fluke, and no wine house in the world, however expensive their product and untiring their efforts, produces great wine year after year. And if they did, the effect would be boring, and a great deal of the romance of wine would be lost.

Simply, you need to seek out good wine for yourself. Read the words, take heed of the recommendations. In the end, you have to decide for yourself.

This new edition will help you. It is virtually a new book. As with the previous books, I have been as much a compiler as an author. On certain matters there are greater experts than I, and today there are so many different small wineries and so many different small pockets within the industry that I felt it was better if local experts were involved. Hence I approached many able wine writers in different states to contribute their wisdom to this volume.

The historical section, so ably researched by Jaki Ilbery in the past, has been extended by Robert Mayne. Graham Gregory and Anders Ousback have developed their respective chapters extensively, and Ian Mackay, Paul Lloyd and John Hanley have done splendid work regarding the wineries and vineyards of Victoria and Tasmania, South Australia, and Western Australia respectively.

Even as I write and edit galley proofs, I hear word of another takeover in the wine world, and thence a change of ownership and management. As this book goes to press, some major wineries are stated to be up for sale, and it is said that more than thirty 'boutiques' are seeking financial assistance. The industry, after a strong showing in the latter half of the 1980s, is said to be in trouble.

Yet all is not lost.

Our winemaking standards have never been higher. More and more attention is being paid to viticulture, and the results are showing. Better vineyards mean better fruit, which equals better wine. The best regions are beginning to work out what they do best, a process which in France, for example, took several hundred years. Planting is no longer being carried out across a broad spectrum of grape varieties — 'Let's establish a vineyard, let's plant everything.' We now know, for example, that Riesling, true Riesling, does not work very well in the Hunter, and that the reds from Coonawarra are better than the whites. It will not be many wine years (which are longer than calendar years) before regions will concentrate on just a few varieties each. This book helps identify these directions.

Above all, Australian wine is still consistently great value. In no other wine country are the best wines so reasonably priced in relation to their quality. In no other country are more variety and excitement available for reasonable prices.

I had the recent privilege of addressing the Master of Wine in England. I made the statement that wine is sold worldwide in four categories — *Fancy, Realistic, Ordinary,* and *Very Ordinary.*

Fancy wines include the greatest wines of the world — Chateau Margaux, Chateau Yquem, Chambertin, le Montrachet, Krug. Most top Bordeaux and Burgundy wines are in this category, and I believe their prices have gone too high. Even the prices of top Rhone wines, and the best of Californian and Italian wines, have reached heights never thought possible.

Well, jolly good luck to them all, for I wish my wines sold as expensively!

The *Very Ordinary* category needs little commentary: there is an awful lot of wine in the world, and a lot of awful wine. I have never been interested in wine just as a beverage.

Australia is important in the other two categories. We do produce *Ordinary* wines — pleasant, low-priced, easy to drink — and we shall continue to do so. However, it is in the realm of the *Realistic* section that we will do best, both nationally and internationally. Dry reds and whites, from cabernet sauvignon, merlot, shiraz and pinot noir, and from riesling, semillon and chardonnay, are among the top five per cent of quality in the world today, and they have the distinction of being far better value than most of those in the *Fancy* section.

There is no such thing as the absolute palate; no such thing as the absolute wine knowlege. Wine is an egocentric indulgence. What pleases one may repel another. In all honesty, it's a darn good thing we don't all like the same wine.

Still we recognise that over the years, some areas, some winemakers and some varieties do emerge as being among the best. This book will help you find the 'good bottles'.

A History of Wine in Australia

Jaki Ilbery

The First Vines

The grapevine is not indigenous to Australia and the history of viticulture in this country begins with the birth of the penal colony in New South Wales. Captain Arthur Phillip, RN, later the first governor, was in command of the expedition and was, in effect, Australia's first vigneron.

The First Fleet, which Phillip led to New South Wales, comprised eleven small ships totalling 3890 tons, and carried an extremely disparate group numbering just over 1000 men, women and children—convicts and free men. The hazardous voyage took eight months with stops at Rio de Janeiro and the Cape of Good Hope, where supplies for the new settlement were taken aboard. Included in these supplies were vine cuttings and grape seeds which were to be planted on arrival.

Phillip was a remarkable leader of great ability, as is shown by the extremely low death rate on the long voyage—at most thirty-two people. The mortality rate in England at the time may have been even higher than this, so Phillip's attention to the diet and living conditions of his party showed a humanitarian and enlightened outlook.

The motley group of settlers disembarked on 26 January 1788 to begin the task of establishing a new gaol for convicts from the British Isles. Australia's drinking heritage began with what Surgeon Bowes recorded as a scene of debauchery and riot, with almost all the sailors drunk. It was the beginning of the abuse of spirits, especially rum, in the colony of Australia.

Phillip faced a huge number of problems at this time—the main task being simply to keep the convicts, soldiers and officials alive. Supplies of food from home were irregular and ignorance of local conditions meant that early agricultural enterprises were often unsuccessful. An adequate supply of food was not easy to obtain. Not least of the problems must have been the convicts themselves. Although historians have never been able to agree about the character of the people who committed offences punishable by transportation, there were undoubtedly some real criminals among them.

Life for all the settlers was hard. And, although Phillip imposed reasonable restrictions on the issue of spirits, from the origins of the colony there is an unfortunate record of widespread drunkenness. Captain Phillip encouraged the brewing of beer, then regarded as an essential item of diet, but he deplored the excessive use of hard spirits. He was a naval officer and schooled in the wine-drinking traditions of the wardroom.

With the First Fleet came cuttings and seeds which were planted on the eastern side of Sydney Cove in Phillip's garden. The diary of the Judge Advocate David Collins notes:

> A portable canvas house was brought over for the Governor and erected on the east side of the Cove . . . Some ground having been prepared near His Excellency's house . . . the plants from Rio de Janeiro and the Cape of Good Hope were safely brought on shore in a few days and we soon had the satisfaction of seeing the grape, the fig, the orange, the pear and the apple taking root and establishing themselves in our New World.

Early records mention that grape seeds of the 'claret grape' (probably cabernet sauvignon) were planted as well. The vines were planted not far from where the Sydney Opera House now stands, and close to the site of the present

Botanic Gardens. Those early settlers had no knowledge of soil or climatic conditions and probably chose the site because of its proximity and ease of clearance of natural vegetation.

But the humid subtropical conditions of Sydney Harbour are not conducive to the cultivation of the vine and, although those early vines grew, they were attacked by the fungoid disease anthracnose or 'black spot' and no wine was made. (In a fitting historic footnote 197 years later, six cabernet sauvignon grapevines, one from each of the Australian states, were planted in the magnificent Royal Botanic Gardens, where they can now be seen growing.)

Governor Phillip did not give up, and on 18 March 1791 Mrs John Macarthur wrote that the grapes were thriving remarkably well and that some bunches the Governor sent were 'as fine as any I ever tasted'. In a dispatch dated 16 October 1791, Phillip reported that he had 3 acres (1.2 hectares) of vineyard at Government House, Parramatta, and that Phillip Schaffer, a German from the Rhinehessen, had planted 1 acre (0.4 hectare) of grapes on the north bank of the Parramatta River. This makes Schaffer Australia's first private vigneron.

Phillip resigned his position as governor in 1792 because of ill health and returned to England. Although local wine was of no significance at that stage, Phillip actually created the Australian wine industry. From that time, things began to move and some vineyards were planted by private settlers, generally as part of mixed-farming operations. The development of new vineyards continued and 'appreciable quantities' of wine were made by the opening years of the nineteenth century.

The British Government appeared to be keen to establish a vine-growing industry, for in 1800 two French prisoners, de Riveau and Landrien, were given their freedom in return for spending three years in New South Wales establishing vineyards and demonstrating winemaking. They were not terribly successful—one was sent back to England and the other reprieved because he 'made good cider from peaches'.

There must have been quite some interest in viticulture in the colony, as the very first issue of an Australian newspaper, the *Sydney Gazette*, dated 5 March 1803, published an article of directions on how to plant a vineyard.

An observer in 1811, after complaining of the high price of spirits, noted that 'wines are not so eagerly sought after and are therefore more reasonable than might be expected'. The populace may not have been over-enthusiastic about wine, preferring spirits or beer, but there are numerous references in early dispatches to the Home Government's expectation of the establishment of a vine-growing industry.

Why should England, not a wine-producing country of any significance, be interested right from the start in making wine in Australia? Furthermore, the British people as a whole were not wine drinkers, and certainly not table wine drinkers. The wealthier classes, who also comprised the governing classes, were, however, used to drinking table wines from France, Germany, Portugal and Spain, and their influence prevailed.

First of all, the imperialistic British wanted their own source of wine, one which could be relied on to supply their needs at all times, without relying on the unpredictable European nations, with whom war was an ever-present possibility. The idea of Australia as a vineyard for the United Kingdom continued for many decades, and is aptly summed up in the title of Hubert de Castella's book *John Bull's Vineyard*, published in 1886. In addition, the British Government naturally wanted its colonies to be successful in establishing primary industries which would not only be able to supply produce but also to create revenue.

At the local level the authorities encouraged the planting of vineyards and the making of wine not merely for the economic value but in an attempt to convert the populace to moderation in drinking. Among the enlightened men who realised the value of drinking wine—as against the debauched and excessive consumption of rum—were Dr John Lang and, at a later date, Dr Lindeman, James Busby and the irrepressible Reverend Dr John Bleasdale, otherwise known as 'Dr Blazes'.

Vines and wines got a slow start, largely because there was little time or social inclination to follow the wine consumption habits of the British ruling classes in the day-by-day struggle for survival in the colony. Some saw the opportunities. The French botanist François Peron, a member of the French explorer Nicholas

Old ruins in Pewsey Vale, South Australia, in a vineyard planted in 1847.

Baudin's 1800–4 expedition, recorded that Australia would eventually provide England with the wines to enable her to stop buying from Continental Europe.

In 1830 Busby wrote that had New South Wales been settled by a colony from France,

> . . . or any other country whose climate is favourable to the growth of the vine, we should at this day have seen few corn fields without their neighbouring vineyards; and the poorest settler, aye, and his meanest servant, would daily have regaled their palates and invigorated their bodies with this first of the blessings which nature bestows upon the more genial climates of the earth.

And the same year he added that light table wine was 'designed to increase the comforts and promote the morality of the lower classes of the colony, and more especially of the native born youth . . . where . . . the unlimited use of ardent spirits and the excitement they produce is more likely to terminate in mischievous results'. This is a theme that persists through much of our nineteenth-century winemaking.

Even though large tracts of Australia had 'a climate with Mediterranean characteristics, the settlers themselves were farming in a new and untried environment and thus aimed to experiment with as many types of agriculture as they could. So, in addition to their sheep and cattle, wheat and other crops, vegetables and orchards, many planted small areas of grapevines for winemaking. The influence of natural conditions combined with the skills of the producers determined the degree of success of these ventures. Further, the modern winemaker and author Dr Max Lake believes that the 'move to winemaking in the last century was a genuine, new and national thing, spurred by revolt against the excesses of the unfortunate rum currency in the new colony'.

The Pioneers
Gregory Blaxland, John and William Macarthur, James Busby

We will not debate here the claims of Blaxland, the Macarthurs or Busby to being the 'father of Australian viticulture'. Each contributed a great deal and it is not necessary to rank them in order of importance.

Gregory Blaxland, an explorer who crossed the barrier of the Blue Mountains of New South Wales in 1813, is also remembered for his pioneering viticultural activities. On his arrival in the colony he purchased from D'Arcy Wentworth 182 hectares in the Parramatta Valley, near the present suburb of Eastwood. He named the property Brush Farm and planted some vines that he had brought from the Cape of Good Hope between 1816 and 1818. His vineyard was largely

An early Australian vineyard.

based on the 'claret' grape which proved most resistant to the troublesome vine blight, anthracnose.

In 1822 Blaxland made history by shipping a pipe (about 340 litres) of red wine fortified with brandy to London, where the Society for the Encouragement of Arts, Manufacture and Commerce awarded him a silver medal in 1823. Five years later Blaxland was awarded the gold 'Ceres Medal' for a further two samples, which were considered to be decidedly better than his first effort. It was at this time that the basic assumption was made that Australian wines could not stand the journey to Britain without fortification.

No more was heard about Blaxland and winemaking, but in those few years he had achieved a great deal. Above all, he had shown that sound, drinkable Australian wine could be made, thus promoting the idea of a colonial wine industry to the English and to local settlers, who were no doubt encouraged by Blaxland's success. He also experimented with varieties of grapes in an attempt to establish 'blight-resistant' vines.

Captain John Macarthur (1767–1834) arrived in Sydney with the New South Wales Corps in 1790 and began a turbulent and colourful career in the colony. Posterity honours him for first importing merino sheep to Australia, but we are more interested in the fact that he was one of the first settlers to plant a vineyard for winemaking on a commercial basis.

From 1809 to 1817, as the result of a violent and bitter quarrel with the Governor (Captain Bligh), Macarthur became an exile in Britain. He took with him his sons James (born 1798) and William (born 1800), and in 1815 and 1816 the three made an eighteen-month tour through France and Switzerland. Macarthur said they were travelling 'for the express purpose of collecting vines, and of obtaining information respecting their culture'.

On their return to the colony the Macarthurs planted their first vineyard at Camden, to Sydney's south-west, in 1820. The ruins of this winery, built on the side of a hill so gravity could move the grapes, juice and then wine through, can still be seen near Camden Park Estate, which is occupied by a descendant of the Macarthurs.

After some trial and error in the 1820s the Macarthurs removed their vineyard to a 9 hectare property on alluvial soil sloping down to the Nepean River near Penrith, west of Sydney. This was Australia's first commercial winemaking enterprise and by 1827 their vintage totalled 90 000 litres. In the 1830s they started another vineyard on a different site.

James Macarthur died in 1867 after an active public life. His brother, Sir William Macarthur, led a distinguished public career as a Member of Parliament and Commissioner for the Paris Exhibition. He exported some of his wine and secured awards for Camden Park wine and brandy in 1841. In 1844, under the pen-name 'Maro', he published *Letters on the Culture of the Vine, Fermentation and the Management of Wine in the Cellar*. An arrogant belief in his superiority shines throughout the book, which mentions that one must select as grape pickers only those 'who are likely to be attentive and obedient'. He also writes of men treading out the grapes by rapid motion of the feet for fourteen to sixteen hours a day! The book nevertheless was, and is, valuable for its detailed descriptions of cellar equipment and vintage procedures—practical information of great importance to the infant wine industry. In the 1850s William Macarthur was instrumental in founding the New South Wales Vineyard Association. He died in 1882.

James Busby has long held the reputation of being the father of Australian viticulture and founder of winemaking in the Hunter Valley. More recent research has, however, cast new light on this pioneer, and it now appears that his role may have been somewhat overstated. Nonetheless, he did have considerable influence as a teacher and theoretician; perhaps he is best described as 'prophet'. Eric Ramsden in *James Busby: The Prophet of Australian Viticulture* (1941), was the first to characterise him thus.

Busby was born in Edinburgh on 7 February 1801 of an old Northumberland family. In 1810 his father took over the management of the Irish estates of the Marquis of Downshire, and it is there that young James first became interested in agriculture. He came to Australia on the *Triton*, arriving in 1824 with his father, John Busby, who was an engineer and mineral surveyor, and other members of the family. Before leaving Scotland he had become convinced that there was a great future for viticulture in the colony—quite an extraordinary conclusion in itself—and to this

Receiving the grapes at the wine-house and unstalking the bunches preparatory to pressing.

end spent some months studying viticulture and winemaking in France.

On 8 May 1824, Grant 125 of 2000 acres (800 hectares) on the Hunter River between Branxton and Singleton was made to John Busby. It was named Kirkton. Later, under the management of James Busby's brother-in-law, William Kelman, it became well known for its wines.

Shortly after his arrival in 1824, James Busby was engaged to teach viticulture to the boys of the Male Orphan School at Bull's Hill, near Liverpool (south-west of Sydney). His job involved taking charge of the 5000 hectare estate and organising an agricultural institute there. He was to teach cultivation of the vine and other suitable but previously neglected products. In March of the following year Busby planted a vineyard at the orphan school which, under the management of Richard Sadlier, yielded in 1829 a 'sound wine of Burgundy character'.

In passing, it is interesting to note how the colonials described their new wines with the familiar European nomenclature—the only names with which they could equate them. Names such as 'Burgundy', 'Hock', 'Champagne' and 'Hermitage'—all related to French and German regions —abound in the early literature about Australian wines. 'Claret' (the wines of Bordeaux in France) and 'Port' (from Oporto in Portugal) are others. This very understandable adoption of names dear to European hearts would lead to acrimony

and litigation almost two centuries later.

In 1825, after he had been in New South Wales only a short time, Busby's first book was published, a work of 270 pages titled *A Treatise on the Culture of the Vine*. The book consisted largely of translations of the writings of Chaptal and other French authorities. Although quite an achievement in view of his youth, the book had a less than favourable reception if some articles in *The New South Wales Magazine* are any indication. The anonymous reviewer was hostile to the treatise, accusing Busby of lack of practical knowledge and of giving an abstruse scientific discourse instead of simple directions.

Busby had his troubles in other areas. When the Corporation of the Clergy and School Lands took control of the school in 1826 they decided, in view of the running costs, to close the school down, and Busby was involved in a wrangle about a financial settlement. The Corporation kept the vineyard going but there is no evidence that Busby himself actually made any wine there. His career for the next few years did not go smoothly. He held various government offices, such as Collector of Internal Revenue, but considered that he was badly treated.

Busby did find time between his other activities to publish in 1830 his most successful book, *A Manual of Plain Directions for Planting and Cultivating Vineyards and for Making Wine in New South Wales*. The 96-page book was aimed at the small farmers and was well received by the press critics. In the book Busby extolled the virtues of the daily drinking of light wine, as against the excessive consumption of spirits with its unfortunate consequences. He also gave detailed instructions on grapegrowing and winemaking, pointing out the need for cleanliness. He believed that there should be a vine arbour in every home and wrote in an oft-quoted passage:

> The man who could sit under the shade of his own vine, with his wife and children about him, and the ripe clusters hanging within their reach, in such a climate as this, and not feel the highest enjoyment, is incapable of happiness and does not know what the word means.

The year after the publication of the manual, 1831, Busby left for Britain to attempt to redress his grievances. However, more than self-interest was involved, for he took the opportunity to tour the wine areas of Spain and France to examine the influence of climate, soil and viticultural practices on the wine of each area, and to collect samples of different varieties of vines. Busby spent four months travelling, starting from Cadiz and ending in Paris. The bulk of his collection (of which there are various estimates of the number), 433 vines, came from the Botanic Gardens at Montpellier, but 110 came from the Luxembourg Gardens, 44 from Sion House near Kew Gardens in England, and 91 from other parts of France and Spain. Busby generously donated the collection to the government 'for the purpose . . . of forming an Experimental Garden at Sydney, to prove their different qualities, and propagate, for general distribution, those which may appear most suitable to the climate'.

Early in 1832 the cuttings were packed in cases of moss and shipped to Australia. The collection was planted in the Botanic Gardens, where Busby's enthusiasm was not shared; and after initial successes the vines were neglected and subsequently lost. Fortunately, distributions from the collection were made to Kirkton, Camden and the Adelaide Botanic Gardens, from which thousands of clippings were taken and spread throughout South Australia. The Adelaide collection was also neglected and ultimately destroyed, but some cuttings were taken at the time to Spring Vale and to Watervale, and thus Busby's efforts were not wasted, even though

their potential was not fully realised.

In 1833 Busby published a work of great importance to ampelography (the science of grapevine identification) entitled *Journals of a Tour through Some of the Vineyards of Spain and France*. The book lists a catalogue of all the vines he collected on his tour. That year he left for New Zealand, where he took up the post of British Resident. He felt in later years that his efforts on behalf of the wine industry were not appreciated.

James Busby died in England in 1871, but posterity at least has recognised his achievements. As W.P. Driscoll writes: 'His enthusiasm and ardent propaganda, his publications and collections of vines were of great importance to the infant industry.' Indeed, it seems likely that he was responsible for introducing into Australia the variety which he listed as 'Pineau Blanc or Chaudeny', describing it as the only variety of white grape cultivated in the best vineyards of Burgundy. There, of course, it makes the great white burgundies of France, and it was from Burgundy that Murray Tyrrell and others obtained the inspiration for the plantings of chardonnay in the early 1970s. Tyrrell's cuttings came from Mudgee, which in turn were almost certainly descended from Busby's 'Chaudeny' vine cuttings.

The Hunter Valley

By the time of Busby's departure to New Zealand there were more than 8 hectares under vine in the Hunter Valley, 160 km north of Sydney. This district was to become one of the fine wine regions of Australia.

In the very early days of the colony, around 1797, Lieutenant Shortland discovered and named Hunter's River while searching for escaped convicts. Four years later Lieutenant-Colonel Paterson led an expedition which mapped the meandering Hunter, William and Paterson Rivers, and a convict settlement was established at Maitland in the Hunter Valley.

The vast coal deposits Shortland had discovered were not considered of much importance but timber was, and lumbering operations were soon established inland from Newcastle. At that time the only way to get to the area was by sea, but in 1820 John Howe discovered a way through the mountains from Windsor to the Singleton district. In April 1823 Major Morriset made the first overland journey from Newcastle to Sydney, establishing the feasibility of overland passage. In 1826 the area was opened up with the construction of a roadway.

The first significant numbers of settlers arrived in the Valley in the late 1820s and turned to grazing and agriculture. We have no records of who planted the first vines there, although they would have been part of mixed farm holdings.

Among the earliest vineyards which were to achieve impressive reputations were George Wyndham's Dalwood and James Busby's Kirkton, managed by William Kelman. What Max Lake has called 'the first grape rush' began, and by 1843 the Hunter had 106 hectares of vines which produced 75 000 litres of wine and 636 litres of brandy. Seven years later, in 1850, there were more than 200 hectares owned by thirty-two vine growers. The pattern in the Hunter was for large properties of 200 to 800 hectares. Small areas were used but mostly for growing vines as a hobby.

One of the earliest vignerons was George Wyndham, a settler from Wiltshire who first attempted to grow vines on his grant Dalwood in 1830. His first vintage was 1835; it was not successful and Wyndham noted in his diary that the wine 'should make good vinegar'. The following year his vintage was 7500 litres. (More is said of Wyndham later—see Wyndham Estate, Hunter Valley, New South Wales.)

Busby's connection with the Hunter was chiefly through William Kelman, a fellow passenger on the *Triton*, who married Busby's sister, Catherine. Kelman planted Kirkton with some of Busby's vines in 1830, and in 1834 boldly decided to extend his vines to 4 hectares. After years of experimentation Kelman did quite well. By 1843 he had further increased his vines and was having particular success with the white hermitage variety (probably what we now know to be trebbiano).

Another successful settler was James King, one of the most prominent vignerons of the nineteenth century. King was born in Hertfordshire in 1800 and arrived in New South Wales in 1826 as a free settler. He took up a grant of 800 hectares on the Williams River, a tributary of the Hunter. On this property, which he named Irrawang, he grew grain and raised cattle, but for some years his main interest was in establishing himself as a merchant in Sydney. In 1832, however, King planted a vineyard on the property near Raymond Terrace, and made his first wine in 1836.

King was a cautious man. He had only 6 hectares under vine in 1854, of which 2.4 hectares was an experimental vineyard, and only then

Irrawang Vineyard and Pottery (Mitchell Library).

would he expand with another 3.6 hectares. His most successful variety was Shepherd's Riesling, later known as Hunter riesling but more accurately as the white grape variety semillon, the main white wine variety of the Lower Hunter district.

King was fully aware of the value of experimentation and scientific study. He carried out an extensive correspondence with Baron J. von Liebig, a great German chemist and philosopher. This had a twofold effect: King learned a great deal from von Liebig, and his correspondence helped to publicise the industry overseas. Further attention was gained by King during a trip to Europe, where his wine won a medal at the Paris Exhibition of 1855, and was chosen with some wine of Macarthur's to be 'placed on the table in front of the Emperor (Napoleon III) during the ceremony of closing'. Although James King did not record what became of the wine, he was 'well satisfied' with the compliment. On the same trip King showed his wines to von Liebig and the Duke of Nassau who approved of them.

King never returned to Australia from his European trip. He was seriously ill but managed to publish a slim volume in Edinburgh in 1857 titled *Australia may be an Extensive Wine-producing Country*, in which he shared the belief of Busby and others that the consumption of light wines was far more desirable than hard spirits. He died very soon after the publication of his book.

King's intelligence and enthusiasm have earned him an honoured place in Australian wine history. He was instrumental in founding the Hunter River Vineyard Association (of which more will be said later) and passed on a great deal of the knowledge he had gained.

One of the other great pioneers was Dr Henry John Lindeman, who planted Cawarra in 1843 and thereby founded one of Australia's great winemaking enterprises. His life and career are dealt with in the entry on Lindemans in the Hunter Valley section (New South Wales).

The decade of the 1840s was one of consolidation. Although the colony passed through a severe depression, winemaking was not adversely affected and there were about 120 hectares of vines in the Hunter Valley in 1846. In January 1843 the Maitland *Mercury* newspaper was established. It became a most important medium of communication on all facets of winemaking (and incidentally an invaluable primary source for present-day historians). Winemaking in the Hunter Valley made such strides that by 1847 an association of those interested in winemaking was formed. This organisation arose largely from the conflict between the pastoralists and vignerons in the Hunter River Agricultural Society—shades of the enmity between the American cattle barons and sheep men!

Those credited with the formation of the new Hunter River Vineyard Association were James King; Henry (later Reverend) Carmichael, MA, Government Surveyor for Gloucester, Durham and Brisbane, or Porphyry vineyard; and Dr Andrew Lang of Dunmore. The inaugural meeting was held on 19 May 1847 at the Northumberland Hotel, with James King in the chair, and the Association was formed 'for the purpose of promoting the culture of the vine and turning its products to the most profitable account'. The Association met twice annually, with members submitting samples of their wine for inspection. These meetings were precursors of today's national wine shows. One of the Association's successful campaigns was in having Australian wines accepted as 'Colonial' or 'Empire' wines in Britain, so that they could compete under the same conditions as Cape wines (South African) on the UK market.

In 1847 the British Government allowed non-British immigration to the colony, which meant that trained European labourers could be employed. William Kirchner (a German living in Sydney) visited Germany after consultation with the vine-growers and arranged for two groups of vine dressers to go to the Hunter district. Although there were problems with the Germans —they had troubles with heat, language and lack of familiarity with soils, seasons and climate —their long-term influence was undoubtedly beneficial.

By mid-century the fledgling industry was established well enough to survive labour scarcities and other problems associated with the gold rushes. By 1852 the Hunter River district had 186 hectares (461 acres) of vines from which 268 000 litres of wine and 5000 litres of brandy were made. A wave of new plantings began. The Land Act of 1861 reorganised the system of land allocation with the result that settlers paid £1 an acre for their selection. Vineyards sprang up all over the Pokolbin area in the Hunter Valley.

Martin Bouffier from Nassau, Germany, is credited with being the first vigneron in nearby Cessnock. His vineyard, north of the Wollombi Road, was planted in 1866. Another of the earliest settlers at Pokolbin was John McDonald, who built the house and winery at Ben Ean in 1870. George Campbell, an Irishman, had a vineyard on his 80 hectare property Daisy Hill, where he built fine red-brick cellars. Many of the names of these vignerons have faded into obscurity. Long forgotten are J.F. Doyle of Kaludah, Frederick Wilkinson of Cote d'Or, J.D. Brown of Colestoun and Dr John Glennie of Orindinna to name but a few. From around this time, however, some of the now-familiar Hunter names began to crop up: Tyrrell, Drayton, Elliott, as well as the early established Lindeman.

It is interesting that such a similar boom should recur almost exactly one hundred years later. Let us hope that the events of the following years do not also parallel those of the nineteenth century. There was a major economic depression and bank crash in the early 1890s. But, although the effects of this were severe, they were not nearly as devastating to the vignerons of the Hunter as the effects of Australian Federation. With the formation of the Commonwealth of Australia in 1901, customs barriers between the states were removed and the winemakers of South Australia took full advantage of the situation. There was a veritable flood of all types of wine from there and, as these were cheaper, the Hunter wines could not compete. Many vineyards were uprooted and lost to winemaking —the boom had bust in the Hunter.

On 20 September 1901 the Pokolbin District Vinegrowers' Association was formed to replace the Hunter River Vineyard Association and at its peak had more than forty independent growers as members. The new Association held local wine exhibitions and was active in protecting the district against the phylloxera infestation. (The Phylloxera Disaster, caused by a root-sucking insect, had a catastrophic effect on the vineyards of Europe and later on a number of parts of Australia, and is described in more detail later.) The Association also achieved some legal measures to discourage unadulterated wine coming in from other states.

Thus the turn of the century saw the Hunter Valley down but not out. In fact, the Valley was to fall further before the revival sixty years later.

Corowa and Albury

Winemaking in New South Wales in the nineteenth century was not solely confined to the Hunter Valley. The towns of Corowa and Albury in the far south of the state, on the Murray River, were the centre of quite an extensive winemaking district in the 1890s.

Winemaking at Corowa began in the mid-nineteenth century when many small vineyards were established there. The Lindeman name was prominent in the area. Large-scale winemaking began there with Dr Lindeman's purchase of a property known as Haffner's Vineyard in 1872. The phylloxera epidemic at the end of the nineteenth century devastated the district and many of the smaller vineyards were lost.

An important vigneron of the times was J.T. Fallon, who had an extensive vineyard at Ettamogah, a few kilometres from Albury. In 1873 Mr Fallon read a paper on New South Wales wines before the Royal Society of Arts in London (the same body addressed by Blaxland in 1823). When phylloxera attacked his vines in 1906 Mr Fallon did not replace the vineyards. A Mr L. Frere attempted to make sparkling wine at Albury in the belief that some of the lighter soils of the district would produce light wines of quality. Unfortunately, phylloxera interrupted his plans and we have never discovered just how accurate Mr Frere's ideas were.

A well-known identity of the district was John Delappe Lankester, born in Lichfield, Staffordshire, on 20 September 1837. He arrived in Sydney with his father in 1849, and spent his adult life working in the wine industry. In 1860 he opened and managed a wine business for Dr Lindeman in Sydney. Lankester was manager of J.T. Fallon's vineyards when they were destroyed by phylloxera. He then cultivated his own vineyards at Ettamogah, where he had a grant of 65 hectares of land. Lankester died in January 1938 at the age of 101.

The Sydney Area

After the early attempts at growing grapes for wine at Parramatta, there were no serious plantings in the Sydney area. Among the early pioneers no mention has been made of James Ruse (the ex-convict who, in 1791, became one of the first settlers to support himself through agriculture), who planted at Rosehill on the outskirts of Parramatta, or of Dr Robert Townson who cultivated the muscatel grape at Bunbury Curran near Campbelltown and made a sweet wine.

A vineyard was planted early in the nineteenth century at Rooty Hill, near Sydney. This was named Minchinbury and became renowned for its sparkling wines. The land was originally acquired as a grant by Captain William Minchin in 1819, and passed to a Dr McKay after the Captain's death in 1821. Dr McKay planted the first vines there and built a winery. The property was acquired by Penfolds in the early 1900s. Minchinbury is discussed in detail in the entry on Penfolds.

Thomas Henry Fiaschi, yet another wine doctor, established a vineyard on the banks of the Hawkesbury River, near the Sackville Reach, in the 1880s. Dr Fiaschi was born in Florence in 1853, the son of a professor of literature who had wine interests. Fiaschi graduated in medicine from Pisa and Florence and then did postgraduate study in England. After his arrival in Sydney in 1874, the doctor began practice in Macquarie Street and eventually became senior surgeon at Sydney Hospital. After some years in Sydney Dr Fiaschi decided to make wine in a personal effort to improve the standard of the local wine, and in 1886 he started planting a vineyard which he called Tizzana, after the family property in Italy. He designed and built a two-storey winery like those he had known in his homeland, and the stone shell still stands. Dr Fiaschi imported French and Italian varieties and appointed a French manager, Mr Sarar. Their wines became better known, especially the light wines, and were sold at the family cellars in the heart of Sydney. He died in 1927 and the firm went out of business about twenty-five years later.

Mudgee

Vines were first planted in Mudgee at Craigmoor in 1858 by Adam Roth, a German immigrant. By the 1880s there were thirteen established wineries in the area and more than 160 hectares under grapes. In 1881 a Mudgee red (probably a shiraz)

won a diploma of honour at a Paris wine show. By 1892 there were fifty-five grapegrowers in the Mudgee area. Dr Fiaschi of Tizzana was one who bought a vineyard at Mudgee. This district has been revived in recent years after a long period in the wine doldrums.

Victoria: The Early Days

As the founding of the two colonies was so different, so the making of wine in Victoria began in quite different circumstances to those in New South Wales. John Batman founded the settlement of Melbourne in 1834 and, according to the *Port Phillip Patriot*, the new settlement owed its existence 'to the skill and enterprise of the individual colonists', whereas other colonies depended on government decisions. Free settlers flocked to the surrounding districts almost immediately. Governor Bourke proclaimed jurisdiction over the settlement in 1836, but there was a strong separatist movement right from the beginning.

The growth of vineyards in the new colony was rapid. In the absence of intensive divisions in the community over the abuse of spirits and with government encouragement in the form of subsidies, Victoria soon became prominent as a wine-producing state, with thousands of hectares under vine.

Edward Henty has always been credited with the planting of the first vineyard when he settled at Portland, in the western part of Victoria, in 1834, the year of the founding of the colony. He arrived from Launceston, Tasmania, on the schooner *Thistle*. His effects are quoted as including 'one cask of grape cuttings'—although there is no further mention in any records of what became of these vines.

Four years later William Ryrie, a pastoralist who came overland from New South Wales, planted the first vines in the Yarra Valley at Yering. Ryrie planted 12 hectares in this fertile area, which was only 50 km from Melbourne. The first wine was made there in 1845. By this time, however, Ryrie was no longer alone in practising viticulture. The rush to plant grapes in the area was immediate and on a large scale. By 1848 there were 40 hectares under vine and over the following twenty years this increased to 1200 hectares.

In September 1839, Charles Joseph La Trobe became superintendent of the new settlement. By a fortunate chance for Victorian winemaking, he had lived for some years at Neuchatel in Switzerland, where he acquired some knowledge and a real appreciation of wine. During his Swiss sojourn La Trobe married Sophie, the daughter of Frederick August de Montmillon, Swiss Counsellor of State.

On their arrival in Victoria the La Trobes named their house Jolimont, after Sophie's country family estate, and planted a small vineyard in what was to be the garden of the first Government House in Melbourne. La Trobe encouraged other settlers to follow suit and directed, for example, the planting of vines at Mayfield, the home of the McCrae family. It is also probable that he advised Skene Craig, Commissariat Officer, who had a vineyard in what is now Collins Street West, in the centre of Melbourne. Amiet Pelet, the husband of La Trobe's housekeeper Rose, had his own vineyard in what is also now the centre of the city. In fact, his wine was honoured by being served at the ball given on 28 November 1850 to celebrate the separation of the colony of Victoria from New South Wales.

Although these activities were significant, La Trobe's great contribution to Australian winemaking was to influence some of the people of Neuchatel to come out to the colony and practise their viticultural skills there. Five years after La Trobe's arrival in Melbourne, eleven men had started from the canton of Neuchatel for Australia. They settled near each other in the district of Geelong and all planted vineyards around their homes.

A number of people clearly saw the promise of Victoria and there is much to suggest that it is being realised today. One was John Ignatius Bleasdale. He was the Catholic gadfly of his day, a man of pugnacious and untamed ideas who vociferously advocated wine and its civilising influence on everyday life. He was born in Lancashire in 1822 and went to the Victorian colony in 1851.

The Reverend Doctor followed the wine debate, perhaps even led it, and he watched the work of people like the Macarthurs in New South Wales with great interest. He was an outspoken advocate of the Victorian wine industry and in 1867 delivered a paper to the Royal Society 'On Colonial Wines'. His sober remarks about the benefits of wine earned him opprobrium in the magazine *Melbourne Punch* as 'Dr Blazes'—a sort of drunken prelate of booze.

Sadly, Bleasdale's thoughtful comments—he had an outstanding mind—were wasted and he went to California to live out his days. He died in 1884 but his name lives on in the Bleasdale winery at Langhorne Creek in South Australia.

The de Castellas and the Fabled Wines of the Yarra Valley

The early Swiss migrants had an influence which far outweighed their numbers, as they were better educated than most and also had a thorough knowledge and understanding of winemaking and viticulture. Among the Swiss settlers were Clement Deschamps (the son of a head vigneron at Neuchatel), Baron de Pury, and his cousins the de Castella brothers who were to make immense contributions to the wine industry of Australia.

The first of the de Castellas to come to Australia was Paul, son of the chief physician of the Pourtales Hospital at Neuchatel, who arrived in 1848 with Adolphe de Meuron. Paul bought part of Ryrie's cattle station, Yering, at Lilydale and began to plant a vineyard, for which he obtained 20 000 cuttings (principally cabernet sauvignon) from Château Lafite. Most of these struck and Yering soon had a reputation for good red wine.

Paul invited his brothers to join him and in 1854 Hubert de Castella arrived in Australia. In turn, Hubert established a second vineyard which he called St Hubert's. This vineyard eventually reached 100 hectares with a vintage of 318 000 litres. Legend grew about the quality of the Lilydale wines, which were apparently of extraordinary finesse and of a quality never before seen in Australia.

At the great Melbourne International Exhibition of 1881, St Hubert's triumphed by being awarded the prize for the most meritorious exhibit in the entire show. This prize, a silver table set of seven silver-gilt epergnes worth 25 000 francs or £800, was awarded by Emperor Wilhelm I of Germany. How the judges could decide between such diverse items as steam engines, felt hats and wine is difficult to understand. St Hubert's wine was also honoured with the award of Grand Prix at the Paris Exposition of 1889. This was one of only fourteen such prizes given to wines from all over the world, so the quality of the wine must have been very high.

Yet another part of the Yering cattle station was bought and planted to vines by Guillaume, Baron de Pury, who called it Yeringberg and from all accounts produced first-class white wines.

Hubert de Castella not only made wine, he wrote books about it. South Australian wine historian Valmai Hankel describes him as the 'most lyrical and charming of our nineteenth-century oenographers'. De Castella published *Notes d'un vigneron Australien* (Melbourne, 1882) and *John Bull's Vineyard* (Melbourne, 1886). In the latter he deplores the winemaking practices of those growers who drank no wine, describing 'one amateur vigneron who had his grapes carried on the zinc roofs of his shed and cellars and, previous to crushing them, left them for two days *improving* under a burning sun'. The book records that Yering vineyard then occupied 40 hectares. Yeringberg on the same bank of the Yarra was 28 hectares, and his own St Hubert's 105 hectares. As de Castella wrote: 'Wine growing is an enticing pursuit. It is an art, a bond of hospitality, pride to the host and good humour to the friend.' A noble testament.

St Hubert's vineyard later came into the possession of David Mitchell, the father of Dame Nellie Melba. Unfortunately, a variety of factors put the Lilydale vineyards out of production in the 1920s, one of the last vintages at Yeringberg being made in 1921. The noxious phylloxera bug was not responsible for the failure of winemaking in the Lilydale area—the reasons were wholly economic. The grape harvest was small compared with other Victorian areas, partly because the choice vines were low yielders, partly because spring frosts became an undue hazard through the clearing of timber, and partly because of the decline in fertility through neglect of manuring. Further, in those days the number of wine lovers was too small and most Australians were not prepared to pay the necessary price for quality. The overriding factor, however, was the growth in the fortified wine market. The addition of alcohol stabilised the wines and most people apparently preferred the sherries, ports and mus-

cats freely available from other areas. Some properties were bought by people more interested in dairying than viticulture; and, finally, rising land values made it uneconomic to continue with the vineyards.

In the late 1970s and the 1980s there was a strong wine revival in the Yarra Valley. The recognition that suitable soil and climate provided a perfect partnership for excellent table wines was a belated acknowledgment that the vignerons of the nineteenth century were right.

Other Nineteenth-century Victorian Vineyards

About a hundred years ago vineyards covered thousands of hectares of what is now South Yarra, Hawthorn, Brighton and other suburbs of Melbourne, as well as Geelong and Bendigo. The *Illustrated Australian News* proclaimed in 1866:

> The notable increase of private vineyards is one of the most cheering signs of the times, a few years hence and every country resident will be enabled to entertain his visitors with the produce of his own little vineyard.

In 1840 John Fawkner put in 4 hectares at Pascoe Vale near Flemington and eight years later had a vintage of 9000 litres of 'excellent wine'. Hawthorn was another suburb noted for its wine. Count Alinant de Dollon cultivated 12 hectares, and adjoining these were the vineyards of I. McKinnon and Neil McLean. Edward Khull, the goldbroker, owned the Tooronga vineyard nearby. The now-fashionable suburb of South Yarra was also a winemaking centre in the nineteenth century. A contemporary writer recorded that a young Swiss, Mr Wisewould, made 1350 litres of 'exceedingly good' wine there, including a riesling from the 1861 vintage.

Many vineyards were planted at Sunbury, including Mr J.S. Johnston's famous Craiglee, which ceased production in 1926. The four-storey bluestone winery and cellars survived, however, and Victorian wine writer James Halliday—who now operates a very successful vineyard and winery in the Yarra Valley—records that a cache of 1872 Sunbury wine was discovered in 1951, and that 'at their best the wines were superb'.

At Whittlesea the Glenlinton vineyard was established towards the close of the century by

H.E. Dawson, a solicitor-turned-vigneron, and a Mr Gilchrist, who was chief Hansard reporter. The Dawson wines were high-quality reds, but wine production was terminated at Glenlinton when the vineyard was turned over to grazing in the 1930s.

There were a number of vineyards in the Gippsland area in the nineteenth century, including those of the Costellos and Luis Wuillemin, whose cellar buildings still stand.

Ebenezer Ward also described a vineyard near Ballarat, owned by Monsieur Fleischhauer, which was planted in 1859. At Avoca the pioneer viticulturist was Mr Mackereth, who planted vines in 1848—an enterprise which was passed to his son, who finally sold out in 1929 to a Methodist minister. Sadly, the winery was closed and the 20 hectares of vineyards pulled out.

Geelong

The first vineyard in the Geelong area was planted in 1842 at Pollock's Ford, where David Louis Pettavel and Frederick Breuget established the Neuchatel vineyard on high land near the Barwon with cuttings brought from Dijon. In 1845 they made their first wine.

Most of the Geelong vineyards were small holdings, with the Ballarat goldfields providing a ready market for both table grapes and wine during the 1850s in particular. By 1858 there were nine thriving cooperages providing casks and vats. In 1864 Geelong was one of the most important winemaking areas in Victoria, and Ebenezer Ward gave a detailed description of more than fifty vineyards there. More than 400 hectares were under vine by 1870.

Like the vineyards round Lilydale, the Geelong district was best suited to the production of light dry table wines. The many Swiss settlers mentioned earlier were followed by Germans, at the appropriately named German Town (now known as Marshall), and they probably would have encouraged this style of wine anyway.

Geelong wines were acclaimed at Intercolonial exhibitions and shows and as far away as Bordeaux and Paris. The 1860s were the great years, highlighted by the visit in 1867 of the Duke of Edinburgh to Pettavel's Prince Albert vineyards at Waurn Ponds.

Bendigo

There is no historical certainty as to who planted the first vines at Bendigo. A claim has been staked for a Frenchman, Bladier, and a German, Delscher, in 1856. Ebenezer Ward, however, in 1864 believed that Yarraberb station on Myers Creek was one of the oldest and best-known vineyards in the area, and wrote: 'There are six acres of vines, the oldest from 10 to 11 years of age.'

Ward wrote about approximately forty vineyards in the Bendigo area, mostly of recent origin. The area boomed first with the gold rush and then a vine rush. By the end of the 1880s there were more than 130 vineyards and 450 hectares under vine in the district.

One Bendigo wine of distinction was entered in the 1873 Vienna Exhibition. François de Castella relates that the French judges withdrew in protest as they did not believe that the Bendigo Hermitage was an Australian wine—its quality was such that it could only have been French!

Winemaking at Bendigo suffered the same fate as at Geelong. Phylloxera and the 1890s economic depression wiped the area off the wine map until the Victorian revival which began in the late 1960s.

Rutherglen

Rutherglen, in the north-east of Victoria, originally sprang into prominence as a goldmining centre in the 1850s. Gold trebled the population in ten years, brought enormous and sudden wealth and gave a greater complexity to colonial society. Merchants and food producers, pastoralists and transport operators shared in the prosperity brought about by the rich gold discoveries of the next decade. But it did not take very long for the surface alluvial gold to be worked out, and many of the disenchanted miners turned to a new industry—viticulture.

Vines were first planted in the Rutherglen district by Lindsay Brown at Gooramadda in 1851 with cuttings from Albury (where German growers were already making wine on a small scale). Brown was persuaded to venture into viticulture by three German employees—Frauenfelder, Rau and Schumbach.

From then the growth of vineyards was rapid and within a decade Rutherglen was in the fore-

Phylloxera, and Other Disasters

In 1875 the vine grape louse *Phylloxera vastatrix*, a parasitic aphid which lives on and destroys grapevines, was discovered at the village of Fyansford in the Geelong area, soon spreading to Geelong itself. This discovery marked the beginning of one of the great natural disasters of Australian winemaking history.

Grapevines, in this case the grape-bearing plant *vitis Vinifera*, are subject to a number of diseases, like most plants. The early and middle decades of the nineteenth century saw a fungal disease, oidium, hit Europe's vineyards. Later, sprays were developed which did, and continue to, control this problem.

Phylloxera, however, was a greater peril. It was appropriately described in 1989 as 'the AIDS of grapevines'. And so it must have appeared to European and Australian vine-growers from the second half of the nineteenth century through to the early part of the twentieth century. Its menace is by no means gone today.

The phylloxera insect was detected in the vast vineyards of France in 1860. It obviously came from North America, which had its own indigenous grapevines (including *vitis Labrusca*), and these vines were resistant to the embrace of the louse, which has a complex life pattern, maybe with as many as eighteen cycles. These include that of a grub, an insect and an airborne form. Lacking an understanding of the potential biological menace of the louse, it was presumably transported across the Atlantic in soil, probably around the roots of vines carried from America. It spread like wildfire among grapevines unable to cope with it. They were weakened by its effects, which did not kill the vine itself, though it poisoned the roots of the vines, welcoming the attack of other predators and diseases.

It did not take long for phylloxera to make its way by sea to Australia in cuttings and perhaps on agricultural equipment, or by other means. And as Victoria's wine industry was growing rapidly in the latter half of the nineteenth century, the state was worst hit by the louse.

There was, and is, no known treatment, though many drastic cures were tried. The insect finds it difficult to move through sandy soil. But to this day the only real answer appears to be to graft vines onto resistant rootstock, or to plant vines already grafted onto resistant rootstock. American vines are resistant to phylloxera's fatal attraction.

As the unfolding disaster of phylloxera's spread became apparent, the Victorian Government ordered the destruction of all Geelong vines, and an extensive soil sterilisation program, in which the vineyard sites were fumigated with carbon sulphide gas, was undertaken. The aim was to prevent the disease reaching Rutherglen—then the principal wine-growing area of the state. The policy was totally unsuccessful. The louse got to Rutherglen anyway and the vineyards of Geelong were totally ruined. As the market for dry table wines had collapsed, the vineyards were not re-established. A few holdings continued into the early decades of the twentieth century, but there was a lapse of many decades before any new vines were planted at Geelong.

It is worth pointing out that phylloxera could wreak yet more havoc on Australia's vineyards. Careless planting and interstate transfer of grapes, agricultural machinery and cuttings could well trigger a new disaster.

front of wine production in Victoria. Many of the great winemaking concerns were founded in that era—the Sutherland Smiths of All Saints, Morris of Fairfield, Chambers, Campbells and Gehrigs. Mr P.B. Burgoyne then owned the Mt Ophir vineyard near Chiltern, where he built a beautiful winery in 1893. Mt Ophir produced some legendary wines of a 'Burgundy' style. Unfortunately, in the middle of this century the property was given over to other agricultural pursuits and Mt Ophir wines were no more.

Anthony Ruche, a German vigneron, had a great influence on the district with the sale in 1879 of ten years' output of wine to a Melbourne merchant for £1680. Within six months it had been resold at ten shillings a gallon, more than twice the price Ruche had been paid. When the news spread, more vineyards went in and within four years planting had increased from 300 hectares to almost five times that area. Ruche ultimately sold his business to Chambers.

By the 1880s Rutherglen was surrounded by some thousands of hectares of vines, although the actual area is still a controversial statistic. Whatever, in those joyous days the future looked bright indeed. North-east Victorian wines were amassing prizes all over the world. In 1883 the Murray District Vinegrowers' Association was formed with George Sutherland Smith as its first president. At the time, Rutherglen had more than half of all the area under vine in Australia. The main reason for the vast expansion after 1880 was the connection of Rutherglen and Melbourne by rail in 1879. This granted ready access to a waiting market. Previously, wine had to be shipped to Echuca by riverboat, which had greatly hindered the young industry.

At the end of the decade in 1889 the Victorian Government passed a bill designed to encourage the expansion of the rapidly burgeoning industry, and in doing so helped to bring about its downfall. The Planting Bonus Bill gave a bonus of £2 for every acre of vines planted in Victoria after that date. This encouraged the planting of vines by farmers who had little or no knowledge of viticulture; a huge quantity of often inferior wine was made by them, with consequent harmful effects, especially on the reputation of Australian wine in London.

In the 1890s Australia passed through an acute economic depression from which the Victorian wine industry did not escape. After agitation by the Rutherglen Vinegrowers' Association, the State Government subsidised the growers to the tune of a bonus of one shilling a gallon on Victorian brandy. In the same year, 1896, the Viticultural College was established at Chiltern to instruct young men in the science of vine-growing. But the zenith had been reached. In the late 1890s there were 5600 hectares under vine at Rutherglen.

In 1897 phylloxera was discovered. It did not take long to devastate the vineyards and ruin the growers of the district. By 1904 the blight had made rapid progress through the clayey loam of vineyards to the east of Rutherglen; in 1906 there were less than 2800 hectares of vines left; by 1911 less than 2000 hectares.

Under the advice and direction of Francois de Castella, the Government Viticulturist, the State Government began a policy of assisting the Rutherglen growers to rehabilitate their vineyards. At the time the cure was a new discovery—the replanting of European scions grafted on to resistant American rootstocks. De Castella, among others, and the Chiltern Viticultural College did valiant work in advising growers and distributing resistant stocks, but the damage had been done. Many growers decided to abandon vine-growing—some vineyards were replanted with other crops, and others were turned into grazing land for sheep. The Rutherglen district never regained its former importance for volume of wine. At least the destruction was not complete, as at Bendigo and Geelong, and some excellent wines have continued to be made in the north-east of the state; notably, marvellous fortified wines such as 'Liqueur' Muscats and Tokays, and some excellent table wines.

Great Western

Australian history is more notable for floods, fires, droughts and strikes than romance. So the story of the beginnings of winemaking at Great Western is one of the more picturesque episodes in our history.

It all began in France in 1825 in the province of Lorraine, where Anne Marie Blampied was born to a farming family. She must have been an adventurous girl, for at the age of twenty-eight she and her brother Emile (aged fifteen) left for Australia to seek their fortune on the goldfields. They arrived at Beechworth in Victoria in 1853, and went into business transporting supplies to the miners with another Frenchman, Jean Pierre Trouette. Anne Marie married Jean Pierre and they moved to the goldfields at Great Western in about 1858, accompanied by young Emile.

The gold was soon worked out. Jean Trouette bought land near the Central Victorian village of Great Western, apparently because the area reminded Trouette of his home (the department of Gers). In 1863 he began planting vines from Geelong on the property which was named St Peters, in partnership with Emile Blampied. The following year they increased their plantings and by 1867 they had about 50 000 vines and 2000 fruit trees. That year 2275 litres of wine were made and awards were gained at home and abroad.

Jean Trouette died in November 1885 at the age of fifty-two. The following year his only son Nicholas was killed while attempting to rescue a workman from an underground wine tank. (This is an ongoing risk of the winemaking business, as noxious gases left over from fermentation, or from vat cleaning, have killed many winery workers right up to recent times). Bad fortune continued to plague Anne Marie and after a series of poor seasons and crop failures St Peters was sold in 1897 to an English family named Merton. Anne Marie Trouette died in December 1905 leaving her daughter Marie, who lived until 1927. St Peters lapsed into obscurity, and wine was no longer made there.

Although St Peters has not existed as a vineyard for many years, the Trouettes and Blampied were the founders of winemaking at Great Western. They were also the inspiration which led the brothers Joseph and Henry Best to plant their vineyards, which have survived, in the Great Western area. These days Great Western is well known for its champagnes. The history of Hans Irvine and the House of Seppelt, who are responsible for this, is recounted in the section on the vineyards of Great Western. Briefly, in 1865 Joseph Best planted grapes from St Peters on his property which he called Great Western. Best sold out to businessman and politician Hans Irvine in 1888, who expended a great deal of effort on the venture and succeeded in making first-class sparkling wine. Seppelts took over at Great Western in 1918, and have continued to make wine there. In 1866 Joseph Best's brother Henry planted a vineyard on the banks of Concongella Creek, which is now operated by the Thomsons.

Great Western is another winemaking area of Victoria which is now but a shadow of its former self. In the early years of this century there were more than 800 hectares of vines in the area from Glenorchy in the north to about 15 km below Ararat in the south. The decline was not caused by phylloxera but by economics. Great Western produces wines of high quality, but the soils are quite poor and the climate, with its frequent frosts, is such that yields are often low. Although many vineyards were uprooted and turned over to sheep, Seppelts and Best's have survived.

Central Goulburn Valley

Major Mitchell was the first to explore Victoria's Goulburn Valley, which later became a grazing area and, in the 1850s, a wine-growing area as well. The viticultural history of the area is inextricably bound up with the history of Chateau Tahbilk, whose vineyards were first planted near the town of Nagambie in 1860 by a Melbourne syndicate. These were eventually bought out by John Pinney Bear.

In the 1880s phylloxera struck Tahbilk and wiped out all but 55 hectares which were planted on moist, sandy soil. The vineyard then went into a decline until it was bought in 1925 by the Purbrick family, who own it today. The chronicle of Chateau Tahbilk is detailed in the section on the vineyards of the Goulburn Valley, Victoria.

Near the town of Shepparton, Dalmation-born Trojano Darveniza planted the Excelsior vineyards in 1875 and had numerous successes at overseas exhibitions.

Mildura

The town of Mildura on the Murray River depends on the water of that river for its existence. The men who first harnessed the Murray waters were the Canadian-born brothers Ben (W.B.) and George Chaffey, who came to Australia at the request of Alfred Deakin in the 1880s. The account of the development of the irrigation settlement at Mildura is firmly linked with the history of Renmark, 144 km from Mildura but 320 km down river.

The Chaffey brothers had been invited to undertake the irrigation projects by the Victorian and South Australian Governments. Politicking meant that they ended up looking after the two big projects at once—and the problems they encountered were legion.

In 1887 irrigation from the Murray was begun. The first planting of 65 hectares of vines at Irymple (which is now part of the First Mildura Irrigation Trust administered area) in 1888 and 1889 consisted of the following varieties: cabernet sauvignon, 2 hectares; hermitage, 6 hectares; white hermitage, 2 hectares; malbec,

2 hectares; sherry grapes, 2 hectares; gordo blanco, 8 hectares; mataro, 38 hectares; and doradillo, 4 hectares.

The first small vintage was crushed in 1891 in a bough-roofed shed—crushed, moreover, by bare feet, a method that was used until 1897 when 'W.B.' (Chaffey) brought a Chaffey Bros steam traction engine to the site to operate a mechanical crusher. A substantial brick building with cellars and ample storage was completed for the 1892 and subsequent vintages, and this original structure is still in use today. The bricks were made on the site and the cellars excavated with a horse-drawn scoop.

The first commercial harvest was in 1893. Unfortunately, that year the Murray dried up earlier than usual and without transport the fruit and grapes were left to rot on the wharves. The Chaffeys had established Chateau Mildura and, despite an impressive output of wine and brandy in terms of quantity, were declared bankrupt in 1893.

The man in charge of the vineyards and winemaking was Pierre Joseph Mari Mazou who had come from southern France via South Australia, where he had gained experience in viticulture as practised in this new land. Peter Mazou left in 1901 and was succeeded by a relative, Florentin Jean Louie Gelly. Gelly, also a native of southern France, had come to Mildura from the job of managing one of the Hardy Cellars in South Australia.

By 1900 the industry was in a very depressed state and W.B. Chaffey could see no future for his table wines. He took the decision to graft all his wine grapes over to drying varieties, and Florentin Gelly's first job was to supervise this. By 1901 the task was completed and Gelly's duties were then confined to vineyard management and the care and delivery of wines from stock.

About 1908 W.B. Chaffey sold the balance of the wine stocks to a Melbourne firm whose identity is not recorded. So ended the first attempt to establish Mildura as a premium wine area.

Winemaking at Mildura thus began in rather strange circumstances. This, combined with the Victorian Government's planting bonus, did not help the reputation of Australian wine. The situation did eventually improve, however. Further details of the Chaffey saga are given in the history of the Murray Valley, South Australia, and in the entry on Mildara Wines in North-west Victoria.

South Australia
The Founding Years

South Australia, by a combination of the blessings of nature, the enterprise of its settlers and some plain good luck, has long assumed the dominant position in the Australian wine industry. The abundance of grapevines and olive trees (many self-sown) reinforces the image of South Australia as having the Mediterranean climate of the Southern Hemisphere—described by some as the 'Athens of the South'.

Soon after the founding of the colony in 1836 it was realised that the wine industry could be important. In the *Almanac* of 1849 George McEwin, a pioneer horticulturist, forecast that wine would become 'a source of great wealth to the colony, the climate and soil being ideal' and affirmed that wine 'rivalling the most famous growths of the old world will be produced in South Australia as soon as we gain the requisite knowledge and the practical experience necessary to success'.

Vines were planted almost at the beginning— the undisputed first by John Barton Hack, who planted vines obtained at Launceston in lower North Adelaide in 1837. This vineyard made way for urban development (a portent of things to come) and was destroyed by 1840, by which time Hack had 700 vines planted at Echunga Springs. Another early figure of note was George Stevenson, who had 1.6 hectares in North Adelaide where he grew vines imported in 1838. From these he provided cuttings to many other colonists.

There has long been a dispute among wine historians and the companies concerned as to who made the first wine in South Australia. The rival claimants are John Reynell and Richard Hamilton, although recent research supports the previously unheralded Walter Duffield, who in 1845 sent Queen Victoria a case of 1844 white wine made in the Adelaide Hills and described as 'Echunga Hock'. Whether Her Majesty was amused by this presumption is not recorded, though the wine did make it to Buckingham Palace.

The old wine cellar at Reynella, excavated by John Reynell in 1838.

Richard Hamilton arrived in the colony first, on 17 October 1837, and took up his land on 6 June 1838—before Reynell had arrived. John Reynell landed in South Australia on 16 October 1838 and took up his land on 6 July 1839. With regard to winemaking, the only extant proof is an entry in John Reynell's diary which says he planted vine cuttings from Tasmania in 1838. The historical waters are muddied, however, but it does appear Duffield wins the 'first winemaker' contest. What really matters is that Duffield, Reynell and Hamilton all planted vineyards and made wine in the early days of South Australia and were thus instrumental in laying the foundations of the wine industry.

The Adelaide Environs

The first vines in South Australia were, naturally enough, planted in the vicinity of the capital city of Adelaide. As the city has grown, most of these vineyards have disappeared. These include the first vineyards of what have become leading winemaking companies. Foremost among these is Penfolds, which in 1844 had its origins at Magill,

some 6 km east of the city at the foot of the Mount Lofty Ranges. Dr Christopher Rawson Penfold originally began to make wine for its tonic properties in aiding the health of his patients, and in so doing shaped the beginnings of the largest wine company in Australia.

In 1854 Patrick Auld began to plant the Auldana vineyard (long owned by Penfolds). In 1862 Mr Auld formed the Australian Wine Company in London to sell the produce of his vineyards there. A report in the London *Wine and Spirit Gazette* in 1869 noted that although Australia could not then be considered as an exporting country the wines of Auldana were being sold in London and 'deserve the highest praise of connoisseurs'. The article went on to say that Mr Auld was 'dead against any attempt at artificial fortifying, and his ambition is to obtain the pure juice of the grape without the slightest addition of spirit'. Would that more vignerons of those and later days had thought similarly! Incidentally, Patrick Auld's London company later became incorporated in the Emu Wine Company.

Woodley House and part of vineyard.

Other early Adelaide vineyards were those of Osmond Gilles at Glen Osmond (1856), which was later owned by Woodley Wines; H.S. Clark at Stonyfell (1858), later owned by H.M. Martin and Son; Dr W.T. Angove at Tea Tree Gully (1884); Douglas A. Tolley at Hope Valley (1893); and Hamilton's Ewell vineyard near Glenelg.

The now-prominent firm of Thomas Hardy & Sons had its beginnings when Thomas Hardy emigrated from Devon (also the home county of John Reynell) in 1850 and got his first job in South Australia with Mr Reynell, 'gentleman farmer', at his Reynella farm 23 km south of Adelaide. It was here Hardy became interested in wine-growing.

Hardy was employed by Reynell 'for seven shillings a week with a prospect of a rise in a short time'. Hardy wrote at the time:

This is splendid country indeed. Things seem very strange at first but one soon gets used to the ways of the country. Everything is looking prosperous. The bark is used for tanning and it becomes an article of export. The fruit trees are finely in blossom. Master has just finished pruning the vines.

He learnt about vines, and winemaking in Reynell's Old Cave cellar. In 1851 Hardy trekked off to the Victorian goldfields to make some money. He succeeded, and returned to South Australia and bought land at Bankside, on the banks of the River Torrens near Adelaide in 1853. He began clearing and planting almost immediately. Thomas Hardy & Sons Ltd prospered, and wine was made at Bankside until the early 1920s, when the vineyard became a casualty of the city's expansion. In the intervening years Hardy's, under the far-sighted guidance of this eminent Australian winemaker and businessman, expanded enormously in South Australia, buying into McLaren Vale to the south, and moving into markets in other states and overseas. Thomas Hardy's direct descendants bought Chateau Reynella in late 1982 and restored it as their corporate headquarters.

A number of attempts were made in the early days to grow grapes on a commercial scale in the wetter parts of the Adelaide Hills, but all failed with the exception of the vineyard planted at Clarendon in 1849 by John Edward Peake. Peake is remembered now because it was he who first imported direct from Spain the palomino, pedro ximenez, doradillo, temprana and mollar negro grapes, some of which have been important in South Australia ever since.

Dr R.M. Schomburgk, later well known as Director of the Adelaide Botanic Gardens, planted a small vineyard in 1857 at Buchfelde (now called Loos), west of Gawler on the Para River. Dr Schomburgk was responsible for introducing to South Australia the sultana grape, which was to assume major importance in the irrigation areas of the Murray.

The Southern Vales

The Southern Vales area south of Adelaide, on the plains between the Mount Lofty Ranges and the sea, was established early on as a major centre of wine production. The first of the vineyards in the area was John Reynell's, planted in 1839 near the township which was later to bear his name.

He was soon followed by Dr Alexander Charles Kelly who planted a vineyard which he called Trinity, near Morphett Vale in the early 1840s. This vineyard was later owned by John B. MacMahon, but the property was sold and is now covered by houses. About twenty years later Dr Kelly was responsible for founding a company which bought a property near McLaren Vale, where there was a vineyard that had been planted by Mr W. Manning in 1850. Dr Kelly expanded the plantings and named the property Tintara. Eventually Thomas Hardy bought the holding. Dr Kelly was a firm believer in the value of wine and had great faith in the future of the wine industry. He published a book, *The Vine in Australia*, in 1861, in which he emphasised the need for a scientific approach to winemaking and the use of suitable grape varieties. The book is a detailed and thorough account of both the theory and practice of winemaking. This was followed in 1867 by *Wine-growing in Australia and the Teachings of Modern Writers on Vine-culture and Winemaking*. Both books were outstanding for their research and clarity, as well as their originality and presentation. They would have been of inestimable value to vignerons of the time. More is said of Dr Kelly in the account of Hardy's Tintara vineyard.

The Seaview vineyard near McLaren Vale was originally planted in 1850 by George Manning, who called it Hope Farm. The late nineteenth century saw the beginnings of many vineyards whose names we know well today. In 1892 a Mrs Horn planted a vineyard at O'Halloran Hill, south of Adelaide, which became Glenloth. In the McLaren Vale area the Ryecroft vineyard was established by Frederick Wilkinson in 1884; the Kay brothers began planting at the Amery vineyards in 1890; and Mr A.C. Johnston of Pirramimma bought his property in 1892, and it is still run by his descendants.

For many years most Southern Vales wines were 'big' and 'jammy' and sold in bulk only. Things began to change in the early 1960s, when some makers started to lighten the style of reds and to produce light, clean whites. In the 1970s the area virtually exploded with boutique wineries—they literally popped up like mushrooms after rain. Two-thirds of the fifty wineries in the Southern Vales area fall into this category—and all sorts of revolutionary wines are being produced.

Nature has been particularly kind to viticulture in the Southern Vales. Frosts are not a problem, droughts are few, the climate is generally moderate, and vine diseases (notably phylloxera) have not been a serious worry. Little wonder then that the area—despite the southern march of Adelaide suburbia, and a very long period with no spectacular developments—has gone from strength to strength.

The Barossa Valley

The Barossa Valley, an hour or so's drive to the north-east of Adelaide, has long been one of Australia's largest and most important wine areas. This area was totally unexplored by white men when Colonel William Light led the first party of exploration there in December 1837. It was Light, the first Surveyor-General of South Australia, who named the valley after an area in the south of Spain—Ba Rosa, or Hill of Roses. One of the far-sighted (though eccentric) early explorers was Johann Menge, geologist, who reported:

> I am certain that we shall see the place flourish, and vineyards and orchards and immense fields of corn throughout. It will furnish huge quantities of wine; it will yield timber for our towns, and superior stone and marble abounds for buildings.

The man who was responsible more than any other individual for the early development of the area is George Fife Angas, the 'father' of the Barossa Valley. Angas, who was born in Newcastle, England, in 1789, was largely responsible for founding the South Australia Company and was appointed its director. The company was formed with private capital to develop the new colony and did much to advance its agricultural settlement. George Angas settled in the valley and became something of a feudal lord. The village of Angaston (initially Angas Town) was sur-

Barossa Valley, South Australia.

veyed in 1841 and named after him. Angas needed labour for his orchards and, being both practical and humanitarian, he realised that the ideal solution would be to bring to Australia some Silesian Lutherans, who were being persecuted at the time. Since 1822 the religious Lutherans of Silesia had been oppressed for refusing to annex their church to the State Church of King Frederick III of Prussia. Angas saw them as highly suitable migrants, being hardworking and sufficiently idealistic to resist tyranny. He thus arranged with Pastor August Ludwig Christian Kavel to bring out the first three boatloads of German migrants from Silesia in 1838, and provided the finance for the venture. The first German settlement of twenty-eight Lutheran families took place in 1842 at Bethany, sometimes called Neuschlesien: New Silesia.

Many others followed these first migrants to the new land, where they settled in the Barossa Valley, worked hard and prospered. Naturally, many of the Silesians turned to viticulture, and among the German settlers were men whose

names are household words today. The first man to plant vines in the Barossa was Johann Gramp, who in 1847 established a small vineyard at Jacob's Creek, just 2 km from the present giant Orlando winery. The same year Samuel Hoffmann settled at Tanunda. Joseph Seppelt arrived in Australia from Germany in 1849 and settled in the Barossa Valley in 1851 with the intention of growing tobacco. He soon switched his interests to viticulture. So began the House of Seppelt.

Although the German settlers were of major importance, the English colonists also did their bit. Samuel Smith founded the Yalumba winery in 1849, and William Salter began his vineyard near Angaston ten years later, in 1859 (Saltrams).

Thus within two decades from the time the first European set foot in the Barossa Valley, the foundations of the industry that was to be so much a part of the story of Australian wine were firmly laid.

The Barossa Valley has enjoyed good fortune

and is today recognised as the key growth area of the Australian wine industry, with some of the biggest and best-known wineries based there. Above all, it escaped the horrors of phylloxera, which did such damage in the neighbouring state of Victoria. This was not only good luck; rigid vine quarantine measures were enforced by Act of Parliament. The vintners of the Barossa have worked for their success, but they could not have done it without the natural advantages of the area—plus a dash of good luck.

Clare-Watervale

The Clare area is the most northerly of the South Australian wine districts, about 130 km from Adelaide. The countryside is hilly and no doubt would have reminded the early German settlers of parts of the Rhine Valley, where grapes had been grown for centuries. The only survivor of the early Clare vineyards is the Sevenhills College Vineyard, originally planted by a group of Austrian Jesuit fathers in 1848. Other vineyards in the same area, such as the one planted by John Ward in 1854 and another planted by Valentine Mayr in 1859, no longer exist.

Seven Hill Vineyards and Winery, Clare
— one of the oldest in South Australia.

Clare Valley, South Australia.

The first vineyard at Springvale was a small one planted by Francis Treloar in 1865. In 1889 the firm of H. Buring and Sobels bought the Quelltaler property. Wine is still being made there, although several companies, most recently Wolf Blass, have taken over the company and the property.

In 1896 the Stanley Wine Company was founded, as was the family concern of A.P. Birks. Both these companies are still in existence, though again under different control. Stanley-Leasingham passed into the hands of H.J. Heinz of Pittsburgh, Pennsylvania, in the early 1970s, and into the hands of Hardy's in early 1988.

Langhorne Creek

In 1860 Mr Frank Potts planted the Bleasdale vineyard 50 km south-east of Adelaide at Langhorne Creek on the Bremer River. The Bleasdale vineyards are still owned by the Potts family and continue to produce wines, especially reds, sought after for their flavour.

Coonawarra

Coonawarra, from the Aboriginal 'place of wild honeysuckle', is some 350 km south-east of Adelaide, close to the state's border with Victoria. The area is not only isolated geographically, but also historically. The history of the area is most interesting—being quite different and not nearly as smooth running as the other South Australian wine areas. The name of John Riddoch features prominently in the Coonawarra story but another man, whom history has largely forgotten, was the first to plant fruit trees and vines in the area. In fact, his success was Riddoch's inspiration.

William Wilson, born 1819 in Scotland, came to Australia after some years as a soldier in the Mediterranean. It was he who discovered, without really knowing it, the unique red 'terra rossa' soil of Coonawarra.

After a modest gold strike at Ballarat, Wilson bought just under a hectare at Penola. The climate there reminded him of the Mediterranean regions of Spain and France where he had been stationed. Wilson planted fruit trees and vines, and they flourished.

Enter John Riddoch, the Scottish-born 'Squire of Penola'. He came to Australia with the gold rush but discovered that running trading posts was a better way of making money. He bought Yallum Park (Yallum being an Aboriginal word for 'grassy') outside Penola in 1861 and gradually extended his holding to 250 sq. km. Riddoch became a member for the Victoria district in the South Australian Parliament from 1865 to 1873. He was also a close friend of the poet Adam Lindsay Gordon. In 1881 Riddoch built a magnificent sandstone mansion, which was at the time compared to the palace of Versailles, and this was surrounded by a deer park, splendid gardens and an orchard. Sheep were always John Riddoch's main interest, and it was from these that he made his money. He and his brother George built up enormous flocks.

In about 1890 Riddoch decided the land should be thrown open for closer settlement. Acting on the advice of Professor Perkins, agriculturist with the State Government, he resolved to establish a fruit colony in the belief that 'with intense cultivation the land might be made to support a large population, combining the advantages of rural, healthy life with the pleasures of social intercourse'. Acting on William Wilson's advice, Riddoch determined that it should be started on the stretch of red soil Wilson had done so well on.

In June 1890 Riddoch advertised the intended Coonawarra Fruit Colony subdivisions of 4 hectare (10 acre) blocks at £10 per acre with 5 per cent per annum interest. The offer involved 464 hectares, 75 per cent of which were taken up. Originally twenty-six colonists took up Riddoch's offer, and planted apples, peaches and apricots, and grapes. Riddoch himself planted 140 hectares of vines—shiraz, cabernet sauvignon, pinot noir and malbec—and encouraged the colonists to plant in the proportion of one-third cabernet to two-thirds shiraz. In the first season 95 000 vines were established.

Riddoch built a winery with cellars which held 340 000 litres, and he bought the colonists' grapes. This building, which was built in the 1890s, is still used and is well known throughout Australia from its black-and-white and black-and-red stylised representation on Wynn's Coonawarra labels. Riddoch also intended to build a jam factory, though this never eventuated.

The growers formed the Coonawarra Fruit and Winegrowers' Association. Early vintages at

Coonawarra showed the area's capabilities. The wines of 1895 and 1896 were of 'superior quality'. However, Coonawarra grapes were never much good for brandy because of their low spirit yield, and thus the area suffered greatly when there was a lack of demand for table wine. By the beginning of the twentieth century Riddoch had thousands of litres of wine on his hands and could not sell it.

Riddoch died in 1901 at the age of seventy-three, only ten years after the foundation of the fruit colony—a practical visionary whose scheme did not work out the way he had planned. His brother George died three years later and their huge land holdings were divided by the government.

John Riddoch died in the year of the federation of the Australian states—and also the year that Bill Redman arrived at Coonawarra. Redman was to have more influence on the wines of Coonawarra this century than any other individual.

The history of Coonawarra in the twentieth century is one of crisis after crisis. Although the area made dry red wines of outstanding quality, only a few people appreciated them; and it was only in the 1950s that Coonawarra began to come into its own. It is curious that the three areas (the Hunter, Coonawarra and Great Western), which have made many of Australia's top table wines, have shared long stretches of hard times and crisis before achieving widespread recognition. The later history of the Coonawarra area is given in the Redman and Wynn entries, but it's fair to say that most wine authorities now acknowledge that Coonawarra is Australia's greatest red wine district, and one of the best producers of great reds in the world.

The Murray Valley

Water is the lifeblood of the settlement along the Murray River. When Captain Charles Sturt first explored the area in 1830 he found only red sandy alluvial flats, sandhills with 'not a blade of grass', stunted box-trees, some blue gums and scattered Aboriginal tribes. Now, of course, the river has been put to use for irrigation, and the vines of the Murray Valley have yielded millions and millions of litres of wines and spirits.

The story of this transformation began with Alfred Deakin, later Prime Minister of Australia,

who was travelling in the United States as a Royal Commissioner on Water Supply for the Victorian Government in the 1880s. There he met the Chaffey brothers, George and William Benjamin, who were involved in establishing an irrigation settlement in California. He persuaded them to come to Australia to begin a similar project. To his eternal credit, Deakin realised that the Murray Valley was ideal for such a development—and that the Chaffeys were the right people for the job.

George and William Benjamin Chaffey were born in Canada at Brockville, Ontario, but came to Australia as Americans following their most successful venture in California, where a second Ontario became famous as an irrigated paradise in the Cucamonga Valley. The partnership of Chaffey Bros, with George as the creator and engineer of irrigation settlements, and W.B. as convenor, adviser and administrator, looked to the dry but potentially fertile banks of the Murray River. George, the older brother, then aged thirty-eight, arrived in Australia first and saw the Renmark area, then a part of the Bookmark sheep station, which was nothing but a flat, hot, barren slab of land.

In February 1887 the brothers signed an agreement with the South Australian Government and later a similar agreement with the Victorian Government. The plan was that the Chaffeys would prepare and irrigate land, sell it in blocks on time payment and use the revenue for further development. Two settlements were started—first at Renmark and then at Mildura in Victoria. Within a year, land was on offer at £20 an acre for orchard blocks, £20 each for town allotments, and £100 for residential sites, with ten years to pay. In South Australia the Chaffeys were to receive an acre of land freehold for every £4 spent by them or property owners in development.

Settlers were encouraged to the area, and many came from England in response to highly-coloured descriptions of the glorious future of the area. Life in those pioneering days was hard, and it became harder when the Chaffeys went bankrupt with the bank crash of 1893. At that time a Royal Commission, in an extraordinary finding, found them guilty of mismanagement. With the crash, development stopped dead and many settlers abandoned their properties. George

Chaffey borrowed enough for his fare and went back to the United States, where he later completed irrigation works that made Renmark and Mildura seem insignificant.

W.B. Chaffey stayed on at his vineyard at Mildura. During this dark period the Renmark Irrigation Trust was created by Act of Parliament in 1893. The Trust was set up to administer the area and was controlled by the growers themselves. The early years of the Irrigation Trust's control were tough going, but they persevered and eventually made it work.

Before prosperity, Renmark had to face the drought of 1914, when the Murray dried to a mere trickle. Without water the settlement was doomed, and it was realised that a system of locks was essential. An agreement was made between the New South Wales, Victorian and South Australian Governments to erect a series of locks which would ensure that the level of the river was maintained throughout the year.

The story of how winemaking began in the irrigation settlements, in an attempt to make use of the unwanted gordo grapes that had been grown for drying, is told in a later chapter.

South Australia from 1870

It was clear from early days that this state, established without the dubious benefit of convict labour, could grow grapes successfully for winemaking, drying and the table. Many of the vineyard areas of South Australia were established rapidly after the founding of the colony. From 1846 to 1852 the colony's area under vines was quadrupled and by 1856 the vintage exceeded 450 000 litres from about 300 hectares of vines. Expansion continued at a remarkable rate, and from 1861 to 1867 the area under vines had grown from 1600 hectares to 2500 hectares, and the vintage from 2.1 million litres to 4 million litres. South Australian wine was by then finding its way to other states, and there was even some exported to England.

In its rapid expansion, the South Australian wine industry took no heed of economic limits and by 1870 saturation point was reached. The home market was glutted and interstate markets offered little promise, for both Victoria and New South Wales imposed stiff discriminatory tariffs against South Australian wines to protect their own makers. The bottom fell out of the London market—in haste for profits, considerable quantities of poor-quality, raw young wine had been shipped to England, and the long voyage did not help either. Some of this wine was sold at only one shilling and fourpence a gallon, and some had to be shipped back at the owner's expense. As a result, scores of unprofitable vineyards were uprooted, and between 1865 and 1885 the area of vines in the colony fell by a third. It took twenty years before the original ground was recovered.

The 1880s and 1890s were great years for South Australian viticulture. Through the first of the decades the industry gradually overcame its slump, confidence returned and planting was resumed. By 1889 more than 3000 hectares were under vine, the vintage topped 4.5 million litres, and there were seventy recognised winemakers in the colony, half of them in a substantial way. Five years later the vintage was climbing rapidly towards 9 million litres, which it reached at the turn of the century. Increased volume was accompanied by increased attention to quality. An incentive to improve standards were the colonial and overseas exhibitions of the period, at which the best Australian wines competed with those of European vineyards, and were far from disgraced.

By the end of the century Victorian vineyards were being ravaged by phylloxera, which South Australia had escaped. In 1899 the South Australian Parliament promptly passed an act which imposed rigid quarantine measures under the supervision of a newly established Phylloxera Board. The Act put a levy on winemakers for the creation of a fund to assist the industry with replantings should the need arise. The introduction of any vines or plants from infected areas was prohibited, and a nursery of resistant stocks was established in Victoria in case of need. Whether by good management or good fortune, South Australia was kept free of disease for over a century.

During the latter half of the nineteenth century, family wine dynasties prospered. They included names such as Seppelt, Gramp (of Orlando fame), Hardy, Reynell, Tolley, Smith (of Yalumba), and Hamilton.

At the turn of the nineteenth century the South Australian wine industry was riding the crest of a vinous wave. The area under vines had increased to 8440 hectares, yielding almost 10 million litres of wine. With Federation the customs barriers between the states were removed and South Australia was poised to expand its interstate markets and establish itself as the premier wine state of the Commonwealth.

It remains that way to this day.

Western Australia

The history of viticulture in Western Australia goes back almost to the founding of the colony, which officially came into being on 18 June 1829 when a special proclamation was read aloud on the banks of the Swan River. Once again we run into a historical controversy on 'firsts'. Who planted the first vines in the west? The contenders are Thomas Waters of Olive Farm and Captain John Septimus Roe of Sandalford.

Captain Roe was one of the original settlers of the colony, who arrived on the *Parmelia* in June 1829. He became the colony's first Surveyor-General and in 1840 was granted a property he called Sandalford. Assuming he planted his vines immediately, he would still have been later than Thomas Waters, who appears to have a far stronger case. Further, Roe's vines were for table grapes and currants only.

Waters arrived in Western Australia just later than Roe in September 1829. He was a botanist who brought all sorts of seeds and plants with him from South Africa, and was granted a property on the banks of the Swan River on his arrival. The annual report of the Western Australian Agricultural Society in 1834 reported that one settler had one-fifth of a hectare of vines planted—in all probability this was Thomas Waters. He had learned to make wine from the Boers in South Africa, and a letter dated 1842 records that he used wine made at Olive Farm to barter for other goods. This is the earliest proof of wine being made there. In the absence of further evidence, it is reasonable to suppose that Thomas Waters planted the first grapevines in Western Australia soon after his arrival in 1829. Vines were also planted at the Houghton property in 1836, according to recent research.

Interestingly, it follows then that Western Australia has a longer viticultural history than either Victoria or South Australia: Edward Henty planted the first vines at Portland in

Victoria in 1834; while John Barton Hack was first in South Australia with his North Adelaide vineyard in 1837.

Houghton claims to be the first vineyard in which wine was made commercially. There is evidence that the then owner, Dr John Ferguson, made 135 litres of wine in 1859. Whether this was more 'commercial' than Thomas Waters' wine, which was used for barter, remains a matter of conjecture.

The centre of viticultural activity in Western Australia has always been the Swan Valley, north-east of Perth, from where the bulk of the production has come. There are records of early developments in other areas, however, such as the Bussells at Ellenbrook in the 1830s, although whether these were table or wine grapes we do not know. In the Mount Barker area, F. and C. Piesse planted a vineyard at Katanning in the 1880s, which disappeared by the end of World War I. Bunbury was represented in the early days by Ephraim Clark, who planted vines just south of there in 1890.

Back in the Swan expansion continued, particularly after 1860. Houghton, the winery best known outside Western Australia, had its first commercial vintage in 1859 from vines planted more than two decades earlier. Valencia, a long-renowned name phased out in the early 1980s, was first planted to grapes in the 1890s by a partnership which included the skilled viticulturist Adrian d'Espeissis. The large companies have continued making wine since then.

This century has seen many Swan Valley wineries run by European settlers, many from Yugoslavia. Only in recent years has the West Australian wine scene expanded dramatically. New areas have come into being, notably Mount Barker, Margaret River and Moondah Brook.

Houghton was bought in 1976 by Hardy's, from South Australia, after a takeover tussle with local entrepreneur Robert Holmes à Court. Hardy's won (reportedly because Mr Holmes à Court was himself tussling with the mumps), and after extensive investment Houghton easily remains the biggest winemaker in Western Australia. The state produces only a very small proportion of the nation's wine, but commands a larger slice of history—and clearly has a lot to offer in the quality area.

Queensland

The hot Queensland climate is not generally suitable for growing grapes for wine, so it is not surprising that little wine has been made there. However, there has been a small winemaking industry there since the 1850s—the time of Queensland's separation from New South Wales.

The first recorded grapevine to be planted in the Stanthorpe area on the 'Granite Belt' was a white syrian planted near the town of Ballandean in 1859. The planting was to mark the establishment of Queensland as a colony in its own right, so that grapegrowing has been at least a small part of the district's heritage since this time. The vine still exists and has produced as much as 680 kg of fruit per vintage.

Winemaking was started by Father Davadi, a Roman Catholic priest, in the late 1870s. The district was at that time almost entirely dependent on the alluvial tin-mining industry, and Father Davadi realised that mineral reserves were declining. Seeing the resemblance between the climate and terrain of the district and those of his native Italy, Father Davadi conducted a campaign to persuade landowners and others to enter the fruit and wine industries. He planted his first vineyard in the house paddock of the presbytery. This planting, and a larger one at the foot of Mt Marley, was successful. Father Davadi later sold the larger vineyard to the Vichie family, also of Italian origin. The remains of the original Vichie wine cellars are still in existence.

Winemaking, except for personal use and for the bulk trade, declined some decades later with only a few Italian makers carrying on small businesses. It was only some ten years ago that the commercial production of quality bottled wines was re-introduced to the Granite Belt. A memorial to Father Davadi and his contribution to the wine and fruit industries was recently erected outside the Stanthorpe Catholic Church.

The other centre of winemaking in Queensland has been at Roma, some distance northwest of Stanthorpe. Samuel S. Bassett, a Cornishman, established a vineyard there in 1863, which for many years was the dominant force in the Queensland winemaking industry. The company was owned by the family for more than one hundred years.

Some good table wines have emerged from the Granite Belt in recent years and, over a longer period, some superb fortified wines from the Roma district.

Tasmania

Little wine has been made in Tasmania in the past, probably mainly because the climate, with its low heat summations, is unsuitable for the production of fortified wine. It is also probable that early attempts to grow grapes were frustrated by the inability to control powdery mildew and downy mildew and some of the vine pests.

Clearly, though, a few valiant aspiring vignerons recognised that Tasmania, lying between 41° and 43° south of the Equator, had something geographically in common with the great northern wine areas of France and Germany. So they set out to establish vineyards in Tasmania in the early nineteenth century.

The first commercial plantings were made by Bartholomew Broughton at his Prospect Farm in the early 1820s. Broughton was a convict, who became a Treasury clerk, gained a pardon and purchased a substantial property—no mean feat for the time (though it would hardly be unusual today!). Although the exact date of his first plantings is unknown, *The Times* of London reported from Van Diemen's Land in 1824 that 'grapes, in particular, had succeeded beyond expectation'. By 1827 Broughton's wines were eliciting much local praise, such as from the *Colonial Times*, which recorded that one local judge declared Mr Broughton's wine as superior to Mr Blaxland's as 'fine Port to Blackstrap'.

Broughton died in 1828 at the age of thirty-two. Captain Charles Swanston purchased the property and carried on the wine production Broughton had started. Swanston has been described as a 'commercial adventurer', who planted further vines and increased production to 7300 litres by 1848. He was, perhaps, a marketer born in the wrong century, as he also sold some exotically-named liqueurs such as Chinois, Eau d'Or and Angelique. Despite his success, Swanston's death in 1850 brought an end to wine production on the property, the new owner showing no interest in viticulture.

In the 1840s Dr Mathias Gaunt of Windemere, East Tamar (just to the north of Laun-

ceston on the island state), was making his own wine from grapes growing on his property. Around the 1830s William Effingham Lawrence had approximately 1.5 hectares of vines planted near the junction of the South Esk and Tamar Rivers within the city of Launceston. There are a number of indications that other grapevines were grown for wine at this time, but none of the planted areas was extensive. However, at the Melbourne Intercolonial Exhibition of 1866 there were eight Tasmanian vignerons entered in the appropriate section.

From that time, the industry went into a decline until the arrival of Diego Bernacchi in 1884. An Italian silk merchant, Bernacchi formed the Maria Island Company and had 16 hectares under vine in 1886. He had grand plans of producing 440 000 litres by 1894, but his venture on the isolated, rocky outpost off the east coast of Tasmania collapsed for want of financial support, and went into liquidation.

Perhaps influenced by Bernacchi's aspirations, the Tasmanian Government debated a Bill in 1893 to regulate the sale of locally manufactured wine. It was introduced by W. Gill in an attempt to encourage a wine industry to provide jobs and also encourage temperance. It is a matter of record that this legislation did not eventuate.

Thus, in the end, all nineteenth-century Tasmanian winemaking ventures failed, and by Federation in 1901 Tasmania stood out as the only state that had not achieved and maintained a commercial level of wine production. The major reason for this was probably climatic—the island is not suitable for the fortified wines that were in demand—and the local population preferred beer and spirits anyway. There was to be a long lull until the period between the late 1950s and 1970s, when Tasmania was recognised as an area where high-quality red and white table wines, and very good sparkling wines, could be made—by those willing to chance their arm against the elements, and plant vines in an untried viticultural area.

Australian Wine in the Twentieth Century

The opening years of the new century were particularly favourable for the wine industry of South Australia. A sequence of dry years ended, and in 1902 the vintage mounted to about 11 million litres.

There was a temporary halt in about 1904–5 when there was a slump for a season or two. The vintage was down by nearly half and many vines were affected with diseases, the causes of which were not understood. Growers sold for as low as fifteen shillings a ton or fed their grapes to pigs. The crisis passed fairly quickly and by 1906 the production figures were rising again.

Many of the South Australian wine families understood that to continue successfully in business they would need to develop their markets in the most populous states to the east: New South Wales and Victoria. After Federation in 1901, and the subsequent removal of trade barriers, South Australian wine had free access, and the big companies such as Penfolds and Hardy's were quick to take full advantage of this. In four years the volume exported rose to nearly 4.5 million litres, of which the other Australian states took 3.8 million litres, while interstate sales of spirits mounted nearly tenfold.

This was good for the South Australians but it hit the Hunter Valley winemakers hard. They simply could not compete in price with the South Australian wine, which was cheaper principally because of subsidies to growers by the South Australian Government. As a result, in the next ten years or so more vines were uprooted in the Hunter than at any other time. All this led to rather frosty feelings between the winemakers of the Hunter and South Australia.

The outbreak of World War I severely affected the rising exports of wine to Britain. The effects of this were only felt badly from 1916, though there was an immediate rise in exports after the war. On the home front, the war led to a tremendous amount of hostile feeling to the German settlers, and indeed anything Germanic. This was especially evident in the Barossa Valley of South Australia, where there were many settlers of German descent. There was little ill-will at the outset, but animosity grew with the intensity of the struggle and the increasing Australian casualties. Prejudice was shown in employment, many Germans in public life were subjected to attack, and the South Australian Parliament passed an Act to wipe out German associations by a wholesale changing of place names. By this Act, Kaiser-Stuhl near the Barossa Valley became Mt Kitchener, Siegersdorf ('Conqueror's Village') became Dorrien, and Gnadenfrei became Marananga. (When cooler counsel prevailed years later, some of these names were changed back.)

In the post-war years the government instituted a policy of settling repatriated soldiers on the land. The initial success of the Murray River settlements beckoned governments searching for land on which to settle returned soldiers. In the five years after 1919 there was a record expansion of the irrigation settlements along the Murray and Murrumbidgee Rivers in South Australia, Victoria (at Redcliffs and Merbein) and in New South Wales. Thousands of ex-servicemen, not all suitable for the work, were placed on river blocks planted with vines (many of them doradillo grapes), which promised a quick return, principally from spirit making. Many of these land blocks, whose occupants became known as 'blockers' were not economically viable for this type of cultivation—a problem that became much worse decades later.

In New South Wales, the Hunter Valley shared in the repatriation scheme. Twenty hectares was considered to be a suitable subdivision, and several such blocks at Fordwich were given to returned men. For a variety of reasons the plan failed and the vineyards were later taken over by Tulloch and by Elliott.

Also in New South Wales, the Murrumbidgee Irrigation Area (MIA) underwent enormous expansion at this time. The development of the area had begun only a few years previously with the construction upstream of the Burrinjuck Dam. The first farms in the Griffith area were

Irrigated vines near Griffith.

Vineyard and windmill in the Riverina, New South Wales.

taken up in 1912 and irrigation and planting began in 1913. With the arrival in the area of large numbers of inexperienced farmers, numerous problems had to be overcome. Unsuitable grape varieties were planted, and unsatisfactory methods of cultivation and irrigation adopted.

In a few years the new wine-producing areas on the Murray grew to rank near the top in terms of quantity. South Australia, for long the leading wine state producing 60 to 70 per cent of the commonwealth vintage, went still further ahead to provide up to 75 or 80 per cent of the Australian total. In 1919–20 the South Australian vintage was 22.5 million litres; by 1923–24 it passed 45 million litres for the first time.

The expansion was too rapid to be digested, and it was realised that wine was being made which could not be sold. Before 1924 was over, reaction had set in. Its first manifestation was a glut of doradillos—fat white grapes of neutral flavour which yielded heavily and were suitable for distillation and maybe for sherry-making. Grapes that two or three years before had been selling at £12–£14 a ton fell rapidly to fetch only £4 a ton or less. It was a story of excessive enthusiasm and optimism that led to production far in excess of demand. The industry was to feel the effects of this over-production for decades.

World War I and what followed was no help to the Rutherglen area. The early years of the century had seen something of a revival there, although few growers took part in it. After the war, costs of production rose and the land was put to other uses, notably wool. The decline was to continue for many years.

After the slump following the over-production of the early 1920s, expansion followed a somewhat more orderly and judicious program. The area under vines increased each year by an average of about 200 hectares, so that in the next ten years South Australia's area of vineyards rose gradually to 21 000 hectares. In 1927 its vintage exceeded 73 million litres.

The decade of the 1920s was not the happiest in the Hunter Valley. World War I helped the vineyards recover to some extent from the problems of the previous years; in 1922 there were 1000 hectares in full bearing. But soon downy mildew hit badly. In 1925 this disease destroyed three-quarters of the crop, the following year a similar loss was caused by drought, and in 1927

extensive hail virtually wiped out the entire vintage. After a great year in 1928 (there is always a little silver lining), disaster struck from another direction. In 1929 there was enormous industrial unrest in the mines with a sixteen-month lockout and considerable civil strife. The local wine market collapsed a year ahead of the world depression of the early 1930s.

From the late 1920s there were many portents of the coming economic storm. Australian rural industries were facing serious difficulties, with apparent over-production, under-consumption and a disastrous decline in export prices. Other industries, notably the New South Wales coal industry, also showed symptoms of worsening economic conditions. With the real onset of the depression the wine industry passed through one of its worst crises. Export to England fell, and the local market faded away—Australian consumption of wine declined by 60 per cent. The price of grapes fell to £2 a ton for cheaper varieties and real disaster faced the industry.

Many vineyards were torn out and given over to sheep and cattle for, although a fortune could not be made from them, at least they offered a living. During a glut at Coonawarra the State Government intervened and agreed to pay all soldier-settlers with a fruit block a subsidy of £4–£10 an acre to pull out their grapes and start dairy farms. As a result many Coonawarra vineyards disappeared. Of the original 300 hectares only 120 remained. Victoria lost thousands of hectares of vines around Ararat and Stawell. It lost them in the Yarra Valley and in Central Victoria.

In South Australia the Barossa vignerons survived by concentrating on fortified and sweet wines to fill what demand there was for wine. The demand was largely for sweet fortified wine simply because this was the cheapest form of alcohol available.

Partly as a response to these problems, and to problems in the United Kingdom market, the Commonwealth Government established the Australian Wine Board in 1929 under the Wine Overseas Marketing Act of that year. Its charter was to supervise and promote exports of Australian wine and to promote wine quality and research. It succeeded well, both with exports and with solving some of the spoilage problems which faced the industry. In 1937, for example, more Australian wine was exported, mainly to the UK, than was consumed at home (18 million litres against 16 million litres drunk in Australia).

Tragedy, War and Opportunity

Recovery from the depression was slow, and although the situation gradually improved from 1932 to 1938 the industry was in a generally unstable position.

There was a tragic note for the winemaking industry in 1938 when three leading industry figures were killed in a plane crash on their way to a Wine Board meeting with the government in Canberra. They were all chief executives of their companies, Tom Mayfield Hardy of Hardy's, Hugo Gramp of Orlando and Sidney Hill Smith of Yalumba. The DC-2 'Kyeema', trying to find Essendon airport near Melbourne, flew into the fog-bound slopes of the Dandenong Ranges.

World War II gave the wine industry a much-needed fillip. Exports were naturally severely curtailed—they fell from 17 million litres in 1939 to 7 million litres in 1945. Home consumption increased tremendously in the same period, from 16 million litres to nearly 40.5 million litres. The reason for the increased consumption during the war years may have been partly because wine was sold on a quota system, which made most people battle for their allowance. It seems more likely that the presence of local and visiting servicemen had a strong influence on sales of wine. The bulk of this wine was fortified, but gradually table wine (that is, unfortified) became more popular, and by 1946 about 40 per cent of wine was in this category.

At war's end the government again had a policy of settling returning soldiers on the land, often hard land. It was at this time that the Loxton irrigation area near Renmark in South Australia was established, as was the Robinvale settlement in Victoria. In other places, however, the decline in vineyard area continued. In the Hunter Valley in 1947 only about 445 hectares of vines remained (compared with the 1866 peak of more than five times that amount). In Victoria the area under vine also continued to fall.

With the ending of World War II came a notable change in the marketing of wine. Before this, wine (along with many other food commodities) had largely been unlabelled and sold in bulk. Hotels and other outlets bought in bulk and sold from the cask by the glass, in the customers' containers or bottled under their own labels. With temporary shortages after the war, the big wine companies seized the opportunity to sell in bottles under their own labels so that their names became more widely known. While this marketing change led to an increase in wine quality, it was also largely responsible for the increased cost of wine.

In the post-war period the Australian community became more affluent. The 1946 initiative of Immigration Minister Arthur Calwell also saw the beginning—very significantly for the Australian wine industry—of a stream of millions of displaced and dispossessed European immigrants seeking new homes Down Under.

The Decades of Sweeping Change

For several decades after World War II the industry was still based around fortified wines, but enormous and probably lasting changes in public taste were on the way. Until 1959 Australians drank more fortified wines, sherries, ports and so on, than table wines. But some of the makers saw the signs of change. The first signs of a revival were there: Wynns and Mildara moved into the Coonawarra area; different grape varieties were being tried; investments were made in new technology, which was to be the key to the future.

The most significant arbiter of change came from Orlando. This company installed temperature control equipment in their Barossa Valley winery to enable them to make more white wines in the Germanic style in the early to mid-1950s. The first was the epochal 1953 Barossa Rhine Riesling, a white wine that showed that Australian white wines could have strong and vibrant fruit flavours. It would take other makers some years to grasp the enormous marketing impact the application of this technology offered. And nearby in the Barossa Valley a young winemaker called Ian Hickinbotham used similar technology to make a sparkling, fruity wine described as 'Pearl', which would take young Australia by storm and start a new wine boom.

The boom came with the 1960s. Annual consumption of wine increased from 5 litres a head in the early 1960s to 8.2 litres a head in 1969, and this increase was almost entirely because of the greater popularity of table wines. Evidence of this boom was everywhere—the proliferation of books and articles on wine, the shortage of premium wines and the unbelievably high prices they commanded, and a wave of new plantings all over the country, many in previously untried areas. Why? Why after so many years did wine drinking become the 'in' thing?

People now had more money to spend on the good things of life and discovered that wine was a very good thing indeed—especially with the better and more varied food that the European immigration had introduced. This affluence brought with it widespread ownership of the motor car, enabling many to take advantage of the proximity of the vineyards to Australia's capital cities. It became a commonly enjoyed weekend pastime to drive out to the vineyards, sample their offerings, and buy a bottle or two. A 'cellar', not an inexpensive investment by any means, became a status symbol.

The Australian Wine Bureau, some writers and other personalities made an organised effort to educate people about drinking and enjoying Australian wine. The wine companies increased the volume of their advertising and changed the nature of their promotion. They began to stress the no-nonsense theme, 'drink what you like with what you like', and aimed to appeal to young people. And it all worked.

'Cellarmaster' in *The Bulletin* began the first regular wine column in 1962. In 1965 the Wine Bureau began to put editors and writers together, and from about that time things really began to move. Writers and journalists such as Frank Margan, Frank Doherty, Jack Ludbrook, Neville Baker, Dan Murphy, Keith Dunstan and, of course, Len Evans all had an inestimable influence in popularising table wine. By informing the public and providing an interesting background to wine and how to enjoy it, they introduced a great many people to the pleasures of drinking wine with a meal.

Len's efforts are now multiplied a hundred times by wine columnists in almost all of the newspapers and many of the national magazines, even some radio and television stations; today Australians know more about wine than ever before.

Their efforts were backed and encouraged by Wine and Brandy Producers' Associations and the Australian Wine and Brandy Corporation (successor to the Australian Wine Board), a commonwealth statutory authority which deserves recognition for its long-term efforts in the promotion of Australian wines within Australia and overseas.

Various wine and food societies were an additional cause and effect of the wine boom. The senior bodies, such as The Bacchus Club in South Australia and the Wine and Food Societies of New South Wales and Victoria, played an important role in spreading the appreciation of good food and wine in the community. With this increased awareness many new societies sprung up, and so the snowball effect continued.

The White Wine Boom

Perhaps most important of all, the quality of the wines being offered by wineries was increasing dramatically. White wines were at the forefront in the 1970s and, in mid-1975, for the first time white wine sales surpassed the sales of reds. The white wine boom was happening as Australia itself changed, matured and started enjoying itself. As a team of university researchers from Newcastle, New South Wales said, in effect 'the men and women of Australia got to know each other over a glass of mutually appreciated white wine'.

If wine became 'trendy' in the 1970s, a decade of tremendous change, the single most dramatic happening was the swing to white wine, and the virtual collapse of the red wine market. Conversely in the late 1970s and 1980s the sales of 'cask' wines (4 litre collapsible plastic bags inside cardboard boxes) rocketed. The public's familiarity with wine and price were dominant factors in this boom, as was the high quality, compared with *vin ordinaire* wines of Europe and elsewhere, brought about by the high level of Australian winemaking technology.

The effects of the white wine boom of this period on the industry were traumatic. Some companies went under, marketing strategies had to be changed and plantings altered—drastically. It was boom-bust-boom, before some semblance of stability appeared in the late 1980s.

A major factor in the increased popularity of whites was the new technology of closed and temperature-controlled fermentation in stainless steel tanks. This resulted in fresher, more aromatic and consistent white wines. Further, the introduction of the residual sugar style (meaning some natural grape sugar could be left in the finished wine), begun with Orlando's Barossa Rhine Riesling and Yalumba's Pewsey Vale, ensured the continued success of white wines. Today Australian wine drinkers accept whites such as these and other major brands as the norm.

Wine casks, which now have a place in thousands of Australian refrigerators, appeared in the 1970s. The first cardboard 4 litre box was introduced by Wynns in 1971. Despite some initial technical problems, the advantages of having a glass or two of wine readily available at low cost were rapidly appreciated. Now over a half of all Australian wine sales are in casks (the industry calls them 'bag-in-box', the public sometimes know them as 'Chateau Cardboard'!).

The Trade Practices Act of 1975 opened the way for a subsequent price-discounting war which appeared on the surface to be of benefit to the consumer, but was hard on profitability in the industry. Costs were such that many companies lost money on cask and flagon wines, but discounting continued.

The industry remains increasingly divided: the mass market, with casks and flagons which involve volume drinking at a lower price; and the premium end, with an emphasis on quality varietals from top areas. And this led to another trend—the dramatic growth in boutique wineries in areas such as the Hunter Valley, Western Australia and many areas of Victoria. These are small concerns often run by enthusiastic amateurs on a part-time basis, many of whom intend to produce top varietal wines (with varying degrees of success).

A whole new atlas of winemaking areas was written in the 1970s and 1980s—the Upper Hunter and Mudgee took off in New South Wales, and Clare emerged as an area in its own right. The really outstanding moves occurred in Victoria and Western Australia. In Victoria, the Yarra Valley and the Pyrenees began to make their presence felt with some top-quality wines, with other areas such as Gippsland in their infancy. In Western Australia a host of new names such as Margaret River and Mount Barker appeared, bringing with them a promise of some exciting wines to come. Even Tasmania and Queensland, states that were earlier not considered to be good viticultural prospects, now have growing wine businesses.

The late 1970s and 1980s could be called the 'decades of the varietals'. All sorts of experimental plantings were carried out, and chardonnay, led by Tyrrells, became *the* white grape. Sauvignon blanc, cabernet sauvignon, pinot noir and blends of reds such as cabernet–malbec–merlot and cabernet–cabernet franc, introduced wine drinkers to the delights of complexity in red wines.

There have been many other developments—a very strong growth in bottle-fermented sparkling wines, a decline in the fortified-wine market, the emergence of a new generation of young winemakers, some moves towards 'appellation' control, company amalgamations and takeovers . . . years of ferment for an ever-changing industry.

In recent times, governments have appeared more likely to intervene, in one way or another, as the anti-alcohol lobby gains strength, refusing to acknowledge that moderate wine consumption is good for us. There was an increasing clamour to control liquor consumption by taxation and other means, such as label warnings, similar to those adopted in some parts of the United States. In 1989 South Australian Premier John Bannon, representing the state still growing almost two-thirds of the nation's wine grapes, persuaded the industry to agree to the formation of a new 'umbrella' industry body, the Federation of Australian Winemaker Organisations, to present governments, both state and federal, with a more unified view of the wine industry's position on import issues such as taxation, health and other bureaucratic controls.

At the end of the 1980s and the beginning of the 1990s, the Australian wine industry appeared to be slowly settling down. About 85 per cent of Australia's wine was being sold by about ten or a dozen of the country's 560 winemakers, leaving the other 550 makers to split up the specialised, higher priced, high-quality, cellar door end. Red wine sales rose in 750 ml glass bottles, as sparkling wines continued to rise too. Overall consumption of wine fell from a peak in the late

1980s of almost 23 litres per person a year down to the present level of about 19 litres.

Even though there are more Australian wineries than ever before, the battle to grab market share has become increasingly more fierce. The business of brand management—major makers producing large quantities of wine and advertising their brands aggressively—is now par for the course in order to make required profits for shareholders. Takeover raiders are always on the lookout for brands, for cash flow and for disposable assets, and more family names (such as Seppelt) have disappeared from the boards, even though they remain the company names.

Grape prices rose dramatically as the export boom of the 1980s and better profits fuelled the interest of competitors. Australia's biggest winemaker, Penfolds, is controlled by Adsteam, which also owns interests as diverse as major retail chains and food manufacturers; several overseas players, presumably disillusioned with profitability, have sold their stakes in the Australian wine industry. H.J. Heinz sold Stanley, and Reckitt & Colman sold Orlando to a management buy-out team. A year later, the French liquor giant Pernod Ricard bought Orlando, which then acquired Hunter Valley maker, The Wyndham Estate. Further changes are expected as the race for performance continues.

The big have become bigger, and may yet get bigger, with more takeover activity forecast. The middle-sized companies are finding the going rough, and the small winemakers, including people from many other walks of life, still enjoy the vigneron lifestyle and work hard to produce even more diverse wines.

Australian Wines Abroad

As we have seen, it was intended from the earliest days that Australia would supply at least part of the demand for wine in Britain. A flood of Australian wine has been sold in Britain over the years, but its quality and the prejudices of the British people have been such that Australia's reputation as a winemaking country has for long been distinctly unfavourable.

The first wine shipped to London was Gregory Blaxland's 1822 vintage, which The Royal Society of Arts honoured with the award of a gold 'Ceres Medal'. The committee of the Society found the wine to be 'a light but sound wine with much of the odour and flavour of Claret, or rather holding an intermediate place between that wine and the red of Nice'. So, from the beginning Australian wine was considered not on its own terms, but rather in comparison with the wines of Europe. This is not surprising, given Australia's geographical isolation and the then 'unknown' quality of its products.

In the early 1840s John Macarthur received prizes for wine exhibited in London, but it was not until the mid-century that any significant quantities of wine were exported. The first year that the Department of Customs and Excise recorded Australian wine in bond in the United Kingdom was 1854. That year the amount noted was 6300 litres but from then on there was a steady increase, until 230 000 litres entered Britain in 1864. The 1860s marked the beginning of a new era in the export of Australian wine, with quite a lot coming from South Australia, where companies were established to supply this perceived market. From the beginning of the nineteenth century, Cape wines enjoyed a preferential tariff in the UK. This ended in February 1860 when the import of South African wines declined considerably, to the advantage of the Australian wine industry.

Exhibitions

In the nineteenth century numerous 'great exhibitions' were held all over the world as a grand form of trade fair. Australian wines were exhibited at many of these and the results were mixed. The first recorded success was at the Paris Exhibition of 1851, after which Australian wine was reputed to be 'in high demand among connoisseurs' abroad. An exhibition at which considerable controversy arose was at Vienna in 1873, when some judges refused to judge the Australian entry because it was felt that 'wines of this quality must clearly be French'.

Australian wine was also exhibited at the Bordeaux Exhibition of 1882, and was awarded some prizes there. In a critical report on these wines, however, M. Emile Dubois noted that 'in general the wines have not been properly clarified before bottling and the bottling has not been done properly'. He found that the grapes were harvested when too ripe and that the jurors

Fruit of the vine.

'believe that you put brandy in the wine'. They found the wines have a 'curious taste of bitterness' and believed that the grapes were planted in brackish soil. The highest number of points awarded any wine was 16 out of 25, and several scored no points at all.

These exhibitions did serve a purpose in bringing attention to Australian wine. The wines usually competed in an 'Empire' or 'Colonial' wines division, and not in open competition with the European products. The awards they won, however numerous, did therefore not mean much to the British.

The colonial 'cultural cringe' in seeking approbation from overseas had its echoes down the years as Australian winemakers constantly sought to show that they could gain medals and awards in 'international' wine competitions, many of them spurious. Today, Australian wineries can boast of successes in places as diverse as Yugoslavia, Britain, the USA and Japan.

The Emu Wine Company

In 1862 the Australian Wine Company was registered in London. The proprietors of this company were Patrick Auld of Auldana vineyards and a Mr Burton, formerly an employee of the Department of Customs and Excise. Their aim was primarily to sell Auldana wine but also to sell Australian wines generally. The Australian Wine Company was the first to popularise and distribute Australian wines in the United Kingdom. In 1883 the manager of the company, James Cox, registered the trade mark 'Emu'. Two years later the company was bought by Aylwin Whately Pownall.

The Emu Wine Company continued to grow and by 1925 was the largest importer of Australian wines in both the United Kingdom and Canada. Five years later, in 1930, the company acquired its first vineyards with the purchase of R.C.H. Walker's property at Morphett Vale, 30 km south of Adelaide.

In 1945 the Emu Wine Company expanded into Western Australia with the purchase of the Valencia Wine Company, and five years later they bought Houghton, one of Western Australia's oldest winemakers. Commonwealth trade preferences saw good markets for this company's wines, initially fortified but later table wines, in the UK and particularly in Canada, where a system of provincial government liquor monopolies exist.

In 1976 Thomas Hardy & Sons acquired the Emu Wine Holdings, the London-based parent of the Emu Wine Company, and retain it to this day, selling wines under this brand in several overseas markets, notably in Canada.

World War I and After
Did it travel well?

During World War I, exports fell considerably because of the lack of shipping. In 1918 only 800 000 litres were exported, but after the war the figures went up again. Practically all Australian wine imported into the United Kingdom up to this time was of the full-bodied dry red type, with an alcoholic strength of about 27 per cent proof spirit (and that's high!). The quality was, at best, uneven.

In 1914 the New South Wales Department of Agriculture held a blind tasting by leading Australian wine merchants of wines that were available at retail shops in London. Of the thirty-seven wines examined, eighteen were considered good (some excellent), six of medium quality, nine indifferent and four bad. Some of their comments are illuminating. Of a 'burgundy' which sold for nineteen shillings a dozen: *Taster 1*: 'A rather rough wine, but otherwise a very good wine for the English market.' *Taster 2*: 'Very rough, sound, good; would not appeal to any wine drinker being too rough.' *Taster 3*: 'Rough, sound, full bodied; typical for the English market.'!

By the early 1920s Australia was faced with a glut of fortified wine, mainly resulting from the over-production of the newly planted irrigation areas. With the home market saturated, it was natural for the local winemakers to turn to the United Kingdom. Unfortunately for them, however, Britain had signed a treaty with Portugal in 1916 which legally reserved the names 'Port' and 'Madeira' for the wines of Portugal and Madeira.

According to H.E. Laffer, who wrote the authoritative *The Wine Industry of Australia* (1949), 'the vital need for Australia was to get rid of bulk stocks representing good, sound, and palatable wines which ultimately proved to the liking of the people in the mass'. The Federal Government then passed The Wine Export Bounty Act of 1924. This applied only to wines of at least 34 per cent proof spirit, as the glut consisted mainly of sweet fortified wine. The bounty was two shillings and ninepence a gallon, to which was added a refund of one shilling and threepence a gallon paid in excise for the fortifying spirit used.

The following year, 1925, the British Government decided that blood was thicker than water and granted Empire wine a 50 per cent preferential margin over foreign wine. This meant, for example, that when foreign wine paid eight shillings a gallon duty, Empire wine only paid four shillings. This was a tremendous help to the Australian industry. Then in 1927, when the situation was looking a little brighter, the Commonwealth Government reduced the bounty by one shilling per gallon.

Consider for a moment what sort of Australian wine was being sold in Britain. The wine was sold at a lower price than the European product, partly because it was regarded as inferior to the wines of Europe. The cheap fortified sweet red 'port style' wines sold well compared to more expensive Port from Portugal. Heavy, fruity Australian reds were sold as 'Australian Burgundy', which was advertised as being good for the health. This burgundy was alleged to contain lots of iron and thus be good for anaemia and invalids. (Dr Penfold had thought the same thing eighty years before. Surely medicine had made more progress than that!) Australian 'boarding-house burgundy' had a lowly reputation in Britain, and obviously the main reason it was bought was because it was a cheap form of alcohol.

In 1929 the Wine Overseas Marketing Act was passed, which set up a Wine Overseas Marketing Board (this later became the Australian Wine Board), with Mr J. Wallace Sandford elected as its first chairman. The following year a London office was opened under the management of Mr H.E. Laffer.

In 1930 the Federal Government imposed steep increases up to 83 per cent in the rate of excise duty on fortifying spirit, and the wine industry successfully pressed the government to place the revenue in a special trust fund for payment of the bounty on exports.

The outbreak of World War II gravely affected the Australian wine industry. In the preceding year some 16 million litres had been exported to Britain, but with war more urgent cargo took priority. In addition, of course, shipping became extremely hazardous. From 1941 the British Government issued an embargo on all imports of wine and spirits, and in the following years very small quotas were imposed—only about 1000 tonnes in 1943.

During the war years, when exports were slight, a considerable balance was built up in the Wine Export Encouragement Trust Account, and by the end of 1946 it was worth £1 000 000 ($2.2 million at a straight conversion rate). The government decided in 1947 to discontinue the bounty, because they claimed higher prices being paid overseas for wine and the increased local consumption made it unnecessary. A sum of £500 000 ($1 million) from the Trust Account was made available for use by the wine industry (which was used in 1955 to set up the Australian Wine Research Institute, a highly successful industry research body based in Adelaide). The balance disappeared into Consolidated Revenue.

Exports to Britain continued during the 1950s and in 1960 the Wine Board opened the Australian Wine Centre in Soho. This was financed by the Board and seventeen leading Australian wine companies, to act as a central supply point in the United Kingdom. The Wine Centre was closed in March 1982, and subsequently many major exporters to the UK operated through their own representatives or through agents. In 1990 the sales of Australian wine in the United Kingdom were growing steadily.

Exporting Australian Wine Today

The 1980s saw a strong boom for Australian wine exports, partly because several key world markets recognised the inherent quality and flavour of Australian wines, and partly because Australia itself gained recognition for a number of reasons and went out selling. In a number of overseas wine competitions wines by aggressive marketers such as Tyrrells, Rosemount and Wolf Blass also gained considerable plaudits. Varietal wines such as chardonnay and cabernet sauvignon were in strong demand in North America, but the boom slowed at the end of the decade for exchange reasons, and probably also because Australian winemakers failed to make an impact in these markets.

Many Australian companies realised the benefits of exporting, if only as a safety valve against a static or government-depressed domestic wine market through taxation. The two major exporters in the 1980s and early 1990s were the Penfolds Group (Penfold, Kaiser Stuhl, Wynn's, TST, Lindeman and Tulloch) and the Hardy Wine Company (Hardy's, Chateau Reynella, Stanley-Leasingham, Houghton). They had the lion's share of the slowing export growth, with vigorous competition from Seppelt, Orlando, Mildara, Berri-Renmano, Wolf Blass, Rosemount and the Wyndham Estate.

As the decade turned, the key overseas markets for Australian wine were in Scandinavia (mainly Sweden, where a government liquor monopoly also exists), the United Kingdom, North America, New Zealand, South-East Asia and Pacific Oceania. The problem that loomed at the beginning of the 1990s was the tariff unification of Europe in 1992; the biggest opportunities appeared to be the imminent relaxation of the trans-Tasman market under Closer Economic Relations with New Zealand, and the likelihood of an expanding Japanese market.

The Australian Wine and Brandy Corporation moved in the late 1980s to regulate exports more strictly, acting against one Hunter winemaker, Tyrrells, for adding an illegal substance, sorbitol, in wine submitted for export. The need to maintain a high standard and police it rigorously was proclaimed.

And the Next 200 Years . . .

As a nation, Australians are today drinking better wines, and more wines from 750 ml glass bottles. We are becoming more discriminating, which is a sign of maturity. Today Australians are the largest wine consumers in the English-speaking world, at around 19 litres a head a year—roughly double that of our American cousins, and our British founders, but still a fair way behind our European educators. The French drink about four times this amount of wine, as do the Italians and the Spaniards and even the Latin nations of South America!

Grapevines and winemaking—not to mention wine drinking—have been around for 6000 years. Australia's 200 years or so of winemaking is not significant in this long history, and many believe that the best Australian wines are yet to come. The improvements are to be made in the vineyard—the winery itself having been brought under the winemaker's full control.

Currently, Australian winemakers are producing the best across-the-board, value-for-money range of wines in the world. As consumers, we now enjoy sound, light wines as part of our everyday lives, without worrying which side of the hill the grapes came from. James Busby would be delighted.

Australian winemakers can look back on what has been done in a young industry, and on a vast continent, with justifiable pride.

GUIDE TO THE REGIONAL MAPS

New South Wales

Len Evans

The Lower Hunter Valley

The Hunter Valley is, without question, one of the great wine-producing areas of Australia. Its wines have not always been fully appreciated, but in recent years the reputation of the Valley has been greatly enhanced as more and more wine lovers discover for themselves the delights of both the area and its wines.

The chequered early history of the Hunter Valley has been described in the section on the history of Australian wine. After Federation in 1901 the Valley went into a long period of decline. It could not compete with the flood of state-government subsidised wines from South Australia. Hectares of once-famous vineyards disappeared, mostly to be used for grazing land. By 1956 only 466 hectares of vineyards remained, in which semillon, hermitage and white shiraz comprised almost the only varieties. The reason for this was, again, economic. The market demand was for fortified wines, for which Hunter material was not especially suitable. Grape varieties were selected to produce well, not for delicacy of varietal character.

The latest Hunter boom began in the 1960s, in which context Max Lake must be mentioned: in 1963 he planted the first new vineyard in the Valley for many years. And then it all took off—big money was poured in by big companies, the Upper Hunter became a new winemaking area, and boutique wineries appeared in profusion. By 1977 the area under vine had increased to 4126 hectares—from which high point there has been a decline. In the mid-1970s the demand for red wine took a serious downturn and the Hunter was severely shaken, with a number of companies going under. However, by the end of the

Max Lake.

1980s there were 2821 bearing hectares from 114 growers.

Why the Hunter Valley has been so successful for wine cultivation is probably because of a combination of factors—soils, climate and, not least, the efforts of the winemakers. Success begets success, and legends of great wines and great winemakers, notably Maurice O'Shea, have developed. This has had a two-way effect. It has perhaps stimulated old and new winemakers to recreate and possibly exaggerate past glories. The 'Hunter mystique' has also encouraged wine lovers to be interested in the area—to visit it to see the renowned vineyards for themselves, but above all to buy, cellar and eventually drink the wines, and in turn to develop new legends of their experiences.

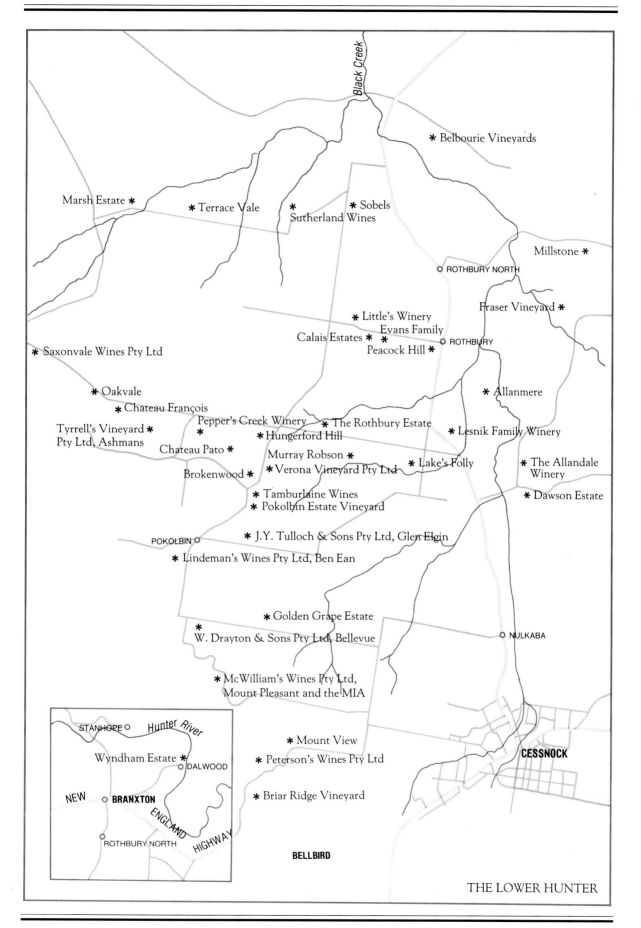

* Belbourie Vineyards

Marsh Estate *

* Terrace Vale   * Sobels
Sutherland Wines

Millstone *

O ROTHBURY NORTH

* Little's Winery
Evans Family
Calais Estates * *
Peacock Hill *   O ROTHBURY

Fraser Vineyard *

* Saxonvale Wines Pty Ltd

* Allanmere

* Oakvale
* Chateau François
Pepper's Creek Winery   * The Rothbury Estate
Tyrrell's Vineyard *   * Hungerford Hill   * Lesnik Family Winery
Pty Ltd, Ashmans
Chateau Pato *
Murray Robson *   * The Allandale
* Verona Vineyard Pty Ltd * Lake's Folly   Winery
Brokenwood *
* Dawson Estate
* Tamburlaine Wines
* Pokolbin Estate Vineyard

POKOLBIN O   * J.Y. Tulloch & Sons Pty Ltd, Glen Elgin
* Lindeman's Wines Pty Ltd, Ben Ean

* Golden Grape Estate
*
W. Drayton & Sons Pty Ltd, Bellevue   O NULKABA

* McWilliam's Wines Pty Ltd,
Mount Pleasant and the MIA

STANHOPE O   Hunter River
* Mount View
Wyndham Estate *   * Peterson's Wines Pty Ltd
O DALWOOD
CESSNOCK
NEW   O BRANXTON
* Briar Ridge Vineyard
ENGLAND
O
ROTHBURY NORTH   HIGHWAY
BELLBIRD

THE LOWER HUNTER

51

The Hunter Valley can be divided into two main vineyard areas. The newer area is the Upper Hunter, west of Muswellbrook. The older vineyards are centred in the parishes of Pokolbin and Rothbury, a short distance from the coal town of Cessnock; the fame of the Hunter has been built on this area, which is the one discussed here.

The Hunter Valley is the largest area of lowland on the east coast of New South Wales. With the exception of the coastal break at Newcastle, it is bounded by uplands from 450 to 1200 m altitude. The Hunter Valley region is about 26 000 sq. km, but grapegrowing is concentrated in a relatively small part of the central lowlands.

Geologically speaking, shale, tuffs, sandstone and conglomerates are the principal constituents, with some lava beds in the basal portions. They form most of the lowland area of the Valley, giving rise to undulating country. There is sandstone plateau to the south, with hilly country and alluvial river flats to the north.

The soils are mostly podsolic, with an absence of free lime in the subsoil. They are fine textured, and generally very dark brown to grey-brown. This type of soil is friable when moist, and soft to hard when dry. There are also some areas of loams, which have concentrations of limestone and vary from red to chocolate in colour. The third type of soil is found in the alluvial river flats. (These differences in soil all have their effects on the grapes produced from them, although the nuances in the wines may not be apparent to any but the real experts.) The most important feature of the soils of the Hunter vineyards is the evidence of the remains of volcanic activity. This is found in a long strip east of the Mount View Range, and in small areas which run in a line north of Mount Pleasant. The majority of top-quality red wines of the Pokolbin area come from this weathered volcanic soil, red clay loam.

Climate has an enormous influence on grape cultivation, and thus on the wine made from them. The average annual rainfall in the Hunter Valley is about 685 mm, but this varies considerably from year to year. The rain is heaviest in summer, with a secondary peak in early winter. There is an average of eighty wet days per year.

Temperatures are moderate. In summer, of which January is usually the hottest month, the mean daily temperature exceeds 21.1°C. In winter the mean minimum is about 4.4°C, with July having the lowest temperatures.

It has been said in the past, especially abroad, that vintage years mean very little in Australia—that all years are similar. This is not so, especially in the Hunter area where climatic conditions can and do alter considerably from year to year.

Too much rain is often a problem, particularly at vintage time. This may cause the grapes to split open and decrease the sugar content of the berries. It also increases the likelihood of mildew diseases. The end result may be very light wines.

Unfortunately floods and droughts have been frequent. Between 1908 and 1962 thirty-one years were either flood or drought years, and in one-third of those years the area has suffered both floods and drought. Particularly severe floods have occurred in 1893, 1913 and five very wet years in the early 1950s, with further bad floods in 1955 and 1963. 1990 promised to be a superb vintage, until just after picking started. When 40 cm of rain fell in eight days, it became a vintage to 'rescue' rather than celebrate. Fortunately frost is generally not a problem.

Hail, however, is one of the major worries of the Hunter winemakers. It can completely destroy an entire year's crop in a matter of minutes. Severe hail damages the vine as well as the grapes and can affect the vintages of the following few years. Not all vineyards are hit by a single hailstorm. In recent times 1963 was the worst year for hail. There is usually very little warning of impending hail, although there is little anyway that can be done as a preventative.

Bushfires must be added to the catalogue of woes. In 1968 fires badly affected some of the vineyards such as Tyrrells and Elliotts, destroying many of the vines especially at the perimeters.

Vine diseases present further hazards. The Hunter is one of the few areas to have escaped the dreaded phylloxera, which devastated many Australian vineyards in other states in the latter part of the nineteenth century. The area is (perhaps as some form of divine compensation?) susceptible to downy mildew, a fungus that withers leaves and berries. A wet summer and lack of sunshine favour the disease, which the vignerons attempt to combat by spraying with copper and other chemical compounds. Downy mildew first

Semillon juices prior to fermentation, Rothbury Estate.

struck in 1917 and did a great deal of damage over the following years, entirely wiping out some vineyards.

The two traditional varieties of the Hunter have long been semillon and shiraz (often called Hunter riesling and hermitage). To this today must be added chardonnay, which is now by far the most important variety, and pinot noir with which makers are still struggling. Cabernet sauvignon is also available, but is assuming less importance, especially in dry seasons. Traminer still has an important role among 'commodity' winemakers. Towards the end of the 1980s, in a typical crush of 20–21 000 tonnes, the respective quantities crushed of these major varieties was approximately: semillon, 6500 tonnes; chardonnay, 4500 tonnes; shiraz, 3500 tonnes; traminer, 1500 tonnes; cabernet, 1200 tonnes; and pinot noir, 500 tonnes, nearly 18 000 tonnes or 90 per cent of the total. Though there are other varieties—merlot has caused some enthusiasm, also verdelho and then sauvignon blanc among others—it would appear that the big five will continue to dominate for years.

·The fame of the Hunter rests on its unfortified wines—its dry reds and dry whites. Traditionally the justly famous whites have been made from semillon. They tend to be soft, round wines with extraordinary bouquet and flavour. They have a honey character, and some see 'sweaty saddle'. As elsewhere in Australia, changes in winemaking techniques have greatly changed the traditional style. The trend now is for delicate, fresh, more acid wines, and the techniques of controlled temperature fermentation and refrigeration have made this possible. As stated, by the end of the 1980s chardonnay was far more important, and the national and international fame of the district was largely dependent on this variety.

New oak barriques and puncheons now play a much more important role in wine maturation, with reds as well as whites but especially with chardonnay. New cold rooms for prolonged maturation in these vessels is now a feature of the major wineries of the district.

Towards the end of the 1980s, and before the increased interest rates of 1989 curtailed investment, the district was in yet another boom. This time it was the increase in land values, especially in relation to its use for tourism. Auction signs and development applications were rampant, though the degree of auction activity was somewhat less.

However, since the Lower Hunter is now less than two hours car travel from the Sydney Harbour Bridge, there is little doubt, in good times, that it will become a playground of Sydney. Some even predict that, by the turn of the century, it will be a tourist area with vineyards, rather than the other way around.

And there you have the Hunter—an area that has seen the good times and the bad, and throughout all has continued to produce at least some wines of unqualified excellence.

The Allandale Winery

The Allandale name goes back a long way in the history of the Hunter Valley. The original Allandale was prominent in the late nineteenth century, but only the name lives on. The present winery is of recent origin.

The force behind the Allandale Winery was Edward Jouault, a former chartered accountant who gained considerable experience in various parts of the wine industry. He established and built the winery in 1977, for vintage the following year. It is a modern small-batch winery situated on 12 hectares of gently sloping hillside with views across Pokolbin to the Brokenback Ranges.

While Ed Jouault was at the winery he had firm views about many things. Unfortunately this led to differences with his partner, Wally Atallah, a Sydney businessman, which resulted in Ed leaving in 1986 and Mr Atallah assuming full ownership. However, there is little doubt that Ed made a great contribution to the founding of Allandale and his name lives on.

The 7 hectares he planted in 1989 are now flourishing, comprising largely chardonnay with semillon and pinot noir. Most of the fruit for the 260 tonne crush is purchased from local growers, and altogether about 20 000 cases are produced. Sauvignon blanc, gewurztraminer, shiraz and cabernet sauvignon are other wines and there is also a sparkling wine.

Cellar door sales are brisk and visitors are always welcome. They have good export sales, chiefly to the UK market, and they have distributors in Sydney, Brisbane and Melbourne.

Bill Sneddon, who was assistant winemaker to Ed Jouault, took over as chief winemaker on his departure.

Allanmere

Situated in the Lower Hunter and owned by the gregarious Dr Newton Potter, an anaesthetist and wine lover, and his wife Virginia, who virtually runs the place. Geoff Broadfield helps Newton with the wine, of which they are quite proud (especially the chardonnay and the cabernet sauvignon). Their first vintage was in 1986, and they are still delighted with it. The grapes mainly came from other growers, since their own vineyards were not fully established. They still buy in some material for their 50 tonne crush.

The present vineyard area is split up into 2.5 hectares of cabernet sauvignon, 2 hectares of shiraz and one each of trebbiano and semillon. They blend a wine called Trinity from chardonnay, semillon and sauvignon blanc, which Newton reckons is a claim to fame.

Of their 3000 case production, nearly all goes to cellar door and mail order sales, though a little slips down to restaurants in Sydney.

Allanmere has a growing reputation, much of it due to the dedication and friendliness of the Potters.

Belbourie Vineyards

Belbourie is one of the most ardently individualistic small vineyards established in the Hunter in the 1960s. It was started by James Roberts and his wife Janet. Jim Roberts was born in Maitland in 1923, the son of a schoolteacher-turned-farmer. He had a Bachelor of Science degree from the University of Sydney and spent some time as an oil geologist. Janet Roberts is a daughter of the previous owner of the property, the late Norman E. Wright of Merriwa. She breeds pheasants as a hobby.

Belbourie, a property of 50 hectares between Rothbury and Allandale, runs along the lower slopes of the Molly Morgan Range on the northern side of Black Creek. Until 1964 it was used solely for grazing.

In 1964 Jim Roberts planted a hectare of grape cuttings. They struck well, and planting began on a larger scale, eventually 30 hectares being under vine. Some of this was sold, and others were let go, and now there are 6 hectares of good-quality vines, with more being planted. Varieties include semillon, trebbiano, traminer, shiraz and cabernet sauvignon. Yields are low, and something over 1000 cases is produced, most of which is sold at cellar door.

The winery at Belbourie is an interesting building, being made from convict-cut sandstone taken from Wyndham's original winery at Dalwood. There are also the remains of one of Molly Morgan's wineshops on the property. It also boasts the largest fireplace in the Hunter Valley.

Aboriginal names are used for some styles, notably Belah, and Jim Roberts did a series of finger paintings which are still used for labels. He used to claim that these were his expression of the character and style of the wine.

Jim died in 1987, but he did leave a legacy of individuality. This is still carried on by Bob Davies and Jim's son John. They make large-flavoured wines of totally idiosyncratic style. In this age of homogeneity, the Roberts have always been eccentric, doing what they believed in, and for that they should be commended.

Briar Ridge Vineyard

This is the former Murray Robson operation, which he started in 1972. Always immaculate, it is one of the prettiest of the Hunter Valley's small wineries. (Murray is a great asset to the Valley and now operates from the old Audrey Wilkinson property, having had to dispose of this, his original operation.)

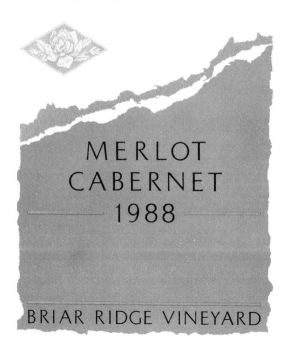

MERLOT
CABERNET
1988

BRIAR RIDGE VINEYARD

In 1988 a syndicate bought the vineyards and winery. This was headed by Dr John Davis, now the chairman, who bought the Seppelt vineyard known as Pokolbin Creek, on the Allandale Road, in 1982. Trevor Drayton of the well-known wine family is also a member, independent of his family; and Kees Vandescheur, who worked for Murray for ten years, is the third.

Their fruit comes from their own 9 hectare vineyard; a varietal mix of chardonnay (almost 2 hectares), cabernet sauvignon (the same), shiraz (1 hectare) and parcels of merlot, pinot noir, traminer and sauvignon blanc, plus that available from the 15 hectare Pokolbin Creek vineyard. Further plantings are being made to take the crush from the usual 100 tonne level to 200 tonnes, which the partners consider to be an intelligent, workable amount. Kees Vandescheur started his career at Rothbury Estate before assisting in a winemaking capacity at Robson's for ten vintages. He is now the chief executive and winemaker of Briar Ridge. Kees says they intend to pursue vigorously the policy of making high-quality table wines that reflect true varietal identity. Of his vintages he likes the 1989 year for whites, particularly chardonnay.

Over 50 per cent of all sales are made at cellar door. Mail order is also popular.

Brokenwood

This small vineyard and winery, in the heart of the classic Hunter, was the dream of three Sydney lawyers with no previous experience in viticulture. Tony Albert, John Beeston and James Halliday were the trinity behind the venture. They bought the original 4.05 hectare block in October 1970 with unbounded enthusiasm. The first plantings of cabernet sauvignon were made by the principals and helpers in July 1971 in heavy clay that was once a playing field, complete with cricket pitch. Over the next three winters the area under vine was increased to 3.4 hectares: 1.5 hectares of cabernet, with the rest a mixture of hermitage (shiraz), pinot noir, cabernet franc, merlot and malbec. The first crop was picked in 1973 and yielded for release seventy-five dozen hermitage–cabernet sauvignon.

By January 1975 the attractive winery, designed by John Rourke, was built. The wines produced meanwhile were meeting with out-

Brokenwood smallwood storage.

standing success in open competition and at tastings. The vineyard area was expanded in 1978 with the purchase of an adjoining block (known as the Graveyard) from Hungerford Hill. Six new partners, holding smaller shares, were taken in at that stage. A further rationalisation occurred when James Halliday sold his share in 1983. Extra capital was also needed and today there are twenty partners including Ian Riggs, an Honours graduate from Roseworthy College, who is chairman, managing director, winemaker and chief dog walker. He is one of the more thoughtful of the personalities who have become part of the Hunter during the past few years.

Brokenwood now has 19 hectares under vine, with hermitage (7 hectares) and cabernet sauvignon (6 hectares) being the predominant varieties. The partners plan to progressively replace hermitage with cabernet sauvignon until the proportions are about two to one in favour of cabernet. There are also small quantities of pinot noir, cabernet franc, merlot and malbec. There is only one white variety, chardonnay, of which there are a couple of hectares. Other fruit is purchased, including all the requirements for

their greatest commercial success, a lean, fresh, crisp dry white from semillon. In all, about 12 500 cases are produced; 6000 of semillon, 2500 of chardonnay (which matures excellently with bottle age), 1500 cases of a unique cabernet blend which includes material from Coonawarra, and the balance being sundry reds.

The Brokenwood partners aim for nothing less than excellence—insofar as the vagaries of the Hunter climate permit. Their intention is to produce premium-quality wines which are clean, elegant and complex. The extremely heavy clay soil, low yields and meticulous vinification techniques result in a distinctive style of wine which has been extremely well received by critics.

An extraordinary feature of winemaking at Brokenwood is that all winery tasks are carried out by regular volunteers. Partners are allocated weekends in rotation and are responsible for organising the roster of helpers. The operation is deliberately labour intensive as the partners believe that this is the only way to guarantee the individuality of their wines. It would be impossible to conduct a commercial winery on such a basis.

They make very good wines at Brokenwood and the partnership has a top spot among the frontrunners of the Hunter Valley pack. They have won many well-deserved golds, trophies and international accolades with various wines.

It is rare to see such singlemindedness (and plain hard yakka) put into the realisation of a dream.

Calais Estates

Calais Estates, formerly Wollundry Winery, on Palmer's Lane in Pokolbin, was founded by Ron and Kay Hansen. They bought the property in 1971 and had their first vintage in 1975 in a machinery shed.

In 1976 a winery was constructed, and masses of sandstone organised to build tasting rooms. These were never completed because the Hansens decided to sell for private reasons.

In January 1987 Colin Peterson (son of Ian Peterson) bought the property. He finished the tasting room facility in the style of an old bush hotel, and set about refurbishing the winery.

They have 20 hectares on the property; 6 hectares of semillon, 3 hectares of chardonnay, 8 hectares of shiraz, 2 hectares of cabernet sauvignon and 1 hectare of pinot noir. This provides a third of their potential crush of 300 tonnes, the rest being purchased from local growers.

Sales are divided between the cellar door and distribution in Sydney. The chardonnay and semillon have both won golds and trophies at local shows and form the backbone of acceptance of their output.

Chateau François

Chateau François is owned and operated by the energetic Dr Don François, who used to be Director of Fisheries for New South Wales, and who made a great contribution in that capacity. He has always been a wine enthusiast, and started making wine many years ago in suburban Sydney before establishing his own vineyard.

Among the smallest vineyards in the Hunter, Chateau François has 2.5 hectares under vine in the shadow of the mountains behind Tyrrells. A small winery was built in 1973, extended in 1977, and a larger winery was erected in 1982.

Chateau François produces semillon, chardonnay and shiraz–pinot wines. Don usually does well at local wine shows, picking up the odd gold and almost always a silver or two. His output is small, with only about 18 tonnes being crushed and 1200 cases made. Most is sold by mail order, but tastings may be made by appointment. Occasionally Dr Don holds an open weekend, when he welcomes visitors, and these can be great fun. He also grows and bottles the best olives in the area.

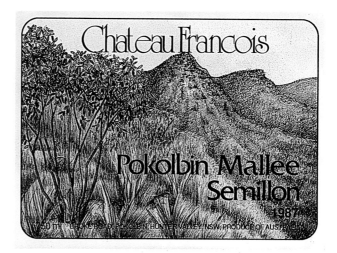

Chateau Pato

On Thompson's Road in the Lower Hunter, behind the Hungerford Hill complex, is the idiosyncratic dream of national radio personality and omnipresent television voice-over, David Paterson, who drives the tractor, and Helen Paterson, who is far more efficient.

They planted their vineyard in 1981, the hares got to the young shoots; they shot and ate the hares and planted again in 1982. The winery followed in 1986.

Chateau Pato is not big. Not even big enough to make industry listings, yet they make their presence felt. Only 600–700 cases come from 3 hectares of shiraz, half of malbec and a scrap of pinot noir; and 1 hectare of traminer. David's wines are very carefully made, always have good colour, are entirely sound and redolent of their variety.

Since they crush less than 10 tonnes they pay no industry levy, a non-contribution dear to the heart of 'Pato'.

Of his vintages, he thinks 1985 outstanding (a lovely rich, soft, full shiraz), 1986 and 1987 are also very good.

Incidentally, one has to make an appointment to enter the hallowed halls of Chateau Pato; that keeps you honest and means one rarely leaves without something.

Dawson Estate

This 7 hectare vineyard at Nulkaba in the Hunter Valley was established in 1980 by Ben Dawson. The 85 tonne crush produces 4500 cases of chardonnay and 400 cases of traminer. Although the Dawson Estate does not have its own winery, wine has been made under contract for them each year from 1979 on.

Cellar door and mail order are the chief means of sale. The Dawson chardonnay is extremely popular and sells out fairly quickly.

W. Drayton & Sons Pty Ltd, Bellevue

This is a relatively small family concern, but the Draytons have a long association with the Hunter. Theirs is the only name still actively concerned with the area that is to be found on

Reg Drayton tests a wine's sugar content.

the original maps of the land grants in the Pokolbin area. Only two family concerns that survived the 1930s depression still independently make wine today; the Draytons are one of these.

The founder of the enterprise was Joseph Drayton, who was born in 1820 at Bellevue in England, and emigrated to New South Wales where he took up a grant of land at Pokolbin on 9 February 1852. Joseph intended establishing a small farm on the 16 hectare block, and it was not until 1857 that he decided to plant a vineyard. His first wine was made in 1860.

The Draytons were a prolific family—Joseph had four sons and two daughters by his second wife. One of his sons, William, did even better by producing nine boys and a girl (William, Joseph, Lewis, Walter, Ernest, Wesley, Reginald, Edgar, Ivy and Len). William was a practical man; his son Len described him as 'a winegrower, cooper, carpenter and blacksmith'. The youngest son, Len was born at Pokolbin in 1905. For many years he was the chief winemaker, and became managing director of the company until his retirement in 1973. As senior wine man of the Hunter, with his life-long association with winemaking there, his knowledge and experience are keenly sought after by younger vignerons.

The boom of the 1960s brought a measure of

prosperity to the Draytons. Life for any primary producer is never plain sailing, and the Draytons lost 50 per cent of their crop in a short but severe hailstorm in 1963. They were also affected by bushfires at the end of 1968 which nearly destroyed the old family homestead.

The Bellevue vineyard is located in the foothills of the Mt View range, just north-west of Mt Pleasant. Much of the soil is light grey loam, which is apparently alluvial (rather than the volcanic soil that is largely found in the area).

Although there was once a wide variety of grapes planted, they now have mostly hermitage (shiraz) for the reds, with the addition of some cabernet sauvignon in recent years. The dominant variety for the whites is semillon (Hunter riesling) and there are good plantings of chardonnay and some verdelho, traminer and Rhine riesling.

Draytons expanded during the late 1960s and 1970s by planting the Lambkin Estate next to Lake's Folly and by purchasing the old Ivanhoe property in 1969 (the ancient fermenters, last used in 1928, may still be seen among the pepper trees opposite Reg Drayton's house). Part of McDonald's Flat, across the road from the

winery, was purchased in 1982 and a vineyard was established there.

In January 1989 there was a rationalisation of the company. Max and his three sons, Trevor, John and Greg, took over completely, and Reg, who had worked so long and hard as the winemaker and manager, retired from the company, taking with him the Lambkin and Ivanhoe Estates as settlement.

Whatever the family ownership mix, Draytons have been, and I'm sure will remain, among the most honest, direct and traditional of the 'old' makers. Many of their wines may also be considered slightly old-fashioned, with fairly solid semillons and hearty reds to the forefront. Yet their welcome is old-fashioned too, and cellar tastings are a feature. Become a regular customer and you'll experience their barbecues and cask tastings.

Some of their chardonnays and some small wood-matured reds have shown very modern characters, however. The thing to do is to go and find out for yourself, for you are sure to find a Drayton somewhere to help you—and you can't say that for many today in a valley that was once dominated by family companies.

Vintage at Drayton's Bellevue vineyard.

Evans Family

Somewhat close to home, to say the least. Owned by Trish, Sally, Jodie and Toby Evans (though Daddy has all the 'A' shares).

Four hectares of chardonnay were planted on the lower slopes of the hill on which the family home sits. The aspect of the vineyard is south and south-east. Plantings were made in 1976, 1977 and 1978.

The wines are now made at Rothbury under contract. With the exception of the 1983, which flattened quickly, they tend to be more delicate than others made at Rothbury, and have a long aftertaste which develops very well in the bottle. Outstanding vintages were 1982 (made by Murray Tyrrell), 1984 and 1986. Also good were 1985 and 1987; 1988 and 1989 are both rather more delicate and will need extra bottle age.

There are also 2.5 hectares of pinot noir, planted in 1985, and half a hectare of gamay, planted in 1988. Though some pleasant light reds have been made, plus a sparkling wine in 1989, little has been sold. One ambition is to produce a soft, 'slippery-smooth' light red of high fruit character, but this is proving to be difficult.

Of the chardonnay, up to half is exported to the UK and USA, and the rest is sold in Australia on demand. A cellar-door sales area, featuring a cloistered courtyard, offers quiet contemplation for dedicated wine lovers. Small group tastings by appointment.

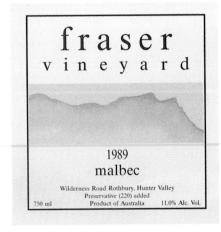

Fraser Vineyard

This relatively small vineyard was established in 1987, although the winery itself was built in 1986.

Peter Fraser is the winemaker at Fraser Vineyard, which has about 7 hectares of vines. The varieties Peter includes are semillon, chardonnay, shiraz, cabernet sauvignon, chenin blanc, malbec and sauvignon blanc. From the malbec and the sauvignon blanc, Peter produces some esoteric wines in small quantities which are very popular. These, along with the other more traditional table wines, have meant an output for 1989 of about 2500 cases and Peter is hopeful of increasing this to 3000 cases. Fraser Vineyard wines are available by mail order.

Golden Grape Estate

The Golden Grape Estate in Pokolbin is a complex which has grown dramatically since its change of ownership in 1985. It is now owned by Pieroth, the German company devoted to at-home wine tastings. Previously known as Happy Valley, this vineyard has a long history dating back to 1824, the present winery being about thirty years old.

The complex covers 43 hectares with 29 hectares of vines. The varieties included are semillon, chardonnay, shiraz, cabernet sauvignon and muscat, with a crush of about 3 tonnes per hectare. Of the table, sparkling and fortified wines available, most outstanding have been the 1985 cabernet sauvignon, the 1986 pinot noir and the 1988 chardonnay.

Sales have been increasing in New South Wales, Queensland and Western Australia over the last three years. As well as cellar door and mail order, direct national sales are made through nationally conducted wine tastings.

Hungerford Hill

Hungerford Hill was another of the boom babies of the late 1960s. The company was formed to develop vineyards in the Hunter, and in 1967 it began operations by buying Allan Hungerford's Friesian stud, hence the origin of the company name.

From 1968 over 60 hectares were planted, but changing fashions, and changes of direction and ownership, have resulted in a reduction of this to 24 hectares, made up mostly of chardonnay, followed by semillon, shiraz, merlot and pinot noir. Perhaps more importantly, the company has a source of fruit in Coonawarra, where it part owns and operates 80 hectares of vineyard comprising Rhine riesling, chardonnay, cabernet sauvignon, cabernet franc and merlot.

They also purchase fruit from other growers in the Hunter Valley, and buy both must and wine from other areas, all of which is processed at their winery in the Hunter. The total crush is 1400 tonnes, which results in 100 000 cases of premium wine. Of this, 20 per cent is exported, and the balance is sold wholesale, chiefly on the eastern seaboard of Australia.

The ownership of the company has changed and at present Hooper Baillie, once a subsidiary of the New Zealand group Richmond Smart, owns the entire shareholding of Hungerford Hill.

David Hammond became the general manager in 1984 and has guided the company to profitability. Adrian Sheridan became the winemaker in 1988 following the departure of Ralph Fowler from the Hunter Valley.

The main thrust of the company's promotion is through their premium range, the Merchant label. Of this the most important is the chardonnay—usually a rich, complex wine of good fruit and oak flavours, which matures very well in the bottle. There is also a semillon- sauvignon blanc blend, a cabernet merlot and a shiraz, all from the Hunter Valley, and a Rhine riesling and cabernet sauvignon from Coonawarra.

Lake's Folly

Lake's Folly is a small vineyard, but its influence and the quality of wine it produces have given it an importance that greatly outweighs its size. Its owner, Dr Max Lake, was born in July 1924, graduated in medicine from Sydney University in 1946, and was a surgeon eight years later. He became a serious student and lover of wine, and has written some very good books on Australian wine, with a special contribution to research on the Hunter.

Dr Lake decided that he wanted to make his own wine and establish his own vineyard; and this in itself was a remarkable decision. In 1961 he began searching the Hunter for the ideal land. In 1963 he bought 25.5 hectares near McWilliam's Rosehill paddock, of which he is aiming to have 10 hectares under vine. He built an A-frame winery, which is locally referred to by some as the 'Pokolbin Opera House'. This was

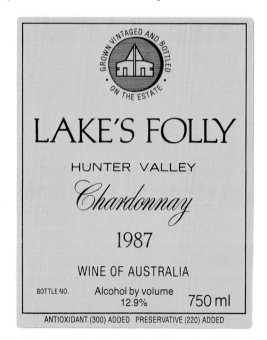

Lake's Folly.

the first new vineyard to be planted in the Hunter for many years, and probably did much to influence others to follow his example. In effect he pioneered the trend to boutique wineries there, and certainly influenced the Hunter revival of the 1960s and 1970s.

The chief variety planted was cabernet sauvignon, the great grape of Bordeaux, with about one-quarter red hermitage. (Some malbec and a little merlot was later added.) This was a radical departure from the traditions of the Hunter, where hermitage (shiraz) had long been the most popular variety. The vineyards are planted in 3 m rows, with the vines 2 m apart. All the vines were planted by Lake's friends, who also picked the grapes at the first vintage in 1966. The quantity of grapes was small, and the wine was made by the ancient method of treading out the juice by bare feet (to the accompaniment of 'Zorba the Greek' played on the piano by Lake himself). This historic grape-treading force was Marie Schmid, David and Stephen Lake, Len Evans and David Lynch. Stephen became assistant winemaker in the 1977 vintage, and winemaker-manager in the early 1980s.

Max was also very early with his plantings of chardonnay in 1969, and they now have 4.5 hectares. These wines can be quite steely and closed when young but they develop extremely well with bottle age. The reds are idiosyncratic and variable, some suffering, perhaps, from an excess of Hunter Valley sweaty saddle, or a form of H_2S (hydrogen sulphide). Yet all the wines have a devoted following and sell remarkably quickly. Overall, some 4000 cases are made. Good chardonnay vintages are 1974, 1979, 1981, 1983, 1986 and 1989, and good years for the reds are 1969, 1972, 1978, 1981, 1985, 1987 and 1989.

Lesnik Family Winery

Situated on the main road between Cessnock and Branxton, opposite the turn-off into the main vineyard area. Josef (Joe) Lesnik is a character who has operated in the district for years, chiefly as a grapegrower, establishing his winery in 1986. His vineyards are on the Wilderness Road and around the winery. They comprise merlot (3 hectares), shiraz (2), cabernet sauvignon (2), pinot noir (1), malbec (1), verdelho (3), almost the same of chardonnay and 2 hectares of semillon—a considerable varietal mix.

He processes his own material only, at present about 70–80 tonnes, and all the varietal styles emerge plus some sparkling wine.

Joe specialises in cellar door sales and is providing broader facilities for casual visitors, including barbecues and a children's play area.

Lindeman's Wines Pty Ltd, Ben Ean

The influence of the Lindeman name now extends far beyond the confines of the Hunter Valley where it all started. It now is one of the major winemakers of Australia, and is closely bound up with the whole industry of wine in Australia.

The founder of this viticultural giant was Henry John Lindeman, who was born in London in 1811, the son of a doctor. In 1834, aged twenty-three, he graduated from St Bartholomew's Hospital as a surgeon and joined the Royal Navy. Lindeman married Eliza Bramhall in 1840, left the Navy, and decided to emigrate to Australia. They arrived in Sydney in September 1840, and Dr Lindeman set up as a general practitioner at Gresford on the Paterson River, a tributary of the Hunter River.

On 12 January 1842 he purchased a property at auction which was originally part of a grant to George Townshend of Trevallyn. Called Cawarra (which is an Aboriginal word for 'by running waters'), he commenced planting it as a vineyard in 1843.

Dr Lindeman was successful for some years, and built up a large stock of maturing wines, reputed to have been of high quality. In 1850 Dr Lindeman joined the Hunter River Valley Association, and later became its president. Disaster struck in 1851, when a fire completely destroyed the doctor's wooden storage shack and winery.

At this stage, Lindeman left for the Victorian goldfields, where he worked as a surgeon and a miner, and, incidentally, studied winemaking in the Corowa and Rutherglen areas. He returned to Cawarra with his fortunes restored, and subsequently rebuilt the winery and expanded his plantings. In 1870 he established the headquarters of his company and his winery in Pitt Street, Sydney—the first Hunter wine company to do so.

In order to supplement the dry wine produced from Cawarra with sweet ones, for which there was a great demand, he extended his holdings to Corowa. In 1872 he bought Haffners' vineyard at Corowa, on the banks of the Murray River, the border between New South Wales and Victoria. The Felton and Southern Cross vineyards there were also acquired.

The old Ben Ean winery at Pokolbin.

Dr Henry John Lindeman died at Cawarra on 23 May 1881, and was buried at St Anne's Anglican Church, Gresford. He had been a strong exponent of the value of drinking table wine as a deterrent to rum and spirit drinking (with its attendant drunkenness), and his influence in the Hunter Valley and at Corowa was huge. In 1879 Dr Lindeman had made his three sons partners in the firm. Charles Frederick Lindeman became manager after his father's death, and built on the foundations he had laid.

In 1896 a writer in the Maitland *Mercury*, H.M. McKenzie, was most impressed by the 'immense storage capacity' at Cawarra. He noted that all the casks there (which were made of 3-inch oak) were imported from Germany and cost £26 each to set up in the Cawarra cellars. There were then about 10 hectares under vine. Mr McKenzie wrote: 'It is a recognised fact that Cawarra is the best vineyard in the district, the wine, especially a light claret which I tasted and found excellent, being bottled at the premises.' The Cawarra clarets were 'light, sound and free from acid, and by no means, as so many colonial clarets are, rough on the tongue'. The Lindemans had an 'invariable rule' that no wine left the vineyard for at least four years; it was then rested for at least one year in the cellars in Sydney before sale. The wines were mostly Madeira and Black Hermitage.

In 1901, at the Sydney Commonwealth Exhibition, Cawarra wines gained a record number of forty-two awards, including two championships and nineteen first prizes. The company was prospering under the management of Dr Lindeman's sons: as mentioned, Charles Frederick was the manager, Arthur Henry was the winemaker and Herbert was the 'taster'.

In 1906 Herbert was bought out, and a limited liability company was formed. At that time Arthur Lindeman took the Cawarra vineyards separately, but continued to supply wine to the company until at least 1912.

By 1907 Lindeman's had moved their Sydney headquarters to the Queen Victoria Building where they remained almost until the Second World War. The operation there was on a large scale, with the main cellar 60 m by 27 m.

The company continued to expand, although the number of vineyards in the Hunter began to decline from the turn of the century. The Ben Ean vineyard was purchased by Lindeman Ltd in 1912 from John H. McDonald, who had planted it in 1870. Apart from being a household word as the brand name of a moselle, it is now the site of an impressive winery and is Lindeman's chief base in the Hunter Valley.

Coolalta, which is at the back of Ben Ean, was sold by the Wilkinson family to Lindeman's. Coolalta had been planted in 1866 and is possibly the oldest vineyard in the Pokolbin area. This was followed by the acquisition of Catawba from the Cappers, and Warrawee.

In 1914 Lindeman's purchased Kirkton from James Kelman and his sister Catherine. This historic property, situated 7 km from Branxton, was a land grant to John Busby in 1824. When James left for New Zealand in 1833, his father John settled on the property, where he died in 1857 aged ninety-two. The control of the property passed to James Kelman, who was James Busby's nephew. James Kelman had married Dr Henry Lindeman's daughter Matilda many years before.

At the turn of the century there were 26 hectares of vines on the sandy reddish soil, which produced 4000 to 6000 litres per hectare each year. According to Mr McKenzie in the Maitland *Mercury*. Kirkton produced

a delicate wine in the shape of hocks and clarets, amongst which the red hermitage seems to suit the soil better than the majority. The verdelho and riesling are also a very suitable kind for the Kirkton soil.

In 1924, 455 litres each of chablis and burgundy were made from the remaining Busby vines and were served at the centenary celebrations of Kirkton in 1930. There was a certain irony in those celebrations, in that the vineyard had been sold after the 1924 vintage as being uneconomic.

'Porphyry' is now well known as the name of a sweet white wine. It was indeed also the name of a wine served to Queen Victoria in 1851 (history does not record whether she was amused). That wine was named after the property from whence it came: the vineyard planted in 1838 by the Reverend Henry Carmichael, near Raymond Terrace, in the Newcastle district. The vineyard remained in the Carmichael family, and in 1915 the trade name Porphyry and the wine stocks were sold by the attorneys of Gavin Dixon

Carmichael to Lindemans Ltd. The vines were abandoned; and when Gavin Carmichael was killed in France in 1917, G.V. Ralston inherited the property.

The next acquisition in 1920, was a property known as Sunshine, near Branxton on the Cessnock Road. It is now an important vineyard in Lindeman's Hunter holdings.

Meanwhile, Charles Lindeman had suffered a stroke before 1916 and, although he lived to 1931, he no longer played an active role in the business. The company's rapid expansion produced severe financial problems, and in 1923 its bank insisted that its nominee be appointed manager. Leo Buring was appointed, and he was in sole charge until 1930, while the company's financial situation steadily grew worse. At that time, Lindemans was forced into receivership, and a Mr Nelson was appointed to that role. The combined effects of the depression, World War II and the company's debts meant that it remained in receivership until 1947, when a new era of expansion began. Bert Bear was manager through the 1940s and 1950s, to be succeeded by Ray Kidd.

In 1953 Lindeman's became a public company, and underwent a major reconstruction in 1959. In 1960 it established headquarters at Marrickville, Sydney, but later moved to Nyrang Street, Lidcombe.

Lindemans acquired Chateau Leonay, formerly Leo Buring's concern, in 1962—an ironic twist in view of Buring's earlier management of the now parent company. Lindeman's further increased its influence on the wine scene when it took over Rouge Homme Wines in 1965.

In one of the most significant events in its corporate history, Lindeman's was itself taken over by the American tobacco company, Philip Morris, in 1971 and is now a wholly owned subsidiary of that company.

The Ben Ean vineyard is on rich volcanic soil. The white wines from Ben Ean are particularly famous, especially the semillons, which really set the standard for all other wines of this style in the Hunter. The company has a policy of maturing these whites for future 'classic' releases, and wine lovers all over the world have become aware of the superb qualities of a mature Lindeman's semillon of some ten to twenty years bottle age. I've tasted whites well over thirty-years-old

which are quite magnificent. The reds are no slouches either, and Bin 1590 of the 1959 vintage remains a benchmark of Hunter red quality.

The crush is now in the vicinity of 2000 tonnes, almost half of which is red. In fact, shiraz is now the dominant variety crushed. Semillon makes up 35 per cent of the total, with 10 per cent chardonnay and 5 per cent verdelho. There are tiny percentages of other varieties.

Although their Hunter wines are only a small proportion of their overall production, Lindeman's take great pride in their quality. They have a policy of releasing fine wines with some years' age, which gives those wine lovers who have not had their own cellars (or are perhaps too young) an opportunity to taste very good wines of some years past.

Lindeman's were the leaders in changing the style of white wines to the more delicate, fresh style common today. In the Hunter, in 1956, they installed pressure fermentation tanks, which allow the winemaker to control the temperature of fermentation. It was in 1965, however, that Lindeman's really began to modernise the equipment at Ben Ean. They installed a German Wilmes air-bag press, which gets the maximum delicacy and flavour from the grapes, and much other modern machinery which ensures maximum quality in their wines. Lindeman's emphasise complete cleanliness as being essential to good winemaking.

Lindeman's are constantly expanding in the Hunter. New plantings are being made, and old areas replanted with premium varieties. They have also added to their Hunter holdings. In 1967, 37 hectares at Rothbury, known as the Steven vineyard, were acquired and 10 hectares were planted in 1968–69. At Broke, in 1972, Lindeman's purchased a 124 hectare property, of which 100 hectares are planted.

With regard to the present position of Lindeman's wines, the contributions made by two of their outstanding winemakers—Hans Mollenhauer and Karl Stockhausen—should not be overlooked. Hans Mollenhauer, a German food technologist who emigrated to Australia shortly after World War II, was winemaker at Ben Ean in the 1950s. Some of the wines that he made are now part of the Hunter legend. He also published research papers on winemaking, developing a theory on the rate of maturation of grapes, and on local history. He returned to Germany in 1959.

Mollenhauer was succeeded by Karl Stockhausen. Born in Hamburg, Germany, in 1930, he came to Australia in 1955 and studied accountancy while staying at the Greta migrant camp. He joined Lindeman's as a casual worker, and after a year moved to their headquarters in Sydney where he worked as a clerk while completing his accountancy studies. Stockhausen passed his degree in 1961. When Mollenhauer returned to Germany, Karl Stockhausen was offered his job. His experience at that stage was not large, but with much care and meticulous attention to detail, he has succeeded in producing wines of very high quality. Early in 1980, Karl moved to take charge of the Leo Buring winery at Chateau Leonay in the Barossa Valley.

Chris Buring took over for the 1980, 1981 and 1982 vintages, when some very promising wines were made. In mid-1982 Chris was moved to become senior winemaker at the Nyrang Cellars in Sydney, and Karl Stockhausen returned to the Hunter, no doubt with added experience from his time in the Barossa.

In December 1985 Karl was moved again, this time to a head-office position in Sydney. Gerry Sissingh, who had returned to Lindeman's in 1979 after a ten-year stint at Rothbury, took over as chief winemaker in 1985. He resigned in 1990 when Penfold's took over Lindeman's and amalgamated these holdings with those of Tulloch's, a previous acquisition.

Cellar door sales were commenced in 1979, and the Ben Ean cellars now feature a winemaking museum. The shop area remains one of the few places in the Hunter from which old wines may be purchased, albeit at prices commensurate with their age.

Little's Winery

My near neighbour, Ian Little, got going for the 1984 vintage after he and his father had been 'scouring' the area for a while. His winery in Palmer's Lane is workmanlike and it seems to attract more than a fair portion of wine-loving visitors.

They crush about 75 tonnes, of which 60–65 tonnes are from their own or leased vineyards. Their own varietals include 2.5 hectares of

cabernet sauvignon, 2 hectares of shiraz, the same of pinot noir and a mixed hectare of cabernet franc, merlot and malbec; 3 hectares of chardonnay, 2.5 hectares of semillon and 2 hectares of traminer plus a touch of clairette. The world of wine in two small areas. In all, 6000 cases are produced, a little of which goes to export, some to restaurants in Sydney and Brisbane, more to mail order and most to cellar door sales. They do very well with both chardonnay and cabernet, the eternal favourites, though there is unusual demand for a vintage port made from shiraz.

Of the various vintages of the 1980s, 1986 stands out, though 1989 was 'very good'.

The Littles are very nice people and they and their wines have settled well into the district.

Marsh Estate

The Marsh Estate was so named by Peter Marsh when he took over the winery in late 1978 from Dr Quentin Taperell, who had begun planting vines on the property in 1971. Peter, a graduate of pharmacy from the University of Sydney, brought his analytical skills to winemaking with considerable success, winning the Best Small Winemaker (crush, not height) at the Hunter Valley Show at Singleton on consecutive years, 1987 and 1988.

He and his wife very much enjoy the lifestyle of the small vigneron, and all wine sales are made at cellar door, which is fairly rare today. Consequently, there's always a warm welcome at Marsh Estate.

They have 21 hectares under vine: including, in order of area, shiraz, semillon, chardonnay, cabernet sauvignon, pinot noir and a little traminer. Some merlot has been planted and further chardonnay plantings are underway. This provides a range of 100 per cent authentic varieties, plus a sparkling wine from chardonnay and pinot and a small quantity of vintage port. The total available each year is from 5000 to 6000 cases.

McWilliam's Wines Pty Ltd, Mount Pleasant and the MIA

McWilliam's have huge wineries at Yenda, Hanwood and Beelbangera in New South Wales, and at Robinvale in Victoria; but most of

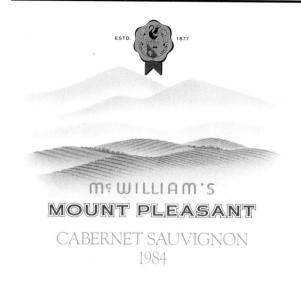

McWILLIAM'S
MOUNT PLEASANT
CABERNET SAUVIGNON
1984

PREMIUM HUNTER VALLEY WINE 750ml

McWilliam's top-quality wines come from their Hunter Valley vineyards and are sold under the Mount Pleasant label.

McWilliam's have been involved in the Hunter only since 1932, but the Mount Pleasant label and wines have a much longer history than that. The small original vineyard of Mount Pleasant, in the Pokolbin area near Cessnock, was planted in 1880 by Charles King on a Crown grant. The soil there is weathered volcanic loam, which is very fertile.

Some years later the vineyard was acquired by John Augustus O'Shea, an Irish immigrant married to a Frenchwoman. After his son Maurice had finished school in Australia, John O'Shea sent him to France, where he studied viticulture, first at the agricultural college at Grignon, and later at the University of Montpellier.

Maurice O'Shea returned to Australia in 1921 with an extensive knowledge and feeling for food and wines. In 1925, when the vineyard was about 48 hectares in area, he named it Mount Pleasant. On taking over as winemaker, Maurice O'Shea extended the vineyards and began making wine of such quality that he has assumed nothing short of legendary status in Australian wine history.

In 1932 the McWilliam family, interested in dry table wines and recognising the potential of the estate, combined with O'Shea in the equal ownership of a company known as Mount Pleasant Wines Pty Ltd. The O'Shea family later sold their shares to McWilliam's Wines. Maurice was retained as vineyard manager and director until he died.

O'Shea was given a free hand by McWilliam's and, with their capital behind him, began to extend their holdings. They acquired Lovedale on the Cessnock–Branxton road. Vines were planted, but at the outbreak of World War II the government took over the property and converted it into an emergency landing field for the duration. In 1950 the government released the area, and Maurice and McWilliam's started again. They planted the area mainly with semillon. The Lovedale soils are mainly alluvial silt with yellow clay, and this vineyard is the source of the dry white wine known as Anne Riesling.

In about 1950 O'Shea planted the vineyard known as Rosehill, which is situated along the Broke Road, opposite the present Lake's Folly. Rosehill has volcanic soil and is the source of the Robert series of reds and much of the Philip series.

Maurice O'Shea died in May 1956, and is buried in a neglected grave in the cemetery at Gore Hill, Sydney. His reputation, however, lives on, and a legendary aura has developed about his name. He had superb judgment of wine, and with the company's financial resources backing him he was able to buy the pick of the wine made by other vignerons, to be blended as he saw fit. O'Shea certainly made some of the most magnificent wines ever seen from the Hunter, and was largely instrumental in putting the area and the Mount Pleasant name firmly on the viticultural map.

Brian Walsh took over after O'Shea's death. Walsh was born in Sydney in November 1931 and graduated from Sydney Technical College as an industrial chemist. He joined McWilliam's as a laboratory assistant in 1952 and three years later was sent by them to Newcastle to learn winemaking from O'Shea. Walsh helped O'Shea with the 1956 vintage, and in June 1957 he moved to Mount Pleasant.

From Walsh's time on, until he retired and was replaced by Phillip Ryan in the early 1980s, the vineyard size increased quite dramatically. Though they purchase material from other growers, there are 160 hectares of semillon, chardonnay, shiraz and pinot noir, including a little Rhine riesling and cabernet sauvignon.

In 1989 the company bought Barwang, the Robertson property at Young, to grow more chardonnay, and also an extensive tract of land at Broke, near the Lindemans' vineyards, to further increase white variety plantings—an indication of their belief in the future of premium regional varieties in Australia.

The Mount Pleasant winery, built in 1960, is modern and well equipped with the latest winemaking facilities and both oak and stainless steel storage. A refrigerated cellar has been constructed to maintain all the white table wines at a constant low temperature until bottled. This has helped to produce wines with a greater varietal aroma and flavour. It is all vastly different to O'Shea's old winery, l'Hermitage, which was pulled down to make room for the expansion of the new winery.

The wines from Mount Pleasant enjoy the reputation of being readily available. They are the saviour of many an inadequate restaurant wine list.

In any discussion of the Murrumbidgee Irrigation Area, the name McWilliam is the one that immediately springs to mind. The McWilliams were the first in the area and dominated it for the years of its early development. McWilliam's have also been leaders in producing quality table wines in an irrigation area.

Samuel McWilliam, the founder of the company, first planted a few hectares of vines at Corowa, on the Murray River, in 1877. It was his son John James, however, who began the expansion of the family enterprise which has grown to become one of the major winemaking companies of Australia.

In the MIA the McWilliam empire really flourished. In 1912, almost before the main irrigation canal reached Hanwood, 6 km from Griffith, 20 hectare blocks were bought and planted with about 35 000 cuttings. From 1916 their grapes were processed at the Junee winery. In 1917 the McWilliams built themselves a winery at Hanwood and crushed 170 tonnes. Three years later, in 1920, another winery was built at Yenda, near Griffith. A distillery was also installed there, and later on cellars for the storage of their sparkling wines.

McWilliam's Wines is still a family concern, with many of the McWilliams playing active roles in the organisation. Various relatives of the four brothers who were sons of the original founder are doing different jobs for the company.

McWilliam's have a huge centre at Chullora, having sold their celebrated Pyrmont headquarters in Sydney.

Much of the credit for the MIA winemaking revolution—that is, the transformation of the area into a producer of well-made, ready-drinking quality table wines—must go to the McWilliam family and the succession of highly competent technical directors, Glen, Jim and Doug (all McWilliams), who showed just how well it could be done.

The sheer size of the McWilliam's operation is staggering. They have four 450 000 litre stainless steel tanks at Hanwood and even some stainless steel rail tankers. McWilliam's produce 24 million litres of wine a year; a sizeable percentage of Australia's total output for a single maker.

The Hanwood Winery has storage for 22.5 million litres! It has the capacity to crush 12 000 tonnes. Yenda is the centre of sparkling wine production, and also has two brandy stills in operation. It puts through 10 000 tonnes of grapes each year. Beelbangera was acquired as a going concern, and it specialises in fortified wines with an annual crush of 9000 tonnes. All centres are versatile and produce a range of wines.

Despite the huge quantities of wine involved, quality has by no means been overlooked. The McWilliams have actively encouraged local growers to plant better varieties, even providing them with the new vines. They have cooperated with the CSIRO and Department of Agriculture in the first significant trials on the scientific control of irrigation to improve wine quality, and these efforts have begun to pay off. In the late 1960s McWilliam's Cabernet Sauvignon from Hanwood began winning many gold medals. They followed these successes with other gold medals for local Rhine riesling. These breakthroughs were evidence to prove that irrigation areas can make top wines.

Of all the McWilliam's wines, there is little doubt that the Mount Pleasant Hunter bottlings, direct descendants of O'Shea's, are the standard bearers of the company. During the 1950s and early 1960s they were among the most important reds and whites on offer in Australia. There were all sorts of 'name' wines available: Richard,

Frederick, Henry, Charles, Stephen, Robert, Anne, and so on; plus OP and OH (Old Paddock and Old Hermitage), P and OP (Pinot and Old Paddock), RH (Rosehill), *et al*, most of them from single casks of wine that were a connoisseur's dream and a marketer's nightmare. Then the company seemed to dismiss these, though there would be the odd resurrection as a special wine demanded attention, as it concentrated on the two Mount Pleasant staples, Philip and Elizabeth, the red and white respectively. Before the advent of Tyrrell's Long Flat Dry Red and White, these were the largest volume lines sold from the Hunter. In the late 1970s there was a softening of demand for these, however, as the styles, particularly the red, seemed to lose their way. However, the success of the 1981 and 1982 Elizabeth Riesling (semillon) and the increased demand for red wines have witnessed a new awareness of their traditional qualities, and the company has been sensible in keeping suggested retail prices to a realistic level. I find these wines to be very dependable and well priced and I often find myself ordering them from restaurant wine lists for these reasons.

Millstone

This property was started by Peter and Vivienne Dobinson. Peter had been a potter working in stoneware for years. In 1965, while working in the rubber industry, Peter was test-driving for wear on tyres near the vineyards of the Murray Valley. He was struck by the appearance of the vines, seeing them as 'old people standing in a paddock'. He says this inspired him to grow vines and make wine.

In 1971 the Dobinson family moved to Allandale, settling on 40 hectares at back of Jim Roberts' Belbourie. The family built a home and a pottery kiln and began planting a vineyard on their property. Between 1973 and 1980 about 8 hectares were planted with cabernet sauvignon (2.6 hectares), sauvignon blanc (1.8 hectares) and other varieties such as chardonnay (1.2 hectares), plus shiraz, pinot noir, ruby cabernet and semillon. First vintage was in 1976, with the first commercial vintage in 1978.

In 1985 the Dobinsons decided to move on and they sold to the Ross family, who immediately settled well in the district. Unfortunately, Mr Ross became ill and was forbidden any form

of alcohol. Unhappily, he was forced to sell the winery, though it's a pleasure to record that he fully recovered from his illness.

In December 1988 Michael and Rae Tate took over. Michael, an Englishman, trained as an agriculturalist though he worked in Sydney as a financial planner. He is now in charge of finance at Australian Poultry (formerly Steggles). Rae Tate was a therapy radiographer before children took over, and she says she's delighted now to be in charge of the vineyards and winery, though she does seek consultant help from time to time.

Of their whites, sauvignon blanc and chardonnay are the most important. They were thrilled with their first vintage and look forward very much to the next few years. They crush about 40 tonnes, producing 3000 cases—most of which is sold at the cellar.

Mount View

Harry Tulloch, proprietor of Mount View, is a member of the famous Tulloch family. He is a thoroughly experienced viticulturist, with an unsurpassed knowledge of clonal selection of vines and vineyard planting techniques.

He established his own Mount View vineyard, 9 km west of Cessnock, in 1970, having previously been responsible for the establishment of the Hollydene and Seppelt Vineyards in the Hunter Valley.

A small winery was constructed prior to the 1980 vintage, and since then Harry has been making his own wine, helped from 1983 by son Keith, on a part-time basis. Six hectares of verdelho, semillon, traminer, sauvignon blanc, cabernet sauvignon and hermitage produce a useful 60 tonnes, of which part is sold as fruit. Three thousand cases are made from that retained and chiefly sold at cellar door.

Murray Robson

Murray Robson is a perfectionist who has brought a great deal of style to the Hunter Valley. His winery and operation at Mount View was a joy. Unfortunately, an intended public float and issue did not take place because of the 1987 October Crash. The property was sold to a syndicate and renamed Briar Ridge.

Murray then took over the old Audrey Wilkinson property for a while. However, he is now concentrating his efforts on his home property, down Hall's Lane, which runs off the Broke Road opposite Rothbury Estate.

Oakvale

Barry Shields, a Sydney solicitor, together with his wife, Jan, bought the old Oakvale property, on the Broke Road in the Lower Hunter, in 1985. This was the famous property of the Elliotts, one of the oldest Hunter families, and a spot at which I've enjoyed many a steak with a glass of red while on buying trips in the old days.

But times change. Doug Elliott sold to Hermitage, who were taken over by Wyndham. The Belford vineyard was retained by John Elliott, Doug's son, who sells his grapes to other makers. Meanwhile, Barry Shields is working hard to re-establish the Oakvale name.

He has only 4 hectares under vine at present,

3 hectares of chardonnay and 1 hectare of shiraz, though another 8 hectares will soon be bearing. He buys the rest of his material from local growers and crushes altogether about 100 tonnes, resulting in just over 7000 cases.

The main wines are the traditional semillon and shiraz, with chardonnay the third, and cabernet sauvignon the other main line. Barry has done quite well at major and local shows; he is extremely keen to make his wine mark and has already become very much involved in the affairs of the Hunter Valley.

Most sales are made at cellar door and keen buyers are made very welcome. There is a Sydney distributor for restaurants.

Surprisingly, Barry cites 1987 as his best year among those of his first few vintages. His semillon is a very good, well-balanced wine, leaning towards the older, slightly heavier style that matures so well in the bottle.

Oakvale winery.

Peacock Hill

The Peacock Hill vineyard is attached to the Herlstone Estate vineyard of Rothbury in the Lower Hunter. It is owned by Fred Renton and Harry Terrett. The 5 hectare property is leased by them to a syndicate involving themselves, Denis Power and David Lowe.

There are 2 hectares of chardonnay, half a hectare of pinot noir, 1 hectare of cabernet sauvignon and 1.5 hectares of shiraz.

The wines are processed under contract at Rothbury and are sold at Pokolbin Estate, limited licensed trade and export sales. Peacock Hill's 1987 reds were very good.

Pepper's Creek Winery and Antiques

Peter Ireland runs the wine side of the operation while his wife, Pam, concentrates on the antiques. They operate from charming stone buildings that Peter built in 1986 and 1987 in front of Pepper's Guest House, on Broke Road, in the Lower Hunter.

There's only 1 hectare under merlot, and fruit is purchased from local growers. The crush is generally 10–15 tonnes and 1000 cases are produced, all sold at cellar door. A straight semillon, a semillon–chardonnay and a shiraz are the main wines. Peter is very interested in merlot and intends to specialise in this variety.

Peterson's Wines Pty Ltd

This is one of the most successful of the more recent wave of Hunter winemakers. Run by the amiable Ian Peterson and his charming wife, Shirley, the vineyard was established in 1971 and the winery added in 1981.

There are 15 hectares of vineyard, made up of almost 6 hectares of semillon, 2 hectares of chardonnay; 5 hectares of shiraz, 2 hectares of pinot noir and some cabernet sauvignon. Altogether approximately 100 tonnes are processed.

Peterson's sprang to prominence in the mid-1980s with gold medals being won at major shows plus trophies for 'Small maker' success at the Hunter Valley Show. One remarkable achievement was the 1984 Chardonnay, which tied for gold medal at a special international judging in Melbourne (Victorian International Exhibition of Wine 1985). The 1986 Chardonnay

won the gold medal for being the best chardonnay on the day of the QANTAS Wine Cup 1987, held between the USA and Australia.

All this has firmly established the name, and Peterson's are now one of the most visited of the smaller wineries in the Hunter. Sales are normally at cellar door with some mail order. About twenty Sydney restaurants feature the wines.

Pokolbin Estate Vineyard

Situated in the Lower Hunter on McDonald's Road in between Brokenwood and Tulloch's. This was the Macdougall property on which they re-assembled a handsome old stone cottage from Belford. A Sydney company bought the vineyard and property and it is now operated by John Furlong. The vineyards—8 hectares of shiraz, 2 hectares of Rhine riesling and half a hectare of semillon—had become rather run down, and yields were fairly low, the crush being made under contract at Drayton's. The returned wine is sold under the Pokolbin Estate label. However, in addition to this, wines from other small vineyards are featured, among them Lake's Folly, Pothana, Peacock Hill and Callatoota.

The vineyards are now being brought back to full working order and chardonnay is being planted.

Pothana Vineyard

Situated just off the New England Highway at Belford in the Lower Hunter. Owned by the Hook family, David Hook being a science graduate from Sydney University. There are 4 hectares of vineyard, two of which are chardonnay, with 1 hectare each of semillon and pinot noir.

Over 20 tonnes is crushed from which 1500

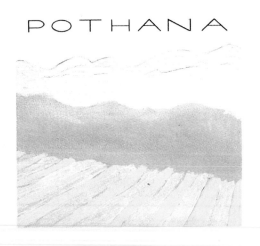

1989 SEMILLON

cases plus are made. Up to and including the 1989 vintage, the wines have been made, with David's help, at Hungerford Hill and Rothbury.

A winery was built for the 1990 vintage and there are now cellar door sales. A chardonnay and a semillon are the main wines (1987 being a very good year), and the wines are sold through local distributors.

Richmond Grove (see Wyndham Estate)

Not to be confused with the Old Richmond Grove property in the Upper Hunter which is now Richmond Vale.

The winery is in the Lower Hunter near the Hermitage Estate. It is situated on the Old Homestead Hill block once owned by the

Rothbury Group. An ultra-modern winery was built for the 1988 vintage. Mark Cashmore is the executive winemaker and Ian Scarborough the winemaker. Almost 200 000 cases of wine are produced, from the usual Hunter varietals, though sometimes it is difficult to understand the interplay between the Wyndham group's various Hunter wineries. They have 16 hectares of vineyards on the property and a further 36 hectares are coming into bearing.

Highly attractive tasting room facilities are a feature of this operation. Wines include Oak Matured Chablis, French Cask Chardonnay, Fumé Blanc, Nouvelle Chardonnay, White Bordeaux, White Burgundy, Cabernet Merlot, Nouvelle Cabernet Merlot and Cabernet Sauvignon.

The Rothbury Estate

The Rothbury Estate, one of the largest estate vineyards in the Hunter Valley, was begun in 1968 under the guidance of Len Evans and the celebrated vigneron Murray Tyrrell. The original team consisted of Dr Alan Burgess, Dr John Burgess, Peter Davidson, Len Evans, Alan Grainger, Ted Gowing, Rudy Komon, John McDowell, Frank Mills, Bob Sanders and Murray Tyrrell. The intention was to grow 100 hectares or so of vines. However, the financial euphoria of the late 1960s and requests from other investors led to three associate vine-growing syndicates being formed—Herlstone, Homestead Hill and Brokenback. Eventually the area under vine grew to 280 hectares.

In 1974 the syndicates were amalgamated, and a successful issue of shares was made to wine lovers who wished to be a part of the venture. A further reorganisation followed in 1977, which led to interests associated with Len Evans, the late Peter Fox and Daniel Chen having a controlling interest in Rothbury. The major lender, the Australian Industry Development Corporation, retired their funds in 1980, when a further 1000 or so members of the Rothbury Estate Society elected to become shareholders.

An outstanding feature of the Rothbury Estate is its impressive winery, situated on the Broke Road in the heart of Pokolbin/Rothbury parishes. Designed by Keith Cottier, it won the prestigious Blackett Award for Architecture in 1970. The spectacular Cask Hall seats more than 200 people for a meal. It also holds sixty-two 4500 litre casks, and was fully air-conditioned in 1982 to assist in the maturation of wines. The best modern equipment has been installed: including enclosed fermenters, centrifugal filters, must coolers, ultracoolers and Bucher Guyer presses, which are CO_2 jacketed to prevent oxidation.

After some viticultural rationalisation—involving the uprooting of unsuitable experimental varieties and low-yield, uneconomic vineyards, and the further planting of more successful ones—the Hunter Valley vineyards now comprise 111 hectares of vines: shiraz (37 hectares), pinot noir (10), cabernet sauvignon (5), merlot (2), chardonnay (33), semillon (20) and sauvignon blanc (4). The vineyard areas are the home paddock, Rothbury, plus Brokenback and Herlstone, all within close proximity.

In addition, in 1982 Rothbury purchased the 90 hectare Lachlan Valley vineyard, at Cowra in central New South Wales, to supplement its crush. The vineyard mix there comprises 38 hectares of chardonnay, 4 hectares of sauvignon blanc and 2 hectares of semillon.

In 1988 Rothbury purchased the Denman

Cask storage, Rothbury Estate.

Estate in the Upper Hunter and, after some rationalisation of the vineyard, there are now 8 hectares of shiraz, 6 cabernet sauvignon, 2 pinot noir, 1 gamay; 22 hectares of chardonnay, 15 semillon, 11 Rhine riesling, 9 traminer and 7 sauvignon blanc.

Rothbury's annual crush varies considerably. In 1979 it was 1900 tonnes, yet because of a prolonged drought which followed, this fell to 1300 tonnes in 1980, and only 500 tonnes in 1981. The crush was 1400 tonnes in 1982, and it is hoped that eventually a stable figure of 1800 to 2000 tonnes will be achieved.

Few grapes are brought in, in the belief that only total control can result in the best wines. And the Rothbury Estate does make every effort to make the very best wine. However, since this is not possible in any vintage, there is a vigorous selection program conducted by the winemakers and a selection tasting committee.

There are several categories of wine sold under the unique label designed by artist Fred Williams. The top wines are black label 'individual paddock' wines, which come from a particular block that in any year provides an exceptional wine. The next are individual vineyard wines, which come from particular vineyard areas. Wines not selected for these two series may be sold under varietal labels or under lesser designations. The white wines of Rothbury, in particular, have established a fine reputation.

Much of the wine is sold directly to shareholders and members of the Rothbury Estate Society, a unique wine club. All wine is released to them initially through a monthly newsletter. In addition, there are numerous dinners and other functions in the Cask Hall of the winery, as well as tastings, wine schools, seminars, auctions and other functions. An educational system of ribbon-award dinners operates, and nearly 10 000 members possess ribbons achieved through palate success—the ultimate being the Purple Ribbon, worn by fewer than a hundred tasters. The Society has done more in wine terms for its followers than any other wine group in Australia. Recently, part of Rothbury's production has been sold through quality shareholders. A variety of wines are bought in from different areas for the mail order program and these appear under other labels.

From the mid-1980s, the company embarked upon an ambitious wholesale and export program, particularly as chardonnay availabilities grew and demand increased. By the end of the decade, almost a third of total production was being exported to Sweden, the UK and the USA, in particular, as well as other countries.

In 1989 a new administration building was incorporated in a new Stage 3 of the winery, which also included a cool-storage area for bottled wine for 150 000 cases, and a cool-storage area for 5000 small barrels.

Rothbury has always been celebrated for the quality of its dry white wines, though the emphasis has changed from semillon to chardonnay. Top years for semillon (which is still held in high regard) are 1972, 1974, 1976, 1979, 1984, 1986 and 1989. Two styles of chardonnay are made, a quite rich and full-flavoured Hunter and an even more concentrated example from Cowra. From 1986 a Reserve program was instituted for small cask selections of these wines, chiefly for export. The 1986 was named by *Decanter* magazine, in the UK, as Australia's top chardonnay (and one of the best in the world). The 1987 won the gold medal at the QANTAS Wine Cup held in the Napa Valley in October 1988, being the best on the day of the ten top chardonnays of both the USA and Australia.

The reds are more mixed. Top years are 1973, 1975, 1979, 1983, 1986 and 1989. However, in some vintages there was probably too much effort directed towards the traditional lighter styles of the Hunter, and a more vigorous, richer wine is now being produced in suitable years.

After some trials and tribulations, Rothbury has become an important wine company. It does not intend to grow beyond a 2000 tonne crush and will always emphasise the pursuit of excellence in wine qualities.

Saxonvale Wines Pty Ltd (see Wyndham Estate)

Saxonvale was formed as a public company in 1970, and was part of the development boom in the Hunter at the time. The company was founded with substantial assistance from the AIDC (Australian Industry Development Corporation), a body set up by the Commonwealth Government to help the development of Australian companies.

The major upheaval in its existence occurred when the company was forced into receivership. Unfortunately for Saxonvale, it had been acquired by Gollin and Co shortly before the collapse of that company. The Macdougall brothers acquired the Saxonvale enterprise in 1978, and in turn sold to Wyndham in 1987.

The home of Saxonvale is the Fordwich Estate near Broke, where the winery (built in 1973) is situated. They have 100 hectares of volcanic reddish-chocolate soils there. Spring Mountain Estate (formerly Mount Leonard) is the second of Saxonvale's Lower Hunter holdings. The 115 hectare property has rich alluvial soils and weathered rock from the mountains behind the vineyards. Both these vineyards have a trickle-irrigation system installed to provide relief to the vines during the pre-vintage dry periods.

The vineyard mix at Fordwich and Spring Mountain includes semillon, cabernet, chardonnay, traminer, shiraz, and smaller plantings of pinot noir, Rhine riesling, chenin blanc and sauvignon blanc.

John Baruzzi is now the winemaker in charge of a 3500 tonne crush.

There are two distinct ranges of wine: the Premium Bin range, chardonnay, semillon, hermitage and cabernet sauvignon (all named Bin 1); and the Spring Mountain varietal range. Distribution is mainly through Cellarmasters (American Express) and restaurant sales through Mark Fesq. At least 200 000 cases are sold under the above labels.

Sobels

Sobels is situated on McDonald's Road in the Rothbury parish of the Lower Hunter, next door to the giant Vintage Country Club resort. This was the Tamalee winery, before that Macpherson's, and was bought by Kevin Sobels in March 1986.

Kevin Sobels, a member of the family who owned Quelltaler, has wide experience in the South Australian wine industry, where he worked for Hardy's, Saltram and Seppelt at Tanunda. He came to the Hunter in 1972 to establish Denman Estate's new winery—and made his own first vintage in 1974.

He then moved to Queldinburg, on the New England Highway, before selling out to move to the Lower Hunter.

To the 18 hectares of vineyard, he added, by purchase, the Leonard property in Palmers Lane. The total area under vineyard is now over 50 hectares: comprising 30 hectares of shiraz, 2 of cabernet sauvignon, 2 of pinot noir, and 2 of merlot; 16 hectares of chardonnay, 8 of semillon and 2 of sauvignon blanc. This, plus material purchased locally, gives Kevin a total of about 400 tonnes, which he hopes to increase to 600. In the meantime, he sells some of his own fruit and makes in excess of 20 000 cases, with a 40 000 case output being the eventual aim. All his wines are single varietals, plus a sparkling wine, and at present nearly 20 per cent is exported. The rest is sold at cellar door and a thriving mail order business, with some local distribution.

During 1989 and 1990 the winery was remodelled, a brick façade was added, complete with tower; new equipment was installed and a restaurant developed. All this with the help of Stan Parker, a Sydney businessman, who has become Kevin's equal partner in the enterprise.

Sutherland Wines

Sutherland Wines, established 1979, is a family concern at Pokolbin. Visitors are likely to meet the ebullient Neil Sutherland or his charming wife, Caroline. The winery, built for the 1983 crush, normally processes just under 100 tonnes.

There are 18 hectares of vineyard: semillon (7 hectares), chardonnay (5), chenin blanc (2); pinot noir (1.5) and shiraz (2.5).

Although the chardonnay has received the most accolades in the past, recently a 1988 semillon received a Benchmark award.

While cellar door and mail order sales have

been the most popular, now some wines go to Sydney restaurants and a 40 per cent export trade has been developed.

Tamburlaine Wines

The Tamburlaine vineyard and winery was founded by a Cessnock doctor, Dr J.A.L. Allen, and his family. It was started as a hobby in 1967 with the planting of shiraz, cabernet sauvignon and semillon varieties in red clay podsol in the low, undulating hill country of Pokolbin, between the Hungerford Hill and Tulloch vineyards. At that time, there were only three new small winemakers in the Hunter—Lake's Folly and Belbourie being the other two. The winery was built in 1977.

In 1986 Tamburlaine was bought by Mark Davidson and Greg Silkman. They now have 10 hectares under vine, 7.5 hectares of which is shiraz, the rest being cabernet sauvignon and semillon. Two hectares of chardonnay at Broke are also purchased under contract. A total of 80 tonnes is crushed, resulting in up to 6000 cases, of which half is sold at cellar door and 1000 exported to the UK. The balance is distributed in New South Wales and Western Australia.

Mark and Greg are great enthusiasts, interested only in quality production, and are already respected members of the group of smaller producers in the Lower Hunter.

Terrace Vale

Terrace Vale is the realisation of a romantic idea of a group of friends—wine and food enthusiasts—to recreate a small, old-fashioned, quality winery in place of all those that were being lost to big business. It owes its existence to a group of Touche Ross accountants who got together with the Tyrrells 'for a bit of fun'. Dick Tiley is still involved, as is Peter Wood, and Bruce Tyrrell also remains a shareholder. Winemaker Alain le Prince also bought into the partnership.

The idea became reality with the purchase, in 1971, of a property situated a few kilometres south and east of the Terrace Ranges, and adjacent to Rothbury Creek, which meanders through the vineyard. The Terrace Ranges are a range of hills of unpretentious dimensions north of the Pokolbin district. It was from this range that the winery took its name.

The vineyard was planted in stages over four years, commencing in 1972. This approach allowed a slower build-up of wine, so that wine stocks grew in balance with development of product awareness. The wine and food club background had a telling influence on the grape varieties selected for planting—only climatically suitable premium dry varieties. Chardonnay and cabernet sauvignon were selected as essential. More whites than reds were planted, anticipating the white wine boom (bold stuff in 1971). The land selected was mainly white wine country, being loamy creek flats with a watertable only a couple of metres below.

The outward appearance of Terrace Vale had to be of 'character'—the labour of artisans. The winery was designed to be practical while incorporating as much of the Hunter 'old shed' tradition as good winemaking practice would permit. In 1981 a small tasting pavilion with accommodation facilities above was completed. These are linked with the winery by a courtyard dressed with a pergola and muscat grapevines.

The 35 hectare vineyard is now at full maturity, comprising 12.5 hectares of shiraz, 2.5 of cabernet sauvignon, 1.5 of pinot noir, and just over half a hectare of merlot; 10 hectares of semillon, 5 of chardonnay, 2.5 of traminer and half a hectare of sauvignon blanc, which is made into a dessert wine.

Of the material available, about 100 tonnes is the usual crush, resulting in 7000 plus cases. The balance of the fruit is sold to Tyrrells.

Terrace Vale white wines, in particular, made by winemaker Alain le Prince, have already established a considerable reputation. The plan has been to make only specific varietal wines, rather than wines of a particular style. There are single examples of each varietal, with the exception of semillon, of which there are two, a flinty Bin 1 and a rounder, softer B1A.

Mainly cellar door sales.

J.Y. Tulloch & Sons Pty Ltd, Glen Elgin

For many years the Tullochs had the largest family vineyard in the Hunter. They are one of the four original families who survived the 1930s depression which wiped out so many of the vignerons of the time. Today, the Tullochs are no longer a family concern.

The story begins with John Younie Tulloch, the Methodist owner of the general store in Branxton. He was quite a prosperous man, for he also had grazing interests. In the style of the times he had a large family—nine children, of whom five were boys (Hector, Roy, James, Alec, Keith) and four girls (Dorothy, Marjory, Jean and Kath).

In what must be one of the most extraordinary business transactions in the history of the Hunter, Tulloch accepted a 20 hectare vineyard at Glen Elgin 'in satisfaction of an overdue debt'. The name of the customer who had no cash is not known, but he had ceased cultivation at Glen Elgin, and no wine had been made for a year when Tulloch took over in 1893. The vineyard was neglected, but, with no experience, John Tulloch made one hogshead of wine from the 2 hectares under vine in 1897. He sought advice from Professor J. Blunno of the New South Wales Department of Agriculture, and planted shiraz vines on the red and yellow clay podsolic soil.

John Tulloch had an uncle, J.A. Russell, who was a wine traveller. Russell sold his nephew's wine in Newcastle and the Cessnock district. Thus encouraged, Tulloch began to expand and plant more grapes. He moved his family from Branxton to live at Glen Elgin, when wine became his way of life.

With Federation in 1901 and the removal of trade barriers between states, Tulloch, along with other New South Wales vignerons, faced a flood of cheap government-subsidised wine from South Australia. He made fortified wine at Glen Elgin for the first time, but also continued to make dry reds.

After World War I, John Tulloch began to buy grapes from repatriated soldiers the government had settled on various 20 hectare properties at Fordwich, in the nearby Broke district. He later acquired six of those blocks, and eventually had a second vineyard of 120 hectares on sandy soil with basalt subsoil and clay. The grapes from Fordwich have always been processed at the home winery at Glen Elgin.

J.Y. Tulloch held on through the 1930s depression and in 1939 formed his business into a limited liability company. Through the 1920s and 1930s most of Tulloch's wine was sold under the Caldwell label, and thereafter to Douglas Lamb and Leo Buring.

When J.Y. died in 1940, Hector Tulloch, his eldest son, became manager of the Glen Elgin winery, with his brother Keith as his assistant. Another brother, Jim, took over the management of the Fordwich vineyard, while brother Alec was given control of the company's cattle properties. At the end of World War II it was decided to sell under the Tulloch label, instead of in bulk to big companies. It was a most successful move.

Hector Tulloch and his wife Eileen were well known in the Pokolbin district for their hospitality. He was chief winemaker until his death in 1965. Hector was especially proud of his 1954 Pokolbin Dry Red, which won first prize in both the Claret and Burgundy classes of the Sydney Show—it rather made nonsense of the claret and burgundy distinctions, which are not really applicable in Australia.

Keith, one of Hector's brothers, was chief winemaker from Hector's death until his retirement in 1970. He never married, and was assisted by Hector's son Jay. Keith was one of the vignerons of the Hunter district who had a great knowledge of winemaking in the local conditions and was willing to share that knowledge. Hector and Keith Tulloch made good wine, and with their efforts Tulloch Pokolbin Riesling and Tulloch Pokolbin Dry Red competed successfully in wine shows throughout Australia.

In November 1969 the company was taken

over by Reed Consolidated Industries, a huge Australian public company with strong British connections. The Tulloch name was not lost entirely—with Jay Tulloch and his cousin John S. Tulloch (also a grandson of the founder J.Y. Tulloch) staying on. Reeds built a new winery, replacing the old one which has been described as an 'iron structure resembling a cow-shed'. They installed a considerable amount of new equipment, such as modern presses and stainless steel tanks. Under the supervision of a new manager, Dickson Morris (previously winemaker at Berri), more wine was produced and great effort was made to ensure that production was of the highest possible quality.

In 1970 a further 120 hectares of land was purchased adjoining the Glen Elgin winery. This area was planted with cabernet sauvignon and hermitage grapes, which in turn, under new ownership, were either grubbed out or sold, illustrating the rather difficult situation for management during this time.

John Younie Tulloch (Jay), the grandson and namesake of the founder, was appointed general manager when Dickson Morris left the company in 1973, and Ian Scarborough (a Roseworthy graduate) was appointed winemaker.

In another notable move, Gilbeys Australia, the company's wine marketers, acquired a controlling interest in J.Y. Tulloch & Sons Pty Ltd from the Reed group in 1974. Wynn's in turn purchased the company in 1983 and itself was absorbed by Penfolds in 1985.

These changes must have been quite unsettling over this period, as different owners wanted different things, and it must be said that the company appeared to lose some direction during the 1970s and early 1980s. The famous reds of the 1950s were occasionally emulated and the whites suffered comparison with other emerging styles. However, by the late 1980s things had settled down, and Tulloch's were allowed to act from a largely autonomous point of view, leaving the marketing of their product to Penfolds.

The company is now mostly a white wine producer, with only 30 hectares of vineyard supplemented by purchases from local growers. Five hundred tonnes is an average crush, with semillon, verdelho and chardonnay the main varieties, plus some shiraz also being made. The year 1987 was an excellent chardonnay vintage,

1986 very good for semillon and 1983, 1986 and 1987 produced deep, rich reds.

Following Ian Scarborough's decision to go into his own business, Patrick Auld was appointed Tulloch's winemaker. His family is very well known in the industry. He is a sixth-generation winemaker whose great-great-great-grandfather started Auldana in South Australia. His grandfather on his mother's side owned Seaview for many years.

My first trip to the Hunter was on 4 July 1966, which coincided with the birth of my son Toby. It was a day spent with the late Johnny Walker of Bistro fame. We finished up having a steak dinner that night seated between the rows of old casks at Tulloch's and enjoyed various vintages of Tulloch red, the 1964, 1962, 1961, 1959, 1958, 1957, 1955, 1954, 1952, 1947, and finally the 1931! All remarkable wines and a tribute to Hector and Keith Tulloch and the glory that was there. One day may it return.

Tyrrell's Vineyard Pty Ltd, Ashmans

Tyrrell's are the oldest family company still producing wine in the Hunter Valley. The Tyrrell name is now well known, owing to the enthusiastic promotional efforts of the present proprietor, Murray Tyrrell.

The Ashmans story began with Edward Tyrrell, a nephew of the first Anglican bishop of Newcastle, who, in 1858, bought the land where the vineyards are now. The original holding, which he called Ashmans, was 130 hectares. First, Edward put up a shack of gum-tree slabs, in which he lived. This small hut still stands, adjacent to the present winery. He then cleared some of the land and planted grapevines. The first vintage was in 1864, from a 20 hectare patch of vines descended from the Rhône Valley. For nearly twenty years Edward Tyrrell increased and improved his property. A strip of his vines planted in 1879 and still bearing fruit are believed to be the oldest vineyards in production in the Hunter Valley.

One of his sons, Dan (whose full name was Edward George Tyrrell), took over in 1883 at the age of fourteen. He was the oldest of Edward's ten children. Dan Tyrrell is a part of the Hunter legend. He built up the Tyrrell name and added considerably to the family holdings.

Dan had very strong views on winemaking and believed simply in good basic equipment and methods. He was convinced that the earth floor of the winery contributed to the quality of his wine and that the fluctuating temperatures in the slab-and-iron winery helped to make the wines unique. He was a firm traditionalist, who would never use anything but wild yeasts and was quite opposed to the use of sulphur. Dan sold his wine in bulk, to be bottled by others. Maurice O'Shea was one of the buyers, and some of his great wines were, in fact, Tyrrell's. Dan Tyrrell, who never married, died in April 1959.

Murray Tyrrell, the son of Dan's brother Avery, was born in February 1922 in Cessnock. At the end of World War II, on his return from overseas service, he became associated with the vineyard; he took over as winemaker on Dan's death in 1959. The early years of his management were not easy. Severe hailstorms almost wiped out the crops in 1958 and 1960, and also hit in 1962, while the 1959 and 1961 vintages were affected by the hail of the previous years.

Murray Tyrrell began tentatively bottling wine in 1962. It is perhaps remarkable that a company which has been to the forefront of recognition as a premium-wine producer, in part supported by a depth of tradition, is in fact a comparative 'newcomer' as far as bottled wine is concerned. Tulloch's, for example, were far better established by the 1950s or even the late 1940s, as makers of high-quality bottled wines. Tyrrell's were still selling in bulk. It is a testimony to the talent and drive of Murray Tyrrell that his company has become so important.

Sales at present are approaching the 400 000 case mark. Yet I can remember buying sixty cases of wine in 1963 and Murray Tyrrell being flabbergasted at the size of the order.

Tyrrell's were also pioneers of chardonnay and pinot noir, and their show successes with these varieties, plus the traditional semillon and shiraz, stress the thoroughness and completeness of this establishment as one of the most important wine producers in Australia.

By the late 1970s, within twenty years of their first bottlings, this had been achieved. Then, in the early to mid-1980s, there appeared to be a diminution of this effort. First, the leasing and then purchase of the Chateau Douglas vineyards in the Upper Hunter provided quantities of good sound material which went into the Long Flat series. A great effort was made to create this easy-drinking, relatively low-priced line, first in red and then in white, for both wholesale distribution and export sales. Successful they were, for Long Flat Red is now second only to Jacob's Creek Claret in terms of red wine sale volumes, and the Long Flat White has climbed into the top ten of volume case sales. Bruce Tyrrell, who has virtually managed the day-to-day business of the company since the mid-1980s, is delighted with these 'bread and butter' volumes. He feels that they will enable the company to put more money and time back into the pursuit of highest qualities, including the retention of quantities of the top reds for on-site maturation.

Murray still keeps a benevolent eye on everything, though his purchase of a large cattle property at Quirindi (over 1000 hectares), and the more recent acquisition of a huge property near Rockhampton, Queensland (7500 hectares), has meant that his time is limited.

Of the wines, Vat 1 and Vat 18 are the pick of the semillon variety, the latter being slightly heavier and rounder than the other. Though these were called Hunter riesling for years (incorrectly for the purists), the true varietal name, semillon, is now being used. The Vat 47 pinot chardonnay (another varietal bloomer, just chardonnay being sufficient) has long been among the most important of Australian chardonnays. The 1973 led the way and won almost country-wide show recognition. There followed the 1975, 1977 and 1979—all multi-gold winners.

After the 'hot' vintages of 1981, 1982 and 1983, there was a slight departure from style in 1984, and Limousin oak was used for maturation instead of Nevers, the wine being a trifle lighter and more delicate. The 1986 and 1987 are both good examples of this style.

Of the reds, Vats 5, 9 and 11 are of traditional shiraz regional style—rich, soft, earthy, and matured in large old oak; and Vat 8 is of a newer style, kept cooler and on stalks, spliced with some cabernet and matured in new oak barriques.

Tyrrell has done extremely well with Pinot Noir, 1976, 1981, 1983 and 1987 being outstanding examples. These wines are unlike their more aromatic brothers from the south. They need from three to five years in the bottle and they emerge as highly flavoured soft dry reds that are of regional character firstly, and varietal character secondly. Yet they are lovely soft wines that do not taste typically of shiraz—they are different, and have to be understood. The 1976, incidentally, won its division in the Wine Olympics held in Paris in 1979, at which I was a judge, and did a great deal to put Australia on the wine map.

There was also an excellent sparkling wine made in 1982 from pinot noir. Tyrrell's made the base wine, and the second fermentation and maturation on yeast lees was done elsewhere under contract. However, from 1986 they have completed the whole process there and the 1986 Pinot Noir Brut is a wine of considerable quality.

In all, Tyrrell's, though no longer a small company, continue to make batches of wine of an idiosyncratic character, many of which have great appeal. We trust that their drive for a place in the quantitative market will never usurp the quest for individualism in regional and varietal wines.

Verona Vineyard Pty Ltd

Verona Vineyard, planted on the banks of the Hunter River, immediately north of Muswellbrook, is owned by a Muswellbrook family, the Yores of Negoa. The vineyard takes its name from the area first planted with grapes. In 1890 it belonged to two butchers from England, Mr Abraham Clark and Mr Joe Gillies, who, considering themselves gentlemen of learning and with a knowledge of Shakespeare, took the name for their property from his play *Two Gentlemen of Verona*.

Interestingly, the vineyard started as a demonstration nursery for a drip-irrigation system designed by engineer Keith Yore. The first grapes were picked in 1973, when what is described as a 'fun day' was held and the fruit trodden by foot with a small amount of wine being made. It was then that the decision was made to enlarge the vineyard, and now 30 hectares are in production.

Varieties planted at Verona in Muswellbrook are verdelho, semillon, chardonnay, sauvignon blanc, Rhine riesling, cabernet sauvignon and shiraz. At Pokolbin they have 5 hectares of shiraz and 1 hectare of chardonnay.

The first wine under the Verona label was made in 1974, in the winery alongside the New England Highway near Muswellbrook. In 1981 another winery was built at Pokolbin, on Macdonald's Road, opposite Brokenwood.

Altogether some 60 to 70 tonnes are processed, to make approximately 5000 cases, mostly for sale at either cellar door. The balance of the fruit is sold to other companies.

Wyndham Estate

Wyndham Estate has been through several changes in name, ownership and prosperity in its long history. It is now the oldest established vineyard still operating in Australia (though claims that the Wyndham of today is Australia's oldest are somewhat specious), and as such warrants a full recounting of its story.

George Wyndham was born in Wiltshire in 1801 to a wealthy family. He was educated at Eton and Harrow before travelling through Canada, then France and Italy, where he studied the culture and production of wine. He came to New South Wales in 1827 with £3000 borrowed from his father, some servants and a range of stock animals.

On 15 January 1828 George Wyndham purchased a 485 hectare property at a bankrupt's auction and christened it Dalwood, after one of his father's farms in England. He added considerably to his land holdings, eventually holding thousands of hectares. He planted 600 vine cuttings given to him by James Busby in 1830, as part of a farming venture which attracted more than its share of natural disasters. This makes him a contender with Busby in the 'who planted the first Hunter vines?' contest. His first vintage, which he recorded 'promised to make good vinegar', was in 1835.

The situation improved, and in the late 1850s Wyndham's son John took over the management of the property and, with his brother Alexander, extended plantings to a total of 30 hectares by 1886. John Wyndham has a place as one of the real pioneers of the Australian wine industry; he was Australia's first wine merchandiser. He promoted Dalwood as a show place of the Australian industry, with auctions that became famous. In its heyday, the late 1880s, Dalwood was the second largest vineyard in the colony, and its wines won various trophies and medals in Bordeaux, Amsterdam, London and Bombay.

With John Wyndham's early death in 1887 and the economic recession of the 1890s, Dalwood collapsed and the Commercial Banking Co ran the business until it was sold to J.F.M. Wilkinson of Coolalta in 1901. He split Dalwood into two properties, selling the house, with 52 hectares, to a Mr McNamara.

A new era began in 1904, when Frank Astor Penfold Hyland bought the other 56 hectare property for Penfolds. Under Penfold management, Dalwood became a household word, and many champion red and white table wines were made there until the early 1960s, when they decided to move to Wybong in the Upper Hunter.

Perc McGuigan, who had been Penfold's winemaker for more than twenty years, bought the Dalwood Estate property, though not the name, for £12 000. Perc's son Brian, with Jim Allen and Digby Matheson, founded Wyndham

Estate Pty Ltd and in 1971 acquired the original house block, thus reuniting the property. In 1976 the Australian Guarantee Corporation Ltd bought Matheson's 40 per cent interest, and later Anglo Thai bought into the consortium, so that AGC and Anglo Thai had 44 per cent each and Brian McGuigan 12 per cent.

Under Brian McGuigan's guidance, Wyndham Estate has been developed to the showplace standard that it held in John Wyndham's time a century ago. Many of the historic buildings have been preserved. Dalwood is now the administrative base of Wyndham's operations.

The vineyards, right on the banks of the Hunter River, have been planted three times. Penfolds replanted over the years and removed the last of the old vines in 1961. Wyndham Estate uprooted Penfold's vines, partly because they were too close for modern machinery, and partly to establish new clones of the white varieties they had imported through the Department of Agriculture. Replanting took place from 1970 to 1972, and included semillon, chardonnay, sylvaner, traminer, Rhine riesling, blanquette, sauvignon blanc, tokay and white frontignac. For reds, cabernet sauvignon, pinot noir, malbec and mataro were planted.

In a major development in 1975 Wyndham acquired Hollydene, in the Upper Hunter, after it had been through troubled times financially since its establishment in 1967. Total plantings are now 41 hectares, over half of which are white varieties; mainly semillon with chardonnay and sauvignon blanc.

In 1978 Wyndham took over the Hermitage Estate, a large-scale vineyard development which ended in the ignominy of receivership, and renamed it the Hunter Estate. It began, however, as long ago as 1901 under the name Mistletoe Farm, when grapes were first planted at the vineyard situated towards the base of the Brokenback Range. Hermitage Estate was formed at the time of the wine boom in 1967, and 300 hectares of grapes were planted during the next five years. Much of these were red varieties planted on tough clay. In 1973 a winery of advanced design was built, housing the latest winemaking equipment, including two of the three Rotatank fermenters in Australia. The winery is capable of handling up to 7000 tonnes of grapes each vintage. Wines include char-

The old winery at Wyndham Estate.

donnay, fumé blanc, pinot noir and cabernet sauvignon. Neil McGuigan, Brian's younger brother, is winemaker there.

Richmond Grove in the Upper Hunter became part of the group (see Richmond Grove) and then, on 1 January 1987, Saxonvale, another of the Hunter giants of the late 1960s boom, was taken over (see Saxonvale Wines). Brian McGuigan seemed to be doing deals in every direction. But there was more to come.

Stan Hamley had been an executive with AGC. In 1984 he and Brian bought Wyndham from AGC and Anglo Thai. They listed in 1985 and a $4 million dollar issue was fully subscribed. There was a further $2 million dollar float in 1987.

Since going public, profitability has been good and is growing rapidly. Wyndham now processes 500 000 cases, and the whole group 1 million cases, 10 per cent of which are export sales, under the direction of the hard-working (Mrs) Fay McGuigan. Group turnover exceeds $50 million annually. In 1990, Orlando, the Barossa Valley giant, took over the Wyndham group, giving it a substantial holding in NSW, and a very strong market acceptance in that state.

Wyndham market a substantial range of red and white table wines in three distinct price categories. Benchmark Accredited wines, Bin 888 Cabernet Merlot, Hunter Chardonnay and the recently released Verdelho and Chardonnay Cuvée are the flagship wines. These are followed by Oak Chardonnay, Bin 444 Cabernet Sauvignon, Limited Release Semillon, Pinot Noir, and Bin 222 Chardonnay Semillon. A wide range of more popular styles is available, including Chablis Superior, Bin 777 Graves Exceptional, Bin 555 Hermitage, TR2 Traminer Riesling, GT Bin 6 Gewurztraminer and White Burgundy.

One suspects that having achieved such commercial success, Brian now wants to make the best wine in Australia. To questions regarding his ambitions, he will give stock answers:

We want to service the changing market, in order to provide an honest return for shareholders . . . We want to broaden our base in Australia and not just be a Hunter Valley Company . . . Huge vineyards and advanced technology mean that we can help Australia provide a great deal of the needs of the world at an economical price.

There is little doubt that Wyndham intends to continue to expand, as the following list of vineyard holdings show. (Prospective plantings included both definite acquisitions and those still in negotiation.)

Yet, when pressed, Brian finally did weaken to reveal an ambition that I suspected had been part of his recent thinking. 'I would like,' he told me, 'to make a really ball-tearing wine.'

WYNDHAM GROUP VINEYARD HOLDINGS—EXISTING AND PLANNED			
	Existing	Prospective Plantings	Total Hectares
Hunter			
Dalwood	42	—	42
Casuarina	25	—	25
Golden Grape	17	—	17
Hunter Estate	96	—	96
Richmond Grove	16	36	52
Spring Mountain	48	—	48
Hawthorn Glen	34	—	34
Fordwich	76	—	76
Hollydene	41	—	41
Richmond Vale	100	—	100
Mudgee			
Montrose	10	—	10
Amberton	39	—	39
Craigmoor Winery	9	—	9
Craigmoor House	90	—	90
Stoney Creek	31	—	31
Oakfield	56	—	56
Michaels	8	—	8
Cowra			
Cooraminta	224	—	224
Canowindra	—	320	320
Victoria			
Tslepsis	20	60	80
Mitchelstown	—	100	100
Yarra Valley	—	40	40
South Australia			
Siegersdorf	32	—	32
Fullers	31	—	31
Angle Vale	36	20	56
Coonawarra-Padthaway	—	80	80
McLaren Vale	48	—	48
Totals	1129	656	1785

The Upper Hunter

This is a fairly broad appellation for a number of wineries scattered around an area south of Muswellbrook and Singleton. Broke/Fordwich, separated from the Pokolbin/Rothbury parishes by the Army firing range, is not part of it; Arrowfield, across the Putty Road that links Singleton and Windsor, is.

This does not mean that the area is devoid of viticultural history. In 1864 Karl Brecht planted

a vineyard which he named 'Rosemount'—a name which has come back into prominence today. Brecht, a German, had been brought to New South Wales as a 'wine dresser' to work for William Dangar, which he did until 1860, when he bought his own property. He had 10 hectares under vine in 1862 and produced a wide range of wines, including champagne, for which he won many awards at exhibitions—among them a gold medal at the Bordeaux International Exhibition of 1882 for his 1880 Hermitage. There were scattered German vignerons in the area in the second half of the nineteenth century, and they survived until the 1930s depression, their plantings being mainly on the rocky hilly outcrops.

The Upper Hunter became all the rage again in the 1960s when Penfold's, wishing to expand their Hunter holdings, sent Perc McGuigan and John Davoren scouring the area for suitable land. I do not know the full story of recommendation and acceptance, but I do know that there was a tremendous amount of ballyhoo about the rich, black soils and unlimited irrigation. Whatever, they bought over 500 hectares, planted all sorts of varieties, built a modern winery and installed a young Brian McGuigan as winemaker/manager. I was at the opening in the mid 1960s when the late Harold Holt amiably presided, and it was to be one of the major advances in wine production of the century.

What went wrong? It would take a skilled historian of investigation a great deal of time to completely identify the answer. Sufficient to say there were too many varieties, many of them unsuitable for the area; the soil was not suitable for varieties that may have been useful; Penfold's changed direction and grew tired of the project. Whatever, very few wines of distinction emerged from Penfold's Wybong, and eventually changes in ownership and management at Penfold's resulted first in closure of the winery and subsequently in a sale to Rosemount.

Yet their enthusiasm and size of investment had lured others, notable among them being Rosemount, Chateau Douglas, Richmond Grove and Arrowfield. Today only Rosemount has survived the market shake-outs, turnovers and take-overs. There are still sturdy independent vignerons, such as the Cruickshanks of Callatoota Estate, a rare cabernet specialist, but

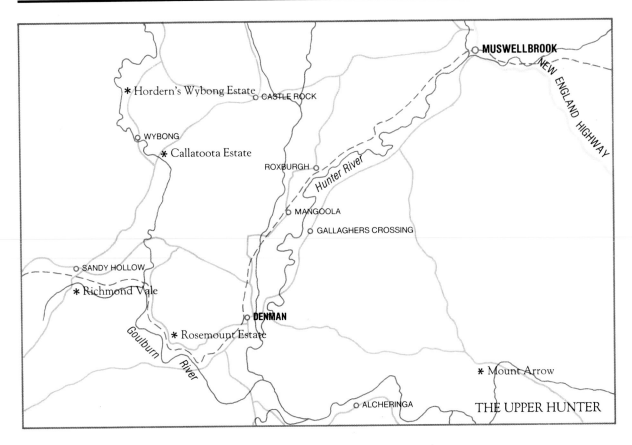

THE UPPER HUNTER

most of the others have been incorporated into either the Wyndham, Tyrrell or Rosemount maws, though there have been other new owners appearing. For example, Denman Estate was partly sold to Rosemount, who developed their Roxburgh vineyard into an outstanding producer of chardonnay, the rest of the vineyard and winery later being taken over by Rothbury.

Rosemount, who own and purchase material from different parts of Australia, still have their main winemaking facility and most of their own vineyards in the area and that is sufficient to prove the viability of it. For I feel that, in spite of the boom and doom nature of the region, enough has been shown in the last twenty-five years to prove that once again the Upper Hunter could become an important area.

There are suitable fertile soils, land is comparatively cheap, and there is plenty of water. Excellent whites and flavoursome reds have been made, though I am inclined to support the specialisation of effort into rich, soft whites, particularly from chardonnay.

It will only take another wine sales boom, which is probably to be one of export, to witness further developments.

Callatoota Estate

A small winery on Wybong Creek in the Upper Hunter, Callatoota Estate was unique in that I believe it was the only one in Australia devoted to a single variety: cabernet sauvignon. They rather spoiled this when they added a little cabernet franc.

John Cruickshank, a Sydney management consultant, planted 4 hectares in 1974 and subsequently another 5 hectares on this 16 hectare property. The varieties grown are 90 per cent cabernet sauvignon and 10 per cent cabernet franc. The winery was built in 1981 and, although at present producing a 50 tonne crush, when the new vineyard is in full production this is expected to become 100 tonnes. Production is 4000 cases and will rise to 7000 cases.

Andrew, John's son, is the winemaker and viticulturist, and he processes only his own material. The resultant red has good colour, full fruit and flesh and a soft tannin finish. The oak can be assertive, but examples I've seen of recent vintages indicate that this is diminishing in force.

The Cruickshanks welcome visitors to see their operation and vineyard and to taste their

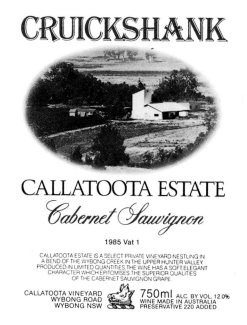

CRUICKSHANK

CALLATOOTA ESTATE
Cabernet Sauvignon

1985 Vat 1

CALLATOOTA ESTATE IS A SELECT PRIVATE VINEYARD NESTLING IN
A BEND OF THE WYBONG CREEK IN THE UPPER HUNTER VALLEY.
PRODUCED IN LIMITED QUANTITIES. THE WINE HAS A SOFT ELEGANT
CHARACTER WHICH EPITOMISES THE SUPERIOR QUALITIES
OF THE CABERNET SAUVIGNON GRAPE.

CALLATOOTA VINEYARD
WYBONG ROAD
WYBONG NSW
750ml ALC. BY VOL. 12.0%
WINE MADE IN AUSTRALIA
PRESERVATIVE 220 ADDED

wine, the best vintages being 1982, 1985, 1986 and 1989. The bottle sales are mainly cellar door and mail order though one may find them at shops and restaurants in Sydney, Melbourne and Canberra.

Hordern's Wybong Estate

David Hordern, grazier and owner of the Hereford stud at Brogheda, was the first private individual to plant vines in the Upper Hunter when he planted some 3 hectares with shiraz cuttings in 1965. Two years later Dr Bob Smith, a Sydney orthopaedic surgeon, established Wybong Estate on Wybong Creek in the south-west corner of Brogheda. In 1969 they joined forces to establish the Wybong winery.

Their winery is both beautiful and unusual—it is a reconstructed gaol. The enterprising pair moved the 1840 stone prison from Bengalla, piece by piece, and it was rebuilt in a different shape using the ironbark supports, bearers and joists from the century-old Dalgety wool stores to support a cedar-lined roof. They added an ironbark slab winemakers' quarters lined with shingles hand-made from King Billy pine.

The first vintage was 1971, after which Bob Smith gained practical experience by working a season at Wachenheim on the Rhine in 1972 and in the Napa Valley in 1973. In the early 1980s Bob Smith bought out David Hordern.

The Estate puts out a range of varietal whites and blended reds which have collected an impressive range of medals on the show circuit.

John Reynolds, whose career progressed from Rothbury to Wyndham, bought the property from Bob and Theo Smith in early 1990. He is a fine winemaker, and I have no doubt he will work very hard to achieve Bob's 'corner of paradise' dream. We will eventually see many fine wines from his first commercial venture.

Mount Arrow

The history of this property goes back to 1824, when Governor Macquarie granted several fertile tracts of land in the Upper Hunter to George Bowman.

Bowman based the names of his properties on variations of the family name: Arrowfield, Bowfield, and Archerfield. He planted a vineyard on Archerfield, made wine and obtained a licence to distill brandy. (All three properties survive today. W.R. Carpenter later bought the Arrowfield holding.) Bowman, a magistrate, was assigned seven convicts, and in 1832 they completed a two-storey sandstone block cottage on Arrowfield, which included an underground lock-up with six leg irons fastened to the walls. The cottage and the lock-up (including leg irons) still stand.

There were several changes of ownership, including a long term under the Moses brothers, who put Arrowfield on the map as a horse stud. Such horses as the 1920 Melbourne Cup winner, Poitrel, and 1926 Caulfield Cup winner, Manfred, were bred there.

ARROWFIELD
——— ESTABLISHED 1824 ———

'THE BLUFF' BY ASHLEIGH MANLEY

Sauvignon Blanc
HAWKES BAY
750ml, 11.0% ALC/VOL, ARROWFIELD WINES PTY LTD
PRODUCE OF NEW ZEALAND / AUSTRALIA

Young vines at Arrowfield.

The vineyard development at Arrowfield occurred between 1969 and 1974 and 460 hectares of vines were planted by W.R. Carpenter Holdings Pty Ltd. Each vine was supplied with supplementary water through a large trickle irrigation system. The plantings at Arrowfield consisted of chardonnay, Rhine riesling, traminer, semillon, clairette (blanquette); and for the reds, shiraz and cabernet sauvignon. There is a wide range of soil types, from heavy black alluvial river flats to the lighter hilly sandstone-type soils.

In 1975 a large modern winery was constructed under the direction of winemaker 'Scotty' Ireland, who had become well known as a champagne-maker for McWilliams and Seppelts. The attractive winery was built on two levels, the lower and larger cellar being almost two-thirds below ground level to create ideal cellar conditions. An enormous amount of money was invested in the venture; apart from the land, vineyard development and winery construction, the sheer scale and extent of winery equipment boggles the mind. There is 5 million litres of stainless steel storage, for example.

The impressive scale of the operation did not prevent severe problems for the company in the late 1970s. One could say, in fact, it was the cause. The huge output of wines became something of an embarrassment when the public swing away from red wines became evident. Thus in mid-1979, Arrowfield, under the direction of chief winemaker Gary Baldwin, changed direction. Red plantings were substantially reduced, the operational vineyard was reduced to less than 300 hectares, and the use of the trickle irrigation curtailed to maximise flavour and quality.

This was not enough, however, as the pendulum of demand swung, first to riesling and then to chardonnay. By the mid-1980s losses were substantial, to say the least. Baldwin left for greener fields, to be replaced by Simon Gilbert in 1985. He made further rationalisations, particularly with the winery, selling off large tanks and surplus equipment, though both a new press and modern bottling machinery were installed.

In 1986 the Australian Racing and Breeding Stables (ARABS) bought the entire property from Carpenter; they in turn changed their name to the Arrowfield Group Pty Ltd in 1987.

In 1987–88 the winery 'broke even' and things started looking a little better. However, the racing people realised that the wine game was some-

Arrowfield winery laboratory.

what tougher than their winning sport, so in turn they sold lock, stock and barrel, but not the winery or vineyards, to a group headed by Nick Whitlam. This was in April 1989, with the group having an option to buy both winery and/or vineyards. Nick Whitlam became the chairman, Andrew Simon the managing director and Simon Gilbert the winemaker and manager. There are a number of other 'sleeping' partners.

They own a limited range of vineyards, 12.5 hectares of chardonnay, plus 14 hectares of mixed varietals—chardonnay, semillon, sauvignon blanc, pinot noir, cabernet franc and merlot —and, of course, have access to the huge vineyards there, helping market the product. They also buy other material from the Hunter, Cowra and Mudgee.

The crush has returned to almost 2000 tonnes, the majority being contract wine (for other wine companies), though they keep 80–100 000 cases for their own marketing purposes. Chardonnay and a semillon chardonnay are the major lines. Recent top years include 1986 and 1987, some latter years being wetter and producing more delicate wines. Besides cellar door sales, Arrowfield wines have wide distribution and export.

The Mount Arrow group, which owns the new Arrowfield, will also market wines under the Simon Whitlam, Woolombi Brook and Simon Gilbert labels. In 1990, a Japanese company bought a controlling interest in the group, but apparently will leave the running of the operation to the present management.

Richmond Vale (formerly Richmond Grove, see Wyndham Estate)

As Richmond Grove, this was situated on the banks of the Goulburn River at Denman, south of Sandy Hollow. The property was originally owned by John and Mary Muddle, of the poker machine business Nutt & Muddle, who sold the first Richmond Grove grapes to Penfolds in 1973. This material was made into Penfolds 1973 Bin 6K Riesling, which won the trophy for the best wine at the Melbourne show. In view of the potential of their grapes, the Muddles decided to make their own wine rather than sell the fruit to other wineries.

In April 1982 Richmond Grove came under

the management of the talented Mark Cashmore and Richard Warland, who formed a new wine venture, Australian Vintners. Wyndham Estate was also involved. Later, it bought the other two partners out, thus becoming the owner.

The 433 hectare property is covered in a 12 m deep, rich alluvial loam deposited by the river. The annual rainfall is 710 mm, and the property is under drip irrigation, enabling each vine to receive a carefully controlled amount of water. The richness of the soil and degree of root penetration insulates the grapes from the negative effects of drought. The grapes easily reach full maturity, and desirable acid/sugar levels are consistently achieved.

Plantings now exceed 100 hectares, with the main variety planted being 24 hectares of chardonnay. As well, the vineyard comprises gewurztraminer (15 hectares), shiraz (15), semillon (13), Rhine riesling (9), sauvignon blanc (8), French colombard (6.5), blanquette (3), mataro (2.5), cabernet sauvignon (2), ruby cabernet (1) and merlot (1).

When Wyndham bought the Homestead Hill property in the Lower Hunter (formerly part of the Rothbury Group), they re-named it Richmond Grove and changed the name of the Upper Hunter property to Richmond Vale. All a little confusing.

Even more confusing is that material from the Richmond Vale still goes into wine which sells as Richmond Grove. These are among the premium labels of the Wyndham group.

Rosemount Estate

There is little doubt that Rosemount is one of the great success stories of the Australian wine industry. Born during the wine boom of the 1970s, it was an idea of Bob Oatley's, whose Angco company had been involved in coffee and cocoa production in New Guinea. The company, formed in 1969, selected the 600 hectare Rosemount property, near the junction of the Goulburn and Hunter Rivers in the Upper Hunter Valley, as a cattle property. Charolais cattle and stud horses still graze near the vineyards.

But Rosemount, named after a village near Stirling, in Scotland, has an historic link with viticulture. In the 1840s a settler named Karl Brecht was brought to the area as a shepherd by

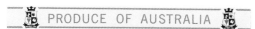

William Dangar. He was granted land near the junction of Wybong Creek and the Goulburn River, where he planted grapes. His first wines were made at Rosemount in the early 1860s. These won several international awards—at the American Centennial in 1876 in Philadelphia one of his 'Burgundy' wines won a gold medal, and other gold medals were awarded at Paris and Montpellier. Sadly, as was so often the case, his successors sold the land, and it became a dairy farm from the time of World War I until the Oatley family replanted vineyards from 1970.

The Rosemount home property on which the winery is built was originally notable for success with traminer and Rhine riesling. In fact, early show success during the mid-1970s was responsible for the name becoming well established. However, it was as a producer of chardonnay that Rosemount became a household name. They bought whatever fruit and wine they could, while establishing and buying vineyards as quickly as possible.

Edinglassie, a property near Muswellbrook, was bought and planted, plus properties nearer Rosemount, Yarrawa and Roseglen.

A significant move was the 1977 acquisition of Penfold's Wybong Estate vineyards and winery. Further expansion occurred with the purchase of the Roxburgh vineyard from Denman Estate. The plantings are heavily inclined to the premium white wines so much in demand. A number of the vineyards are irrigated.

In December 1981 Rosemount moved into Coonawarra, with the acquisition of the last piece of terra rossa land there. This property is now called Kirri Billi and has 25 hectares of cabernet sauvignon, cabernet franc, merlot, malbec, pinot noir and chardonnay. In 1983 the large Mount Dangar vineyard at Sandy Hollow was added to the total.

The Hunter vineyards now total something over 500 hectares, over half of which is chardonnay, the rest being Rhine riesling, sauvignon blanc and semillon; shiraz, pinot noir, cabernet sauvignon and malbec. Total production now stands at almost 6000 tonnes, producing 80 per cent of their total sales of 500 000 cases. Of this, 170 000 cases are sold overseas, a remarkable achievement.

Rosemount have been to the fore as far as export is concerned and much of Australia's present success in the United Kingdom must be attributed to them.

Of the wines, Roxburgh Chardonnay has a special place, being consistently among the very best produced in Australia. The Show Reserve Chardonnay is next; part of their top range also includes a semillon, a Coonawarra cabernet, a Coonawarra merlot and a pinot noir.

However, the 'bread and butter' line is the Diamond Label Chardonnay, sometimes erratic in quality, part of a range which includes a fumé blanc, a semillon, cabernet sauvignon, shiraz and pinot noir.

Chief winemaker since 1982 has been Philip Shaw, an agreeable if somewhat eccentric style of chap who has a very good palate and a deep desire to make great wine.

One feels that Rosemount, having done so well in such a short space of time, will now consolidate for a number of years, matching demand but not pushing it, preferring instead to polish qualities in order to maintain their special place overseas and their wide acceptance in Australia.

The Murrumbidgee Irrigation Area (Riverina)

In terms of volume alone, the Murrumbidgee Irrigation Area (MIA) has been very important in the production of Australian wine, supplying the major part of the wine made in New South Wales and about one-tenth of Australia's total

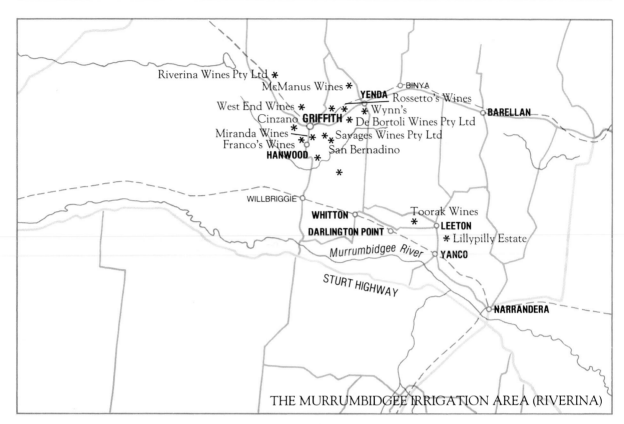

Riverina Wines Pty Ltd *
McManus Wines *
YENDA ○ BINYA
Rossetto's Wines
West End Wines * * * Wynn's
Cinzano **GRIFFITH** * De Bortoli Wines Pty Ltd
Miranda Wines * * * Savages Wines Pty Ltd
Franco's Wines * * San Bernadino
HANWOOD *
*
BARELLAN
WILLBRIGGIE ○
WHITTON ○
DARLINGTON POINT ○
Toorak Wines *
LEETON
* Lillypilly Estate
Murrumbidgee River ○ **YANCO**
STURT HIGHWAY
NARRANDERA

THE MURRUMBIDGEE IRRIGATION AREA (RIVERINA)

annual vintage. With the increasing demand for light 'table' (that is, unfortified) wines, the winemakers in the MIA have made full use of modern technology and are producing some wines of gold-medal-winning quality.

The MIA, or Riverina, is a large area in the south-west of New South Wales, around the towns of Griffith, Leeton and Yenda. Murrumbidgee is an Aboriginal word for 'big water', which is really most appropriate. The development of the area began only in the first decade of this century, after the New South Wales Government passed an Act in 1906 authorising the construction of the Barren Jack (now Burrinjuck) Dam, near Yass. The waters of the Murrumbidgee River are stored and regulated at the dam, whence they flow along the natural channel of the stream for about 380 km to the Berembed Weir. Here water is diverted into the man-made canal which supplies an area of 182 581 hectares.

The New South Wales Conservation and Irrigation Commission has been mainly responsible for land development in the area. Irrigable land is not allowed to be held by companies, but only by individuals, with a maximum permitted holding of 30 hectares of land for fruit cultivation, or 120 hectares for grazing.

After World War I the government settled repatriated soldiers in the area. There were many problems with totally inexperienced farmers in an untried area. Some unsuitable varieties were planted, and unsatisfactory methods of cultivation and irrigation adopted. Gradually, with experience, things improved and better techniques were implemented.

The population grew as cultivation expanded. The early 1920s saw the first wave of Italian migration arrive in Griffith. They came from Treviso in the north of Italy and Calabria in the south, bringing with them skills in grapegrowing and winemaking and the traditional involvement of the whole family in all operations from vineyard to table.

The second wave of migrants, also principally from Italy, arrived after World War II. These settlers have had considerable impact on the area as a whole, often achieving impressive success.

Griffith is 633 km from Sydney by rail, at an altitude of 128 m. As well as its pastoral industries (rice, wheat and oats, sheep, pigs, cattle, citrus, and of course, grapes) Griffith developed secondary industries, such as rice mills and dried-fruit processing plants. Temperatures can be very hot in Griffith (an average of more

Orchards and vineyards, Griffith.

Pastures and irrigation canals in the MIA.

than 32°C in February) and cold too (down to 3.8°C in July). The region has the characteristic inland climate of hot days and cool nights, which helps the balance of degree heat summation. Average annual rainfall is only about 400 mm, but in view of the irrigation system this is not really important. The growers boast that they have never had a crop failure.

Soils of the MIA vary considerably, ranging from heavy clay to light sandy loams with occasional patches of sandy soils. The subsoil is mostly clay, which holds the irrigation water. There are no rocks in the area. Generally the soil types are quite heavy, and the grapes there produce more flavour under irrigation than the grapes from lighter irrigated soils in other regions.

The region grows practically every known grape variety. There are more shiraz, semillon and trebbiano (white hermitage) grown in Griffith than in the rest of Australia. A higher proportion of white grapes than red are planted. Sultana, malaga and muscat are used for sweet and fortified wines. During the last twenty years cabernet sauvignon, Rhine riesling and then chardonnay, became extremely important.

The MIA, as can be seen from the governmental regulations on the size of properties, is an area of small farmers, most of whom sell their grapes to one of the winemakers for processing. This is a fragmented system, but the big companies are now exercising greater pressure on the growers, on such matters as the time of picking and desirability of planting certain varieties. Some coordination is exercised by the Irrigation Research and Extension Committee (IREC). This body was set up in 1947 under the auspices of the various governmental authorities concerned with the area, such as the Commonwealth Scientific and Industrial Research Organisation and the NSW Department of Agriculture. Mr Vivian Charles Williams, a leading vine and citrus grower, was its first chairman. The IREC has set up a conference on plantings which makes recommendations to growers on the planting of the most suitable varieties.

The winemakers group together as the MIA Winemakers' Association, while the grape growers are organised under the title of MIA Wine Grape Marketing Board. These two organisations link very closely to the Viticultural Research Station.

The irrigation of vineyards increases their yields between three and seven times those of non-irrigated areas. The average yield for all wine varieties in the MIA is about 18 tonnes per hectare, a very high figure compared to non-irrigated areas where yields are perhaps 2 tonnes per hectare. In 1969, the total area in the MIA under wine grapes was 2662 hectares. In the period from 1960 to 1968, the area under vine expanded by fifty per cent: production doubled in the same period. In the 1969 vintage, 42 786 tonnes of wine grapes were harvested in the MIA, out of the total New South Wales crop of 53 775 tonnes. In 1970, 53 323 tonnes were harvested. The figure is constantly increasing. By the early 1990s, this was over 100 000 tonnes.

The problem with irrigation in the past has been that the quality has tended to suffer somewhat. The berries of irrigated grapes tend to be fuller, and lighter wines result. Traditionally great wines have not come from irrigated areas, with most of the material being used for the sweet fortified styles and making spirits for brandy. Thus, although in quantity terms these wines were of great importance, it was widely believed that good wine could not be produced by irrigation methods. The early mistakes of the inexperienced returned soldiers who were the original growers helped to perpetuate this idea. The winemakers of the MIA, led by McWilliams, are rapidly changing this image by giving increasing attention to the planting of classic wine grape varieties and by using the most modern techniques of winemaking. The most outstanding feature of winemaking in the MIA in recent years has been the transformation of its wines: from emphasis on the sweet fortified styles and spirit for brandy, to concentration on light table wines of as high a quality as possible. To achieve this, winemakers have encouraged the planting of premium grape varieties. The introduction of earlier picking of grapes, especially of the white wine varieties, has been most important, as a better balance of acid and sugar has resulted in improved quality wines. As excessive heat at vintage time is a great problem, the introduction of refrigeration techniques to control the temperature of fermentation has allowed more delicate wines to be made—the esters and aromatic flavour substances not being destroyed by the heat of fermentation. Other technological advances such as centrifuges have also helped the production of good wines.

During the decade of the 1980s the emphasis was on two developments (though one other very important quality programme was evolved).

First, the forgiving white variety that appears to do so well in nearly all wine-growing areas, chardonnay, became very important to the MIA. It grows well under irrigation, produces extremely good yields, and can be made into extremely well-priced drinking wine of good flavour—witness the success of the well made and very reasonably priced Orlando RFI Chardonnay. Further developments in the cultivation of this variety, in harness with specialised making and maturation techniques, could result in the extensive sales overseas of a product that would have a tremendous quality/price ratio, something which is very necessary in all international markets if any volume is to be achieved.

Secondly, there have been tremendous advances in viticultural techniques, particularly with canopy training, minimal pruning, alternative irrigation methods and fertilisation. The vine selection work means that only the best disease-free and profit-producing clones are being planted. In short, the area is being transformed

from a provider of a ragbag of styles and cocktails, to one with greater quality emphasis and hence potential.

Evidence of this is the spectacular success of the De Bortoli Sauternes, a high-priced wine made from botrytis-infected semillon, which has won all sorts of Show awards during the 1980s and has met with much international acclaim. This success story, coming from a company not previously associated with international recognition, demonstrates that quality can be achieved.

Casella's Wines

Casella's is a small Italian family concern. The vineyard is situated on Farm 1471, just outside the township of Yenda, in the Murrumbidgee Irrigation Area (MIA). Fillipo Casella bought the farm from a Mr Shaw in 1965, and began making wine in a very small way four years later. Using time-honoured techniques, the first wine to be made there was crushed by foot. Time marches on, however, and now modern equipment is used. Winemaking has been expanding, with a crush of 200 tonnes normal. Storage at the winery is about 80 per cent stainless steel, and the balance oak vats.

The 19 hectare vineyard is planted to the following varieties: shiraz (4 hectares), trebbiano (3), grenache (3), chardonnay (2), pedro (2), cabernet sauvignon (1) and troia (1). The shiraz, grenache and pedro vines are those planted by the original soldier-settlers.

The winemaker at Casella's is John Casella, son of Fillipo, who is a graduate of the wine science course at the Riverina College.

Their wine is, at present, sold in bulk to consumers for home bottling. The Casellas do plan to bottle their better quality varietal wines in the near future. They are currently marketing a brand of spumante called Yendalla.

Cinzano

The first Italian company to invest in this country, Cinzano has come a long way since its foundation in 1757 in the city of Turin. The opening in Australia came after almost two centuries of successful business and expansion throughout the world. In 1931 Cinzano established its own company in Sydney and pioneered the vermouth market in Australia with Sweet and Fontorice (a dry) vermouth.

In 1976 Cinzano opened their Griffith winery and manufacturing plant, which now produces the bulk of the base wines for Cinzano vermouth, plus a huge amount of bulk wine, mostly from premium varieties such as semillon, chardonnay, French colombard, shiraz and cabernet sauvignon, for bulk supply to the industry. The vast array of equipment at Griffith means that only nine people (six in the factory and three in administration) are required to produce the huge quantities of vermouth and bulk wine sold by Cinzano Australia every year.

For years now, Cinzano has had the lion's share of the vermouth market in Australia. Vermouths produced are Rosso, Bianco and Dry plus Cinzano Fernet. Various imported products are also marketed by the company.

De Bortoli Wines Pty Ltd

The founder, Vittorio de Bortoli, arrived in Griffith from Italy in 1923 and worked at various jobs until 1927, when he obtained a plot of land to start a winery. The first two vats of 3000 litres each were built in 1928, the year the first wine was made. De Bortoli's battled through the 1930s depression and by 1936 had a capacity of 114 000 litres. Since 1963 tremendous strides have been made at the company.

De Bortoli's winery now has a storage capacity of more than 18 million litres, including 500 000 litres of wood storage. The company also owns 50 hectares of vineyard at Nericorn, about 32 km from the Bilbul Cellars, as well as the 30 hectares which are there.

De Bortoli's is one of the oldest and largest of the family-owned Griffith wineries. It markets more than fifty different wines and spirits, which are produced at their winery. The table wines tend to be of the soft style for immediate drinking. In the early 1980s, Deen de Bortoli, who is now the managing director, and Darren, the production director, experimented with botrytis culture, encouraging its development on the semillon left on the vine after the normal harvest. This led to the 1982 sauternes, which won all sorts of trophies, medals and rave reviews. This line has now become part of Australian wine lore, for the 1984 repeated this success, and the 1987 threatens to surpass them all with

sufficient bottle age. The 1988 was another top vintage. There was no wine of this style in 1989 due to the wet weather.

Only 1000 to 2000 cases of this wine are made and it sells for a rewardingly high price. Small parcels of it are sold overseas, where it is very well received.

In 1988 de Bortoli's bought the Chateau Yarrinya cellars in the Yarra Valley (see Victoria).

Franco's Wines

This small winery is situated about 5 km south of Griffith. The enterprise began in 1933 when the Franco family bought the fruit farm and small vineyard on the site of the present winery. They began to make wine in small quantities (about 430 litres annually) for their own and their friends' needs.

The wines became popular, and in 1959 the present owner, Salvatore Franco, converted a fruit-packing shed into a winery, and produced 6800 litres from his own grapes. From 1964 grapes were bought in from other growers to expand production.

Shortly afterwards, Louis Delpiano was appointed winemaker. He was born in Alba (Piedmont) and trained at the School of Oenology there. He worked in Italy, France and Spain before emigrating to Australia in 1956. Here he worked at a large Griffith winery until 1967. Delpiano believes white wines should be consumed while very young, and that most reds are at their best when three- to four-years-old.

Franco's Wines has expanded to the stage where 1500 tonnes of grapes are crushed each vintage. The company makes thirty different styles of wine.

Lillypilly Estate

One of the relative newcomers to the Griffith area, the Lillypilly Estate, is named after the Australian native trees of the same name. The winery is located just off the main road between Leeton and Yanco. It was established in February 1982 by the Fiumara family. Robert Fiumara is the manager and winemaker, while his father and brothers run the vineyard.

All grapes crushed come from the Estate's own vineyard. There are 17 hectares of vineyards,

LILLYPILLY ESTATE

Noble Muscat of Alexandria

1987

SWEET WHITE WINE MADE FROM MUSCAT OF ALEXANDRIA
AFFECTED BY NOBLE ROT. 11.0% ALC/VOL
PRESERVATIVE (220) ADDED
PRODUCT OF AUSTRALIA
375 mL

made up of chardonnay, semillon, traminer, sauvignon blanc, muscat of Alexandria; cabernet sauvignon and shiraz. There's also an experimental vineyard with another ten varieties planted.

The initial crush was just over 50 tonnes. When in full production it should reach about 200 tonnes. The winery is well equipped, with the aim of producing premium table wines. The white wines show distinct varietal character. Some chardonnay and sauvignon blanc is now being fermented in new French oak, the barrels later being used to mature cabernet sauvignon.

Almost 10 000 cases are produced from the varieties listed, plus good stocks of vintage port.

Sales are by cellar door which has built up to a healthy subscription mail order list.

McManus Wines

Dr David McManus is operating a small (tiny by MIA standards) vineyard and winery at Yenda in the Riverina district. He has 12 hectares of vines, including hermitage, cabernet, malbec, merlot and pinot noir; semillon, chardonnay, pinot blanc and trebbiano. The first vintage was 1973.

The winery is a family affair—Dr McManus is winemaker and Miss Marguerite McManus is manageress. The wines are named after members of the family, including Thelmay, Raghnall and John Bruce.

David McManus' approach to winemaking is individualistic. His yields are kept down by pruning and controlled irrigation—the vines being given far less water than usual in the district. He

has installed cold fermentation to increase the delicacy of the whites, and is experimenting with a shiraz which has been given heat extraction treatment. The wines are matured in stainless steel with oak chips added where necessary.

One of his better known wines is Catherine Marie, a sweet red which is very popular locally. David McManus also produces a range of other wines, all of which are reputed to show more body and fruit than other MIA wines. Interestingly, they don't always make a vintage. Most of the fruit is sold anyway, about 1000 cases being the limit of ambition. But in 1989, for example, David thought it was too wet and that the grapes didn't fully ripen. Hence no wine that year.

The good doctor adds some interesting advice for those worried about cholesterol. Eat porridge (rolled oats) to help the blood cholesterols stay down, the sugars to level out and for healthy bowel function. American research suggests that porridge cleans 25 per cent of cholesterol out of the body via the bowel (or so he says), with red wine.

Miranda Wines

Francisco Miranda, a migrant fresh from Italy, crushed his first vintage by foot, in the Griffith area in 1940. Today the multi-million dollar company crushes 11 000 tonnes of grapes annually. This makes it one of Australia's largest wholly owned family wine companies. Who says Australia is not a land of opportunity?

1987 SEMILLON SAUTERNE

GOLD MEDAL CLASS 15 1988 RUTHERGLEN WINE SHOW
GOLD MEDAL CLASS 34 1988 HOBART WINE SHOW
GOLD MEDAL CLASS 14 1988 COWRA WINE SHOW
TROPHY BEST OPEN SWEET WINE COWRA WINE SHOW

WYANGAN ESTATE

PRODUCT OF AUSTRALIA 750ml

The Miranda family has, however, made the most of that opportunity by forward thinking in terms of new technology. In 1958 they installed an ion-exchange column to lower pH, and claim to be the first to do so in Australia. Ron Potter (who has given his name to the fermenter he invented) was winemaker there for many years. Jim Miranda is now the chief executive and John Griffiths the winemaker.

In 1978 Miranda began making sparkling wines and now produces more than 150 000 cases per year. The company has traditionally produced mainly bulk wines, but in recent years has been producing some quality table wines.

A huge range of wines is now produced, including Charmat-fermented spumantes, marsalas and cocktail nips. More and more emphasis, however, is being placed on dry reds and whites. They have done well in shows with cabernet sauvignon, shiraz, chardonnay and semillon. A botrytised sweet white is also made.

Orlando Wickham Hill Cellars

Winemakers are David Morris and John Wilson. This is basically a large processing facility for local material purchased for Orlando products. There is a range of Wickham Hill wines in the lower price bracket.

No cellar sales.

Riverina Wines Pty Ltd

This was formerly Sergi's Wines. Antonio Sergi is still the chief executive and John Casella the winemaker. Situated on the western edge of the Griffith township, they began commercial production in 1971. The winery, which James Halliday subtly describes as a 'long, in-line

winery, built in tasteful feature-brick in Hispano-Griffith architectural style', was completed in 1975. They now have a total capacity of 10 million litres.

The crush has now grown to 13 000 tonnes, with fifteen or more varieties being processed. The majority of the wines are sold in bulk to the industry, though there are two ranges of bottled wine, Riverina Wines and Ballingal Estate.

Rossetto's Wines

This family-owned winery is at Beelbangera, 8 km from Griffith. The company was founded by the late Angelo Rossetto, in 1930. He had emigrated from Treviso in the north of Italy in 1922, and settled on his present site in 1928.

Angelo's son, John, was in charge of the company until May 1988, when he collapsed and died at a local dance. His wife and sons, Garry and Brian, now run the business.

Though they have only 15 hectares of their own vineyard (shiraz, semillon, trebbiano and grenache), they crush 7500 tonnes of grapes purchased locally. This all goes into a vast range of wines and liqueurs (Mt Bingar, Beelgara, Rossetto, St Jacques du Mont) in flagons, bottles, 4.5 litre casks and so on.

San Bernadino

San Bernadino Wines was established in 1973 by two families: the Pilloni family and the Aliprandi family. The driving force behind the venture is

Stan Aliprandi, a Griffith businessman and indefatigable promoter of the area.

San Bernadino has expanded every year since its inception and is now crushing over 6000 tonnes annually. They produce a dazzling array of wines and liqueurs and make large bulk sales to the industry.

However, their thrust is now into bottled premium wines made from classic varietals, and the demand for their reasonably priced products is growing rapidly. Sparkling wines too are very much in demand.

Winemaker is Walter Santesso, who comes from Italy. Their own farm, a 15 hectare block, is a vineyard of the usual varieties: semillon, chardonnay, trebbiano, palomino, gordo, marsanne; cabernet sauvignon and shiraz.

There are big cellar door and mail order sales. Wholesale sales are nationwide and exports are growing.

Savages Wines Pty Ltd

The letterhead of Savages Wines quotes from Louis Pasteur: 'Wine is the most healthful and most hygienic of all beverages', which is as convincing a recommendation as any.

Evan and Stewart Savage, the two principals of the company, established their winery near Griffith in 1947. Since then, they have been making bulk wine for licensed merchants. They purchase all their grapes from growers in the Murrumbidgee Valley, as well as settlements along the Murray River, in Victoria and New South Wales.

Toorak Wines

Toorak Wines is situated not in the well-known Melbourne suburb, but in Leeton in the heart of the Riverina. The partnership was formed between Frank and Vince Bruno in 1965, and by the end of the 1980s, 2000 tonnes were being processed, much of which is sold in bulk to other companies.

The company has an impressive array of winemaking equipment, and has had continued success in shows, particularly with a liqueur muscat made from their own brown frontignan grapes. Altogether they have 30 hectares at their Amesbury Estate, semillon, Rhine riesling, chardonnay, sauvignon blanc, cabernet sauvignon and shiraz. Ninety per cent of all

wines processed are table varietals.

They make the equivalent of 20 000 cases for local sale, chiefly cellar door and mail order.

West End Wines

The West End winery was first opened at Griffith in 1948. Twenty years later Bill and Tony Calabria, sons of the company's founder, took over. Bill is now winemaker and Tony is sales manager.

The winery crushes 500 tonnes of grapes a year, 20 per cent of which come from their own 14 hectare vineyard. It has storage for 750 000 litres—concrete, stainless steel and wood storage.

The Calabria brothers market an extensive range of wines, including red and white varietals which have been successful at recent local wine shows. There are also two spumantes.

Most of the production goes into flagons and bottles (no 4.5 litre casks).

Wynn's, Yenda

The old Caldwell's winery, bought and later modernised by Wynn's, later taken over by Penfolds. Now, with Roger Black in charge and Harold Davoren (Jr) the winemaker, Penfolds process between 10 000 and 20 000 tonnes there each year, of gordo, semillon, chardonnay, sauvignon blanc, cabernet sauvignon, shiraz and more, for varietal and fortified wine use, including premium port base. This bulk is transported to Nuriootpa in the Barossa Valley.

There are no local cellar door sales.

Mudgee

Mudgee is located on the central-western tablelands of New South Wales, 256 km by road north-west of Sydney. The town was settled in 1836 and is now the centre of a growing agricultural and pastoral district. The site of the boyhood home of one of Australia's best-known writers, Henry Lawson, is a monument on the road to several wineries.

Adam Roth and Dr Fraschi were among the pioneer winemakers in the area, and at one time in the late nineteenth century there were 13 established wineries and over 400 acres under vine. For most of this century the winemaking industry was almost non-existent. In the 1960s,

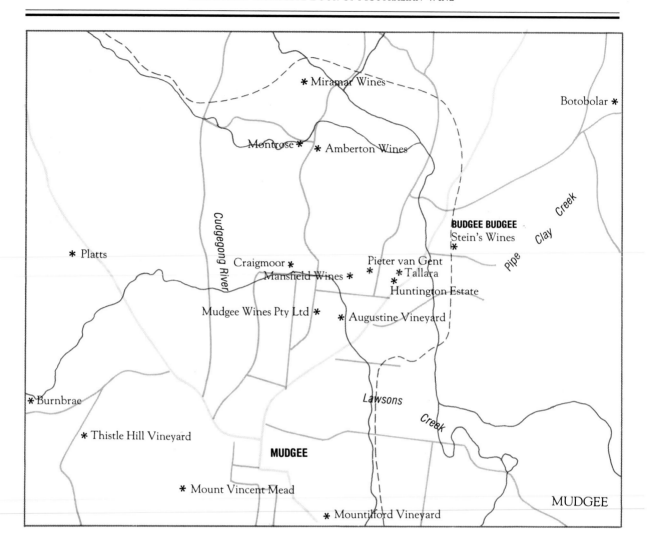

however, the renaissance began, and the reputation of the area as a source of quality wines has been rapidly growing since. The pattern of development has been small holdings of premium varieties.

Although the area is only 30 km from the Hunter as the crow flies, the climate at Mudgee is very different. A major difference is the altitude, with most Mudgee vineyards at high altitudes between 450 and 600 m above sea level. The effect of this is a slower ripening period and a harvest some six weeks later than the Hunter Valley. Being on the same latitude as the Hunter, Mudgee enjoys the same summer-dominant rainfall pattern; however, its position on the western slopes of the Great Dividing Range means that the total summer rainfall is less, and rain is not such a problem at vintage time. The average annual rainfall is 600–660 mm. Generally the climate is moderate, although the area is subject to occasional floods and frost.

The soils are generally red loam containing limestone and ironstone. The subsoil is heavy clay, which retains moisture but needs to be ploughed to a depth of at least 150–230 mm to enable young vine roots to strike successfully.

I started going to Mudgee in the early 1960s, and from what I can remember only one winery remained from the old days—Craigmoor—and there was a new tiny operation, Mudgee Wines, owned by the late Alf Kurtz, who pioneered chardonnay in the district. The reason for my visit was a 1961 Craigmoor Red, with an excruciating purple grape bunch label, which had been exhibited by Jack Roth and which won First Prize (this was before Gold Medals) at the Sydney Show. This led to further visits with Graham Gregory, who was then Government viticulturist for NSW, and Bob Roberts, a wine-buff solicitor who, together with his wife Wendy, has subsequently done so much for the area.

Bob and Wendy settled there and established Huntington, and they were followed by others, the most expansive of them being the people from Transfield who built and operated Montrose before it was sold to the Wyndham group.

However, small holdings dominated, and there was much early success with chardonnay in the early 1970s, the variety being positively identified in Alf Kurtz's Mudgee Wines vineyard. This clone is also certainly a direct descendant of James Busby's cuttings, having followed a circuitous route from Kirkton (Arthur Kelman's nineteenth-century Hunter winery) to Smithfield on the outskirts of Sydney, to Mudgee. There are further descendants of these clones in the Rothbury Cowra vineyard.

Yet it appears to me that the area is more successful with red table wine, though some very good chardonnays are still made. As an occasional Chairman of the Mudgee Wine Show judging, I have always thought the red wine classes showed consistent higher qualities, and that the best reds came, not from single varietals, but from blends of varieties—cabernet sauvignon and shiraz, or, à la Bordeaux, cabernet sauvignon and merlot.

Mudgee claims to be the first established district to declare a disciplined appellation classification system for its wines; in fact a similar arrangement began in the young Margaret River area of Western Australia a year earlier. The scheme began in 1979, the aim being to guarantee, beyond reasonable doubt, the origin and authenticity of wines that bear the accredited mark of the Society for the Appellation of Wines of Mudgee. The controls of the society have been examined by trademark authorities in Canberra, and the mark now has the same status as the Standards Association mark.

Control is by a chartered accountant, who has access to confidential records. There are statutory declarations by grape growers and winemakers on production, and controls on label printers. The minimum standard accepted to carry the appellation tends to correspond broadly to bronze-medal standard in Royal shows. Although participation in the scheme is purely voluntary, it shines out as a most worthy step in the possible wider system of appellation for Australia as a whole.

Amberton Wines (Also see Montrose and Wyndham Estate)

Amberton Wines was conceived by a group of wine lovers in the mid-1970s. Notable among these was Manuel Damien, a well-known Sydney restaurateur. Familiar with the area, they bought some 120 hectares of gently undulating land on Henry Lawson Drive, planted a vineyard and eventually built a winery.

About 20 hectares were planted to vine in 1975 and 1976 on two gently sloping vineyard sites. These were carefully chosen in regard to soil, aspect and freedom from frosts. The plantings were 60 per cent white and 40 per cent red to meet the demands of the market. Only premium varieties were selected—chardonnay, traminer, Rhine riesling, semillon and sauvignon blanc in the whites, and cabernet sauvignon and shiraz in the reds. In 1981 another 2 hectares of chardonnay were planted, with a further 3 hectares each of chardonnay and sauvignon blanc anticipated for 1982.

Two small vintages were processed in 1978 and 1979 at neighbouring wineries. In 1980 it was decided to build a modern winery, and John Rozentals was appointed winemaker. He was a wine science graduate of Riverina College of Advanced Education, with the college medal for academic achievement.

Amberton was taken over by Montrose, who in turn was taken over by Wyndham Estate. The winemaker is now Robert Paul, and 20 000 cases of wine are produced under this label, including semillon, sauvignon blanc, traminer, chardonnay, shiraz and cabernet sauvignon. These wines are sold at cellar door and to members of American Express wine club through Cellarmasters.

Augustine Vineyard

The Augustine Vineyard at Mudgee is the revival of Dr Fiaschi's vineyard which was established in 1918 and abandoned in the mid-1940s. In 1969 the only surviving vines were of the aleatico grape (a variety imported from Italy), and a replanting program was carried out. There are now 38 hectares under vines. Varieties include cabernet sauvignon, merlot, pinot noir, semillon, traminer, chardonnay, trebbiano and aleatico. Most are made as straight varietals.

The altitude of 500 m and the degree of ultra-violet sunlight lead to high colour and flavour in the grapes, and enable them to be picked at peak condition in falling temperatures. The Mudgee district character comes through in all varieties. Both red and white wines are full bodied and flavoured. The winery complex has a fully licensed restaurant.

In 1984 a syndicate which included the well-known wine judge and Wine and Food Society man Dr Ray Healey bought into the company, taking it over completely in 1988. Their own Settler's Creek vineyard, which adjoins Augustine, is predominantly of chardonnay.

Their total production is now 600 tonnes or more. This is bought and processed by other wine companies on a 'buy-back' system in which a small part is returned in bottle. At present this amounts to only 2000 cases for local cellar door sales, but this is likely to rise to approximately 5000 cases dependent on the success of their label.

Botobolar

The highest vineyard in the Mudgee district is at Botobolar, 600 m above sea level. The vineyard's owners are Gil and Vincie Wahlquist.

Since 1970, 27 hectares have been planted. The vines are contour-planted on a north-east slope and include the varieties shiraz, cabernet sauvignon, pinot noir, mataro, marsanne, chardonnay, gewurztraminer, Rhine riesling and crouchen. The first wine was made in 1974.

An old woolshed with a fine view of the vineyard comprises the Botobolar winery. Noteworthy is the Wahlquists' bottle-sealing method —the necks are hand-dipped in local beeswax.

An exceptional feature of the vineyard management is the elimination of pesticides and herbicides, all grapes being grown according to organic farming principles. Birds are encouraged at the vineyard, the theory being that resident birds will chase away visiting fruit eaters at harvest time.

The Wahlquists have made such a feature of this organic approach that they achieved a Grade 1 listing by NASA, the National Association of Sustainable Agriculture (Aust), which is recognised worldwide. Of their 8000 cases, over 20 per cent is exported, mostly to devotees of organic farming in the UK.

Another feature is the 'Botobolar Bugle', a lively newsletter put out by Gil, sent to regular purchasers of their wines.

Botobolar vineyard.

Burnbrae

Burnbrae is situated 10 km west of Mudgee on the Hill End Road, in an area that is proving to be a microclimate within the traditional Mudgee region. The site was chosen in the early 1970s for its viticultural advantages. These include altitude (600 m, with a cooling climatic effect), good seasonal rainfall (600 mm average) and well-drained red soils derived from slate and shale. The climate allows for cool, slow ripening of the grapes, giving rise to a good balance of components. Vintage is normally March, April and even May.

Paul Tumminello was the first winemaker of Burnbrae, but he and his partners sold out to Robert and Pamela Mace in 1983, though Paul remained on until 1986 as winemaker. Robert Mace now crushes about 36 tonnes of low-yielding fruit from his vineyards, making an average of about 2300 cases.

The vineyard comprises 3 hectares of shiraz, 2 hectares of cabernet sauvignon, a touch of malbec; 1.5 hectares of chardonnay plus some semillon, trebbiano and riesling. There are 6 hectares of black muscatel, half of which is being grafted to shiraz.

Why shiraz? Robert Mace is a vintage port man, and his wines have won golds and Best Wine of Class at the respectable Mudgee Show. There is also a softer red—a shiraz, cabernet and malbec blend, which can impress.

Cellar door sales take up most of the output, though the wines may be found in some Sydney wine merchants' outlets.

Craigmoor (Also see Montrose and Wyndham Estate)

Craigmoor is by far the oldest of the Mudgee vineyards. It was established in 1858 by Adam Roth, a German immigrant who settled at Mudgee within a few months of his arrival in Australia. His original grant of land was 47 hectares on the banks of the Pipeclay or Eurunderee Creek. The first vineyards were planted in the same year, and the land has been in continuous cultivation to vines ever since.

The business became firmly established in 1872 when gold was found at Home Rule, and before long the closest diggings were a mere kilo-metre from the Rothview Vineyard. The family prospered, supplying wine, fruit and vegetables to the miners. By the 1880s there were thirteen established wineries in the Mudgee district and more than 160 hectares under grapes. The Roth family operated six of these wineries, with five of Adam's six sons having been established in separate ventures of their own, while the youngest helped his father manage the principal business. The largest winery in the Mudgee district in this period was Fredericksburg, which adjoined Rothview and had nearly 80 hectares under grapes.

The 1890s depression was a severe blow to these wine producers, and the Fredericksburg Winery collapsed financially. From then on, the wine industry in Mudgee went into a gradual decline which was reinforced by the fact that most of the younger members of the wine-producing families moved out of the industry, into grazing, share-cropping and fruit production. By the 1930s there were only two significant wineries left in the district: Craigmoor and Dr Fiaschi's vineyard at Bumberra, some 3 km away. In 1935 Craigmoor passed into the hands of Adam Roth's grandson, Alan S. (Jack) Roth, who ran the business until his death in 1969. The business was then sold to van Heyst family interests in Sydney.

Pieter van Gent was winemaker at Craigmoor in the 1970s. He was followed by Barry Platt.

Craigmoor has vineyards of about 99 hectares, of which some 60 per cent are planted to white varieties, mainly chardonnay, semillon, traminer, muscat of Alexandria and other minor plantings. The balance are red varieties, mainly shiraz and cabernet sauvignon with smaller plantings of pinot noir and merlot.

The chardonnay plantings are especially significant. Some of the first plantings of chardonnay in New South Wales were at Mudgee in 1930, when several hectares were planted to this variety. Craigmoor's chardonnay has been very well received since the first straight varietal was bottled in 1971.

In recent years Craigmoor has been marketing a wide range of quality varietal wines. In addition to their quality table wines, fortifieds are also made—the Rummy Port being especially well known.

Eventually Craigmoor was taken over by Montrose, who in turn were taken over by

Wyndham, and they in turn were taken over by Orlando. The winemaker is Robert Paul, and 15 000 cases of wine are produced under this label: including chablis, semillon, chardonnay, semillon–chardonnay, shiraz, cabernet sauvignon, liqueur muscat and port, which are mainly distributed nationally on a wholesale basis.

Huntington Estate

Bob and Wendy Roberts were amongst the first to establish a vineyard near Mudgee at the time of the area's wine renaissance. Bob has a Diploma in Agriculture from Wagga Wagga and later completed a law degree. He became interested in the Mudgee area in 1967, and even more interested when he saw an old Craigmoor red beat a top Coonawarra and Chateau Latour at a blind tasting. Thus convinced, he and Wendy bought two parcels of land in the Mudgee district totalling 56 hectares, of a fairly mediocre quality. The name Huntington Estate was one of those originally considered by Rothbury. Bob and Wendy Roberts selected it for want of a better alternative.

Planting of the 40 hectare vineyard commenced in 1969, and further plantings on a small 8 hectare vineyard adjoining the nursery were made in 1972. Only premium table wine varieties have been planted. The vineyard mix has been changed over the years by grafting, but is now as follows: shiraz, 43 per cent; cabernet sauvignon, 26 per cent; pinot noir, 5 per cent; merlot, 4 per cent; chardonnay, 10 per cent; semillon, 10 per cent and sauvignon blanc, 2 per cent.

In the early 1970s Bob Roberts enrolled in the English-speaking correspondence course from the Oenological Research Institute in Surrey, England. At the same time he designed and built his winery himself, at the now incredible cost of $30 000, in time for his first vintage in 1973. The wines, both red and white, are made under enclosed fermentation and are also cold-fermented. The reds are given from eighteen months to two-and-a-half years maturation before bottling.

The majority of Huntington Estate wines are sold by mail order and at cellar door. Bob Roberts does not see his vineyard and winery growing any larger, finding his current crush of about 300–400 tonnes comfortable from both a winemaking and merchandising point of view.

Bob Roberts has had little formal training as

Casks, Huntington Estate winery.

Huntington Estate vineyard, Mudgee.

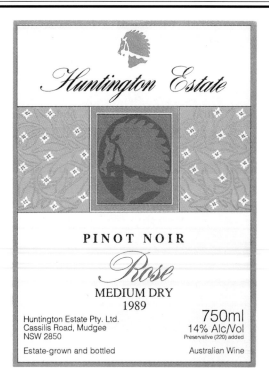

Huntington Estate

PINOT NOIR
Rose
MEDIUM DRY
1989

Huntington Estate Pty. Ltd.
Cassilis Road, Mudgee
NSW 2850

750ml
14% Alc/Vol
Preservative (220) added

Estate-grown and bottled

Australian Wine

a winemaker, but as a dedicated enthusiast has produced wines of outstanding quality. His semillons and chardonnays have been very well received, and Huntington Estate red wines are of excellent quality. He has dominated as Most Successful Exhibitor for years at the Mudgee Show, his reds in particular winning class after class.

During the late 1970s it was discovered that the winery had wonderful acoustics. The Roberts, both dedicated music lovers, and their daughter, Susan, took advantage of the situation by holding small concerts. These have now grown into a full-blown festival, held in November or December, which features up to thirty musicians and singers, offering up to ten different concerts over a five-day period. The mixture of great music, fine wine and hearty food in intimate surroundings has great appeal. In fact, some unkind people now suggest that Bob Roberts cares more for the music than the wine.

Mansfield Wines

Peter Mansfield is a scion of one of the two leading Mudgee winemaking families. His great-great-grandfather, Andreas Kurtz, began growing grapes in the district when he settled there after emigrating from Wurttemberg in the 1860s (the Roth family is the other).

Mansfield Wines was struck with disaster in its early years when a fire, in October 1979, destroyed all the wine maturing from its first vintage the year before. Peter Mansfield had spent five years gaining practical experience with his uncle, Alf Kurtz, at Mudgee Wines before starting out on his own. He now has 22 hectares of vineyard, including chardonnay, semillon, traminer, pinot noir and cabernet sauvignon. Seventy tonnes are produced. Interestingly, Peter sells most of this to other makers, preferring to buy bulk and cleanskin for his mainly local trade, specialising in sweeter table and fortified wines.

Miramar Wines

Miramar, a relative newcomer to the Mudgee district, has proved to be a most worthwhile one.

Sydney architect Ken Digby planted the first vines at Miramar in 1974, on a site 12 km north of Mudgee on Henry Lawson Drive. The vineyard is at an altitude of 570 m, on an eastern slope surrounded by granite hills. The soil is a generally rich red loam overlying a deep, well-drained friable clay subsoil, grading up to a shaley tree-covered ridge on top of the hill. Several outcroppings of quartz dot the area.

When winemaker Ian MacRae joined Ken Digby in 1976, some further plantings were undertaken, which resulted in a total of 30 hectares: the original cabernet sauvignon and shiraz, chardonnay and semillon, plus sauvignon blanc and a little tokay.

Ian MacRae was born at Berri in 1940, and went on to graduate with honours in 1962 from Roseworthy College. He has had extensive experience in the wine industry, having worked for Penfolds, Hardy's, Loxton and Kaiser Stuhl. In addition, he has been responsible for the design of many of the newer wineries, including Hungerford Hill at Buronga and Krondorf. He later formed his own company, Wine and Industrial Development, which was involved in the design and construction of many of the wineries built in the 1970s Pokolbin boom, including Hungerford Hill, Tullochs, McPhersons and Hermitage. MacRae was winemaker at Montrose Wines at Mudgee from 1975 to mid-1976, when he joined Ken Digby. He firmly believes that Mudgee is potentially the best area in Australia to make good wine.

Ken Digby ceased to be involved at Miramar

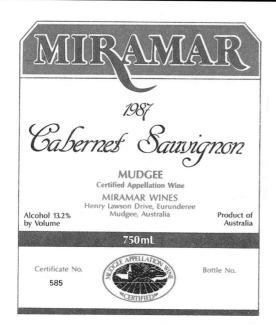

in 1981. Ian MacRae now owns 95 per cent of the operation, with one overseas friend having the balance.

The Miramar philosophy is to crush no more than 150 tonnes of grapes, all from the Mudgee area and to produce high-quality wines of a distinct style. Along with Bob Roberts, Ian MacRae was one of the most enthusiastic supporters of the formation of the Society for the Appellation of the Wines of Mudgee.

Ian MacRae's wines have had considerable show success, in the local Mudgee Show and in various interstate shows and overseas. Each year 10 000 cases of wine are made. These include a chardonnay, of which he is justly proud and which regularly wins Best White at the Mudgee Show, a semillon–chardonnay, a semillon, fumé blanc, cabernet sauvignon and a rosé. There is also a sweet wine called Doux Blanc which has appeal.

Sales are mostly at cellar door, though there is some export and interstate distribution.

Montrose

Montrose is the largest winery in the Mudgee district. It was built in 1975 by Franco Belgiorno-Nettis and Carlo Salteri of Transfield fame. Indeed, one of its problems was this very size, for they never processed the 2000 tonnes for which the winery was designed. The market was never strong enough for the ensuing 150 000 cases; consequently, available grapes went elsewhere.

Their own winery and Stoney Creek vineyards, planted since 1974, include chardonnay (12 hectares), Rhine riesling (5), traminer (4), semillon (3), cabernet sauvignon (11), shiraz (5), pinot noir (3) and 3 hectares of sangiovese and nebbiolo barbero. There are another 50 hectares of the Oakfield vineyard.

The modern winery is well equipped with a capacity of 1000 tonnes. In 1982 they crushed about 400 tonnes. Montrose has a storage capacity of 500 000 litres stainless steel, with American casks and French puncheons.

Winemaker and manager Carlo Corino's first vintage was 1977. Italian-born, he graduated from the Institute of Oenology at Alba in Piedmont, and later worked for Noilly Prat in Ethiopia and a local winery in Alba, where he played a significant part in the rebirth of the dry white wine Arneis. Carlo brought an Italian and individual touch to Montrose wines. He produced reds using the carbonic maceration technique, and many of his other ideas have resulted in some very good and also quite different wines.

In 1984 Montrose bought Craigmoor Wines, followed by Amberton in 1986 to combine a total crush of 1600 tonnes. (Amberton having 40 hectares of vineyard and Craigmoor 63 hectares. There is also the Elvina vineyard of 30 hectares.) This greater size, and the diversity of labels, proved too tempting for Wyndham Estate, who bought the company on 1 April 1988.

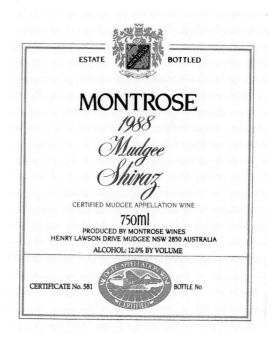

Carlo Corino, who had done so much to establish and promote Mudgee wines in his thirteen years there, departed in July 1989 to manage a huge (50 000 tonne crush) winery in Italy, leaving the winemaking in the hands of Robert Paul, his assistant for the previous two years. A new chapter in the Montrose book is presently being written.

Mountilford Vineyard

The Mountilford Winery itself was established in 1981, with grapes coming from vineyards at Mt Ilford and Rylstone. The varieties grown in almost equal proportions are Rhine riesling, traminer, chardonnay, sylvaner; cabernet sauvignon, pinot noir and shiraz.

With a crush of about 20 tonnes producing table wines and some port, sales are by cellar door and mail order only.

Mount Vincent Mead

Although mead has been made at Kinlochleven in Mudgee by Mount Vincent Mead since 1972, wines have only been made from 1982 on.

About 1 hectare of vines are coming into production soon and they include semillon, chardonnay, and Rhine riesling. The present crush of 3 tonnes is from bought-in grapes.

The wines are a cabernet sauvignon, a Rhine riesling and a liqueur muscat, which is made from cane spirit and is very popular. An exciting innovation is a dry, crisp honey wine made from muscat grapes and honey. Sales are at cellar door and selected outlets.

There is a music bowl, which provides an ideal site for listening to medieval music and supping mead, whilst strollers can dine out-of-doors, gaze at the fernery or hark to the bee-keeping hints.

Mudgee Wines Pty Ltd

Mudgee Wines, the smallest vineyard in the district, was established by Alf Kurtz in the early 1960s, and pioneered dry varietal table wines in the Mudgee area. When Alf Kurtz retired in early 1977, Jerry Winston and Jennifer Meek took over the 10 hectare property. John McArthy, a metallurgist, later became a shareholder.

Mudgee Wines is unusual in at least two aspects. Firstly, its resident manager and winemaker is a woman—Jennifer Meek; secondly, no pesticides are used. The theory is that slashing of grasses between the vines reduces moisture loss, and provides an area for mice, worms and beetles, encouraging predator birds which drive off birds that would otherwise damage the grapes. Wasps and spiders in the vines control caterpillars and moths. We are assured that the grapes are picked by hand 'so the beasties don't end up in the wine'.

Varieties planted include chardonnay, traminer, malvasia bianca, shiraz, crouchen, trebbiano, muscat, cabernet sauvignon and pinot noir. About 10 tonnes are crushed each year. From this, the winery produces some 750 cases per year using a 100-year-old hand press and a lot of help from friends.

Mudgee Wines produce a remarkably large number of styles (in small quantities) for a vineyard of its size. Of these, Jennifer recommends the chardonnay, traminer, pinot noir and cabernet sauvignon.

Cellar door sales only.

Pieter van Gent

Pieter van Gent is one of the most experienced winemakers in the Mudgee district. He was chief winemaker at Craigmoor from 1971, in the period when it was making a name for its wines, and had worked for Penfolds for ten years prior to that.

His present venture, a winery be built of natural materials to harmonise with the landscape, is 8 km north-east of the Mudgee township.

With an annual crush of between 50 and 100 tonnes, Pieter specialises in port, a four-year-old, full-bodied wine of late-bottled, vintage style called Pipeclay Port, and a white port. A dry chardonnay, matured in 100-year-old 4500 litre casks is also made, and a soft shiraz.

Most of the wine is sold at cellar door.

Platts

Platts is the only winery in the historic country town of Gulgong. This is owned and operated by winemaker Barry Platt. He has 10 hectares of vineyard at Gulgong itself, and 20 hectares of vineyard at Mudgee. These comprise semillon, chardonnay, sauvignon blanc, traminer; shiraz, cabernet sauvignon and pinot noir.

A hundred tonnes or more are produced. The semillon, chardonnay, shiraz and cabernet sauvignon is retained and 80–90 tonnes of these varieties are crushed to make the four main wine styles. The balance is sold as fruit to other makers.

Cellar door sales utilise a third of the 6–7000 cases made. There is a little export and the balance is distributed by agents in New South Wales, Victoria and Queensland.

B. Seppelt & Sons, Barooga

In the late 1920s Seppelt acquired a property at Barooga in New South Wales, just down the Murray River from Rutherglen. The main purpose was to establish a nursery for phylloxera-resistant stocks which could be used for South Australian vineyards should the need arise. There were also supplementary objectives of vineyard research and viticultural experimentation. Its proximity enabled Barooga to be worked in conjunction with the Rutherglen wine areas.

There are now over 125 hectares of vines at Barooga, which produces over 2000 tonnes, of which 75 per cent is chardonnay; the balance being Ondenc (Irvine's white), chenin blanc, pinot noir and muscat of Alexandria. This is processed on site and taken as chilled must to the Great Western Cellars, where much of it is made into base wine for Great Western Champagne.

Stein's Wines

Formerly the Sandal Park Estate in Mudgee, owned and operated by Robert Stein. He started planting in 1976, made his first wine in 1980, and opened the winery for cellar door sales in 1986. They have 4.5 hectares under vine: chardonnay, Rhine riesling, traminer, shiraz, black muscat (frontignan) and gordo muscat.

They pick between 40 and 60 tonnes, and sell some grapes and buy some grapes, depending on their need. Altogether between 3000 and 4000 cases are produced.

Though Robert is very serious about his table wine, particularly the chardonnay and shiraz, he enjoys making and selling fortified wines, vintage and rum-barrel aged ports and liqueur muscats. The winery is being expanded as there is a very strong local demand for the best fortified wines. Prices are reasonable and all visitors are welcome. Robert has done well at local shows with his port entries.

Tallara

Rick Turner, a Sydney chartered accountant, started developing a vineyard on the Cassilis Road at Mudgee, next door to Huntington Estate, in 1970.

Over the years this has grown to 35 hectares: cabernet sauvignon (10 hectares), shiraz (10), chardonnay (8), semillon (4) and sauvignon blanc (2) with 1 hectare of table grapes. This is all sold to Rosemount, and Rick receives a few hundred cases of chardonnay and cabernet sauvignon back from Phillip Shaw, the chief winemaker there. This is sold privately. Eventually a winery will be built for cellar door sales.

Thistle Hill Vineyard

This vineyard was established in 1976 at Mudgee, with the winery being built in 1984. David Robertson is about to take up full-time

occupancy at the vineyard after thirteen years absentee ownership.

On the 10.8 hectares, there are 1.2 hectares of riesling, 3.2 hectares of chardonnay, 5.2 hectares of cabernet sauvignon and 1.2 hectares of pinot noir vines.

The winery crushes up to 40 tonnes, resulting in 2500 cases, 95 per cent of which is table wine; the rest is fortified wine.

Cellar door sales and mail order are the main methods of sale.

Other Districts

Historically there have been vineyards scattered through various parts of New South Wales, such as Port Macquarie, Bathurst, Camden and Inverell. The Sydney area has contained some vineyard activity since the First Fleet, and this has persisted until today.

The following details about the various producers indicate the incredible range of practice in NSW. There are highly professional large-scale operations such as Buronga Hill on the Murray River, the Stanley Wine Company operation at Buronga (not to be confused with the former) and Cassegrain at Port Macquarie. These three alone crush over 60 000 tonnes in total. There is much development at Cowra. Yet all the rest of the widespread wine operations—'other districts' —range from the small to the minute. Some are

so small that they never answer their listed telephone number, or the letters sent to them. One may only conclude that they are too small to bother, are hobby farmers who are rarely there, have given it up, or are one-person operations without relatives or friends, who have been pinned under an overturned tractor for the past few months. Whatever, these are my excuses for the non-inclusion of some winemakers in this book. One can only do so much.

This, however, is one of the joys of the 'small' wine industry of Australia. The figures vary, but it is quoted that ten wine companies produce nearly 90 per cent of all Australian wines, the rest being produced by over 400 other makers. The small winemakers (many of them really just hobby farmers doing it all themselves, and in some cases just scratching a living, even, indeed, doing other work to subsidise their dreams) still, however, make a great contribution. At their wineries the wine-lover and would-be connoisseur come face to face with wine reality. Someone once suggested the small winemakers are the wine peasants of Australia—a fanciful thought, since so many of them are doctors, dentists, pharmacists, restaurateurs, musicians, journalists etc. Amusingly, few of them are accountants, which may tell us all something.

Whatever, they are becoming as evident in NSW as they are in South Australia, Victoria and Western Australia, and they dot the landscape almost anywhere that there is sufficient rainfall. Some of them have succeeded for many years; not all are very small; some produce very fine wines; others service local needs. Most, however, contain interest and charm, and testify to the incredible range of involvement in the Australian wine industry.

Benfield Estate

Owned and run by solicitor David Fetherston, who would dearly love to be a full-time wine man, this is one of those operations that are a tribute to dreams and the tenacity that comes from reality when the dreams aren't immediately fulfilled.

Initially David planted some 11 hectares on his Yass property. Maintaining this proved to be too difficult for a part-time operator and it became almost a start again project. For example, from 6 hectares of vines (2 Rhine riesling, 1.5

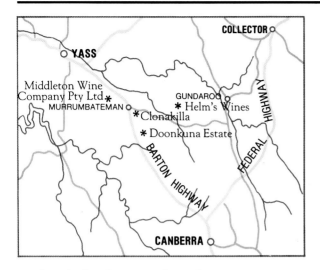

merlot, 1 chardonnay, plus cabernet sauvignon, cabernet franc and shiraz), only 2 tonnes were picked in 1988 and 6 tonnes in 1989. Yet David perseveres and eventually hopes to pick 60–70 tonnes from 20 hectares.

Of his wines, he is particularly proud of his merlot, which he thinks has a great future. The chardonnay is lean and fruity; and as for the Rhine riesling—'we get botrytis here. In fact, at Yass we never have any trouble getting botrytis.'

Buronga Hill Pty Ltd

Situated at Buronga, near the Murray River in New South Wales, this is one of those almost covert operations that few get to hear about. The main partners, Rob McLeod (managing director), Terry Hill (operations director), and Sam Cross (winemaker), all worked at the Buronga plant of Hungerford Hill, and when a series of takeovers occurred with that company saw an opportunity and took it.

Their first vintage was in 1985. Within a few years their crush had grown to nearly 30 000 tonnes, most of it sultana and gordo muscat, which is sold entirely in bulk to other wine companies. Consequently, there are no bottles and no visitors, though the partners are running a very successful and needed operation.

Camden Estate

Norm Hanckel, the well-known wine figure of the 1960s and 1970s, reckons that he has finished up closer to the heart of the industry than anyone else, being only 1.5 km from where Macarthur first claimed wine fame for Australia in the 1820s.

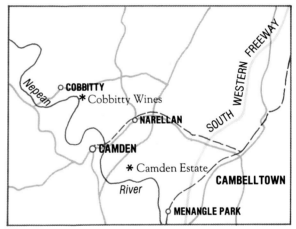

Norm planted his vineyard in 1974. In 1980 a crushing facility became the bones of a winery, but different winemakers have made his wine, with Vicary at Luddenham, near Penrith, doing it towards the end of the 1980s under the auspices of winemaker Chris Nicol.

There are 17 hectares under vine: 11 hectares of chardonnay, 2 hectares of traminer, 2 hectares of trebbiano and 2 hectares of cabernet sauvignon. All in all, about 110 tonnes are produced and the larger part of the wine crushed is sold in bulk as a cash crop. However, Norm retains 4000 cases to bottle, 90 per cent of which is a chardonnay of very rich fruit character.

Each year a third of the chardonnay is fermented in new French wood and the rest is matured in second and third year oak, the lot finally being blended together. This is a very consistent dry white and deserves wider exposure.

Cartobe

A unique winery on Young Road at Boorowa, which lies in a triangle of the towns of Yass, Young and Cowra.

Geoff Carter, the owner and winemaker (he started the course at the Riverina College in Wagga Wagga during the last year of Brian Croser's reign in 1978), was given the winery. It came from Rye Park, 30 km away, where they made wine and distilled spirits from 1856 to 1908. At the turn of the century the Methodists moved into the area, and closed down the hotel and eventually the winery. (It became known to

the locals as 'Dry Park'.) Geoff located the old slab-sided winery, and they let him take it away to rebuild it.

Geoff crushes between 40 and 50 tonnes of fruit from his Cartobe and Boorowa vineyards, which total 4 hectares of chardonnay, 3 hectares of Rhine riesling, 1 hectare each of sauvignon blanc and pinot noir and some cabernet sauvignon and merlot. The result is 3000 cases of wine, distributed by two agents and Geoff himself (in Canberra). Cellar door sales comprise about half of all sales.

Of his vintages, Geoff says 1986 was outstanding, with 1989 a close second.

Cassegrain

Port Macquarie has a winemaking history dating back to the nineteenth century, boasting vineyards and vignerons who exhibited in London, Amsterdam, Bordeaux and Calcutta (colonial and Indian Exhibitions), where medals and certificates of excellence were won.

In 1882 the *Port Macquarie News* reported that wines which had left for Bordeaux arrived at their destination and were highly commended. The paper further commended Messrs Francis and Fern from Port Macquarie on their enterprising spirit in bringing local wines before the markets of the world. This was at a time when the wines of France and Germany dominated these markets and Australia was just becoming recognised as a wine-producing country.

The later 1800s saw a peak in the fortunes of the winemaking industry of the Hastings Valley where it was second only to the timber industry in its importance to the region.

The last record of wine being made was in

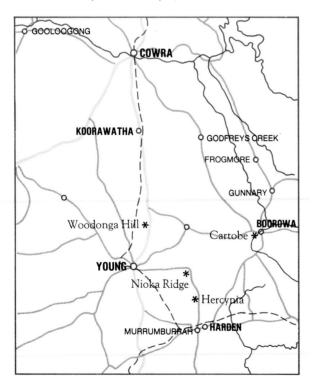

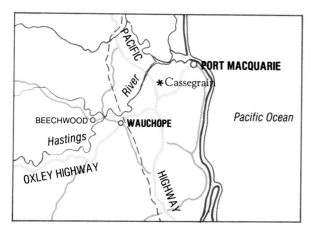

1919. From this time to 1956 the vineyards were still functioning but sadly only for the purpose of jam-making. The decline and final collapse of the wine industry was due to many things; the depression of the early 1900s, changes in consumer habits and the breakdown in state trading barriers, and the subsequent flow of subsidised South Australian wine into New South Wales.

In 1980 John and Eva Cassegrain established the Cassegrain Vineyards alongside the Pacific Highway, just 10 km west of Port Macquarie.

John Cassegrain completed his studies at Roseworthy Agricultural College, South Australia, and obtained his Bachelor of Applied Science in Oenology in 1978. In 1980 he presented his thesis on natural fermentation to the World Oenology Conference held at Davis University, California. The research he did in collaboration with Roseworthy College for his thesis continues at the winery today, and his practical training was with Murray Tyrrell of Tyrrell's Vineyard in the Hunter Valley. John also worked in Burgundy to gain traditional experience. In 1989 they bought vineyards in the Lower Hunter, no doubt because of John's regard for the area.

The winery is designed to crush a maximum 1000 tonnes and it is supplied with the very best equipment available.

The region has a temperate climate with regular rainfall throughout the year. Being close to the coast it is subject to cool breezes that limit the mean summer temperatures, but it is also subject to relatively high humidity which is good for the development of the vines. Irrigation is not necessary.

Soils around the Hastings Valley vary greatly in fertility, depth and structure. There are rich alluvial soils, volcanic free-draining soils, and heavy clay soils. Some are very deep, some overlie gravel, while others overlie limestone.

Initial planting took place in 1981 and the first wines were released in 1985. The vineyards are: Hastings Valley Winery, 16 hectares, planted in 1981 (Hastings Valley); Le Clos Sancrox, 64 hectares, planted in 1987 (Hastings Valley); Le Clos Verdun, 90 hectares, planted in 1988/89 (Hastings Valley); Le Clos Colline, 16 hectares, purchased in 1989 (Lower Hunter).

In addition, grapes are purchased from independent grapegrowers from the Lower Hunter, McLaren Vale, Tenterfield, Moombi (in the New England), Coonawarra and the Hastings Valley. Grape varieties include chardonnay, sauvignon blanc, semillon, trebbiano, pinot noir, shiraz, chambourcin, merlot and cabernet sauvignon.

John Cassegrain is in charge of all winemaking.

Production is climbing! By the end of the 1980s they were crushing 500 tonnes, and as the new vineyards come into bearing they intend to go as high as 3000 tonnes, with two specialist wineries.

Their tasting rooms and public facilities are of an extremely high standard and there is a roaring cellar door trade in the Hastings district. Distribution of their wines is quite wide.

Of all the wines made at this stage of development, the company has already a considerable reputation for their top chardonnays, which feature quite heavy new oak treatment.

This is a relatively new company showing high energy and great promise.

Clonakilla

Clonakilla, at Murrumbateman, was in the vanguard of an emerging confidence in this new wine area. Believed to be the first commercial vineyard in the area, their first vintage was in 1976, when the winery was also set up.

Of the 1.5 hectares of vines presently in production, the main varieties are cabernet sauvignon, riesling and cabernet franc with 'a little bit of everything' in the remainder. Dr Kirk (the vineyard principal) describes the riesling as a reliable, nice, fragrant and very drinkable wine created from a grape which appears well suited to the district—it grows well and yields well. The

cabernet sauvignon is good too and the pinot and semillon are evolving nicely. Not forgotten are the vintage port and muscat, giving this trail-blazing enterprise a wide range of products. Most sales are cellar door but the pick of the crop can be enjoyed in some Canberra Hotels.

Cobbitty Wines

The Cogno family has been making wines for five generations at the Alba Winery in the province of Piedmont, in northern Italy, which is famous for its Barbera, Barolo and Spumante.

After arriving in Australia in 1950, the Cogno family eventually decided to carry on the old business in the new country. In 1964 Mrs Cogno and her sons Giovanni and Secondo planted a vineyard on the 5.6 hectare property at

Cobbitty, 8 km north-west of Camden. Barbera, muscat, trebbiano, shiraz and chardonnay are grown, and South Australian grapes are bought in. There are now 10 hectares of vineyard.

Business has grown rapidly, to the extent that buildings were erected in 1972 and 1976. A modern winery was erected in 1982. Currently 150 tonnes are processed, plus bulk wine purchased interstate. Table, fortified, and sparkling wines are sold at the winery, which has extensive tasting and public facilities.

College Winery, Charles Sturt University—Riverina

Previously known as the Riverina-Murray Institute of Higher Education, the College Winery is now part of the new Charles Sturt University.

A viticultural course at Wagga Wagga was originally proposed in the 1880s to be part of the Agriculture Experiment Farm. But the 1890s recession delayed the establishment of the course until 1975, when the Ron Potter Centre for Teaching and Research in the Wine and Grape Industries began teaching students at Wagga Wagga. Since then the Charles Sturt University has been making an increasingly important contribution to the wine industry—in the training of winemakers, the provision of technological support to the industry, and in applied research. The University is in rolling hills, 9 km from the centre of Wagga Wagga.

The importance of integrating the teaching program with practical aspects of commercial production was recognised, and a winery and vineyard were established at the University for this purpose. Both are managed on a commercial basis and, as well as being important in the practical teaching of wine science and viticulture courses, they provide a basis for applied research in winemaking and grapegrowing.

The University's vineyard is named Booranga and has 12 hectares of grapevines. In 1989 a total of 164 tonnes were harvested, including grapes from chardonnay, cabernet sauvignon, riesling, traminer, sauvignon blanc and small quantities of fortified varieties. It is already apparent that the use of clonally selected vines, carefully controlled drip irrigation and high trellising are providing good-quality fruit and sound economic yields. This is particularly pleasing to the

University because Wagga Wagga must be classified as a warm to hot grapegrowing area.

In addition to the commercial planting, the vineyard includes a small-scale planting of table grapes and rootstocks; an ampelographic collection; demonstration plantings of pruning, trickle irrigation and trellising techniques and vine propagation facilities that include the capability to produce grafted rootlings.

During 1976 and 1977, staff and students in the wine science course were involved in the setting up of the University's winery. The main function of the winery is to increase the practical experience of wine science students by introducing them to grape varieties, regions and techniques outside their own vocational circum-

'Old Cask Hall' Muscat

Made and Bottled by
The College Winery, Boorooma St., Wagga Wagga NSW 2650
18% ALC/VOL   PRODUCE OF AUSTRALIA   750 ML

CELLAR DOOR RELEASE

stances. This is done by involving students in the monitoring of grape maturity of different varieties from regions throughout New South Wales, Victoria and South Australia. Since 1977, the University has obtained grapes or must from these regions and, although extensive plantings of grapes have been made in the University's vineyard, it is expected that grapes will continue to be purchased in different areas for teaching purposes on a commercially realistic scale.

The University's winery has a capacity of approximately 250 tonnes of grapes and it produces about 7000 dozen bottles of premium varietal wines each year. For its size, the winery is one of the best equipped and most versatile wineries in Australia. It includes some valuable

features such as the ability to chill must immediately after crushing, the use of cold settling and earth filtration in juice and wine clarification. Refrigeration and inert gas allow juice and wine to be stored indefinitely. An underground barrel fermentation storage area has been installed. There is also an air-conditioned bottling hall which includes facilities for the production of bottle-fermented sparkling wines. This impressive range of resources is situated in a converted fruit-packing shed, surrounded by olive trees which were planted around the turn of the century— the parent stock for olive plantings in Australia.

Techniques used in production of the small commercial batches of wine are innovative and relevant to industry requirements. The commercial operation of the University's winery enables wine.making and viticultural research projects to be undertaken on a practical scale.

The excellent quality of the University's wines has been acclaimed by wine judges and wine writers. More than 292 medals and three championship trophies have been awarded to the wines at major Australian wine shows since 1977. This success reflects the outstanding ability of the staff and the graduates, who are now occupying senior positions in wineries and vineyards throughout Australia and New Zealand.

A feature of wine production is the practice of acquiring grapes from a variety of grapegrowing regions. By processing grapes from a variety of regions, under the same controlled fermentation conditions, students are provided with a unique opportunity to compare climatic and regional differences.

Staff expertise encompasses all facets of winemaking and viticulture, with depth in the areas of chemistry, ampelography and vine physiology. The research interests of the group include grape and wine flavour development, evaluation of vine varieties, finger-printing grapevine varieties and new trellising and training systems. The grape flavour or pyrazine work of Dr Malcolm Allen has received international acclaim.

Celebrated winemaker Brian Croser was winery director, and his position is now held by Dr Brian Freeman. He is backed up by an enthusiastic team including Rodney Hooper as winemaker and Libby Tassie as vineyard manager.

The University offers training in viticulture and wine science both by either external or correspondence teaching and full-time, on-campus teaching. The teaching program also offers a Masters degree for graduates of other courses who wish to specialise in viticulture or wine science.

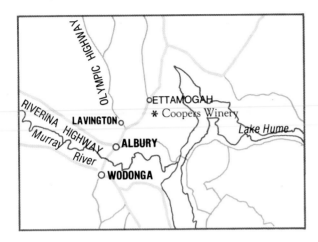

Coopers Winery

Coopers Winery, established fifteen years ago at Tabletop near Lavington, was formerly known as Table Top Cellars.

The 15 hectare vineyard includes riesling, semillon, chardonnay; cabernet sauvignon and muscat. A 60 tonne crush produces table wines, fortified wines and sparkling wines. Their best wines to date are the cabernet sauvignon and late-picked Rhine riesling.

The manager Bob Harris would like to continue to meet the cellar door demand for sweeter varieties whilst continuing to introduce more quality wines. To this end, Brian Wilson, who has come to Coopers from San Bernadino where he devised the very popular Mother Machree's Shamrock Cream, is keen to create a similar success for Coopers with a different base and style.

Because of its situation next door to the Ettamogah Public Hotel complex, most sales are cellar door catering to a variety of palates which favour the sweeter wines. There are barbecue facilities and a restaurant.

Cowra Wines

Cowra Wines were established in 1963 on the outskirts of the town of Cowra and have 50 hectares of vineyard, 50 per cent of which is planted with chardonnay, the rest include riesling,

sauvignon blanc, traminer; pinot noir, merlot, cabernet franc and cabernet sauvignon.

The table wines produced are made at Arrowfield by winemaker Simon Gilbert. One of the best wines produced is the 1987 chardonnay. Sales are cellar door or mail order.

Cubbaroo Vineyards, Burren Junction

Cubbaroo Wines, which was established in 1970, stands all alone in terms of its location. The vineyard is situated on Cubbaroo Station near Burren Junction, on the road from Narrabri to Walgett, in north-western New South Wales.

The Namoi Valley, with its rich black-soil plains, is more famous for cotton and wheat than grapes. Nonetheless, there are 16 hectares under vine at Cubbaroo, as part of a large holding owned by Ron Radford, in the area where he grew cotton, sunflower and other crops.

The winemaker is Brian McGuigan of Wyndham Estate, who crushes about 110 tonnes annually for Cubbaroo. The grapes are bought and processed by Wyndham Estate, who return an amount of bottled wine to Ron Radford for sale in hotels and at cellar door.

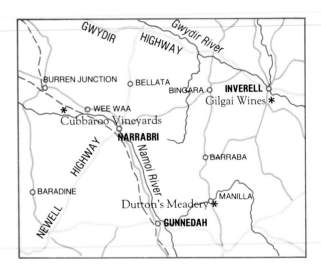

D'Aquino Bros Pty Ltd, Orange

D'Aquino Bros at Orange is a family concern which was established in 1949 by Charlie d'Aquino, a third-generation winemaker from Italy. In 1952 he was licensed to distill spirits. His first crush was 10 tonnes, which increased slightly every year; by 1956, when his son Leo took over, the annual crush was 20 tonnes. The

third generation, Rex d'Aquino, is a graduate of the oenology course at Roseworthy College, and the family now crush about 100 tonnes.

They have none of their own grapes, except for a contract with 2.5 hectares, called Garrallan, in the Cowra district. All the rest are bought in.

A full range of fortified and table wines is produced. The winery is situated at the back of the premises, the front of which is a retail wine and spirits shop.

Doonkuna Estate

Doonkuna Estate, on the Barton Highway outside Canberra, was established in 1973 when half a hectare of vines were planted. Progressive plantings to 1983 have brought the vineyard size to 5.5 hectares. A new winery was built in 1982.

Doonkuna Estate is owned by Sir Brian and Lady Murray. Sir Brian, a naval man, was a former Governor of Victoria and Jan, Lady Murray, is an extremely keen student of wine.

Grape varieties are 1 hectare of riesling, 1.5 hectares of chardonnay, 1 hectare each of cabernet sauvignon and pinot noir and small amounts of semillon, sauvignon blanc and shiraz.

A normal crush is 40 tonnes, producing exclusively table wines. Named in the top hundred in the 1988 Small Winemakers Awards were the 1987 cabernet sauvignon and the 1987 shiraz, and in the 1989 Small Winemakers Awards the 1988 riesling was in the top hundred.

Most sales are by mail order with limited cellar door only.

Dutton's Meadery

Ian Dutton, a celebrated apiarist and mead-maker, is something of a character. He has worked hard for recognition, and his meadery at Manilla in New England is now a member of the Wine and Brandy Producers' Association.

He does grow vines, a small vineyard of 1.5 hectares of muscat and merlot, with some 'very vigorous' chardonnay. The juice of these grapes is mixed with honey to make a product he calls Pyment, an ancient name for the process.

The remarkable thing is that a protein in the honey acts as a stabiliser and anti-oxidant, and no sulphur is needed in the winemaking process. A honey-wine product would have a considerable future on the 'organic' market.

Gilgai Wines, Inverell

Keith Whish was not really a pioneer when he established the Gilgai Red Vineyard at Inverell in 1968. In fact, Inverell was the centre of a wine-growing district from the 1850s.

In 1849 Charles Wyndham, son of George, took vines from George's Dalwood vineyard in the Hunter Valley to Inverell by pack horse and planted them at Bukkulla Station. To keep the cuttings alive on the journey he dipped them into each creek and river he passed on the way. Bukkulla became a major wine producer, noted for its immense wines. The wine-growing industry expanded from the 1850s to peak in the 1890s. The *Inverell Times* of 1875 stated: 'If there is one thing more than another that finds a congenial home within the district it is the vine.' The industry declined in World War I and ceased to exist in World War II.

Keith Whish revived the industry when he returned to Dalwood for his first cuttings in 1968. A number of different varieties were planted on an experimental basis.

'Gilgai' is an Aboriginal word meaning water-hole or place of refreshment. Varieties grown at Gilgai Wines, 10 km south of Inverell, include semillon, trebbiano, Rhine riesling and sauvignon blanc for the whites. Red varieties are shiraz, malbec, cabernet sauvignon, mataro, grenache and pinot noir.

The soil on which the vines are grown is red laterite, and the rainfall about 750 mm per year. The vineyard is well drained and situated at an altitude of 760 m. The autumn weather is kind to ripening grapes—dry warm days followed by cool to cold nights. Vintage is mid-March, and lasts about three weeks. The current crush is between 10 and 20 tonnes, since some fruit is sold. Thirty tonnes is the total production.

The grapes are hand-picked, mechanically crushed and hand-pressed. The reds are matured in French oak casks for eighteen months. The white wine is made in stainless steel vats from the free-run juice and is bottled and marketed within six months. They make a port for local sales.

The winemaker is Dr Keith Whish and he has help from his sons. Jeremy, who is a botanist, does vineyard work and Charles, a winemaker at Rosemount, helps with the wine side.

Glenfinlass Wines, Wellington

It is impossible to imagine a more beautifully romantic glen than that in which we lay. There was just level space on either side of the stream for the horses to travel along, the rocks rising almost perpendicularly from it to a towering height, covered with flowering acacia of various species, whose bright yellow flowers were contracted and mingled with the more sombre foliage of the blue gum and cyprus trees. We named it Glenfinlass; it might, perhaps, be properly termed the Glen of Many Windings.

This expressive extract from Lieutenant John Oxley's diary of 1817–18, on his journey of exploration along the Macquarie River valley in central-western New South Wales, describes the tiny and charming valley in which the Glenfinlass winery is situated.

The winery, cradled by outcropping rocks and

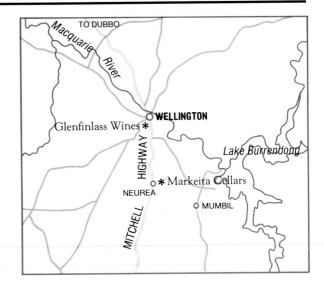

shaded by river gums, is dwarfed by the densely forested ridges of the Catombal Range, 8 km south-west of Wellington on the road to Parkes. The use of convict-made bricks adds to the rural charm of the winery with its chapel-like appearance.

Glenfinlass Wines, one of the smallest commercial vineyards in New South Wales, was established in 1968 by a Wellington solicitor, Brian G. Holmes. It is entirely a family concern, with all the work being done by the Holmes family, Brian, Nyasa and four children, and their friends.

The vineyard comprises only 2.5 hectares of shiraz, cabernet sauvignon and sauvignon blanc. No irrigation is used, thus the annual production is up to 400 dozen only.

Brian Holmes describes his winemaking:

The wines are hand-made in the traditional manner, with natural yeasts being used to a large extent and with fermentation taking place in open tanks with hand plunging. Wines are neither blended nor filtered but are left as natural as possible. Our family believe in the Earth Garden concept of letting nature take its course, and this is evidenced throughout the whole winemaking process including the vineyard where neither pesticides nor insecticides are used and mildew protector sprays are used in a minimal manner only.

Their first vintage was in 1972. The wines have shown quite a deal of vintage variation, drier years producing heavier, full-bodied reds. In 1985 the reds were outstanding, and 1989 was an excellent year for sauvignon blanc.

Glenfinlass has no retail distribution.

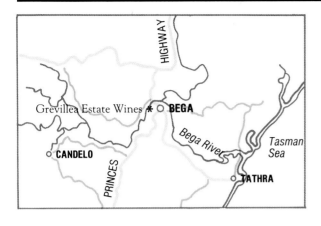

Grevillea Estate Wines

Grevillea Estate Wines, at Bega in Southern New South Wales, is a newly established winery of 7.5 hectares.

They crush 40–60 tonnes of riesling, semillon, chardonnay, sauvignon blanc, traminer; cabernet sauvignon and merlot, including some grapes bought in from the Hilltops. Of the table wines produced from these, the 1988 chardonnay is considered the best. It will not be long before the winery is totally self-sufficient.

Most sales are at cellar door, where the tasting rooms are incorporated into a restaurant.

The Gum Ridge Vineyard

Stephen and Rhonda Doyle are the owners and winemakers at the Gum Ridge Vineyard. The site chosen for their vineyard is 5 km from Orange on gravelly sedimentary soils, not at all typical of the area generally. It has a north-easterly aspect and, surprisingly, seems to be relatively frost free. It is a 6 hectare vineyard quite closely planted with cabernet franc, 1.5 hectares; cabernet sauvignon, 1.5 hectares; chardonnay, 1.4 hectares; riesling, 0.9 hectares and small amounts of merlot, pinot noir and malbec.

Pursuing the ideal of 'a little bit, well done', the normal crush of 30–40 tonnes is to be carefully increased to 60–65 tonnes. Although the other varieties are coming along nicely, the riesling could very well be the surprise—it continues to develop so well. Of the other table wines developed to date, Stephen feels the reds, particularly the cabernet blends, will be the wines to 'make the name' of Orange.

An obvious attention to detail has meant that most wine bottled to date has been pre-sold, but there is a mailing list for keen buyers.

Helm's Wines

Helm's Wines at Murrumbateman is an ever-expanding venture for keen enthusiasts, established in 1974.

Although the home vineyard is just 2 hectares, the crush from these is supplemented by the fruit of 10 hectares of contract growers, all situated within 1 km of the Helm's winery, which has a capacity of 70 tonnes. More grapes bought in from the Canberra district enable the production of a 29 tonne crush, which has been steadily building up since the winery was built in 1977 and crushed half a tonne.

The major varieties are Rhine riesling, gewurztraminer, chardonnay, half a hectare of muller thurgau; cabernet sauvignon and very small amounts of several other varieties.

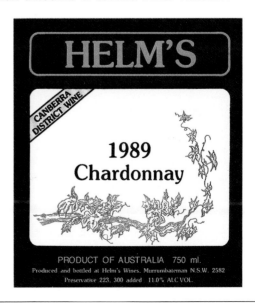

Nearly all the wines produced to date have been table wines, some sherry, and a very interesting muller thurgau—a German varietal. The cabernet sauvignon won top gold in the Small Winemakers Class at the 1988 Sydney Show.

Helm's believe the Canberra and surrounding district has enormous potential for the production of champagne. There has been a batch made each year from 1984 and now a hundred cases of 1989 are the first commercial batch to emerge. It's no wonder that sales, which have previously been cellar door and mail order, now include about fifteen restaurants and major hotels in Canberra and are soon to 'go national'.

Hercynia

Situated in the 'Hilltops' region of New South Wales, this small family-operated winery had its first commercial vintage in 1985.

Lawrence Doldissen is the winemaker and his wife Shirley, who is the great-grand-daughter of Karl Wilhelm (founder of the huge Grieffenhagen Winery in Bendigo in 1871), is his able assistant.

There are 6 tonnes crushed from the 5 hectare vineyard. Varieties include Rhine riesling, chardonnay, sauvignon blanc; cabernet sauvignon and pinot noir with some new plantings of shiraz. Of the pinot noirs, the 1985 was 'good', the 1988 is 'coming up well' and the 1989 is 'looking good'. The late-picked sauvignon blanc is 'very interesting'.

Sales are at cellar door and some mail order.

Hopevale Estate Winery

This is another small family winery at Wagga Wagga, with kids in the kitchen, vines in the paddock and a fine bottle or two stashed away in the cellar. Paul and Gail Jurissen, joint owners, winemakers and bottle washers, planted their first vines in 1987 and are optimistic and excited about their future.

With experience Paul gained from the College Winery at Riverina, he is experimenting with zinfandel grapes, a Californian variety not often tried in Australia. Although only making up 15 per cent of the 2 hectares of vines at the moment, the zinfandels are 'growing vigorously and showing promise'. Chardonnay makes up about 50

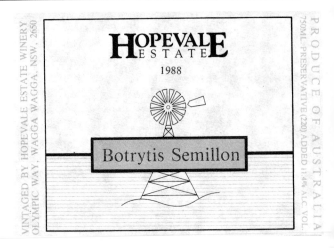

per cent, cabernet sauvignon 20 per cent and merlot the other 15 per cent.

An old tin-shed-style winery, which is in keeping with the homestead, dated 1876, is open to the public; and of the table wines offered, the pinot noir and the chardonnay are well worth trying. From the 1990 crush Hopevale Estate Winery opened as a cellar door sales point.

Jasper Valley Wines, Berry

The most unusual feature about Jasper Valley is its location, at Berry, in the Shoalhaven Valley, 120 km south of Sydney. The vineyards were established in 1976, with the first vintage made in 1978 by the late Mr S.C. Mitchell, who had studied winemaking at the Riverina College.

The 5 hectare vineyard is planted to semillon, Rhine riesling, cabernet sauvignon, shiraz and chardonnay. The rainfall is quite high, at 1500 mm, which necessitates careful spraying to combat mould. Vintage is usually in late February. The annual crush is about 20 tonnes.

In October 1988 the property was bought by John and Pat Wyeth. John, a colonial policeman (Rhodesia), emigrated to Australia in 1966 and worked variously as a policeman and National

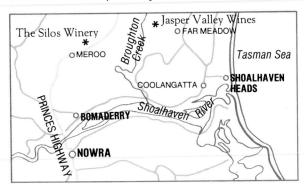

Parks Officer. They sell some wine to restaurants locally but almost all sales are at cellar door, where people are made most welcome. There is a range of ploughman's and steak lunches available which are extremely popular, and Jasper's has become something of a local favourite watering hole.

Lachlan Valley Wines, Forbes

The Chislett family has been making wine in some isolation at their century-old Wandary Lane winery, at Champsaur, 6 km from Forbes, since the 1930s.

Their wines are made from a variety of grapes grown on the family vineyard: gordo, frontignac, shiraz, trebbiano, palomino, cabernet sauvignon, pinot noir, doradillo and semillon—approximately 40 tonnes producing up to 3000 cases.

Frank Chislett, who ran the property for years, still takes a great interest in it. The proprietors are now Frank's son, Les, and his wife, Annette. Winemaking takes place in March and April in the historic winery, which has cellars, storage and sales area below ground. Their wines have won a number of awards at regional and national shows.

Sales are mostly at cellar door and include varietal table wines, and a range of fortifieds of which port is the most popular.

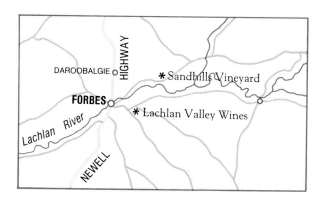

Lake George Winery

This is the rather private folly of Dr Edgar F. Riek, a wine devotee who has done more than any other person to impose the National Wine Show held in Canberra upon the wine industry. Edgar has been untiring in his efforts in developing and promoting this event, and the success of the show is due to his great foresight and innovativeness.

View of Lake George, by Joseph Lycett (28th October 1820)

LAKE GEORGE

TAWNY PORT
Wood-Aged Fortified Pinot noir

Grown and Vintaged by
EDGAR F. RIEK, CULLARIN, COLLECTOR, 2581

PRESERVATIVE (220) ADDED

750 ml PRODUCE OF AUSTRALIA 19.0% ALC/VOL

His own little vineyard and winery is on the side of Lake George. The vineyard's 3.5 hectares—one each of pinot noir and chardonnay, half each of cabernet sauvignon and merlot, the rest being semillon and others— produce an average of 20 tonnes of fruit, most of which is sold as such. He keeps enough to make 100 cases each of cabernet sauvignon, pinot noir, merlot, semillon and chardonnay, which he sells to local licensees.

There are no cellar door or mail order sales. He planted in 1971, made his first wine in 1975 and built the winery in 1979. His best years are 1986, 1987 and 1988 'when the grapes were ripe', which does not always happen by the side of Lake George.

Lark Hill

This vineyard overlooking Lake George, near Canberra, has been producing since 1978. The winemaker is Sue Carpenter (who completed her degree in wine science at Riverina College in 1989).

The total vineyard area is 10 hectares, of which 25 per cent is chardonnay, 25 per cent riesling, 25 per cent pinot noir; the balance is cabernet sauvignon, merlot and a little semillon.

Winery equipment has been recently upgraded, enabling the leasing of a further 2 hectares of chardonnay and cabernet sauvignon (also overlooking Lake George).

Specialising in production of table wines, especially chardonnay, has brought some success.

Autumn mists, Lark Hill's riesling block.

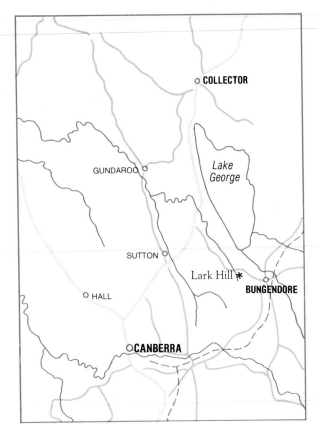

The chardonnay wines were among the top hundred in the Small Winemaker Awards of 1988. The cabernet merlot has also done well.

It is interesting to note that Sue and her husband, Dr D. Carpenter, are grafting much of the cabernet sauvignon to cabernet franc because they've found it a little cool for cabernet sauvignon in their area. This will enable earlier picking.

Although most of their sales are cellar door or mail order, they do supply some retailers in Sydney and Melbourne.

Markeita Cellars, Neurea

Markeita Cellars are situated at Neurea, a tiny settlement between Molong and Wellington, in central-western New South Wales. The winery was established in 1974 by Keith and Margherita Reinhard on their property, which has been in the family for more than forty years. Vines were first planted there in 1950 for the dried-fruit trade, and limited quantities of wine grapes were added later. The name 'Markeita' is a combination of the names Keith and Margherita, and the property has always been known as such.

Cellar manager is the Reinhards' eldest son, Bradley, who is also joint winemaker with his father. Vineyard management is Keith's responsibility.

The vineyards are on soils ranging from black river flats to gentle, sloping reds. The vines can all be irrigated from wells on the property in dry years.

From their own vineyards they process about 20 tonnes of cabernet sauvignon, shiraz and frontignac. Their specialties are big gutsy reds from shiraz, and a surprisingly large range of ports, vintage and tawny, for which they have a prominent name locally. They buy in bulk material as well and sell at cellar door 'all shapes and sizes' in bulk and bottle.

Middleton Wine Company Pty Ltd, Murrumbateman

The Murrumbateman Winery, owned and operated by the Middleton Wine Company, is situated on the Barton Highway between Canberra and Yass. Vineyards in this area are about 600 m above sea level.

Grapes were first planted by Geoff Middleton in 1973. Varieties planted include shiraz, cabernet sauvignon, sauvignon blanc, chardonnay and Rhine riesling—a total of 2 hectares. Total crush is only about 15 tonnes. The winery was completed in 1980 and, although small, is well equipped for production of red and white wines. In addition to their own grapes, some are bought in from other growers. The winery also produces mead made from local honey.

Geoff Middleton offers good picnic and barbecue facilities and operates a restaurant which serves very good food (open Friday and Saturday nights and for Sunday lunch).

Nioka Ridge

Nioka Ridge, at Young, has been established as a vineyard since 1979. Dr Phil Price is the winemaker and Keren Bissett the company secretary. Recently, Karl and Annette Robertson have joined the team and they now live on the vineyard and manage it.

The present 35 tonne crush will be increased to 40 tonnes. Varieties are riesling, semillon, chardonnay; shiraz, cabernet sauvignon,

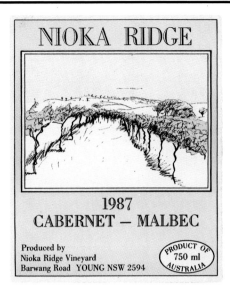

cabernet franc, merlot and malbec. Of these, the best wines produced are the rieslings and the cabernet malbec, and most sales are made at cellar door.

Sandhills Vineyard, Forbes

This vineyard was formerly owned by Jacques Genet, who sold in February 1989 to John Anthony Saleh, a Sydney businessman. John developed his interest in wine to the level of becoming a Purple Ribbon Holder at Rothbury.

John, with the help of his son Mark, intends to rejuvenate the property, concentrating on table wine production. At present there are 11 hectares, which are made up of riesling, muscadelle, shiraz and mataro. They are planting chardonnay and pinot noir.

Nearly all sales are at cellar door.

Silos' cabernet shiraz.

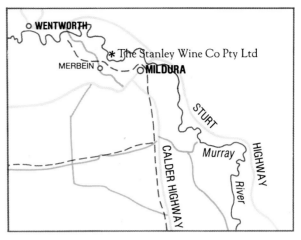

The Silos winery.

The Silos Winery

A nice idea, in that this is a development of a restaurant on an old dairy farm with a vineyard supporting it. Alan Bamfield and his sister Marie bought the property at Jasper's Brush, on the Princes Highway, near Nowra in Southern New South Wales, and started planting in 1978. Development of the vineyard has been intentionally slow, since they were also converting and running a restaurant.

Now they have 8 hectares of semillon, chardonnay, sauvignon blanc; shiraz, cabernet sauvignon, malbec and merlot, of which at present they make approximately 1000 dozen of straight varietals and one blend, a cabernet-shiraz.

The restaurant is open five days a week in winter and every day in summer. The old cow bales room is the tasting area, the old cattle feed shed is the restaurant, and one silo is the cellar. All the wine is sold either in the restaurant or at cellar door.

The Stanley Wine Co Pty Ltd, Buronga

This was the Hungerford Hill bulk plant at Buronga in New South Wales, near Mildura in Victoria, purchased by the Stanley Wine Co who in turn were taken over by the Thomas Hardy group. Incidentally, the old Stanley Winery at Clare is now named the Leasingham Winery (Leasingham, bottles; Stanley, casks). They crush 30 000 tonnes here, a lot of gordo muscat and sultana, plus all the classic varietals, for 2 litre and 4 litre casks, and for base wine material for sparkling wine. Actually, they process and package all the casks on the spot, which is far more efficient than carting it around all over the place.

The manager is Bob Smith, and the winemaker Richard Rowe. There are cellar door sales on site.

Tilba Valley Wines

This winery is situated in the foothills of Mt Dromedary, about 2.5 km from the ocean. It is in undulating country surrounded by beautiful blue gum forest overlooking Corunna Lake. A family concern, the vines were established in 1978 and the winery built in 1983. Barry Field is the winemaker and Val, his wife, an active assistant with son Robert as vineyard manager.

Of the 8 hectares under vine, riesling, semillon and cabernet sauvignon make up the largest part; with chardonnay, traminer and shiraz the remainder. Added to this, they have a grower at Victoria Creek who provides the fruit from 1 hectare of cabernet sauvignon and 1 hectare of chardonnay for them.

A crush of 30 tonnes produces both red and white table wines as well as a Tilba Tawny Port. Barry considers his best wines to be his cabernet sauvignon–shiraz blend and, for a sweeter palate, his traminer riesling. However, all wine made sells within twelve months of release either at cellar door or the few local restaurants who receive it.

There are picnic and barbecue facilities available with views over the lake.

Vicarys

Vicarys, on a ridge overlooking the Blue Mountains in New South Wales, is an elaborate complex catering for many activities. The vineyard itself dates from 1915 and the winery from 1923. Although retaining its 'old look', the winery has been updated to complement the picnic grounds, woolshed and function rooms. A lively addition to the charming surrounds are the percheron draught horses which are bred on the property.

The 3 hectares of vines are divided between chardonnay and traminer plantings. To make up to the normal 80–100 tonne crush, grapes are selected from the Hunter, Mudgee and Camden. The table wines produced from this crush are chardonnay, cabernet blanc, semillon and traminer in the whites; and a shiraz and a cabernet sauvignon in the reds. The most successful of these is the 1985 cabernet sauvignon.

Cellar door still accounts for most sales, where, as well as the table wines, a vintage port and tawny port are available.

Woodonga Hill

Owned by Phil and Jill Lindsay, the Woodonga Hill vineyard is situated on the Cowra Road outside Young. It was started in 1981 and now comprises 5 hectares of semillon, Rhine riesling, sauvignon blanc, chardonnay, traminer; shiraz, merlot, cabernet sauvignon and pinot meunier.

Jill is the winemaker, a graduate of the Riverina College in Wagga Wagga, and the first wine was made in 1986. The crush is small, 10 tonnes and growing. Mostly straight varietals are sold at cellar door.

Jill's best are Rhine riesling and cabernet sauvignon, and she is interested in developing lighter style reds.

Yass Valley Wines

Yass Valley Wines at Murrumbateman is a small vineyard. It was established in 1978, with a winery which was converted from an old shed in 1983.

The present owner, winemaker Peter Griffiths, has half a hectare in production with 1.25 hec-

tares in preparation. Peter has planted five hundred Rhine riesling vines and a hundred traminer, with cabernet sauvignon, shiraz and sauvignon blanc to come.

The present crush is 1.5 tonnes and, with a little extra bought in for the reds, production is about eight hundred bottles. Of the table wines and mead wines produced the Rhine riesling is the best, especially the 1988.

Most sales are private.

Australian Capital Territory

Kyeema Wines

A bit of a roving vagabond type of operation conducted by geophysicist Andrew McEwin, a wine enthusiast who was a graduate of Riverina College in Wagga Wagga in 1986. He works in Canberra, but has a New South Wales vigneron's licence near Young. He buys grapes from New South Wales growers scattered around the ACT, and makes four wines: a semillon, a chardonnay, a cabernet sauvignon–cabernet franc–merlot mix, and a shiraz. These wines are made at Young and other makers' wineries around the area, depending on where the fruit comes from.

Wines are sold by mail order or to restaurants around the ACT. Only 7–10 tonnes are processed, resulting in 400–600 cases. Andrew's wines have scored well at local wine shows.

Warralonga Vineyards, ACT

An experimental vineyard and operation that claims to be the first in the ACT itself. Situated along Sutton Road, about 5 km north of Canberra, it is owned by John Rees, a woolgrower who also happens to own a computer company.

One hectare, half each of chardonnay and pinot noir, was planted in 1986 and 1987. The wine made thus far is in small quantities and has been consumed among friends.

John has had help from people like David Lowe and viticulturist William Gray, and a production manager is even listed! Obviously great things are expected of ACT's first.

VICTORIA

Ian Mackay

The North-West

Pivotal to the history of winemaking in the desert-like north-west of Victoria is the growth of Mildura and the role of the Canadian-born Chaffey brothers in the development of irrigation from the Murray River, which forms the state's boundary with New South Wales. Under their ministration, water brought life to the desert, and today this vital area of riverland produces more than 80 per cent of all grapes grown in Victoria for wine, and more than 90 per cent of its white wine grapes.

Ben (W.B.) and George Chaffey came to Australia in the 1880s at the request of Alfred Deakin, and they were invited to undertake major irrigation projects by the governments of both South Australia and Victoria. In the Victorian riverland irrigation from the Murray began in 1887, and during the next two years 65 hectares of vines were planted at Irymple, in what is now part of the First Mildura Irrigation Trust administered area. Grape varieties included cabernet sauvignon, hermitage (shiraz), white hermitage, malbec, various sherry varieties, gordo blanco, mataro and doradillo.

The first small vintage was crushed in 1891 in a bough-roofed shed, and it was crushed by bare feet, the method used until 1897 when Ben Chaffey brought a Chaffey steam engine to the site to operate a mechanical crusher. By 1892, a substantial brick building with cellars and ample storage was completed, and the original structure is in use to this day. The bricks were made on the site, and the cellars excavated with a horse-drawn scoop.

The first commercial harvest was in 1893. Unfortunately the river dried up, and without riverboat transport, the grapes were left to rot on the wharf. The harsh summer that year also had a devastating effect on the Chaffeys' own venture, Chateau Mildura, which was declared bankrupt despite an impressive output of quality wine and brandy.

In charge of the vineyards and winemaking at Chateau Mildura was Pierre Joseph Mari Mazou, a southern Frenchman who had reached the riverland via South Australia, where he had gained some experience in viticulture. 'Peter' Mazou left in 1901, to be succeeded by a relative, Florentin Jean Louie Gelly. Gelly, also from southern France, arrived in Mildura after managing one of Thomas Hardy's cellars in South Australia.

By the turn of the century the industry was in a very depressed state, and W.B. Chaffey could see no future in table wines. He decided to graft his vines to drying varieties such as gordo and sultana, a task supervised and completed by Florentin Gelly in 1901. By 1908 Chaffey had sold all of his stocks of wine to a merchant in Melbourne and, for the time being, the role of Mildura as a centre of premium wine production was over.

The renaissance came at the end of World War I, when irrigated settlements for ex-servicemen were established at Red Cliffs and Merbein, and there was similar expansion at Robinvale after World War II. Mildura itself continued to grow, and is now Victoria's northernmost city with a population of 20 000. It is a popular tourist town with a lovely winter climate—the centre of extensive plantings of citrus, stone fruit and vegetables as well as grapes for the table, for drying, and for wine. Away from the river the landscape is undulating and

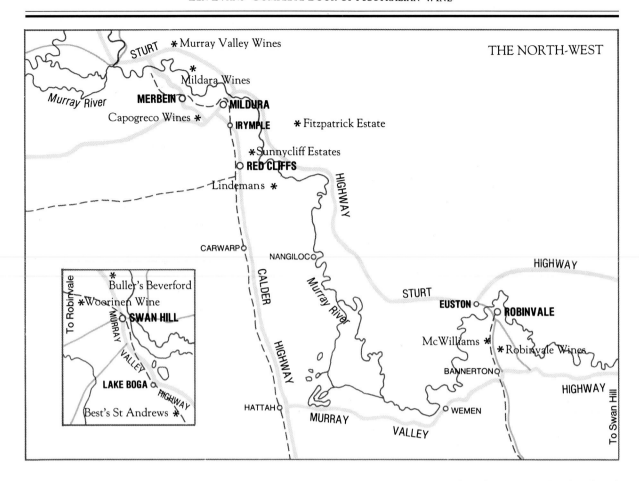

THE NORTH-WEST

monotonous, with an altitude generally less than 100 m above sea level.

Summers are long and hot; but severe spring frosts can be a problem, with oil burners and overhead sprinklers used to protect the vines. The area has been phylloxera free, but spraying is necessary to control insect pests, and problems such as mildew and mould. The soils are typical mallee pink-brown loams, red surface sand and underlying limestone and clay, which can cause drainage problems.

The main grapegrowing settlements are in the Mildura–Merbein–Red Cliffs area, but they extend also to Lake Boga, Swan Hill and Robinvale. Over the years growers have tended to produce fruit for major wine companies, but the pattern is changing somewhat and many smaller winemakers are now in operation. Statistics show, however, that premium red and white varieties are very much in the minority in the riverland. Sultana constitutes more than 25 per cent of the crush and muscat gordo a further 24 per cent, with red varieties making up less than 10 per cent of the total crush. These figures tell their own story. Although there is evidence

that whites such as chardonnay and colombard are increasing rapidly, most of the wine being made in the region is going into the big companies' white wine casks. Brandy and fortifying spirit is also made in large quantities.

Best's St Andrews

We have mentioned in this book's section on Best's Wines, Great Western, how in 1930 Frederick Thomson and his son Eric were forced off their properties by the economic depression, and their purchase of what they called the St Andrews vineyard at Lake Boga. It was an inspired buy which eventually led to better things for the Thomson family; today St Andrews still remains a vital part of their whole winemaking enterprise. In volume terms, it provides the major part of total Best's output.

The vineyard is now 25 hectares, and varieties include cabernet sauvignon, shiraz, Rhine riesling, muscat and chenin blanc. The St Andrews wines are made there and taken to Great Western for maturation and bottling. Small amounts of brandy and fortifying spirit are also made there in a pot still. In 1988 Simon Clayfield took over as winemaker when Trevor Mast, who had worked with Viv Thomson for a number of years, left to pursue his own considerable wine interests.

Vintage at Lake Boga is quite a bit earlier than at Great Western, and the wines are significantly different. They do not have the depth and complexity of their Great Western cousins, but what they do have is lightness and freshness which comes from the way the grapes ripen and from some clever winemaking. The chenin blanc, for instance, ripens well but retains good acid structure; it is matured in American oak to make a very pleasant and drinkable white wine indeed. The cabernet sauvignon also shows lighter varietal character than at Great Western, but with a year or two of bottle age it comes up as a very consistent, very drinkable red.

Buller's Beverford

We have also written elsewhere in this book about the Buller family of Rutherglen, and their move to Beverford, 15 km north of Swan Hill, in 1952. The idea was to provide more wine to complement that of their famous Calliope vineyard, and the project has worked extremely well.

They have 15 hectares of vines at Beverford, including shiraz, cabernet sauvignon, muscat of Alexandria, gordo, semillon and pedro. They also purchase extensively from other growers in the district, all of whom are encouraged to cultivate premium table wine varieties. Dick Buller junior is the winemaker and he makes a full range of red and white table wines, some of which are sold in bulk. At the top of the line are good varietals, a big solid cabernet sauvignon with quite a distinctive character of its own; and chenin blanc and semillon as whites. Dick also has a distillery, which provides fortifying spirit for the famous Buller Rutherglen muscats and other fortifieds, and which is much in demand from other winemakers around the country. Beverford cabernet port is different from the Calliope version, but a very good buy nevertheless.

Capogreco Wines

Bruno and Elvira Capogreco came to Australia in 1954 from Calabria, in southern Italy, where Bruno's family had a small winery. In 1976 they established a 20 hectare estate in Riverside Avenue, Mildura, and planted shiraz, Rhine riesling, sultana, cabernet sauvignon, mataro, palamino and black and white muscatel. They also have some of the lovely Italian variety, barbera.

The Capogrecos make their wines very much in the traditional Italian way, picking the grapes when they are very ripe then fermenting and maturing the wine in large oak casks. Most of them retain some sweetness, as they do in southern Italy, and Bruno promises that they are made without the use of any chemical additives. His elder son, Vicenzo, studied oenology at Roseworthy Agricultural College, and now he helps make the wine in what is very much a family business.

They have a wide range of wines, sparkling to fortified, and some good varietal reds and whites including barbera, cabernet sauvignon and a mataro–shiraz blend. The wines are all sold at the cellar door, and are very, very popular with the local Italian community.

Fitzpatrick Estate

Previously known as Bonnonee Wines, Fitzpatrick Estate was established in 1974 by Michael Fitzpatrick, a local grower, and winemaker Richard Cirami. Now run by Michael and his wife Sandi, it is quite a large operation producing significant amounts of wine.

The 30 hectare vineyard, in Campbell Avenue, Irymple, is planted to shiraz, ruby cabernet, barbera, sultana, Rhine riesling, chardonnay, gewurztraminer, colombard, gordo and crouchen. Each year they crush about 600 tonnes of their own grapes, and another 2000 tonnes or so of grapes from other growers. This gives them about 2 million litres of wine a year, the top 10 per cent or so of which is bottled and sold under Fitzpatrick's own label.

The winemaker is Neville Hudson, and he produces a wide range of Fitzpatrick Estate wines, including Old Borer and Belya Light Red, some cheap fortifieds and even a spumante. His best varietals are Rhine riesling and traminer, both of which have won show medals, and a light but very pleasant red blend of ruby cabernet and barbera. Most of them are sold at cellar door, but they are now being more widely distributed in Melbourne.

Lindemans, Karadoc

In 1973 Lindemans, owned at the time by the Philip Morris company and one of Australia's biggest wine companies, bought 141 hectares of land at Karadoc, 28 km south-east of Mildura and 10 km upstream from Redcliffs, and built what is probably Australia's biggest winery. It is of modular design and grand proportions, and uses the most modern techniques, equipment and material-handling systems in the world to produce high-quality table wine from fruit grown in the Sunraysia district. As it grew out of the desert landscape locals were wont to speculate about whether it was a winery or, in fact, a refinery.

Adjacent to it is a large production facility where Lindemans' range of 'Cellar pack' cask wines, said to be the largest in the country, are filled; and around it all is a 110 hectare vineyard planted to chardonnay, Rhine riesling and muscat. Chief winemaker there is Wayne Falkenberg, and he has the enormous task each year of processing between 40 000 and 50 000 tonnes of grapes from their own vineyard and from other growers in the district. Karadoc, under his care, has become chief production centre for the Lindeman–Leo Buring empire.

As well as 'soft packs', this huge volume of wine goes into the company's wide range of products, including Ben Ean moselle, Leo Buring Liebfrauwine, the Matthew Lang range of chardonnay, fumé blanc and cabernet sauvignon, and others. They also make some straight Karadoc varietals, bottled and matured there for cellar door sales and promotions.

McWilliam's, Robinvale

McWilliam's Wines, founded in 1877 and pioneers in the Murrumbidgee Irrigation Area (MIA) in New South Wales, established a large winery at Robinvale, 80 km south-east of Mildura, in 1961. Under the care of winemakers J.G. McWilliam and A.J. Hooper, it crushes about 15 000 tonnes of grapes a year—all of them bought from local growers, although they have a few hectares of their own grapes around the winery.

Although not in the same league as Lindemans at Karadoc, it is a major operation which produces large amounts of wine for the company's cream sherry, sparkling Bodega, and its range of 4 litre wine casks, including fruity lexia. There are good facilities for visitors, including many items of interest relating to the pioneers of Robinvale housed in a 'Drop Log' cabin tasting and sales room.

Mildara Wines

Mildara is the largest Victorian-based wine company; it has been listed on the Stock Exchanges of Australia since 1976. In recent years it has truly become a national company, both through acquisitions of operations such as Krondorf, Hamilton Ewell, Yellowglen and Balgownie, and through expansion of its operations in Coonawarra and elsewhere. Its administrative headquarters are in Melbourne, but its processing and distribution centre is still at Merbein, 11 km from Mildura, up on the cliffs overlooking the Murray River where Canadian irrigation expert William Benjamin Chaffey established a home for the company in 1913.

Part of the story of Ben Chaffey and his brother George is told in the introduction to this section, and elsewhere in the book. Sufficient now to recall that Mildura was founded in 1887, and that the Chaffeys planted a vineyard the following year and built a winery at Irymple, just south of the town. They called the property Chateau Mildura. They made their first wine in 1891 and three years later were declared bankrupt. A Royal Commission found the Chaffeys guilty of mismanaging the irrigation schemes they had been brought to Australia to establish. After this finding George Chaffey returned to the United States.

Ben Chaffey hung on at Chateau Mildura; however, it became clear that there was no demand for the kinds of wine he was making, so he grafted his vineyard over to drying grape varieties and closed the winery. By 1911 things had begun to improve, and in that year he formed Mildura Winery Pty Ltd. Within two years he had begun construction of a winery at Merbein, but again business slumped and both Irymple and Merbein wineries were offered for sale. There were no takers.

Ever resilient, Chaffey formed another company in 1922, this time called Mildara Wines. It took over the remaining assets of the first company, and by 1924 he was making wine again.

Cask Storage, Mildara Wines — original winery, Irymple, Victoria.

Flor sherry casks, Mildara.

The company profited by the export boom of the 1920s, and Chateau Mildura, with its vineyards, winery and distillery, was a major winemaking force in the area.

In 1933, export sales were threatened by technical and marketing problems in the UK, where its wine and brandy had been sold under the prosaic Emu Wine Company label. The Mildara trademark was registered, new labels designed, and in 1935 Roseworthy College graduate Ron Haselgrove, who had worked in Europe in the cognac trade, was appointed technical adviser with the task of significantly raising the standard of the company's products.

One of the biggest problems at the time was the spoilage of fortified wine at Merbein by the bacteria known as 'tourne', so Haselgrove persuaded the Waite Research Institute in Adelaide to try to come up with some answers. Scientist John Fornachon undertook a research project under the joint sponsorship of Adelaide University and the Australian Wine Board. His report in 1943, 'Bacterial Spoilage of Fortified Wines', not only helped solve Chateau Mildura's problems, but won world recognition.

In the next two decades enormous effort was put into fortified wine production at Merbein, particularly sherry. John Fornachon had also done definitive work on the flor sherry process, and with his technical assistance winemaker Jack Schultz was able to install a flor sherry-making process which was easily one of the best and most efficient in Australia. Supreme dry sherry, first laid down in 1936, became a commercial success, and so did George, an ultra-dry fino developed specifically for George Caro, a diabetic who was chairman of the liquor merchants Gollin & Company Pty Ltd. George, still a wine for the cognoscenti, was first released in 1954.

In 1955, Ron Haselgrove—by then a director of the company—decided to broaden Mildara's table-wine options and bought 5 hectares of land in the famous 'terra rossa' strip in Coonawarra, in south-east South Australia. Planting began the same year, with cabernet sauvignon, shiraz, palamino, and a few experimental rows of semillon, sauvignon blanc and crouchen. Today, of course, Coonawarra reds are the jewel in Mildara's table-wine crown, and the company has 200 hectares of vines and a major winery there.

In 1976 Mildara was listed on the stock exchange. Three years later, increased capital through a rights issue financed the purchase of Hamilton's Ewell Vineyards, Fesq & Company Pty Ltd and John Woods & Company Pty Ltd. It also allowed the establishment of Haselgrove's Pty Ltd as a national marketing subsidiary. Ron Haselgrove resigned in 1974, and was succeeded as managing director by his son, Richard, who

had joined Mildara in 1960 as technical manager.

The winery at Merbein, high on a bluff overlooking the river, is one of the best-kept and smartest in Australia—although it lost a bit of its shine, and many millions of dollars worth of maturing wine, when fire swept through one of its major storage areas in 1989. It is home for all the company's many products (the top Coonawarra reds are oak-matured in Coonawarra but are taken to Merbein for bottling and bottle ageing); chief winemaker Mike Press spends a good deal of his time travelling between its various outposts. The company retains its connections with Irymple, where it has storage cellars and 56 hectares of vineyards which include 25 hectares of a specially-selected Spanish strain of palamino, used to make high-quality sherry.

About 400 growers provide the balance of Mildara's Sunraysia crush of about 17 000 tonnes. About one-fifth of this goes into brandy, 45 per cent into sherry, and the balance into table wine—including Mildara's well-known Church Block series and the very popular Windsor Brut Chardonnay sparkling wine. A good deal of these wines go towards satisfying Mildara's growing export trade.

Murray Valley Wines

One of the older and more unusual wineries in the riverland, Murray Valley Wines was set up in 1920 by Greek immigrant George Kalamastrakis to make the kinds of wines he and many of his Greek friends in the area love.

He planted 5 hectares of vines on his block in 15th Street, Mildura; shiraz, gordo, Rhine riesling, cabernet sauvignon and muscat. He makes a range of fortified wines and a Greek-style Kokkinelli red which is quite sweet and is best drunk chilled! He makes a lighter red from shiraz and grenache, a riesling hock and a semillon moselle. He also uses riesling and pine resin to make a pretty good imitation of authentic Greek retsina.

Robinvale Wines

This is another Greek-inspired winery, established in Robinvale South in 1976 by the Caracatsanoudis family. With its Greek temple facade, columns, arches and doorways, it could

Jamiesons Run
CHARDONNAY
1989 COONAWARRA   750 ml

have been shipped straight to Australia from the eastern Mediterranean.

They have 30 hectares under vine, but a good deal of their production is for the table and for dried fruit. They make quite a range of wine, however, including both still and sparkling non-alcoholic wine for a growing market in Melbourne. Among these are various grape juice blends, plus sparkling passionfruit and grape juice and a sparkling ginger and grape juice. Their table wines have a distinct Greek flavour, and include such things as white rozake, retsina and mavrodaphne.

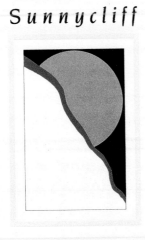

Sunnycliff

VICTORIAN
Sauvignon Blanc

750 ML PRODUCE OF AUSTRALIA 12.0% ALC/VOL

Sunnycliff Estates

Sunnycliff Estates, one of Victoria's largest winemaking enterprises, is owned and operated by Rentiers Pty Ltd, the company which also owns a large slice of the action in Coonawarra, including Katnook Estate and the Coonawarra Machinery Company Pty Ltd. By Victorian standards it is a massive operation—250 hectares of vineyards and a large and ultra-modern winery in Nangiloc Road, Iraak, near Red Cliffs in the Murray River valley region now widely known as Sunraysia.

The property was established originally in 1972 to grow grapes for other wine companies; but in 1980 the winery was built and Sunnycliff began making wine and clarified grape juice which was also sold to the trade. In 1989, however, it started to bottle wine under its own label, and to sell stainless steel containers of its very

fine products to hotels, bars and larger restaurants. The managing director of Sunnycliff is Geoff Thompson, and he believes the Sunraysia region has come a long way in quality wine production in the last decade; and this is reflected in the style of the wine his company is now distributing around Australia.

In 1989, for instance, Sunnycliff won a gold medal for its chardonnay vintage 1988 at the Royal Melbourne Wine Show, and the estate is the second largest producer of chardonnay in Australia. Sunnycliff's 'chardonnay-on-tap' was very well received by the trade and public at the Exhibition of Victorian Winemakers soon after it was launched in 1989. This was an occasion which revealed a good deal about just how much of this classic variety will be appearing on the Australian scene in the 1990s and beyond. The combination of quality, volume and price (the 1989 chardonnay, also a medal winner, was introduced at just over $7 per bottle) was good news for consumers, but perhaps not for 'boutique' producers. Other wines in the range, available both in bottle and on-tap, were sauvignon blanc, chablis (a blend of chardonnay and colombard), and Rhine riesling. At just over $5, the latter two wines were significant bargains.

Geoff Thompson points out that plantings of chardonnay and sauvignon blanc have supplemented the original vineyards of Rhine riesling, colombard, cabernet sauvignon and ruby cabernet, and that well over 7000 tonnes of grapes are crushed each year. The grapes are mechanically harvested at night and crushed immediately, and the wines are fermented and stored under refrigeration to minimise the effects of the Sunraysia's burning summers.

Science, technology and super-efficiency are bywords at Sunnycliff, and there is no doubt that the effect of its wine on the bulk and retail markets will continue to be significant. In a state where the small tend to be very small and the big few and far between, Sunnycliff is in a league of its own.

Woorinen Wine Estates

Before it went into receivership in 1985, Woorinen was the third largest winery in Victoria. Established in 1968 in Palmer Street, Woorinen South, 11 km west of Swan Hill, it was owned by the state's only producers' cooperative.

What was known as Woorinen Wine Estate (Victoria) Pty Ltd had 200 shareholders cultivating some 2000 hectares of vines. Winemaker Wayne Dutschke made a wide range of table and fortified wines, most of them for sale in bulk but also under Woorinen's own label. Outstanding among them was Mellifera Noble Rot, a late-picked, botrytis-affected Rhine riesling of great quality.

In 1986 it was taken over by the Valmorbida group, owners of the winery operation at Mitchelton, in the Goulburn Valley. Most of the grower-shareholders now sell their grapes to other producers; but Mitchelton's chief winemaker, Don Lewis, uses the winery as a valuable adjunct in the production of the company's rapidly expanding second label, Thomas Mitchell.

The North-East

The north-east of Victoria is an historic wine-growing region which has perhaps seen more than its share of fortune and misfortune. It survived the rigours of the gold rush only to become the first major viticultural area in Australia to fall to phylloxera; in more recent years, a decline in demand for its great fortified wines and table reds 'built for heroes' led to straitened economic times. New winemaking technology and increased viticultural expertise, however, appear to have ushered in a new age for the north-east, and the quality and quantity of wine being made there is increasing rapidly.

This region, which pioneering viticulturist Hubert de Castella thought had the potential to become what he called 'John Bull's vineyard', is roughly triangular in shape, bounded on the north by the Murray River, on the east by the beautiful river valleys which reach up into the Great Divide, and on the west by the sweeping Oxley Plains. Winemaking is centred around Rutherglen, but on the edges of the triangle are other wine settlements such as Corowa (in fact, over the Murray in New South Wales), Glenrowan, Milawa, Taminick and Barnawartha.

Rutherglen, once a booming goldmining town, is now a centre for tourism in the north-east; and motels, and born-again hotels, cater for

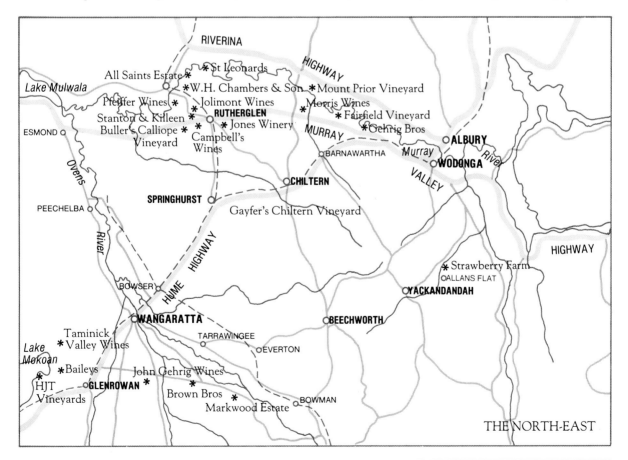

THE NORTH-EAST

visitors from all over the country. In recent years, major producers Seppelt and Lindemans have closed their operations in Rutherglen because of a downturn in fortified wine production; but both premises have been re-occupied by smaller companies interested in entertaining visitors as much as they are in making and selling wine. The importance of providing activities for visitors is reflected in the annual North-east Winery Walkabout, a Queen's birthday long-weekend holiday given over to eating, drinking and having the kind of fun that only wine people seem to be able to turn on. For several years, the Walkabout has been voted Victoria's leading provincial festival.

From an historical point of view one of the most satisfying factors in this prosperous renaissance has been the survival of the pioneering families; the Campbells, the Browns, the Sutherland Smiths, the Chambers, Gehrigs and so on—fifth- and sixth-generation settlers who followed the gold to Rutherglen and turned it to their own advantage. Not only have the names and properties survived, but other great properties such as Fairfield, created magnificently from the wealth of gold, have been restored to remind us of the heritage of this remarkable region.

In viticultural terms, the mountains that overlook the north-east have a moderating effect on climate, which varies little from year to year. Conjecture on the so-called Greenhouse Effect has been stimulated by recent summers, warmer and wetter than usual; but generally the rainfall is about 635 mm per year and falls largely in winter and spring. The nights in winter are cold and frequently frosty, but the warm, sunny days are part of a picture which visitors from Melbourne and beyond find irresistible.

A Roseworthy Agricultural College study shows north-east Victoria to have the coldest winter temperature of any mainland viticultural region. Spring temperatures are lower than in South Australian table wine areas, while maximum temperatures in January, the height of summer, are similar. The total heat summations and aridity are almost identical to the Clare Valley, but ripening can be up to two weeks later in the north-east. Fungal damage is not usually a problem because the vintage period is normally dry. In 1989, however, unseasonal rains plagued so much of the picking season that growers had to be careful to avoid mildew and bunch rot.

Rutherglen has an altitude of 170 m above sea level, and most of the wine-producing country is lower than that. Vineyards lie mainly in the flat, sandy loam valleys created by the King, Ovens and Kiewa Rivers flowing down to the mighty Murray from the rain and snow catchments in the Great Divide. The Murray River itself is a major source of irrigation. What is remarkable about the region is the enormous increase in vineyards in the upper reaches of these streams, many of them dairy and tobacco farms given over to a more profitable pursuit.

There are now more than twenty producers in the region, with approximately 700 hectares under cultivation. Many of the vineyards which traditionally produce red and fortified wines have been replanted in recent years, and now vineyard managers are as likely to be talking about chardonnay, sauvignon blanc, pinot noir, merlot and cabernet franc, as about cabernet sauvignon and shiraz. Some splendid new table wines are being produced, and they contrast remarkably to the big, dark, highly alcoholic wines of the past. Drinking habits have changed (most will say for the better), and the north-east has reacted appropriately with cold fermentation, small-oak fermentation and maturation, and other thoroughly modern winery techniques which have helped overcome some of the problems of the past. Style and delicacy is the thing, and north-east producers are supplying it in plenty.

The fame of the Rutherglen area has rested on its fortified wines, great ports, sherries, tokays and muscats. The Rutherglen brown muscat has virtually become recognised worldwide as a subspecies in its own right, creating luscious and unique wines. These wines are all expensive to make and, particularly in recent years, difficult to sell at anything resembling a reasonable return for all the effort. Declining sales led many producers to fear the extinction of the style, but the vigorous rebirth of the region now probably means it will survive. Indeed, production at some wineries is increasing to cope with demand finally being shown overseas. That half-a-dozen Rutherglen producers should club together to promote liqueur muscat at the London Wine Show as they did in 1989 is a very good sign for the future.

All Saints Vineyard (built 1869), Wahgunyah, Victoria.

All Saints Estate

In May 1989, All Saints at Wahgunyah celebrated its 125th birthday with a dinner which also served to introduce the new owners of this historic estate. Ownership had passed from G. Sutherland Smith & Sons to All Saints Estate Wines, a company headed by Adelaide financier and Barossa Valley producer, Mr Brian Anders. Strong family ties remain, however. George Sutherland Smith is the group's corporate director and his son, Andrew, a fifth-generation Sutherland Smith, is chief winemaker. And new owners or not, the great turreted red-brick winery of All Saints stands as a living monument to the man who founded one of Victoria's winemaking dynasties.

George Sutherland Smith was a Scot, born into a family of carpenters in Caithness who had worked for generations on the maintenance of the Castle of Mey in the parish of All Saints. He made his way to Australia as a young man in the 1850s, and by 1860 was running a riverboat between Echuca and Wahgunyah with his brother-in-law, John Banks. In 1864 he and some partners, aware that the river trade was dwindling, bought a large riverfront block in Wahgunyah and began planting vines. They had no winemaking experience, but within less than

a decade George Sutherland Smith had been awarded a Diploma of Honour at the Vienna Exhibition and a gold medal at the London Wine Show.

His previous work in the building trade stood him in good stead, and in the 1880s he began making bricks on the property for the construction of the present winery, which was modelled on the Castle of Mey (now owned by the Queen Mother). George died soon after the winery was completed in 1884. His son, David Banks Smith, was already an experienced vigneron when he inherited the property, and he set about vigorous expansion of the vineyards and winemaking facilities. In the 1890s, however, phylloxera swept through the Rutherglen region, and even vines not infected by the root-attacking louse were destroyed as part of a government-sponsored, vine-pull program.

David steadfastly set about replanting All Saints, and cellar extensions were underway at the turn of the century. Massive storage capacity was installed by way of 'Sullivans', massive oak casks made by cooper Peter Sullivan who worked in the Barnawartha region until 1905 and who won world fame for the quality of his work. Eventually All Saints had storage capacity for more than 2.25 million litres of wine—the largest in the Southern Hemisphere in the early part of the century.

David Banks Smith was succeeded by his sons David and George, under whose management a bottling plant and offices were opened in Selbourne Place, in the heart of Melbourne. In 1960, a modern bottling plant and distribution centre was set up in North Melbourne. David's son, Ian Sutherland Smith, became sales and marketing director in Melbourne while George's sons, George and Peter, looked after the winery and the vineyards respectively. The property had always been run as a mixed farm, and it still includes a prize Murray Grey cattle stud.

All Saints continued in family hands into the 1980s, but appeared to be facing an unequal struggle in the increasingly competitive wine-marketing business. It began to fall behind in the way its wines were being made and sold, and it needed a dose of capital to make it competitive. Eventually these resources had to come from outside, and the formation of the new All Saints Estate's group was the result. Immediate changes included the clearing out of a lot of unsuitable old oak storage and the acquisition of small French and American oak barrels, a new wine press and new stainless steel fermenters. Andrew Sutherland Smith made his first vintage in 1989 in his great-great-grandfather's winery, and proclaimed that the future looked bright.

The 150 hectares of All Saints vineyards have been subject to an extensive replanting program which extended throughout most of the 1980s. Some phylloxera still existed on the property so all new plantings were made on resistant rootstocks, and the replanted areas were set up for mechanical harvesting. Traditional plantings of cabernet sauvignon and shiraz were invigorated with new clones of these famous varieties, and work was begun on producing disease-resistant strains of marsanne, the Rhône Valley white variety which had long been an All Saints favourite.

New plantings included chardonnay, sauvignon blanc, Rhine riesling, chenin blanc, merlot, cabernet franc and pinot noir—all top varieties which Andrew Sutherland Smith believes will take All Saints table wine production through to the turn of the century. Fortified wines are not being ignored. Huge stocks of sherry, muscat, port and tokay have been classified into new soleras which Mr Michael Fallon, managing director of All Saints Estate Wines, believes will provide the basis for some exciting production in the future under the once-famous All Saints Black Swan and Lyrebird labels. This is indeed a new era for an historic company.

Baileys of Glenrowan

Legends and wine promotion go well together, so perhaps it was natural that Bailey's Bundarra should now be more closely associated with Glenrowan, where Ned Kelly made his name. As James Halliday has pointed out, Baileys make blood-and-thunder wines which would probably have met with the lamented Ned's complete approval. In fact, Bundarra was the name of what was one of the oldest vineyards in Australia, 5 km west of the township of Glenrowan at the foot of the Warby ranges and overlooking Lake Mokoan.

The hearty Bailey traditions began when Richard Bailey, who ran a coaching business in Manchester, came to Australia and set up a horse-drawn transport business in Melbourne in the 1830s. Gold took him to the north-east where Richard and his son Varley ran the first general store in Glenrowan. Business flourished and around 1875 the Baileys bought land for running sheep and cattle. They planted grain crops and vines as well, and those that survived phylloxera and later plantings on resistant rootstocks, produced rich red wines which reflected the red granite loam and the dry Warby summers.

Four generations of Baileys followed in these footsteps, and it was Alan Bailey who produced the first of the now-famous liqueur muscats in 1934. He had seen that in some years the brown muscat (often called 'frontignac' locally) ripened with enormous sugar content, sometimes reaching in excess of 30° baumé (1° baumé being equal to 1.8 per cent of sugar by volume), and that the wines could be bottled at up to 14° baumé after maturing for many years in oak casks.

In 1972 the property went the way of many other family wineries at the time—sold to a multinational company with little or no previous connection with the wine industry. In this case the buyer was the Australian company, Davis Consolidated Industries, which installed one of its senior research and development executives as general manager and winemaker. Harry J. Tinson had no experience in making wine, but being of scientific bent soon settled into the Bailey tradition of producing regional and highly individualistic wines. Harry and his wife Catherine, assistant winemaker and excellent cook (who used liqueur muscat in a profusion of recipes), were also responsible for the introduction of refrigeration and fermentation in pressurised stainless steel tanks in which they made a new range of white wines.

These wines complemented the amazing Bundarra reds which over the years had created a mythology all their own. Melbourne medico and author, Dr Sam Benwell, referred to them as 'nothing less than a tour-de-force . . . they are red wines in another language'. He quoted a visiting Frenchman who in turn had described them as 'food, wine and a good cigar'. To Keith Dunstan they were 'liquid steak and eggs', while Hugh Johnson remarked, 'If they made wine like this in the Rhône Valley they would be declaring it the vintage of the century'.

In 1986 Harry Tinson left to run his own HJT vineyard several kilometres away, and Steve Goodwin, formerly of Yalumba, took over as winemaker. The fruit at Baileys is as deep as ever, but technology, and the winemaking style, have changed. The reds are rich without being muscular, and there are some interesting barrel-fermented whites, including a good chardonnay. He has Rhine riesling, aucerot, chasselas and

traminer included in his 94 hectares or so of vines, and shiraz and cabernet sauvignon for his reds. But the power and the glory are still Rutherglen brown muscat and tokay, the source of superb material and of fortified wines which, at their best, are probably unequalled.

Brown Bros Milawa Vineyard

One of the outstanding new vineyards in Australia is Whitlands, a sculptured piece of mountainside in the Great Dividing Range overlooking the King Valley and in turn the Oxley Plains, which stretch beyond Rutherglen to the Murray River. With an elevation of some 800 m it is one of the highest, coolest vineyards in the country, a bold experiment by the Brown Bros of Milawa to seek out quality wherever it might be.

The pursuit of quality has been a Brown Bros trademark for just on a century. The story of what has become a winemaking dynasty began in 1857, when a Scot by the name of John Graham bought 50 hectares of land and started planting vines at Milawa, in the beautiful Ovens Valley between the Ovens and King Rivers. In 1852 a young law clerk, George Brown, arrived in Melbourne in time to join the gold rush. Eventually he bought land at Hurdle Creek and married John Graham's schoolteacher daughter, Rebecca. On the death of her father they moved to

Wood storage at Brown Bros Milawa Vineyard.

Milawa, began a family, and started making wine in 1889.

They built a new winery in 1900; but between 1915 and 1919 the vineyard was devastated by phylloxera, and all of their vines were destroyed. John Francis Brown, the second son, set about replanting Milawa on American rootstocks, and by 1920 some 16 hectares of new vines were coming into production. His son, John Charles Brown, became winemaker in 1934, and he expanded the vineyards and winery. Since the death of his father in 1943, John Brown II has presided calmly over the affairs of the company, tempering an adventurous outlook with the practical ability to understand new grape varieties and advanced winemaking techniques.

The vineyard at Whitlands is a perfect example of this. John Brown II had been keeping an eye on what was a dairy farm for some years, and when the 68 hectare property came up for sale he was soon on the spot. In 1986–87 it was planted to chardonnay, pinot noir, cabernet sauvignon, traminer, Rhine riesling and sauvignon blanc; and some stunning young wines have been the result. What is important

about Whitlands is not merely the quality of its fruit but also that, a century down the track, Brown Bros is showing itself to be one of the most forward-looking and innovative companies in Australia.

John Brown II and his wife produced four sons, all of whom are now fully involved in the family company. John Graham Brown is now chief winemaker, and Peter Brown is vineyard manager and viticultural adviser to the rapidly increasing number of growers contracted to supply Brown Bros. Ross Brown is the sales and marketing director, and Roger Brown, the baby of the family, is in charge of the plant propagation division which is so vital to the company's continued expansion.

The Milawa vineyard and winery are situated 16 km east of Wangaratta on the so-called 'Snow Road', which carries thousands of skiers each winter from Melbourne to the snowfields of Mt Buller and Falls Creek. The soil is deep red loam overlaying river gravel which contains large reserves of water useful in dry seasons. Average rainfall is 650 mm, and the summers are warm enough to ensure good ripening. Frost can be a problem, and the winery was once destroyed in a cyclone; but a more welcome pest these days is the fungus botrytis cinerea or 'noble rot', which results in great sweetness and lusciousness and can be seen from year to year in Brown's famous Noble Riesling.

A frost which wiped out the Milawa Estate crop in 1967 convinced the Browns that they needed to find alternative sources of supply; and they bought and planted 74 hectares at Mystic Park, now a thriving vineyard on the shores of Kangaroo Lake between Kerang and Swan Hill. In addition to the 74 hectares at Milawa they now have 25 hectares on the original property at Hurdle Creek, 37 hectares at Whitlands and half-a-dozen more producers in the King Valley producing high-quality grapes exclusively for their use.

Brown Bros produce a large and very fine range of varietal white and red table wines; of special interest are their very popular Rhine riesling, chardonnay, shiraz and the famous SMC blend of shiraz, mondeuse and cabernet. In 1988 they added to the range the first new red wine for ten years, a lovely Bordeaux-style blend of cabernet franc and merlot from the King Valley.

Making wine at Buller's, Rutherglen.

Buller's Calliope Vineyard

Calliope was the Greek muse of epic poetry, mother of Orpheus, the lyre player. It was also the name of a property taken up as a soldier settlement in 1921 by Reginald Buller, late of the Royal Navy. With no previous experience in viticulture he bought 24 hectares of vines planted off the Murray Valley Highway in Rutherglen by the Callen family, who had worked the land more or less successfully until the outbreak of phylloxera. The sandy loam over clay subsoil was replanted to typical north-eastern varieties, shiraz, blue imperial, muscat, frontignac plus one or two white wine and sherry varieties.

Reginald's son Dick Buller went to a post-World War II course at Roseworthy Agricultural College and started work on the property in 1947. Under his care the vineyard was expanded to 32 hectares, and his sons, Richard, Graham and Andrew, were also involved in running Calliope. In 1952 they established their Beverford vineyard and winery near Swan Hill, and that is referred to elsewhere in this book. Andrew is the third-generation Buller making the wine at Calliope, and although he makes some distinctive reds, he shares his father's view that the low-yielding, non-irrigation vineyards in the Rutherglen area are best suited for fortifieds.

He has spent some time in Portugal making vintage ports, and his Calliope vintage port is one of the few to be seen in the north-east. It invariably has dense, purple-blue colour, a complex bouquet of fine spirit and ripe fruit, and a well-balanced palate—not over-sweet, and with a hint of spicy tannin. It is a consistent medal winner.

Campbell's Wines

Campbell's winery is only a kilometre or so out of Rutherglen on the Murray Valley Highway, an oasis-like settlement with a spread of green lawn and a modern facade, the main buildings set back from the road behind a clump of eucalypts. The shiny new tasting, sales and office area is itself a front to a much more traditional Rutherglen scene—gloomy rows of dusty oak in which golden fortifieds reach towards a state of grace.

Like other Rutherglen pioneers the Campbells were Scots, John Campbell leaving his home at St Andrews at the age of twenty-four to emigrate to Australia. He arrived in the good ship *Mer-*

chant Prince in 1857, and like many young people of his time went prospecting for gold. He worked for some time in the Beechworth area where he met and married Jessie Robb, and eventually they moved to Rutherlgen and settled on 32 hectares of land adjoining the Bobbie Burns goldmine. They followed the lead of other farmers in the area and planted vines, the first of them in 1870, and they had their own wine cellar by 1885.

John Campbell died in despair after seeing his vines destroyed by phylloxera, but his son David persisted, replanting the vineyard on rootstocks and finally seeing it flourish again. He died in 1933, and his son Allen took over and battled on through the depression. He and his wife Isabel bought more land in the 1940s, and their sons Malcolm and Colin eventually combined forces to make Campbells the thoroughly go-ahead concern it is today.

Colin Campbell worked for Lindemans at Corowa after graduating from Roseworthy College, but finally decided that he would continue the family line. These days he makes the wine and Malcolm runs the vineyards. They have a modern winery with the kind of refrigeration and other equipment needed to produce the necessary delicacy—for their white wines in particular; and 61 hectares of vines which also reflect the swing away from complete dependence on fortifieds in the north-east to quality red and white table wines. The vineyard is planted to one-third each of muscat and shiraz, with the other third a mixture of white varietals and a patch of old sherry grapes which still provide an excellent chablis-style white.

Colin Campbell is particularly proud of what is called 'classic regional Rhine riesling', which in 1980 won a trophy in Melbourne as best Victorian dry white; however, his most popular and distinctive wines are the inimitable Bobbie Burns shiraz and Old Rutherglen muscat. This is a lighter and more elegant style than many others in the region, and a true classic by any standards.

W.H. Chambers & Son, Rosewood

This is another small Rutherglen family vineyard and winery, 1 km out on the road to Corowa but now virtually part of the town itself—not quite subdivision country yet, but the houses of the expanding township are getting closer and closer. Rosewood includes what is probably the oldest surviving planting in the Rutherglen area, that of German-born recluse Anthony Ruche, whose 2.4 hectare vineyard was there before the gold rush. It was bought in 1870 by William Chambers, an emigrant from Norfolk who took up land near Corowa in 1850. He planted more vines, but the whole place was then destroyed by phylloxera, and he had to start again.

The Chambers family still run Rosewood, where the winemaker is great-grandson Bill Chambers. Over the road and closer to the river, near a lagoon known locally as Lake Moodemere, Bill's brother Peter has another Chambers' vineyard called 'Lakeside'. Over the years both vineyards have been replanted to provide more table wine varieties, but the emphasis is still on the kinds of fortified wines that have long made the north-east famous. Altogether they have some 48 hectares providing about 5 tonnes of grapes to the hectare—fruit which is processed in a little winery which hasn't changed too much since Ruche's day.

A basket press of enormous age stands by a stainless steel Potter fermenter, and other antique equipment comes into play from time to time. This by no means affects the quality of the wine produced. Bill Chambers topped his year at Roseworthy Agricultural College, and for a number of years has been chairman of judges in the wine section of the Melbourne show. He is also a popular judge in Sydney and Adelaide.

His red varieties are cabernet sauvignon, shiraz and a local favourite, blue imperial; and these make typically robust Rutherglen wines with plenty of rich berry character. His whites include a blend of riesling and gouais (better known as 'gouais blanc' in its native Jura region of north-east France). The grandeur of Rosewood is in its fortifieds, however; a vintage port of great character and Old Liqueur Muscat and Old

Liqueur Tokay are superb wines of great age that are the very essence of the Rutherglen style.

Fairfield Vineyard

Fairfield is an historic winery on the Murray Valley Highway near Rutherglen which, after a period of more than sixty years, was returned to the Morris family. Mrs Melba Slamen, a great-grand-daughter of G.F. Morris, bought the property in 1973 and since then it has been extensively restored and returned to a wine-making role.

The career of George Frederick Morris (known as G.F.) is described later in this chapter (see Morris Wines). Melba Slamen casts further light on the career of her illustrious forbear. She points out that his fare was paid to Australia by a customer of his father's shop in Manchester, a Mrs Hughes—this was a prudent gesture which removed him immediately from the affections of her daughter, Sarah. Nevertheless, Sarah later joined him in Victoria, and they married, established Fairfield, and had no fewer than seventeen children.

The rise of Fairfield coincided with the rising importance of Victoria as a wine-producing area. Eventually there were more than 240 hectares under vine—a very large vineyard by any standards—and the cellars held the equivalent of three vintages of 900 000 litres each. Constructed of hollow brick to insulate against extremes of temperature, they incorporated the most modern crushing and fermenting equipment in the world.

More than three-quarters of Australian wine was being exported at the time, most of it to London for distribution throughout the empire. In 1886 the Victorian Government appointed G.F. as a wine commissioner to the Colonial and Indian Exhibition in London, where his task was to promote his and other Victorian wines. For months after G.F.'s trips to London all hands at Fairfield worked until 10 pm filling, labelling and dispatching casks of wine to fill his English orders. The casks went by dray to Rutherglen, and then by train to the wharves in Melbourne.

Fairfield was the biggest winery in the Southern Hemisphere and one of the largest in the world. Its workforce was numerous, including one Billy Gill, the cellarmaster who could carry a 270 litre hogshead on his head, and 120 Chinese who worked in the cellars and among the vines. Grapes were bought also from neighbours, and Mrs Slamen was told that at the height of vintage, growers were queued up a kilometre along the road. There were so many grapes that the 180 000 litre fermenting vats were soon filled, and fruit was left piled on the floor awaiting crushing. Pressings were discarded for lack of storage space.

Eventually phylloxera ruined the great vineyards, and the so-called 'colonial' wine market all but disappeared. Fairfield was left to vandals and sheep, and virtually deserted until Mrs Slamen ignored architectural advice and acquired it after Reckitt & Colman had bought the family's Mia Mia winery.

Now the place has again assumed at least the spirit of its former grandeur. Much of the original winemaking equipment has survived, and Stephen Morris uses it to produce a dry red in the old style. During fermentation, for instance, the must is pumped more than a metre above the fermenting tanks then allowed to cascade over wide boards back into the tanks. Stephen says this doesn't cause oxidation because there is so much carbon dioxide there, created by the fermentation. Fairfield reds, bearing a copy of the original label, have been doing well in local shows.

Gayfer's Chiltern Vineyard

Chiltern was one of the leading gold-producing areas of the golden north-east, and between 1872 and 1900 some 12 tonnes of gold were won from the Chiltern Valley mine. The galvanised iron vault which is now the winery at Keith Gayfer's Chiltern winery was the engineroom which helped bring that wealth to the surface.

When the gold in the area started to run out around the turn of the century, many people drifted away from the district. In an effort to establish new industry and regain some prosperity for the area, a group of Chiltern towns-people formed a company under the leadership of local physician, Dr C.F. Harkin. It was decided winemaking was the right way to go, and 60 hectares of land on the Hume Highway, 5 km south of the town, was chosen for a vineyard.

Mr R.N. Gayfer was appointed to manage the business, and he planted the first cuttings there in 1913. He had grown grapes before but never made wine, and the first vintage, from the initial

26 hectares of vines, was made in the former engineroom. Construction went on as vintage proceeded, and by the time it was over the place still didn't have a roof. That wasn't added until the following year, and the building itself wasn't completed until 1922.

Over the years Dr Harkin bought out all of the original partners, finally selling out himself to the Gayfer family in 1948. Keith Gayfer is the present owner and winemaker, and he has 18 hectares of vines still at Chiltern, and a further 6 hectares at Katunga, near Cobram. He grows duriff (elsewhere in the north-east it carries only one 'f') and shiraz for his dry red; other varieties are alicante bouschet, pedro, mondeuse, trebbiano, grenache and muscat. Most of his duriff, however, goes into vintage port, a lovely deep scarlet wine fortified with Buller brandy. He also makes a range of tawny ports and sherries.

Gehrig Brothers, Barnawartha

Barnawartha is a small settlement between Rutherglen and Wodonga and one of its original inhabitants was Phillip George Gehrig, who settled there around 1858. The Gehrig vineyards there now, run by Barney Gehrig and his son Bernard, were planted originally by a joint stock company. The Barnawatha [sic] Vineyard Company, and eventually Phillip Gehrig bought them out. A contemporary noted: 'The present owner is working the vineyards profitably and producing some excellent wine.' He had more than 40 hectares of vines before phylloxera wiped them out, and his son, Frederick, replanted some 24 hectares.

The present generation of Gehrigs have about 20 hectares of vines on clay loam soils, and use irrigation from the Murray River. Varieties there include shiraz, trebbiano, cabernet sauvignon, Rhine riesling, chardonnay and pinot noir. The chardonnay cuttings were bought by Barney Gehrig from the Rutherglen Viticultural Research Station in 1966 with the idea of selling the wine to Seppelt for their champagne. This didn't happen (there is some suspicion that the chardonnay was either a poor clone or chenin blanc), but the overall emphasis at Gehrigs is on table wines rather than fortifieds.

This is a bit unusual in the north-east, but that doesn't concern Barney Gehrig. He's a great Rutherglen character, presiding over what has been described as a fairly ramshackle domain, which nevertheless houses the kind of high-technology equipment needed to provide refrigeration. and other winemaking necessities. The problems with chardonnay certainly haven't affected Barney and Bernard's enthusiasm for table wines, and one of their recent successes has been with pinot noir. They have extended their plantings of the variety, and are producing a nicely coloured, full-flavoured pinot that has triggered much interest and comment. The slightly cooler conditions at Barnawartha, brought about by air coming down the mountains at night, mean that in most years vintage is two weeks later than in Rutherglen. Although this tends to favour table wine production, the Gehrigs also make a very good vintage port.

John Gehrig Wines

John Gehrig is the fourth generation of his family to make wine in the north-east of Victoria; he is also one of the few people in the past decade to start from scratch with a new vineyard and a new winery. He worked with his father, Barney, at Barnawartha before moving to Oxley, where he and his wife Elizabeth began planting 8 hectares of vines near the banks of the King River in 1976.

He planted Rhine riesling, chenin blanc, chardonnay, pinot noir, merlot and cabernet sauvignon; and while his vines were growing he worked as a cellar hand at Brown Bros at Milawa, several kilometres away. He made his first wines in 1980 with the help of David Traeger, who in turn worked for Mitchelton before setting up a consultancy and his own winery at Seymour. By 1986 the range of John Gehrig wines was settling down: two reds, two whites, and an impressive *méthode champenoise* brut blanc de noir made from pinot noir.

The bulk of John's pinot noir, however, goes into a straight red varietal, the 1986 version of which was a fifty-fifty blend of warm and cool ferment, thereby retaining colour as well as producing plenty of good plums-and-cherries flavour. His other red is a fifty-fifty blend of merlot and cabernet sauvignon, some of the cabernet coming from Cliff Booth at Taminick. John Gehrig whites are a very elegant chardonnay and a Rhine riesling which has a little residual sugar but is well backed by good acid structure.

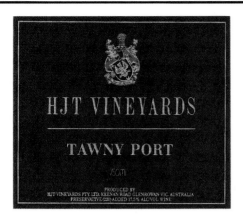

HJT Vineyards

Harry J. Tinson, as noted elsewhere in this book, was the man who took over as winemaker at Baileys of Glenrowan when the famous old vineyard and winery was bought from Alan Bailey by Davis Consolidated Industries in 1972. At the time, Harry—by training a research chemist and then a corporate planner—had no plans to change his discipline; however, when Alan decided to retire the company had no hesitation in appointing Harry Tinson in his place.

After fourteen years at Baileys—a period in which he played a major role in the lightening of table wine styles and the promotion of Baileys' marvellous muscats and tokays—Harry Tinson retired. That was in 1986. He said his greatest thrill at the time was the national wine show in Canberra in 1984, when a Baileys liqueur muscat was awarded the highest score recorded to that time by an Australian wine, 58.5 out of a possible 60 points.

When he retired, however, he decided that fortified wines were no longer for him. English-born Harry and his wife Catherine had in 1979 bought a property in Keenan Road, Rutherglen, with a 7 km frontage to Lake Mokoan, and planted cabernet sauvignon, chardonnay, pinot noir and Rhine riesling. Since his retirement they have been able to concentrate on the production of very fine table wines in limited quantities (about 13 000 litres a year), using modern, small-winery techniques.

They are avoiding such bruising equipment as must pumps, for instance, and are refrigerating the air in the winery rather than chilling the wine itself during stabilisation. They are not de-stemming their bunches because they feel the process leads to the introduction of bitter, stalky

characters. Early results have shown promise; the first commercial HJT Chardonnay (1984) won the trophy for the best district white wine at the Rutherglen Show in 1985, and HJT pinot noir is showing some very Burgundian characteristics.

Jolimont Wines

When the large and impressive Clydeside Cellars were built in the centre of Rutherglen in 1886 they were something of a mockery. They were filled with what was then modern winemaking equipment, but because of phylloxera there were simply no grapes to be had. Replanting of major vineyards on to American rootstocks had begun, however, and as an insurance against the plague spreading to South Australia Oscar Seppelt bought the place, with its neigbouring vineyards, in 1914.

In fact, it was not until 1929 that wine was made on the property; but for the next sixty years or so the cellars became the home of Seppelt Rutherglen muscats and other fortifieds. In the late 1960s a nearby vineyard of 20 hectares, known as the Tuileries, was purchased and part of it was planted with chardonnay. In combination with grapes from Barooga, Seppelt produced a varietal reserve bin chardonnay and a private bin white burgundy there. Faced with dwindling fortified sales, however, Seppelt sold the property in 1984, and since then it has been completely renovated and reopened as Jolimont Wines. The name Tuileries lives on in a fine restaurant in the building.

The winemaker is Howard Anderson, and he has 12 hectares of vines next to the winery; a patch of the port varieties corniseto, xeries and caracosa, Rutherglen brown muscat, and chardonnay and sauvignon blanc for his own varietal whites. Premium reds are bought in from

Harvesting the grapes, Jolimont Wines.

the Rutherglen district. The name Jolimont, incidentally, was that given by Governor Charles Latrobe to Melbourne's first vineyard, planted in 1839 on the site of what is now Government House.

Jones Winery

The Jones vineyard, about 2 km from Rutherglen on the road to Chiltern, has a long history. It was originally planted by the Rhue family who came from Germany and are thought to have settled on the property in the 1860s. An interesting remnant of that era is still to be found there in a barn of handmade bricks which is now used as a cellar and winery. The original bark roof remains beneath a new one, and provides a most effective means of insulation.

An unenviable distinction for the property is

that it was here phylloxera was discovered for the first time in the Rutherglen district in 1897. All the vines were destroyed. Les Jones bought the replanted 17 hectare vineyard in 1927, and his son, also Les Jones, now runs the business and makes the wine. The grapes are shiraz, Rutherglen pedro and white hermitage, and traditional winemaking practices are followed.

There is no stainless steel, for instance, and all the wines are hand-pressed then fermented in the original nineteenth-century oaken vats. The wines are also in traditional style; full-bodied dry red shiraz, shiraz vintage and ruby ports, and a range of sherries from flor to sweet.

Markwood Estate Vineyard

When Reckitt & Colman took over the Morris family's Mia Mia operation in 1970, Mick Morris decided to stay on as winemaker but Rick Morris decided to go off on his own. He headed for the

Morris Wines

The famous Mia Mia vineyard and winery off the Murray Valley Highway, 15 km north of Rutherglen, was established in 1887 by Charles Hughes Morris, son of the remarkable G.F. Morris whose exploits in the north-east of Victoria are examined elsewhere (see Fairfield Vineyard). At one stage Charles sold his grapes to Fairfield, and when phylloxera and the subsequent collapse of the colonial market had all but destroyed that unique enterprise, the Morris family's attentions were focused on Mia Mia.

Phylloxera struck there also, and the vineyard had to be replanted between 1918 and 1920. No sooner were the vines in bearing than the depression dealt another blow to the wine industry; but the tenacious Morris family wasn't easily dislodged. Charles had three sons, Charles, Gerald and Frederick, and all worked in the business. Charles, born in 1928, was better known as Mick, and after graduating from Scotch College he gained a BSc from Melbourne University and then a winemaker's diploma from Roseworthy Agricultural College.

In 1971 Reckitt & Colman took over Mia Mia, and Mick Morris was a vital part of the acquisition. He has remained in charge since

Ovens Valley country beyond Milawa, and now has 5 hectares under vine in well-named Morris Lane off the so-called 'Snow Road', which takes skiers from Glenrowan to Myrtleford. In conditions cooler and damper than in Rutherglen, he grows cabernet sauvignon, shiraz, chardonnay, gewurztraminer, semillon and trebbiano —with perhaps the inevitable patch of Rutherglen brown muscat thrown in for good luck.

Rick Morris's aim has been to produce European-style wines in style and balance, and with this in mind he has concentrated on small quantities of chardonnay as a premium white, and cabernet and shiraz as reds. He makes several fortifieds, including a white port, and has installed a pot still which provides high-quality brandy spirit from the well-recognised Cognac varieties, colombard and trebbiano. If you want to drop in and see him, Rick also has a 1000 m airstrip on the property.

Mick Morris, Rutherglen.

then, still dedicated to the magical fortified mus-cats of the region for which Morris is almost a synonym; but in recent years he has turned also to surprisingly elegant white wines and the pro-duction demands of the enormous Orlando–Morris cask wine market.

The Mia Mia vineyard is about 44 hectares, the soils consisting of red clay loam with yellow pebbly clay subsoil. Main varieties are muscat, tokay, white hermitage, cinsaut, shiraz, cabernet sauvignon and durif. In 1908 the remarkable C.H. Morris, observing that the dreaded phyl-loxera was less vehement in its attack on vines planted in sandy soil, acquired land and planted a vineyard at Balldale, across the Murray River in New South Wales. Another 40 hectares fur-ther west along the Murray Valley Highway from Mia Mia also supplies high-quality fruit.

Mick Morris produces some fine table wines, including semillon and chardonnay, and tremen-dous dry reds such as Durif and Blue Imperial. But the greatness of Mia Mia is muscat, and Morris Premium Liqueur Muscat is one of the great wines of the world.

Mount Prior Vineyard

Mount Prior, on the Howlong Road 14 km east of Rutherglen, is another historic vineyard—established in 1860, but another victim of phyl-loxera. It was replanted in 1974 by Dr Hugh Catchlove; 51 hectares of carignan, grenache,

cabernet sauvignon, cabernet franc, malbec, durif, shiraz, chardonnay, traminer and chenin blanc. The winemaker is Rick Kinzbrunner, and wines are sold at cellar door.

He has a good chardonnay which is fermented in oak, and a typically spicy gewurztraminer. He makes varietal reds from cabernet and shiraz, and distinctive, light-bodied wines from both malbec and cabernet franc. A light red Beaujolais-style wine is made from carignan.

Pfeiffer Wines

Chris Pfeiffer was a winemaker for Lindemans at Corowa, and when operations there slowed down in 1984 he and his wife Robyn took over the old Seppelt distillery in Wahgunyah and turned it into a winery. The historic building is made of hand-made bricks, and it provides a pic-turesque setting for cellar door sales and tastings on the banks of Sunday Creek.

They have 22 hectares of vines; chardonnay, tokay, muscat, cabernet sauvignon, pinot noir and a patch of Portuguese port varieties. Of par-ticular note is Chris's pinor noir—a good, ruby-coloured wine with excellent depth of flavour. His most unusual wines are a Beaujolais-style red made from gamay, a fruity, easy-drinking wine with a nice dry finish; and an auslese tokay—rich, luscious, and with honey-like characters which go perfectly with desserts and cheese. Developments at Pfeiffers will be watched with interest.

St Leonards

St Leonards has had more than its share of ups and downs in the past 160 years or so, and after a few decades in the wilderness has emerged as a north-east producer with a handsome style of its own. It is a subsidiary of Brown Bros of Milawa, who still make most of the wine, but it has quite an autonomous existence and manager–wine-maker Roland Kaval is convinced this indepen-dence of operation will continue to pay off.

Vines were first planted at St Leonards—situ-ated in a picturesque bend of the Murray River near Wahgunyah—in 1866 by James Scott, who named it after his birthplace in Scotland. He sold it to a New Zealander, Henry Ireland, who increased plantings there, but between 1900 and 1905 saw phylloxera take its toll. He eventually replanted the vineyard and extended it to some

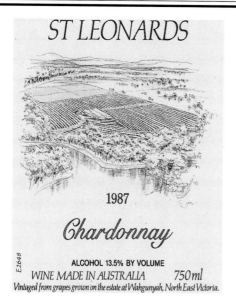

ST LEONARDS

1987

Chardonnay

ALCOHOL 13.5% BY VOLUME
WINE MADE IN AUSTRALIA   750 ml
Vintaged from grapes grown on the estate at Wahgunyah, North East Victoria.

E.2648

95 hectares. At that time, the annual crush was 400 tonnes of grapes, mainly for dry red, most of which was exported to the UK.

In 1919 Ireland sold the property to a local syndicate, and Seppelt, Chambers, Masterton and Dobbin (operators of the distillery later taken over by Seppelt and now owned by Chris Pfeiffer), together with George Gehrig and Frank Herman, were the major shareholders. Most of the wine was sold to Melbourne merchants, W.J. Seabrook and John Connell & Co in particular, and this market continued well into the 1930s.

The depression then brought hard times, and when World War II broke out, there were only three men there to handle St Leonard's 93 hectares. Business hobbled along until 1959 when it was sold to a farmer who pulled most of the vines out. Remaining grapes were usually sold to the influx of Italian tobacco growers in the Myrtleford area who made their own wine at home. In 1973 the artist John Darbyshire bought the property and set about replanting, this time to premium table wine varieties chosen for their suitability to the region and its soils.

In 1978 Brown Bros was approached to make the wine from the new vines, and two years later Brown family members formed a syndicate to buy the property. Today there are 40 hectares of chenin blanc, semillon, gewurztraminer, chardonnay, sauvignon blanc, cabernet sauvignon, shiraz, merlot and orange muscat. There is also some fetyaska, a Rumanian variety. The vines are planted in deep rich alluvial soils, ranging from sandy loams through to red clay loams. The

vineyard is set up for mechanical harvesting, which can be done at night to reduce the threat of oxidation in the hot, north-eastern summers.

All of the wine is made at Browns, 60 km away at Milawa, but all of the grapes are kept separate and the Browns and St Leonards styles have distinctive differences. Roland Kaval plays a major consulting winemaker's role, sustaining those regional strengths and differences; and in the past few years St Leonards has gained an impressive market niche. Although their chardonnay is popular it is not as good a white as either the St Leonards semillon or chenin blanc, both of which benefit from having better acid structure in such a warm climate. Ahead of both of these is St Leonards shiraz, however, a splendidly rich north-eastern wine given surprising elegance by clever use of oak.

Stanton & Killeen

Jack Stanton is a legendary figure in the north-east. He was born in 1895, when there were still goldminers around Rutherglen, and before phylloxera had completed its destructive work. Although he has now retired, he has been associated with the winery which bears his name all of this century, an historical fact which goes some way to explaining the regard in which he is held locally. But the Stantons are a long-lived lot. Jack's father, John Richard Stanton, died in 1956, and his grandfather John Lewis Stanton in 1926. His great-grandfather, Timothy, died in 1895, and all of them lived well into their eighties.

Timothy Stanton had come to Australia from his native East Anglia in 1855 in search of gold. He turned instead to farming, and he and his family took up a selection of land at Black Dog Creek near Rutherglen in 1865, which was about the time that viticultural pioneer Anthony Ruche was planting at 'Rosewood'. Timothy and his son John began planting vines around 1875 on a property known as Park View, about 2 km south-west of Rutherglen, but these were destroyed by phylloxera and had to be replanted around the turn of the century.

In 1925, fourth-generation winemaker John Charles Stanton—known to all and sundry as Jack—established the Gracerray vineyard as an offshoot to his father's business on land owned by the Hughes family and known locally as

Quandong. Hughes's vineyard had been wiped out by phylloxera, and of their original winery, built in about 1890, only concrete fermenting and storage vats remained. Jack Stanton built a new winery around them, and they remained in use until new fermenters were installed several years ago.

In 1948, Jack's daughter Joan Stanton married Norman Killeen, who for the previous thirteen years had been a field officer (specialising in fat lambs) with the Victorian Department of Agriculture's research station in Rutherglen. The partnership of Stanton & Killeen was founded in 1953, and Norm left the department to help run the Stanton's 360 hectare farm. In the 1960s the economic balance swung from agriculture to viticulture, and Norm Killeen put his Bachelor of Agricultural Science degree to good use and took over the role of winemaker from his father-in-law.

Norman and Joan's son, Christopher Killeen, joined the team in 1972, and in subsequent years studied oenology at the Riverina College of Advanced Education in Wagga Wagga. Until two or three years ago, Jack Stanton continued to come to work every day, assisting in the office and providing advice based on a lifetime of experience. Chris Killeen took over as winemaker in 1981, although father Norman still has an active advisory role.

There are now two distinct vineyard areas. Gracerray, about 20 hectares surrounding the winery, is planted to muscat, tokay and touriga, and produces traditional fortified wine styles. Moodemere, several kilometres west and named after the lake nearby, was begun in 1968 and contains shiraz and cabernet sauvignon as well as some fortified varieties.

A new vineyard was started in 1978, planted to durif, tokay and muscat. Durif is ideally suited to Rutherglen and is used for making big, full-bodied reds.

It was not until 1970 that Stanton & Killeen began bottling wine under their own name, but it is now one highly respected in the north-east and beyond. Norman Killeen regards their vineyard soils as unsuitable for the classic white varieties, but they do make a delightful spicy, slightly sweet white from early-picked muscats. Otherwise they concentrate mainly on reds and fortifieds.

The Moodemere cabernet and shiraz blends are very good wines indeed. The grapes tend to be picked earlier than elsewhere in the region, and with clever treatment in small German and French oak casks they retain good varietal character, with some local peppermint overtones.

The fortified wines also tend to be lighter in style than many of their local competitors, the muscats fresh and clean with good spirit, and the vintage port richly structured for long life but not over-sweet. It is clear that the old company is in very good hands.

Taminick Valley Wines

This small vineyard, 5 km north-west of Glenrowan on the Taminick–Glenrowan Road, was planted in the early 1960s by Vicenzo Bordignon, who called the place Taminick Springs. In 1969 the property was bought by Allan Watson, who succeeded his father as proprietor of the famous Jimmy Watson's Wine Bar in Melbourne. Both father and son bought substantial amounts of wine from the north-east which they bottled and sold in the wine bar, and Taminick Springs was seen as both a hobby and a future source of supply.

At the time there was an old winery and about 4 hectares of vines on the property, most of which had been given over to sheep. Allan Watson and a small army of friends cleaned up the vineyard, tended the vines, and harvested a crop in 1970. They coaxed the old winemaking equipment back to life and John Brown senior came over from Milawa to offer advice and help make the wine—a straight shiraz which astonished everyone, the owner included, by taking out a silver medal in the Melbourne Wine Show in 1971.

Watson continued to make the wine, and a shiraz–cinsaut blend, until 1979 when because of pressure of business he decided to sell the place. The new proprietors are Gerald and Angela Baker, who live in Melbourne and operate the winery at weekends. They renamed it Taminick Valley Wines, and at the moment have 4 hectares of shiraz and cabernet sauvignon. They make a cabernet, a shiraz, and a blend of the two, and have one or two retail outlets in Melbourne.

Great Western

The history of European occupation of Australia is more notable for floods, fires, droughts and strikes than romance. The story of the beginnings of winemaking at Great Western in Victoria is thus one of the more picturesque episodes.

It began in France in 1825, in the province of Lorraine where Anne Marie Blampied was born into a farming family. She must have been an adventurous girl, for at the age of twenty-eight she and her fifteen-year-old brother, Emile, left for Australia to seek their fortune in the goldfields. They arrived at Beechworth in 1853, and went into business transporting supplies for miners with another Frenchman, Jean Pierre Trouette. Anne Marie and Jean Pierre were married, and with young Emile in tow they moved to Great Western, then a booming gold settlement, in 1858.

The gold in the area was soon worked out; but the land around Great Western so reminded Jean Pierre of his home in the department of Gers, that he bought some land in partnership with

Emile, and called the property St Peters. In 1863 they began planting vine cuttings they got from Geelong, and within four years they had 50 000 vines and 2000 fruit trees. In 1867 they made 2275 litres of wine, which won prizes at home and abroad.

Jean Pierre died in 1885 at the age of fifty-two. The following year his only son, Nicholas, died tragically trying to rescue a workman from an underground wine tank. Bad fortune continued to plague Ann Marie, and after a series of poor seasons St Peters was sold in 1897 to an English family named Merton. The property lapsed into obscurity after the death of Anne Marie in 1905, and her daughter Marie, in 1927.

Despite the demise of St Peters there is no doubt that it served as an inspiration to the wine industry in western Victoria. It led to Joseph and Henry Best planting vineyards which survive to this day, and to Hans Irvine establishing Great Western as one of the great champagne-producing areas of Australia.

The names champagne and Great Western are now almost automatically associated, but the township itself is a modest place on the Western

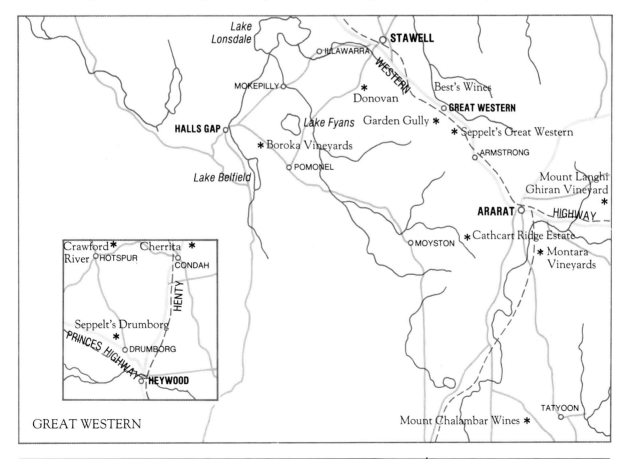

GREAT WESTERN

Highway, 218 km west of Melbourne, and midway between Stawell and Ararat. The country is hilly, with the Grampian Mountains 40 km to the west, and generally poor—with severe frosts, insufficient rainfall for good viticulture and low yields. Nevertheless, over the years Great Western has produced some of the finest wines in Australia.

Height above sea level varies roughly between 280 and 360 m, and this and the latitude, 37° south, gives the cool conditions desirable for the slow ripening of fruit and retention of acid. The average mean temperature in the hottest month is 20°C, and this, along with the pattern of ripening and harvesting, is similar to classic areas in Europe.

Rainfall is about 500–600 mm a year, mainly in winter, so drip irrigation is widely used. Frost is a major hazard, which every three or four years destroys young shoots and causes significant economic loss. Soils are volcanic but quite poor for viticulture, varying from red-brown gravelly loam to grey granitic sand. Some flats along Concongella Creek have deeper and richer soil.

Vine disease is rare but low yields are one of the major problems in Great Western, often only 2.5 tonnes to the hectare, with 10 tonnes at very best. Unlike frost, however, this can be overcome to a certain extent by better viticulture—close selection of vines, for instance, and planting of better clones of more suitable varieties. All of this means that the best Great Western wines are, justifiably, not cheap.

Best's Wines

We have already mentioned the historical role played in the development of the Great Western region by the brothers, Joseph and Henry Best. It was Joseph who in 1865 laid the foundations of what became the Seppelt empire in the area (see Seppelt's Great Western); Henry, in the following year, set about establishing his own vineyard on the banks of Concongella Creek, a property which has carried into history the lovely Concongella name.

The brothers, natives of Surrey, came as children to Van Diemen's Land in 1834, sailing shortly thereafter with their parents for Melbourne, where the boys went to school at St James's. In the 1850s they followed the miners to Ararat and, after scratching around unsuccess-

Vaslin press at Best's Concongella winery.

fully for gold, set up a meat wholesaling business which brought them the prosperity the goldfields had denied them.

Inspired by the winemaking success of St Peters, they decided winemaking was the ideal way of compounding their fortunes, and while Joseph was doing his thing at Great Western, Henry was clearing his 30 hectare property on the banks of Concongella Creek. In either a fit of enthusiasm or a desire to see which grapes would grow best on his new domain, Henry planted almost every variety he could lay his hands on. To this day the so-called 'fruit salad block' is planted with cuttings from James Busby's collection in Sydney; this historic block delighted French ampelographer Paul Truel on his visit to Australia several years ago.

Prominent among his grapes were frontignac, burgundy, esparte, hermitage, black prince, muscatel, malbec, sweetwater and chasselas. Henry Best aimed at making light-bodied, elegant table wines rather than the fortifieds so popular at the time, and he succeeded pretty well. Most of his wine was sold in the UK and Europe, and in some vintages his entire production was shipped overseas.

Henry Best died in 1913 at the age of eighty-one, and was buried beside his brother Joseph in the Great Western cemetery. His son, Charles, carried on making wine at Concongella until 1920, when he sold the winery and the Best name to Frederick Pinchon Thomson.

Thomson's father, Scotsman William Thomson, had been a mail carrier in the Ballarat district and then a very successful baker in Melbourne. He finally took up a property at Rhymney, in the hills near Ararat, where he established a large orchard and vineyard he called 'St Andrews'.

He didn't know anything about winemaking, but in those days, few people did. Between 1892 and 1920 the Thomson family became significant producers of wine, both at St Andrews and at a neighbouring vineyard called Fairview, which they bought in 1911. Some of their best whites were sold to Hans Irvine at Great Western for champagne. Concongella was their third vineyard, and Frederick Thomson hoped to be able to work it successfully with his two young sons, Frederick (who became known as Eric), and William.

Parlous economic times were at hand, however, and in 1925 F.P. Thomson was forced to sell St Andrews and Fairview, and Concongella went into the hands of receivers. In 1930, Frederick looked northward for further opportunity, and by chance encountered a patch of vines on Lake Boga which he bought and renamed St Andrews. He also managed to buy back Concongella from the receivers, and from then until now the Thomson name has survived on the strength of both of them.

In 1949, Frederick Thomson died while on a cruise to Hong Kong (coincidentally, both his mother and father had died on a voyage back to Scotland in 1924), and his properties were inherited by his sons, E.F.H. and W.H. Thomson. E.F.H.'s son was E.V.H. (Viv) Thomson, a Roseworthy College graduate, and today he continues to run the business and make the wine with help from Simon Clayfield.

Best's Wines now have some 30 hectares of vines at Concongella, including hermitage (shiraz), pinot meunier, esparte, dolcetto, Rhine riesling, ondenc, chardonnay, chasselas, gewurztraminer and cabernet sauvignon. The first Concongella cabernet (1987 vintage) was released in 1989, and was instantly hailed as an excellent red in the Great Western style, with firm fruit and tannin character and great depth of flavour. Concongella Claret No. 0, a blend of hermitage and esparte, has been a favourite Best's wine for many years; so has its pinot meunier—one of the lightest and fruitiest 'lunch-eon' wines made in Victoria. With the help of consultant Trevor Mast, Viv Thomson was able to make much of his white varieties, and his Great Western chardonnay, matured in new French oak, has been outstanding.

Concongella is still a marvellous place to visit. The lovely old wooden-slab winery overlooking a 120-year-old vineyard is a significant piece of Victorian history, and the Thomsons always have a warm welcome in store.

Boroka Vineyards

Boroka was established in 1969 by Stawell man David McCracken, on cool yet frost-free land 5 km from Halls Gap. It was planted with shiraz and cabernet sauvignon, and a smaller patch of Rhine riesling, malbec, trebbiano, chasselas, aleatico and grey riesling. A small winery was built; early problems included an invasion of wild deer from a nearby national park who proved very fond of young vine shoots.

Bernie Breen, an industrial chemist, and his wife Cordelia bought the place in 1981, and since then have increased plantings to about 9 hectares with the addition of sauvignon blanc and chardonnay. Rainfall appears adequate at around 750 mm a year, but yields are low. This is compensated for in the quality of Boroka wines, with a particularly good shiraz, and the potential for the property appears quite high. Eventually Bernie Breen hopes to have 12 hectares in production, concentrating on shiraz and cabernet as reds, and chardonnay, Rhine riesling and sauvignon blanc as whites. We hope the deer keep away.

The 1976 vintage of the Boroka Shiraz won medals at Lilydale, Canberra and Melbourne shows, and although the current owners have not repeated that success the potential is undoubtedly there.

Cathcart Ridge Estate

Dr Graeme Bertuch is a general practitioner in Ararat, who established what is now a very pretty vineyard and small, functional winery in the rolling hills of Cathcart in 1977. It was meant to be a hobby, but as the strains of practice increased, he was tempted several times to sell out. In 1988 he was faced with crushing something like 80 tonnes of fruit from his own vineyard and from Westage Vineyard nearby,

but found that too much to handle. He has now decided to keep the crush at about 25 tonnes from his own plantings of Rhine riesling, chardonnay, shiraz, cabernet sauvignon, merlot and cabernet franc. In 1989, in fact, owing to hot weather his crop was only 16 tonnes, but it helped confirm his view that he could hang on as both a medico and a winemaker at that level.

He had some help in early vintages from Trevor Mast, the guru of Great Western, and made some excellent wines—both red and white. In fact he made a red and a white blend; one batch of shiraz showed excessively heavy, ripe fruit so he added chenin blanc for its acid and the result was a very good wine indeed. In 1985 he won the Victorian Wine Press Club trophy for the best young Victorian red in the Melbourne Wine Show with an excellent 1984 Cathcart Ridge Shiraz.

Cherrita Wines

Branxholme is a little town in south-western Victoria 25 km south of Hamilton, where what must be Australia's only eel-skinning championship is an annual attraction. It is good grazing country for cattle and sheep, and the Sobey family is one of a number in the district who have planted vines as an adjunct to other farming pursuits.

In this case, John Sobey planted 4 hectares of shiraz and Rhine riesling on part of his 400 hectare farm in 1969, and since then has been making small quantities of wine, usually sold at cellar door. There are usually three wines, Cherrita hermitage and Rhine riesling, and a shiraz port.

Winemaking takes a back seat when extra effort is needed with the livestock; no wine at all was made in 1989, for instance, because there was no time to spare.

Crawford River Wines

The Crawford River runs between Dartmoor and the Condah swamp in the south-western corner of Victoria, giving its name to the Thompson family property 8 km north-west of Condah on the Hotspur Road. In 1975 John Thompson began planting grapes there, and now he has some 7 hectares of vines producing around 35 tonnes of fruit each year.

He grows Rhine riesling, sauvignon blanc, semillon, cabernet sauvignon and merlot; according to John in the past two or three years the vineyard has become a worthwhile commercial addition to his sheep and cattle interests. He did the winemaking course at Riverina College in Wagga Wagga, and although he says he could do with laboratory help at vintage time he has made some very good and rather adventurous wines.

His delight with sauternes, for instance, has led him to experiment a lot with botrytised white grapes and in 1988 he made an extremely elegant sauvignon blanc semillon blend. He also gets botrytis in riesling, and on several occasions has made beerenauslese. He has also been experimenting with riesling in new French oak, and thinks the results are very pleasing. He sees riesling as his main variety, coming up every year with intense citrus characters, grapefruit and lime, and with around 8.5 g per litre of natural acidity they are wines that age well.

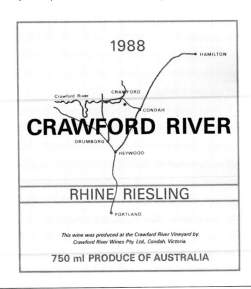

Semillon is proving more difficult as it is hard to get it ripe in those southerly climes; but the sauvignon blanc has been ripening well, up to 12.5° baumé in most years, and the two varieties go well when blended together. John is also justifiably proud of his cabernet sauvignon, which he crushes with a small amount of merlot. It shows lovely cool-climate herbaceous and berry character. After a visit to Europe in 1986 he has been very conscious of the need for canopy control in the vineyard so that the green characters of the cabernet and semillon are not overdone. One third of his cabernet each year goes into new French oak and two thirds into one-year-old oak. The final blend is allowed to settle in bottle before sale through mail order and one or two retail outlets and restaurants in Melbourne. John does all the vineyard and winemaking work himself, although the wine is contract-bottled by Trevor Mast at Mount Langhi Ghiran Vineyard.

Donovan

This small, family-owned vineyard and winery, situated 4 km south of Stawell on the Pomonal Road, was known previously as Donoview. It was established in 1977 by Peter Donovan, a great-grandson of Peter Pola, a Swiss immigrant who was one of the pioneer vignerons of the Great Western–Grampians district. He arrived in the area in 1864, and planted vines on his property at Rhymney, near Ararat. Eventually he had four vineyards, St Mark's, St Dominic's, St Paul's and St Andrew's.

Most of the vines disappeared during the depression when grazing and other forms of farming became more economic, but the remains of the old winery and cellars can still be seen on the Donovan property. Peter and his family have re-established some of the old plantings in the rocky slopes of the Black Ranges, in an area running from Stawell in the north to Moyston in the south. Varieties include Rhine riesling, shiraz, traminer, crouchen, chardonnay and a small patch of frontignac. In addition, the Donovans lease the new Calawadda vineyard north of Stawell, where first pickings of pinot noir, semillon and Rhine riesling in 1989 showed great promise.

Donoview shiraz has proved to be an excellent wine over the years, and the first blended red

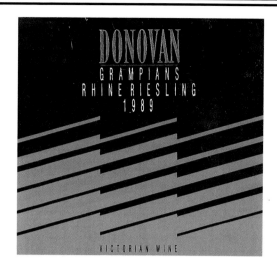

under new Donovan labels was due for release in 1990. Donovan whites are Rhine riesling, which shows good regional character in a firm acid and fruit base, and classic dry white, a blend of its other white varieties. A new winery and cellar door sales area, designed to take the Donovan name into the 1990s and beyond, is on the drawing boards.

Garden Gully

Garden Gully is one of the newest wineries in the Great Western region of Victoria; it is, at the same time, part of one of the oldest. In 1984 Seppelts began a rationalisation of their operations at Great Western; this included the decision to expand its champagne-making capacity and to do away with some of its locally-made table wines. In the days of the great Colin Preece this was the home of such well-known wines as Chalambar burgundy, Rhymney chablis and so on; but as the nation's appetite for Great Western champagne increased, these famous names were allowed to fall by the wayside.

The rationalisation of the 1980s meant a greater commitment to the sparkling white varieties, chardonnay and pinot noir in particular, and Seppelts found themselves with some fine bearing vineyards of such varieties as shiraz and Rhine riesling which they simply didn't need any more. A group of staff members saw the opportunity to broaden their horizons somewhat, and set up a company they called Garden Gully Great Western Vineyards Pty Ltd to buy the vineyards and to make wine of their own. Part of the property was the site of the original Salinger's Hockheim winery, built in the 1870s from local stone, mud and straw. Salingers operated it there until 1945 when it was sold to Seppelts. The old winery crumbled, but original underground tanks remained and were put into operation when the Garden Gully winery and cellar rose on the site in 1986.

Since then Garden Gully, with a few changes in its board of shareholders, has begun to flourish, and now produces a very fine range of wines in the inimitable Great Western style. There are 7 hectares under vine, including most of the famous old Chalambar vineyard of thirty- to forty-year-old shiraz, and another 2 hectares was due to be planted in 1990. Another block is leased from Seppelts and that contains some very good traminer vines; other varieties are chardonnay, pinot noir and Rhine riesling.

One of the original shareholders was Warren Randall, chief sparkling winemaker at Seppelts until he left in 1989 to run Andrew Garrett Wines in McLaren Vale. He continues to make Garden Gully Chardonnay–Pinot Noir, a 'true brut' style of *méthode champenoise* sparkling wine first laid down in 1984. Another was Brian Fletcher, who was chief white winemaker at Seppelts before going to St Hubert's in 1987. These days he is Garden Gully's main winemaker as well. Vintage is usually much earlier in Great Western than in the Yarra Valley, so the grapes are chilled and trucked all the way from Garden Gully to St Hubert's where they are crushed and fermented. Once settled down they return to Great Western for maturation and eventual bottling.

As well as the sparkling wine, there are four Garden Gully table wines, each of which has been a success in either regional or state wine shows. Wines bearing the Great Western appellation are made from either their own fruit or from that bought elsewhere in Great Western, and there are four of these: Classic Dry, a straight gewurztraminer; Rhine Riesling, from fruit on the Chalambar block; and Shiraz, also from Chalambar. Garden Gully Chardonnay is a blended wine with 20 per cent Great Western material, the local component being barrel-fermented in new Seguin Moreau barriques and then given full malolactic fermentation. The 1987 wine was aged for eighteen months in bottle before being released; it was a wonderfully complex wine which obviously needed more age before showing its best.

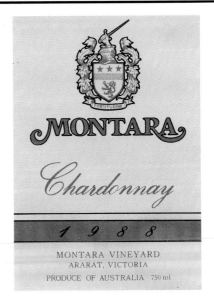

Montara Vineyards

Montara is one of the larger of the new wave of Great Western vineyards, 13 hectares of vines planted in 1970 by the McRae family on a beautiful eastern slope of Mt Chalambar, 3 km south of Ararat. John McRae was a retired engineer, and he put many of his professional skills to work designing and building a handsome house and colonial-style winery on the property, and a good deal of ingenious winemaking equipment as well. Among his 'inventions' is a mobile crusher built in 1980, which follows the pickers and means a speedy journey between vineyard and fermenter. The winemaker is John's son, Michael McRae.

The grape varieties chosen were considered most suitable for the red loam soil, and initial plantings included cabernet sauvignon, shiraz and pinot noir; with chasselas and ondenc (Irvine's white) for the whites. Rhine riesling and chardonnay have been planted more recently. What is unusual about Montara is that the vineyard is frost free. It is sited high up on a hillside (altitude 340 m above sea level) overlooking the broad valley which stretches northeastward towards Mt Langhi Ghiran. The height and slope is such that frost, which acts rather like water, simply rolls down the hill.

This is cold comfort for Trevor Mast, whose Mt Chalambar vineyard lies at the foot of the hill, and which more than once has been totally devastated by spring frost. The McRaes make quite a range of varietal table wines which Thelma McRae sells at cellar door. In recent years they have also made a good vintage port.

Mount Chalambar Wines

Trevor Mast is one of the most remarkable young winemakers in Australia. He studied oenology at Geisenheim, in Germany, for four years, gaining his degree in 1974. During this time he worked at various European wineries and then went to South Africa where he worked with the Stellenbosch Farmers' Winery in their microbiology and quality-control laboratories. He returned to Australia in 1975 and worked for a short period at Seppelts at Great Western before becoming consultant winemaker at Best's.

While still working with Viv Thomson he was looking around the Great Western area and elsewhere for a property of his own; in 1978 he bought 4 hectares of land on the eastern slope of Mt Chalambar 3 km from Ararat. There, in what he describes as friable ironstone clay overlaying soft, mineral-rich schist, he planted chardonnay and Rhine riesling. He made his first Mount Chalambar wines in 1983 at Best's, the Rhine riesling as a straight varietal and the chardonnay as base wine for what has become Trevor Mast's dream—production of a *méthode champenoise* sparkling wine of the very highest quality.

In 1987 he released the first of these wines, 1984 Mount Chalambar Brut Sauvage, which was very quickly hailed as one of the best wines of its type ever made in Australia. By then he was seeking to both consolidate the style of the wine and increase its production. With the help of the Victorian Department of Agriculture, the geology department at Melbourne University and the geological survey division of the Department of Minerals and Energy, he began to comb central and western Victoria for the combination of soil and weather he believed would best suit his purposes.

After testing no fewer than twenty-three properties, he settled on two—both of which were leased in 1985 and planted with pinot noir. The first was 700 m up Mt Edgarton, overlooking Lal Lal reservoir, and the second at Mt Hollowback, near Clunes. They also selected a vineyard at Norval, an old goldmining area between Ararat and Moyston, run by a grower who in the past had supplied fruit to both Seppelts and Best's. Trevor Mast said the Norval fruit was some of the best pinot he had ever seen.

The fourth site involved was Trevor's own Mt Chalambar vineyard, and this now provides the chardonnay component of Brut Sauvage. The first wine, 1984 vintage, spent two-and-a-half years on lees; it contained some 1983 material, and about 10 per cent of the chardonnay was fermented in oak. Later releases have shown greater complexity as the percentage of pinot noir in the blend increases, and so good has been the wine from the Norval block that in future it might be kept aside as a separate cuvée.

Mount Langhi Ghiran Vineyard

'Langhi Ghiran' is an Aboriginal name for the yellow-tailed black cockatoo, and the name also of a great bluff which marks the end of the Pyrenees Ranges and the beginning of the flat western plain which stretches from Stawell to Horsham and beyond. In 1970, the three Fratin brothers, whose parents had come from Italy, bought 23 hectares of land in a valley on the eastern slopes of Mt Langhi Ghiran, on the Warrak to Buangor Road. They planted 16 hectares of shiraz, cabernet sauvignon, Rhine riesling and chardonnay, and made a comfortable living selling their grapes to local winemakers.

Trevor Mast, then at Best's and in the process of establishing his own vineyard at Mt Chalambar, convinced the Fratins that the fruit was so good they should be producing wine of their own. This they did in 1979 (with Trevor acting as consultant), and their red wines in particular were soon noted for their intense fruit and local character. The 1983 Langhi Ghiran cabernet sauvignon and shiraz both won Victorian export awards (in a competition judged in London in 1985), and so convinced was

Trevor Mast of the future of the company that he bought a major shareholding in it. Mount Langhi Ghiran shiraz, with its distinctive peppery style, remains outstanding.

Seppelt's Great Western

B. Seppelt & Sons have been the dominating force at Great Western for most of this century. They have been there since 1918, although the history of their vineyards and their remarkable winery, where an impressive percentage of Australia's 'champagne' is made, goes back much further than that.

It was Joseph Best, born in Richmond, Surrey, in 1830, who planted the first of what were to become Seppelt's Great Western vineyards. He arrived in Australia as a child with his brother, Henry, their builder-father, David, his brother, George, and their wives. That was in 1834. In the 1850s they followed many other immigrants to the western Victorian goldfields where they made their fortunes by supplying miners with meat rather than competing with them in the mines. As the gold rush subsided so did trade in their slaughterhouse; inspired by the French pioneer vignerons, Blampied and Trouette, Joseph and Henry Best planted vineyards of their own.

Henry founded what is still known as Best's Great Western, on the banks of the Concongella Creek. Joseph bought a property south of the township of Great Western, and in 1865 began clearing and fencing the gently rising land. He began planting the following year with cuttings obtained from the Trouettes and others, including the de Castellas at Yering, in the Yarra Valley. He had his first vintage in 1868, all 170 litres of it, but by 1877 his plantings had increased and vintage was 32 000 litres.

In 1870 he began excavating cellars, and discovered in the subsoil a soft granite stratum which proved ideal for tunnelling. There were plenty of under-employed and unemployed goldminers still in the district, so Joseph Best employed them to excavate a system of tunnels, or drives, 2 m high and a metre or so wide, in which he could store his maturing wine. Best prospered, and his wines took prizes all over the world.

Joseph Best never married, and lived with his father and sister, Elizabeth, in a plain four-roomed cottage. He died at the height of his success on 8 January 1887 at the age of fifty-seven, and was buried in Great Western cemetery. He had died intestate, so the Great Western property was sold up and the proceeds divided among family members.

Great Western Vineyards.

PRESERVATIVE (220) ADDED. ANTIOXIDANT (301) ADDED

SBL119   750ML   WINE MADE IN AUSTRALIA   12.0% ALC/VOL

B. SEPPELT & SONS LTD GREAT WESTERN VICTORIA 3377

SEPPELT
GREAT WESTERN

HANS IRVINE 1979
Champagne

A traditional Australian Champagne named in honour of Hans Irvine who pioneered the style in 1891. The wine was made from the grape variety Irvines White (Ondenc) grown at Seppelt Great Western Vineyards.

The purchaser was Hans Irvine, a Ballarat businessman, who paid the considerable sum of £12 000 for 22 hectares of vines, 180 hectares of grazing land and the stock of wine in the unique cellars. Hans Irvine was a remarkable and sophisticated man. He wanted to make champagne, not just sparkling wine but champagne to equal the best from France, and he spared no effort in attaining this end. He made several trips to France (no mean effort in those slow-travelling days), and brought back a skilled team of champagne-makers headed by Charles Pierlot, an expert of considerable repute from the great Champagne house, Pommery.

In 1890, the same year Pierlot came to Australia, Irvine began planting at Arawatta, 3 km south of the cellars, where he had purchased 58 hectares. 'Arawatta' was local Aboriginal dialect for 'water hole', and it was there Irvine planted what he called white pinot—the variety later known as 'Irvine's white' and which, in fact, was probably ondenc. The classic grape of Champagne is pinot noir. So, even though it was subject to disease at Great Western, what was thought to be the white version was tried and persisted with for many years.

In an effort to take his wine directly to the British rather than through the hands of merchants, in July 1905 Irvine opened a depot at Dowgate Hill, near Cannon Street, in London. This considerable investment of energy and money was rewarded with the success Great Western wines achieved at exhibitions throughout Europe. This did not go unnoticed in Victoria, where Irvine was making a political name for himself as well. He was elected to the Legislative Assembly in the 1890s, and in 1903 became Member of the House of Representatives for the seat of Grampians in the new Federal Parliament. He was also president at the time of the Viticultural Society.

While all this was going on, Irvine was not neglecting his winemaking. By 1907 some 1.5 km of drives had been dug under the winery, and he was buying grapes from other growers, mainly for distillation and brandy. He acquired the St George's winery and vineyard from a Mr Skyrmes, and stole a march on all of his competitors by actually going to the trouble to advertise his Great Western wines. But all this effort was becoming tiring. In 1918, at the age of sixty-two, he decided to retire, and Seppelts became Great Western's third owners. Henry Irvine, who had done so much for the wine industry nationally as well as locally, died four years later while on a visit to London.

A new era began at Great Western with the resource and experience of the new owners. Reginald Mowatt, a Roseworthy College graduate, was appointed manager, and he held the post until resigning in 1932. The depression was then at its height, and it was hardly an auspicious beginning for the new manager, Colin Preece. Born in Adelaide in 1903 and dux of Roseworthy College in 1923, Preece joined Seppelts and worked at Seppeltsfield before being promoted to Great Western. It is sufficient to say here than Colin Preece went on to become one of the greatest Australian winemakers of this century.

During the next twenty years, 137 hectares of new vineyards were established and 32 hectares replanted. Holdings were extended in 1945 with the purchase from Maria Salinger (after whom the brilliant new Seppelt Salinger champagne is named) of the St Ethel's and Hockheim properties about 2 km south-east of the cellars. The first stage of an impressive new building was begun in 1946, and a second floor added thirteen years later. By 1964, increasing sales made it necessary to extend the cellar area, and a modern fermentation cellar was completed in time for the 1965 vintage.

During this time the famous drives were given over to the storage of sparkling wine. Famous people, including Dame Nellie Melba, opened and gave their names to new drives, which now total some 5.5 km and are classified 'A' by the National Trust of Victoria. Technology marches on, however, and conditions in the drives have now been bettered in enormous air-conditioned sheds which provide easier handling and storage.

Millions of bottles of fine Australian champagne mature in the cool underground drives at Seppelt's Great Western.

Colin Preece retired in 1963 because of poor health. To many of his peers he was the master, ranked with other such great winemakers as Maurice O'Shea and Roger Warren. Under Colin Preece's management, Great Western champagne far outstripped its competitors. In the 1940s he also began making wine which led to the successful commercial range from Great Western—Moyston claret (named after a village south of the winery); Chalambar burgundy (from Mt Chalambar); Rhymney chablis (from nearby gold diggings); and Arawatta riesling (named after the best-known Great Western vineyard). Colin Preece died in December 1979 after spending most of his retirement nearby in Ararat, and having maintained close ties with the Victorian wine industry through his work as a consultant in such major projects as Mitchelton.

In 1978, Seppelts recruited Dominique Landragin, a young champagne-maker from Verzenay, as chief sparkling winemaker at Great Western. Under his guidance the foundations of the styles which still give the company its great dominance in the field were laid. Much work was done on new plantings of chardonnay, pinot noir and pinot meunier, the planning of new cuvées, the use of yeast cultures from Champagne and so on.

In 1982 Dominique Landragin left Seppelts to join Yellowglen (in 1987 he opened his own company, Landragin Australia, to make sparkling wine), and was succeeded by Warren Randall, who continued the good work. In 1987, all four of Seppelt's Great Western sparkling wines—Salinger, Fleur de Lys, Great Western Brut and Blanc de Blanc—won gold medals in the Sydney Wine Show. The 1984 Salinger Brut won the Thorp Trophy for the best champagne in the show. Warren Randall has now also gone on his way (to Andrew Garrett Wines in McLaren Vale), but the sparkling styles of Seppelt's Great Western, born in the days of Hans Irvine and nurtured by the likes of Colin Preece and Dominique Landragin, are well and truly set.

Seppelt's Drumborg

In 1964, B. Seppelt & Sons wanted to expand its Victorian operations, but it was difficult to find suitable land in the vicinity of Great Western. It was not possible to plant any of the Great West-

ern vines in South Australia because of the phylloxera quarantine regulations, so eventually the company settled on a 190 hectare farming property at Drumborg, on the Princes Highway 6 km from Heywood.

The red-brown volcanic soil, with its ironstone gravel, was similar to that of the Arawatta vineyard; and although Drumborg was cooler than Great Western, it also had better rainfall, about 750 mm a year. More than 110 hectares were planted there to cabernet sauvignon, Rhine riesling, tokay, miller's burgundy, gewurztraminer, chardonnay and pinot noir. All of the fruit is processed at the Great Western winery, most of it for sparkling wine production, but also for a very fine range of Great Western and separate Drumborg label table wines.

The Pyrenees

The relatively new Pyrenees wine-growing region of Victoria takes its name from the gently picturesque Pyrenees ranges, which could be seen as the western-most extremity of the Great Dividing Range. It flanks the Pyrenees Highway between Ararat and Avoca, then tends northwards along the Sunraysia Highway on its way beyond Redbank to St Arnaud. It lies between the Great Western region and the southern Central Victorian region which extends roughly from Ballarat to Bendigo, and although it takes

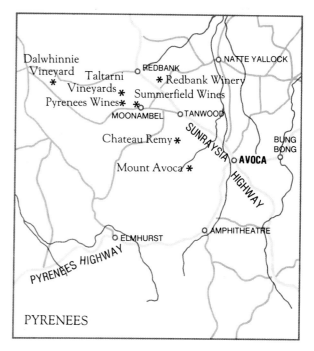

PYRENEES

something from each it has an identity of its own which its producers are exploiting very well. There is a mintiness to the wines, even a hint of chocolate and of the eucalypt scrub which covers many of the rolling hills, and Pyrenees style is now something recognisable and desired.

This was goldmining country in the middle of last century, and around many of today's vineyards are the remains of shafts and open cuts and well-dredged creeks. As in other parts of the state the vignerons followed the miners, and in 1848 a man by the name of Mackereth planted vines near Avoca. His sons, Edward, John and Charles Mackereth tended the 'pinneau' vines (we presume pinot noir), and made red table wine and port, both of which won their share of prizes. The winery was closed in the 1930s and the property turned over to grazing, a familiar scenario elsewhere in the state.

Further north, at Moonambel, a settler named Adams established what became known as Kofoeds Mountain Creek Vineyard, and production continued there until about 1945. There are still a few bottles of Kofoeds wine in private cellars; dry white muscat, for instance, bottled in heavy, dark-green champagne bottles, and a white port. The rebirth of the district came with the establishment of Chateau Remy in 1963, and now there are more than half-a-dozen wineries and a swag of mainly small growers producing fruit and wine of great character.

Unlike their European counterpart, the Victorian Pyrenees are hills rather than mountains—not much more than 600 m above sea level with most of the vineyards at around 400 m. The climate is mild and temperate (although there are photographs of Taltarni and Redbank blanketed in snow), and frosts are infrequent. Rainfall is 500–600 mm, mainly in winter and spring. This is not particularly high, and many vineyards have supplementary watering. Mould and fungus are rare but, as elsewhere in 'the garden state', birds are a problem.

The soils are generally alluvial gravels over clay, which is why the miners went there in the first place, and soil varies in colour through bright red at Redbank, orange at Moonambel to yellow at Avoca. The clay retains moisture during summer, but the fertility of the soil is not high, with the result that vines can take up to four or five years to produce their first crop, and

bear only lightly after that. But quality is the thing, and most of the Pyrenees producers are delighted with the progress made there in the past twenty years.

Chateau Remy

The Victorian connection with the French Cognac giant, Remy Martin, dates back to the 1920s when the Melbourne firm of Nathan and Wyeth were appointed Remy's agents in Australia. Over the years, Remy president, Andre Heriard-Dubreuil, developed a great love for Australia, and during one of his frequent visits floated the idea of having a vineyard for the local production of Remy brandy. Supplies from France had been interrupted by World War II, so this was felt to be a very good idea.

Colin Jones, a director of Nathan and Wyeth, was brought up in Avoca, and remembering that wine had still been in production there when he was a boy in the 1920s, set about finding a suitable site. After several years of negotiation (which required the Victorian Government to rezone a portion of state forest), what was originally one square mile of undulating country 7 km west of the little township of Avoca was made available. Winemaker John Robb, who had worked for a time in the Hunter Valley with the legendary Maurice O'Shea, moved in to create Chateau Remy.

Half of the original 96 hectare vineyard was

planted to white hermitage (ugni blanc) grapes for champagne, and half to doradillo, the high-yielding variety most used in Australia for brandy distillation. The white hermitage flourished but the doradillo did not. There was plenty of vine growth in the doras, but sugar content was too low to make distillation worthwhile. After some breast-beating the doradillo vines were pulled out and replaced with red varieties, cabernet sauvignon, shiraz, merlot and pinot noir. It was an excellent decision. By the early 1980s Chateau Remy reds had developed distinct regional character and triggered the emergence of the Pyrenees as a premium red wine-producing district.

In 1982 the vineyard was doubled in size with new plantings of chardonnay and pinot noir for champagne. To cope with this extra fruit the champagne cellar, opened in 1981, was also doubled in size. This included installation of a brand new French production line to streamline the time and labour-consuming classical *méthode champenoise* process. These days about 650 tonnes of fruit are crushed each year for champagne, providing about 600 000 bottles. There are three products in the Chateau Remy sparkling range; Cuvée Speciale Brut, Royal Vintage (made only in exceptional vintages and matured on lees for four years), and Rosé Premier Brut.

John Robb, who retired in 1983, was confident that Avoca would also distinguish itself as a red wine area. He compared it favourably with Coonawarra, pointing out that its cool conditions went hand in hand with brilliant colour, good acidity and reasonable alcoholic strength. He was succeeded as winemaker by Christian Morlaes, from Bordeaux, one of two young winemakers brought to Australia by Remy. The other was Michel Dietrich, a native of Alsace, who worked at Quelltaler, the beautiful property in the Clare Valley which had also been owned by Nathan and Wyeth and which was eventually sold to Wolf Blass in 1988.

Some brilliant red wines emerged under Christian Morlaes's direction: Blue Pyrenees Estate, a blend of cabernet sauvignon, shiraz and merlot; and Australis, a limited edition shiraz from Remy's Australis vineyard which was planted in 1973 and which produces only 4 tonnes to the hectare of particularly fine fruit each year. Christian left in 1986 to move to Sandalford, in Western Australia. He was replaced by another young Frenchman, Vincent Gere, who did one vintage with Christian and one with Michel Dietrich before taking over the reins completely. In 1987, Christian returned to Remy's operations in Bordeaux.

Chateau Remy is now fully owned by Remy Martin. Part of the deal when Quelltaler was sold to Wolf Blass was that Chateau Remy would have access to some of the top fruit grown there, and this now makes its appearance in three wines: a premium sauvignon blanc called Clos St Charles, and a wood-matured semillon and a botrytised semillon—both simply labelled 'S'. These wines are fermented in Clare, but then returned to Avoca for further treatment, bottling and maturing.

In 1989 some $1.6 million was spent on upgrading the main winery at Avoca, installing a new press, new stainless steel fermenting and storage equipment, and a new laboratory. In the preceding three years there had also been a lot of work done in the vineyard, replanting and grafting the old ugni blanc vines over to premium sparkling varieties, chardonnay, pinot noir and pinot meunier. It is now a thoroughly modern operation producing the kinds of wines that have taken the Pyrenees name to all parts of Australia, and to markets around the world.

Dalwhinnie Vineyard

Architect Ewan Jones, from Ballarat, established Dalwhinnie in 1973 on a 130 hectare block in Taltarni Road, Moonambel, 16 km north of Avoca. Gary Farr, from Bannockburn, supervised the planting of 3.3 hectares of cabernet sauvignon, merlot and shiraz. Mr Jones built a handsome weekender on the property but the wine was to be made at Yellowglen, the boutique champagne winery at Smythesdale, near Ballarat. This was owned at the time by his brother-in-law Ian Home, a Ballarat supermarket owner. A third figure in what was a triumvirate of new wine producers was Stuart Hooper, who owned supermarkets in Geelong and whose ultra-modern winery at Bannockburn was designed by Ewan Jones!

In 1981 chardonnay was planted at Dalwhinnie, taking the total vineyard area to 10 hectares. By then the Farr-made Dalwhinnie reds were on sale. There is now quite a range of varietals of the very highest quality being made in small quantities; Dalwhinnie shiraz, cabernet sauvignon and chardonnay, Dalwhinnie Pyrenees cabernet, and 'Eagle' cabernet and shiraz. They sell through new cellar door sales facilities (with a beautiful view of the Pyrenees), and through the company's headquarters in Ballarat.

Mount Avoca

Melbourne stockbroker John Barry had barely heard of Avoca until 1968 when by chance he met John Robb, the hands-on founder of Chateau Remy. John and his architect wife, Arda, had a love of good wine and for some time had been looking for somewhere in Victoria to establish a vineyard of their own. Rutherglen was an early choice, but the director of the Viticultural Research Station pointed them in the direction of John Robb, and the Barrys were impressed by his enthusiasm for the natural beauty of the place and the wines it was producing.

In 1970 they purchased 81 hectares of land in Moates Lane, Avoca, not far from Chateau Remy; and in 1972 began planting 15 hectares to cabernet sauvignon, shiraz, trebbiano and semillon. The first grapes from what they called Mount Avoca were sold to Seppelts at Great Western, although John made small batches of wine in 1976 and 1977. The following year they built a small winery (to Arda's design), and made their first commercial vintage, which included a very silky cabernet sauvignon filled with the minty, eucalyptus character for which the region is now so well known. In 1981 they slightly corrected the red-white imbalance in the vineyard by planting 1.2 hectares of chardonnay and 2 hectares of sauvignon blanc.

In the meantime, John had been doing the correspondence winemaker's course at Riverina College in Wagga Wagga, and while doing some practical work there he met Guy Stanford, who in 1980 became winemaker at Mount Avoca. He made several vintages before being succeeded by Rodney Morrish, formerly of Seppelts. While he remains resident winemaker, John Barry—a regular commuter from Melbourne—continues to play an active role, particularly during vintage.

There are now six Mount Avoca wines. The shiraz is a lovely peppery wine with strong regional character. John Barry is so impressed with the way it has developed in the past few years that he feels the Pyrenees will eventually become known as home of some of the greatest shiraz wines in the world. Mount Avoca cabernet is also developing well; in recent vintages John and Rodney Morrish have been looking for a less assertive style, less tannic, and concentrating more on the complex minty, blackcurrant fruit character that Avoca imparts.

But it is the quality of the white Mount Avoca wines which has brought most praise in recent vintages. Pyrenees Dry White is made from trebbiano—a firm, clean wine with excellent flavour. The Mount Avoca Chardonnay and Semillon are outstanding, both are oak-fermented and matured, and share great depth of fruit flavour and very firm, crisp acid character. Perhaps the biggest surprise of the 1989 releases was the 1988 Sauvignon Blanc, which had the characteristic bouquet but backed it up with excellent acid balance and much more depth of fruit than was expected. It certainly challenged the proposition that the Pyrenees was exclusively red wine country.

Pyrenees Wines, Warrenmang Vineyard

The story of Warrenmang is very much the story of the emergence of the Pyrenees as a quality winemaking district. It began with Wal Henning, a former mayor of Stawell and the earth-moving contractor who did much of the land clearing and drainage work at Chateau Remy in 1963. That job alerted him to the potential for vineyard development in the area, and in 1969 he bought a large tract of land 5 km north of Moonambel. With the help of a local farmer, Jack Clark, he began planting grapes. The sheer size of the operation proved its undoing, however, and in 1972 he sold 110 hectares of it to the French–American proprietors of what is now Taltarni.

Not completely disheartened, Mr Henning held on to 10 hectares of the property and called it Warrenmang. In partnership with Maryborough businessman Russell Branton and Leo Hurley, who had been cellarmaster and winemaker at Seppelt's Great Western from 1923 to 1973, he continued work on the property and their first Pyrenees Wines, as they called them, were released in 1977.

Mr Hurley retired a couple of years later and Neill Robb, son of Chateau Remy's John Robb and proprietor of his own Redbank Winery, helped make the wine. Mr Henning was replaced in the partnership in 1977 by Luigi Bassani, who ran the renowned Copper Pot restaurant in Bendigo and then the equally well-regarded La Scala restaurant in Ballarat. Russell Branton was already partner in the Melbourne wine merchants Duke & Moorfield, and when he later took over W.J. Seabrook & Son, Luigi Bassani became involved in operations at Warrenmang. Luigi took over completely in 1986, and since then the property has become very much part of the Bassani style.

Luigi and his wife Athalie built a country retreat at Warrenmang but they didn't have much time to spend there. Luigi designed and built two restaurants in Melbourne and a nightclub complex in Warrnambool, and then built and operated the highly successful bar and restaurant complex in the National Wool Centre in Geelong. In 1988–89 he built what he calls his Pyrenees Vintage Village on the property, a $1 million combination of retreat, restaurant, conference centre, cellar door sales area and a dozen two-storey country cottages overlooking the rolling Pyrenees hills and vineyard.

Through all of this he has not neglected his role of winemaker. He now has 10 hectares of cabernet sauvignon, shiraz, malbec and chardonnay, and a small patch of sauvignon blanc. The winery is dug into the side of a hill—a final piece of fine earth-moving by Wal Henning —and there Luigi produces a small but quality range of reds and whites, which all display the now well-known Pyrenees trademarks of depth and character.

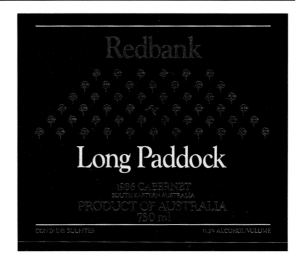

Redbank Winery

Neill Robb and his wife Sally migrated to the Pyrenees several years after Neill's father, John Robb, was appointed estate manager for the Chateau Remy project at Avoca in 1963. Neill had worked at wineries in the Hunter Valley and in South Australia, and he spent several years at Chateau Remy before finding some land of his own just outside the little township of Redbank, 22 km northwards along the Sunraysia Highway from Avoca. He and Sally began planting vines in 1973 and, because they were both confirmed red wine lovers, they stuck exclusively to red varieties—cabernet sauvignon, shiraz, merlot, malbec, cabernet franc and pinot noir.

While the vines were maturing they built a very handsome house and winery from 100-year-old bricks they found in the district. The first release of Redbank wines followed in 1976. With only 10 hectares of vines yielding a very miserly 1.2 tonnes per hectare, the Robbs were forced to buy in grapes from other areas—Avoca, Moonambel, Marong, Ballarat, Nagambie and so on—and these are released under their particular origin labels. Their best-known wine is Sally's Paddock, which comes from their main vineyard and is a mixture of shiraz, cabernet and malbec crushed together then aged in good French oak.

The winery was specifically designed to cope with small batches of grapes, using techniques which combine Californian technology with European tradition. Cap plunging is carried out by hand, for instance, and pressing is in hand-operated cage presses. Fermentation is in open vats and there is no sign of the massive refrigeration plants which now seem part and parcel of

Redbank Winery.

every modern winery. This is a red wine winery after all, and temperatures during vintage, usually in April, are generally so low that stuck ferments are often more troublesome than any risks of oxidation. Production is only around 2000 cases per year, but demand is high and sale is usually through cellar door or by mailing list.

Summerfield Wines

Ian Summerfield's property on the outskirts of Moonambel is one of the smaller Pyrenees vineyards; he began planting the 4.5 hectares of shiraz, cabernet sauvignon and trebbiano in 1970. Early crops were sold to other wineries in the district but a small winery was built in time for the 1979 vintage, when 8 tonnes were crushed and Ian made the wine with the help of a few local friends. The first release was a shiraz, but since then the range has broadened to include trebbiano, semillon, shiraz, a cabernet–shiraz blend and a sparkling white *méthode champenoise* wine. Distribution is through cellar door, the Moonambel Hotel (250 m away), and a couple of outlets in Melbourne.

Taltarni Vineyards

The Taltarni story is a remarkable one by any standards. It goes back some thirty years to the Medoc, where André Portet was estate manager and a winemaker at Chateau Lafite, one of the great wineries of Bordeaux. His sons Dominique and Bernard were the sixth generation of vignerons in the family. Both sons realised that given the strict French government controls over the wine industry and the virtual impossibility of expansion in Bordeaux, they were faced with a future which promised a rather regimented existence as French vignerons.

In 1972 Bernard Portet migrated to the United States, where he became involved in the development of Clos du Val vineyard in California's Napa Valley. The property was owned by millionaire banker and businessman John Goelet, whose family had been important Bordeaux wine merchants. He had been searching the world for properties capable of producing wine up to the best French standards, and while the vines at Clos du Val were maturing Bernard Portet extended the quest to Australia. At Moonambool he saw the vineyard which had been established by Wal Henning, earthmover and former mayor of Stawell, in 1969, and arranged Mr Goelet's purchase of about 100 hectares of it.

In 1973 brilliant young Western Australian winemaker David Hohnen, who had trained at Fresno State University in California, was appointed to oversee operations at Taltarni. When he left in 1976 to become a partner and winemaker at Cape Mentelle, in Margaret River, Bernard's younger brother Dominique arrived to take over. He made the first wine bottled under the Taltarni label in 1977, and since then Taltarni and Clos du Val have operated hand in hand, and half a world apart.

When it came to setting up operations at Moonambool no expense was spared; having a millionare owner was a great comfort.

Dominique Portet studied viticultural science at Montpellier University and worked in the Medoc, the Rhône Valley and Provence before moving to the Napa Valley and eventually to Australia. In 1978 he was joined at Taltarni by Greg Gallagher, a Roseworthy College graduate who had worked at Seppelts, and together they set up a winery which almost literally lacked nothing. They had access to the best equipment and the most expensive French oak, while in the vineyard work was completed on a complex series of dams and watering systems which made the property virtually drought-proof. In 1982, the company celebrated the tenth anniversary of its arrival in the Pyrenees with the opening of a handsome new office block and tasting room.

Winemaking there is what Dominique has described as a blend of conservative French tradition and high technology. The winery is fully air-conditioned, and all fermentations are strictly temperature-controlled. All red wines are stored in small Nevers oak for one to two years, and over the years they have changed as Dominique adapted to the conditions. His first reds were enormous wines, rich in flavour and tannin, to last for generations. Because of the Australian conditions they were much richer and bigger than their recent Bordeaux equivalents. In 1987 a vertical tasting of all of the red wines from Taltarni demonstrated not only how they had become more complex and elegant over the years, but also how well the older wines had held their colour and structure.

It was a decade also in which Taltarni wines received international recognition. In 1979 cabernet sauvignon was voted 'Best of Reds' at a worldwide judging by the *Los Angeles Times* in 1983, and three successive vintages of the wine were acclaimed as 'Critics Choice' wines by *Wine Spectator* magazine in New York. This recognition, plus an entrée to the US market via Clos du Val had, by 1989, seen an encouraging growth in export sales.

The vineyard is now around 112 hectares, planted on grey and red oxidised clay ('Taltarni' is said to be local Aboriginal dialect for 'red earth') which is high in iron and low in potassium and therefore conducive to low pH levels in the grapes. Red varieties are cabernet sauvignon, cabernet franc, malbec, merlot and shiraz (since 1984 Taltarni shiraz has been referred to as 'French syrah' because of marketing problems with the name shiraz). White varieties are sauvignon blanc, ugni blanc, chardonnay, Rhine riesling and chenin blanc. Production is between 30 000 and 35 000 cases per year, divided between four sparkling wines (Blanc de Blanc, Brut, Brut Tache and Royal), three whites (fumé blanc, Rhine riesling and Blanc de Pyrenees), and four reds (cabernet sauvignon, French syrah, merlot and Reserve des Pyrenees, which is a cabernet–malbec blend). All of the wines come from the estate, and there is no doubt that at Taltarni the Portets have fulfilled their stated aim of balance, complexity and finesse with ageing potential and grace at the table.

Central Victoria

This important agricultural area of Victoria is also attracting an increasing share of viticulture; in some cases in regions which have not seen vines before, and in others the rebirth of famous nineteenth-century vineyards and wineries. It extends from Ballarat to Bendigo, both historic goldmining towns, and is flanked to the east by the Goulburn Valley wine-producing region and to the west by the Pyrenees. It includes Sunbury, where both Goonawarra and Craiglee flourished a hundred years ago, and the Macedon region, where half-a-dozen new properties have sprung up in the last decade.

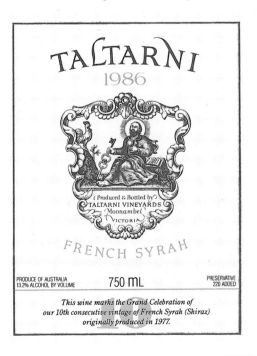

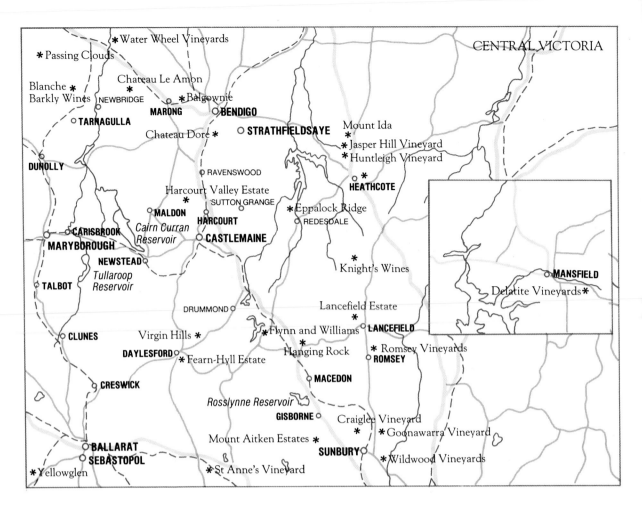

History tells us that vines were planted near Ballarat by Monsieur Fleischauer in 1859, and near Bendigo three years before that by a German called Delscher and a Frenchman by the name of Bladier. In 1864 Ebenezer Ward wrote that Yarraberb Station on Myers Creek was one of the oldest and best-known vineyards in the Bendigo area, with 'six acres of vines, the oldest from 10 to 11 years of age'.

The area boomed, first with gold and then with vines, and by the end of the 1880s there were more than 130 vineyards around Bendigo, covering more than 450 hectares. One Bendigo wine of distinction was entered in the 1873 Vienna Exhibition, and François de Castella related that the French judges withdrew in protest because they did not believe the wine, a Hermitage, could have been anything other than French.

As happened in so many areas of Victoria, phylloxera and economic depression combined to wipe out most of the pioneer vignerons, and it was not until Stuart Anderson planted his Balgownie vineyard near Bendigo in 1969 that a revival began. A problem around Bendigo as far as vines are concerned is low rainfall, about

500–550 mm per year. Winemakers cope in different ways; some use irrigation, some are helped by an underground water drift which allegedly follows the old goldmines, and others depend on moisture-retentive subsoil. The area is prone to spring frosts, and birds are a problem.

Ballarat, 130 km south of Bendigo and 120 km north-west of Melbourne, is higher, colder and wetter; and in the depths of winter, with the prevailing south-westerlies blowing, it can be one of the most inhospitable places on this earth. Nevertheless, conditions such as these have some perverse reflection in the quality of wine produced, and winemakers of the calibre of Dominique Landragin and Gary Farr believe it produces the best base material for *méthode champenoise* sparkling wines in Australia.

Balgownie

Stuart Anderson studied pharmacy at the old Victorian Pharmacy College in Swanston Street, Melbourne, where the Royal Melbourne Institute of Technology now stands. Over the road was (and is) the Oxford Hotel, and at the time publican Maurice Johnston had one of the best tables in Melbourne, and certainly one of the best cellars. The young Stuart Anderson fell in love with the Maurice O'Shea reds which Johnston stocked, and when he returned to his home town, Bendigo, to practise pharmacy he had been well and truly bitten by the wine bug.

Outward symptoms did not erupt until 1968, however, when he bought an old farm at Maiden Gully, south of Bendigo, and called it Balgownie after the village near Aberdeen where earlier generations of Andersons had lived before joining the gold rush of the 1850s. Stuart began planting vines the following year—cabernet sauvignon, shiraz, pinot noir, riesling, traminer and chardonnay; and while his vines were maturing he set about learning at least some of the techniques of making wine. He spent a couple of vintages with that other inspired amateur, Max Lake, at Lake's Folly, and travelled to France where he worked during vintage at Château Cissac in Bordeaux.

His 13 hectare vineyard was planted on alluvial sand and clay loam overlaying a clay and ironstone gravel subsoil; although early frosts proved a problem he had his first vintage in 1972 and his first commercial release in the following year. His early reds, cabernet and shiraz, were matured in large oak barrels; but in 1977 he bought some 225 litre French oak barriques for his cabernet, and Limousin oak for his chardonnay and pinot noir. There were thus some changes in style in the first few years at Balgownie, but the quality of his cabernet, in particular, was so outstanding that a whole new generation of Victorian boutique wine producers was practically born on the spot. His ambition to make wine in the French style was reflected also in the quality of his chardonnay and pinot— always made in small quantities and always very much in demand. A 1974 cabernet tasted in 1987 was in superb condition, very much like a top Pauillac in its prime.

In 1985, Balgownie was taken over by the rapidly-expanding Mildara Wines, and Stuart Anderson was made a director of the company and retained as supervising winemaker. In 1987 a new range of Balgownie 'Premier Cuvée' wines was introduced as distinct from the original Balgownie Estate label. These were made from fruit produced elsewhere in Mildara's empire, but the wines were all made under Stuart's supervision and priced slightly below the Estate range.

Blanche Barkly Wines

Blanche Barkly takes its name from an enormous 1880-ounce gold nugget found in the beautiful Kingower Valley, some 60 km north-west of Bendigo, in 1857. The nugget was named after Blanche, daughter of the then Governor of Victoria, Sir Henry Barkly. In 1972, Kingower brothers David and Alvin Reimers planted 4 hectares of grapes around the spot where the nugget was found, and eventually built a small winery there.

The valley soil is rich and lies on the southern slopes of undulating ranges where winters are cold and the autumn ripening period is long and cool. It is also dry, at best about 450 mm of rain per year, but the vines feed deep and irrigation is unnecessary. Varieties are cabernet sauvignon, with smaller quantities of shiraz, mondeuse, pinot noir and Rhine riesling. It is so cool at Blanche Barkly that the grapes are usually picked around Easter, and yields are such that only 12–13 tonnes are picked each year.

Nevertheless, fruit quality is rich, and the Reimers, who learned winemaking at Reynella in South Australia, tend to pick early and ferment the grapes cold. The resultant wines are soft, generous and complex; Blanche Barkly cabernet sauvignon, in particular, has a depth of flavour which suggests many years of life. There are usually three wines each year: Mary Eileen shiraz named after Maisie Reimers, Alvin's mother; Alexander cabernet sauvignon named after their grandfather; and George Henry cabernet sauvignon, the top-of-the-line red named after a goldmining great-uncle. From time to time they also make Hermitage Nouveau, a cool-fermented shiraz which is taken off the skins early and aged briefly in new Nevers oak.

Chateau Dore

Chateau Dore vineyard is at Mandurang, 8 km south of Bendigo. It was initially established by Jean de Ravin in 1866. He also built a handsome winery in local bluestone which stands today in remarkably good condition. The vineyard was replanted in 1975 by de Ravin's great-grandson, Ivan Grose, who now has 7 hectares of shiraz, cabernet sauvignon, Rhine riesling and chardonnay. Wines are sold at cellar door by Ivan and his wife, Jan.

Chateau Le Amon

Various comparisons can be made between Chateau Le Amon, 10 km south-west of Bendigo, and Balgownie, 8 km west of the once golden provincial city. Both Phillip Leamon and Stuart Anderson came to winemaking relatively late in life. Both chose a cool-climate region of Central Victoria, and both very quickly established reputations for brilliant red wines, cabernet sauvignon in particular. There are some differences in style, but Balgownie and Chateau Le Amon remain benchmarks (and inspirational ones at that) for small winemakers throughout the state.

Phillip Leamon worked for the State Electricity Commission in Victoria before being promoted into an administrative role he found thoroughly boring. In 1973 he started looking around for a site for a vineyard, settling eventually on 5 hectares of land on the northern slopes of Big Hill, overlooking the Calder Highway. With the help of relatives and friends, he planted 1.2 hectares each of cabernet sauvignon and shiraz, and 0.6 hectares each of semillon and Rhine riesling. The vineyard, at an elevation of 300 m, received only 580 mm of rain per year, but with the aid of a water right which went with the property, arrangements were made to flood-irrigate it several times a year.

While the vines were maturing, Phil Leamon (Leamon is an anglicised version of his family name, Le Amon) studied textbooks, attended seminars, completed a course in inorganic chemistry and, just before his first vintage in 1977, attended a wine quality-control workshop at Riverina College in Wagga Wagga. He must have been a good student because his first wine, cabernet sauvignon, won a gold medal and the small vineyard trophy at the First National Wine Show in Canberra in 1978.

Since then the Le Amon style has consolidated, and four wines are produced each year; cabernet sauvignon, shiraz, semillon and Rhine riesling. All show the natural depth and elegance of the area. The red wines are brilliantly coloured yet soft and pleasant on the palate, and the whites are robust and full-flavoured. The star of the line-up is still the cabernet sauvignon, a rich and complex wine which ages well, although it also drinks beautifully when young. It is very reasonably priced in these days when 'boutique' quality can also mean premium prices.

Craiglee Vineyard

Craiglee is an historic property reborn. It was planted originally in Sunbury, 40 km north-west of Melbourne, by Scotsman James Stewart Johnston, a Melbourne businessman who had many interests, horseracing among them. He was Chief Stipendiary Magistrate of the Victorian Racing Club for a time, and his name is commemorated there in the annual Craiglee Stakes. He was born in Edinburgh in 1811, and was fifty-two years old in 1863 when he began planting his vines in Sunbury, at the time a fashionable part of outer Melbourne. His neighbour was James Goodall Francis, a former premier of Victoria, and they both turned to viticulture in the hope of cashing in on what was then a valuable wine export trade to Britain and New Zealand. In this venture, Johnston survived and Francis failed; practically all of the Craiglee wine was sold in London, but Francis's Goonawarra vineyard was turned over to grazing around the turn of the century.

Johnston's plantings were of verdelho, riesling, hermitage (shiraz), and pinot, although some doubt remains about whether the 'pineau' referred to in winery records was in fact pinot noir. Eventually only hermitage and riesling were used for winemaking, which ended in 1927. A few rows of grapes were retained by the Johnston family for the table, but practically the entire vineyard, which had been around 200 hectares at its peak, had been pulled out by 1940 to make way for general farming.

In 1951, ten cases of Craiglee 1872 Hermitage

were found behind a brick wall in the four-storey bluestone cellar building, which at the time was being used as a farm storage shed by Dr William Johnston, the founder's grandson. He kept some for himself and the rest went to Tom Seabrook, the well-known Melbourne wine merchant, who sold it for ten shillings a bottle, no refund for faults. By all accounts the wine was in good condition, and since then bottles have popped up from time to time—interesting reminders of what wine was like in those feisty colonial days. In October 1988 what was thought to be the last remaining bottle was handed to Melbourne auctioneer Stewart Langton, who sold it for $2500.

The Carmody family, who bought Craiglee from the Johnstons in 1961, were not among the bidders. They didn't find any more old wine although they rebuilt the cellars and replanted 6 hectares of vineyard to shiraz, cabernet sauvignon and chardonnay, and a small experimental patch of pinot noir. While all this was going on Pat Carmody graduated in science and then did the oenology course at Riverina College in Wagga Wagga. He had his first vintage, 7 tonnes of cabernet and shiraz, in 1981. Because of health regulations, ironically, he couldn't make his wine in the splendid bluestone winery, but used a new one built further away from the nearby creek.

The crush is now around 50 tonnes and Craiglee is up and running again as a commercial proposition. The new Craiglee labels are practically identical to those of Johnston's days, and other similarities remain. The founder was an assiduous keeper of records, and Pat Carmody has unearthed many of these in the Victorian State Archives. Today's harvest times and yields are almost identical with what they were a century ago, and so are rainfall and other weather conditions.

The 'new' wines are also very similar to others now being made in the area called the Macedon region. This is a narrow strip of fairly hilly country which extends from Keilor, on the western outskirts of Melbourne on either side of the Calder Highway to Kyneton. Craiglee shiraz and cabernet share an interesting depth and intensity of flavour quite different from that emerging in the Yarra Valley, for example; and the chardonnay also has a beguiling fullness and richness which bespeaks considerable life.

Delatite Vineyards

Delatite takes its name from the Delatite River, a little trout stream which flows down from the slopes of Mount Buller in the Victorian Alps to Lake Eildon. This is the beautiful country in which *The Man from Snowy River* was filmed; indeed, Delatite is the pride and joy of the Ritchie family, which has been running cattle on these red-gum hills out of Mansfield, some 200 km north-east of Melbourne, for four generations. (Delatite is not strictly in Central Victoria; in fact, at the moment it can be considered geographically unique!)

Robert Ritchie, grandson of the original settler on the property, had diversified over the years away from complete reliance on cattle and sheep into such crops as rye grass and peas. He hadn't thought about vines until one night his friend Doug Escott, the warden on Mount Buller, dropped in with Jim Irvine, the well-known South Australian winemaker and consultant who was also a regular visitor to the Victorian ski slopes. At the time, Irvine remarked that it looked like good wine country. The Ritchies didn't think any more about it until several months later when Jim returned with a car full of vine cuttings from McLaren Vale.

That was in 1968. The cuttings were planted in a small plot near the homestead, and to the Ritchies' surprise, they all struck. There was Rhine riesling, carignan and cabernet sauvignon; and the following year they planted more riesling and some gewürztraminer. During the 1970s small amounts of wine were made for them by Brown Bros at Milawa, but by 1980 Browns had grown too large to have time for other people's

169

small batches so the Ritchies were faced with building a winery and finding a winemaker.

Fortunately Robert and Vivienne Ritchie's daughter Rosalind decided to do the oenology course at Roseworthy Agricultural College. During her course she worked at the Southern Vales Cooperative, Browns, and after graduation with Bill Chambers in Rutherglen. The new winery at Delatite was ready for her to make her first vintage in 1982, and since then Delatite has gone from strength to strength.

There are now 20 hectares of vines, and cattle and sheep have taken a back seat. Robert Ritchie and his sons look after the vineyard, Rosalind makes the wine and Vivienne sells it—and the vagaries of the livestock market are no longer a problem. Ros won a gold medal with her very first gewurztraminer at Brisbane in 1982, and the Delatite version of this difficult variety continues to be remarkable for its delicacy and beauty.

Her Rhine riesling has developed a strong cellar style, strong acid structure and delicate, floral character in the palate (since 1988 it has included fruit from the Goulburn Valley); and Delatite chardonnay, matured in Nevers, Troncais and Vosges oak, has also become a lovely style—the 1988 filled with intense fruit flavours but quite firm and elegant. Red wines include New Shiraz, which is taken off the skins midway through fermentation and bottled soon after without any oak contact; and pinot noir, a delightful wine with bright ruby colour and full, rich flavour. The cabernet goes into Devil's River blend with some merlot, the first of these being released in 1988—very up-front fruit flavours providing easy and immediate drinking but also a wine which will keep.

Eppalock Ridge

This small estate, originally known as Romany Rye, was established in 1978 by Rod and Sue Hourigan at Redesdale, 121 km north of Melbourne and 23 km south-west of Heathcote. They planted pinot noir, cabernet sauvignon, chardonnay, merlot and semillon, and now have 12 hectares of vines in two vineyards, at Heathcote and near picturesque Lake Eppalock.

The winery was once a hayshed, and there Rod Hourigan makes three wines which are usually sold by mailing list, at cellar door, or through one or two outlets in Melbourne. His

Heathcote shiraz is a typical wine of the district—peppery, intense, showing lovely rounded fruit character as it ages; and cabernet sauvignon-merlot is a blend of small parcels of fruit from both the Redesdale and Heathcote vineyards. Eppalock Ridge chardonnay comes entirely from the so-called winery vineyard at Redesdale, and it is an elegant wine very much in the style of a true white Burgundy.

Fearn-Hyll Estate

Fearn-Hyll Estate is David and Ann Marie Farnhill's vineyard, winery and restaurant on the Ballan Road 4 km south of Daylesford, a charming little town known for its natural springs. David had worked in the wine industry in Tasmania before moving to Central Victoria in 1974, and he and Ann Marie began planting what is now 8 hectares of vines including cabernet sauvignon, shiraz, pinot noir, malbec, Rhine riesling and chardonnay.

They make four wines: shiraz, cabernet and riesling as straight varietals; and a white burgundy which includes some later-picked riesling. Production in 1989 was around 50 000 litres, most of it sold through their own restaurant and other restaurants around Daylesford and Ballarat.

Frost is a problem, and in the older part of the vineyard watering is done by overhead sprinklers which provide some relief. Drip irrigation has been installed in the newer plantings of chardonnay and riesling. Birds, particularly currawongs, are an absolute menace according to David. In 1989 he estimates he lost between 6 and 7 tonnes of fruit to bird damage, and in 1990

was installing netting over the entire vineyard. Picking continues most years through April and May and sometimes even into June, and this very long season also increases vulnerability to birds.

Flynn and Williams

Silversmith John Flynn and winemaker Laurie Williams, who had been Tom Lazar's offsider at Virgin Hills, established a small vineyard on the northern outskirts of Kyneton, on the Calder Highway 20 km north of Woodend, in 1983. Like Tom Lazar they concentrated on cabernet sauvignon, and released their first wine to an admiring public in 1985. Production remains strictly limited. F&W has become highly sought after for its unique, Central Victorian eucalypt and mint character which, when complemented by the natural herbaceousness of cabernet, provides a surprisingly Bordeaux-style wine of great elegance and finesse. So impressed was Melbourne wine merchant Nick Chlebnikowski when he first tasted the 1965 version at the Macedon region dinner at Goonawarra recently that he ordered twenty cases on the spot—all that John and Laurie could spare.

Laurie Williams puts enormous effort into the care of his vines, favouring a traditional 'clean cultivation' technique which leaves bare earth between and around the vines. The wine is also made traditionally—open-fermented then matured in small French oak—with as much time as possible in bottle before being released. The winery is set in an incredible garden of fountains and roaming peacocks; it is all a part of the very interesting Flynn and Williams experience.

Goonawarra Vineyard

In the 1860s Goonawarra was the most grandiose of the eight vineyards which flourished in the Sunbury region 40 km north-west of Melbourne. It was the country seat of one-time Victorian premier, James Goodall Francis, who in 1858 began setting up a wine estate in the grand European manner. Planting vines on extensive stone terraces cost him a staggering £150 per acre, and a further small fortune was spent in 1863 on a massive bluestone winery. As recounted already (see Craiglee Vineyard), Mr Francis hoped to get a good return from what at the time was a burgeoning export market for col-

onial wine; but by the time of his death in 1884 the enormous costs of the project and the decline in the English market had brought about its demise. By the turn of the century the property had been given over to grazing.

Nevertheless, Goonawarra (meaning 'black swan' in local Aboriginal dialect, and not to be confused with Coonawarra, which translates as 'honeysuckle'), produced some good wines in its time—particularly 'pineau' which was probably pinot chardonnay or simply chardonnay. Chardonnay is, in fact, among new plantings begun at Goonawarra in 1983, when the property was bought by Melbourne solicitor John Barnier and his wife Elizabeth.

They did a massive refurbishment job on the old winery, turning it into a very impressive restaurant, and built a new winery in which Graham Durie made the first Goonawarra wines this century in 1986. There were further plantings in that year; pinot noir, cabernet franc, semillon and viognier, and the vineyard is now 5 hectares. The first cabernet franc was released in 1989, and the range of Goonawarra wines will increase as the newer vines come into bearing.

Hanging Rock

John Ellis had a significant impact on the Victorian wine scene when he left the Hunter Valley in 1978 to join Dr Peter Tisdall in setting up Tisdall Wines at Echuca. With the good doctor's blessing he explored the cooler-climate regions of the state, eventually helping establish Tisdall's remarkable successful Mt Helen vineyards high up in the Strathbogie Range. In

The cellar, Goonawarra Vineyard.

1984 he left Tisdall to put in more work on land he had bought for himself on the Jim Jim at Newham—a rugged hill 3 km north of legendary Hanging Rock and 10 km from Woodend.

At an elevation of about 700 m this was mountainous country indeed, and during the time he was planting vines and getting his new vineyard into shape, John Ellis was often brushing away the snow. He built a winery in 1987 and started making wine with fruit from various growers in the district whom he had been helping on a consultancy basis; shiraz from Heathcote, for instance, chardonnay from Faraday and Rhine riesling from the King Valley.

In his own vineyard he had concentrated on cold-weather varieties such as pinot noir, chardonnay and semillon; in 1989 he released the first of the Jim Jim wines, a 1988 semillon with classic cool-climate elegance and depth of character. With his skills, and the kind of fruit now being produced by an ever-increasing number of vineyards in this area, John Ellis's Hanging Rock Winery will be watched with great expectation.

Harcourt Valley Estate

Established in 1976 by Ray and Barbara Broughton on the Calder Highway at Harcourt, 188 km north of Melbourne, this small vineyard and winery was bought by Philip Honeyman in 1988. The property, at 425 m above sea level, was originally a prime apple and pear orchard. Rainfall is 650 mm per year, and extra water from the Coliban system of reservoirs is essential in summer to keep the vines growing in what is porous granitic sand.

The Broughton's first vintage was in 1980 when Ray, an engineer, made the wine; the following year the vineyard was doubled in size to 4 hectares. Varieties now include cabernet sauvignon, Rhine riesling, shiraz, chardonnay, malbec and pinot noir; and these will be supplemented by fruit from Philip Honeyman's own vineyard at Metcalfe. There is a very nice winery built from local grey granite quarried on Mount Alexander, and most of the wines are available from the sales and tasting area on the mezzanine floor of the winery with its dramatic views of the surrounding countryside.

Heathcote Winery

The Heathcote Winery is a high-tech establishment behind an authentic 1850s miners' store facade in the main street of Heathcote, a pleasing small town on the confluence of the Northern and McIvor Highways 110 km north of Melbourne. It was established in 1982 by local veterinarian Dr Kenneth Tudhope and his wife Doris, who in 1978 had planted some 16 hectares of vines on their property 7 km south of the town.

Grape varieties are chardonnay, pinot noir, traminer, chenin blanc and viognier. Winemaker Peter Florance produces a stylish range of wine which includes very good chardonnay and a wood-matured chenin blanc. Reds include pinot noir, shiraz, cabernet, and a shiraz and cabernet blend. For many years the Heathcote area was a source of grapes for a number of wineries and for enthusiastic home winemakers in Melbourne, particularly those of Italian extraction. Now, however, there are several wineries there which are showing that the area has quite a distinct and very pleasing regional style of its own, and one we will be hearing a lot more about.

Huntleigh Vineyard

Leigh Hunt, a Melbourne stockbroker, was one of a number of wine enthusiasts inspired to try winemaking himself by Bendigo pharmacist-turned-vigneron Stuart Anderson. In the 1970s Leigh began looking for some land in the Bendigo area to grow vines, eventually buying 24 hectares in Tunnecliff's Lane, 8 km north of Heathcote, in 1975. During the next few years he planted just over 5 hectares of traminer, cabernet sauvignon (which now includes some small patches of merlot and cabernet franc), Rhine riesling and shiraz.

While his vines were maturing he did a few vintages with Stuart Anderson at Balgownie and a couple of courses at Riverina College, and made his first wine, Huntleigh cabernet sauvignon, in 1979. Ten years later, he said, it still tasted like a young wine. He now makes two white wines, Rhine riesling and a traminer which he ferments quite dry and which is most impressive with its spicy odours and flavours. He makes a typically peppery Heathcote shiraz, and his cabernet now includes about 5 per cent of merlot and cabernet franc. Production is small, and sold at cellar door and by mail order.

Jasper Hill Vineyard

Located just north of Heathcote in the foothills of the Great Dividing Range are the two separate vineyards of Jasper Hill, Georgia's Paddock and Emily's Paddock. They are named after Ron and Elva Laughton's daughters, and indeed Jasper Hill has been a family business since plantings began in 1976. Shiraz is the main variety, with much smaller plantings of Rhine riesling, cabernet franc and sauvignon blanc. Jasper Hill shiraz has certainly made a name for itself since the first commercial wines were made in 1982. Jasper Hill Georgia's Paddock shiraz, for instance, was judged best red wine at the Exhibition of Victorian Winemakers three years in a row from 1985.

The red gravelly soil, elevation and natural rainfall in the area produce low yields; but the grapes have a naturally low pH and produce soft, full-flavoured and elegant wines. To conserve what rainfall there is, Ron Laughton mulches his vines using natural weed growth. None of his 15 hectares is irrigated.

By 1987 he and Elva had built a handsome, two-storey winery and were on the way to finishing their own mudbrick house when the 12 hectare Georgia's Paddock was devastated by bushfires which also destroyed 6 hectares of vines next door at Mount Ida vineyard. From being a seller of grapes (he had sold 30 tonnes in 1986 to help finance expansion), he had to become a buyer to get any volume of wine in 1987, and even a year after the fire it was not clear how many of his charred vines would regenerate.

Knight's Wines

Granite Hills is an appropriate name for the Knight family's vineyard in the Great Dividing Range at Baynton, 25 km east of Kyneton. It is a cold and blustery place where even sheep and cattle display heroic tendencies. In 1971 Gordon and Heather Knight planted an experimental patch of vines to see if viticulture might provide a hedge against the wild fluctuations in the livestock market at that time. This led to annual plantings of vines (the 1973–74 effort was lost to marauding locusts), until the current area of 6 hectares was reached, including Rhine riesling, shiraz, cabernet sauvignon, chardonnay, merlot and cabernet franc.

At 550 m above sea level Granite Hills is one of the most elevated vineyards in Australia, and this combines with its southerly latitude to ensure a very cool climate. This means in turn that vintage is late, from the end of April to mid-May, and even extends into June in particularly cool years. The advantage of fruit ripening in these cooler months of the year is that there is more time for the berry to develop fruit flavours in balance with sugar accumulation, and at the same time maintain a high natural acidity.

Fruit picked at this time of the year is also cool, typically between 6° and 10°, which means it is less susceptible to oxidation and spoilage. Rainfall averages 750 mm per year to which some supplementary watering is added. Because of the deep, well-drained granitic sandy loam soil and low humidity there is little frost and few mildew problems.

Small crops in 1975 and 1976 were made by neighbour Tom Lazar and went into his Virgin Hills red, and Gordon Knight made his 1978 vintage at Virgin Hills. His major piece of winemaking equipment at the time, said Gordon, was the telephone. In 1979 son Lew Knight returned after completing the winemaking course at Riverina College in Wagga Wagga and a year learning the ropes at Kaiser Stuhl in the Barossa Valley. He built a winery, and has guided the fortunes of Granite Hills ever since.

Gentle handling is the simple philosophy behind all of Lew's winemaking procedures. Hand-picked fruit ensures that only sound, intact bunches arrive at the winery, where an elevated crushing area allows grapes to be gently gravity-fed from bucket to press. During juice settling, fermentation and oak maturation, protection of fruit characters is paramount. As well as their own estate wines (Granite Hills cabernet sauvignon has been a consistent medal winner both inside Australia and out), Knights make wines from other vineyards, including a very fine Heathcote shiraz and Arthurs Creek chardonnay and semillon.

Like most others in the region he is particularly impressed by Heathcote shiraz, and its very marked pepper character. There are times, he says, when the smell of pepper seems to come up out of the crusher; it is a herbaceous character sometimes seen in cabernet sauvignon, but never as intensely as in shiraz. He thinks it probably comes from the amount of stress the vines grow under, conditions in which it is very windy and very cold, and the vines suffer considerable damage. 'It might be the soil, it might be cool-climate character, but when I smell it coming out of the crusher I know we have something special on our hands.'

Lancefield Estate

Lancefield is a small town in the gold-and-granite country which rises from the western side of the

Goulburn Valley with Mount Macedon in the south and Heathcote to the north. Some stately old buildings reflect its gold-rush wealth, and one of its oldest farming properties is now the home of one of an increasing number of vineyards, Lancefield Estate. Its first vines, chardonnay, were planted by Roger and Ann Hart in 1982, and they had a very small first vintage two years later. In the meantime they had planted pinot noir, traminer and merlot; eventually expanding the vineyard to some 6.5 hectares.

They began building a small winery in 1985, but the following year sold the property to Ann and Andrew Pattison, a couple of wine lovers who until then had been proprietors of the Troubadour Restaurant and Music House in the Melbourne suburb of Fitzroy. Andrew followed the Harts' example of buying in extra fruit from other vineyards in the area, and their wine was made with the help of Lew Knight, their neighbour at nearby Granite Hills. Production is continuing to expand as vineyard yield grows, and the former restaurateurs now supplement their incomes by providing picnic and barbecue meals at weekends and holidays.

Landragin Australia

Dominique Landragin has become something of a rarity in the Australian wine scene, a major producer without a vine of his own. He is one of the country's leading exponents of the *méthode champenoise* production of sparkling wine, and since 1989 he has been putting together a range of blended table wines which defy geographic definition. He is based in Victoria, at Mt Helen on the western outskirts of Ballarat, and many of the wines which go into his blends are Victorian. He is very much part of the Victorian wine-making scene, and has been ever since he left France in 1978 to become chief sparkling wine-maker at Seppelt's Great Western.

He was head-hunted by Seppelts, and for several good reasons. The company had been involved in sparkling wine production at Great Western since 1918, and by the mid-1970s had collared a very fair share of what was a growing Australian market. Other companies could see a bright future for the product, and Seppelts, in an effort to maintain their lead, had undertaken a widespread program in both winery and vineyard to ensure their No. 1 position could be kept. Dominique Landragin was an important single figure in the revolution, if that is indeed the word, and the company's continued dominance in the lucrative bubbly market seems to suggest that the choice was a wise one.

Dominique Landragin was a *Champenois*, descendant of Nicholas Landragin who began making champagne in the village of Verzenay in 1772. Dominique's grandfather was vineyard manager for Veuve Clicquot and his father, Pierre, worked for Veuve and for Heidsieck Monopole before establishing his own house, Champagne Landragin, in 1952. Dominique had worked for several companies in Champagne, including his father's, before being recruited by Bill Seppelt; and he and his wife Anna, and their two young sons, arrived in the blazing Australian summer of 1978.

For the next four years he oversaw the swing away from Irvine's white—the main champagne grape at Great Western (properly identified as ondenc)—to chardonnay and pinot noir, and the laying down of new cuvées which have seen Seppelts dominate the sparkling classes in Australian wine shows ever since. In 1982, he left what was Australia's largest 'champagne house' to help establish what was, at the time, the smallest. Ballarat businessman Ian Home had a dream to make an Australian sparkling wine comparable to the best in the world, and he poured money into a vineyard and winery at Smythesdale, 25 km south-west of Ballarat, which he called Yellowglen. Dominique Landragin became his winemaker and partner, and Yellowglen became very important very quickly on the Australian wine scene.

Despite his considerable commitments in Australia, Dominique returned to Verzenay each vintage to lay down the new cuvées of Champagne Landragin. He had been selling small amounts of the wine in Australia, and when his father died in 1985 he was faced with a dilemma. The Champagne house had been left to Dominique and Anna, and his sisters in Verzenay, Anna-Marie and Marie-Elizabeth. He was tempted to return to France, but as both he and Anna and their children had come to feel Australian, they decided to stay.

Dominique left Yellowglen in 1987 and set up his own premises near Ballarat, and began putting down blends for his own sparkling wine which he called Landragin Australia. He continued to sell Champagne Landragin from Verzenay, but the fall of the Australian dollar soon made the idea impractical. Not to be outdone he began to supplement his sparkling wine output with a range of Australian table wine, and in 1989 released Landragin Australia—chardonnay, Rhine riesling, shiraz, cabernet sauvignon and cabernets, a blend of cabernet sauvignon and cabernet franc.

The blend components come from a dozen different districts of southern Australia, and they are all assembled at Fareham Estate winery, in the Clare Valley of South Australia, before being brought to Mount Helen for maturing and distribution. Combined with the growing fortunes of the sparkling side of Landragin Australia it is an operation which will be watched with great interest.

Mount Aitken Estates

Mount Aitken, on the Calder Highway between Sunbury and Gisborne, is part of an expanding wine-producing business run by Roger and Ann McLean. They came to the area in 1974 already having vineyards of their own in McLaren Flat, in South Australia. They built a large winery and sales area which has now been expanded to include a functions room, restaurant, art gallery and port room.

The vineyard surrounding the winery contains 23 hectares of cabernet sauvignon, shiraz and trebbiano, although the emphasis is on cabernet which is bottled and sold under the Gisborne Cabernet label. In recent years they have also had a vineyard at Heathcote, and its wines have now been added to the extensive Mount Aitken range.

Mount Ida

Mount Ida is north of Heathcote and lies adjacent to Ron Laughton's Jasper Hill vineyard. It was established in 1976 by well-known artist Leonard French and his partner, Jim Munro. Len was fond of telling everybody that Mount Ida was there to make the only French wine in Australia. The grape varieties were cabernet sauvignon and shiraz, and in one corner of the 7 hectare vineyard there were small experimental patches of Rhine riesling and chardonnay.

The first vintage was in 1980, with a single

Mount Ida red made by Jeff Clarke at Tisdall. There was no supplementary watering in the vineyard so yields were always low; but the shiraz in particular displayed splendid Heathcote character, and the wine gained quite a following. The bushfire in January 1987 which devastated Jasper Hill also swept over Mount Ida, and no wine at all was made in 1987 or 1988. A single, solitary tonne of grapes was crushed in 1989, by which time Len and Jim had decided that perhaps Mount Ida was not a working proposition any more.

Tisdalls had always taken an interest in the vineyard, and had mentioned to Len French that if ever he decided to sell they would like first option. Decision time came in early 1989, and Mount Ida is now part of Tisdall operations. The plan is to regenerate the vineyard as much as possible, with new trellising and soil conditioning and so on, and to maintain Mount Ida as a separate label. Jeff Clarke has long been impressed by the quality of the Heathcote fruit, and although an option at the time of purchase was to install drip irrigation in an attempt to increase yield, the intensity of the fruit goes hand in hand with the difficult conditions, so watering will be undertaken only as a last resort.

Murrindindi Vineyards

The Cuthbertson family owned the farming and grazing property Murrindindi, off the Melba Highway between Yea and Yarra Glen, for many years before Hugh Cuthbertson persuaded his father, Alan, to plant vines. Hugh had done the marketing and oenology courses at Roseworthy College and was running the former Seabrook offshoot, Talavera, when the first Murrindindi vines were planted in 1979. There were 5 hectares of cabernet sauvignon, merlot, cabernet franc and chardonnay, and Hugh made the first wine in 1984. A further half hectare of sauvignon blanc was planted in 1986.

Production now is 400 cases of cabernet-based red each year, and the chardonnay is sold to Yellowglen as champagne material. The red is very intense, a long-living wine which has a very dedicated following of mail-order clients. Hugh Cuthbertson is now marketing director at Mildara.

Passing Clouds

Graeme Leith was a Melbourne electrical contractor who in the 1960s liked red wine so much he bought grapes from Mildura at the Victoria Market and made his own. In 1970 he and journalist Sue Mackinnon decided to quit the rat-race for a winemaking existence in the country, and they were particularly impressed by land around the township of Kingower, 60 km north-west of Bendigo. Blanche Barkly vineyard was by then up and running, and Graeme and Sue noted that the rich soil on the narrow creek flats had already been turned over and over by the questing goldminers of the 1860s.

The little Kingower valley, sheltered from northerly winds by hills of ironbark forest, seemed to offer the possibility of producing wine from unirrigated fruit of high quality, and they returned to Melbourne to read up on vine-growing and winemaking. A block of land near Kingower came up for sale in 1973 so they bought it, and during 1974–75 began planting what eventually became 7 hectares of vines, cabernet sauvignon, shiraz and pinot noir. It was a tough job, particularly during summer when a huge pile of nearby rocks known as Melville's Caves triggered thermals which seemed to split the banks of summer clouds. Graeme remarked wryly one day that they ought to call the place 'passing clouds'; so they did, and the name has stuck.

They persevered, however, and while the vines were growing Graeme Leith did several short courses at Riverina College and spent the vintage of 1975 at Laira, in Coonawarra. They had their first vintage in 1980, and since then have made some excellent wines; all of them red blends or varietals depending on the quantity and quality of their vines each year. The main wine is cabernet-shiraz, but in some years, and 1987 was one, there was enough shiraz to increase its share of the blend and this left sufficient material for a cabernet sauvignon, which was released in very limited quantities two years later.

Romsey Vineyards

Gordon Cope-Williams, an English-born architect, first planted grapes on Rocky Hill, a windswept series of extinct volcanoes just north

of Romsey and 15 km east of Mount Macedon, in 1977. He planted several hectares of pinot noir and chardonnay in the hope of making base material for a *méthode champenoise* wine, but conditions were so fierce and yields so low, that the dream never reached fruition. Gordon admitted he had learnt from his mistake, and in 1982 be bought a neighbouring dairy farm where he began planting small experimental patches of vines to see which varieties did best under varying conditions.

His painstaking work has paid off, and now he has 20 hectares of vines, predominantly pinot noir and chardonnay; with smaller plantings of sauvignon blanc, merlot, cabernet sauvignon and cabernet blanc. Ten hectares of pinot and chardonnay provide fruit for Domain Chandon's impressive new champagne operations in the Yarra Valley, and now Romsey wines are making their presence felt in their own right. Since 1984 Gordon has been making champagne base in his own winery from pinot and chardonnay, both of which show characteristics markedly different from elsewhere in Victoria.

The first Romsey *méthode champenoise* wine, 1984 chardonnay, was released in 1986; since then the base wines have included increasing amounts of pinot noir. The first release of the blended wine was in November 1987, coinciding with the official opening of the Cope-Williams's new house and a brand new cricket oval—cricket-mad Gordon's pride and joy. Romsey table wines are also making their presence felt. At the 1987 Ballarat Wine Show what was the first commercial chardonnay grown and made in the Macedon Ranges region won a gold medal and the La Scala trophy for the best Victorian white wine. The 1985 chardonnay was made from the first fruit from the 1982 plantings at Romsey, and since then the style, intense fruit and marked cool-weather character have continued to improve.

St Anne's Vineyard

St Anne's, situated eye-catchingly at Myrniong overlooking the Western Freeway which runs between Melbourne and Ballarat, is a successful wine-retailing business which exploits one of the busiest pieces of highway in the state. It is owned and run by Alan McLean and his wife Shirley, and is similar in operation to Mt Aitken Estates, run by Alan's brother Roger on the Calder Highway near Gisborne.

Some grapes are grown around St Anne's, which the McLeans established in 1971, however, most of their wine comes from McLaren Vale in South Australia. Although they sell two reds, cabernet sauvignon and shiraz, they tend to specialise in white wines, and have a large range of Rhine riesling in its various forms—botrytised, spatlese and sauternes. There is also a sauvignon blanc and a classic white blend, and a range of fortifieds including tawny port, muscat and tokay.

Virgin Hills

Years ago Melbourne restaurateur and man-about-town Tom Lazar complained that he couldn't find the wine he liked in Australia—so he decided to make his own. It wasn't an idle threat. While still running his renowned Lazar restaurant this Hungarian-born ex-sculptor and entrepreneur bought a property at Drummond, near Kyneton, on the basis of a promising report from the Victorian Department of Agriculture, and called it Virgin Hills.

Beginning the implementation of his dream in 1968 he planted 18 hectares of vines in the shaly, sandy loam soil; mainly to cabernet sauvignon with smaller amounts of shiraz, malbec and pinot noir. Some whites, chardonnay, Rhine riesling and traminer came later. He learned winemaking from books and a vintage at Redmans Wines in Coonawarra, and built a winery and then a large restaurant (which burnt down). The first vintage was in 1974 when he made a Bordeaux-style red which is still talked about with some awe; but his financial problems were such that two years later the property was bought by Melbourne hotelier,

Marcel Gilbert. Fortunately he retained Tom Lazar as winemaker, and some brilliant Virgin Hills wines were produced under the Lazar label.

In 1986 Tom Lazar left to establish another property at Emerald, in the Dandenong Ranges, and Mark Sheppard was appointed winemaker. He continues to make very characteristic Virgin Hills reds, which make up 90 per cent of production; and a single white wine, a chardonnay.

Water Wheel Vineyards

Water Wheel Vineyards was established in 1972 as a subsidiary of Water Wheel Flour Mills, whose water-driven turbine on the Loddon River at Bridgewater, 37 km north-west of Bendigo, gave the operation its name. This was a large and successful viticultural area last century before the arrival of phylloxera, so the Water Wheel plantings were part of a renaissance which has been remarkably successful.

Plantings on the 10 hectare block were basically to red varieties; cabernet sauvignon, ruby cabernet, cabernet franc, pinot noir, shiraz, and mondeuse. Interestingly enough, there was also a patch of very good Portuguese port varieties, including mourisco preto, tourssea, bastardo, touriga and souzao. In 1975 more cabernet sauvignon and shiraz was planted, and in 1977 Rhine riesling and chardonnay were added.

David von Saldern, German-born and a graduate in 1953 from the Weinsberg Wurttenburg wine college, joined the company in time to make its first wines in 1976, in an annexe of the flour mill. He designed his own winery which was ready for vintage in 1980, and since then has produced a range of wines both varied and variable.

To begin with there were two versions of cabernet sauvignon and hermitage (shiraz), private bin and 'standard'. All of them were characterised by deep flavours and marked varietal differences. They were rich, vinous wines which won a faithful following. The chardonnay, labelled 'pinot chardonnay', saw early blends which included 20 per cent Rhine riesling; but in more recent times the range has sorted itself out to the extent where there is hermitage, cabernet sauvignon, chardonnay, Rhine riesling and a rosé made from cabernet sauvignon. Naturally there are ports too; vintage port which is lighter in body and a touch more elegant than some of those we have been accustomed to from the Rutherglen district, and a liqueur port which is bottled after longer oak maturation.

Wildwood Vineyards

One of the newest of the Macedon region vineyards, and the closest to Melbourne, is Dr Wayne Stott's Wildwood, in St John's Lane, Bulla—just a short hop the other side of Tullamarine Airport. Dr Stott and his family planted the 3 hectare vineyard in 1984, and it produced its first commercial wines in 1988.

The main varieties are chardonnay, shiraz and the 'Bordeaux' reds—cabernet sauvignon, cabernet franc and merlot. These were the three wines made in 1988 and again in 1989. The chardonnay shows nice Nevers oak and apples and almond flavours, while the berry-flavoured shiraz displays vanillan American oak influence. The red blend also goes into new French oak; its medium-weight, complex mulberry flavours and long, elegant finish suggesting interesting things to come from Wildwood in the future.

Yellowglen

Yellowglen takes its name from an old goldmine which prospered during the Ballarat gold rush days of the 1860s, and again in the 1920s when rising gold prices made its drives worth re-exploring. Today, like many others in the area, the mine is flooded and unworkable, yet sur-

rounding mullock heaps are reminders of its glittering past. For some twenty years Yellowglen, at Smythesdale, 25 km south-west of Ballarat and 130 km west of Melbourne, has been the property of Ian Home, a wealthy Ballarat supermarket owner and operator.

In 1969 Mr Home began experimenting with vines on the property. Cabernet sauvignon, merlot, pinot noir and chardonnay were deemed worthy of attention while some poor plantings of shiraz, sylvaner and chenin blanc were done away with. Winemaker and consultant Neill Robb made the first Yellowglen wine in 1974, although the grapes were not from the property. This was a batch of sparkling wine made from chenin blanc and white hermitage (ugni blanc) grapes from around Avoca, and it was the precursor of the successful sparkling wine Yellowglen is now known for.

At around the same time Gary Farr, winemaker for Ian Home's friend Stuart Hooper at Bannockburn, made several Yellowglen reds from cabernet sauvignon and shiraz. By 1980 the decision had been made to concentrate on sparkling wines, and the vineyard began to reflect the needs of champagne-making. In 1981 Mr Home approached Dominique Landragin—who had been brought to Australia from Verzenay to make the sparkling wine at Seppelt's Great Western winery—for help in taking Yellowglen down the right path. Dominique left Seppelts and became a partner in the company in May 1982, taking charge of what at the time was a rarity in Australia—a vineyard and winery devoted to the creation of champagne.

He extended the vineyard to its present 18 hectares of pinot noir, pinot meunier and chardonnay; and Yellowglen wine, made by the authentic *méthode champenoise*, had an enormous impact on the Australian market. In 1984 the company was taken over by Mildara Wines Ltd, which appointed Ian Home as a director.

Dominique Landragin continued to make the wine until 1987, when he left to set up his own company, Landragin Australia. Yellowglen remains a specialist producer of sparkling wine, and an important part of the Mildara group. Winemaker Jeffrey Wilkinson produces a range of products, Non-vintage Brut, Cremant, Rosé and, since 1985, the very popular Cuvée Victoria which has been a prolific show medal winner.

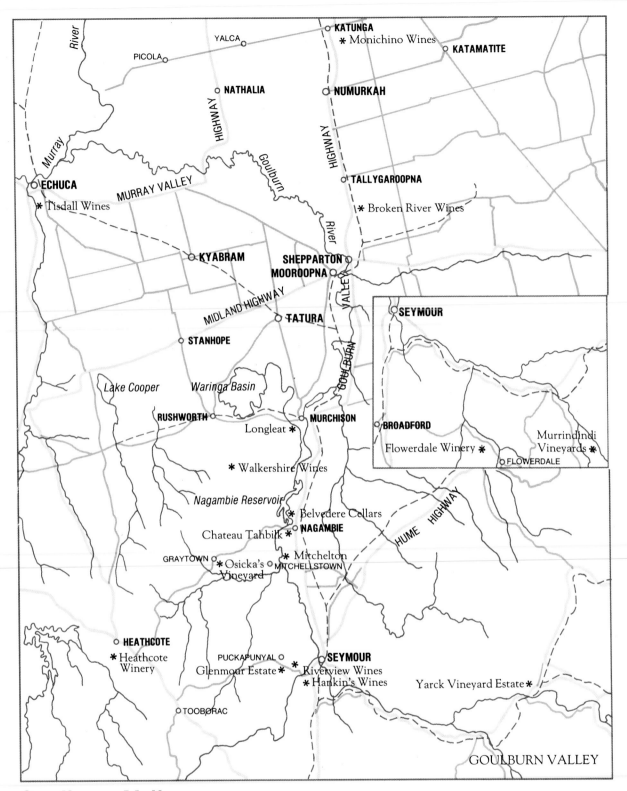

GOULBURN VALLEY

Goulburn Valley

The increasingly fruitful winemaking area of the Goulburn River Valley, 120 km north of Melbourne, covers a roughly triangular area through Seymour to Nagambie and Murchison, and across to Rushworth. To the north, there are several small vineyards near the busy rural centre of Shepparton. The valley was first explored by Major Thomas Michell in 1836. He described the area as 'ready for the plough in many parts, as if specially prepared by the Creator for the industrious hands of Englishmen'. Grazing flourished there, and grapegrowing became popular in the 1850s.

The predominant name over the years in the Goulburn Valley has been Chateau Tahbilk, but the development of the very impressive Mitchelton estate since 1969, and the growth of some small-to-medium-sized wine 'boutiques' has seen the beginning of a new era for this beautiful part of Central Victoria.

The Goulburn River itself, fed by tributaries coming down from the Great Dividing Range, flows into picturesque Nagambie Lake and then, via Goulburn Weir, into the Murray River near Echuca. The climate, the soils and the availability of water make the valley a natural for grapegrowing, and it shares much with many of Australia's famous valleys of wine. The wines are generally full-flavoured and full-bodied, with a unique Goulburn quality—a richness which aptly reflects the sun and the circumstances.

Belvedere Cellars

Nagambie is a pretty little town on the Goulburn Valley Highway about 22 km north of Seymour, with Lake Nagambie curled around its western side. The Hotel Tabilk in the main street is owned these days by the Purbricks of Chateau Tahbilk. A few kilometres away to the south-west, and on the left-hand side as you leave town heading north to Murchison, is a neat cream-brick house and winery salesroom known as Belvedere Cellars.

Between the highway and the Goulburn River lie 2.5 hectares of vines planted about twenty years ago and now owned in partnership by David Traeger. Traeger is one of the bright young winemakers who helped rescue Mitchelton, Chateau Tahbilk's modern neighbour, from financial collapse more than a decade ago. As an employee of Mitchelton, David Traeger was interested in what else was happening in that stretch of the Goulburn Valley, and in 1986 he bought a share of Belvedere, and started making wine there as an interest in the future.

At the same time, he was setting up a winery of his own at Riverview in Seymour (see Riverview Wines), and therefore what promises to be a considerable personal stake in these southern reaches of the Goulburn Valley. Belvedere, he says, is hardly a viable proposition on its own with an annual crush of 20–25 tonnes, but its very presence is an incentive to other growers and producers and an added tourist attraction to Nagambie itself.

The vines are predominantly shiraz and cabernet sauvignon, with a small patch of ries-

ling, semillon and marsanne. At cellar door it is possible to buy a nice fruity dry red at a few dollars per bottle for a very pleasant house wine, or something altogether more sophisticated. Belvedere shiraz, cabernet and merlot is an excellent blend (the merlot bought in from nearby); but David's best wines there are Belvedere Shiraz and Belvedere Cabernet Sauvignon—full-bodied, ripe fruit wines with a touch of elegance.

Broken River Wines

For a number of years Frank Dawson had been growing grapes in his vineyard at Lemnos, 8 km east of Shepparton, and selling them to other winemakers. In 1988 he decided to establish a label of his own, and enlisted the help of two well-known winemakers in the district, Jeff Clarke of Tisdall and David Traeger, formerly of Mitchelton and now running Belvedere, in Nagambie.

In 1988, Jeff made a cabernet franc, the first Broken River dry red, which went straight into new American oak. In 1989, David made three wines—a light red, also from cabernet franc, but made by the carbonic maceration process; a light Frascati-style dry white from chenin blanc; and an aromatic dry white made from chenin blanc and chardonnay. The quality of Frank Dawson's fruit and of these early wines suggest that Broken River is a name to watch for.

Chateau Tahbilk

In 1971, not long after Alister Purbrick had finished matriculation, his parents gave him a party at home and posed the traditional question, 'What do you want to do now?' Being a Purbrick of Tahbilk, he didn't have to consider the matter for long. 'How about being a winemaker?' he replied. 'What do I have to do?' By coincidence his parents had already booked him into Roseworthy Agricultural College and had the enrolment papers all ready there for him to sign!

In the event, he was very happy to go off to Roseworthy College, and he graduated with his Diploma of Oenology in 1975. He went to work for Mildara at Coonawarra during the next two vintages, taking over the family reins at Chateau Tahbilk in 1978, a third-generation winemaker in charge of an historic property which has almost become a Victorian institution.

Chateau Tahbilk is undoubtedly one of the

most picturesque wineries and cellars in Australia. The pride of the Goulburn Valley, it is situated 130 km north of Melbourne and 8 km from the town of Nagambie. The name is derived from a place on the Goulburn River local Aborigines called 'tabilk tabilk' meaning 'a place of many waterholes'. The nearby township is known as Tabilk, and why the Chateau added the extra 'h', no-one really knows.

In 1840, the Manton brothers took up land on the Goulburn River in an area known as Carrick O'Shannesy, and Tabilk was their head station. The huge property was acquired in 1842 by John Purcell and Henry Moore, and in 1852 Hugh Glass, then one of the largest landowners and richest men in Australia, became Purcell's partner. In 1856 the Pre-emptive Right was declared and Glass and Purcell split up, with Glass taking the southern portion of the property which included Tabilk.

Chateau Tahbilk's Cellars near Nagambie.

In 1859, Glass appointed a young Frenchman from Burgundy, Ludovic Marie, as his manager. Marie was well known locally; he owned the general store and ran a ferry service across the Goulburn. Marie planted some grapes, and then convinced Hugh Glass and others that the soil and the climate in their part of the valley were highly suitable for viticulture. On 16 March 1860 the Goulburn Vineyard Proprietary Company was formed with the intention of buying nearby Noorilim Estate to develop as vineyards; the sale fell through, however, with the death of its owner, Andrew Sinclair.

On 6 June 1860 a new company was formed, Tabilk Vineyard Proprietary, with Richard Horne as secretary and Ludovic Marie as manager. An important addition to the board was John Pinney Bear, a rich English gentleman-farmer who proposed the grand idea of placing an advertisement for one million vine cuttings six times in each of the major newspapers in Victoria, New South Wales and South Australia.

On 1 August 1860 the new company, with a capital of £25 000, took over 258 hectares of the Tabilk run, which had been purchased from Hugh Glass at £5-10 per acre. Under the supervision of Bear, 60 hectares of the land was cleared and 26 hectares planted with vines by the end of that historic year. To John Pinney Bear goes the title of first vigneron of Tahbilk, but in fact the honour of planting the first vine went to itinerant man of letters Richard Henry Horne, an Englishman known in the colony variously as Orion and O'Ryan Horne. Although there was no wine, large vaulted underground cellars were built in 1860, and remain in perfect condition to this day.

Ludovic Marie left in 1862, but planting and clearing went on under the control of Bear, who gradually bought out the other shareholders until he owned the whole company in 1877. In 1875 the so-called New Cellars were built, 100 m long extensions designed by Melbourne architect W.A. Zeal, which took storage capacity to some 900 000 litres of wine. A bulge in one corner appeared to endanger the new building, but more than a century later still had suffered no ill effects. To mark the opening of the new cellars a bottle each of 1875 dry red and dry white were sealed in the wall. They were removed in 1947: the red was still in good condition.

Chateau Tahbilk's old winery.

By 1876 the annual vintage was about 315 000 litres, and by 1890, fifty hogsheads a month were being exported to London. Between 1881 and 1888 the winery won fifteen awards in national and international competitions. By then it had become known as Chateau Tahbilk, with its mysterious 'h', and in 1887 François de Coueslant was appointed manager. Copies of letters he wrote as manager give an excellent picture of daily life at the time; he was a far-sighted man, very interested in experimentation, and he put several of his novel ideas into operation.

He planted olive trees, for instance, with the idea of establishing an olive oil industry; and he planted a double row of mulberry trees along the drive leading to the homestead in the vain hope of raising silkworms. The handsome trees remain, and so does the splendid tower (renovated in 1989), which it is believed de Coueslant erected, and which still adorns the labels of Chateau Tahbilk wines.

John Pinney Bear died in 1889 while in his mid-sixties, after an association with Chateau Tahbilk of more than a quarter of a century. Not only had he seen the establishment of the vineyards, he also witnessed the destruction of all but 55 hectares of them by phylloxera. These were planted on moist, sandy soil which pro-

tected them; seven rows of these original shiraz vines have been left to this day for sentimental reasons.

The remaining vines, particularly riesling, were badly affected, but little grafting or replanting was done. Yields declined but no fertilisers were used. Not long after Bear's death, de Coueslant decided the time had come to leave, and the property went into a long period of decline. It was still owned by Bear's widow, who lived in London until her death in 1925 at the age of ninety-two. By then the area under vine was just 46 hectares, and the combined vintages of the four previous years was just half of that recorded in a single year in the 1880s.

The vineyard came on the market in 1925 and was bought by Reginald Purbrick, then Conservative member for Walton in the House of Commons and father of Eric Purbrick, Alister Purbrick's grandfather. Eric was born in Sydney and educated at Melbourne Grammar, and was called to the Bar of the Inner Temple in 1929 after graduating in law from Jesus College, Cambridge, four years earlier. While on holiday in Germany in 1929 he decided to take up his mother's suggestion that he go to Australia and manage Chateau Tahbilk. He arrived in 1931, with no previous winemaking experience, in time to preside over vintage at a rundown winery going through a period of acute economic depression.

He applied himself energetically to learning the new business and its rehabilitation; reading books, listening to the winemaker at the time, a man called McDonald, and to such eminent personalities as T.C. Seabrook and François de Castella. De Castella, the Victorian Government Viticulturist, advised improvement of the soil by deep and early winter ploughing, winter irrigation and manuring, and the replacement of phylloxera-infected vines with grafted rootstocks.

De Castella had faith in the place and so did Tom Seabrook, who asked if he could become agent for Chateau Tahbilk wines, having just two years previously declined the honour because of what he regarded as the inferior quality of the wine. Eric Purbrick himself worked hard at selling, getting one shilling and twopence a gallon for bulk wine delivered to Melbourne, and driving around Victoria in a truck selling direct to the wine bars.

In 1936 most of the old homestead was pulled down, and the well-known architect, Sir Roy Grounds, designed a fine new one. Purbrick added to the atmosphere by erecting a large wrought-iron sign, copied from an eighteenth-century sign he had seen in the Black Forest of Germany, above the main entrance to the cellars.

In 1955 Eric's son, John, took over running the farming side of the property, leaving his father free to concentrate on winemaking. In 1959 the cellars were classified by the National Trust as being of historic and architectural interest, and in 1960, at the celebration of the centenary of Chateau Tahbilk, the then Prime Minister of Australia, Sir Robert Menzies, entombed two bottles of wine for future generations.

These days there are 85 hectares under vine on the 1120 hectare property, planted to shiraz, cabernet sauvignon, marsanne, Rhine riesling, semillon, chardonnay, sauvignon blanc and chenin blanc. Soils vary from sandy loams to grey alluvial types and the presence of the Goulburn River adds subsoil moisture. Rainfall is about 560 mm a year, and vines are irrigated only when young. Older vines are not irrigated, but average yields are still around 10 tonnes per hectare.

A great Tahbilk tradition lives on in the way red wines are made. The crushed juice is run into waxed concrete tanks where it ferments under header boards. When fermentation is complete the wine goes into old casks (although some new oak has been added in recent years) to mature for as long as necessary in the New Cellars (built in 1875). Alister Purbrick believes this is the way to make long-living wines. Obviously there is no oak extraction from the old casks, but he says there is slight oxidation which helps the cabernet sauvignon, in particular, to develop its own complexity. Over the years Chateau Tahbilk cabernets have become one of the quality benchmarks in Australian wine, so the winemaker has to be believed.

White winemaking, on the other hand, is much more modern in concept. In 1978–79 a new white wine fermenting cellar was built to house such paraphernalia as must coolers and temperature and pressure-controlled steel fermenters. This is the home of Tahbilk chardonnay, chenin blanc, Rhine riesling, semillon and marsanne—all of which are treated differently, although they begin life in the same way. The juice is chilled to around 5°C and filtered before fermentation; then comes variation in the time the juice is left on the skins and whether fermentation is in oak or steel. Riesling and chenin blanc tend to go into stainless steel, for instance, whereas chardonnay, semillon and marsanne are fermented in oak.

Over the years Tahbilk has produced some of Australia's greatest reds, both shiraz and cabernet. The 'private bins' stand out, but the standard wines have also been remarkably consistent—always with an elegant fineness and potential for considerable life. With the introduction of new technology the whites have also had remarkable success for what has traditionally been seen as a red wine region, with Gold Label Marsanne, in particular, standing out.

Flowerdale Winery

Melbourne businessman Peter Geary bought what was to become Flowerdale Winery on the Yea Road at Flowerdale, 80 km north of Melbourne, in 1976 as an investment–recreation property. He started planting vines in that same year, and eventually there were 2 hectares of chardonnay, traminer, chenin blanc and a small patch of pinot noir.

David Wakefield looks after the vines, and the wines are made each year at Delatite by Ros Ritchie. The three whites are made as varietals, but the pinot noir has proved less successful and is only made in good years. The average crush is about 8 tonnes. Flowerdale whites have made quite a name for themselves, their character reflecting the geographic position of the town midway between the Goulburn and Yarra Valleys.

David Wakefield says the soil is not as good as in the valleys, which means lower yields, but he is convinced that it is a good viticultural region and in 1989 he was in the process of planting a vineyard of his own just a few kilometres away. The wines are sold mainly at cellar door, and through local hotels and wine stores.

Glenmour Estate

Frank Deak's Glenmour Estate is one of a number of small vineyard properties in the Goulburn

Valley north of Seymour which were originally part of the Fitzpatrick estate. A neighbour in Johnsons Lane, Northwood, is Dr Max Hankin, who also took over Fitzpatrick vines to establish Hankins Wines.

In 1986 Mr Deak was looking for some recreational land in the Goulburn Valley and by chance came across the 20 hectares which is now Glenmour Estate. About half of the land was planted to malbec, mataro, crouchen and trebbiano, and there was a patch of carignan which rapidly succumbed to vine die-back disease.

The rest of the vineyard was in pretty poor shape, but in 1986 enough malbec was picked to make the very first Glenmour Estate red. Since then a lot of time and effort has gone into rehabilitating the property. A lot of the Fitzpatrick vines had been planted on ungrafted rootstocks and a patch of phylloxera was found on the property. This has been isolated and all new plantings have been with grafted vines. Shiraz, cabernet sauvignon and chardonnay were due to be planted in 1989–90.

The wines are made by Alister Purbrick at Chateau Tahbilk, and there are four of them. Malbec is made and bottled as a straight varietal, and mataro goes into a light red style known as Bin 121. A dry white is made from crouchen and trebbiano and in most years a spatlese crouchen is also made. Overall production in 1989 was around 20 000 bottles, and about half of the grapes were sold to Chateau Tahbilk and Mitchelton.

Goulburn Valley Winery

This is quite an historic property in the heart of Shepparton's shopping district, having produced and sold wine since 1908 when it was founded by the Alexander family. It went through some troubled times more recently, closing in 1950 then reopening when Don Phillips bought it in 1979.

With no vineyard of his own, Don has bought grapes from various north Goulburn growers; most recently from Frank Dawson, now proprietor of his own Broken River winery at Lemnos, 8 km from Shepparton; and from another grower on the Shepparton–Dookie road. Given the size of the premises, now surrounded by supermarkets, production is small, with 12

tonnes crushed in 1989. The wine, however, is consistently good. In 1987 a shiraz–cabernet made by Peter Hayes, then a lecturer at Dookie Argricultural College (and in 1989 appointed Victorian Government Viticulturist), won a gold medal in the Victorian Wine Show at Seymour. In 1989 Don Phillips made the wine himself with the help of government oenologist Drew Noon, and it is typical of the Goulburn Valley, with full, ripe fruit flavours and plenty of staying power.

Hankin's Wines

Dr Max Hankin is a general practitioner and a partner in the Thomastown Clinic in the western Melbourne suburb of Lalor. In 1975 he bought part of the Fitzpatrick Estate at Northwood, a little settlement in the Goulburn Valley between Seymour and Nagambie, where distinguished neighbours are Chateau Tahbilk and Mitchelton. The Fitzpatricks, it might be remembered, were the Melbourne liquor wholesalers who, during the wine boom of the 1960s, set about establishing what was planned to be the largest red wine vineyard in Australia. The scheme ended with the property being broken up, and Dr Hankin was one of several buyers—and beneficiaries.

Vines on the block were fairly well established when he bought the place, and he started making his own wine in 1977. It was trial and error to begin with, and Dr Hankin admits he had to pour as much down the drain as down people's throats in the early days. But he started picking up medals in the local Seymour Show, and by mid-1989 was considering giving up medical practice and retiring to full-time winemaking. He makes three wines: a very good cabernet sauvignon, shiraz and malbec blend; a straight shiraz; and a dry white which is a blend of semillon, sauvignon blanc and a little chardonnay. He also grows grenache, which he sells to Mitchelton for their Cab Mac.

Longleat

Johann Samuel Schulz was born in Prussia in 1819. He set sail for a new life in the colony of South Australia in the ship *Prince George*, arriving in Port Adelaide on 21 November 1838, just two years after the colony was proclaimed. By 1842 he had married and saved sufficient money

The Wines
of
LONGLEAT
GOULBURN VALLEY
CABERNET SAUVIGNON
1986
MURCHISON VINEYARD COMPANY,
OLD WEIR ROAD, MURCHISON, VICTORIA
750ml   PRODUCT OF AUSTRALIA   12.0% Alc/Vol

Longleat Vineyards lie in the Goulburn Valley of Central Victoria, some 150 kms north of Melbourne, Australia.

Established in 1975 by Peter Schulz, who was joined by his son Mark in 1979, the total Estate now occupies 100 acres.

This wine, made by Peter Schulz and Alister Purbrick, is produced from 100% estate grown Cabernet Sauvignon and made using the traditional Bordeaux approach with fermentation taking place in open oak vats, then a period of maturation in French Oak for 18 months prior to bottling.

The nose and palate exhibit typical "mint" fruit characters, whilst the finish is long and complex with an excellent balance of fine grape tannins and fresh acidity. This medium bodied wine will benefit with 5-6 years cellaring, during this time a natural fruit crust may form.

Analysis at bottling:
Alcohol: 12.0% Alc/Vol
Acid: 5.8 G/L
pH: 3.50
PRESERVATIVE (220) ADDED.

to buy a farm at Rowlands Flat in the Barossa Valley. He was soon joined in the area by fellow countryman Johann Gramp, who established the first vineyard in the Barossa at Jacob's Creek, and later by Bruno and Hugo Seppelt and Samuel Hoffman.

Johann Schulz developed an appreciation for wine which he passed on to his descendants; it found an outlet 150 years after his arrival in Australia, when Peter Schulz established Longleat 2 km south of Murchison in the heart of the Goulburn Valley. Peter had for some time been a good friend of the Purbricks at nearby Chateau Tahbilk, and in 1975 he and his wife Jenny and their son Mark, decided to replant what had been old vineyard country right on the banks of the Goulburn River.

They planted 6 hectares of shiraz, cabernet sauvignon, Rhine riesling and semillon, and in 1981 made their first wines with the help of Alister Purbrick. Peter Schulz is now winemaker, and Longleat produces three estate-grown wines each year: a medium- to full-bodied shiraz with good peppery fruit character; cabernet sauvignon, a deep and complex wine with minty fruit character; and a delicate, medium-bodied Rhine riesling. They buy in grapes from elsewhere in the Goulburn Valley for both red and white table wines. In 1987 they began developing a vineyard in the King Valley, in north-east Victoria, where they planted sauvignon blanc, chardonnay and pinot noir.

McIvor Creek Winery

McIvor Creek vineyard was established by Jim Hopcroft and Alan Gould in 1973 just to the south of Heathcote on the Heathcote to Nagambie Road. In 1985 it was bought by Peter

and Robyn Turley, and now it is a most attractive property with a local stone winery, tasting room and barbecue facilities. It is also producing some very fine wine.

Peter Turley comes from a long line of winemakers. His mother's side of the family were McWilliams, and after graduating from college Peter worked for several years in the Griffith district of New South Wales. He decided 'the big side of the business' was not for him, so he and Robyn bought McIvor Creek and immediately set about expanding the vineyard and winemaking facilities.

They now have 6 hectares of vines, cabernet sauvignon, merlot and cabernet franc, and in 1989 crushed 100 tonnes of fruit. They buy in grapes from other growers in the area, mainly shiraz but also some white grapes, Rhine riesling and sauvignon blanc. In 1989 they made an auslese from botrytised Rhine riesling brought from Griffith.

Their own vineyard is heavy clay over sandstone and, given the fairly harsh climatic conditions in the area, yields have traditionally been low. In 1989 drip irrigation fed by three dams on the property was used for the first time. Peter is very conscious, however, of the link between yield and quality, and watering will be carried out only when the vines are stressed. He believes, nevertheless, that yield could be doubled to about 7 tonnes per hectare without affecting quality.

As well as the whites he makes each year from bought-in grapes, Peter makes three McIvor Creek reds: cabernet sauvignon, cabernet–shiraz, and cabernet sauvignon–merlot–cabernet franc. They are all excellent wines with the great depth of character which is now becoming a Heathcote regional trademark. Most of production is sold at cellar door.

Mitchelton

Mitchelton is a remarkable property which is producing some remarkable wines. It was one of the newer large developments in Victoria, established as much as a tourist attraction as a winery. After some extremely difficult years, during which it all but foundered, it recovered to the point where it is undoubtedly a great credit to all involved.

In the 1960s Melbourne businessman Ross

Mitchelton Winery, Nagambie.

Shelmerdine had the multi-million dollar dream of making a top vineyard and winery the focal point of an entertainment complex designed to attract visitors in their hundreds of thousands. In 1969, on the advice of Colin Preece, Laradoc Pty Ltd—the pastoral company owned by the Shelmerdine family—bought 200 hectares of land at Mitchellstown, near Nagambie, with 5.5 km frontage to the Goulburn River. There they planted about 92 hectares of vines, mainly cabernet sauvignon and shiraz, to make red wine and trebbiano for sparkling wine.

In 1969 plans were drawn up for the winery and tourist facilities, and no money was spared in building what today remains one of the most extraordinary properties in Victoria. The winery was built in 1973 along heroic lines. Massive red-brick cellars even more like the catacombs of Rome than Colin Preece's famous champagne drives at Great Western extended a couple of hundred metres underground, and even contained a small chapel. The following year the tourist facilities were completed: a massive, four-storey tower which beams over the Goulburn Valley riverflats like a lighthouse; cellar door sales area; two restaurants; swimming pool; wildlife sanctuary; aviary; riverside barbecues—enough to make an Antipodean Walt Disney green with envy.

No sooner were things in place than misfortune followed misfortune. The river rose and flooded the cellars; phylloxera made an unwelcome reappearance in the vineyard; the wine boom flattened and the tourists stayed away in droves. Mitchelton went into receivership after the Victorian Economic Development Corporation wrote off its $332 000 investment in the venture; but 1979 proved a turning point. Consultants—Oentec—were called in to replan the winery complex, which in 1980 was taken over by the well-known Valmorbida family of merchants and businessmen. Laradoc retained ownership of the vineyard, and viticulturist Ian Watson put in a lot of hard work re-establishing phylloxera-affected areas.

Now there are about 104 hectares; the main

Michelton Vineyards in the Goulburn Valley.

varieties are marsanne, semillon, Rhine riesling and cabernet. Some trebbiano and shiraz remain and there is also some chardonnay. The quality of the fruit gives winemaker Don Lewis plenty to work with. About 1000 tonnes are crushed each vintage, with extra fruit and extra must coming from as far afield as Western Australia and South Australia.

Mitchelton wines come as white varietals, Rhine riesling, wood-matured marsanne and wood-matured chardonnay; and red varietals, shiraz, cabernet sauvignon, and in recent years Print Label cabernet sauvignon–merlot, a premium blend whose label bears the winning entry in what is now the annual Mitchelton print competition. Also under the heading of red varietal comes Cab Mac, the remarkable carbonic-maceration wine originally made under licence from the Hickinbotham family.

There is also a very good secondary range of wines under the Thomas Mitchell label, named after the explorer who crossed the Goulburn in 1836 near where the winery now stands. It varies from year to year, but includes good blended red and white table wines at most reasonable prices. Both Mitchelton and Thomas Mitchell wines have been prolific medal winners during the past decade and doubtless there will be plenty more to come.

Monichino Wines

Carlo Monichino was eighteen years old when he left his home near Asti in northern Italy to come to Australia in 1949. He arrived in Melbourne on a grey day in the liner *Sebastiano Cabot*. With a group of friends he met on the boat, he hopped on the train at Spencer Street station and four days later arrived at Ingham, in north Queensland, where he began work as a sugarcane cutter. Carlo worked and saved hard, and in 1962 had enough money to buy a fruit block in the Goulburn Valley near Katunga, 8 km on the Goulburn Valley Highway beyond Numurkah.

Remembering his origins in the distinguished wine-growing country of Piedmont (the Piemonte region), Carlo Monichino enlisted the help of the local Department of Agriculture office when he decided to plant vines alongside his peach trees, and was advised to put in some shiraz for wine, and some gordo for the table. By 1969 the stone-fruit industry had entered a decline, but the vines had prospered. Carlo looked around for better varieties, eventually replacing his peaches with cabernet sauvignon, mataro, brown frontignac and the Californian hybrid, rubired.

Rubired was chosen because of its natural resistance to phylloxera but, although it had good yields in the Goulburn Valley, it had little flavour. Mataro was also unsuitable, so Carlo replaced them both with sauvignon blanc and traminer, then added some semillon and malbec. Eventually he had 15 hectares under vines, including orange muscat, chardonnay and riesling; and he produced a wide range of varietal and blended table wines, with skill and a great deal of verve.

Carlo turned his packing shed and chilling room into a winery with such modern touches as fruit and must chilling and cold stabilisation. Using a disused milk tank he made a refrigerated crusher which could be towed around the vineyard to minimise oxidation. He began fermenting some of his chardonnay in small oak, and called Balgownie's Stuart Anderson in to look at his reds, cabernet sauvignon and malbec, and at his early, intense, Rutherglen-style vintage ports.

His white wines are deceptively delicate for such conditions, yet never lacking in verve and flavour. Carlo Monichino may be a long way from Asti but his dedication to the production of good wine has never wavered.

Osicka's Vineyard

The Osicka family came to Australia from Czechoslovakia in 1955 and settled at Graytown, 24 km west of Nagambie. Paul Osicka's forbears had been vignerons for generations, so it was natural enough that he should plant vines and make a living from wine. With his wife and son, also Paul, he began planting what is now known as Major's Creek Vineyard, some 20 hectares of shiraz, cabernet sauvignon, Rhine riesling and chardonnay.

Early vintages were made in rather a rough shed, but eventually a hand-made brick winery, with arched bottle storage area, was built into the side of a hill—allowing it to remain at a cool and even temperature throughout the year. In fact at Graytown, which is really nothing more than a name on the map, cool-climate and natural rainfall conditions enable slow ripening, although frosts can be a serious problem. In 1978 frost destroyed almost the entire vintage. On the other hand, the sandy Goulburn Valley loam there has probably been a factor in protecting the vineyard from phylloxera.

In the early years the Osicka wines were sold in bulk; one fine wine was bottled by Crittenden's in the early 1960s, and others found their way onto Melbourne palates via such places as Jimmy Watson's wine bar. Since 1973 most of it has been released under Osicka's own label. The Osicka reds, shiraz and cabernet sauvignon with some malbec, have been compared in style with those of nearby Chateau Tahbilk. Certainly they have plenty of regional character and ageing potential. Osicka Vintage Port is also a skilfully made wine, winning its class in the Rutherglen Show three years in a row.

Riverview Wines

The Australian wine industry is littered with broken dreams, and today Riverview Wines, on the southern fringe of Seymour, 100 km north of Melbourne on the Hume Highway, is what is left of several of them. It had its beginnings in the wine boom of the 1960s, when the Fitzpatrick brothers, Melbourne liquor merchants and businessmen, established a venture they called Glengariffe Wines, with a number of what at that stage were experimental vineyards scattered around the southern reaches of the Goulburn Valley.

The vineyards and a modern winery built in Emily Street, Seymour (it was the Hume Highway at the time), were to be at the heart of a $4.5 million project not dissimilar to that taking place at the time further north at Mitchelton. In this case, the funds never materialised. Brian Fitzpatrick, who was also an architect, was involved in an oil search venture with cut-price petrol millionaire Ian Sykes in the nervous days preceding the mining market collapse in 1970. When the crunch came it was Glengariffe, among other interests, which went to the wall.

At the time, Maurice Bourne specialised in company restructuring and debenture lending, and when Glengariffe collapsed he found himself with a debenture over wine held in containers owned by a finance company. It was, he recalled later, a situation straight out of the Merchant of Venice: 'Spill not a drop of my wine!' More than $1 million was needed to keep the place operating, so Maurice Bourne, with no more than the average drinker's knowledge of wine, decided to take over the place himself. With the 1976 vintage on his hands, he hired winemaker Ian Deacon and called the venture Seymour Vineyards.

At the time there were three vineyards: Chinaman's Garden (where Chinese had grown vegetables during the gold rush), on the Hume Highway at Seymour; Northwood, some 5 km north, on the Goulburn River; and Keay's Flat, low land behind the winery itself. Ian Deacon left in 1979 to be replaced by Californian Jim Clendenen. Eventually Maurice Bourne took over the winemaking himself with the help of experts from Riverina College in Wagga Wagga. He won a gold medal for his 1981 cabernet sauvignon at the Melbourne Wine Show the following year.

In the meantime, the Northwood block had been sold to Dr Max Hankin, and in 1987 Maurice Bourne decided it was time to retire, selling out to another doctor and a dentist. They hired consultant David Traeger, who had established a big reputation for his winemaking skills at Mitchelton, and renamed the place Riverview Wines. David spent the next two years re-equipping the winery with his own equipment, and the company is now a joint venture between himself and the owners.

There is a range of Riverview wines, but the best of recent vintages have been the 1987 Rhine riesling, which has a spicy, slightly botrytised green lime bouquet, and what David calls a lolly-sweet palate very well balanced with acid; and the 1987 shiraz, a smoky peppery wine with typical rich soft-berry character with prominent oak likely to soften with age. In 1988 there was also sauvignon blanc, typically grassy with pungent fruit aromas and crisp acidity on the end of the palate.

In addition to the Riverview crop, David Traeger crushed 350 tonnes of his own grapes at the winery in 1989. This will form the basis of his own label, which he was looking forward to releasing towards the end of 1990.

Tisdall Wines

Dr Peter Tisdall is an extraordinarily energetic man, and although he had a very busy general practice in Kyabram, in the rich Murray River dairy country in northern Victoria, he was always looking around for other things to do. He rejected the idea of setting up his own dairy herd, deciding that growing grapes and making wine would be much more creative and satisfying.

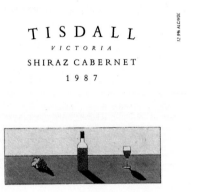

TISDALL
VICTORIA
SHIRAZ CABERNET
1987

750 ml

With this in mind he bought a large estate known as Rosbercon at Picola, in the Murray Valley, about 40 km north-east of Echuca, and in 1971 began planting 80 hectares of it to a variety of vines. Because of the warm and generally dry climate in the area the new vineyard was irrigated, and the first grapes were ready for harvest in 1975.

In 1974, while all this was going on, Dr Tisdall arrived at the view that future success in the wine industry in Australia would have two major components: cool-climate viticulture, and what was then the comparatively rare white wine variety, chardonnay. He began a search for a property where both could be drawn together. Eventually he bought what was known as Jackie Hollaway's scrub, 500 m up in the Strathbogie Ranges, near Avenal. The scrub was cleared, and planting began at Mt Helen in 1976.

In 1978, Dr Tisdall created something of a stir in the industry by luring outstanding young winemaker John Ellis away from Rosemount Estate in the Hunter Valley to Echuca, where his first task was to convert a disused milk factory into a winery. In fact there were certain similarities in making wine and preparing milk for market; lots of stainless steel, for instance, equipment for heating and refrigeration, and large tiled areas which had to be kept scrupulously clean.

The winery opened for business in vintage 1979 with the fruit coming from both Rosbercon and Mt Helen. Since then Tisdall wines have not only succeeded in terms of return for their owner and acclaim for their winemaker, but have also had a vital influence on the industry throughout Victoria. The Rosbercon wines showed that warm, irrigated areas did not necessarily have to produce poor quality, while those from Mt Helen, 120 km away, illustrated quite graphically the fine effects of cooler, later ripening conditions.

In 1983, Jeff Clarke, who had spent the previous four years at Penfolds in the Barossa Valley, joined Tisdall, becoming chief winemaker when John Ellis (who had talked science graduate Clarke into an oenology course several years before) decided in 1984 to buy and begin planting his own property further south at Hanging Rock. Clarke has maintained early standards remarkably well, and Tisdall's swag of show medals is steadily growing.

Today, the 80 hectares at Rosbercon are planted to cabernet sauvignon, merlot, malbec, shiraz, chardonnay, Rhine riesling, colombard, chenin blanc and sauvignon blanc. The wines made from these varieties are marketed as single or blended varietals (the exception being White Burgundy), and are sold under the Tisdall and Chairman's Selection Labels. Mt Helen vineyard is 45 hectares, planted predominantly to chardonnay, but also to pinot noir, merlot, cabernet sauvignon, sauvignon blanc, gewurztraminer and Rhine riesling. All appear under the Mount Helen label.

In 1989 Dr Tisdall increased his holdings with the purchase of Mt Ida vineyard at Heathcote in Central Victoria. Mt Ida, owned previously by Dr Jim Munro and the well-known artist Leonard French, was planted in 1976, and had its first vintage in 1980. The 8 hectares of excellent red volcanic soil were planted with shiraz and some cabernet sauvignon and, with the help of John Ellis and later Jeff Clarke, the harvest produced some excellent wines with fine regional character. The 1982 Mt Ida shiraz won a trophy for best regional red at the 1983 Victorian Wine Show at Seymour. The property was badly damaged by bushfire in 1987 and no wine at all was made that year or in 1988. It now fits very nicely into the Tisdall strategy of using the best possible Victorian fruit; shiraz was the only major variety it didn't produce for its own labels, and that gap has now been filled.

Among Tisdall's outstanding recent wines are: the 1986 Mt Helen cabernet sauvignon–merlot, winner of the Robert Bryce trophy at the 1988 Canberra Wine Show for the best dry red in commercial classes; the 1988 Mt Helen char-

donnay, an excellent example of cool-climate chardonnay, with good fruit flavour and delicate wood treatment; the 1988 Tisdall cabernet merlot, full of flavour and one of the best value-for-money reds on the market; and the 1989 Tisdall chenin blanc, fresh and crisp, with some sweetness, and also excellent value.

Walkershire Wines

John Walker, born in Yorkshire, arrived in Australia in 1972 after travelling overland from London to Perth. Delighted by the price of wine in Australia among other things, he decided to stay, and because he had been a builder he found himself with a foreman's job on the major Collins Place project in Melbourne. That job only lasted a couple of weeks before the development company folded, but by then he knew where he wanted to live. He had tasted some Chateau Tahbilk reds and visited the Goulburn Valley, and in 1975 he and his wife, Megan, started looking around for somewhere to plant a vineyard.

In 1976 they bought what was known as Grandma's Paddock from the Le Deux family at Bailieston, 144 km north of Melbourne and halfway between Nagambie and Rushworth. Old Le Deux had driven steam engines during the gold rush, and the family had owned a wine bar and two hotels in Bailieston. In 1860 his wife (Grandma) selected the 25.5 hectares which more than a century later was to become Walkershire. There the Walkers hand-planted 3.2 hectares of cabernet sauvignon, shiraz and a few rows of merlot. They produced their first vintage, a single red wine blend, in 1980.

In the meantime they had dug a site 12 m by 6 m into the side of a hill where eventually they built their small winery and sales area. In 1982 they decided to live on the property and added

another storey to the premises. John did the winemaking course at Riverina College by correspondence and his wines started picking up medals in local shows. In 1982 he won the trophy for the best varietal red wine at the Victorian Wine Show in Seymour and in 1984 the wine was also voted most popular red by visitors to the Exhibition of Victorian Winemakers in Melbourne.

He tends to pick his grapes late, often when the leaves on the vines have begun to fall, and fermentation is in open concrete tanks. After ten days or so the must is pressed and transferred into a settling tank and from there into Nevers oak casks. Megan does the bottling and labelling. The label of this fine Walkershire wine is emblazoned with the white rose of Yorkshire. They also make a port which they call LPF, for late-picked fortified.

Yarck Vineyard Estate

This small family business is situated in the foothills 4 km from the little town of Yarck, 145 km north of Melbourne on the Goulburn Valley Highway north of Seymour. It was first planted in 1969 by H.C. Henke in red gravel soil, the hills just high enough to be out of danger from spring frosts. There was cabernet sauvignon, shiraz, and small quantities of mataro and grenache for red wine; and semillon, crouchen, Rhine riesling and palamino for whites.

A large dam for supplementary watering was built in 1970, and a small winery and cellar in 1971. The first vintage was in 1974. Early Yarck wines had their share of show success, the 1977 shiraz–cabernet taking the top gold award in its class in the 1978 National Wine Show. Herb Henke retired in 1979, and his daughter Caroline and son-in-law Tim Miller took over the business. They completed work on the winery and cellar door sales area, and the vineyard is now 5 hectares of shiraz, cabernet sauvignon, semillon and crouchen. They concentrate on oak-matured reds, shiraz and cabernet and a blend of the two; and the wines are all good, full-bodied with well-balanced fruit and oak character.

Gippsland

Gippsland is the fertile heartland of eastern Victoria, the watershed of the Great Dividing Range and the Victorian Alps, home of the Latrobe Valley brown coal deposits which provide most of Melbourne's electricity. It is a beautiful stretch of country which extends from virtually the eastern outskirts of the city along the Princes Highway to the shores of the Tasman Sea. Last century there were important vineyards in the Maffra–Bairnsdale region of East Gippsland, and in the eastern escarpment of the Irish-green Strzelecki Range, which at first overlooks then skirts the southern fringes of the Latrobe Valley.

The renaissance began in 1970 when Pauline and Dacre Stubbs began planting Lulgra Vineyard (now known as Wyanga Park) near Lakes Entrance. This was followed in 1971 by Robert Guy's first efforts at Golvinda, near Lindenow. Since then, development has been a little slow and a little spasmodic. East Gippsland suffered droughts in the 1970s and 1980s which obviously had an effect on would-be vignerons; generally, however, there are large areas of Gippsland where soil and weather patterns suggest a good future for vines, and there is no doubt that here, as elsewhere in Victoria, wine will be a product to be seen more and more.

Given its size, it has enormous variations in soil types, rainfall, elevation, wind patterns and so on. Rainfall varies from 1250 mm in South Gippsland to just 450 mm at Seaspray, on the Ninety Mile Beach. Soils range from a deep red volcanic loam around Thorpdale (the colour, at least, rivals the famous 'terra rossa' strip of Coonawarra), to the highly leeched alluvial soil at Nicholson River, some of the oldest soil on the continent. The country around Lakes Entrance provides a benign, often warming maritime environment; whereas north winds, freezing in winter and burning hot in summer, can put any vineyard's survival at risk. Generalisations about Gippsland wines are not encouraged, therefore, and marked regional differences can be expected as the spread of vines continues.

Briagolong Estate

Briagolong Estate, as Gordon McIntosh calls his 16 hectare property, is in pretty country on the road from Briagolong to Valencia, 25 km from

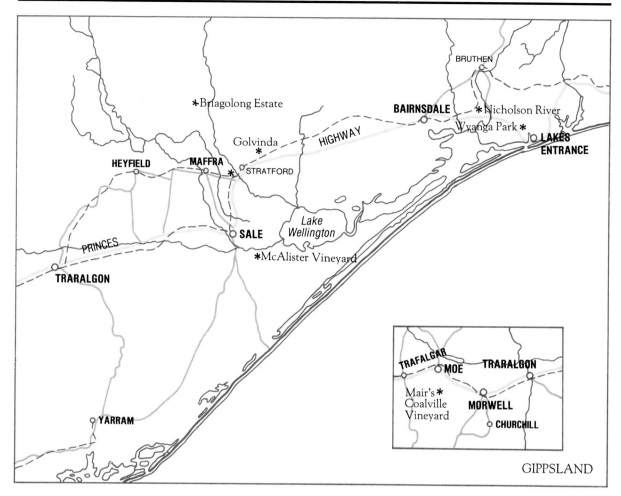

GIPPSLAND

Maffra where Dr McIntosh is in general practice. He bought the place in 1975 and planted 2 hectares of chardonnay and pinot noir. Word got around that he was going to specialise in champagne. In fact, he had in mind to make two wines, a red and a white, and that is what he has done since 1980, despite some awful weather and growing conditions which he believes make this one of the smallest and least productive vineyards in Australia.

'Briagolong' in local Aboriginal dialect means 'land of the rising sun', and Dr McIntosh admits his patch of clay over sandy loam gets more sun than other parts of Gippsland and ripens his grapes earlier than his neighbours at Sale and Bairnsdale. Nevertheless, he can't remember a vintage when the leaves on his vines were not already turning yellow, a symptom of dry-summer stress which he chooses not to alleviate with drip irrigation. He crushes an average of 5 tonnes of fruit each year, and makes the wine himself in a tiny winery with its recycled milk vats and other pre-loved equipment.

His chardonnay has proved to be a remarkably consistent ripener, being ready for picking on almost the same day every year. Pinot noir has proved to be much more difficult. He doesn't really know it is ready until the very last moment, and then there is always a rush to arrange pickers while acid levels drop almost hour by hour. During vintage he and his wife Christine make several trips a day from Maffra to look after the ferments, and the result of their pains is a mere seven or eight barriques of wine which are sold under the Parish Wine label, by mail order or through some good local restaurants.

In 1989 his 1986 pinot noir was rated by *Winestate* magazine as among the top pinots in Victoria, marginally behind James Halliday's 'Three Vineyards' pinot noir from the Yarra Valley. That, of course, made it a very good wine indeed, and Dr McIntosh was happy to see it on the winelists of such posh establishments in Melbourne as Stephanie's and Mietta's.

Golvinda

Robert Guy is quite a character. A graduate of Roseworthy Agricultural College and member of a well-known South Australian grapegrowing family, he settled on East Gippsland as a place to grow grapes for wine after making a painstaking analysis of meteorological data from all over Australia. Perhaps there was something of the astrological about it as well. Rob Guy is a passionate man when it comes to drinking and talking about wine, and there are times when he admits that his stars might have easily led him to Italy or beyond.

He graduated from Roseworthy College in 1965, and after working for a while at Kaiser Stuhl, in the Barossa Valley, he went overseas. During the next ten years he worked in England, Switzerland and the Soviet Union before supervising the construction of a winery in Hyderabad, India. He went to East Gippsland in 1971 and began planting vines in grey, sandy soil near Lindenow South, 20 km west of Bairnsdale: Rhine riesling, chenin blanc, semillon, cabernet sauvignon and (several years later) merlot.

Eventually he had 12 hectares of vines, a small winery he built himself, and a cellar door sales and tasting area which expanded over the years into a place where visiting groups could have a sit-down dinner around an open fire and a roasting spit, surrounded by wall displays of empty wine bottles from all over the world. Golvinda wines had their ups and downs in the early years, but Rob Guy went on to make some severely beautiful white wines from chenin blanc and semillon; and a straight merlot filled with beautiful fruit flavours, which would have been long-lived had it not been practically consumed on the spot.

Rob and his wife Ann provide convivial surroundings for visitors on their way to and from the beautiful Gippsland Lakes, and many a cruiser or yacht has ventured on to those waters with a locker full of Golvinda wine. During a slow period after vintage 1988, Rob Guy bought the block of land over the road and started building his own eighteen-hole golf course, which in years to come will no doubt provide an outlet for the good citizens of the growing town of Bairnsdale. Golvinda wine, of course, will be served in the clubrooms.

McAlister Vineyard

Peter Edwards saw the world as an RAAF officer, and when he served in France he fell in love with the Medoc and its wines. He also spent twelve years at the air force base at East Sale where, unlikely as it might sound, he saw similarities between the passage of the Latrobe River through the little town of Longford into Lake Wellington and the thread of rivers which give the Medoc region of Bordeaux the stable and moderate maritime climate so conducive to the growth of great vineyards.

In 1975 he bought some land in Golden Beach Road, Longford, 9 km from the town, and planted the classic varieties of the Haute Medoc: 2 hectares of cabernet sauvignon, cabernet franc, petit verdot and merlot. The idea was to make one wine only, and since 1979 'The McAlister' has been produced in minute quantities, but for a very faithful retinue of mail-order clients and restaurants.

Over the years Peter has experimented with his wines and made adjustments. For example, he believed that the malic acid level was too high, giving his wine an overly up-front herbaceous character; he also felt that new oak was overpowering the delicate fruit flavours of his grapes. He decided that two-year-old oak was a much better proposition—particularly since he allowed the wine two years in the barrel before bottling. The result is that 'The McAlister' is a beautifully stylish wine, with great intensity of flavour and a complexity which improves greatly with bottle age.

Mair's Coalville Vineyard

Stewart Mair is a specialist physician who works in the Latrobe Valley. He also produces the quite remarkable Mair's Coalville Red from 3 hectares of cabernet sauvignon, cabernet franc and merlot planted around his house on a beautiful green hillside at Moe South, 120 km east of Melbourne. The old coal-mining town of Coalville is only 2 km away so, when their first wines appeared, Stewart and his photographer wife, Mavis, decided to call it Coalville Red.

This may not sound like wine country, but then the Hunter Valley seems able to combine winemaking and coal mining quite well. And vines were growing around Moe at the turn of the century, presumably falling to the government-sponsored vine pull program which followed in the wake of phylloxera. In any case, the Mair's vineyard has flourished, although some unexpected problems have arisen since the first 1.6 hectares of cabernet sauvignon were planted in 1974. Their first wine was made for them at Anakie by the late Stephen Hickinbotham in 1983; he also made the wine for them in 1984 and 1985. In 1986 the vines were wiped out completely by the first attack of downy mildew they had ever experienced.

By then they had bought what had been a small dairy farm next door and planted a further 1.4 hectares of cabernet sauvignon, cabernet franc and merlot. In 1987 they had their best crop to date and the wine was made by Ken Eckersley at Nicholson River. In 1988 there were 2 tonnes of fruit and Stewart made the wine himself in the small winery which used to be his garage. In 1989 the crop had doubled to 4 tonnes, which furnished about 2000 bottles of Coalville Red.

The wines are all aged in good French barriques, and since 1983 they have shown a very interesting consistency in style. The first wines were straight cabernet sauvignons. In later ones the merlot seems to be fleshing out the middle palate to some extent, but there is that same intensity of flavour and ripe berry character. Birds remain a problem in the vineyard, but Stewart now knows how to control mildew. Very early in the piece he also discovered that his hillside, 200 m above sea level, dried out enormously in summer. In 1986 he sank a bore, which provides very good, clear water for drop irrigation when the vines appear stressed.

Nicholson River

Ken Eckersley was a social worker who worked in Bairnsdale and lived with his wife, Juliette,

and family at Nicholson, a little town on the Princes Highway between Bairnsdale and Lakes Entrance. The Nicholson River flows not far from their property in Liddell's Road, a beautiful little stream coursing between grassy banks on its way down to the Gippsland Lakes. Ken started planting grapes in 1978 and now has 7 hectares of cabernet sauvignon, merlot, chardonnay, semillon, pinot noir and Rhine riesling.

By the time his vines had begun to mature, Ken had decided to be a full-time vigneron, and took time off to study winemaking in France. His classical approach is reflected in his Nicholson River cabernets, a Bordeaux-style blend of cabernet sauvignon, cabernet franc and merlot. He also displays some avant-garde technique in his riesling sur-lie, a barrel-fermented wine which spends four months in new French oak before bottling, and which fools most people into believing it is chardonnay. He makes a very fine wood-fermented chardonnay as well (in 1989 the 1987 wine was selling for $31 per bottle). Other Nicholson River wines making their appearance in top Melbourne restaurants are semillon and pinot noir.

Wyanga Park

Wyanga Park was established in 1970 as Lulgra by Pauline and Dacre Stubbs in spectacular country carved out of the Colqhoun State Forest and overlooking the North Arm of the Gippsland Lakes at Lakes Entrance. It was taken over and renamed in 1980 by brothers Andrew and Jonathan Smith and their brother-in-law, Geoff

Mahlook. Since then there has been extensive replanting and grafting of vines. In 1989 there were 7 hectares of cabernet sauvignon, Rhine riesling, chardonnay, pinot noir and sauvignon blanc, but because many of the vines were young, yield was only about 7 tonnes.

Eventually they hope to have about 40 to 45 tonnes of fruit from Wyanga. In the meantime, they have been supplementing their own grapes with wine they make themselves with the help of a mobile crusher they take to other parts of Victoria each year. There are plans in hand to upgrade the present winery and to build a restaurant overlooking North Arm, and to improve tourist access so that visitors can take their boats right up to the property. At the moment they attract about 20 000 tourists a year, and believe the potential for future development, both in winemaking and tourism, is substantial.

Geelong

The migration to the colony of Victoria by relatively wealthy citizens of the canton of Neuchatel in Switzerland, inspired as it was by Charles Latrobe, Superintendent of Port Phillip and first governor of the colony, serves as an introduction to the Yarra Valley section of this book. Not all of Latrobe's friends joined the de Castellas and the de Purys in the mountainous reaches east of the settlement of Melbourne, however. Indeed, David Louis Pettavel and Frederick Breuget established their Neuchatel Vineyard in Geelong as early as 1842, twelve years before the de Castellas arrived.

The Neuchatel plantings were at Pollock's Ford, on high ground overlooking the Barwon River, using cuttings brought from near Dijon. The first wine was made in 1845, by which time other small vineyards were up and running. They all made welcome supplies to the Ballarat goldfields during the 1850s, and the sale of wine boomed almost as much as mining did. There were no fewer than nine cooperages supplying casks and vats in Geelong in 1858. By 1864 it was one of the most important winemaking areas in the colony, with more than fifty vineyards in operation. More than 400 hectares were under vine by 1870.

By all accounts the wines produced by the Swiss, and later by German settlers, were very

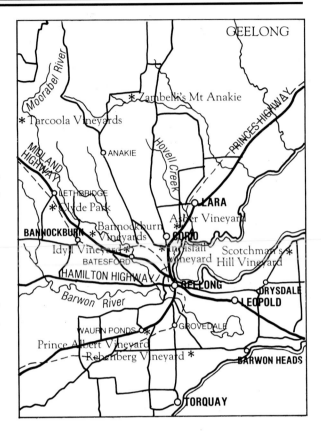

like those made in the Yarra Valley—light, dry table wines different from those which very soon after were to make their presence felt in new areas in the north-east of Victoria. In 1867 the Duke of Edinburgh visited Pettavel's Prince Albert vineyards at Waurn Ponds, and Geelong wines were being acclaimed both locally and in shows as far away as Paris and Bordeaux.

It should be remembered that Geelong was Victoria's main entrepot, so it was perhaps inevitable that vine cuttings bearing the root louse phylloxera (*Phylloxera vastatrix*), which was at the time devastating the great vineyards of Europe, should arrive in the country via Geelong. The first signs of phylloxera in Australia were in 1875 at Fyansford, near Geelong. The battle against the louse, which was to last more than a quarter of a century, was to become the greatest natural disaster in Australian winemaking history.

The Victorian Government ordered the destruction of all vines in the Geelong area, and an extensive soil sterilisation program using the gas carbon disulphide. The aim was to prevent the louse from reaching the Rutherglen region, then the major wine-producing area not only in Victoria but the whole of Australia—but it simply didn't work. Perhaps what they did not know was that during its winged phase, *Phylloxera vastatrix* could travel great distances with the help of prevailing winds. The great westerlies which drove the ships into Geelong also allowed the louse to travel east in vast numbers, and vineyard after vineyard fell in its path.

One or two Geelong vineyards survived into the twentieth century, but by 1947 all traces had vanished. It was not until Daryl Sefton, a great-grandson of Neuchatel emigrants Rosina and Jacob Just, planted vines in the Moorabel Valley north of Geelong in 1966 that the tradition was resumed. Today it is still a small but important cool-climate link in the Victorian wine revival, and some very fine wines are being produced.

Asher Vineyard

Lovely Banks is an outer suburb of Geelong on the road to Moorabool, and in 1976 consulting engineer Brian Moten bought a property there in Goldsworthy Road and named it Asher, after one of the twelve sons of Israel. He planted 2 hectares of vines, cabernet sauvignon and malbec, and made his first wine, a fifty-fifty blend of the two red varieties, from one single tonne of grapes in 1980.

The soil was heavy clay over broken limestone and yields were low; however, after drip irrigation was installed the vines gained heart and by 1989 were producing more than 2 tonnes of fruit. In 1986, 0.4 hectares of sauvignon blanc was planted, and Brian was expecting to make his first white wine in 1990. He is assisted in the small winery by his son Simon, who is a biochemist with Carlton and United Breweries. As Brian admits, they 'do it all the hard way'.

The wine is fermented in steel tanks and matured in wood, and their first 'really good' wine was produced in 1987. Good vintages came also in 1988 and 1989, and now the Asher red has a faithful following, sold by word-of-mouth or by appointment at cellar door.

Bannockburn Vineyards

Stuart Hooper, businessman and landholder in the Geelong district, first planted vines on a residential block in the little township of Bannockburn, 25 km north-east of Geelong on the Midland Highway, in 1973. In 1975 that initial 3 hectares was supplemented by a further 8 hectares on a hillside on his main property several kilometres away. With subsequent plantings the vineyard grew to 16.3 hectares. Varieties were chardonnay and pinot noir in about equal quantities, cabernet sauvignon, merlot, malbec, shiraz, sauvignon blanc and Rhine riesling. Conditions were so dry in the area that many of the vines had to be replaced, so in 1980 a dam was built to provide drip irrigation.

In 1984, 1 hectare of pinot noir was established using the close-planting techniques traditional in Burgundy, 8000 vines to the hectare on a spacing of 1.25 m by 1.25 m with a trellis 0.9 m high. This vineyard is now producing some very fine fruit and Stuart Hooper and his manager-winemaker, Gary Farr, are involved even more deeply in their quest to produce the best possible quality Burgundy-style red wine. Gary Farr, a Roseworthy College graduate, has spent considerable time working in Burgundy, principally at Domaine Dujac in Morey St Denis. In recent years there is no doubt that Bannockburn pinot noir has compared more than favourably with wines from this famous region of France.

An extensive winery was established in 1980, and was first used for vintage 1981 when 17 tonnes of estate-grown fruit was crushed. Total production is aimed at 100 tonnes, 50 per cent white, 50 per cent red. The winery has temperature-controlled fermentation capacity of 49 500 litres, and Gary Farr has enough high-tech equipment on hand to ensure that an entire vintage can be handled by two people. Chardonnay is vinified using traditional French techniques, with fermentation taking place in new Burgundian barriques followed by eight to twelve months storage in the same barriques. Pinot noir is given a cool ferment and then stored in new oak. Gary Farr takes the Burgundian view that if beautiful aromatics are set loose in the winery, as happens with hot ferments, they are not going into the bottle.

There are now five wines in the Bannockburn range, chardonnay, pinot noir, cabernet sauvignon, shiraz and Rhine riesling, and all share the intense fruit characters of this cool region. The cabernet has changed slightly in style with the addition of malbec and merlot, which have lengthened its finish and given it more complexity. The shiraz has gone its own merry way with its distinct spicy nose and lovely balance of fruit and acid. The Rhine riesling is generally fermented dry, and again shows very delicate cool-climate character.

The Burgundian varieties, chardonnay and pinot noir, are outstanding, and very French in style. In 1987 Bannockburn's Melbourne agents, Seabrooks, staged a tasting of 1984 and 1985 pinot noir in a range of Burgundies, including Volnay Clos des Ducs, Faiveley Nuit St George, Echezeaux Domaine Dujac, Leroy Domaine Romanée-Contée and Morey–St Denis cru Clos Sorbes. Both Bannockburn wines came through with flying colours.

Clyde Park

In 1981, having helped Stuart Hooper set up the remarkable Bannockburn Vineyards, winemaker Gary Farr bought Clyde Park, a 56 hectare grazing property next to the Moorabool River and 5 km north of the township of Bannockburn. He planted just under a hectare each of cabernet sauvignon and chardonnay, and in 1987 another 0.8 hectares of pinot noir. Using the ultra-modern facilities at Bannockburn, he began making small batches of his own wine: including barrel-fermented chardonnay, and cabernet sauvignon, which was a blend of traditionally fermented material and some wine made by the carbonic maceration process. In 1985 and 1986 both wines were sold overseas, a particular agent buying his entire output for distribution in the UK, the US and New Zealand.

Gary made his first pinot noir off the block in 1989, a relatively small batch very much in the same, very Burgundian stamp as those made at Bannockburn. The vines are close-planted in rows 1 m apart, and as the vines mature Gary is expecting good yields from the rich volcanic loam over limestone. Production at Clyde Park will always be small, but Gary is aiming at high quality while giving himself room for experimentation both in the winery and the vineyard.

Idyll Vineyard

Among the many Swiss immigrants from the canton of Neuchatel who followed Governor Charles Latrobe to the new colony of Victoria were Rosina and Jacob Just, who in 1874 took over the licence of the Swiss Inn in Geelong. The Inn quickly became a favourite meeting place for other Swiss in the area, particularly vignerons. Rosina Just also planted vines in what was becoming an increasingly important wine-producing region. This region was one of the first to fall to phylloxera, the louse which apparently arrived in Australia on vines landed at the port of Geelong.

Rosina Just's grandson was Dr Daryl Sefton, a veterinary surgeon in Geelong, who heard many tales of the pioneering days during his childhood, and enjoyed visiting the old family property at Tungamah. In 1966 he and his artist wife, Nini, thought it appropriate that they should be part of the rebirth of viticulture in the area, and began planting vines on a beautiful property called Idyll in the valley of the Moorabool River, 10 km north-west of Geelong. They were granted a vigneron's licence in 1974, exactly 100 years after Grandmère Rosina got her wine licence for the Swiss Inn.

The 20 hectares of vines, including cabernet sauvignon, shiraz, gewurztraminer and chardonnay, were planted on the site of an old vineyard, on limestone strata near the major water mass of Corio Bay, where the climate is conducive to slow, cool ripening of the grapes. Vintage is in April and May. Because spring frosts are a problem, Daryl installed a sprinkler system of his own design to lessen their effect. He gave up his veterinary practice when the first vintage came in 1974, and put some hidden engineering skills to work in building and equipping his winery. He learned how to weld stainless steel for instance, and set up his own fermenters and storage vats and many other bits and pieces.

Eventually he built his own mechanical harvester, and designed a trickle irrigation system quite a while before they were readily available.

The original plan was to have two wines, a red and a white, and their cabernet–shiraz blend and gewurztraminer have become well-established Idyll styles. Gewurztraminer has had its ups and downs as a variety in Australia, but the Idyll wine is made firm and dry, and its aromatic spicy qualities compare very well with good wines from its native Alsace. They also make Idyll Blush, a dry, full-bodied rosé which is not as coy as it sounds. It comes off the skins soon after crushing and is fermented in stainless steel. The result is almost perfect colour, which is the only show specification for rosé in Australia, and a refreshingly dry yet fruity palate.

In 1975 they became one of the first small wineries to direct a good portion of their production towards exports. Nini Sefton took a course offered by the Australian Institute of Export and followed it up with a course on export documentation. That year they went to Germany with samples of their wine and so impressed one of Germany's leading wholesalers that Idyll wines have sold well in that country ever since. Nini was a foundation member and later on the committee of the Victorian Wine Exporting Group, and many other Victorian wineries have followed the Seftons' example to their advantage.

Innisfail Vineyard

Batesford is a little town 10 km out of Geelong on the Midland Highway, in a part of the Moorabool Valley through which would-be miners, attracted from around the world by the great Victorian gold rush, passed on their way from Corio Bay to Ballarat and Bendigo nearly 150 years ago. More attracted by the needs of the miners than by the elusive promise of the mines, market gardeners and farmers squatted along the way. In 1852 the Flanagan family settled in Batesford on a property they called Innisfail, and built a handsome bluestone house which today graces the label of some very interesting wines from Ron and Sharon Griffiths' Innisfail Vineyard.

Ron Griffiths was an accountant and company secretary who was working in an engineering works in Geelong when he bought Innisfail in 1980. The lovely old homestead stood on 10 hectares of land, and his friend and neighbour, Gary Farr, manager and winemaker at Bannockburn, several kilometres away, convinced him he should plant some grapes. Ron's company had been involved in building stainless steel tanks and other equipment for the high-tech winery built at Bannockburn several years before, and with Gary Farr's guidance he began planting varieties of grapes which were already showing their worth in the Geelong viticultural area.

There were 4 hectares of cabernet sauvignon, chardonnay and Rhine riesling, and a patch of pinot noir was planted the following year. First vintage was in 1983, with Gary Farr making the wine at Bannockburn. Although the vines were very young, the results showed sufficient promise for Ron to decide that winemaking, as opposed to selling grapes, was worthwhile. A winery was built at Innisfail during 1985–86, and the Griffiths were granted a vigneron's licence in 1988. Although the vines are still maturing, 1000 cases of wine were produced in 1989, sold mainly through retailers and restaurants in Geelong.

Wines produced so far have been chardonnay, Rhine riesling and cabernet sauvignon. The 1984 cabernet was a very good wine, although later vintages showed considerable variation. The chardonnay, which is fermented in small oak and then matured for ten or eleven months before bottling, is quite similar to the very fine chardonnay produced at Bannockburn, with very intense fruit character and obvious lasting qualities. By 1989 there had been two small vintages of pinot noir, and although performance of this difficult variety was mixed as far as growth and yield were concerned, the quality of fruit greatly impressed Gary Farr, a pinot specialist.

Prince Albert Vineyard

Another of Geelong's Swiss pioneer vignerons was David Pettavel, who in the early 1850s planted 10 hectares of vines on what he called the Victoria Vineyard in the Waurn Ponds valley, 10 km west of Geelong. In 1857 he planted a second vineyard, Prince Albert (for a Swiss, he was certainly taken with the British royal family), 5 hectares of vines on a north-facing slope 4 km closer to town. Charles Tetaz bought the Prince Albert vineyard from his uncle several years later, but by 1882 phylloxera had begun its deadly journey across Victoria, and the vineyard and all the winemaking equipment were destroyed by government order.

Enter Bruce Hyett, a Geelong building contractor who always wanted to be a farmer but was so ill after war service in New Guinea that his ambition was never realised. In 1975, however, he bought several hectares of what had been Pettavel's original Prince Albert property, and planted 2 hectares of it to pinot noir. He had read a lot about pinot and Burgundy, and admired what Stuart Anderson was doing at Balgownie and the Seftons at Idyll. He decided he would be a vigneron and produce just one variety and one wine, in the best possible way.

Today Prince Albert is about the same size as the incomparable Domaine de la Romanée-Conti in Burgundy, and there are other similarities. There is the same rich red topsoil, about half a metre over pure limestone marl. The vineyard is frost free, and most of its 550 mm annual rainfall is in winter and spring. Yields are about 8 tonnes per hectare. Primary fermentation takes place in wax-lined concrete fermenters and is completed in stainless steel tanks. Maturation is in small French oak.

Bruce Hyett makes the wine with the help of his partner, Geelong architect Neil Everist, and their first wine was in 1980. The vines were only two-years-old but cropped well, and the wine was very full-bodied with excellent colour and good balance. Apart from 1980, when an unidentified aldehyde emerged after bottling and the entire vintage was recalled, Prince Albert has gone from strength to strength. In a tasting of Australian pinot noir conducted by the *Age* in Melbourne in July 1989, Prince Albert 1987 pinot was judged best wine and, at $17.99 per bottle, also best value for money.

Rebenberg Vineyard

The Swiss were not the only immigrants to settle in and around Geelong last century. There were French, English and Scots, and also a settlement of Germans concentrated around Marshall, which in those days was known as German Town. When Ken and Joy Campbell bought a property nearby, on the Torquay Road 10 km past Geelong on the slopes of Mt Duneed, they felt a German name was appropriate and called the place Rebenberg.

Ken was a biology lecturer at Deakin University in Geelong, and Joy a schoolteacher, and their partner in the 4 hectare property was Peter Caldwell, a computer expert who worked in Melbourne. They planted 2.8 hectares of grapes in 1970: including semillon, sauvignon blanc, muscadelle, cabernet sauvignon, malbec, merlot and shiraz. While the vines were maturing, both Ken and Peter did various wine and viticulture courses by correspondence at Riverina College in Wagga Wagga. Later Ken also visited the Napa Valley in California where he picked up some innovative ideas for trellising vines, which he put to work at Rebenberg.

They built a small winery behind the house Ken and Joy lived in, and in 1976 began making their own wine, producing a red blend of all of their red varieties and a dry white made from semillon with a little sauvignon blanc. They found that the area was susceptible to botrytis, and they now try to make a botrytised semillon each year. Their wines are sold under the Mount Duneed label, and mainly at cellar door. In 1989 they bought the 14 hectare property next door to Rebenberg with a view to planting mainly chardonnay.

Scotchman's Hill Vineyard

This is a comparatively large new development at Drysdale, on the Bellarine Peninsula directly east of Geelong. The vineyard is planted on the remains of an extinct volcano with splendid views over Corio Bay, Port Phillip Bay and the notorious heads between Point Lonsdale and Sorrento. The property was purchased in 1984 by Melbourne financier David Browne and his wife Vivien. Horticulturist Rob Burgess was employed to plant 24 hectares of vines, half of it to chardonnay and pinot noir in equal proportions, and the remainder to cabernet sauvignon, cabernet franc, merlot and Rhine riesling.

Most of the land around Scotchman's Hill is very light sandy loam which over the years has been popular with market gardeners, particularly for growing onions. On the rounded peak of the hill, the highest point on the peninsula, the soil changes dramatically to a dense volcanic black loam, not dissimilar to the legendary Merri Creek soil used in the world-renowned pitches at the Melbourne Cricket Ground.

Rob Burgess realised the great fertility of the soil would produce a profusion of vine growth; at the same time he also felt that the exposed position, with its fierce prevailing westerlies, would provide the kind of balance between bounty and stress which exists in many of the great vineyards of Europe. He had worked in various vineyards in France and Germany where this was the case. His judgment was correct and the vines have developed well; yields are such that fruit quality and quantity are very nicely balanced.

Two wines were produced in 1988 from 4 to 5 tonnes each of Rhine riesling and cabernet franc, and they both sold very quickly after being shown at the Exhibition of Victorian Winemakers. In 1989 the first red was produced, a blend of cabernet sauvignon and cabernet franc plus a little merlot, and put away in small French oak to mature. It is Rob Burgess's dream that, some time in the future, the pinot noir and chardonnay might go into a high-quality sparkling wine.

A winery was built in time for vintage 1989. At the moment it is leased by Hickinbotham Winemakers, whose chief winemaker, Peter Cumming, makes the Scotchman's Hill wines and those of other small producers for whom the redoubtable Ian Hickinbotham acts as consultant.

Tarcoola Vineyards

Tarcoola was established at Lethbridge, on the banks of the Moorabool River, 30 km from Geelong, in 1971. Its owners are Alastair and Hermione Scott, who planted 7 hectares of vines as a retirement activity and investment after working for a number of years running a tea plantation in Sri Lanka. Varieties include shiraz, cabernet sauvignon, Rhine riesling, chasselas and muller thurgau; Tarcoola Rhine riesling, shiraz, and a shiraz–cabernet blend are the wines generally for sale each year. The Moorabool provides a beautiful setting for the vineyard and for visitors to the cellar door sales area; but in bad years it floods, causing considerable damage. At flood time the koalas, which are generally on show, retire to higher trees.

Zambelli's Mt Anakie

The northern slope of Mt Anakie, the remains of a volcanic region 35 km north of Geelong, was first planted to vines by well-known businessman and racehorse owner Tom Maltby in 1968. He had about 15 hectares of shiraz and cabernet sauvignon, and made some very good wines during the 1970s. In 1981 the vineyard and rather ramshackle winery were leased to the Hickinbotham family, Ian and Judy, and their children, Stephen, Jenny and Andrew.

Under their care the vineyard was upgraded, with some replanting and grafting undertaken to include Rhine riesling and chardonnay, with some small patches of cabernet franc, dolcetto, biancone and semillon. Stephen, who had graduated from the national school of winemaking in Bordeaux, made some remarkable wines there, including Cab Mac, a carbonic maceration wine which became immediately popular all around Australia, and which is now made by Mitchelton. In 1986 Stephen died tragically in an air accident, and the Hickinbothams were forced to change direction (see Hickinbotham Winemakers).

In late 1986 this very fine vineyard was sold to Otto and Bronwyn Zambelli, who continue the good work with a range of varietal wines including dolcetto, Rhine riesling, biancone and cabernet sauvignon. They have changed the Anakie label to Zambelli's Mt Anakie, which they sell through Geelong and Melbourne retailers, and at cellar door.

Melbourne and Mornington Peninsula

It is rather difficult to imagine in these days of suburban sprawl that last century hundreds of hectares of what is now the city of Melbourne, including South Yarra, Hawthorn, Brighton and other areas, were covered in vines. The *Illustrated Australian News* proclaimed in 1866, less than thirty years after the settlement on the Yarra River had been named Melbourne:

> The notable increase of private vineyards is one of the most cheering signs of the times, a few years hence and every country resident will be enabled to entertain his visitors with the produce of his own little vineyard.

In 1840 John Fawkner planted 4 hectares of vines at Pascoe Vale near Flemington, and eight

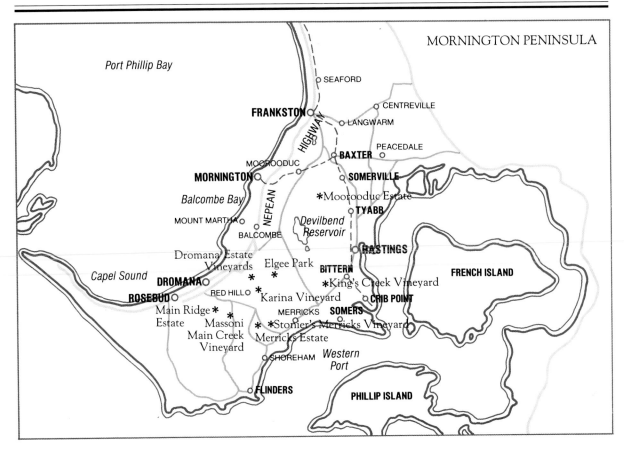

MORNINGTON PENINSULA

Port Phillip Bay

SEAFORD

CENTREVILLE

FRANKSTON

LANGWARM

PEACEDALE

MOOROODUC

BAXTER

MORNINGTON

SOMERVILLE

Balcombe Bay

*Moorooduc Estate

TYABB

MOUNT MARTHA

Devilbend
Reservoir

BALCOMBE

HASTINGS

Dromana Estate
Vineyards

Elgee Park

BITTERN

FRENCH ISLAND

Capel Sound

DROMANA

*King's Creek Vineyard

ROSEBUD

RED HILL

*Karina Vineyard

CRIB POINT

Main Ridge *
Estate   Massoni
Main Creek
Vineyard

MERRICKS

SOMERS

*Stonier's Merricks Vineyard
Merricks Estate

SHOREHAM   Western
Port

FLINDERS

PHILLIP ISLAND

years later had a vintage of 9000 litres of 'excellent wine'. In Hawthorn, Count Alinant de Dollon had a 12 hectare vineyard, and his neighbours, I. McKinnon and Neil McLean, also grew vines in the region of what is now Scotch College and Kooyong Tennis Club. In 1861 T.J. Everish was advertising wine from his Spring Hill vineyard on what is now the intersection of Barkers and Auburn Road at Hawthorn East for twelve shillings a dozen, and some choicer ones at thirty shillings. Mr J. Scott had a fine vineyard between the Hawthorn railway station and St James Park, and Edward Khull, the goldbroker, owned Tooronga vineyard, not far away.

A writer at the time recorded that a young Swiss, Mr Wisewould, made 1350 litres of 'exceedingly good wine' in South Yarra, including an 1861 vintage riesling. David Ogilvie had a vineyard on Punt Hill, South Yarra, which was called Airlie Park, and which ran right down to the river at Alexandra Avenue. It produced a celebrated Red Hermitage, and part of the vineyard remained, in sight of Government House, as late as 1924. A Mr Ross grew vines on the site of what is now St John's Church of England in Toorak Road; and in far-flung

Ivanhoe Charles Mapleston was well known in the 1860s for his reds and a white made from 'Semillion of Saturnes'.

At Moonee Ponds the Ngarveno vineyard owned by John Davies featured a hydraulic press, which was seen by François de Castella as a small boy, although his father, Hubert, wouldn't have one at St Huberts because he had seen a press disintegrate after the cylinder blew up at an earlier vintage. Excellent clarets came from all over Brighton and Caulfield, from Jacob Schneider at Nunawading and others along the Whitehorse Road. By 1880 the total area of these vineyards was about 400 hectares, not much less than is growing today in the Goulburn Valley. The Mornington Peninsula, which lies between Port Phillip and Western Port Bays, had 35 hectares under vines in 1869, producing more than 15 000 litres of wine.

Today the suburban backyards of Melbourne produce grapes for the table and some homemade wine. In 1988 and 1989 John Ellis of Hanging Rock winery collected grapes from all over the metropolitan area and produced a rosé wine which was sold for charity. Something of a revolution has taken place on the Mornington

Peninsula, where more than a dozen vineyards, some with small wineries of their own, have sprung up in the last decade or so. Production hardly shows up in state or national statistics in either varieties or yield, but the quality of both red and white wine coming from this beautiful area on Melbourne's doorstep suggests that a new golden age for 'metropolitan' wine, in quality terms at least, may be dawning.

The peninsula has remarkably similar climatic characteristics to the great wine-producing regions of France. It is cooler than Bordeaux, for instance, and warmer than Burgundy, but during the growing season it has the same average monthly sunshine hours as Burgundy and in summer the monthly average temperatures are similar to those in both Burgundy and Bordeaux. The surrounding ocean mass provides unique conditions with relatively high summer humidity and rainfall. Both of these factors contribute to the great wines of France. Some vineyards are at sea level and others at elevations up to 300 m. The rolling hills provide variation in soil, rainfall and temperature, and regional styles are already starting to emerge.

Chardonnay and cabernet sauvignon are the most widely planted varieties on the Mornington Peninsula, and pinot noir, merlot, Rhine riesling and shiraz are also well established. Wines to date show outstanding fruit flavours, fine structure and soft tannins, and an austerity and acid 'backbone' which means they drink easily while young but can also be expected to age well.

The Mornington Peninsula Vignerons' Association was established in 1987, and by the end of that year had more than fifty members. Many of these were small hobby vineyards, but in 1989 there were thirteen member-growers with commercial releases of wine. The Association also has its own 'guarantee of origin' logo which can be used only on bottles of wine made entirely from grapes grown on the peninsula.

Dromana Estate Vineyards

Crittenden is a well-known name in wine retailing in Melbourne, but Garry Crittenden, who established Dromana Estate in Harrisons Road, Dromana, in 1981, is no relation. He is a horticulturist who comes from a long line of plant nursery proprietors in Victoria. His conversion to wine began in Tasmania in 1977 while he and his wife Margaret were on holiday. He tasted some Moorilla Estate wine for the first time and, fascinated by its obvious cool-climate quality, decided on the spot to one day have a Tasmanian vineyard of his own. For various reasons that didn't happen, but several years later he tasted one of the early Mornington Peninsula wines and his enthusiasm was rekindled.

He bought the 11 hectares of gently sloping land in Dromana and in 1982 began planting 4 hectares of vines in what is grey loam soil overlying clay; cabernet sauvignon and merlot and 1 hectare each of pinot noir and chardonnay. He built an enormous dam which now adds great beauty to the property as well as ensuring reasonable yields. Eventually a small winery was also built, in which he produced his first wine, a 1984 cabernet. It was a beautiful wine which got the kind of publicity it deserved. When it was followed in 1985 by an even better version, plus the first pinot noir and chardonnay, Dromana Estate was well and truly on the map.

In 1986 he sold his remaining nursery interests to concentrate on wine production, and the obvious expertise which had gone into establishing Dromana soon made him a popular figure as a consultant in both vineyard and winery management. By 1989 more chardonnay and pinot noir had come into bearing, and production had risen to a little more than 1000 cases, making it the largest operation on the peninsula to date. Maximum yield will be 50 tonnes or so, and the product line will be four wines each year: Dromana Estate cabernet, merlot, pinot noir and chardonnay.

Elgee Park

The Merricks North property of the Baillieu Myer family was first planted with an experimental block of 400 vines in 1972 on the advice of David Wynn. The vines flourished, and gradually the vineyard was extended to 5 hectares of cabernet sauvignon, merlot, chardonnay, Rhine riesling and sauvignon blanc. Ian and Stephen Hickinbotham made the early Elgee Park wines, Stephen surprising himself and the critics with a very interesting cabernet which contained botrytised fruit. The Hickinbothams continued to make the wine up to and including the 1983 vintage, when a winery was built and the Oentec partner, Dr Tony Jordan, took over as winemaker.

Elaine Tudhope became the resident winemaker in 1986 and produced a very intriguing cabernet–merlot. Since then the wine has been made by another Oentec winemaker, Gary Baldwin. As well as the red blend, small quantities of white varietal wines are made. These are sold by mailing list and through a few retailers and restaurants in Melbourne, the Mornington Peninsula and Sydney.

Hickinbotham Winemakers

The name Hickinbotham has been a major one in the Australian wine scene ever since Alan R. Hickinbotham was appointed lecturer in chemistry at Roseworthy Agricultural College in 1929. In 1936 the Roseworthy Diploma of Oenology was introduced. It was the first formal wine science course in Australia and in many ways set

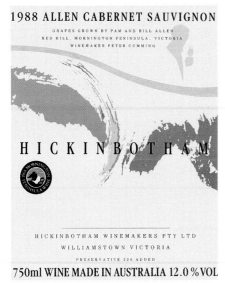

1988 ALLEN CABERNET SAUVIGNON

GRAPES GROWN BY PAM AND BILL ALLEN
RED HILL, MORNINGTON PENINSULA, VICTORIA
WINEMAKER PETER CUMMING

HICKINBOTHAM

HICKINBOTHAM WINEMAKERS PTY LTD
WILLIAMSTOWN VICTORIA
PRESERVATIVE 220 ADDED

750ml WINE MADE IN AUSTRALIA 12.0% VOL

the pattern of winemaking which persists to this day. Hickinbotham himself did extensive work on pH which was widely published overseas, and which is still quoted as original material. His son, Ian Hickinbotham, also became a force in Australian winemaking, arriving in Melbourne in 1963 to work for Penfolds after a spell as general manager of Kaiser Stuhl in the Barossa Valley.

His son Stephen was, ironically, not able to get into Roseworthy College, so he studied French and went off to the National Wine Academy in Bordeaux, where he became one of a handful of Australians to graduate from that distinguished school. On his return to Australia he became the lynchpin of an impressive family winemaking team which took over Tom Maltby's Anakie Vineyard near Geelong in 1981. Ian and Stephen made the wine, sister Jenny and brother Andrew, both qualified viticulturists, ran the vineyard. Despite the rather ramshackle conditions at Anakie they were producing some superb wines and introducing some radical vineyard practices in the way of clonal selection, pruning, trellising and so on.

Stephen's winemaking skills were distinctly French, and he did a lot of significant work with such things as botrytis, yeasts, oak fermentation and carbonic maceration which he used to make Cab Mac. This modified version of the method used in France to make Beaujolais was perfected at Anakie and eventually sold to Remy Australia, and later taken up by Mitchelton. There is no doubt that Cab Mac is still one of the best of the new generation of light red wines made in Australia.

Ian and Stephen also made wine for a number of small producers; grapes arrived in boxes and chillers from as far away as Tasmania and East Gippsland. It was the Hickinbothams who started showing people how good the wines of Mornington Peninsula could be. Another innovative move by Stephen was to convince Ansett Airlines to upgrade the wine carried on flights around Australia. He devised a system whereby small 200 ml bottles could be filled with a wide variety of red and white table wines, easily handled by both air crew and passengers. The secret of the operation's success was a bottling line, built in cooperation with Fareham Estate in South Australia, which allowed a pellet of dry ice to be put into each bottle before filling with wine and sealing with a screwtop Stelvin closure.

The dry ice converted into carbon dioxide, which provided an inert atmosphere for the wine, and the metal screwtop was a sturdy and efficient alternative to cork. The whole package, easily stored and opened, was perfect for the rough-and-tumble life aboard a modern airliner. The system is now used around the world.

Just when it appeared that everything was coming together for the Hickinbotham family in terms of reward for its innovation and hard work, Stephen was killed in an air crash while on holiday in 1986. Being the strong-willed people they are, they carried on. At the end of 1986 they sold the lease of Anakie to the Zambelli family and moved operations to a lovely old house (once a bawdy house, it is said) overlooking the waterfront at Williamstown.

Business now centres on the airline wine bottling and selection, which is carried out at Tisdall Winery at Echuca; the production of the fine Hickinbotham label range of table wines; a wide spread of consultancies in both winemaking and viticulture; and the development of the family's own vineyard on the Nepean Highway at Dromana on the Mornington Peninsula, some 70 km south of Melbourne. Andrew Hickinbotham searched the peninsula for two years before choosing the 16 hectare property; he planted the first 6 hectares of vines in August 1988.

The varieties are mainly cabernet sauvignon with cabernet franc and merlot; two different clones of chardonnay; and two rows of taminga, the CSIRO-developed white variety which is showing considerable promise. The vineyard is close planted, 2.1 m by 0.9 m, and more vines, possibly pinot noir, will be planted as time permits. As well as looking after the new vineyard, Andrew is working as a consultant viticulturist for no fewer than fifteen new vineyard projects on the peninsula, four of them in commercial production in 1989.

Winemaker in the group is Peter Cumming, a Roseworthy College graduate. He works in the fine new winery built in 1989 at Scotchman's Hill Vineyard at Drysdale, on the Bellarine Peninsula north of Geelong. The Hickinbothams helped design the winery, and they lease it from vineyard owner David Browne. There they make the Scotchman's Hill wine and that of half-a-dozen other small producers, as well as their own

range of premium wines, which are the particular province of Jenny Hickinbotham. Wines released in 1989 included the outstanding 1988 Geelong pinot noir, which was declared best red table wine at the 1989 Smallmakers Wine Competition in Sydney. It was the first pinot to win a class traditionally dominated by cabernet sauvignon.

The grapes for the wine were grown by Ian and Wendy Coghill on their Bellarine Estate at Drysdale, and Jenny Hickinbotham believes the true cool climate of the area helps give the pinot fruit tremendous colour and depth because the colour proteins are not affected by heat, as they are in warmer areas of the country. Another fine wine from the Coghill's vineyard was the 1988 Geelong chardonnay labelled Sylvie's chardonnay. During vintage that year French winemaker Sylvie Spielmann worked with the Hickinbothams and produced a wine very much in the style of her native Alsace, oak fermented but with no malolactic fermentation, using French yeasts and allowing some solids to remain in the wine. It was a stylish and brilliant wine, and it very much reflected the great skills the Hickinbothams bring to their work. Their considerable influence in the Australian wine scene continues to be felt.

Karina Vineyard

Karina is a pretty little vineyard next door to Crittenden's Dromana Estate in Harrisons Road, Dromana. It is different from other peninsula vineyards in that it concentrates on white varieties rather than red. Graeme and Jan Pinney planted just over 1 hectare of sauvignon blanc and Rhine riesling in 1984, and by 1987 they had produced a substantial crop of just over 5 tonnes of fruit. They built a small winery and the fruit was processed on the property with the help of winemaker and consultant John Ellis.

In 1988 and 1989 they continued to produce the two varietal whites; the riesling, a particularly aromatic wine with fine acid structure; and the wood-fermented sauvignon blanc, a surprisingly robust wine with good varietal character. The Pinneys were granted a vigneron's licence in 1987, and their wines are available in local restaurants and by mail order.

King's Creek Vineyard

The little township of Bittern lies between Hastings and Balnarring, on the eastern side of Mornington Peninsula overlooking Western Port Bay. If those directions sound confusing it is because the famed navigator, George Bass, discovered and named Western Port before reaching Port Phillip Bay, the entrance to which is 30 km further west. This is good grazing and apple-growing land, and popular with thoroughbred horse stud proprietors; but as yet vineyard development has been sparse.

In 1981, however, Jim and Faye Temple followed the example of some of their more southerly neighbours and planted 2.4 hectares of vines—chardonnay, pinot noir and cabernet sauvignon—on their property in Myers Road, Bittern. The first commercial crop was in 1985; the chardonnay and cabernet were vinified at Elgee Park and the pinot at Prince Albert, west of Geelong, by pinot specialist Bruce Hyett. These were released in 1987, and small amounts of King's Creek wines remain available through local wine shops.

Main Ridge Estate

Nat White, like Garry Crittenden and the Hickinbothams, is a pioneer in viticulture on the Mornington Peninsula and one who has provided inspiration to a number of producers who have followed in his path. While working as a civil engineer he made several visits to Europe in the 1960s and fell in love with the elegant wines of Bordeaux and Burgundy. Recognising the cool-climate quality of these wines he began looking for a suitable area to establish a vineyard of his own. Eventually he chose the Mornington Peninsula in preference to Tasmania, basically because it was closer to home.

In 1975 he and his wife Rosalie began planting

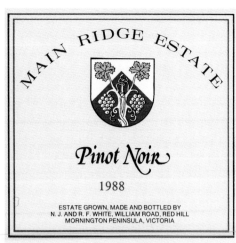

MAIN RIDGE ESTATE

Pinot Noir

1988

ESTATE GROWN, MADE AND BOTTLED BY
N. J. AND R. F. WHITE, WILLIAM ROAD, RED HILL
MORNINGTON PENINSULA, VICTORIA

12.8% Alc. Vol. Produce of Australia 750ml.
PRESERVATIVE (220) ADDED

vines at Red Hill South, in the very heart of the peninsula, adding 0.4 hectares every year until 1981. Their 2.4 hectare vineyard on the deep red well-drained basalt soil of Main Ridge, some 300 m above sea level, now contains chardonnay, pinot noir, pinot meunier, cabernet sauvignon and cabernet franc. With the help of Rosalie's father, retired chemist Gwyn Jones, they built a handsome red brick and timber winery in 1980, and made their first sales in the following year. They were the first commercial releases from this part of the world in the twentieth century.

In the meantime, Nat White had been doing oenology and viticulture courses at Riverina College, and in 1984 he gave away engineering to become a full-time vigneron and winemaker. His wines are now Main Ridge Estate chardonnay, a very beautiful wine much more reminiscent of chablis than most Australian attempts at this variety; and his pinot noir, a very Burgundian wine with a rich fruit nose and a deceptively long palate which gives the impression that it will live and prosper for many years. Main Ridge Estate cabernet sauvignon also has great depth of flavour and regional cabernet character, with a Bordeaux edge to its long, perceptibly acid finish.

Massoni Main Creek Vineyard

Leon Massoni was one of Melbourne's best-known restaurateurs, a member of the so-called 'Spaghetti Mafia', the distinguished group of Italian families who transformed the city's eating habits from the 1930s onwards. The Molinas are still in business but the Triacas and the

Codognottos and Virgonas had all given the game away by 1988 when Leon and Vivienne Massoni retired from their beloved Tolarno in St Kilda to their so-called 'superannuation package' on the Mornington Peninsula.

After selling their restaurant, they bought a tiny vineyard on the Mornington–Flinders Road in Red Hill. The vineyard had been planted in 1984—a single hectare of clone P.58 chardonnay —and, at 300 m up on the basalt slopes of Main Ridge, was one of the most elevated vineyards on the peninsula. The first Massoni wine was made by the Hickinbothams at Scotchman's Hill in 1989, and was due for release in June 1990. Because of great contrasts in temperature during the ripening period it was a difficult vintage on the peninsula, but the wine showed early signs of a stylishness Leon Massoni hopes presages well for the future.

Merricks Estate

Melbourne solicitor George Kefford is another new generation wine lover who wanted a vineyard of his own and chose the Mornington Peninsula, this time Merricks, on the eastern side of Main Ridge and at its highest point, Arthurs Seat, overlooking Western Port Bay. In 1977 he planted his first vines on part of what had been an old dairy farm in Thompson's Lane, Merricks, and now has a vineyard of 2.5 hectares of cabernet sauvignon, shiraz, pinot noir, chardonnay and Rhine riesling.

With the help of Lillydale Vineyard's Alex White, he makes a small range of typical peninsula wine, his reds in particular showing outstanding form. Merricks 1984 cabernet and 1984 shiraz won gold and silver medals respectively at the Seymour and Lilydale shows, and the 1986 cabernet repeated the success at Seymour. In 1987 the chardonnay was an outstanding wine, crafted like most Alec White wines into a very fine chablis style.

Moorfield Vintners

A century ago Melbourne's suburbs were dotted with vineyards, and the inner city had a coterie of wine merchants who bought, blended and bottled wine from all over Victoria for sale at home and overseas. Samuel Wynn was one of the best-known merchants, and others were Max Cohn, George Adams, George Sutherland Smith

and Matthew Lang. In later years there were companies such as Nathan and Wyeth and W.J. Seabrook, but it was not until 1989 that changes in the Victorian licensing law allowed Moorfield Vintners to resurrect the tradition of the 'city winery'.

For a number of years Roy Moorfield had been involved in the business of liquor retailing through his own premises in North Melbourne, while at the same time taking up small parcels of wine from all over the country and wholesaling them under his own Moorfield label. Some notable examples were his 'Western Shiraz' from the redoubtable Roley Birks at Wendouree, near Clare in South Australia, and fortified sherries and muscat from small producers in the Rutherglen region. In 1989, however, he was granted a retailing licence, and his 'winery' in Arden Street, North Melbourne, has facilities to match those of many of the country's so-called 'boutiques'.

Producers large and small have parcels of wine at the end of each vintage which either don't fit in with their own sales patterns, or are simply uneconomic to bottle and sell on their own. Roy Moorfield has made a profitable and interesting business out of gathering such wines together for blending and further maturation either in oak or in bottle. Among his suppliers are such distinguished names as Jack Schulz, Stuart Anderson, Mick Morris, Dominique Portet, Neill Robb, Tim Knappstein and Andrew Mitchell; and his customers in the trade are many. Among house-wine customers, for instance, is the well-known Castaway Island resort in Fiji, for whom he bottles a special blend of Clare shiraz, and a white based on chardonnay from Coonawarra.

Roy Moorfield sees his role as similar to that of the 'negociants' who are the mainstay of the French wine industry in Burgundy and Bordeaux. They are renowned for their capacity to blend great wines from dozens of small producers. Roy Moorfield has shown that he too is able to provide wines which reflect regional character and popular style.

Moorooduc Estate

Dr Richard McIntyre is one of many Melbourne professional people moving into wine production on the Mornington Peninsula. These days the list of growers looks like a roll call from the AMA or the Law Society! In this case, the McIntyre family started planting 2 hectares of vines on a north-facing hillside in Derril Road, Moorooduc, in 1983. The vineyard overlooks Devils Bend Creek, a tributary of Devils Bend reservoir, one of the peninsula's main domestic water sources. The soil is grey sandy loam on a yellow sandy clay subsoil, and the vines are planted in north-south rows with the canopy trained in a vertical curtain to maximise exposure to the sun. The main varieties are cabernet, chardonnay and pinot noir.

In 1987 they built a rammed-earth winery and the wine that year was made with the help of Nat White from Main Ridge Estate. Since then the Moorooduc style has begun to evolve very nicely. There are three wines, the most promising so far being chardonnay, an elegant, obviously cool-climate wine with intense citrus-melon fruit flavours, barrel fermented and matured in good French oak. Small quantities of pinot noir have shown great promise, and a Bordeaux blend dominated by cabernet sauvignon has also shown intense cool-climate fruit character and soft tannins.

St Neot's Vineyard

St Neot was a Cornish-Celtic saint who was said to be a relative of Alfred the Great. He gave his name to a little village in Cornwall, and to an old Gothic mansion in the Melbourne suburb of South Yarra, part of which became the home of Elvala and Philip Ayton. When they bought a property at Red Hill South they were going to call it Pindari, local Aboriginal dialect for 'high place', but there were so many other Pindaris around that instead they settled on the name of St Neot's.

The Aytons began planting vines on the 10 hectare property overlooking Western Port Bay and Phillip Island in 1980, and now have 1.6 hectares of pinot noir, chardonnay, merlot, cabernet sauvignon, semillon and Rhine riesling. Andrew Hickinbotham is the viticultural consultant, and Hickinbotham's winemaker Peter Cumming makes the wine at Scotchman's Hill. The first vintage, in 1987, was made with the help of Adam Wynn, and then the semillon showed outstanding promise. Since then the wines have been produced under the Hickinbotham estate label, the pinot noir and chardonnay being sold exclusively through the well-known chain of Staley restaurants in Melbourne, Sydney and the Gold Coast.

Stonier's Merricks Vineyard

Brian Stonier is another of the Mornington Peninsula pioneers, and with nearly 15 hectares under vines, one of its largest wine producers. He began planting vines in 1978, and now the

Artificial windbreaks in place, awaiting growth of natural windbreaks, at Stonier's Merricks Vineyard.

vineyard is more or less equally divided between cabernet sauvignon, chardonnay and pinot noir, with small plantings of merlot and cabernet franc. The wines were made by Stephen Hickinbotham from 1982 until his death in 1986. In 1987 Taltarni's Dominique Portet undertook the task at Elgee Park, whose facilities the Stoniers still use. The Hickinbotham connection continued through viticultural consultant Andrew Hickinbotham, who supervised later plantings of the Bordeaux varieties cabernet sauvignon, cabernet franc and merlot.

The picturesque vineyard in Thompson's Lane, Merricks, is now producing three wines, all of them very much in the peninsula style of elegant structure, intense fruit and the promise of long life. The cabernet sauvignon is becoming more complex with the addition of merlot and cabernet franc. The chardonnay and pinot noir have been showing absolutely outstanding style—they are beautiful Burgundy-like wines which will doubtless bring many more producers to this part of the world.

Talavera Wines

W.J. Seabrook was a Scot who came to Australia in 1878 and settled in Melbourne, taking over the Little Collins Street premises of Burgoynes, one of the first of the Australian colonial wine shippers. He bought wine from all over Australia for export and for local consumption, and he called his best tawny port Talavera, after the battle in the Peninsula Wars in which Wellington managed to stave off a French attack on British wine interests in the Douro district of Portugal.

Under later generations of Seabrooks the company moved to lovely bluestone premises in Lonsdale Street, still known as Seabrook House (inhabited mainly now by law offices). In 1975 Doug Seabrook, well-known wine judge, sold the company to Hermann Schneider of Two Faces restaurant fame. Three years later Hermann joined forces with the wine merchants Duke and Moorfield (now Moorfield Vintners), and the W.J. Seabrook operation shifted to Erroll Street, North Melbourne.

In 1982 the company was taken over by Hugh Cuthbertson, who had worked for Duke and Moorfield but then went out on his own after completing the oenology course at Roseworthy College. In 1987 he in turn sold his interests to Russell Branton, one of the original partners in Warrenmang Wines at Moonambel, in western Victoria.

The new company, with premises in Queensberry Street, North Melbourne, became known as W.J. Seabrook Tucker & Co., and one of its major cellar operations is still the maintenance of the fortified wine soleras laid down by the Seabrooks so many years ago. Since 1982 they have been sold nationally under the Talavera label—a superb range of nine sherries, ports, muscats and tokays for which the company has gained a well-deserved reputation.

One of the constants in Seabrook operations since 1956 has been Ladislaw Jaciow, the Ukrainian-born cellarmaster simply known as Jack. He learnt the art of blending and maturing wines under Doug Seabrook and practises it to this day, supervising the buying of new wines for the soleras and laying down wines which may make up new blends in the future. Rutherglen muscat and tokay are the only wines in the cellar which come from a specified district. The sherries, and there are five of them, come from places such as Mildura and the Barossa Valley; and similarly the ports, Talavera and VO Tawny, are blends from various districts. Among the sherries is Jack's Blend, a fino with lovely flor character and well-integrated wood which is the result of long storage in Spanish sherry quarter-casks.

Yarra Valley

It is possible that a century ago the Yarra Valley, north and east of Melbourne, was producing the finest wines in Australia. As far as we know, no wines from this period survive so this has to be a subjective judgment. Nevertheless, we know that elsewhere in the colony wine was encouraged as a substitute for the demon rum; winemakers tended to follow goldminers on their quest for riches to many parts of Australia because miners were a thirsty lot, and this basic form of alcohol was an aid to both celebration and commiseration. In the latter part of the nineteenth century wine exports to Europe were booming, but the taste was mainly for fortified wine, as it was at home, and it was here that the great wine estates in north-east Victoria prospered. They were all eventually destroyed by

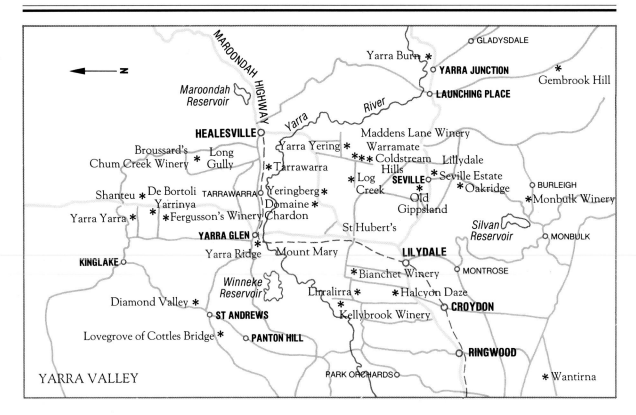

YARRA VALLEY

phylloxera; but the Yarra Valley, which the invading louse bypassed on its hungry way north, fell into decline because its wine was too good, too delicate, too refined and too 'European' for the feisty colonial palate. It is interesting that the Yarra Valley may now be poised once again to assume the mantle we have, perhaps carelessly, thus granted it.

Events in the Yarra Valley, and their connection with the very beginnings of wine production in this country, are well chronicled, but few accounts are as precise as that given by one of the pioneers himself, Hubert de Castella, in his book *John Bull's Vineyard*, first published in 1886. It was subtitled *Australian Sketches*, and here indeed is a detail from a well-wrought portrait of events in those early days:

John Macarthur, who came to Sydney in 1791 as a captain in the New South Wales corps, and to whom Australia is indebted for the introduction of the merino sheep, has also the honour of having been the first to plant an Australian vineyard.

Summoned to England in consequence of his quarrel with Governor Bligh, he was forbidden to return to Sydney from 1811 till 1817, and he devoted that time to the education of his sons, and to travelling with them on the Continent, studying all that could be of advantage to the Colony and

could be introduced on his estate at Camden.

His youngest son, William (afterwards Sir William Macarthur), born at Parramatta in 1800, was placed at school at Vevey in Switzerland. The stay of that young man amid the vines which cover the fair slopes of the Lake of Geneva had an influence, not only on the establishment of the Camden vineyard, but also, indirectly, on Victorian viticulture.

Macarthur's best comrade at Vevey was the Count Louis de Pourtales of Neuchatel, and the latter, from having been the confidante of the young Australian's hopeful tales of his native land, became one of the few on the Continent possessing, as far back as the first quarter of the present century, any special knowledge of the New Holland of these days.

An Englishman, of French extraction, Mr Charles La Trobe, married in 1835 a relative of the Pourtales, Mdlle de Montmollin, and was appointed in 1839 first Superintendent of Port Phillip (afterwards first Governor of the Colony of Victoria). M. Louis de Pourtales' recollections of the sanguine descriptions of his Australian school mate contributed in giving to his cousin, Mrs La Trobe, the courage necessary to start for that distant region.

My parents were living in Neuchatel at the time, and I well remember the astonishment and awe of us little children when told how Mrs La Trobe would be six months on the big sea, how she was to take with her a wooden house in her ship—to live in it in a country peopled with savages.

In a small community, such as Neuchatel was fifty years ago, the departure for the antipodes of a lady belonging to one of the oldest and richest families of the town, created a sensation. Five years after Mr La Trobe's arrival in Melbourne, eleven men had started from the Canton of Neuchatel for Australia. They had settled near each other in the district of Geelong, and, being familiar with the cultivation of the vine, all had planted vineyards around their homes.

In 1848, a nephew of Mrs La Trobe and my brother, both only twenty-one years of age, came to Victoria to be squatters. Another nephew of Mrs La Trobe, Mr G. de Pury, now a Swiss Consul in Melbourne, joined them in 1851, I, myself, in 1854.

My brother had been brought to the station of Yering, thirty miles distant from Melbourne. By a curious coincidence, on that station, as early as 1840, namely before the Geelong settlement, William Ryrie, its original owner, and one of the pioneers of Port Phillip, had planted with vine cuttings from Camden about an acre, the first Victorian vineyard.

Wine growing is an enticing pursuit. It is an art, a bond of hospitality, pride to the host and good humour to his friend. Today the Yering vineyard occupies one hundred acres, and on the same bank of the river Yarra, M de Pury has seventy acres under vines at Yeringberg, and myself 260 acres at St Hubert's.

Official historians have not done much better than that. There is still some doubt about whether William Ryrie was Victoria's first vigneron because of the belief that Edward Henty brought some vine cuttings with him from Tasmania when he settled Portland in 1834; but the records actually talk about Yering wine, whereas there was never any mention of wine at Portland.

Nevertheless, Paul de Castella's acquisition of part of Ryrie's Yering station in 1848 is well documented, as is young brother Hubert's arrival in 1854 and his subsequent establishment of St Hubert's. It is important to note that these were significant plantings, and not merely the work of enthusiastic dilettantes. Yering occupied 40 hectares, de Pury's Yerinberg was 28 hectares, and St Hubert's 105 hectares (now, in replanted form, it is only 18 hectares!).

And by all accounts, the wine was very good.

These were sophisticated European palates, after all, and Paul de Castella had established his vineyard with 20 000 cuttings, most of them cabernet sauvignon, from Château Lafite. Paul was a generous host, and was in the habit of providing his guests with a glass of Pommard—a good Burgundy he was supplied with by a friendly French sea captain whenever his ship sailed into Hobson's Bay. One evening, after a long day in the saddle, a servant announced that there was no Pommard left. As Dr Sam Benwell recounts in his *Journey to Wine in Victoria*, the servant, who had worked previously for Ryrie, appeared with a large china jug containing some of Ryrie's wine. 'Better than Pommard!' the cheerful guests proclaimed.

At the great Melbourne International Exhibition of 1881 St Hubert's was awarded the prize for the most meritorious exhibit in the whole show. The prize, a silver table set of seven silver-gilt epergnes worth 25 000 francs, or £800 was awarded by Emperor Wilhelm I of Germany. In 1889, St Hubert's was honoured again with the Grand Prix at the Paris Exposition. It was one of only fourteen such prizes given to wine from all over the world, so there could not have been much doubt about the quality.

Eventually St Hubert's passed into the hands of David Mitchell, the father of Dame Nellie Melba. By then a great chapter in Australian wine history was drawing to a close. One of the last vintages was made at Yeringberg in 1921, by which time other vineyards in the Lilydale–Yarra Valley area had already passed into disuse.

The problem was not phylloxera but agricultural economics. The grape harvest was small by comparison with other areas in Victoria, partly because the best vines were low yielders, partly because spring frosts became an added hazard as more timber was cleared, and partly because of the decline in soil fertility through neglect of fertilisers. Overwhelmingly, there was the fact that wine lovers were few, and most Australians were unable or unwilling to pay the price necessary for quality.

Tastes had changed; people preferred the fortified wines, sherries, ports and muscats which were readily available from the north-east of the state in particular. As Melbourne continued its spread eastwards, land values increased and dairying and fruit and vegetable growing became a more profitable pursuit than grapegrowing.

The mid-1960s marked a renewal of faith in this beautiful area, however, and if future governments can curb the desire to open the region up for housing development, there is little doubt that it will once again become a major, quality Australian wine-producing area.

Late spring frosts continue to be a problem for the new generation of vignerons, and strong northerly winds are not welcome. Downy and powdery mildew are controlled easily enough by spraying; but birds, attracted by several decades of fruit farmers, are such a major pest that some growers have even experimented with netting their vines.

Rainfall varies between 750 mm and 850 mm, falling chiefly in winter and spring, a good pattern for viticulture. The climate is cool with a slow ripening period during March and April, and soils, varying greatly from red to grey, are generally friable and well drained. The emphasis among the new growers is on premium grape varieties such as cabernet sauvignon, pinot noir and chardonnay; although now the great Bordeaux blending grapes—cabernet franc, merlot, malbec and so on—are appearing. Shiraz, Rhine riesling and sauvignon blanc are grown as well.

Yields are comparatively low, usually under 2 tonnes to the hectare, but quality is high and the future bright. The earlier plantings in this welcome renaissance tended to be small, many of them virtually hobby-farm size with owners working at other jobs and living elsewhere. In 1988 and 1989 there were some remarkable new projects coming into fruition, including the Domain Chandon sparkling wine venture at Coldstream, and very large vineyard developments at Hoddles Creek, Wombat Creek and Healesville.

More and more producers are seeing the complementary aspects of good winemaking and tourism. There is no doubt that future generations of Melburnians will regard the Yarra Valley as fondly as Sydney people now do the Hunter Valley, and citizens of Adelaide their Barossa Valley and Southern Vales.

Bianchet Winery

Lou Bianchet came to Australia from the Veneto region of Italy in 1950 as a twenty-one-year-old cabinet-maker looking to find room for his skills in a new world. By 1953 he had his own subcontracting business in the building trade in and around Melbourne, and by 1974 he was well off enough to shift the business to Lilydale, on the eastern outskirts of the city but still rural enough to be part of the Yarra Valley. Two years later he bought a small farm north of the town, and like any farmer in the Veneto he planted vines.

His first cuttings were cabernet sauvignon and shiraz, and by 1980 Lou was able to make his first, very small commercial vintage. Although he had no formal training in winemaking his early efforts encouraged him to expand production, and in succeeding years he increased his plantings to include pinot noir, merlot, chardonnay, traminer, tokay and the Italian white variety from Friuli, verduzzo. In 1986 he gave up building and turned to winemaking full time, and since then Lou Bianchet and his wines have enjoyed considerable success.

One of the qualities emerging from the Yarra Valley is its ability to produce good pinot noir as a red varietal, and Lou Bianchet has followed the trend. His pinots have all been remarkably similar, quite full-bodied wines which come from a short ferment; hot to begin with, then cooling and slowing to produce a lush, plummy wine with plenty of colour and staying power. It is remarkably similar to that being made nearby by Dr Peter McMahon and Guill de Pury, which suggests the emergence of a strong, lower Yarra Valley style.

In 1980 Lou Bianchet visited the United States, where he saw a lot of plantings of merlot and tasted some straight bottlings of the variety in California. He couldn't wait to get back to Lilydale to plant some of his own, and now he is in the vanguard of a merlot crusade which is gaining more and more followers in that part of the world. His first straight merlot came in very small quantities in 1983, followed by commercial amounts in 1984 which had an exemplary varietal nose, with lots of sweet berry character and herbaceous overtones. It won a silver medal in the merlot class at the Perth Show in 1985 (no gold medal was awarded). His 1985 wine was even better, winning gold in Hobart where it was the most highly rated merlot in the 1987 show. His 1985 pinot noir won the Aberfeldy Trophy for the best pinot (Class 30) in the same show.

These days Lou Bianchet has a partner in his son-in-law, Tony Inglese. They share neighbouring 4 hectare lots in Victoria Road, Lilydale, with a total of 6 hectares under vines. In 1984 they updated their winery and cellar door tasting room, and they are producing a small but very high-quality range of table wines in the Yarra Valley style. Their verduzzo, however, is a Lilydale one-off. Lou got the cuttings from Carlo Corino in Mudgee and it has been a highly successful transplant. The wine is dry, with a rich, honeyed palate not unlike marsanne—it is a beautiful table wine in the chablis style.

Broussard's Chum Creek Winery

Chum Creek is one of the smallest of the small Yarra Valley producers, making small amounts of wine during better seasons, and selling it at cellar door. It was established by Jim Broussard on land he owned in Cunninghams Road, Healesville, where in 1977 he planted 0.4 hectares of pinot noir and chardonnay in a picturesque valley surrounded by the Toolangi State Forest. In 1984 he planted a further 1.6 hectares of cabernet sauvignon. Those vines had their first vintage in 1987.

The climate is cool and mild in the Toolangi hills, which have an altitude of 200 m and an average rainfall of 1000 mm. Yield is not high, but the vineyard is on a moderate slope facing the north-east, meaning more sunlight and less frost. A winery was built in 1987, with earlier vintages being made at Reiner Klapp's Long Gully Estate, several kilometres away.

Jim's cabernet sauvignon is showing good potential, and his 1984 and 1986 pinot noir both won awards at the Lilydale Show.

Coldstream Hills

James Halliday, lawyer, author, wine judge and commentator, had a revivifying effect on the rebirth of the Yarra Valley at a time when it seemed to be losing a little of its 1970s steam. He first visited the area in 1980 to taste its wines and to talk to and write about its winemakers, and he was more than impressed. At the time he was an active partner in Brokenwood vineyard and winery in the Hunter Valley, and had some pretty firm ideas on the way Australian winemaking and viticulture should be going.

In 1983 he moved from Sydney to take up a

1988 *Coldstream Hills*

P I N O T N O I R

R I S I N G V I N E Y A R D

PRODUCT OF AUSTRALIA. 11.5% ALC/VOL

750 ml

partnership in his law firm in Melbourne, and at that time he severed his connections with Brokenwood. Two years later he and his wife, Suzanne, bought Coldstream Hills, nearly 16 hectares of land with a handsome house and 270° views of the Yarra Valley spread beneath, a small dam and some 6 hectares of cleared but otherwise unimproved pasture. Virtually all of the land was steeply sloping, and the remaining 9.8 hectares of forest was subject to a tree preservation order.

In December 1985, 5 hectares of vines were close-planted in rows straight up and down the slopes (of over 20°) in the German or Swiss style. The de Castellas would have undoubtedly approved. The vines, all drop irrigated, were mainly pinot noir, with smaller quantities of cabernet sauvignon, cabernet franc, merlot and chardonnay. That same year the first Coldstream Hills wines were made by James at Elgee Park, on the Mornington Peninsula, using grapes bought from various vineyards in the Yarra Valley. The 7 tonnes of fruit produced 450 cases of what became known as Four Vineyards Cabernet Sauvignon, an intriguing wine which showed there was a good deal more to the Yarra Valley than had been realised for some time.

In 1986 the same four vineyards provided 35 tonnes of fruit, which was processed at Louis Bialkower's Yarra Ridge winery using equipment James was stockpiling for his own winery. The crush produced 2400 cases of wine. This included Three Vineyards Pinot Noir and Three Vineyards Chardonnay, both of which won a swag of medals.

In 1987 James looked to crush about 75 tonnes of fruit, but yields were very much reduced in the valley because of poor fruit set in the cabernet sauvignon and losses caused by birds. The crush was reduced to 50 tonnes. Since then his own Coldstream Hills winery has been in operation, with an immediate capacity of 200 tonnes and room to expand to 400 tonnes.

In 1988, Coldstream Winemakers Ltd was floated on the Australian Stock Exchange, with James and Suzanne Halliday retaining a controlling interest. Long-term contracts for the supply of premium Yarra Valley grapes have been drawn up with Shantell Vineyard, Calulu Park and Hillcrest Vineyard; and Charles Wright's Log Creek Vineyard will also sell its output to Coldstream Hills. The success of the venture so far has been outstanding, and there is no doubt that it will continue to be a quality pacesetter.

De Bortoli Yarrinya Estate

What was known as Chateau Yarrinya was established by Graeme Miller in 1971. Graeme, a graduate of Dookie Agricultural College, had taught agriculture, science and maths for eight years before he and his schoolteacher wife, Denise, settled on the 60 hectare property in Pinnacle Lane, Dixons Creek, 8 km from Yarra Glen and 60 km from Melbourne.

Originally he took up dairy farming but, encouraged by the swing back to vines in the Yarra Valley, he planted 4 hectares of vines with the help of Don and Jan Hall, 3000 rootlings each of cabernet sauvignon and shiraz. They had their first small crop in 1974, and in 1976 their first sizeable vintage of 27 000 litres was made with some difficulty in the cowshed. That same year they began construction of their mock Norman castle winery and cellars, and got their vigneron's licence. They began cellar door sales in 1977, which was to be a very important year. Graeme's 1977 Cabernet Sauvignon won the Jimmy Watson Trophy for the best one-year-old red wine in the 1978 Melbourne Show—the first (and only) Yarra Valley wine to have taken this prestigious award. It was also the first time it had been won by a so-called 'boutique' winery, and sales of new oak in the valley shot up as a result.

Eventually the vineyard grew to 14 hectares with the inclusion of merlot, malbec, pinot noir, Rhine riesling, traminer and chardonnay.

Although Graeme never repeated his Jimmy Watson triumph, his standards remained high and in 1980, at the Adelaide Show, his 1978 malbec blend was the best light red. In 1987 he sold the property to the De Bortoli family of winemakers from Bilbul, in New South Wales, who changed the name and spent a great deal of money rebuilding the sales area to include a large function room. The winery was also rebuilt to include champagne-making facilities.

They also expanded the vineyard to 15 hectares with plantings of more pinot noir and merlot, plus sauvignon blanc and cabernet franc. This made it one of the largest 'estate' vineyards in the valley. The vines are some 160 m above sea level in 300–800 mm of topsoil over a rocky clay subsoil with some quartz. Rainfall averages 720 mm, making irrigation unnecessary. Frosts are rare, but downy mildew can be a problem as Grame Miller found in 1979 when the vintage was devastated. The vines are spaced at 1.5 m in rows 3 m apart, and yields vary a lot, variety to variety, from 5 tonnes per hectare for cabernet, for instance, to 8–10 tonnes for shiraz.

The De Bortolis have kept up the good work. At the 1988 Melbourne Wine Show they won he trophy for best in Class 39 with their 1986 Pinot Noir, and the trophy for best Victorian white wine (Class 43) with their 1987 Chardonnay.

Diamond Valley Vineyards

One of the most successful small ventures in the Yarra Valley has been David and Cathy Lance's Diamond Valley, a beautiful, north-facing hillside of vines overlooking Diamond Creek at St

Andrews, out on the Kinglake Road, 40 km from Melbourne. In recent years they have had a remarkable run at the nation's wine shows. At one stage during 1987 they won no fewer than fifteen gold medals, eleven silver and thirty bronze—culminating at the Melbourne Show that year with the trophy for most successful exhibitor in Victorian classes. Considering that many larger companies are overjoyed when they win a single bronze medal, this was pretty dramatic stuff.

The quest for quality at Diamond Valley had its beginnings many years ago, when David was doing post-graduate work in chemistry in Canada. While overseas he and Cathy encountered French and German wines for the first time. They returned to Melbourne in 1965, David with a new PhD and a job at Carlton and United Breweries, in what was the middle of the Australian wine boom they had been reading about. Local wines seemed to suffer by comparison with those they had tasted overseas, however, and they wondered if it would ever be possible to reproduce those European styles of lightness, fruitiness and elegance.

David, being a microbiologist, felt he knew at least the principles of winemaking, and in 1967 he and some of his like-minded friends made some wine at home with grapes bought by Cathy's father in Mildura. The wine wasn't bad, but David thought he could do better with cool-climate fruit. He and his friends toured the Goulburn Valley unsuccessfully looking for grapes, and finally ended up in the Yarra Valley where the Cester family had, in 1966, replanted part of the once-famous St Hubert's vineyard at

Coldstream. Tom Cester wasn't interested in selling them fruit, but when they persisted he came up with a deal: you provide some scientific expertise and help us get our new winery up and running, and you can have some grapes.

This was the beginning of a relationship which saw David Lance, Alex White and Martin Grinbergs make the wine at St Hubert's (anonymously, because they all had other jobs at the time), and use the facilities at Cesters to make some for themselves as well. It was an arrangement which ended when St Hubert's was sold in 1987, by which time David's Diamond Valley and Alex and Martin's Lillydale Vineyards were both up and running.

While working for Carlton United Breweries and St Hubert's, David had a hankering for a property of his own. After looking around Geelong and other parts of the Yarra Valley, he and Cathy bought their 8 hectares at St Andrews in 1975. During 1976 they terraced half of their pretty hillside, built two dams, and planted 0.8 hectares each of pinot noir, Rhine riesling and 'cabernet'—a mixture of cabernet sauvignon, merlot, cabernet franc and malbec. The first two years brought their shocks. They lost about half of their new vines to a combination of frost, wombats, wallabies, rabbits and lousy weather. As it happened, they had used a grader to do their terracing and the steel blade had polished the surface of the loamy soil to such an extent that it inhibited water absorption. They did a lot of digging, replaced all the 'misses' during 1978–79, and installed drip irrigation from the dams. This worked so well that within another year or so it was impossible to tell the new vines from the old.

They picked their first crop in 1980, which was a very dry year; then came the drought in 1983 when their dams went dry and they had to run a pipe under Kinglake Road to a friend's dam closer to Diamond Creek. The vines were stressed, but provided some beautiful fruit. In fact, winter at St Andrews can be so damp that the vines suffer from 'wet feet', and they appeared to relish the drier conditions of 1983.

David Lance made the first Diamond Valley wine in 1980 at St Hubert's, and quitted Carlton United Breweries the following year when it was available for sale. He planted a further 0.2 hectares to chardonnay and built two more dams,

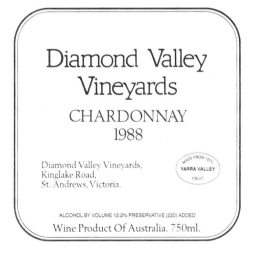

Diamond Valley
Vineyards
CHARDONNAY
1988

Diamond Valley Vineyards,
Kinglake Road,
St. Andrews, Victoria.

MADE FROM 100%
YARRA VALLEY
FRUIT

ALCOHOL BY VOLUME 12.2% PRESERVATIVE (220) ADDED
Wine Product Of Australia. 750ml.

which make the place practically drought-proof. Since leaving St Hubert's in 1987, he has made his wine at David and Chris Fyffe's Yarra Burn. The only expansion he sees now at Diamond Valley is the establishment of its own winery, because the vineyard is as big as he and Cathy can handle themselves. Nevertheless, in 1987 they bought in fruit from other growers in the area to make their Blue Label range of wines, which are also of very high quality and help the cash flow.

Domaine Chandon

One of the more remarkable aspects of the Australian wine industry in the past decade has been the growth in the market for sparkling wine made by the authentic French *méthode champenoise*. In the latter half of the 1980s the fall in value of the Australian dollar and the consequent rise in that of the French franc meant that even the lower rung of French champagnes was becoming increasingly expensive, and a number of Australian companies moved quickly to fill the gap in the market.

Australia was one of the best champagne markets in the world per head of population. The French don't give sales away easily, and working on the 'if you can't beat 'em, join 'em' principle, several of France's major Champagne houses became involved in a series of joint ventures in Australia to make sparkling wine. None has been on the scale of Domaine Chandon, however—an Australian version of the venture which took Moet et Chandon into the United States so successfully in 1973.

In fact, it was John Wright, head of Domaine Chandon in California's Napa Valley, who more or less decided on the Yarra Valley as the site for operations in Australia while on a visit in 1985. He was staggered by the quality of some of the local wines, and at his urging Moet appointed Dr Tony Jordan, then a partner in the well-known consultancy firm, Oentec, to find and establish Domaine Chandon Australia. Dr Jordan, later to become managing director of the new company, went from one end of the valley to the other, from the river flats around Yarra Glen to the mountainous reaches of Hoddles and Wombat Creeks. He finally settled on the 128 hectare Green Point farm at Coldstream.

The farm, which last century had been flanked by St Hubert's and Yeringberg, was purchased in 1987, and Tony Jordan immediately began planting 25 hectares to the great grape varieties of Champagne—chardonnay, pinot noir and pinot meunier. While the vines were maturing he put together two cuvées made from grapes bought from Coonawarra and from several parts of Victoria, the Yarra Valley, Mansfield, Nagambie and Mt Macedon. The first of these, released in June 1989, was a straight chardonnay, and the second, released at the end of the year, included 25 per cent pinot noir. Both non-vintage wines, they came on to the market at around $20 per bottle.

Closely supervising the blending of the wines were Edmund Maudiere, the chief winemaker at Moet et Chandon who also oversees the company's interests in Argentina, California and Spain; and Richard Geffroy, another of Moet's winemakers, who spent vintages 1987 and 1988 in southern Australia racing from vineyard to vineyard ensuring that grapes were picked when they were just right. They were both on hand in March 1989 when Tony Jordan and his assistant winemaker, Wayne Donaldson, crushed their first vintage in their own new winery at Domaine Chandon. At the time the winery had a roof but no walls, but grapes had ripened in a hurry after an unseasonable hot spell, and the show had to go on!

The dramatic, wedge-shaped winery is now the centrepiece of one of the more tourist-oriented winemaking operations in Victoria. The old Green Point farm homestead has been renovated to provide office space and tasting rooms. Due to be opened in 1990 was a restaurant and walled garden designed to lead visitors on through a riddling hall 50 m long to the winery, where galleries have been built for viewing the action on the winery floor.

Although the winery itself is ultra-modern in terms of equipment, there is nothing particularly

Grapevines at Fergusson's in the Yarra Valley.

exotic in the operation. There is no crusher, and whole bunches of grapes are fed straight into a Blucher press. In the case of pinot, the juice is immediately separated from the skins, although some red pinot is retained for future pink cuvées. What is impressive in the winery is the room for manoeuvre. In financing the project (an estimated $7.5 million had gone into the venture by the end of 1989), Moet took the view that future expansion was important. A second Blucher press, for instance, was due to be installed in 1991, and there is room for two more after that.

When completed, Domaine Chandon Australia will be by far the largest winemaking operation in the Yarra Valley, and there are already signs that the size of the French investment has stimulated further growth in the area. Most of the fruit will come from its own vines on the estate but long-term contracts have also been signed with growers elsewhere in the valley and southern Victoria. Growers have been encouraged to plant top varietal clones and to follow French vineyard practices.

Fergusson's Winery

Until it was destroyed by fire just after vintage in 1989, Fergusson's winery and restaurant in Wills Road, Yarra Glen, was one of the showpieces of the valley. The restaurant—in which Peter Fergusson spit-roasted butts of local beef and his wife, Louise, prepared gourmet dishes—had for more than a decade been one of the more joyous places to eat and drink, not merely in the Yarra Valley but anywhere. The good news is that rebuilding is under way, and that a restored Fergussons will soon rise from the ashes.

Among the pioneers in the rebirth of the wine industry in the Yarra Valley, Peter Fergusson, an industrial chemist, and his brother, Michael, a design engineer, bought their property in 1968 and began planting 20 hectares of vines. The only building on the place at the time was a tractor shed in which they ate and slept. As the vineyard grew, more buildings were added. The tractor shed became a restaurant, and eventually the heart of a small village dedicated as much to having a good time as to producing good wine.

The restaurant provided cash flow while the vines matured, and by the time of the first vintage, in 1972, it had established itself as part of Yarra Valley life. The grapes were shiraz and cabernet sauvignon (Rhine riesling, and marsanne, chenin blanc and chardonnay came later), and early winemaking efforts were enthusiastic rather than immediately successful. Neither brother had formal winemaking training, and in 1978 Andrew Forsell joined the team as winemaker. He was immediately successful, his cabernet sauvignon of that year winning a gold medal in the Melbourne Show.

In 1983 Peter bought out his brother's interest in the property, and introduced a new range of Victorian wine to help improve the financial situation. At the time he was suffering from the economies of scale which affect all small producers. His annual crush was 60 tonnes from his own vineyard, producing between 4000 and 5000 cases of wine. Increasing costs meant increasing prices, and at that stage of the game few people were prepared to pay the $40 or so per bottle which the accountants had worked out represented a reasonable return on capital.

In the event, the introduction of the new range, which included chardonnay and 'winter warmer', a ready-mixed mulled wine, (an instant best-seller with the snowfields set), meant prices never went that high. With the help of the restaurant, Fergussons operated very happily. The quality end of production was not forgotten. Kerry Haydon, like Andrew Forsell a graduate of Riverina College in Wagga Wagga, was appointed winemaker in 1985, and she continued the very good work on their Yarra Valley shiraz, cabernet sauvignon and Rhine riesling.

Gembrook Hill Vineyards

In 1983, Melbourne dentist Dr Ian Marks bought some cleared land in Launching Place Road, Gembrook, 40 km south-east of Melbourne, and planted 4 hectares of vines. This is the most southerly vineyard in the Yarra Valley and also one of the most elevated, so Dr Marks chose early ripening varieties, sauvignon blanc, chardonnay and pinot noir. In 1987 he sold his first real crop of grapes to Garry Crittenden at Dromana Estate on the Mornington Peninsula. The following year he made small quantities of

each of his varietals with the help of Reg Egan, of Wantirna Estate. There is a small winery on the property, which Dr Marks runs basically as a weekend concern with the help of his son Andrew and other willing draftees. He hopes that some time in the future it will rescue him from dentistry.

Halcyon Daze Vineyard

Halcyon Daze was established in Uplands Road, Lilydale, by Richard and Cheryl Rackley in the winter of 1982. They planted 3.5 hectares of cabernet sauvignon, merlot, cabernet franc, chardonnay and Rhine riesling, and their aim was to produce hand-crafted wines of the highest standard. Their vineyard, on the northerly slope of an east-west ridge, is not irrigated, and yields so far have been fairly low.

In 1986 their cabernet vines produced only 1.25 tonnes per hectare, and there were very small quantities of merlot and cabernet franc. Richard blended them to make his first commercial release of cabernet sauvignon, however, and it was an impressive wine. It had deep purple colour, rich fruit and soft tannins, and good acid structure which will allow it to live gracefully for many years. He made riesling each year from 1986, and close plantings of pinot noir were expected to yield their first crop in 1990.

In 1989 he released a very fine botrytised Rhine riesling made in 1987, and a 1987 cabernet sauvignon which was a little lighter in body than the heroic 1986. There were also small amounts of 1988 chardonnay which showed promise, but in 1989 the grapes didn't ripen as expected, and the chardonnay was turned into a champagne-base wine. It was a bad year for bunch rot in his corner of Lilydale and, although he picked over his Rhine riesling no fewer than four times and hoped again to make a good botrytised wine, he had to leave about a third of the crop on the vine.

Richard said after such a vintage that he was not discouraged. He now owns the block next-door to his original property and that gives him another 10 hectares which he will plant when time and funds permit. Like many of the small Yarra Valley producers he is having to work hard at being a winemaker-producer, but results have been sufficiently encouraging for him to carry on. Halcyon days may yet be in sight.

Kellybrook Winery

By all accounts, Darren Kelly is the only champagne-cider maker left in the world. Once upon a time this art was practised almost everywhere cider apples were produced—in the west of England, in Normandy and Brittany in France, and at Lilydale in the Yarra Valley. There is plenty of ordinary cider produced, of course, and Darren Kelly does that as well; but he has been unable in his travels to track down anyone making the spare and elegant apple wine in the true *méthode champenoise* as he is doing at Kellybrook, his beautiful property at Wonga Park 30 km east of Melbourne.

Darren Kelly was an accountant, and in 1962 he and his wife, Farley, bought an apple orchard set in 19 hectares of rolling hillside not far from the banks of the Yarra River. They called it Kellybrook, after his ancestors' family home in County Westmeath, Ireland. In 1966 he decided to turn his apples into cider, and made two trips to England and France to study the skills

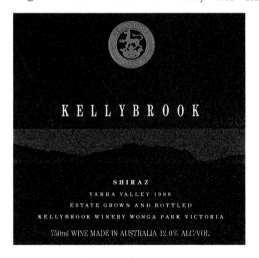

involved. He was given considerable assistance by the Cider Research Station near Bristol.

He was fortunate to have on his property the apple variety kingston black, which he describes as the cabernet sauvignon of cider apples. Apples tend to have a much higher pH than grapes, but the kingston black has acid and tannin and sugar in proportions not dissimilar to wine grapes. Darren, along with a friend at Olinda further up the Yarra Valley, had the only plantings in Australia. He makes his famous champagne cider in very much the same way as the real thing is made, although he has a mincer for his apples rather than a crusher. Thereafter, fermentation, bottling, disgorging and so on continues much as it does in any conventional winery. The result is quite superb—a brilliantly clear Champagne Cider Brut, with a fine bead, clean bouquet, and a long dry palate with a pleasing mix of apple and yeast flavours. At many tastings it has been mistaken for very high-quality sparkling wine, and by experts in the trade.

In 1976 he decided to make wine as well as cider, and replaced a few hectares of apple trees with vines; cabernet sauvignon, shiraz, Rhine riesling, chardonnay, traminer and merlot. While the vines were growing he made several table wines and some port from grapes bought from Bails brothers at Beverford, near Swan Hill. His first Kellybrook wine, which he called Wonga Park red, was made in 1982.

He now has 4 hectares of cider apples and 10 hectares of grapes, a busy winery which handles both cider and wine, and a small and aromatic distillery in which he makes a delicious pot-still, Australian-style Calvados. The property also boasts a large restaurant and reception area, at which the winemaker-cum-cidermaster is likely to burst into loud and melodious song after carving the roast.

Two ciders are made, Champagne Cider Brut and Old Gold English Style Cider (from jonathans and granny smiths). In 1989 Kellybrook released its first 'real' champagne, 1988 pinot noir and chardonnay *méthode champenoise*. Both his Kellybrook cabernet sauvignon and shiraz are excellent reds in typical Yarra Valley style with good flavour and fruit character but distinctly elegant. His 1988 chardonnay was a full-bodied wine showing some oak character and plenty of body.

Lillydale Vineyards

We have already mentioned in the section on Diamond Valley Vineyards that David Lance was one of a small cell of Carlton and United Brewery scientists who for a number of years made the wine at St Hubert's without their bosses being any the wiser. The other two were Alex White and Martin Grinbergs, and just as David Lance struck out on his own, they became partners in another Yarra Valley venture, Lillydale Vineyards.

In 1976, when they had decided that wine was going to be more fun than beer, White and Grinbergs bought land in Davross Court, Seville, off the Warburton Highway, on the way to Yarra Junction. They planted 2.3 hectares of chardonnay and traminer. In 1980 they bought a block across the road and planted Rhine riesling, and in 1984 added a small patch of sauvignon blanc to take their plantings to a total of 5.8 hectares. Further down the road at Coldstream they leased a vineyard of 2 hectares of cabernet sauvignon, merlot and sauvignon blanc.

Part of the deal with St Hubert's was that they could share winemaking facilities there. Their first wines, a chardonnay and a traminer, were made in 1980. The chardonnay, released in 1982, was an immediate success, and was voted 'most popular' wine by visitors to the exhibition of Victorian winemakers in Melbourne. By then both Alex and Martin had decided to become full-time winemakers, and in each subsequent year they produced wines which also met with considerable success.

The first Lillydale (the shire is Lillydale; for some reason the town is Lilydale) cabernet was made in 1983 and the first riesling in 1984, with pinot noir making its debut in 1986 and sauvignon blanc the following year. By then the

chardonnay, in particular, was developing quite a cellar style, becoming a little more austere and elegant—more Montrachet as time went by.

In 1988 St Hubert's was sold, and the three musketeers were told they had to find premises elsewhere. Alex and Martin had always thought that one day they would have a winery of their own, and suddenly, six months or so before vintage, they were forced into taking the momentous step of raising money, drawing up plans and getting builders on site to get the job done.

As it happened, it all turned out very well. Vintage 1988 was made with the walls of the new winery rising around them, and they were faced with crushing a record crop of 170 tonnes from their own vineyards. First of all they had to rescue their Vinomatic red fermenter from St Hubert's, along with a lot of other bits and pieces. At the last minute they were scrounging around the valley for stainless steel to store wine they were not expecting from the abundant harvest. But things went smoothly; the new Blucher tank press did everything expected of it, and by the time fermentation was over the new oak casks had arrived. The winery was, in fact, designed to allow two people to handle 200 tonnes of fruit, and everything went so well they were confident they could handle 300 tonnes without any trouble.

They won't reach that level for some time, but their vineyards are now maturing and yields are generally improving. Things at Lillydale are going very well indeed. The vineyards are on gently sloping land facing the north-east, at an elevation of about 150 m above sea level. Rainfall is 1000 m per year on average, and this is supplemented with drip irrigation, particularly during the warmest part of summer. The soil is grey silty clay loam, and they are keen on regular applications of gypsum.

Birds are a problem, as elsewhere in the Yarra Valley. At one stage Alex experimented with netting the main chardonnay block, and went to enormous trouble and a fair bit of expense to rig a German-made net from 5 m high poles. It appeared to be working until a summer northerly came along and deposited most of it several kilometres away. By winter 1989 he was trying to attract hawks to the property to act as feathered watch-dogs, an experiment his peers were watching with interest.

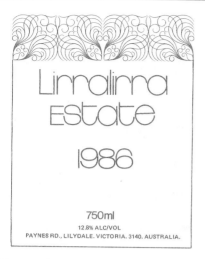

Lirralirra
Estate
1986

750ml
12.8% ALC/VOL
PAYNES RD., LILYDALE. VICTORIA. 3140. AUSTRALIA.

Lirralirra Estate

Lirralirra, in Paynes Road, Lilydale, is a family-owned estate established by Alan Jocelyn Smith with perhaps the unusual ambition of producing sauternes. The Smiths began planting their 4 hectare block with semillon, sauvignon blanc and muscadella in 1981. They were attracted to the idea of making dessert wine by the fact that their proximity to the Yarra River and relatively low altitude provided near perfect conditions for the noble rot, botrytis cinerea. They knew of the superb botrytised riesling produced by Dr Peter McMahon at nearby Seville Estate, and felt that they might do as well with the classic white grape varieties of Sauternes.

In fact their first wine, produced with the help of David Lloyd in 1986, was a dry blend of all varieties, and in 1987 they made a dry semillon–sauvignon blanc. They have yet to release a botrytised wine, but Alan says commercial quantities are not far away.

The vines at Lirralirra are about 80 m above sea-level and are planted on north-east facing slopes in contoured rows 3 m apart. The topsoil is relatively thin, about 10 cm, and overlies a clay shale subsoil in which there are widespread patches of shotty gravel. The vineyard lies in a rain shadow so some drip irrigation is used, and the entire area is netted to guard against bird attack. Expansion plans include the planting of just under a hectare of pinot noir.

Log Creek Vineyard

Log Creek flows through the Gruyere hills near Coldstream, in the Yarra Valley, and the combination of water, and distant misty high country reminded Charles and Jill Wright of Tuscany. The idea of producing their own wine in such circumstances proved irresistible, and in 1984 they began planting 4.5 hectares of vines, chardonnay, cabernet sauvignon and sauvignon blanc. The following year they planted more sauvignon blanc, and in 1987, a small block of pinot noir. In 1989 they put in merlot and cabernet franc, bringing the total vineyard area of picturesque Log Creek to 6.5 hectares.

Grapes are grown on a high trellising system with metre-wide T-cross bars, although experiments are being done with the GDC swing-arm system in the hope of providing maximum sun exposure. The vineyard faces north, and although there is drip irrigation there is no cultivation in the vineyard apart from care of a permanent grass cover between rows. Only organic pesticides are used.

The first full harvest was in 1989, when small amounts of wine were made by David Wollan and Leigh Clarnette at nearby Tarrawarra. Charles, a journalist, was expecting to sell this and subsequent vintages by mailing list once a vigneron's licence was obtained.

Long Gully Estate

Reiner and Irma Klapp say they have always had a strong interest in wine. Irma lived in the Mosel region of West Germany before coming to Australia more than thirty years ago, and it was while they were building their house in Healesville that the idea of having their own winery was sown. Vic Romano was their concrete contractor, and he had been growing vines for some years in the Yarra Valley. He remarked that Klapp's property would make a very suitable vineyard, so they set about planting chardonnay, Rhine riesling and cabernet sauvignon rootlings in 1982.

The vines prospered, so two years later the vineyard was extended to 15.6 hectares with the introduction of new varieties, pinot noir, sauvignon blanc, semillon, cabernet franc, merlot and malbec. The vines have a westerly aspect at an elevation of about 125 m above sea level. The natural slope allows cold air to 'drain' away, thus reducing the risk of frost in the spring growing season. The silty loam topsoil is 1.2 m deep, and annual rainfall of between 800–1000 mm occurs mainly in the winter and spring.

There is drip irrigation if it is needed in summer.

Originally the Klapps were going to have their wine made on a contract basis, but with the expansion of the vineyard they decided to build a winery of their own. In 1986 Mario Marson, who had been working for Dr John Middleton at Mount Mary, was appointed winemaker. Most of the fermentation is carried out in stainless steel, although both chardonnay and sauvignon blanc, which were first made in 1987, were fermented in French oak hogsheads. Both show the influence of this treatment. The chardonnay (which was later matured in American oak) shows up as quite a complex wine which will doubtless age well, and the sauvignon blanc displays grassy, herbal character and a pungent, lemony nose.

The cabernet sauvignon—which after 1987 contained small amounts of the 'Bordeaux' blends, merlot, cabernet franc and malbec—sells out within a very short time of release. Long Gully is one of the newer Yarra Valley 'boutiques' but certainly one of the most promising. When the vineyard is fully bearing total production will be around 12 000 cases.

Lovegrove of Cottles Bridge

Dr Malcolm Lovegrove and his wife Hilde are both psychologists, at La Trobe University and Victoria College respectively. In 1982 they began planting vines on their property at Cottles Bridge, between Kinglake and St Andrews on the northern slopes of the Yarra Valley, and now have 4 hectares of chardonnay, pinot noir, cabernet sauvignon, merlot and sauvignon blanc.

When their vines were young they sold their fruit to David and Cathy Lance at Diamond Valley, to Tarrawarra and to Domain Chandon. By 1988 they had a small winery of their own and their first vintage was made by Ian Leamon, a son of Chateau Leamon's redoubtable Phil Leamon. There were two wines, chardonnay and cabernets, a blend of their own cabernet sauvignon and merlot, and some cabernet franc bought from friends up the road.

The same pattern was followed for the second vintage in 1989, when the wines for a second label to be known as Dunmoochin were also laid down. There were two wines, a dry white and a light red, and the labels were designed by renowned artist and raconteur Clifton Pugh,

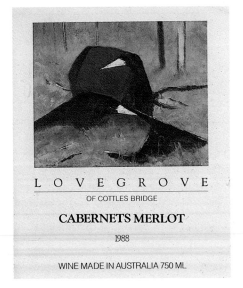

who lives nearby. Pugh, famed for his wombats among many other things, has also decorated the winery lavatory doors in remarkable fashion.

Dr Lovegrove says development at Cottles Bridge will be cautious but sure. In 1989 he planted more chardonnay and sauvignon blanc, and signed contracts with several new vineyard owners in the area to supply grapes during the next decade. Gary Baldwin of Oentec helped Ian Leamon in setting up the winery, and he employs a leading viticultural consultant. It is another very small Yarra Valley operation which is showing enormous promise.

Maddens Lane Winery

What was known as Prigorje Winery in Maddens Lane, Gruyere, was established in 1983 by Ivan Vlasic-Sostaric, who was born in the Prigorje region of Yugoslavia, the country's best-known wine-producing area. He planted 5 hectares of vines, shiraz, pinot noir, semillon and chardonnay; and in 1987 produced his first wines—a blend of reds he called a burgundy, and a dry white made from pinot noir and chardonnay.

In 1988, the property was sold to Geoff Norris, who until then, with the help of his family, had run the very successful Olinda Park Restaurant in Lilydale. The restaurant was a haven for winemakers from the Yarra Valley, and Geoff Norris was one of the enthusiasts who revived the Lilydale Wine Show in 1966. From then until 1972, when larger premises were found, the show was actually held in the restaurant, with a dinner party put on for contestants the following night.

The winery venture is more or less a retirement plan for Geoffrey. In 1989 he sold all of his grapes to other producers in the valley, and was still trying to make up his mind whether or not to label wine of his own.

Monbulk Winery

New Zealanders have been making wine from Kiwifruit, their aptly named strain of the Chinese gooseberry, for a number of years. One of the few commercial exponents of the craft in Australia is the Monbulk Winery, in Macclesfield Road, Monbulk—a pretty berry-growing region on the southern slopes of the Yarra Valley. In 1970 Paul and Ruth Jabornik imported the Hayward variety of Kiwifruit from New Zealand and established a plantation 300 m above sea level in rich red volcanic soil on the north-eastern slope of Stoney Creek.

They were thus one of the first commercial producers of the fruit in Victoria, but it was not until 1980 that they began making Kiwifruit wine. They caught the winemaking bug and in 1982 decided to plant grapes as well. They now have 2.5 hectares of Kiwifruit and 3 hectares of vines, mainly chardonnay but also cabernet franc, shiraz and Rhine riesling. They built a winery in 1984, and since 1986 have been supplementing their Kiwifruit wine with very good chardonnay and riesling. The Kiwifruit wine comes in four grades of sweetness from sweet to extra dry, and it has surprised more than one expert at blind tastings around town!

Mount Mary Vineyard

Dr John Middleton moved to Lilydale after service with the Royal Australian Air Force, setting up as a partner in a general practice in 1951. In 1958 he planted a few vines in his backyard on the advice of Colin Preece, at the time the head of Seppelt's operations at Great Western, and one of the best winemakers in Australia. Preece was very impressed by Middleton's first wine and encouraged him to learn more about both the science and art of winemaking. In 1971 John and his wife Marli bought Mount Mary, 75 hectares of land 5 km north of Lilydale, which had been owned by the Glennon family since the 1850s.

They started planting grapes that same year, 4.8 hectares of the best Bordeaux and Burgundy

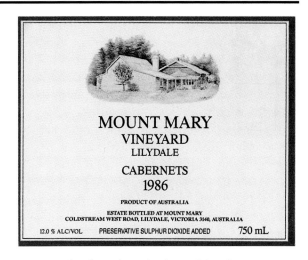

varieties, both red and white. The first vintage was in 1975, and in 1982 more vines were planted, taking the vineyard to 8 hectares. This now provides 25–30 tonnes of grapes each year. The vines are planted on north to north-easterly slopes lying between 85–100 m above sea level. The soil is a sandy clay loam overlaying degenerating Silurian mudstone and clays, and rainfall is about 800 mm a year. The vines are not irrigated but yields are good, the cabernet sauvignon, for example, returning around 7.5 tonnes per hectare.

Dr Middleton retired from medical practice in 1982 to become a full-time vigneron. Since then much has been written about his perfectionist ways in the vineyard and the winery. His winery has been likened to an operating theatre—it is fully air-conditioned and very well organised and equipped. He produces two white wines, chardonnay and a Bordeaux blend of sauvignon blanc, semillon and muscadel; both are cask-fermented, left for a year in oak and then bottled nine months before release. The reds are vat-fermented and temperature-controlled. Mount Mary Cabernets is again a Bordeaux-style blend of cabernet sauvignon, cabernet franc, merlot malbec and petit verdot, and it is left to mature in French oak barriques for two years. His second red, straight pinot noir, is also given eighteen months in new French oak and nine months bottle age.

Robin Bradley has described Mount Mary wines as 'among the most beautiful in the world'. The cabernet has been called the best red wine in Australia; the chardonnay is a complex and elegant wine which has great ageing potential; and his pinot noir also has exceptional character.

James Halliday referred to the 1978 pinot as one of the greatest Australian reds he had ever tasted. Dr Middleton's own assessment of his wines is that they are 'bloody good', and few will disagree. They are all in remarkably short supply and sell mainly through mailing list.

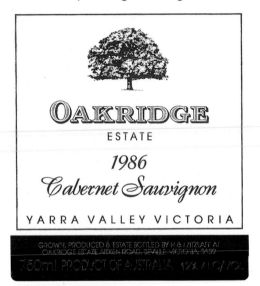

Oakridge Estate

Oakridge Estate, in Aitken Road, Seville, was a cherry orchard when Melbourne businessman Jim Zitzlaff and his wife Irene bought the property in 1974. There was not much which could be done with cherries so Jim decided to try grapegrowing. In 1976 he planted an experimental patch of cabernet sauvignon, shiraz, crouchen, mondeuse and Rhine riesling. Within a year or two it became clear that the cabernet was doing best in the red volcanic soil, so the decision was made to become a specialist cabernet sauvignon producer.

In 1980, 2.4 hectares of cabernet vines were planted, and in 1985 a second property, on the Seville–Monbulk Road, was purchased and a further 1 hectare of cabernet and merlot was planted. There was room also on the 5.2 hectare property for a new house for Jim and Irene, and a winery. Jim and his son, Michael, a Roseworthy College graduate, now make two wines, a straight cabernet sauvignon and a cabernet, merlot and shiraz blend. The first commercial release was in 1984, and since then Oakridge has made quite a name for itself. The 1986 cabernet was a lovely wine which won half-a-dozen gold medals and three trophies, one being for best Yarra Valley red wine in the Lilydale Show in 1987.

Oakridge Estate is one of the more southerly of the Yarra Valley vineyards, and at an altitude of 230 m it is cool and moist most of the year. Rainfall is such that irrigation is not needed, and the red volcanic soils are deep and fertile. One of the major problems is with birds, and the vineyards are now completely netted during the ripening period.

Old Gippsland Estate

Old Gippsland Estate is old indeed. It covers part of what was selection No. 1 in the Parish of Wandin Yallock, near what is now the Yarra Valley township of Seville. It was settled in 1863 by Johann Burgi, a retired schoolteacher from Switzerland who worked for a while for Hubert de Castella at St Hubert's. In 1866, Burgi reported progress on the selection to the Victorian Board of Lands and Works:

I live with my family on this land and have made improvements in clearing, partially fencing, and cultivating the land, digging deep drains, making a dozen underground drains under garden and vineyard, putting up a good comfortable hut, planting about 60 fruit trees, also a thousand of the best sorts of vines on the principle of the Italian high trellis system.

Victoria's first commercial planting of passionfruit was made on what by then had become known as the Haag block in 1892, and it was passionfruit which initially took Garry Evans's interest when he bought the 3 hectare Haag block in 1973. He was also a retired schoolteacher, attracted to the area because of the peace and tranquillity of what was a productive fruit-growing valley. In 1978 he bought the adjoining block, known as Burgi Hill, and began planting vines on high trellises to avoid the frosts common around Wild Cattle Creek, which flowed through the property.

The first 1.2 hectares in 1978 was chardonnay, and there were later plantings of pinot noir, cabernet sauvignon, merlot and sauvignon blanc. Most of the grapes have been sold elsewhere in the valley.

Seville Estate

Dr Peter McMahon followed his father into medical practice in Lilydale, and for thirty years his partner was Dr John Middleton, founder of

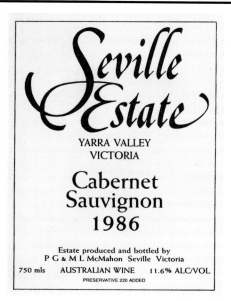

the remarkable Mount Mary Vineyard. Both retired in 1982 to become full-time vignerons; Dr McMahon to his beautiful Seville Estate, 12 km across the Yarra Valley from Mount Mary. Like his partner, Dr McMahon had been dabbling in vine-growing for years. In 1962 he met a Swiss-Italian migrant who had planted a small vineyard at Wandin North, a few kilometres out of Lilydale on the Warburton Highway, and with his encouragement, planted some vines in his backyard. He made some wine in 1964, and by 1970 Dr McMahon and his wife, Margaret, decided their future might be in viticulture.

They bought what was to become Seville Estate, built a beautiful house, and in 1972 planted their first 2.5 hectares of vines. Red varieties were cabernet sauvignon, shiraz and pinot noir, and whites were Rhine riesling and chardonnay. Merlot was planted in 1980 and 1981, and some more chardonnay in 1982. The vineyard now covers 3.7 hectares. The vines face north-east, 200 m above sea level in very fertile soils which range from red volcanic to rich loam over clay. Average rainfall is 827 mm, light frosts occur up to mid-November, and hail storms can be severe in late spring.

Fermentation is carried out in stainless steel fermenters with temperature control. Selected yeast cultures are used and the reds inoculated for malolactic fermentation. Wood maturation of red wines is in small French oak, puncheons, hogsheads and quarter casks. Chardonnay is matured in a mix of French and German oak, and the cask room is air-conditioned so that maturation occurs at an even temperature. Cabernet and shiraz spend twenty-two months in wood, and pinot noir twelve to eighteen months. The wines are bottled about a year before release.

The cooler autumns of the eastern valley slopes (vintage is usually a week or two later than at Mount Mary) are conducive to botrytis mould growth, and Dr McMahon believes the quite extraordinary growth at Seville Estate might be associated with a plum orchard on the property. Rhine riesling in particular is susceptible to the mould, with the happy result that some magnificent botrytised wines have been produced. In various years Seville Estate beerenauslese and even trockenbeerenauslese Rhine rieslings have been produced, and are always in very keen demand.

The McMahon philosophy is to produce wines that compare favourably with their European counterparts. Elegance, finesse and style are hallmarks of Seville Estate. His pinot noir, for example, is very Burgundian in style, and has been a great encouragement to other Yarra Valley producers, who are beginning to believe that they have the best conditions for pinot in Australia. Overall production at Seville Estate is small, however, between 1000 and 1200 cases a year, and sales are mainly through their mailing list.

Shantell Vineyard

Shantell, on the Melba Highway at Dixons Creek in the Yarra Valley, was a block of undeveloped land bought in 1980 as a weekend retreat by surgeon Shan Shanmugam and his university lecturer wife, Turid. In 1981 they planted 1000 vines, and in each of the following four years they planted more until they had a total vineyard of some 5 hectares of cabernet sauvignon, chardonnay, pinot noir and semillon. Both Shan and Turid learned all they could about vine management, training and pruning techniques, trellis design and canopy management, and they produced their first commercial crop in 1985.

They had indeed achieved their first ambition, which was to produce the best fruit possible, and James Halliday was happy to take the grapes for his Coldstream Hills wine. In 1987 they took a step towards the second by building a small winery of their own, and this was completed in time for vintage 1988. Some 10 tonnes were crushed for the first Shantell wines, the rest of the crop again going to Coldstream Hills. By 1990, the crop is expected to be around 50 tonnes, all of which will become Shantell wine.

By then Shan will have completed the science course at Riverina College in Wagga Wagga. In the meantime he has been assisted by consultant winemaker Kathleen Quealy, and their first vintage, 1988, is showing promise. Shantell pinot noir won a gold medal at the Lilydale Show that year, and a silver at the Melbourne Wine Show. The chardonnay won bronze at Melbourne. Both wines were released in September 1989, by which time Turid had given away university duties to manage the medical practice and the winery. The quality of the early wines, and of the fruit which went to Coldstream Hills, suggests that Shantell is a name we will be hearing more of.

St Hubert's

The illustrious history of St Hubert's, founded last century by Hubert de Castella, is described in some detail in the introduction to this section on the Yarra Valley. It is appropriate that it should have been the first vineyard replanted in the renaissance of the area in the 1960s. Much of the original property was owned by the Cester family, who were poultry farmers, when in 1966 Tom Cester began planting 18 hectares of cabernet sauvignon, shiraz, pinot noir and chardonnay. By the time the vines were bearing, the Cesters had phased out the chickens, and in 1974 they produced their first commercial vintage in a winery they had built inside one of the poultry sheds.

The wines were made by Alex White, David Lance and Martin Grinbergs, all of whom had been brewing scientists with Carlton and United Breweries. All three were to use the thoroughly unpretentious but highly efficient winery to make wines of their own during the next decade. The new St Hubert's label (virtually a facsimile of the original one a century before) was an immediate success. By 1980 people were queueing up to pay $20 a bottle for their gold medal-winning cabernet sauvignons. Quality—and price—had returned to the Yarra Valley with a vengeance.

Chardonnay and pinot noir came on the scene in 1980, which added two classy varietals to the range of cabernet, shiraz and Rhine riesling (and some superb late-picked rieslings such as the 1984 St Hubert's Beerenauslese which judges at an international wine show in London 1985 described as 'a brilliant wine'). In 1987 the Cesters sold the property for $1.2 million to a Perth-based public company, Associated Liquor Merchants Ltd, which then operated St Hubert's under a subsidiary, Regional Vineyards (Victoria) Pty Ltd. In June 1989 the company disposed of all of its assets in Western Australia except for its Ironstone Vineyard development at Margaret River, and based all its operations in Victoria.

Laboratory at St Hubert's Winery, Yarra Valley.

In 1988 the company took over Kies Estate in the Barossa Valley, and in 1989 the managing director of the group, Geoff Parkes, announced the development of a new 37 hectare vineyard for St Hubert's in the Yarra Valley at Healesville. Plantings were to be cabernet sauvignon, chardonnay, chenin blanc and merlot. Winemaker since the takeover in 1987 has been Brian Fletcher, who had been chief white winemaker at Seppelts, Great Western. To celebrate the group's move to Victoria he unveiled the first new St Hubert's wine for several years, a *méthode champenoise* sparkling wine made from pinot noir and chardonnay.

Coinciding as it did with several other large vineyard developments in the Yarra Valley and the opening of the French-owned Domain Chandon just 2 km away in Coldstream, this expansion at St Hubert's was another show of confidence in the future of this historic area. Along with his new sparkling wine, Brian Fletcher unveiled two lovely St Hubert's reserve wines, 1988 chardonnay and 1986 cabernet sauvignon. Both showed excellent varietal character and a lot of enigmatic Yarra Valley grace. They indicated very clearly that here was a true renaissance, and not a flash in the pan.

Tarrawarra Vineyard

An 1855 etching by Hubert de Castella entitled *A Picnic at Tarrawarra* and reproduced in his *Notes of an Australian Wine Grower* depicted a pretty spot on the banks of the Yarra River near the site where vines were first planted in the Yarra Valley 150 or so years ago. The property known as Tarrawarra was owned earlier this century by David Syme, founder of the *Age*. It was bought in 1980 by Marc Besen, patron of the arts and founder of a rag-trade empire, who has spared no expense in turning it into one of the most impressive wine estates in the country.

The first 4.5 hectares of chardonnay vines were planted on the 320 hectare property in 1983 and bore their first crop in 1986. A further 1.5 hectares were planted with pinot noir in 1984, and there are plans to plant more pinot as time goes on. David Wollan, a Riverina College graduate who was winery manager and winemaker for Arrowfield Wines in the Hunter Valley, has been associated with the project since

Tarrawarra Vineyard.

227

Wine casks, Tarrawarra Winery.

its inception. Recently he has been assisted by another winemaker, Leigh Clarnette, formerly of Chateau Yarrinya.

The idea of Tarrawarra was to make small amounts of wine of the very highest possible quality, and David Wollan has every conceivable help in achieving this aim, both in the vineyard and in the winery. Vines are planted only on north-facing slopes of the property, which vary in altitude from 76 m to 106 m above sea level. The climate is cool, rainfall about 800 mm per year, and soils are grey silty clay loams over gravelly yellow clay subsoil. The vines are close-planted in 2.1 m to 2.5 m rows, and are trained to various systems including the experimental Te Kauwhata two-tier vertical trellis. Supplementary drip irrigation is installed throughout and a computer is used to monitor soil moisture and other factors.

The winery is as modern as lots of money can make it, and has extensive areas for temperature-controlled wine storage. The first wine from this impressive new estate, 1986 Tarrawarra Chardonnay, was released in 1988. It was a big, complex wine with lots of warm fruit character —figs, melons, peaches, and an overlay of toasty vanillin oak. It was also in excess of $20 a bottle, which put it firmly into the upper boutique class. Future vintages, particularly of pinot noir, will be watched with interest.

Wantirna Estate

Wantirna Estate is technically outside the Yarra Valley because Wantirna South, 20 km from Melbourne, is not within the catchment of the Yarra River. Nevertheless, it lies in Dandenong Creek Valley, just a few kilometres to the south, and for all kinds of reasons it is appropriate that it should be included in this section of the book. James Halliday, for one, has declared Wantirna Estate an honorary Yarra Valley winery on the grounds that it would be a decoration to any region which included it.

Reg Egan is a Melbourne solicitor, and he and his wife, Tina, live surrounded by the vines which provide a hedge against rapidly expanding Melbourne suburbia. They bought the property in 1963 (the same year Dr Max Lake was developing Lake's Folly in the Hunter Valley), and began planting what was the first new commercial vineyard in the Melbourne environs for well

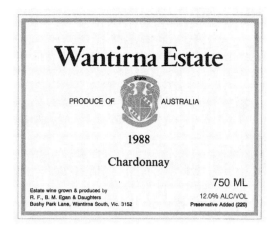

over a century. Their 4 hectares contained cabernet sauvignon, cabernet franc, merlot, pinot noir, Rhine riesling and chardonnay, and Reg made the first vintage himself, in 1969.

He continued to make the wine until 1979 when he retained Ian Deacon as winemaker. In 1984 he took the task on again and is still at it. He has three Estate wines: including pinot noir, cabernet–merlot and chardonnay, all of which show some oak influence and which tend to be a little lighter in body and more elegant than those from the Yarra Valley proper. The cabernet–merlot is aged in French oak barriques for a full two years before bottling, and released about a year after that.

The vineyard, in Bushy Park Lane, Wantirna South, has thin topsoil over heavy yellow clay, and has no supplementary watering. The climate is as cool as that of Melbourne itself, with vintage usually in March or April, and frost is rarely a problem. The annual crush is about 15 tonnes, producing some 1200 cases, and most of the wine is sold by mailing list.

Warramate Vineyard

Warramate, a pretty little property established by the Church family in 1970, is another Yarra Valley vineyard with the desirable address of Maddens Lane, Gruyere. It takes its name from the Warramate Hills, whose lower slopes it graces. Jack Church, a chemist who works in the printing industry, and his sons, David and Ian, doctor and veterinary surgeon respectively, planted 2 hectares of Rhine riesling, chasselas, cabernet sauvignon and shiraz. They had their first commercial vintage in 1977, all 10 tonnes of it, and they immediately won a gold medal in the Lilydale Show.

Warramate faces north, it is 170 m above sea level and just out of the frost line. Rainfall is 800 mm per year so no irrigation is used, and there is 15 cm of grey loam topsoil over clay which contains some stone. The vines are spaced 1.8 m in rows 3 m apart, and trained on a T-bar trellis 1 m high. Birds are a problem as elsewhere in the valley, and nets are erected during the ripening period.

The winery is built in a little log cabin, and the reds are aged in American oak hogsheads. There are three Warramate wines: Rhine riesling, with nice fruit and crisp finish; shiraz, with lots of peppery, berry character in both the nose and the palate; and cabernet sauvignon, a very enticing creature with berries and mint in the bouquet, a rich ripe fruit palate and soft fruity tannins in the finish. The wines are sold by mailing list and weekend cellar door.

Yarra Burn Vineyard

At Yarra Burn, near the township of Wesburn on the Warburton Highway 65 km east of Melbourne, David and Christine Fyffe have one of the most naturally picturesque vineyards in Australia. Surrounded by green hillsides which lead up to Mt Donna Buang and the Warburton Ranges, it is an impressive property with 7 hectares of vines, a modern winery and a lovely bluestone restaurant where an open fire and spit-roasted beef provide splendid accompaniments to good Yarra Valley wine.

David Fyffe was a successful liquor merchant near Lilydale, specialising in wine from Australia's smaller producers. Being very interested in his subject, he spent most vintages helping out one local winemaker or another and he completed several short courses in viticulture and winemaking at Roseworthy and Riverina Colleges. In 1976 he and Christine bought their land in Settlement Road, Yarra Junction, and planted 4 hectares of cabernet sauvignon, merlot, pinot noir and chardonnay. Subsequent plantings increased the vineyard to 7 hectares, the vines spaced at 2 m in rows 3 m apart, red varieties in red loam soil and whites in grey loam. Rainfall is 900 mm per year.

They built themselves a new house while the vines were growing, and what was meant to be a winery from convict-hewn bluestone slabs dating back to 1860. Some cash flow was needed in

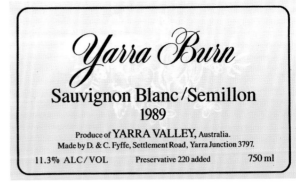

the meantime, however, so the would-be winery became a very fine restaurant, and remains so to this day. The first vintage, in 1980, was made in an extended garage at the rear of the house. Since then a spanking new winery has been built with sufficient capacity to make all Yarra Burn's wine and that of several other Yarra Valley producers. Since 1984 the Fyffes' operation has been one of the most successful small wineries in Victoria.

Their range includes Yarra Burn cabernet sauvignon (the 1984 was Victorian wine of the year in the inaugural Herald Wine Show in 1986), pinot noir, cabernet sauvignon and chardonnay, and each have been prolific medal winners in regional and national wine shows. In 1987 Yarra Burn was the most successful exhibitor in varietal classes in the Victorian Wine Show at Seymour.

In 1983 Yarra Burn made the valley's first serious bubbly, a *méthode champenoise* pinot noir, a lovely, light pink wine which became an immediate best-seller. In 1988 there were two new wines, a sauvignon blanc–semillon blend and a light shiraz. Both were intended as light, easy-drinking styles, and gave another dimension to the premium range of Yarra Burn wines.

Yarra Ridge Vineyard

Louis and Vivienne Bialkower bought Yarra Ridge in 1982. The 22 hectare property in the Christmas Hills at Yarra Glen had been used over the years as a dairy and a market garden. They built a weekender there, and in the winter of 1983 planted 2.8 hectares of chardonnay and 1 hectare each of cabernet sauvignon and pinot noir. In 1984 a little over 2 hectares of sauvignon blanc and a small patch of merlot and cabernet franc were added, and in 1986 a further hectare of pinot noir. This particular planting comprised nine clones of this important but difficult variety, and it is now being used as a source block for Department of Agriculture evaluation trials in the Yarra Valley.

The vineyard runs down the gentle slope of Yarra Ridge within walking distance of the town of Yarra Glen, and it is well drained and exceptionally fertile. Alex White, from Lillydale Vineyards, helped set it up with drip irrigation, no cultivation, and a permanent grass cover in between rows. The vines have grown vigorously, those planted in 1983 yielding almost 50 tonnes of grapes in 1986.

The first vintage in 1986 was a trial 200 or so cases, equally divided between chardonnay, pinot noir and cabernet, which included cabernet sauvignon, cabernet franc and merlot. Louis made the wines himself that year, and in 1987 they were made by James Halliday in the modern, ultra high-tech winery they shared at Yarra Ridge. Since 1988 the wines have been made by Peter Steer. They have all shown excellent varietal character and good depth of fruit. This is another of the new small producers which will be watched with interest.

Yarra Yarra Vineyard

This small vineyard, a mere 2 hectares of grapes, began as a weekend labour of love for Ian and Anne Maclean, and their daughters, Sarah, Phoebe and Charlotte. They bought the 16.5 hectare property at Steels Creek, 10 km out of Yarra Glen on the Glenburn Road, in 1978. Its northerly slopes and well-drained soils made it eminently suitable as a vineyard, and its 360° views and virtual isolation made it the perfect weekend retreat.

They planted Bordeaux varieties, cabernet sauvignon, cabernet franc and merlot to make a red; and sauvignon blanc and semillon to make a white. Ian, an applied scientist, made the first wines himself in 1983, and his first cabernet sauvignon won a silver medal at the Lilydale Wine Show. The vineyard is not irrigated, so the yield is restricted to about 6 tonnes per hectare, and the Macleans continue to make small amounts of very good wine which is sold by mailing list. Both reds and whites are aged in French oak barriques, and the cabernet in particular shows plenty of Yarra Valley character with its low pH and brilliant colour.

Yarra Yering Vineyard

Dr Bailey Carrodus is by training a botanist whose specialty was plant physiology. A decade of wanderings in Europe gave him the dream to one day have a vineyard and make wine of his own. While still based with the CSIRO in Melbourne, he began looking around the Yarra Valley for a suitable site, and after a lengthy search he found a block of land in Briarty Road, Coldstream, which seemed ideal. It had grey silty clay loam with bands of gravel for good drainage, and was situated on a north-facing slope high enough out of the valley floor to avoid late spring frosts.

He began planting vines in 1969, the vineyard eventually extending to 12 hectares. His vintage in 1973 was the first commercial wine produced in the Yarra Valley since 1921. The wines were complex and elegant, and contained the kind of ripe fruit volatility much favoured by Max Schubert in Penfold's famous Grange Hermitage. As was the case with some of the early Granges, the volatility was misunderstood and some critics pointed to the early Yarra Yering reds as having winemaking faults. If Dr Carrodus was worried he didn't show it, and he didn't deviate from his own methods of making wine which many now have called great.

The wines produced are named after the grape variety only if the wine is a 100 per cent varietal, as is the case with Yarra Yering pinot noir and chardonnay. If the wine is blended, the name of the wine is the blend number. Dry Red No. 1, for instance, is made from cabernet sauvignon, malbec and merlot, with a little petit verdot. Half the vineyard is planted to cabernet, so Dry Red No. 1 is the major product. Dry Red No. 2 is made from about 85 per cent shiraz. The blending material has changed over the years and is now moving towards viognier, a fairly rare white grape which in France produces full-bodied, golden wines with an elusive bouquet of apricots and blossom. Its inclusion in a red blend is a reflection of Dr Carrodus's predilection for style rather than custom. The Dry White No. 1 blend has also changed over the years; between 1981 and 1984 it was 100 per cent semillon, but later became semillon and sauvignon blanc.

Dr Carrodus retired from the CSIRO in 1979 to devote himself to Yarra Yering. He still does almost all of the work alone, caring for the

YARRA YERING

DRY RED WINE N° 1
VINTAGE 1987

GROWN MADE & BOTTLED
AT YARRA YERING VINEYARD,
COLDSTREAM, VICTORIA, AUSTRALIA

750 mL   PRESERVATIVE ADDED, SULPHUR DIOXIDE   12.5% ALC/VOL

vineyard—until recently one of the largest in the reborn Yarra Valley—and making the wine in a winery overlooking a lake and a beautiful expanse of the valley. All of his wines are matured in small oak, and all have considerable bottle age before release.

The Dry Red No. 1 has received much critical acclaim from outside the country as well as at home. In 1987 his 1984 wine was judged best wine in the 'new world' section of the Vinexpo competition in Bordeaux. After several tastings of all the No. 1 blends produced in the 1980s, London wine writer and critic Jancis Robinson included it in her book on the top forty wines in the world published in 1989. And yes, Grange Hermitage was one of the other four Australian wines chosen. Despite its fame, Dry Red No. 1 is well priced. The 1987, released in mid-1989, was $18.99, and there were many Yarra Valley wines more expensive than that.

Yeringberg

Yeringberg is the oldest Victorian vineyard still in the hands of the original family, although wine has not been made there continuously. It was established in 1862, near what is now Coldstream, by the present owner's grandfather, Baron Frederic Guillaume de Pury. The Baron was a friend of the de Castellas and one of the famous group who followed Governor Latrobe to the colony of Victoria from Neuchatel in Switzerland.

Vines were planted on about 25 hectares of the de Pury's 450 hectare grazing property, and Yeringberg wines won many awards in exhibitions both in Australia and overseas. With St Hubert's and Yering, it was one of the big three of quality Australian producers, and it helped spread the fame of Lilydale and the Yarra Valley around the world.

After his father's death in 1890, George de Pury continued to make wine until 1921, when the vines were pulled out. Phylloxera had bypassed the valley, but economic times were changing and so was the taste for the elegant table wines its best winemakers produced. The property remained in the family, however, and the carefully preserved timber winery with its adjacent brick stables were classified by the National Trust of Victoria.

In 1969, George's only son, Guillaume de Pury, re-established vines on part of the original vineyard slope, and these were the only plantings in the valley on the exact location of one of those famous nineteenth-century vineyards. Guill, a research scientist, was anxious to see if the old Yeringberg reputation for quality could be revived, and he planted 2 hectares of vines. Some did better than others, and the vineyard now comprises chardonnay, marsanne, rousanne, pinot noir, cabernet sauvignon, cabernet franc, merlot and malbec. These last four varieties are blended to make Yeringberg Cabernet, and the chardonnay, marsanne and pinot noir are made as varietals, although the rousanne will probably find its way into the marsanne.

Guill cranked up the old winery and added some more modern equipment. He now spends his time looking after the grazing side of the property and making small quantities of wine which would have indeed pleased his forbears. The reds are given up to two years in French oak hogsheads, and both of the whites also spend some time maturing in small French oak. Only 200 or so cases of each wine is made, and most of it is sold very quickly by mailing list.

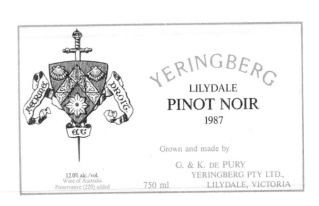

South Australia

Paul Lloyd

Adelaide

Adelaide, gracious queen city of wine, is the capital of the wine state, South Australia—the state that produces well over half of Australia's wine. And that is not just in terms of quantity: at the 1989 Royal Adelaide Championship Wine Show, for example, thirty-four of the forty-two gold medals awarded to table wines were for wines grown in South Australia.

Adelaide plays a vital role in the husbanding of the vine throughout the state. It is the administrative centre of the grape, hosting the headquarters of major industry bodies such as the statutory Australian Wine and Brandy Corporation and the industry's Wine and Brandy Producers' Association; it has the corporate offices of such major producers as Penfolds, Orlando, Seppelt and Wolf Blass; it is the centre of the toughest and biggest annual wine show in the nation; it houses scientific centres such as the Wine Research Institute; and it has proximity to the premier oenology teaching centre, Roseworthy Agricultural College. Adelaide has its own small vineyards and is blessedly close to the major vine-growing areas too, the Barossa Valley and McLaren Vale each being less than an hour's drive from the central business district.

The demands of suburbia have ensured that there are few commercial vineyards left, but Adelaide must still be closer to the vine than any capital city in the world with the exception of Vienna.

Backyard vines flourish. In a remarkable example of the power of the vine in suburbia, the local morning newspaper the *Advertiser* inaugurated the annual Adelaide Vines project in 1989: several thousand readers delivered 15 tonnes of their backyard grapes to the Botanic Garden on 26 February—the amount severely reduced because a fruit fly scare quarantined half the city. The grapes were processed by winemaker Peter Lehmann in the Barossa and the resulting 1100 dozen wines, a pleasantly fruity muscat-style white and a rather eccentric rosé, were sold to aid charity. Roseworthy Agricultural College lecturers and students, who monitored the project, were amazed at the number of grape varieties delivered, some unidentifiable, and some presumed to be survivors of the very first vines planted in Adelaide.

The site for Adelaide was selected by surveyor Colonel William Light, on the Torrens River on the eastern side of Gulf St Vincent at latitude 34°56′S and longitude 138°36′E. The climate was moderate, with generally equable temperatures ranging from 11.6°C in July to 23°C in February, with an average of seven hours of sunshine daily and an annual rainfall of 525-550 mm. White settlers from Britain found the soil moderately fertile with vegetative cover of long grass and widely spaced, tall gum trees. All that remained was the question of what would happen to the Kaurna people of the region. Eventually their land was encroached upon and a city was founded, named after Queen Adelaide, consort of England's King William IV.

As advanced views of lifestyles were prevalent in the new colony, viniculture came naturally, partly because many of the first white settlers came from strata of British society with some knowledge and experience of wine. The growth of the industry in South Australia was enabled partly by other settlers from northern Europe, who brought a pragmatic Teutonic thoroughness to their enterprises.

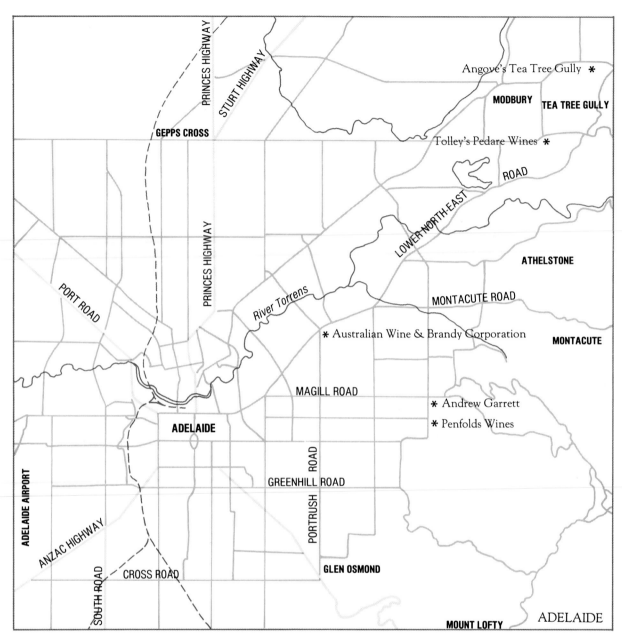

The first vines in Adelaide were planted by John Barton Hack, who in 1805 was born in Chichester, England, and emigrated for health reasons, arriving in 1837, the year after the colony was founded. Hack was a commercial and agricultural pioneer who became a vice-president of the Royal Agricultural and Horticultural Society, a member of the Botanic Garden Board and first president of the Chamber of Commerce. Among his many activities was the planting, in the year of his arrival, of a small vineyard called Chichester Gardens, on the site of what became the expensive inner suburb of North Adelaide.

The South Australia Company, the commercial force behind the establishment of the colony, organised vine cuttings from Hobart Town and the Busby collection in New South Wales, among other sources, and these were propagated in its nursery at Hackney. Early vignerons in that first decade, including George Stephenson in his orchard north of town and Moor's garden down by the Reed Beds, proved that the vine would flourish. Its culture spread to the Adelaide Hills for elegant table wines and to McLaren Vale and the Barossa Valley in short order.

Ebenezer Ward, first wine columnist of the *Advertiser*, reported in 1861 on forty-two vineyards in what is now the Adelaide metropolitan area, and noted at least eighteen others unreported. By 1925 some 1570 hectares of this area were under vine. But then the downturn began as the real estate developers, encouraged by governments, pushed for the suburban sprawl. The pressure continues, and even McLaren Vale and the Barossa come under periodic threats. The most devastating was the ripping out in 1984 of almost the last of the Grange Vineyards on the Magill foothills to build a housing estate. Despite some public passion, the bulldozers moved in on the vineyards which Dr Christopher Rawson Penfold had started planting in 1844, and which had given the world the first Grange Hermitage. Rotary clothes hoists and barbecue kettles replaced the vines, save for a token 20 hectares around the historic winery. These, at least, are used for the Penfolds Magill Estate red wine, which is a beautiful but savage reminder of what was lost. Following, in alphabetical order, is the handful of commercial wine producers primarily associated in modern times with Adelaide.

Anglesey Wine Estate, Angle Vale

Twenty-five minutes drive to the north of Adelaide, on the fertile plain where the city's market gardens flourish, a Sydney stockbroker, Jack Minnert, bought 44 hectares in 1969 and planted his first vines, mostly shiraz with some cabernet sauvignon.

The climate is Mediterranean, with cool winters and hot dry summers necessitating supplementary irrigation. Windbreaks of almonds and olives were planted, these trees being significant crops on the Adelaide Plains where some of the finest olive oil is produced. Following the first harvests off the fertile soil over limestone marls, from 1972 to 1977, semillon and riesling were planted, and in 1978 Anglesey began marketing its own wine, which had earlier been sold in bulk.

The 17 hectare vineyard is planted to cabernet sauvignon, malbec, shiraz and merlot; chenin blanc, chardonnay, sauvignon blanc, semillon and colombard. The estate operation crushes 200 tonnes.

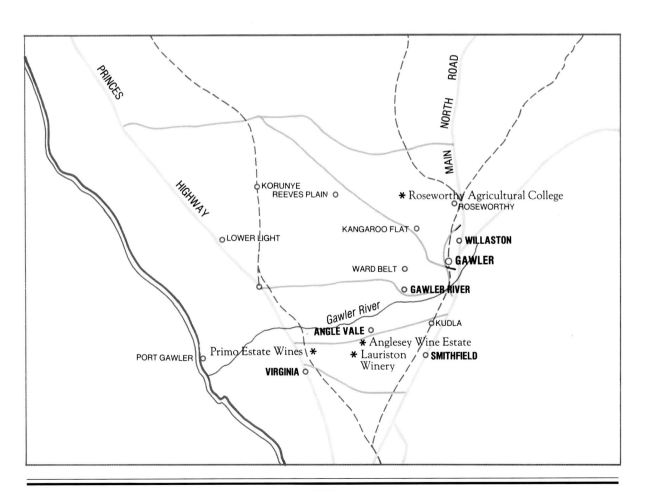

Angove's Tea Tree Gully

Angove's is a major wine producer in the Riverland, making an extensive range of varietal table wines, fortified wines, Marko vermouth, St Agnes brandy and Stone's green ginger wine at its production headquarters at Renmark. It retains a presence, however, with the historic cellars where the company started, at Tea Tree Gully, in what became Adelaide's north-east foothills suburbs.

The company was founded by Dr William T. Angove, born in Cambourne, Cornwall, in May 1854. He practised medicine in Suffolk, married Emma Carlyon in 1880, and three years later emigrated to South Australia. He set up practice at Tea Tree Gully, 19 km from central Adelaide, and made an arrangement with the Reverend George Henry Farr to make wine in Farr's Brightlands cellars, which had been built in the vicinity in the early 1860s. Angove then started planting his own vineyard, in 1886, consisting of 2 hectares of shiraz, riesling and black portugal on steep hills surrounded by almond and olive trees. He later built his own winery and transferred operations there from Brightlands.

By 1903 he was crushing 300 tonnes of grapes, suggesting that a fair bit of the area was under vine to other growers. A correspondent for the newspaper, the *Register*, visited the cellars that year and noted that Dr Angove produced 9000 litres of cabernet sauvignon, which was a 'medium quantity of first-class wine'. About that time a still was installed for the production of fortifying spirit and, on 1 November 1906, Dr Angove took a five-year lease managing the Highercombe vineyards and cellars, one of the most famous of the early Adelaide Hills vineyards, situated up towards the town of Houghton and founded by the self-styled squire George Anstey.

Dr Angove had made a business out of what started as winemaking for the family and for the medicinal use of his patients. When he began making brandy he called it St Agnes after a village in his native Cornwall and also in honour of the patron saint of purity. He died in England in 1912. His eldest son, Thomas Carlyon Angove, had already taken over the business and set up a distillery and processing plant at Renmark. This became the company headquarters.

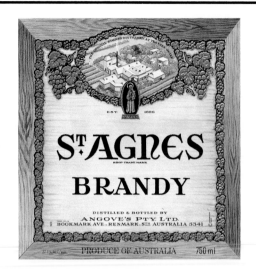

The South Australian State Planning Authority compulsorily acquired most of Angove's Tea Tree Gully vineyards for a residential subdivision in early 1975 and reduced the holdings to a token few hectares. Thus another part of the state's wine heritage was lost in the name of progress. The cellars, however, were converted to an attractive and informative tourist centre where visitors may tour the old winery.

Lauriston Winery, Angle Vale

A cooperative of grapegrowers, the Lauriston Winery, which also trades under the name of Barossa Valley Estates, is part of the Renmano and Berri group under the Consolidated Cooperative Wineries banner, with John Pendrigh as managing director.

The winery has no vineyards of its own. Among many past manifestations, it was the Angle Vale winery, opposite Anglesey Estate. It went broke and was reformed in 1979 as the Munno Para Cooperative of local growers, with such winemakers as Robert O'Callaghan and Stuart Blackwell. The Valley Growers Cooperative was formed in 1984 and the following year entered a joint venture with Consolidated Cooperative Wineries.

Winemaker is Colin Glaetzer, twin brother of Wolf Blass's John Glaetzer, a 1972 graduate of Roseworthy Agricultural College with a diploma in oenology, and formerly with Seppelt in Victoria.

Under the Barossa Valley Estates label, the winery produces 600 cases of premium table wine, including frontignan, riesling, cabernet, shiraz, chardonnay and sauvignon blanc varieties. The best of local fruit, from whatever sources, is reserved for the more expensive Lauriston label, which produces 1200 cases annually of champagne, cabernet–malbec–shiraz, chardonnay, sauvignon blanc, port and muscat. The red blend has a particularly good name.

Penfolds Wines, Magill

Penfolds, Australia's largest wine group, which embraces such brands as Lindemans, Kaiser Stuhl, Wynns, Seaview, Killawarra, Tulloch and Tollana, has its main production centre at Nuriootpa in the Barossa Valley, but it retains a presence exactly where it started, at Magill, in the leafy, upmarket, foothills eastern suburbs of Adelaide. Dr Christopher Rawson Penfold and his wife, Mary, founders of the company, planted their vineyard here; and a token 20 hectares remain, surrounding their original cottage, the Grange, and what was once a major winery.

The son of a Sussex vicar, the Reverend John Penfold, Christopher trained at St Bartholomew's Hospital and worked in private practice, spending some years at Brighton. He married Mary Holt in 1835 and a few years later they emigrated to the colonies. Before leaving England, he arranged the purchase of a grant of land at Magill, for which he paid £1200, a large sum in those days.

The Penfolds arrived at the port of Largs Bay in South Australia with their baby daughter, Georgina, towards the end of 1844, having made the hazardous and uncomfortable voyage on the 350 tonne barque *Taglioni*, under the command of Captain W. Black. The family immediately settled at Magill, building the whitewashed stone cottage called the Grange.

As well as practising medicine and looking after his farm, Dr Penfold planted vine cuttings which he had brought out, their ends dipped in sealing wax to keep the sap in the vines until they were planted. He did not approve the quality of the imported wine of the time so he made his own for the use of his patients with anaemia. Whether the wine was in fact any help to anaemia is debatable, but this now-discredited cure was the start of something big.

The Penfold vineyards expanded and the doctor devoted more of his time to winemaking, in which he was assisted by Mary and her servant, Ellen Tembrell. Women were to play important roles in this family saga, and in the company

The Grange built at Magill in the 1840s by Dr C. R. Penfold.

Penfolds' pot still room at Magill.

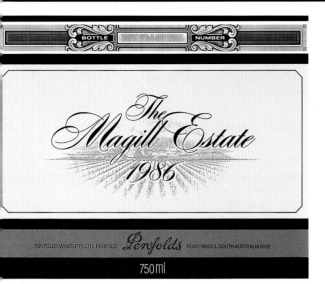

—more than histories reveal. Mary Penfold's diary gives some details of winemaking at Magill and lists some of their maturing wines, which included a white wine ('mixture Sweet Water and Frontignac') and a red wine 'mixture'.

Dr Penfold was well known in the district and became the first mayor of Burnside. In his twenty-six years in the colony he laid the foundations of a dynasty, before dying at the age of fifty-nine in 1870. He was buried at St George's church in Magill.

In 1861 his daughter, Georgina Ann, aged nineteen, married a thirty-year-old Irish officer in the Victoria Civil Service at Castlemaine, Thomas Francis Hyland. The wine business had been experiencing some financial problems at the time of Dr Penfold's death, lacking the capital for necessary expansions. Mary Penfold and Thomas Hyland jointly overcame the difficulties, and he resigned his post in 1880 to devote himself to the family business.

Mary Penfold handed over the management of the vineyards in 1881 to Joseph Gillard, from whom she had just bought vineyards and cellars. She continued to oversee affairs at Magill until her death in 1895.

Penfolds had become an important wine producer. The stock of wine at Magill was 485 000 litres at a time when the total quantity in South Australia was 1.4 million litres. By 1885 trade was flourishing between Magill and all the states, as well as New Zealand. From 404 hectares of land, ports and sherries were made and the expanding range included some table wines.

Georgina and Thomas Hyland had four children; Inez died at the age of twenty-eight and her sister Estelle married a Major Knight and lived in England. Frank Astor Hyland, born 1873, and Herbert Leslie Hyland, born two years later, spent some years at Melbourne Grammar School and finished their education in England. In memory of their mother's father, they changed their names to Penfold Hyland. Frank entered the business in 1892 and spent three years in Europe studying winemaking. With Federation in 1901, trade among the states was made easier and Frank Penfold Hyland opened a branch office in Pitt Street, Sydney.

Joseph Gillard retired in 1905 and Leslie Penfold Hyland took over the management of the South Australian branch. He was active in bringing about the amendment of the 6 o'clock closing law so that wine could be drunk with meals up to 8 pm. During his years of management the company established wineries at McLaren Vale (1910), Nuriootpa in the Barossa Valley and at Eden Valley.

Frank Penfold Hyland supervised the expansion in New South Wales. In 1904 he bought the Dalwood vineyard near Branxton in the Hunter Valley. The company also established a holding at the historic Minchinbury vineyards, originally on a land grant made in 1819 to Captain William Minchin on his retirement from the army. After several changes of ownership, Frank Penfold Hyland bought the vineyards and cellars in 1912. The first manager was Leo Buring, who was there until 1918. This vineyard was the source of the Penfolds' famed Trameah, a traminer varietal wine first marketed in 1920. Minchinbury is gone but the name lives on as the Penfolds' champagne brand, the company's biggest selling line.

In 1920 the Penfolds extended their interests in the Hunter Valley with the purchase of the Sparkling Vale property, from which the first vintage was made in 1924. There were 32 hectares under vine, mostly semillon, before the property was abandoned after rain repeatedly bogged the ground. In 1942 Frank Penfold Hyland bought the vineyards of the old Hunter Valley Distillery, which was the source of Dalwood whites for many years. Six years later the company purchased Penfold Vale, planting it with 20 hectares of white grapes, and the Matthews vineyards of 6 hectares of semillon.

Thomas Hyland, who had remained as a senior partner, retired in 1913 and the business was formed into a company under the governorship of Frank Penfold Hyland.

At about the same time, Penfolds ventured into winemaking in the Murrumbidgee Irrigation Area, building a winery at Griffith in 1913.

Leslie Penfold Hyland died in 1940 after a long illness and the elder of his sons, Francis William, who succeeded him at Magill, died a few years later in 1946. Leslie's second son, Jeffrey, returned from war service and rejoined the company in 1945, becoming a director, later to be managing director.

In South Australia Penfolds expanded to acquire Auldana in 1943, and Modbury and Kalimna two years later. The history of Auldana, neighbouring Magill, goes back to 1842 when Patrick Auld bought two sections of 93 hectares; he started planting vines in 1854. In 1861 Auld floated a company known as the South Auldana Vineyard Association with a capital of £12 000. The Association's first vintage the following year yielded 13 500 litres of wine. This was the first

attempt by an Australian wine producer to establish an independent organisation to sell Australian wine to London. New cellars were built at the foot of the hill in 1897. The Auldana property was sold to Sir Josiah Symon, Senator and Chief Justice of South Australia, before the Penfolds' purchase in 1943. The celebrated St Henri claret line was made at Auldana, for many years under the supervision of John Davoren, whose father Harold had a long asociation with Penfolds at Dalwood.

Frank Penfold Hyland died in 1948 at the age of seventy-four. He had controlled the company for almost fifty years, and during that time was active for the good of the entire wine industry, and had been elected first president of the Federal Viticultural Council. After his death the company was administered by a board of directors; Penfolds became a public company in 1962.

The Penfold family investment company, Francis Investments, sold all interests in Penfolds Wines in 1976 to the New South Wales brewer, Tooth and Co. The other shareholders followed.

In 1973 Penfolds had moved into South Aus-

Auldana Cellars.

tralia's Riverland, purchasing a property at Morgan near Cadell. A broadacre vineyard of 520 hectares was built, and planted with most table wine varieties. But the company was also moving into a period that has variously been interpreted as consolidation or asset stripping. The Minchinbury operations were consolidated into Tempe in 1977, closing one historical chapter. In the same year the Wybong Estate in the Upper Hunter, which had been a bold expansion in 1960, was sold to Rosemount Estate. The Griffith winery was amalgamated into Nuriootpa, as was the Magill bottling line. The Auldana cellars were sold, and the Seaview champagne operation went to Nuriootpa. The cellars next to the Grange vineyards were sold to Andrew Garrett wines, and most of the Grange vineyard was bulldozed for a housing estate.

On the other hand, during this period Penfolds bought a 164 hectare property at Polish Valley, a subregion of the Clare Valley, and established in 1979 a broadacre vineyard of premium riesling, traminer, sauvignon blanc, chardonnay, merlot, malbec, cabernet sauvignon, shiraz and cabernet franc. It also became the nation's largest wine producer, by taking under its wing Kaiser Stuhl (in 1982), Seaview, Wynn's, Killawarra and Tulloch. For Tooths had in turn become part of John Spalvins's aggressive Adelaide Steamship group, putting Penfolds through the most massive shakeup in its history, and giving a huge boost to its image as a quality red wine producer.

Further expansion was the 1990 takeover of its main rival, Lindemans, which like Penfolds had been founded last century by a medical doctor.

By a nice turn of fate, the ultimate ownership of Penfolds is back in Adelaide at the Adelaide Steamship offices on Greenhill Road, just down the hill from the Grange cottage.

Peter Rumball Wines, Adelaide

Winemaker Peter Rumball set himself up in 1988 as a one-person champagne-maker, buying grapes where he could and making the wines at other people's wineries. His first releases of stylishly labelled Peter Rumball (chardonnay–pinot noir) brut, pink and red shiraz champagnes were in 1989 and 1990, while he operated from his home in Adelaide and looked for his own winery and a cellar door sales outlet.

As a Roseworthy graduate in 1973, Rumball was a winemaker with the Stanley Wine Company in Clare before the 1975 establishment, in partnership with Adelaide engineer Stephen Elliott, of Fareham Estate winery in the southern Clare Valley. While making some table wines, the emphasis was on contract bottling for other companies and making champagnes for them. The standards set by Fareham Estate for bottling attracted so much business that in 1985 operations were transferred to Adelaide and the company became Southern Beverage Corporation, for which Rumball consults.

While at Fareham he claimed such innovations as developing a new method of cooling wine tanks using swimming pool solar panels; the development of a system of filling 200 ml single-serve wine bottles for airlines (the application of an idea of the Victorian wine genius, Stephen Hickinbotham); automatic bottling and tank storage systems using programmable controllers; shooting dry ice into wine bottles during the wine-filling operation; pioneering the use of microwave ovens in microlaboratory wine analysis; and developing a special shaking-down bin for sparkling wines.

Primo Estate Wines, Virginia

'The role of the small winemaker is to understand the situation and be innovative, to get away from the mass-market styles and give people something different, interesting and good' says Joe Grilli of Primo Estate Wines, a kilometre north of Virginia on the Adelaide Plains. He certainly understands his situation, in a warm climate, and he certainly innovates. Indeed, he has been one of the nation's brilliant young winemakers since bursting on the scene as dux of Roseworthy Agricultural College's oenology diploma course in 1979. He had a little help from his family too.

Father Primo Grilli grew grapes in the beautiful Marche region of Italy until 1953, when he sought his fortune in Australia. Labouring in the Riverland led to market gardening in Virginia, then to growing grapes again. Primo Grilli, as shown by his gnarled hands and sunshine smile, is in touch with the soil; he built up his planting to 13 hectares, selling the grapes to Barossa wineries. Then he built a winery—neat, white and Mediterranean—and sent his children to

1986

PRIMO ESTATE

Old Port Wakefield Rd., Virginia S.A. 5120

BOTRYTIS RIESLING AUSLESE

375 mL · WINE MADE IN AUSTRALIA

Roseworthy to learn the modern ways.

His son, Joe Grilli, burst out of Roseworthy like a comet, glowing with new ideas. He made botrytis sweet whites in the cellar (as Tim Knappstein was doing at the same time in Clare); he re-pruned the cabernet vines in summer so they would fruit again and ripen in the cooler autumn; he cut vine canes to promote flavour concentration in late-harvested whites; he fermented in oak to get softer integration; he harvested red grapes and left them in the sun to shrivel and concentrate flavours. He made red wines of sensational body and flavour; and mum kept the good food coming while dad tended the vines.

The varieties grown are riesling, colombard, sauvignon blanc, chardonnay, shiraz, cabernet sauvignon and semillon. Mostly hand-pruned and hand-picked, the vines grow on the fertile market garden soil of the plains, the summer heat somewhat tempered by the night breezes from nearby Gulf St Vincent. The crush is 180 tonnes—almost a complete estate operation with only 10 per cent of grapes bought in—and 9000 cases are produced a year in nine table wine styles (plus a few flagon wines for local consumption).

Joe Grilli, who runs the winery with his wife Dina, and is assisted by winemaker Keith Bown, took a head start on many other small wine producers through the 1980s. His experience and skill show in lines that are taking on classic status, such as the botrytis sweet whites and his big but elegant 'Joseph' reds, which have real personality.

Seaview Champagne Cellars, Magill

Andrew Garrett Wines of McLaren Vale in 1988 bought the cellars at Magill, one of the oldest and best known champagne cellars in Australia, after Penfolds had taken over Seaview and shifted its champagne-making operation to Nuriootpa. It has been variously known as Seaview Champagne Cellars and Wynn's Romalo Cellars and Australian Wines Pty Ltd.

The chequered history began with Leon Edmond Mazure, a French cook and former manager of the adjacent Auldana cellars, who in 1919 decided to go into business for himself. He started making champagnes on a property at Rosslyn Park and built the winery at Magill.

Hurtle Walker, who became a renowned champagne-maker, was associated from the beginning. Mazure, then at Auldana, offered the fourteen-year-old Hurtle a job as an errand boy. By the age of twenty-one, he had become a champagne-maker and went with Mazure to the Magill cellars, down the road, where he ended up as manager.

New Zealander Bertam Reginald Collins took over the property in 1920 and coined the name Romalo, combining the name of his daughter Roma and that of Malo, daughter of his friend Charlie Watts. Leo Buring was an adviser for a couple of years and supplied the yeast culture from France. In 1929 Samuel Wynn became the majority shareholder in Australian Wines Ltd, as it was then known.

Wynn's made still wines at the Magill cellars

as well as sparkling and in 1944 Roseworthy graduate Ken Ward was appointed still winemaker, freeing Hurtle Walker to concentrate on champagnes again.

Hurtle Walker had married Ellen Eliza Gratton in 1923 and they had two children: daughter Joyce worked in the winery office before she married, and son Norm, after St Peter's College, graduated from Roseworthy in 1951 with an oenology diploma and the nickname 'Two-storey' because of his height. He joined the company and, for several years, Norm Walker went to Coonawarra each vintage to help Wynn's. Hurtle Walker retired from the managership in September 1963 and was succeeded by Norm Walker, who developed a name as the best champagne-maker in Australia. Wynn's renamed the cellars Seaview, since that was the champagne brand the company was promoting.

One of Norm Walker's most promising apprentices was Warren Randall, who was later to get the plum job as champagne-maker with Seppelt Wines at Great Western, in direct competition with his former master, Norm Walker (who subsequently retired). In 1989 Warren Randall became chief winemaker for Andrew Garrett, the new owner of these fascinating cellars.

Tolley's Pedare Wines, Hope Valley

Within the boundaries of metropolitan Adelaide, Tolley's Pedare Wines continues to function as a winery, as it has done since 1892, even though much of its operations are elsewhere. It is a sizeable operation of 3000 tonnes and is still owned and operated by the Tolley family.

It was founded by Douglas Austral Tolley, and still bears his name in the registered company title of D.A. Tolley Pty Ltd. He was one of the brothers involved in setting up the distillation company, Tolley, Scott and Tolley, which was to become known as Tollana.

In addition to the family distillation interests, he established his own vineyard and winery in 1892 in the foothills of the ranges at Hope Valley, so named by a journalist who lived there and whose house was burnt down in 1851. The suburb, as it became, is also known as part of Tea

Tree Gully, several kilometres north-east of Adelaide.

A contemporary writer noted that it was a beautiful vineyard 'some hundred or more acres in extent . . . considered one of the show wineries of the state, where he had made some very fine wines especially of the drier variety'. He also bought wine and was the first outside champion of Coonawarra. The Hope Valley burgundy, made by Bill Redman, is one of the great reds of Australia. But Douglas Tolley found the market, especially in Britain, was so seduced by the Coonawarra reds that his own looked poor in comparison, and he dropped Redman, leaving Coonawarra to decay for several decades.

Douglas Tolley died in 1932 and his son Leonard J. Tolley, an esteemed figure in Adelaide sporting and commercial circles, looked after the affairs of the vineyards and winery, developing the business substantially. He sold most of the wine in bulk, to be bottled all over Australia.

When Leonard died in 1965 his three sons, Peter, David and Reginald took over. They hit on the idea of renaming the wines Pedare, the first two letters of each of the three names, a name which Len had used for a boat in the 1940s. The name Pedare has become so accepted that a Christian college in the vicinity adopted it for its title. The fourth generation moved into the business and the fifth is on its way.

The company, which employs forty people, has extended holdings of 230 hectares, on its Medlands Estate at Dorrien in the Barossa (where it has a tasting and sales outlet in parallel with the head office at Hope Valley, as well as a small fermentation cellar), and near Qualco in the Riverland. It is planting land it purchased in

1989 in Padthaway as a major investment in the company's future; and it has a small vineyard remaining around the winery, the balance of those vines having been eaten up by housing developers. The vineyard manager is David Tolley.

Company vineyards provide 75 per cent of the crush, which was scaled back in the 1980s for a greater concentration on premium table wines and is about 3000 tonnes, producing 150 000 cases out of the Hope Valley winery. The winemaker is fourth-generation Chris Tolley and Rob Scapin is his assistant in a winery that has historic charm combined with modern technology.

The Tolleys have two ranges of table wines: the budget Cellar Reserve range and the premium Selected Harvest lines, which are still quite modestly priced. The company has developed a name for a sophisticated and spicy gewurztraminer, but it is also not recognised enough for the quality of its reds, especially the Selected Harvest cabernet sauvignon.

Woodley Wines, Adelaide

Woodley, as a company, is integrated with Seppelt Wines in everything but marketplace identity. Its personnel are Seppelt's personnel, its vineyards are Seppelt's vineyards, all over three states, and the wines are made at Seppelt production centres, at Seppeltsfield in the Barossa and at Great Western. However, Woodley is part of the history of Adelaide, and its Queen Adelaide label, one of the most graceful and commercially successful in Australia, speaks of the city of Adelaide.

The wine company started in 1858 but had its origins in 1844, in a house built by the first treasurer of the colony of South Australia, Osmond Gilles, on the dress circle foothills of the Mount Lofty Ranges, 6 km south-west of Adelaide's centre. He named it Woodley, in memory of his brother's wife, Mary Woodley Horne. Gilles planted a vineyard around the house in 1858.

It was not easy. The land had been considered by J.W. Bull, author of *Early Experience of Colonial Life in South Australia*, who took an option in 1838 to buy, but reckoned the land was too stony for easy clearance and planting.

When silver-lead deposits were discovered on the property, Gilles quit as treasurer and leased the land to the Woodley Company, formed to mine the land, from which he received considerable royalties each year. Having planted his vineyard, he appointed his friend J.W. Bull to manage the vines and the winery. By his spellings, the varieties planted were tokay, riesling, mourastie, clarignan, gouais, verdelho, malbec, shiraz, grenache and mataro.

The miners departed after a few years, leaving a system of underground workings about 4 km long, with occasional ventilation shafts. Gilles found that the tunnels maintained a natural temperature of 15°C and were ideal for wine storage.

The business changed hands several times after Osmond Gilles' death. First his nephew, Osmond Horne Gilles, inherited the property, and after his death it passed into the hands of Lewis W. Gilles. In 1892 Benno Weidenbach bought the concern and extended the vineyards as far as Milne's Road. The president of the Vignerons' Association, H.V. Pridmore, bought the property in 1894. In 1922 the vineyards were sold for suburban building blocks but, in 1924, the cellar itself was bought by Lieutenant-Colonel David Fulton, who had been commanding officer of the Third Light Horse during World War I, before which he had studied at Roseworthy Agricultural College. Captain C.E. Hawker joined the firm in 1926 and Woodley Wines was floated as a limited liability company.

It was Colonel Fulton, a significant figure in the history of South Australian wine, who encouraged Bill Redman of Coonawarra to stick with his trade and to make a lighter claret-style wine instead of his heavier, riper style. Bill Redman regarded Fulton as one of the great influences on his winemaking. Woodley, of course, bought Redman's wines, and the history of the Woodley company has essentially been one of buying other wines and blending them to marketable styles or simply repackaging them. Among Fulton's products were an award-winning, Redman-made St Adele claret (the name perhaps being a portent of a name yet to come), and a sweet sparkling wine named Est! which he believed would appeal to the feminine palate. J.A. 'Tony' Nelson, a Viennese-born refugee and wine chemist, joined the company in July 1940 and took over as managing director when Fulton retired.

Although Woodley was located at Glen Osmond, it was in Coonawarra that Nelson really exerted himself. He bought Chateau Comaum for Woodley in 1946, when Coonawarra was a virtually unknown wine-producing district, and sold it to David Wynn in 1952, who made it into the famous Wynn's Coonawarra Estate. In that period Nelson greatly championed Coonawarra to anybody who would listen.

Tony Nelson was responsible for originating a unique series of eight clarets covering the vintages 1949 to 1956. The first four were called the Treasure Chest series, the second four the Vintage Box series, and all were magnificently labelled with designs by the gifted Wytt Morro. The most delicate and refined of these great wines (most of them made by Redman) was Woodley's Coonawarra Vintage 1952. It featured an illustration entitled Her Majesty, the Queen Dowager, Amelia-Adelaide-Louise-Therese-Carolina-Wilhelmina, drawn by H. Dawe esq, engraved by H. Cook.

This was the Queen Adelaide who was consort of William IV when South Australia was founded and after whom the city of Adelaide was named. But it was to be another decade before Woodley used the label again, this time actually calling the wines Queen Adelaide.

Woodley Wines was taken over by a Melbourne chain-store company, Crooks National (Holdings). Tony Nelson, who was retained as a consultant, retired soon after. The company was again taken over by Industrial Equity Ltd in 1971. While the Queen Adelaide name and label held their magic sway over consumers, not just sentimentalists in Adelaide but nationally, the wines went into decline. This was slowly reversed when ownership reverted to a wine company, Seppelt Wines, in 1986.

The Queen Adelaide range is riesling, chardonnay, claret, white burgundy, chablis, spatlese lexia and champagne. The chardonnay is usually a very fine wine at a budget price.

The Adelaide Hills

'The best viticultural land in Australia' says the pioneer of modern viticulture in the Adelaide Hills, Brian Croser. The early settlers of South Australia, a century and a half earlier, thought similarly. The surprise of the late twentieth century is not that the Adelaide Hills should be sprouting vineyards and producing so many magnificent wines, but that they should have been disregarded for so long.

John Barton Hack planted Adelaide's first vines in 1837, the year after the colony was founded, and the vine flourished on the Adelaide Plains. It wasn't long, however, before it was realised that better and cooler sites would have to be found if colonial wines were to compete successfully with imports. So the settlers moved up into the hills which crowd upon Adelaide, firstly to establish summer homes away from the February heat of the plains, and secondly, in many cases, to establish better quality vineyards for red and white table wines.

The Adelaide Hills were alive with vineyards in the nineteenth century. However, with the hindsight of viticultural experience, it can be seen that some of them made a basic mistake: they planted on the western slopes, perhaps because they wanted to live with marvellous views of the city and Gulf St Vincent, perhaps because they wanted for their grapes the disease-free security of ripening in late afternoon sun.

They also fell victim to changing tastes for big-bodied wines that could stand the sea voyage to the export markets of Britain and satisfy local demands for fortified wines. These were better produced by the vignerons of McLaren Vale and the Barossa Valley, with their warmer climates. Even such great vineyards as Highercombe at Houghton petered out early in the twentieth century.

Some wine producers survive from these early Hills vineyards, such as Yalumba at Angaston, Henschke at Kyneton and the vineyards of Eden Valley and Clarendon; but they identified themselves with the Barossa or McLaren Vale. This was very clearly a matter of marketing survival, as well as cultural affinity.

It was not until the 1970s, when the taste for fortified wines had given way to table wines and that in turn to wines of some elegance, that the Hills renaissance started. The force was Brian Croser.

A farmer's son from the south-east of the state, he had a vision from schooldays of making wine. And for him that meant the best wine. He studied science and acquired practical experi-

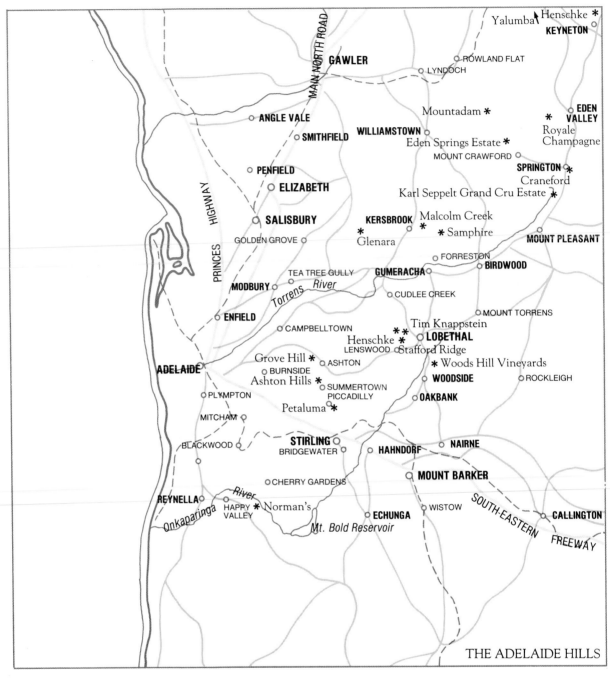

THE ADELAIDE HILLS

ence, and came to realise that Australia's essential viticultural problems were related to warmth. In 1971, when he was quality-control officer with the Hardy Wine Company, he thought of planting in the Adelaide Hills around Mount Lofty. At that time he lived in North Adelaide with his wife, Anne, and used to work on Saturday mornings at the liquor store, then owned by the Caon brothers, in order to taste a range of imported wines and new releases. He would joke with wine merchant Primo Caon about a Mount Lofty chardonnay. After surveying land in the Yarra

Valley, Geelong, Tasmania and Clare however, he opted for home territory. Mount Lofty was not a joke any more when he set up the Petaluma wine company on the eastern side of Mount Lofty, in the picture-postcard Piccadilly Valley.

Croser argued that within a decade the Hills would be as big as Cooonawarra. The official statisticians might not yet have caught up with what is happening, but it seems he was right.

He formed a Hills development company to help private investors buy land; he developed and managed the vineyards for them and contracted to buy their fruit for his champagnes and table wines. He was followed by progressive winemakers from other regions, such as Geoff Weaver of Hardy, Stephen Henschke from Kyneton and Tim Knappstein from Clare, who set up vineyards in the central Adelaide Hills. The growers and winemakers of Eden Valley started to get the idea. And the 'fringe' companies, such as Yalumba to the north and Norman's to the south, started to join in regional promotions for the Adelaide Hills.

This time around the viticultural renaissance may continue to flourish. The Hills' vignerons are learning about such critically important matters as aspect, which their predecessors did not seem to understand.

The Hills area is the central part of the Mount Lofty Ranges, which run rising and dipping from Kangaroo Island to Leigh Creek in the outback. The Hills area is an uplift of sedimentary rock strata which may have been a river plain or under the sea. It was lifted like a piece of cardboard from the west side, now the coastal side occupied by the city of Adelaide. The jagged rocks face west, with the poor soil on these skeletal slopes made poorer by exposure to the prevailing weather, washing them down onto the now fertile Adelaide Plains. On the east side, however, the process was more orderly, with the deep fertile soil flowing off only very gradually towards the Murray River plain. By a happy accident of this fault's flowing north-south, it is the east slopes that face the morning sun, warming up earlier in the day and giving a longer photosynthetic action on the plants. These are the ripening slopes for grapes. With the difficulty of ripening grapes at all in such a cool climate, aspect is critical in viticulture.

Soils are similarly important. With a high rainfall, they become claybound if they are not fertile and free-drained, and the result is root rot.

The dominant Mount Lofty dictates the weather patterns for the area, ensuring that most of the rain gets dumped on the eastern slopes rather than on the Adelaide side. The vine can survive, even flourish, with drip irrigation, but in dry air it is putting too much of its energy into pumping up the water from the soil. In an environment of humid air, such as a high rainfall area, the vine is more likely to put its energy into creating sugar and flavour. To control vigour, by which the plant puts more into growth of shoots than growth of grapes, most Adelaide Hills vignerons have adopted close spacing, giving each plant a smaller amount of the fertile soil to exploit so it doesn't have the luxury of growth. Brian Croser has planted, typically, 3200 vines to the hectare, which is double the density of most vineyards in Australia.

Any of these factors alone might not make a noticeable difference to the resultant wine quality, but added together they can. They can also mean that in some particularly cold years the grapes have trouble achieving sufficient ripeness for table wines of substance (since Australian law, the opposite of European law, permits the addition of acid in winemaking but not sugar, which can bump up the fermentation). Brian Croser's answer to this is to concentrate on making champagne, where the greener grapes that can be expected every year or two find their perfect use. Along the way, some superb table wines, particularly those made from the classic champagne grapes of pinot noir and chardonnay, can be expected; and many small producers of the Hills showed this in the 1980s.

Much of the foregoing applies particularly to the central Adelaide Hills area around Mount Lofty; but by a broad definition the wine region extends much further.

So serious are most Australian vignerons about their wines, especially with the widespread technocratic influence of such institutions as Roseworthy Agricultural College, that old concepts of cultural history, such as those which bind the Barossa, are not enough. The simplest modern way of defining the Adelaide Hills would be to look at a map, observe the easterly watersheds and impose on it heat summation readings. Heat summation, although it has its weaknesses, is increasingly being used to indicate how slowly grapes will ripen, dictating their acid/sugar balances and the character of the resulting wines. Viticulture in Australia ranges from the hot with about 1800°C/days (Mildura, Renmark, Griffith, the Hunter Valley); to the warm at 1550°C to 1700°C (McLaren Vale, Clare); to the traditionally cool at 1400°C to 1550°C (Langhorne Creek, Margaret River); to the true cool such as Coonawarra, the Yarra Valley and Geelong at about 1285°C, the same as Bordeaux in France. Piccadilly, in the Hills, like Drumborg in Victoria and Pipers Brook in Tasmania, is ultracool by this scale, at 1150°C/days. If a true cool standard of about 1300°C is taken, superimposed on a geological structure, the Adelaide Hills can be defined as extending from Clarendon in the south, through Piccadilly, High Eden, Eden Valley and Springton, and petering out about Angaston.

With its consistent coolness for ripening, its range of microclimates suitable for several wine styles, the vinous traditions of nearby Adelaide, the muscle of some established companies, and the enthusiastic dynamics of the new pioneers, the Adelaide Hills region promises to become increasingly important as Australian wine enters the twenty-first century.

Ashton Hills, Summertown

Stephen George was born into wine, to the George family which used to own Skillogalee in the Clare Valley. He even worked for a while at Skillogalee and took a bachelor of agricultural economics, then an oenology diploma at Roseworthy Agricultural College. But he and his parents were to take different paths in life and, after making something of a name for himself as a winemaker at Rothbury in the Hunter Valley and particularly at Wendouree in Clare, the iconoclastic Stephen chose the fields on Tregarthen Road, Summertown, for his own Ashton Hills vineyard.

He was attracted by the cool climate, high humidity and well-drained soils, even though he knew, as he put it, that it would take 'forty years before the area defines the wines. With so many pinot noir clones yet to try and experiments with irrigation, pruning, picking and oaking, this is real frontier stuff. That's why I'm here. It's exciting'.

In 1983 he started planting 3 hectares of riesling, chardonnay, cabernet sauvignon and pinot noir, with dashes of merlot and cabernet sauvignon.

While they were growing, Stephen George set up a business by which he bought various wines from other regions, blended them, and sold them by mail order to customers prepared to trust his palate. The business was called Galah Wines, a name that belied the elegance of the market niche they found.

The first Ashton Hills wines were the real

excitement, and not just for their 360° labels. His chardonnays are generous of flavour and the pinot noir is a red of deep character with cherry and anise flavours.

Craneford, Springton

Colin Forbes, a career winemaker most notably with Saltram in the Barossa, and his wife, Jenny, started attracting attention in the late 1970s with Craneford riesling, made 'on the run' from sixty-year-old vines at Springton. Colin Forbes's founding philosophy was that wines at the time of drinking should be full-flavoured, complex and distinctive enough to enjoy with a diversity of food dishes. He operated in partnership with Robert Forbes until forming a company in 1988 and buying Holmes Estate in Springton (the owners of which, Leon and Leonie Holmes, settled for being grapegrowers).

The public face of Craneford is in the main street of Springton: Cafe C, a restaurant where Mardi Palmer's cooking of local ingredients reflects the Forbes's beliefs in wine and food, with cellar door tastings and sales in a former blacksmith's shop, vintage 1892.

The private face of Craneford is a 6 hectare vineyard at Springton, where Forbes grows riesling and chardonnay, with newer vines of cabernet sauvignon, cabernet franc and merlot. Crop levels are kept low to give high flavour, and Forbes buys in grapes to make up his 45 tonne crush.

The biggest selling Craneford wine is the fleshy riesling, which ages particularly gracefully. Forbes, among his range of wines, also occasionally makes a sparkling burgundy, which is sought after by cognoscenti of that rare style.

Eden Springs Estate, High Eden

On Boehm Springs Road out of Springton, Peter and Karolina Thompson have an old Melbourne tram for wine sales, a barbecue area, lamb-on-the-spit on Sundays and nature walks. They also have an estate wine operation of a 60 tonne crush, handled by contract winemaker Rob Dundon. It all comes from their own vineyards, 500 m above sea level, contoured and facing due east, close by Mountadam. The Thompsons have 17.6 hectares of riesling, cabernet sauvignon and shiraz, with another 8 hectares on the way. The company was founded in July 1988, the first vintage was 1989 and Peter Thompson says: 'Just started. Give us time.'

Glenara, Upper Hermitage

In a picturesque Hills Face Zone valley above Adelaide's northern suburbs live kangaroos with excellent taste. 'They eat only the chardonnay grapes' lament Leigh Verrall and his wife Jan. The first of the vines were planted in 1971 and also include shiraz, cabernet sauvignon, riesling, merlot, cabernet franc and pinot noir varieties. The vines have also suffered from supply gluts and bushfires; but the Verralls have persevered.

The property, once owned by George Percival Verrall, has been used for woodcutting, orchard fruits, market garden vegetables, dairying and premium strawberries. It was put to vines by George's son Ken and his son Leigh almost by accident. They became involved by growing up cuttings from Angove's St Agnes vineyards to rootling stage for other vignerons. On Wednesday 15 September 1971 the Glenara vineyard was born when the Verralls tried planting a few shiraz vines for themselves. Later that year, as fate would have it, an order for 3000 cabernet rootlings was cancelled and the Verralls were stuck with them. They decided quickly to go all the way as vignerons. The grapes which eventually resulted were sold to wineries, including Tolley's, Yalumba, Roseworthy Agricultural College and Kellermeister.

The winemaker at the last, Trevor Jones, also helped them produce their own wines, and in September 1988 Glenara opened to the public. They had a headstart over many small new producers in being able to release some already-mature wines including a berry-flavoured cabernet and a crisp riesling.

Grove Hill, Norton Summit

Adelaide dentist Andrew Cottell, well known in food and wine club circles, went back to running an apple orchard belonging to his wife's family, on a magnificent hilly Norton Summit property with century-old camellia trees. He re-established vineyards that were first grown in 1846 on the steep slopes, with a north-easterly aspect at 450 m. The first release, a chardonnay 1986, showed technical flair and promise.

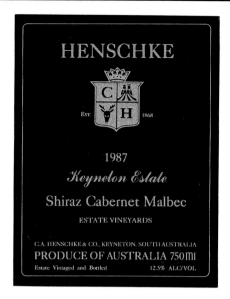

Henschke, Keyneton

Few small and fashionable names in Australian winemaking could boast the depth of heritage and experience of C.A. Henschke and Son. And none could have such an established reputation as this maker of Australian classics, including the Hill of Grace and Mount Edelstone reds.

Stephen Henschke has it in the blood. And he and his wife, noted viticulturist Prue, have it in an excellent range of vineyards, totalling 84 hectares: at Lenswood in the central Adelaide Hills, at Eden Valley and around their historic stone cellars at Keyneton.

The village of Keyneton, 13 km south-east of Angaston, has been considered a cultural part of the Barossa Valley, but it is geographically separate—with sparsely wooded country, poor soils, high altitudes, average rainfall of 433 mm and winter frosts. Early in the twentieth century there were five wineries in the Keyneton area, then known as North Rhine, more for the nostalgic connotations of the name than for any real resemblance to Europe. It is likely that these wineries could not survive against the Barossa Valley vintners, who had better yields and better access to the markets of Adelaide. Only one survived.

The origins of that survival lie with Johann Christian Henschke, wheelwright and builder, who was born in Kutschlau in Silesia in 1803. He arrived in Australia in 1842 on the *Skjold* and settled at Bethay near Tanunda before taking to farming on a small holding near Keyneton. His son, Paul Gotthardt Henschke, born 1847,

Henschke Cellars, established 1868.

planted the first vines on the family property to make wines for local consumption. He had his first vintage in 1868, and the wine company dates from this time.

Paul Gotthard Henschke died in 1914 and was succeeded by his son Paul Alfred Henschke, who extended the property and the cellars. He began making fortified wines, then in demand, but in the drought and the depression of the 1920s farming again became the major family pursuit. Of Paul Alfred's seven daughters and four sons, Cyril Alfred Henschke, born 1924, grew up to become interested in winemaking. Together they extended the cellars in 1949 and turned to making dry table wines. Cyril took charge after his father's death in 1964, and became a well-known Barossa identity and the winner of a Churchill Fellowship.

Cyril Henschke died in 1979, shot accidentally by his wife Doris, and his younger son Stephen became the fifth generation of Henschkes running the property.

Stephen had taken a science degree at the University of Adelaide and studied winemaking

and viticulture at Geisenheim in Germany, where Prue also studied under Dr Becker.

The Henschkes have exceptionally cool and wet vineyards, newly established on former apple orchards at Lenswood, near those of Tim Knappstein from Clare. These, like the other Henschke vineyards, were run by Prue in a hands-on style before she had children. She replanted Lenswood when the first vines were destroyed by Ash Wednesday bushfires. The Henschkes also have an excellent, frost-free riesling and cabernet area of 28 hectares at Eden Valley. But the key vineyards are those near the winery, which is 5 km north of the village of Keyneton, on clay loams, podsols and rich silt.

The most famous are those which have given their euphonious names to the shiraz wines they produce: the Hill of Grace, named after the nearby Gnadenberg Lutheran church where 100-year-old shiraz vines still grow; and Mount Edelstone, meaning noble stone, which has some seventy-year-old shiraz vines. Together with the Keyneton Estate red and a recent addition to the range, a blended red to honour Cyril Henschke and named after him, these are eagerly sought by connoisseurs. Henschke also makes a range of varietals, the most popular being the Eden Valley riesling.

The rustic charm of the Henschke cellars, which resonate to a spine-tingling octet of cellos during the Barossa Gourmet Weekend each August, conceals storage space for more than 45 000 litres, the equipment to crush 650 tonnes of grapes and drives that hold 200 000 maturing bottles. It also conceals a fair bit of the technology that points to the winemaking of the future. For Stephen and Prue Henschke intend the family traditions to extend into future generations of Henschkes.

Karl Seppelt Grand Cru Estate, Springton

Karl Seppelt's family background is told in the section on Seppelt Wines of Seppeltsfield. He is another part of the Seppelt family, which fragmented when the company went into the hands of the South Australian Brewing Company. In 1981 he had started planning for his personal future by planting a vineyard of 8 hectares (with four more coming on stream), growing mainly cabernet sauvignon and chardonnay on contoured north-east slopes near Springton. It is probably no coincidence that he chose this region for his own operation; he had been instrumental in the Seppelt company's visionary establishment of a large cool-climate vineyard nearby at Partalunga.

The stone cellars are 4 km west of Springton and 8 km north of Mount Pleasant, with picnic grounds. (Because this is bushfire country barbecues are not encouraged during summer.) The wines, from a crush of 25 tonnes, are made under contract at Petaluma and Yalumba; they include cabernet, hermitage (shiraz), riesling and chardonnay, with champagne on the way. The cabernet found quick favour with its rich chocolatey flavours.

Malcolm Creek, Kersbrook

Reg Tolley, of the Tolley wine family of Hope Valley in Adelaide, and his wife, Elizabeth, moved to live in the Adelaide Hills in 1980 at a property called Ashwood, between Kersbrook and Williamstown. The Malcolm Creek

meanders through their undulating property and gave its name to the wine they grow. Their first commercial crop was in 1986, and harvest is a family affair. This small operation, backed with the Tolley experience, produces a fine, light claret.

MOUNTADAM
CABERNET SAUVIGNON 1987

12.4% ALC/VOL AUSTRALIAN WINE 750 ml

Mountadam, High Eden

David Wynn, an elder statesman of the Australian wine industry and founder with his father of Wynn's Coonawarra Estate, had time and money on his hands when he sold the substantial S. Wynn & Co. Pty Ltd to the Toohey's brewery conglomerate in 1972. He put both the time and the money, and his considerable experience, into Mountadam, an estate dedicated to uncompromising excellence.

The Mountadam project actually had its genesis in 1969, more than a decade before the first full vintage, when David Wynn established a propagation unit at the Wynn company's Modbury Estate, where Adelaide suburbs now grow. He was multiplying the wine grape varieties being released from quarantine by the South Australian Department of Agriculture. It was the first time new material had been released since the state was sealed off to outside vines early in the century; David Wynn was thus the first in South Australia to handle chardonnay vines.

At the same time, he began a search by car and light aircraft for the suitable combination of soil, climate and topography for the new vine stocks. The answer was in the South Mount Lofty Ranges between Eden Valley and Williamstown, at the headwaters of the River

Marne (which before World War I had been called the Rhine). The area is spectacular country, now known as High Eden, about 600 m above sea level—spectacular country where eagles dare.

Viticulturist Lloyd Portis tends 32 hectares of low-yield, slow-ripening vines, planted between 1972 and 1981, mostly of chardonnay, with pinot noir, cabernet sauvignon and riesling.

The first experimental vintage was 1979, made by Jeff Anderson at Roseworthy Agricultural College. The college exhibited the 1981 chardonnay in the National Wine Show in Canberra and took the trophy for the best current-vintage white of the show.

Meanwhile, David's son, Adam Wynn, having studied agricultural science at the University of Adelaide, had been in France for three years at Bordeaux University—where he topped the oenology class while studying in a foreign language—and worked at Meursault and Montrachet. He also investigated California before returning to Australia in 1982, bristling with ideas. He built and equipped the Mountadam winery with state-of-the-art technology for the 1984 vintage. The technology almost seems redundant when the wine comes from such good fruit and is handled by such consummate natural artistry as Adam Wynn shows. The winery crushes 400 tonnes.

David Wynn, who remains a partner in the family company as well as being a prominent patron of the arts, produces the David Wynn range of interesting, accessible and fashionably labelled wines, much of it fruit bought in from elsewhere. His unwooded chardonnay is an object lesson in the taste of chardonnay and his shiraz is a happy riot of fresh fruitiness.

Adam Wynn, with the Mountadam label, specialises in chardonnay and pinot noir table wines from the cream of the estate's grapes, made to some of the highest Australian standards, although with obvious reference to Burgundy, which had such a strong influence on the winemaker. Mountadam champagne has also captivated the critics.

Mountadam cask cellar.

Norman's, Chandlers Hill

Lloyd Light, to introduce the Norman's story obliquely, was a foundation director of the Southern Vales Cooperative at McLaren Vale in 1965. Vigneron Light knew that the fruit from his own vineyard at Happy Valley, between Clarendon and Reynella, was excellent, so in 1979 he started making his own wines. He expanded with vineyards down on the plains at Murray Bridge and in the region of the winery, the vines being tended by David Light. From 1975, another son, Brian Light, was winemaker. He had graduated with a Roseworthy diploma of oenology, dux of the class of 1973, and had worked for experience elsewhere in the wine industry.

The company, which produced a full range of table wines and fortifieds, was originally known as Light Wines until the ramifications of that name were realised, in an era when lightness in wines was equated with wimpishness, and its name was changed to Coolawin. In the mid-1980s its name was to change again when it was taken over by Norman's Wine Estates—but that side of the vinous story goes back to the last century.

Jesse Norman, a brewer from Cambridge in England, arrived in South Australia in 1851 and two years later planted a vineyard at Underdale, and eventually built a winery. His son Arthur expanded the business and in 1911 acquired vineyards at nearby Sturt. These were eventually acquired by the Government Housing Trust of South Australia and, to compensate, the Normans set up vineyards on the fertile market garden soils of the Adelaide Plains at Evanston. At the same time as Arthur Norman had been establishing the Sturt vineyards, he purchased more land on Holbrooks Road, Underdale, and in 1921 built a new winery.

Arthur's three sons, Herbert, Hurtle and Reg, continued in the business, followed by Reg's sons, Leonard and Ronald. Then came the fifth generation, with Trevor Norman as winemaker. His concentration was on the 57 hectares at Evanston, including such unusual varieties for the time as pinot noir. Norman's was probably the first company in South Australia to release a varietal gewurztraminer of consistent quality.

Another strand to the story entered on 1 March 1982, when the winemaker dynasty ended and Norman's was taken over by the Horlin-Smith family, who had for three generations been involved with the liquor industry, mostly hotels and liquor stores. Robert Horlin-Smith is managing director with John, Donald, David and Murray as directors.

The Horlin-Smiths expanded by taking over Coolawin Estate—with Brian Light, who by this time was starting to win quite a few awards, as winemaker—and made the Chandlers Hill winery the company headquarters.

The image of Coolawin had, historically, been McLaren Vale, and Norman's of the Adelaide Plains. With the realisation that Chandlers Hill and the important Clarendon vineyards had the advantages of the South Mount Lofty Ranges elevation, Norman's began, in the late 1980s, to be considered fundamentally an Adelaide Hills company.

The principal vineyard remains the Evanston Estate on the plains, 52 hectares on rich river alluvial soil and loam over sandstone. Principal varieties are chardonnay, pinot noir, traminer, riesling, chenin blanc, shiraz, cabernet franc, merlot, cabernet sauvignon and sauvignon blanc.

The Clarendon Estate, 6.6 hectares at a high altitude with an easterly aspect, is planted with pinot noir, chardonnay and riesling, and produces, among other wines, the company's champagne.

Norman's makes a full range of wine styles, the top quality being released under the Chais Clarendon label, and also buys grapes from growers in Clarendon, McLaren Vale and Coonawarra. The biggest supplier is Lloyd Light at Baker's Gully.

Petaluma, Piccadilly

Brian Croser is the controversial myth-making leader of a generation of Australian winemakers trying to understand the confluence of art and science in the late twentieth century. He has relentlessly pursued a vision since he was a schoolboy at Adelaide's Scotch College—the making of excellent wine. It is a philosophy he puts thus:

make no compromises . . . eliminate the uncontrolled variables . . . concentrate on what the fruit will do rather than what can be done with it . . . It is a matter of policy that we have total control over the vineyards.

If this philosophy has become something of a religion among many modern Australian winemakers, the high-tech temple is the Petaluma winery in the central Adelaide Hills. Here, in the Piccadilly Valley, Brian Croser has become one of the most influential figures in Australian wine, and in industry politics.

The farmer's son from Millicent pursued his vision purposively by studying agricultural science at the University of Adelaide, a path that has been taken by many other serious South Australian winemakers; but he then bypassed the usual course of Roseworthy College to study oenology at Davis in California. There he encountered the name Petaluma in the Napa Valley and took it for his eventual winemaking operation in Australia, not for the town's associations with chicken farming but for the name's prettiness.

Back in Australia, after making the early Seigersdorf rieslings for Hardy as a hint of the new technologies he was to champion, he made small batches of his own wine while he was senior oenology lecturer at the Riverina College of Advanced Education in Wagga Wagga. These included the Chardonnay 1977 with fruit from the Rothbury Estate's Cowra vineyard. The following year he became a consultant to the Evans Wine Company—and consultancy became, through Croser's Oenotec, the main way he spread his influence and standards throughout Australia—and a relationship with Len Evans was cemented. The Evans company bought vineyards at Clare and Coonawarra and a modern winery was built at Piccadilly.

Brian Croser chose Piccadilly specifically to plant the Tiers vineyard—the tears of angels? or is that Keats's 'beaded bubbles winking at the brim'?—with chardonnay and pinot noir for champagne-making after assessing various cool-climate areas throughout southern Australia. He also knew the area's geomorphology and viticultural history.

The first vintage at Petaluma, in 1979, stimulated the formation of a company which came to have Brian Croser as managing director, Len Evans as chairman, and C. Ryan and the French

Champagne house of Bollinger as the other partners.

In 1986 Brian Croser bought and renovated an 1860 flour mill nearby. The Bridgewater Mill is the Petaluma tasting and sales area, a restaurant, arts complex and champagne-maturation centre for his upmarket Croser champagne.

Piccadilly remains the production centre for the company's yellow-labelled riesling, chardonnay, Coonawarra red and botrytis riesling. It also makes Croser base wine from the surrounding vineyards and a second range of more accessibly priced wines under the Bridgewater Mill label. Petaluma does a considerable amount of contract winemaking for other companies.

If Petaluma is the head of the company, the heart remains the vineyards—47 hectares in the Adelaide Hills, 32 hectares in Coonawarra and 32 hectares in Clare.

Clare is a northern extension of the Mount Lofty Ranges. Petaluma's vineyards are on the western face of the ancient range, overlooking those of Tim Knappstein, 500 m above sea level with a reliable 625 mm annual rainfall and coolish nights. Riesling vines cling to the red-brown earth slopes, which are littered with the blue-grey parent slate. These twenty-year-old vines are arranged in knee-high contours, waving across the slopes in traditional Australian dryland viticultural fashion, and producing a riesling which, for floral aromas and fleshy strength, epitomises the Clare character.

The cabernet and merlot grapes which make the Petaluma Coonawarra, as the red is simply titled, grow on a strip of red soil in the south-east of South Australia, one of the most distinguished strips of red wine grapegrowing soil in the world. This is chilly country, where the grapes ripen slowly, helped by the maternal influence of the Southern Ocean 60 km away.

The soil is nutritious without being garden-fertile and is free-draining and aerobic with abundant subterranean water beneath its limestone foundations. Changing viticultural techniques meant that the complex Petaluma Coonawarra, which has become established as an Australian classic, underwent a subtle change in the mid–1980s to become even firmer and longer lived.

The newest Petaluma vineyards, the Tiers,

surround the winery in a fertile, market-gardening oasis amid old mountains, with 1400 mm annual rainfall and a very cool, humid European climate. The friable loams of the Piccadilly Valley are based on shale, quartzite and ironstone and they support chardonnay and pinot noir in neat hedgerows up and down the steep internal slopes of the valley. They represent a radical approach to viticulture in Australia, being among the first densely planted, manicured, European-style vineyards on the old continental surface which is Australia.

These are the vineyards that make Petaluma wines—these and Brian Croser.

Royale Champagne, Eden Valley

James Irvine is the son of an itinerant baker, brought up around country towns of South Australia. His interest in champagne doubtless goes back to those heady childhood smells of fermenting yeasts, even though he was somewhat surprised, on leaving Adelaide's Scotch College in 1949, to find himself actually working in a winery—as a laboratory assistant at Glenloth. Irvine acknowledges three great training courses for winemakers in Australia: Roseworthy, Riverina and experience. He took the last course, working around the industry in production and marketing until he became winemaker at Augustine (Krondorf) in the Barossa, where he had the freedom to experiment, especially with champagnes.

Irvine works as a consultant winemaker for several companies, but his future is in the small family operation he and his wife and partner, Marjorie, established in the Adelaide Hills. Jim wanted to call it the Giggle Factory; Marge objected. It is called Royale Champagne, dedicated with unashamed elitism to deluxe blanc-de-blanc champagnes (and a highly specialised merlot dry red).

The Irvines started planting chardonnay, merlot and pinot meunier in 1980 on 8.5 cool-climate hectares on Basil Roeslers Road, Eden Valley.

The soils are skeletal-type, grey-brown podsols, and the vines are on a two-trellis system. The Irvines hand-pick 44 tonnes and buy no other grapes, aiming for an eventual production of 3000 cases. Royale Champagne hit the top end of the market in November 1989.

Samphire, Kersbrook

Tom and Rosemary Miller have what they call the smallest of commercial wine operations—less than a hectare of riesling and cabernet sauvignon—growing near Kersbrook. Rosemary sells her pottery at the winery on Watts Gully Road, and Tom has persevered since 1982 in making wines, despite the vineyard depredations of ducks, rosellas, foxes and kangaroos. One of his most remarkable rieslings, the 1988, had an alcohol content of 15 per cent and unexpected tropical passionfruit flavours.

Samuel Smith and Son, Angaston

Yalumba, as the company is generally called even though that is only one of its brand names, is one of the major names of Australian wine, for its heritage, its size, its quality and its role in the ethos of wine. It was in a position of some regional schizophrenia in the 1980s. Culturally, it has a longstanding involvement with the Barossa Valley; at the same time, from its vast spread of fruit sources, it was putting a special emphasis on its Hills Smith Estate, Heggies and Pewsey Vale wines, which are from the Adelaide Hills. Meanwhile, the bluestone clocktower stands oblivious, saying this is S. Smith and Son.

Samuel Smith, who in 1849 founded the company, would surely have approved of the progressive attitudes of his descendant, the current managing director Robert Hill Smith, now overseeing a crush of 10 000 tonnes a year. Samuel Smith would not understand the computers which are used in all phases of operations, but he would appreciate the feeling of continuity which endures in the gracious example of a European wine house, solidly built of local bluestone and set among exotic trees and lawns reminiscent of an English country estate. Samuel Smith was English, a successful brewer from Dorset, born at Wareham in 1812, who immigrated to Australia with his wife, Frances, and five children in 1847. The family moved 80 km from Adelaide by bullock wagon to the emergent township of Angaston, where Smith worked in the garden and orchard of George Fife Angas, then virtually a feudal lord.

Samuel Smith, who might just have seen the last of English viticulture of that era back in Dorset, saw cool Angaston's potential for grapes and he bought 5 hectares for his own vineyard. He named it Yalumba, sometimes Yealumba, which was thought to be an indigenous word for 'all the country around'. In 1849—from which year the company is dated—he began planting the vineyard by night, working during the day for Angas. He later recalled it as a year of struggle, 'but God gave me wonderful strength and my wife helped in every way'.

Smith and his son joined the rush to the Victorian goldfields. On his sixteenth shaft he struck gold and after four months he returned to South Australia £300 richer. He spent £80 on more land, 32 hectares, which he let out; £100 on a plough, two horses and a harness; and the rest he kept for future cellars and another house.

He made his first wine in 1852, and by 1862 he had 3.6 hectares planted with shiraz, also giving cuttings to his neighbours so that he might eventually buy the grapes for wine. In 1862 he produced sixty hogsheads and Yalumba wines won repute, gaining a bronze medal at the 1866 Intercolonial Exhibition in Melbourne, and a silver medal at the 1878 Paris Universal Exhibition.

Samuel Smith was a prominent member of the Angaston Congregational church and was for many years superintendent of the Sunday school. He died of chronic Brights disease in 1889, survived by his wife, four daughters and a son. His estate was sworn for probate at £11 178.

His son Sidney, born in 1837 in Morden,

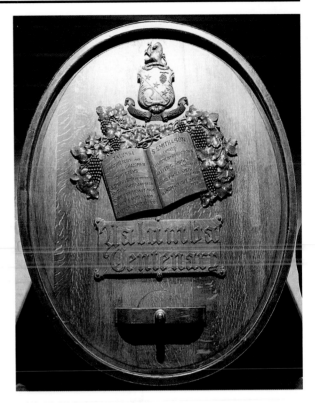

A commemorative plaque at Yalumba.

England, had married Eleanor Caley in 1862 and was his father's business partner and heir. He replaced the thatched cellar with the bluestone winery of today, with its clocktower as a symbol of the family's faith in the future. By 1900 he had 48 hectares under vine.

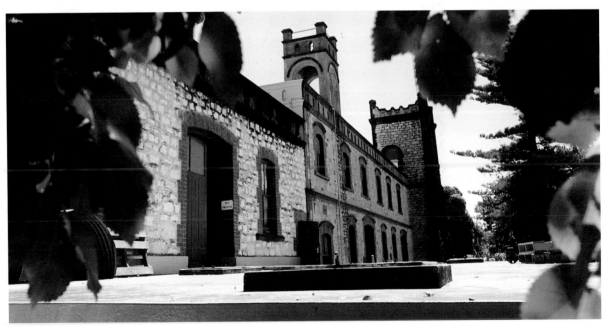

The facade of the old winery at Yalumba

Sidney was chairman of the Angaston District Council and today his descendants are prominent figures in the social and political life of the town. He died of renal disease in 1908, survived by five sons and three daughters. He had retired some years earlier because of failing health, transferring the business to two of his sons.

Percival took charge of the winemaking and cellar operations and Walter supervised marketing, building up exports to England and India. In 1923 Percy Smith retired and a private company was formed with two of Walter's sons as directors, Sidney Hill Smith and Wyndham Hill Smith.

Sidney was killed in the Kyeema air crash of 1938 and brother Wyndham, then aged twenty-eight and looking after the company's affairs in Perth, returned to Angaston to become chairman and managing director. 'Windy' as he is affectionately called behind his back on his visits to the winery today, is a man of charm with a love for wine, horses, cricket and yarning. He is also something of a painter and his works have featured on some company wine labels.

Sidney's eldest son, Mark Hill Smith, returned from war service in the navy, which must be where he developed his polished style, and joined the company as the first of the fifth generation, eventually becoming managing director. His sons Michael and Matthew are the sixth generation, while Windy's sons, Robert and Samuel, are the seventh. Robert Hill Smith is managing director—and there will be more Hill Smiths.

Since World War II, Yalumba has grown rapidly, with such winemakers as the generous-spirited Peter Lehmann, and Peter Wall. Winemakers Brian Walsh, Alan Hoey and Geoff Linton continue the traditions. They crush 10 000 tonnes of grapes, producing a quarter of a million cases of wine a year, 60 per cent of it from the company's own vineyards. These, in the hands of Ray Bartsch and Russell Johnson, total 400 hectares.

In volume terms the principal vineyards are at Oxford Landing in the Riverland, growing riesling, shiraz, tokay, cabernet sauvignon and chardonnay. But the big excitement for the company's leap towards the future was the establishment, in 1961, of vineyards at Pewsey Vale, 540 m up in the Mount Lofty Ranges. It started as a partnership with Geoffrey Angas Parsons,

then proprietor of Pewsey Vale Station, but Yalumba subsequently bought his share. It had been under vines once before, having been planted by pioneer Joseph Gilbert in 1847. His wines were praised abroad and in 1864 the London *Medical Times* mentioned their powerful vinous flavours. Yalumba believed that Pewsey Vale had enormous potential for growing top-quality wines and under the supervision of Norman Hankel more than 56 hectares were contour-banked and planted with riesling, cabernet sauvignon and some semillon. The climate is cool, with 700–750 mm annual rainfall. Pewsey Vale has some rocky outcrops and the soil is podsolic, mostly gravelly sandy loam over a pebbly subsoil. The riesling, distinctively labelled as a separate brand from Yalumba, has proved to be one of the company's outstanding successes in restaurants.

The rapid success of the Pewsey Vale vineyard led to the planting in 1971 of the Heggies vineyard, which had been a sheep property owned by Walter Grandy Smith's former schoolmate, Jim Heggie. Their sons and successors, Colin Heggie and Wyndham Hill Smith, were also mates at St Peter's College and many a bottle of wine was emptied as the two discussed land, cattle, horses, wine, life and, occasionally, selling the property. Finally, they did the deed and the Smith company had what proved to be one of the most viticulturally exciting bits of dirt in the state. It is high in the ranges, at an altitude of 500 m and, of its 200 hectares, 48 hectares were planted to pinot noir, cabernet sauvignon, merlot, chardonnay, riesling, cabernet franc and traminer. The vines were clonally selected and grafted, with higher trellises than normal, close-planted and handled for low productivity. The first release of a Heggies riesling, which like Pewsey Vale is kept as a separate brand, was from the 1979 vintage. It was immediately impressive for its label, featuring a Barry Tucker inkwash drawing of a stockman, said to be Colin Heggie's son. The label is classically Australian and the wine has become an Australian classic for its consistency of character and its uncompromisingly firm spine, needing some years of cellaring to show itself fully. Subsequent cabernet blends from the Heggies vineyard have shown magnificently similar style, and could be to the Smith company what Grange is to Penfolds, Steingarten is to Orlando and Limestone Ridge is to Lindemans.

Pewsey Vale and Heggies vineyards are mechanically harvested at night to achieve lower berry temperatures before crushing. All planting material is from the Smith company's own nursery, which also produces grafted vines for local growers who supply to the company, according to what is considered best for the specific location. The nursery is responsible for nematode-resistant stock which is important for the Riverland vineyards. Attention is paid to grafted vines which have high flavour characteristics, good set, even flowering, disease resistance and desirable growth and vigour for the appropriate area. At the other end of the process, Yalumba pays attention to wine maturation in its cellars and has its own resident cooper, Harry Mahlo, making and repairing barrels.

The Smith company makes a full range of wines, although Commonwealth Government tax policies in the 1980s cut the production of fortified wines for which Yalumba had developed a great name. From March 1982 the top table wines were released as Hill Smith Estate rather than Yalumba. The company resisted the temptation to enter the bag-in-the-box cask market, but in the late 1980s found some success with smaller, 2 litre casks of varietal wines. Yalumba produces Martini vermouth under licence to the original company in Italy and is national agent for a range of imported wines and spirits.

A specialisation is the production of champagne and it was for a while in a joint venture with the French Champagne house of Deut and Gelderman. A legacy of this period is Yalumba's sophisticated champagne called simply 'D'. The company's biggest selling lines are champagnes— Angas brut and cuvée select non-vintage—but its greatest interest, and that of drinkers, must be in such Adelaide Hills' wines as those from Heggies.

SPRINGTON

RHINE RIESLING

PRODUCT OF AUSTRALIA   750 ml
VINTAGED BY ROBERT HAMILTON & SON   SPRINGTON WINE ESTATE
HAMILTON'S ROAD SPRINGTON SOUTH AUSTRALIA   12.0% ALC/VOL

Springton in 1981 have almost as much history involved. The land was leased by John Bollard in 1873 to build a winery, having an agreement with Oscar Benno Seppelt of the Barossa. The property went to the Rayner family and in 1944 it was purchased by the Hamilton wine family, with whom it remained until 1979 when Mildara Wines took over Hamilton Ewell. The Mildara reign was brief and in June 1981 Robert and Mark Hamilton bought back the Springton Wine Estate. They have made wine there since 1982 and also trade under the name of Robert Hamilton and Son.

Almost all their 60 tonne crush, used to produce a wide range of styles, comes from 20 hectares of grenache, riesling, cabernet sauvignon, shiraz, white frontignac, semillon and malbec varieties growing on alluvial sandstones at an altitude of 400 m. The vineyards are being expanded with chardonnay and more riesling.

Outside the winery are two pedro ximenes vines which were transplanted from the now razed Ewell vineyards in Marion—a direct link to the early plantings by Richard Hamilton.

Springton Wine Estate, Springton

Robert Hamilton and his son Mark are of the fifth and sixth generations of the famous and diverse Hamilton winemaking family. Their ancestor Richard Hamilton was one of the first to plant vines in South Australia, at Glenelg in about 1837.

The bluestone cellars they purchased at

Stafford Ridge, Lenswood

No winery, no cellar door, but vineyards devoted to distinctive excellence from the Lenswood region in the central Adelaide Hills. The artist is Geoff Weaver, a senior winemaker with the Hardy Wine Company, who in his spare time started planting 7.5 hectares of cabernet sauvignon, chardonnay, riesling, merlot and

Stafford Ridge

RHINE RIESLING

1988

ASHBOURNE WINE CO LENSWOOD SOUTH AUSTRALIA 5240

750 ml

sauvignon blanc—closely planted to de-vigour the vines, with high trellising—in this cold, wet area at an elevation of 540 m.

Geoff Weaver, still with Hardy, has made some beautiful wines from other sources under his Ashbourne label, but the emphasis is on those from the Stafford Ridge vineyard with 50 tonnes of grapes producing 1000 cases of spendidly crafted dry whites and dry reds. This is small winemaking, with excellence.

Woods Hill Vineyards

Ian Wilson is determined to be part of the revolution that Australian sparkling wines are undergoing, and he is doing it by sharing the faith and enthusiasm of Brian Croser in the Adelaide Hills. He set up Woods Hill Vineyards with a former winemaking colleague, Charles Hargreaves. The aim is to have a string of vineyards between Piccadilly and Summertown totalling 40 hectares by 1994, some owned by the company, some as joint developments with private investors.

Ian Wilson was a Roseworthy oenology graduate, following Urrbrae High School in Adelaide, and his first winemaking job was with the Southern Vales Cooperative in McLaren Vale. There he learnt the importance of vineyards and met Grant Burge, a winemaker from a Barossa family. There was born one of the great double acts—Wilson's urbane sense of style and Burge's solidity—and in 1978 Burge and Wilson bought the Krondorf winery in the Barossa. That was bought by Mildara in 1986 and Wilson quietly

took to the hills to plan his own champagne venture.

The champagnes, labelled Ian Wilson, are made with Brian Croser's facilities at the Bridgewater Mill. For the first couple of years, while Wood Hill's first pinot noir, pinot meunier and chardonnay vines were maturing, grapes from elsewhere were used for Ian Wilson champagnes; but already a new style was being stamped on them.

The Barossa Valley

The Barossa Valley is the powerhouse of Australian winemaking. No other wine region can boast the production headquarters of so many major companies—names such as Penfolds, Kaiser Stuhl, Tollana, Seppelt, Woodley, Wolf Blass, Leo Buring, Orlando, Saltram, Peter Lehmann—or such an extraordinarily high proportion of the medals and trophies won at wine shows. Many of the popular wines of Australia, and some of the finest, have come from the Barossa, even if they were not necessarily grown there. The Barossa Valley also has a deep reservoir of wine heritage, a culture unique in Australia and a major tourist attraction. It is the best known winemaking area of Australia, and can be promoted internationally on a par with other uniquely Australian attractions such as Kakadu National Park, the Great Barrier Reef and the Sydney Opera House.

This beautiful valley is less than an hour's drive north of Adelaide, its floor averaging 300 m above sea level. The highest point is Pewsey Peak at 620 m on the Barossa Range, which is a parallel extension of the South Mount Lofty Ranges, with Eden Valley between the two (although this area is viticulturally part of the Adelaide Hills region); the lowest point is at Lyndoch, at 178 m. The valley varies from 3 km to 11 km wide and extends northwards from Williamstown for 32 km to Kalimna and Koonunga at latitude 34'S, embracing a wide range of viticultural conditions. The principal towns are Tanunda, the historic cultural capital; Nuriootpa, the more modern administrative centre; and Angaston in the hills, which is quite English in character. Each town has a population of more than 1000. There are several smaller settlements, such as Lyndoch, Rowland Flat,

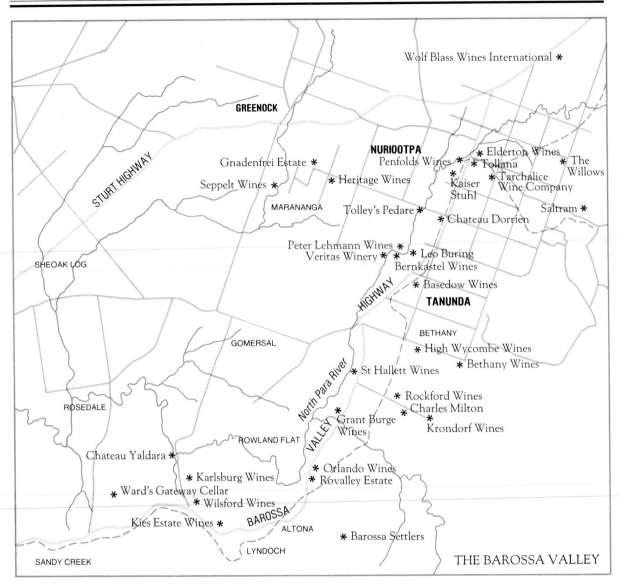

THE BAROSSA VALLEY

Bethany, Seppeltsfield, Marananga and Stockwell. Many of them, and many vineyards, follow the course of the North Para River as it flows or dribbles (depending on the season) southwards through the valley and out to the Adelaide Plains.

Viticulturally, the Barossa is considered a hot region, akin perhaps to Portugal in Europe, and this is why it found early success with fortified wines. Average rainfall is 500 mm, but this varies considerably and is low in summer when the vines can become heat-stressed without supplementary irrigation. The average mean January–February temperature at Nuriootpa is 20.5°C, but 30°C days are not uncommon in summer.

The soil types on the valley floor are diverse, varying from heavy loams to light sandy soils.

The most fertile are the red-brown earths, which consist of loam over clay subsoil and contain some lime. Also commonly found are grey-red soils known as solodized solonetz, which have yellow-brown to grey subsoils containing limestone. There are also patches of terra rossa and rendzinas.

The Barossa escaped the scourge of the louse phylloxera, which destroyed many Australian vineyards last century, and for this it can thank strict South Australian Government quarantine regulations and good luck. The vines are thus not grafted on to other roots, as in so many areas of the world.

The region grows all varieties of wine grapes, for all styles of wines are made here: table, sparkling, fortified and flavoured. Of the 43 000 tonnes of grapes harvested from 5200 hectares

Barossa Valley vineyards above Bethany.

of yielding vines, the most numerous are (in descending order): grenache, used principally for ports and simple reds; shiraz, for the great traditional reds of the Barossa; riesling, for firm-flavoured whites; palomino and pedro, for distillation, fortified whites and cask whites; semillon, for one of the emergent great white table wine styles of the area; and cabernet sauvignon, for firm reds.

All the grapes grown do not total the output of the Barossa. Most of the large companies have large vineyards elsewhere as well, in the Riverland, Clare, Padthaway and Coonawarra. Some of these supply the anonymous wine-cask market; sometimes they help make the truly great wines, such as Penfold's Grange Hermitage, which typically might add to local Kalimna shiraz some Coonawarra and McLaren Vale fruit. And all but the small specialist companies will buy grapes from the Hills, from McLaren Vale, Langhorne Creek, Clare and Coonawarra for flexibility in blending. This is not to suggest that all Barossa wine is somehow false, however, for the Barossa winemakers are invariably honest with their labelling, specifying where the grapes were grown, if it is a premium wine.

The Barossa Wine Show, which is the most important regional wine exposition held annually outside the capital cities, has categories for wines made in the Barossa, regardless of where they are grown; it also has categories for wines made only of Barossa grapes, and some of these are magnificent, for the area has many excellent microclimates and some great individual vineyards, such as the Willows at Light Pass.

The secret of what made the Barossa great, however, is not to be found in the vineyards so much as in the people that tend them. Most of the early settlers were Silesians, Prussians and Brandenburgers, who, if they had to be called anything else, would rather it be Polish than German. These settlers brought with them no great wine-growing traditions but an important community togetherness, a strong religious foundation in the Lutheran church, which still dominates the valley, the capacity for hard and meticulous work and a deep respect for the land that was offering them a new and free or lucrative life. This was the spirit behind the methodical vineyard practices which fuelled the growth of most of the big, modern wine companies.

Grapepickers near Lyndoch.

The first grapes in the Barossa were planted at the village of Bethany early in the 1840s by either Ferdinand and Marno Aldenhoven from Denmark, or Johann Fiedler from Prussia. Within less than two decades many of today's significant names had set up business with wine grapes, including Johann Gramp, Samuel Hoffmann, Joseph Seppelt, Samuel Smith and William Salter.

English some of them might have been but the dominant culture is northern European, and despite Australian monocultural tendencies, examples of this background abound in the Barossa. A form of German language, called Barossa Deutsch, which is almost a pure time-warp encapsulation of dialects long since corrupted in Europe, is still spoken. Germanic family names abound, although many place names were anglicised by Act of Parliament in World War I. The settlements are neat and

orderly, with unique stone houses and scrupulously maintained Lutheran churches. At times it is only the gum trees and the stunningly blue sky that remind one that this is Australia.

Northern European eating habits endure strongly, with cakes such as strueselkuchen and bienenstich; sausages such as mettwurst, leberwurst and blutwurst; preserved meats such as kassler; and the pickled dill cucumbers and real breads that gourmets will drive from Adelaide to buy. They might also drive to eat in the Barossa restaurants, such as Maggie Beer's Pheasant Farm, which is rated one of the finest in Australia (even if it is in the country).

The love of music remains, not only in the churches and in the male choral society founded in 1861, the Liedertafel, but also in the competitive brass bands. It is not surprising to find a euphonium in the back of a winemaker's one-tonne utility truck, ready for band practice in the evening; and under local bandmaster Neville Alderslade the Tanunda Town Band has been a consistent national champion.

The biennial Barossa Valley Vintage Festival, a carnival held every second Easter at vintage time, is reminiscent of northern Europe. The community is involved in setting it up on a massive scale and benefits as proceeds go to local charities. Numerous functions are held in a week of music, theatre, dancing, drinking, feasting, art shows, grape-picking contests, processions, wine auctions, church services, heritage displays and much more. Although the Barossa has taken to the gourmet weekend concept, in which restaurants and wineries combine for annual upmarket promotions of their best wares to quite a discriminating clientele, the vintage festival remains the dominant image of the Barossa, with some 200 000 visitors swamping the 13 000 residents. It shows a valley 'big, bold and brassy' in a well organised and well attended harvest festival that is undoubtedly Australia's most convincing demonstration of a community spirit, and undoubtedly one of the world's largest wine festivals.

This emphasis on 'big' has disturbed some

Vineyards in the Lyndoch area.

people in the Barossa and there was a growing mood in the late 1980s that the Barossa was facing a twofold threat: that it would develop a reputation for only anonymous mass-market blends produced by the big wine companies; and that its heritage and wine potential would be swamped by expanding suburbia from Adelaide and unsupervised tourism development, especially as the valley was the subject of six different local government regions, each with its own agenda. The first threat was rather hollow, given that the big companies are also known for producing some of the truly great wines of Australia; the second was a matter for lobbying of state governments, which at election times are only too keen to talk about heritage and environment and about wine as a great tourist attraction. But to a point, some winemakers in the Barossa tackled both perceived threats directly by a back-to-the-Barossa movement. The result was a flowering of concern for heritage and the establishment of many small, highly individual family wine operations, concerned with giving

personal attention to visitors and hand-crafting their wine, usually from their own Barossa vineyards. Thus 'boutique' wineries, as they are called, sprang up in the cracks between the large companies. This in the long run can only help add diversity to the Barossa, confirm its status as a national treasure and remind wine drinkers that the Barossa can grow many fine wines as well as make them.

Barossa Settlers, Lyndoch

Howard and Joan Haese are fourth-generation Barossa born. They've seen much change and enjoy telling visitors about it in their 1860 stone horse-stable, which is used as a museum of old artifacts and agricultural implements. Almost incidentally, it seems, they also offer a taste of their wine.

The Haeses, who in mid-1983 set up the Barossa Settlers wine company on Trial Hill Road between Lyndoch and Rowland Flat, are surrounded by 26 hectares of vines; growing riesling, chardonnay, chenin blanc, madeira, tokay,

shiraz, cabernet sauvignon and grenache.

Howard Haese, with Doug Lehmann of Basedows as consultant, makes a range of dry, medium and sweet rieslings, shiraz, cabernet sauvignon, port and champagne, sold exclusively at cellar door.

Basedow Wines, Tanunda

Basedow's white burgundy, heavily marketed and widely popular, is an appropriate vinous symbol of the modern Barossa Valley. It might more seriously be titled a wood-matured semillon, one of the leading wine grapes of the region and, despite its modest price, it is a line which consistently wins medals and trophies in Australian wine shows. Its dual success, with sales and honours, is the product of winemaker Doug Lehmann and the heritage he has inherited at Basedow Wines in Murray Street, which runs through the middle of Tanunda.

Martin Peter Freidrich Basedow migrated from Dreckharbourg and settled in Tanunda in 1848. He founded a Lutheran school and later became Minister of Education for South Australia. He also founded Australische Zeitung in 1863, the

only German-language newspaper in the state, and it published until 1914. In 1883 the Honourable Martin Basedow moved to establish a College of Agriculture associated with the University of Adelaide. This became Roseworthy Agricultural College, eventually a dominant force in training Australian winemakers.

The son of Martin's second marriage, Bernhard Basedow, was one of the first Roseworthy graduates to travel overseas to study wine. He graduated in 1887 and left for Montpellier, France, in 1890. Bernhard was behind the establishment of Horndale distillery in McLaren Vale, which he controlled from 1899 and purchased in 1909. It was well known for its brandy and it is claimed that the secret recipe (including prune juice?) died with him.

Alfred Basedow, Bernhard's step-brother, was manager of the Stanley Wine Company in the Clare Valley, and he also worked at Horndale. Another of Martin's sons was Dr Herbert Basedow, an early authority on Australian Aboriginal people; the Basedow Ranges and Basedow River in central Australia were named after him.

Martin Basedow and one of his brothers, Christian, who was a building supervisor and large shareholder of Chateau Tanunda, founded Basedow Wines in 1896. At first it was a hobby, but by the time of Martin's death in 1902 it was a sizeable complex involving both vineyards and winery. Martin's first son, Oscar, became manager and sold red wine and a wide range of fortifieds.

Oscar's two sons, Fritz and Hans, continued to work in the winery and Fritz's son, John, was the last member of the original family making wine in Tanunda. He won a Melbourne Wine Show trophy for his red wine in 1970.

Two years later, Basedow Wines became a public company and was eventually owned by M.S. McLeod Holdings, which also owns Peter Lehmann Wines.

The Basedows' drive comes largely from Doug Lehmann, who happens to be Peter Lehmann's son and therefore has Barossa culture deep in his blood. His assistant winemaker is Roger Harbord, who brought a keen mind from Quelltaler Estate in Clare.

Basedow Wines has no vineyards but purchases grapes from selected growers in the Barossa, and occasionally from outside the

Barossa. The crush is 500 tonnes to produce 35 000 cases, but the winery handles considerably more. Its high technical standards are in demand for contract winemaking for other companies.

The company makes a range of premium table wines and old ports, but is best known for its white burgundy.

Bernkastel Wines, Tanunda

Bernkastel is a small company, with most of its produce sold locally. It was founded in 1932, operating out of a winery built in 1879 by the Petras family, to the west of Tanunda. It has undergone many ownership changes.

Bethany Wines, Bethany

Bethany is a charming, historic hamlet out of Tanunda, where signs of the earliest white settlement in the Barossa Valley can be easily seen. Bethany Wines is on a hill overlooking the village and its pretty creek, peeking out from a former stone quarry.

It was established in 1977 by Geoff and Robert Schrapel, who make the wines and tend 25 hectares of vines. They grow chardonnay, riesling,

tokay, white frontignac, shiraz and cabernet sauvignon, and use only these grapes for their crush of 92 tonnes. They produce chardonnay, fumé blanc, Bethany Reserve riesling, Steinbruch spatlese riesling, auslese riesling, Schlenkes Gully shiraz, cabernet sauvignon, Old Quarry port and a rather delectable white port—thus combining the region's future and its past in one small family operation.

Bethany Wines, Bethany.

Charles Melton Wines, Tanunda

Graeme Melton, formerly a winemaker with Peter Lehmann, set up his own stylish little operation in 1984, in partnership with Virginia Weckert, as a red wine specialist. Here is the modern and elegant face of the Barossa, despite the owner's rather characteristic blunder of registering the winery name as Charles Melton. This was because Graeme Melton was called a Charlie when he was younger. The nickname stuck and when it came to getting his vigneron's licence he thought Charles sounded more up-market than Charlie!

Melton has 4.5 hectares of grenache, cabernet franc and merlot growing on bay of biscay soil around the modern winery and these provide a fifth of his crush of 32 tonnes. He produces cabernet sauvignon, pinot hermitage, Nine Popes (a Rhône-style red blend), sparkling burgundy and rosé. All are distinguished for cleanly capturing attractive fruit characters.

Melton's location is on Krondorf Road, south of Tanunda, with views down the road towards Rockford and the rejuvenated St Hallett. With Grant Burge Wines around the corner, this is the fashionable part of the Barossa for the early 1990s.

Chateau Dorrien, Dorrien

In 1984 Fernando and Jeanette Martin bought Seppelt's imposing old Dorrien storage facility on the corner of Barossa Valley Way and Seppeltsfield Road, and made it into a tourist facility, with restaurant, bar, flea markets and so forth. One of its features is a set of murals depicting the heritage of the valley painted on a row of concrete wine vats.

They also have 3.5 hectares at Dorrien and Stockwell: including cabernet sauvignon, riesling and shiraz grapes. These go towards reds and whites which the company sells at cellar door only, as well as a mead made from fermented honey.

Elderton Wines, Nuriootpa

Neil Ashmead, working as an engineer in Saudi Arabia, tried making his own champagne in a bathtub as a way of getting some (prohibited) alcohol. It was apparently a disaster; but it was enough to give him the taste. When he returned

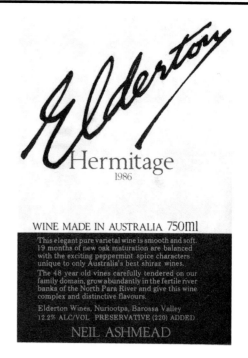

to Australia he and his wife, Lorraine, bought a vineyard in the town of Nuriootpa and in 1985 set up Elderton Wines in the main street.

Just about everything has been painted a bold, burgundy colour, and the unmissable cellar door offers a playground for children, bike and moke hire, friendly service and conducted tours of the vineyards. The Ashmeads, who quickly found a place in Barossa life and its wine industry, understand publicity; they are also producing some good wines to back it up.

The 36 hectares of vines, some very old, are on deep alluvial soil on the banks of the North Para River. Murray Smith tends shiraz, cabernet sauvignon, riesling, pinot noir, merlot and chardonnay. These vines produce 330 tonnes.

Neil Ashmead, with winemakers James Irvine and Adam Chapman, specialises in red wines, such as a shiraz (labelled hermitage), which matures big and soft; and Elderton Domain Nouveau, a frivolous but attractive light red for easy drinking. As well as these, there are dry whites and some interesting champagnes.

Gnadenfrei Estate, Marananga

On a hill above the historic hamlet of Marananga, Malcolm Seppelt and his wife, Joylene, set up Gnadenfrei Estate on 14 April 1979, after Malcolm left the family company of Seppelt. The attractively located winery features barbecue facilities, picnic grounds and a daytime restaurant, and provides picnic baskets for tourists.

Five hectares of vineyards grow shiraz, riesling, cabernet sauvignon and grenache, and these give a quarter of the 45 tonne crush. Gnadenfrei is best known for its ports and white frontignan, and also produces dry reds and whites and a champagne.

Grant Burge Wines, Jacobs Creek

Like his ancestors, who have been growing grapes in the Barossa for more than a century, Grant Burge keeps his feet in the soil. That is what made him such a successful partner with the mercurially sharp Ian Wilson when they were winemakers together at the Southern Vales Cooperative, and when they owned Krondorf from 1978 to 1986. When Mildara took over Krondorf, Burge was not the type to sit in the boardroom—he quit Mildara. The aces up his sleeve were not only the money he made from the sale but also his canny personal ownership of some Krondorf vineyards in the Barossa.

In 1988 Grant Burge and his wife, Helen, bought the 120-year-old Moorooroo Cellars on Jacob's Creek, better known then as the Weinkellar Restaurant. The Cellars were run by

Colin Gramp, who had invented Barossa Pearl for Orlando in the 1950s. Burge, who is also chairman of Ryecroft in McLaren Vale, spent big on stylish renovations and modern equipment. Grant Burge Wines immediately joined the 'boutique boom' of this subregion, including St Hallett, Rockford and Charles Melton, overlooked by Krondorf itself on the hill and presenting a new image for the Barossa Valley.

'The vineyard is the cradle of quality,' says

Grant Burge Wines.

Burge, who has 168 hectares at his disposal. The Nicolai vineyard, overlooking the village of Bethany, produces flavoursome, full-palate sauvignon blanc from light loam over a clay base. Lily Farm vineyard, near Krondorf, has riesling, white frontignac, sauvignon blanc and semillon and red loam on a clay base. The Railway vineyard, in the same vicinity, has cabernet sauvignon, shiraz, grenache, chardonnay and semillon. The microclimate and the red loam and black bay of biscay soils give big, robust reds and richly rounded whites.

To the west of Lyndoch are the original Wilsford vineyards of 15 hectares and the Hilcot vineyards, planted in 1968 to cabernet sauvignon, cabernet franc and merlot on light loam over gravel to give elegant styles.

South of Lyndoch and up towards Williamstown is the Cameron Vale vineyard, with cabernet sauvignon and shiraz on red-brown earth over limestone producing a full, fruity character; the Filsels vineyard of sixty-year-old shiraz and young merlot; and the Miamba vineyards with pinot noir, cabernet sauvignon and semillon on alluvial flats, which give complex flavours.

Burge also has a vineyard in Eden Valley in the Adelaide Hills which he bought in 1986 and named Summer's Hill after a great friend. It is planted with riesling at high elevation and with high rainfall, and with chardonnay and pinot noir for champagne.

While the winery was being set up, the first wines were processed by Doug Lehmann and Roger Harbord at Basedows. Burge got into full swing in 1988 and is now making a range of fine wines which will make him a force to be reckoned with again in the industry.

Heritage Wines, Marananga

Winemaker Stephen Hoff, who set up his own wine company in 1984, first operated as Heritage Wines in the Clare Valley then set up in the Barossa, near the village of Marananga. He uses contract growers in the Barossa and Clare to provide 35 tonnes of grapes, from which he makes chardonnay, semillon, riesling, shiraz, cabernet franc and cabernet sauvignon table wines, the specialty being chardonnay. About 10 per cent of his 2500 case production is exported.

High Wycombe Wines, Bethany

Colin and Angela Davis established their tiny wine operation, High Wycombe, in 1976 at the village of Bethany, 3 km east of Tanunda. They planted 12 hectares of cabernet sauvignon and also buy in other grapes to make up their 30–40 tonne crush.

Karlsburg Winery, Lyndoch.

Karlsburg Wines, Lyndoch

The most immediately noticeable feature of Karlsburg is the fantasy building. The personal creation of the Czechoslovak-born Karl Cimicky, it is castellated with spires and battlements and set in formal gardens. The winery, completed in 1973, is surrounded by 30 hectares of vineyards planted mainly to riesling, shiraz and cabernet sauvignon on sandy loam over a limestone base. A range of wines is produced, of constantly improving quality.

Kies Estate Wines, Lyndoch

The Kies family has been growing grapes in the Lyndoch area all this century, but it was only in 1969 that Ken Kies decided to make his own wine instead of selling the grapes to other companies. The results were mixed and the winery was bought by Regional Vineyards (South Australia), which also owns St Hubert's in the Yarra Valley.

The cellar door is on the flats just out of Lyndoch, in a restored colonial stone building with playground and barbecue facilities.

The Kies family tends 48 hectares of vineyards on river flats loam around Lyndoch, growing chardonnay, chenin blanc, shiraz, cabernet franc, cabernet sauvignon, semillon, riesling and sauvignon blanc. It is an estate operation, these grapes providing all of the 650 tonne crush, which is handled by winemaker Nigel Logos. Brian Fletcher, winemaker at St Hubert's, is also involved.

A range of dry white and red table wines is produced under the Kies Estate label, mostly quite delectable wines, with the classic dry white as the best known. Some of both the Kies and St Hubert's wines are blended into the Andrew Rowan range of products.

Krondorf Wines, Tanunda

Krondorf, which gained an important presence and a very modern image in the marketplace from the blaze of glory of owners Ian Wilson and Grant Burge in the late 1970s and early 1980s, dates back to the mid-1800s.

The Falkenberg family, headed by Gottlieb Falkenberg and his wife Johanna, left Silesia and settled in the eastern Barossa foothills, south of Tanunda. They established a mixed farm and one of the first wine cellars in the valley.

In 1869 Gottlieb died and was buried in the family cemetery in Krondorf village, half a kilometre from the existing winery. His son August, then aged fourteen, was sent to Roseworthy Agricultural College to learn farming, and learnt winemaking as part of his studies. The first winemaking area at Krondorf ('crown village') was a lean-to shed at the end of the Falkenberg horse stables, but over the years it was developed. When August died in 1934, the winery went to one of his sons, P.T. Falkenberg, and he renamed it Glenview.

The winery changed hands several times before Dalgety Wine Estates took it over in the early 1970s. Winemaker James Irvine, who went on to found his own champagne operation in the Adelaide Hills, revamped and updated the complex, which was also known as the Augustine winery at one stage. Irvine left it very well equipped for its time.

In 1978 it was bought by Grant Burge, who came from the Barossa wine family which has Wilsford Wines, and Ian Wilson, a city sophisticate who graduated from Roseworthy in 1973. They had teamed up when winemakers together at the Southern Vales Cooperative in McLaren Vale, and they continued their award-winning run with Krondorf. They gave the label not only technical excellence but carefully considered marketing, advertising and packaging. They not only expanded the winery, pushing the crush up to 3000 tonnes, but the whole operation, buying

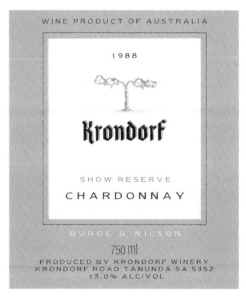

Ryecroft and Merrivale in McLaren Vale.

Burge and Wilson sold Krondorf to the Victoria-based Mildara group for $6.16 million in 1986. The highly experienced, former Seppelt winemaker Mike Press is in charge of twenty employees and the production of 180 000 cases of wine.

Viticulturist Syd Kyloh tends 78 hectares of valley-floor grapes, grown using traditional methods, and 24 hectares at Eden Valley using modern techniques. Principal varieties are chardonnay, semillon, riesling, muscadelle, shiraz and cabernet sauvignon. These provide a third of the crush; the balance comes from other growers and from McLaren Vale, Langhorne Creek and Coonawarra.

Winemaker Nick Walker specialises in white wines at Krondorf, and the chablis (a Barossa semillon) is one of the best known products. Krondorf has also shown consistent excellence with its Eden Valley rieslings.

Leo Buring, Tanunda

Leo Buring has an important role to play as part of one of Australia's largest wine companies, the Lindemans group which, in turn, is part of the Penfolds group; it also has its own importance, especially with the rieslings made by John Vickery. And in its name of Leo Buring and its setting of Chateau Leonay, it perpetuates the memory of a significant person in the history of Australian wine.

Hermann Paul Leopold Buring was born in 1876 in South Australia, of German parents. He graduated in 1896 as dux of Roseworthy Agricultural College, then studied oenology at Geisenheim on the Rhine and at Montpellier in France. Two years later he returned to Australia, where he worked for several companies before joining Minchinbury Cellars in 1902. In the seventeen years he spent there, Leo Buring produced the first Minchinbury champagne and won many medals abroad. He left Penfolds in 1919 and spent five years as a consultant before becoming governing director of Lindemans, appointed by the company's bankers to be unofficial receiver. (It is a twist of fate, paralleling Hardy's purchase of Chateau Reynella, that Lindemans was eventually to acquire the Barossa chateau that Buring rebuilt.)

In 1931 Buring went into business for himself.

With Reginald Mowat of Great Western, he formed Leo Buring & Co., a Sydney-based wine merchant. The first wine, from Emu Plains, 62 km west of Sydney, appeared on the market in 1934. Buring's semi-sweet white, Ringolde, was almost a synonym for wine in the 1930s. The name came from the German 'reines geld' meaning pure gold. Thus it referred to the colour of the wine, and perhaps to what Buring's bankers must have thought of it, and not to the Rhine river in Germany. Buring took all of the Phillip's Hunter Valley production of 45 000 litres or more and used this with other material to make Ringolde. The main Hunter vineyards became the Brokenback Estate. World War II was a big stimulus to the demand for wine, which American soldiers especially bought large quantities of. Building his fame on Ringolde, Buring prospered and expanded, taking over the Melbourne company of Matthew Lang in 1941.

Leo Buring came seriously to the Barossa in 1945 when, at the age of sixty-eight, he bought the small Orange Grove winery which had been built by Gottlieb Hoffmann in 1897. Chateau Leonay, as it became, is on the east bank of the North Para River about 2 km north of Tanunda. Buring extensively rebuilt the winery, adding turrets to the corners of the building. He planned to build Flemish towers and designed a label with a drawing of his dream winery. The towers were never built. Even today there are people at Lindemans who will occasionally muse on how they should be built someday, but still nothing has happened.

In the beginning Buring had handled vintages of 300 to 400 tonnes in small fermenting vats, 1.5 m square by 1.5 m deep. By 1953 he was able to afford a Coq mill crusher (the company went public in 1950). In 1955, a year before Buring retired, winemaker John Vickery joined the company and struggled to make fine wines from equipment that by then was inadequate. In 1959 a second-hand bottling plant was installed.

Leo Buring died in 1965 at the age of eighty-five. He has been called a true 'ambassador of wine'. He made a great contribution to Australian wine through his influence on the many companies with which he was associated, by introducing thousands to wine through Ringolde, and through his establishment of Chateau Leonay.

Lindemans took over the company in 1962 and upgraded equipment. After improving a cooling plant in 1962, refrigerated equipment was installed in time for the 1963 vintage. It was followed by a continuous pneumatic press, air bag presses and stainless steel tanks.

In his own way, Leo Buring winemaker John Vickery has been as important as Leo Buring, for he made Australian rieslings into great wines and powerfully influenced a generation of younger winemakers. Ask almost any winemaker to nominate their favourite wines, and they are likely to reply: one of the great aged rieslings made by the legendary Vickery.

Vickery, a gentleman, does not see himself as a legend, or as a repository of any unique wine secrets. He says he has done it by paying attention to details and by the hands-on experience that many modern winemakers do not get, certainly not in large companies, because of trade union demarcations or because of an emphasis on academic learning.

He was brought up, a teacher's son, in the Mallee of South Australia, then in the historical working-class region of Port Adelaide, and was packed off to study at Roseworthy Agricultural College. He's still not sure why he went on from agricultural studies to the oenology diploma, but he had fun and graduated in 1955 with such other subsequently prominent names as Dr Bailey Carrodus, Harold Tulloch, Harold Davoren and Grahame Williams.

During vacations Vickery worked at the Emu winery in McLaren Vale, in the Hunter and at Valencia in Western Australia, and came under the influence of winemakers Tony Nelson and Colin Haselgrove. In 1955 he joined Leo Buring and Reg Shipster at Chateau Leonay, where he has been ever since, except for a spell away in the 1970s. He went down to Lindemans Rouge Homme in Coonawarra for a time to prove that he could make great red wines as well as great whites—such as the Limestone Ridge 1976, and the St George cabernet sauvignon 1980, which won a much-publicised trophy at the Melbourne Wine Show.

The stylish rieslings at Burings started in 1963, after Ray Kidd of Lindemans ploughed in new equipment, and with the introduction of carbon-dioxide blanketing, which Gunther Prass had developed down the road at Orlando.

Leo Buring's personal concept of white labels and bin numbers was retained and these were to include legendary wines. The numbering system is: 'DR', or 'DW' (for dry red or dry white), then a letter for the vintage year (starting with A for 1945 and going through the alphabet—thus starting at A again with 1971), then a bin number. Varietal wines have a two-figure number starting with first wine crushed in the vintage, while blends have three-figure numbers and drop the year letter. Perhaps this was too complicated for the marketing department at Lindemans Sydney head office, and, sadly, the Leo Buring rieslings were re-packaged to look like any cheap wine. However, the Vickery touch remains in the full but delicate flavours and the architecturally sound structures of the wines.

Leo Buring, which has vineyards at Tanunda and at Broke in the Hunter Valley, called the Wollombi Brook Estate, takes most of its grapes from private growers in the Barossa and, of course, is part of the Lindemans network, giving it access to the fine varieties of Padthaway. For a while it had the Florita vineyard at Watervale in Clare, so called because Leo Buring had it planted with grapes for making flor sherry, but this was auctioned to Jim Barry Wines as part of a Lindemans rationalisation prior to the company's sale to Penfolds.

The company produces a range of table wines, with its Liebfrauwine moselle style being the best known. The DW rieslings, however, remain the great wines.

Orlando Wines, Rowland Flat

Orlando products are known throughout Australia to even the most casual drinkers of wine. In modern times, even through ownership and management changes, it has remained a dominant and pioneering force—with such names as Barossa Pearl, Coolabah casks and the Jacob's Creek range—while also scaling heights of vinous mangificence with Steingarten rieslings, Flaxman's traminer and the Saints range of table wines. All this is due largely to a culture of Teutonic thoroughness running through the company, laid down by Johann Gramp, who was born in 1819 at Eichig near Kulmbach, the son of a Bavarian landowner and farmer.

Johann Gramp left home at the age of eighteen and sailed on the 400 tonne barque *Solway*

Grape reception at the Orlando winery, Rowland Flat.

with fifty-two other migrants to Kangaroo Island, off the coast of South Australia. He went to work with the South Australian Company on the mainland then took a job with a banking business before taking up land at Yatala, near Port Adelaide, where be built a log cottage.

In 1947 Gramp moved to Jacob's Creek, a small tributary of the North Para River in the Barossa, a kilometre north of the present Orlando winery and near where Grant Burge Wines operates. Here he planted a small vineyard, probably of riesling, and harvested his first grapes in 1980, making one octave of a hock-style white wine. His son Gustav was born in that year.

Gradually, the area under wines and the scope of operations increased and in 1887 Gustav Gramp took over management of the vineyards and moved the winery to the higher ground of Rowland Flat, where it sprawls massively today. By 1912 the business had become an established success and a limited company was formed. In 1920 Gustav's son Hugo became managing director.

On 25 October 1938 the company suffered a setback, as did the Hardy and Yalumba companies, when the aircraft Kyeema crashed at Mount Dandenong near Melbourne, killing Hugo Gramp, Tom Hardy and Sid Hill Smith, along with Charles Hawker, a Commonwealth Minister. Hugo's only brother, Fred, took over as managing director and management remained with the family after Fred retired, with sons Sid and Keith and their cousin, Hugo's son Colin.

In December 1970, Orlando—formally known then as G. Gramp and Sons Pty Ltd—was bought by the Australian arm of the English corporation Reckitt & Colman. It left the running of the business to the 'wine men' but contributed its expertise in marketing, financial and control procedures. Throughout the 1970s Orlando was most enthusiastically promoted by public relations manager Bob 'Lunchtime' McLean (who has returned to the Barossa as a partner in St Hallett Wines, up the road from Orlando). During that decade Orlando capitalised on the technical expertise developed by such people as Guenter Prass and Mark Tummel, who in 1953 were leaders of the Australian wine revolution with the adoption of cold pressure-controlled fermentation systems developed in Western Germany and Austria. The result was white wines which captured full bouquet and flavour; and two years later Barossa Pearl, a naturally sweet sparkling wine, was launched. This had a huge impact on the Australian market and on Australian lifestyles. The popular discovery of wine—swinging away from the taste for forti-

Colin Gramp in the Steingarten vineyard.

Equipment at the Orlando winery.

fieds—can be dated from the introduction of Barossa Pearl, and all serious winemakers should hold this wine in a place of honour, for it enabled so many of them to practise their craft.

Prass and Tummel continued to lead in complex and often expensive technology, pioneering such machines as centrifuges, gravity separators, thermovinification and the use of pure strains of yeast culture in winemaking. As a result, in the late 1970s Orlando was able to blitz almost every Australian wine show as the most successful exhibitor. Content with this extraordinary record, the company policy changed from spending so many resources on preparing wines specifically for wine shows—for so many of the medals and trophies were awarded to rare blends of

fortifieds—and entered only the wines which were going on to the market commercially. This left the 'most successful exhibitor' title to be fought over between Lindemans and Seppelt. Orlando, however, was happy in the knowledge that all the trophies and medals its wines did continue to win could be directly related to the marketplace.

In the next major development, a $75 million management buyout brought ownership back to South Australia in 1988. This was the year in which Orlando, by now turning over $145 million a year, embarked on a $10 million expansion at Rowland Flat, with new warehousing and filling facilities; and on the $6.5 million development of a 162 hectare vineyard at Padthaway in the state's south-east. The following year, the French multinational Pernod Ricard, one of the world's five largest wine and spirit groups, bought a stake in the company, giving it international marketing muscle again. More than 15 per cent of its produce is exported and the aim is to reach 25 per cent. Orlando took over Morris Wines in Victoria and, in 1990, the Wyndham estate group in New South Wales, making it the nation's second largest wine company.

Chris Roberts, as chairman and chief executive, oversees 400 employees from the company's highly efficient, if not exactly beautiful, headquarters at Rowland Flat.

Orlando has 500 hectares of vines at Padthaway, Eden Valley, Ramco and in the Barossa, growing a wide range of varieties, mainly classics for table wines. The Barossa vineyards are planted at 1000 to 1500 vines to the hectare, usually on the 4.4 m by 2 m plan and using supplementary drip irrigation. The soils at Rowland Flat are mainly gravelly sandy loam over red and yellow clay.

In 1962 Colin Gramp supervised an experiment in the planting of a hectare of riesling on the eastern face of the Mount Lofty Range behind Rowland Flat, at an altitude of 490 m. The soil is almost pure rock, known as schist, which is a soft shale. It had to be broken up—first mechanically, then by hand with stone hammers—before planting could commence. There is no trellising; each vine is supported by a tall stake in the German way. The vineyard is appropriately called Steingarten (stone garden). This was a costly experiment because such cool temperatures are unreliable; however, when there is a harvest it results in wines of delicacy and finesse, and Orlando's Steingarten rieslings are rare examples of great Australian white wines.

Colin Gramp purchased 102 hectares in Eden Valley in 1969. This had been a currant vineyard and pear orchard early in the twentieth century, planted by Charles Stephens. After World War I, at the request of Walter Smith of Yalumba, Stephens planted 4 hectares of riesling, which was the beginning of the Eden Valley riesling. His son, Eric Stephens, planted more riesling and, as a shareholder/director of the Kaiser Stuhl Cooperative, provided the Wyncroft individual label riesling. Gramp cleared more land

and planted more riesling and traminer. This is the vineyard that produces Orlando Flaxman's traminer, a rich, spicy white wine of remarkable character.

The 500 hectares of company vines, tended by Don Lester, Peter Stephens, John McCarthy, Graham Wellman and Mark Sheridan, provide less than 5 per cent of Orlando's 88 000 tonne crush. So most grapes are bought from other growers.

The large output covers all styles, from the Coolabah cask wines through the Carrington champagne lines, to the highly popular Jacob's Creek range of budget-priced bottled wines, and to the elegant Gramps Five Generations range of table wines. While there are also many individual lines, range marketing extends even to the top of the scale, where the St Helga Riesling, the St Hilary Chardonnay and the St Hugo Cabernet Sauvignon represent the consistent excellence of Orlando. The winemaking team, led by Robin Day, includes Ivan Limb, Leon Deans, Bernie Hickin, David Morris and Tom van der Hoek. Teamwork is a vital part of the Orlando organisation, which is Australia's second biggest single wine producer. It is a far cry from the young German immigrant with his octave of hock down by Jacob's Creek; but it was Johann Gramp who laid down the thorough foundation that continues to mark the Orlando company.

Penfolds Wines, Nuriootpa

The history of the various arms of the Penfolds group, Australia's largest wine-producing organisation, can be considered separately, and Penfolds, Lindemans, Kaiser Stuhl, Wynns (see Coonawarra), Seaview (see McLaren Vale), Tollana, Tulloch and Killawarra do retain their own identities in the marketplace; but in terms of production, administration and even the face presented to visitors to the Barossa Valley, many of them have become closely intertwined.

The origins of the Penfolds company itself, the spiritual home of which remains at Magill, is told elsewhere (see Adelaide). In the Barossa, the three adjacent wineries of Penfolds, Kaiser Stuhl and Tollana are joint production headquarters for the company, a wholly owned subsidiary of Tooth and Co., which is in turn part of the Adelaide Steamship group.

Warren Ward is production director, John

Duval is chief winemaker of a large team, and Andrew Pike is group vineyards manager, overseeing some 2500 hectares in the Barossa, Coonawarra, Padthaway, Clare, McLaren Vale, the Riverland, the Hunter Valley and what remains of the Magill vineyards. Every useful variety of grape is grown somewhere, with the emphasis on the classic table wine varieties such as shiraz, cabernet sauvignon, merlot, malbec, pinot noir, chardonnay, riesling, semillon, sauvignon blanc and traminer. The company vineyards supply about a third of the company's 100 000 tonne crush. The result is a bewildering array of wine styles and labels, ranging from simple coolers and cask wines; through Minchinbury champagne (which is, incidentally, the company's biggest selling line); ports and other dessert wines; premium white and red table wines; to the grandeur of some of Australia's finest red wines, for which Penfolds has a special name, such as Grange Hermitage, Magill Estate and Bin 707 Cabernet Sauvignon.

Penfolds began operations in the Barossa in 1911 when the local growers guaranteed they would deliver at least 1000 tonnes of grapes a year to the new winery. Penfolds guaranteed a minimum price of £4 a tonne. A 6 hectare vineyard at Nuriootpa, formerly owned by J. Lange, was bought and the building of a winery commenced. At that time it was planned that the new winery would be subsidiary to the one at Magill, but the Barossa operation soon overtook it in size.

By 1913 a cellar was completed to handle the

grapes but storage was limited and the company built a large distillation plant to convert part of the vintage into rectified spirit and brandy. This plant included a 23 000 litre still, the largest pot still in Australia. In 1920 Penfolds built a cellar and distillery at Eden Valley, 25 km from Nuriootpa. The wine was taken by road to Nuriootpa for blending, but as road transport improved the grapes were taken to the valley for processing, and the Eden Valley cellars were left as a maturation centre for flor sherry. Expansion of the business made further building necessary at Nuriootpa and a hectare of land adjacent to the winery was purchased in 1948. At one stage Penfolds had a variety of wineries, stores and vineyards scattered all over the place.

The Nuriootpa winery, on Tanunda Road at the southern end of the town, is no oil painting; it is a huge, functional factory covering 3 hectares, with a storage capacity of 33 million litres, a railway siding within the premises, and an efficient laboratory where scientific staff keep a check on the wines at all stages of manufacture and maturation. It was in this laboratory in 1931 that a lad from Nuriootpa High School, Max Schubert, had his first job, leading to his becoming the inventor of Grange Hermitage and the most honoured winemaker of modern Australian wine history.

The lad impressed his superiors by grasping innovations. We suspect that the handsome young man was also skilled at company politics and doubtless put a few older noses out of joint with his radicalism, as subsequent innovators Brian Croser and Wolf Blass did in the essentially conservative Australian wine industry.

Schubert's big bombshell was to come when, after a trip to Bordeaux, he made a red wine in 1951 that spearheaded Australia's red wine revolution—Penfolds Grange Hermitage, named after the original Penfolds cottage at Magill, the Grange, and called hermitage as a frenchified synonym for the shiraz grape which was its basis. The first release of Grange, which was to become the Penfolds flagship, was the 1952. The craggy-faced maestro later recalled,

> It was controversial, and I had to battle with both the company and the public to get it accepted. It had an overwhelming power of flavour and character and it wasn't until it had mellowed with years of cellaring that people could accept it.

Grange was the product of certain techniques, such as controlled volatile acidity and the extensive use of good oak, although these must be in harmony with a richness of fruit. The hugeness of the wine's flavour might also have had something to do with Max Schubert's copious smoking at the time of unfiltered French cigarettes. To Schubert, however, it was simply a matter of 'getting the right grapes from the right area and getting the most out of them. I saw it all in the Medoc in France, where it was laid out like an open book'. Schubert was the one man with the courage to read that book and to apply its lessons to winemaking in Australia. He went out into the vineyards, where—as he points out—wine is essentially made, and selected the right grapes, originally using the Magill vineyard as the base and then Kalimna. The 'mix' varies over the years, to maintain a reasonable consistency of style, with the grapes from the Barossa, from McLaren Vale and increasingly from Coonawarra, frequently with the addition of some cabernet sauvignon.

Grange and Schubert had a huge effect on Penfolds, and the wines' characteristic rich fruit and harmonised oakiness became a Penfolds trademark in red wines across the range. There was a huge effect on other winemakers. Once Grange had become accepted, as it did when the doubting Thomases saw it again with a few years' age, it gave Australian winemakers the confidence to have a go at making great red table wines of new dimensions. The styles changed, of course, to much lighter reds in the 1970s and 1980s, but the inspiration remained and, like Orlando Barossa Pearl at the other end of the price spectrum, Penfolds Grange Hermitage deserves to remain honoured for at least its inspirational value.

Back at the Nuriootpa centre where Max Schubert had started work, the emphasis was shifting—with the wine boom of the 1960s—from ports and other fortified wines to the production of table wines.

Paul A. Scholz, who joined as a cellar hand in 1913, was prominent in the Penfolds story until he retired fifty-one years later. He was succeeded in 1935 by Ray Beckwith, who had graduated from Roseworthy Agricultural College in 1932 and, failing to find work, remained at the college as a cadet, working with Alan Hickinbotham on wine yeasts and acidity. Subsequently, while Beckwith was working with Hardy, he published a scientific paper on the subject in the Australian Brewing and Wine Journal. This attracted the attention of Leslie Penfold Hyland, who offered him a job as a wine chemist at Nuriootpa.

Beckwith became chief chemist in 1951 and did an enormous amount to improve the quality of Penfold's wines. He was responsible for the first commercial application in Australia of pH control in wines, and he retired in October 1973—the first Australian-trained graduate to have held such a specialised position in a wine company.

Now it is almost routine for any wine company of any size to have such specialised scientists in their laboratories. They do not get much public exposure, because the image of a laboratory, with test tubes bubbling away, does not exactly square with the romantic image of sunny vineyards and cobwebbed cellars; but chemical analysis plays a vital role in maintaining wine quality.

The principal Penfolds vineyard in the Barossa is Kalimna, towards Moppa and Koonunga, a few kilometres north of Nuriootpa. It had been run at the turn of the century by William Salter and was bought by Penfolds in May 1945 from D. and J. Fowler Ltd, a grocery firm which had been making wines for export to Britain. This famous vineyard was the source of the cabernet sauvignon used by John Davoren at Magill to develop the St Henri line; and its shiraz, especially, with its warm and rich flavours is the backbone of most Penfolds reds, including Grange.

Next door to the Penfolds complex at Nuriootpa is a former rival, the Kaiser Stuhl chateau, known also as the Barossa Cooperative Winery Ltd, which became part of the group in January 1982. To the cooperative this was only the latest, but the most significant, of the many changes it had undergone since it was set up in May 1931.

That year, eight Barossa grapegrowers, suffering the effects of economic depression, banded together for security. It was a struggle to keep going in the early years but they managed to keep solvent and in 1933 put up their first building. Their main market was Britain but the outbreak of World War II had a disastrous effect on the export trade. The cooperative survived these trials and continued to sell its output in bulk, mostly to other wineries.

In 1958 the company developed its own label, Kaiser Stuhl (seat of kings), which is also the name of a flat-topped mountain peak and conservation park in the Mount Lofty Ranges, visible from the winery. The new label soon became a force in the marketplace. This was due in no small measure to the enthusiastic and well-qualified managerial and technical team running the organisation on behalf of the grower-members. Oscar Semmler, whose family had settled in the Barossa Valley a century earlier, was the chairman, and one of the 520 share-holders, for many years.

It was Semmler and the visionary general manager Ian Hickinbotham who had the foresight to see in the 1950s that with the decline of bulk markets the cooperative had to develop a market for table wines under the Kaiser Stuhl label. This was a radical step for a company that served existing markets of other wineries; it had to get out and establish its own markets, although it did also retain a large business making wines in bulk.

One of the many distinguished names to have passed through Kaiser Stuhl was a young German immigrant, who in 1961 brought to Australia some experience in French champagne-making. He was employed to make Kaiser Stuhl Pineapple Pearl, in its handgrenade-shaped bottle—now a prize among collections of Australia kitsch. That young winemaker was Wolf Blass.

Another key person was George Kolarovich, who joined as a winemaker also in 1961, took over as technical manager in 1964 and was general manager from 1974 to 1977. Kolarovich had entrepreneurial style and it was through his imaginative thinking that the unmissable chateau building, standing back from the Tanunda Road, was born.

The cooperative expanded beyond merely taking members' grapes as it developed markets in Australia and abroad. In the 1970s it entered agreements with the Waikerie Cooperative and the Clarevale Cooperative to take selected material. It also bought fruit from Langhorne Creek and Coonawarra. This enabled it to make some complex, award-winning wines.

Kaiser Stuhl is best known for sparkling Summer Wine, for many years the biggest selling wine in Australia, and for its Gold Medal rosé, a style that the cooperative was the first to market seriously in Australia. Along with other commercial lines, it also produces some rare examples of excellence, such as wines from individual members' vineyards and the Red Ribbon Shiraz, which, at quite a budget price, has varied according to vintage conditions from excellent to outstanding.

Across the road from the Penfolds headquarters is one of the latest acquisitions, Tollana Wines. Although Tollana had concentrated on brandy and commercial wines and never made a great impact on the quality wine market, it had nevertheless developed a specialisation in rieslings, and had a fine name for its Woodbury reds from Eden Valley. Much of this was the result of Wolf Blass as winemaker for the company from 1968 to 1973 (during which time he was also setting up his own label).

The origins of Tollana lie, obliquely, in the formation on 23 August 1858 of the East Torrens Winemaking and Distillation Company, formed with a capital of £2000 in 400 shares of £2 each with Thomas Mildred as chairman. Its purpose was purchasing grapes and manufacturing brandy and spirit for fortifying wines and methylating. After a few years the distillery at Nelson Street in the inner Adelaide suburb of Stepney was closed down. It was later purchased by H. Linde who called the business the Phoenix Distilling Company.

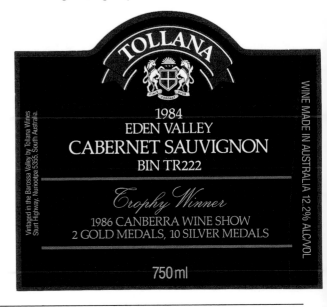

Thomas Scott, Ernest Tolley and Douglas Tolley bought the distillery in 1888 and began trading as Tolley, Scott and Tolley, which was to become the company name producing Tollana wines. Scott had distillation experience in England and Peru and organised the business soundly, fitting new equipment to specialise in the manufacture of brandy, gin and rectified spirit for fortifying wine. He eventually sold his London distillery and settled in Australia.

Ernest A. Tolley was born in Adelaide in 1862, and was educated at St Peters College before going to Europe in 1879 to study at Kings College, London, and to learn about winemaking in Epernay and Narbonne in France. He joined the Abbey Street Distillery in Bermondsey, South London, which was owned by his future partner, Thomas Scott. The other Tolley brother, Douglas A. Tolley, was also to set up a wine company best known by the acronym Pedare.

Another early personality in the company was John Linnett, a London-born banker who had emigrated to Melbourne in 1875. Linnett returned to London to spend seven years with Thomas Scott before joining Tolley, Scott and Tolley in Australia.

In 1904 a modern distillery was erected at Angas Park, Nuriootpa, and four years later the company purchased a winery that had belonged to S. and W. Sage at Nuriootpa, with 16 hectares of vines. The holdings were gradually extended until there was 240 hectares under vine.

The company was formed into a limited liability company in January 1921, with John Linnett as secretary and a capital of £150 000. The reformation was to allow the members of respective families to participate in the business. Albion James Tolley, father of Ernest and Douglas, put some capital into the venture, as did two of his brothers, Albion Edward and Frederic Osborne. Ernest's son, Sam, and Douglas's son, Len, followed their fathers into the business and later the next generation also joined the board.

United Distillers Pty Ltd of Britain took over the company in 1961 and a new era began. In 1966 it was decided to create Tollana Wines, in addition to the extensive distillation business, and within two years Wolf Blass had been hired as winemaker. More vineyards were bought,

including 400 hectares at Waikerie in the Riverland; and the Eden Valley vineyards were established, the principal being Woodbury.

This Adelaide Hills area has an annual rainfall of 686 mm and the vineyards are 450–520 m above sea level. The vines are contoured on the slopes to retain soil moisture during the summer months. Soil is podsolic sandy loam with outcrops of quartz and mica shiltz; the upper slopes are shallow loam intermixed with clay and gravel; in the valleys the soil is deeper and retains more moisture. Vine growth and fruit yield are relatively low but the slow ripening delivers intense varietal bouquet and colour. Tollana planted 140 hectares of the 200 hectare property to riesling, shiraz, cabernet sauvignon, traminer and chardonnay. Also at Eden Valley, Roesler's Vineyard was planted with 20 hectares of riesling, shiraz and experimental varieties.

Tollana achieved a national first in 1971 when it imported a mechanical harvester, an Upright Selma, from California. This changed grape harvesting around the nation. There remain arguments that mechanical harvesting damages the grapes more than hand harvesting does and that this affects premium wine quality; however, there can be no argument with the fact that it enables commercial wines to be harvested in the cool of night, which enhances quality. It also enables a vineyard to be stripped rapidly at the time of optimum maturity, and saves considerably on labour costs.

In 1982, when Robin Sinclair was manager and Alan Hoey was making some marvellous whites for Tollana, a new, versatile and modern winemaking and distillery complex was completed. This, too, the Penfolds group inherited.

Peter Lehmann Wines, Tanunda

If one man can be said to express both the vinous and cultural soul of the Barossa Valley it is Peter Lehmann. Behind the label that bears his name is one of the most technically advanced large wineries in the valley, some 80 per cent of the production of which is sold anonymously in bulk to other wineries.

Peter Lehmann, or PL as he is widely known, is a fifth-generation Barossan, born in Angaston in 1930, the son of a Lutheran pastor, who died when the lad was fifteen. He became a winemaker, partly to escape boarding school, and in

1947 joined Yalumba to train under the great Austrian oenologist Rudi Kronberger. Here he learnt his craft for thirteen years, together with Peter Wall. He rose to prominence after joining Saltram as winemaker in 1959.

Over the next two decades, PL made smiling reds and set legendary standards of hospitality, running the vintage from the weighbridge where black-tie society guests from all over Australia would rub shoulders with the dour local growers, delivering their grapes and staying around for a 'schluck' or taste of port with PL. He had a special rapport with the growers, and took their grapes—good year or not—knowing that eventually he could always do something with the wine.

In 1977, following a remote and anonymous boardroom decision, Dalgety Wine Estates, which had bought Saltram, said the company had too much wine and would not be buying any grapes. PL got permission to take the grapes personally. He made the wine and sold it off in bulk, keeping faith with the growers.

Saltram was then sold to the United States multinational, Seagram, which was not quite as understanding as Dalgety had been; PL had little choice but to leave. He quickly found backers, took the growers with him and set up Masterson Barossa Vineyards. The name refers to a character in 'Guys and Dolls', the inveterate Runyonesque gambler Skye Masterson; and the gambler's card, the ace of clubs, was adopted as the new company's symbol.

On 11 November 1979 the foundation stone was laid for the marble and brick weighbridge at the new high-tech winery, just out of Tanunda. It is no coincidence that some of the most individual architectural design should have gone into the small weighbridge building, for it is here that PL runs the vintage, maintaining a hands-on style and yarning with the growers delivering grapes. Beethoven blares as the schlucks are dispensed.

It is no coincidence that the foundation stone should have been laid not by a politician or any of the society guests, but by Albert A. Schmidt, a Barossa grapegrower. It is part of the biblical, bacchanalian and bountiful personality of the big-hearted Lehmann to eschew pomposities. During a Royal tour Queen Elizabeth in Canberra presented him with an Australian Order of Merit for his services to the wine industry, and a week later he found himself presented to her again. 'So you work in the wine industry do you?' the Queen enquired pleasantly. Lehmann replied: 'Surely you haven't forgotten me already, your highness? You pinned a gong on me only last week.' Queen Elizabeth was amused.

This basic approach to life conceals the complex logistics of the Masterson philosophy of selling all the growers' wine in bulk to other companies. PL, however, could not resist wanting to put the best into bottles, and this he does with Peter Lehmann Wines, as the company became known, which is owned 8 per cent by the Lehmann family and 92 per cent by M.S. McLeod Holdings (which also owns Basedow Wines in Tanunda).

The operation has also absorbed Hoffmann Wines, down the hill on the bank of the North Para River. This was land taken up in 1947 by Samuel Hoffmann, a trooper in the Prussian army, who had fought at the Battle of Waterloo and then taken up farming before emigrating to South Australia. It was a prolific family and the winery, which developed a name for fine old ports, stayed in family hands for six generations.

Peter Lehmann Wines, which crushes 9000 tonnes of grapes—with winemakers Andrew Wigan, Peter Scholz and Leonie Bain working under PL—produces a range of riesling, semillon, chardonnay, fumé blanc, chenin blanc, botrytis sweet whites, cabernet sauvignon, shiraz, pinot noir, vintage port and a Brut Absolu champagne. The dry semillon and the vital, earthy shiraz found ready acceptance in the marketplace; and the pinot noirs, which come from the Willows Vineyard at Light Pass, might yet be some of the finest wines Peter Lehmann has made in his long and distinguished career—ranking with the great reds from the Saltram days.

To honour Peter Lehmann, and the sixth generation, son Doug Lehmann of Basedows, the McLeod group in 1989 launched the Lehmann Wines Foundation, to provide scholarships for the children of grapegrowers to attend Roseworthy Agricultural College.

Rockford Wines, Tanunda

Robert O'Callaghan regards himself as a guardian of the heritage of Australian wine. His small winery on Krondorf Road, south of Tanunda, is a stone complex he saved from demolition, and one of the rash of small wineries tackling the modern mass-production image of the Barossa. O'Callaghan collects old equipment, such as slate open-fermenters from Quelltaler and a hand-operated crusher from the defunct Petras winery. It is not just a museum; it is all used to make wine in a turn-of-the-century manner. O'Callaghan is no mere reactionary, however; he uses the facilities of other wineries to process his whites, which need the benefit of high-tech treatment. But, for the reds, he is convinced that one day he will win wine show awards against all the modern reds for one made his way.

Robert (variously known as Rocky or Rockford) O'Callaghan brings to this business a keen intelligence and a heart that comes from being, so he says, conceived under a grapevine. His grandfather, Jack O'Callaghan, came from Ireland to clear land on the Murray River after World War I. He set up a vineyard and became an original shareholder in the Berri Cooperative. Jack's son was vineyards manager for Seppelt at Buronga.

Grandson O'Callaghan grew up with the magic of the old River wineries and became a trainee with Seppelt at Rutherglen in 1965. He came under the influence of the big Great Western styles of reds made by the legendary Colin Preece.

He worked at eight wineries, including St Hallett (where he made some outstanding reds and ports), and Bernkastel in the Barossa, before setting up Rockford Wines which was opened on 26 October 1984.

His philosophy focuses on premium varietal wines with fidelity to the vineyard, which is a legacy of his growing up amid vines. His Vine Vale riesling, made from 100-year-old vines, his Basket Press shiraz and his Black Shiraz (a sparkling burgundy) are outstanding examples of flavour and character in wine that will mature to refinement with cellaring. Rockford Wines is a form of guarantee that the soul of the Barossa is alive.

Roseworthy Agricultural College, Roseworthy

Roseworthy College has developed a public profile as a wine producer, but its chief legacy is the

generations of winemakers it has trained. Nineteenth-century wine scribe Dr. A.C. Kelly wrote in 1861: 'It is a notorious fact that modern science has not found its way into the cellar of the vigneron, who follows exactly the same routine his fathers have pursued for centuries.' This situation began to change in Australia with the establishment in 1883 of Roseworthy Agricultural College, 56 km north of Adelaide and near enough to the Barossa Valley to be considered in this chapter. It was to become the major Australian centre of training in oenology, the science of winemaking.

Oenology and viticulture were at first part of the agriculture course; in 1936 Dr A.R. Callaghan, the principal, established the diploma course in oenology, with Alan R. Hickinbotham in charge of constructing, developing and directing the course. 'Hick' as he was known, was described by one of his students as a seeker of truth, a most exact and precise man of science who continually refused to accept what was traditionally taught unless it could be proved scientifically. This, through the students he trained from 1936 to 1948 and the feeling he left within the college, is his legacy to the Australian wine industry.

Increasing demands for skills, as the wine boom gripped Australia, led in 1978 to the conversion of this course to a bachelor of applied science in oenology. It is often taken as a postgraduate course following university degrees in science or agricultural science.

The graduations boards at Roseworthy record most of the celebrated names of the Australian and New Zealand wine industry for a century.

The oenology course emphasises the technical side of winemaking and viticulture as a training for the practical winemaker. Students are required to complete three years of training, covering principles and practices of winemaking, quality control and evaluation, viticulture, microbiology, chemistry, engineering and business management. During the course, they also spend a vintage working in the college's cellars and another working in the industry.

An associate diploma in wine marketing was introduced in 1975 to meet industry needs. This two-year course offers training in the principles and practices of wine marketing and business management for men and women working in the industry, or intending to. A brief one-year graduate diploma in wine was introduced in 1980. About 120 students are entrolled in the three courses and women are increasingly entering —correcting a traditional imbalance in an industry that has long failed to realise that the majority of wine purchasers are, in fact, female.

There is a recognition perhaps that in the generally warm climate of Australia, which necessitates greater care in making fine wine, winemaking in the late twentieth century has become a complex combination of science and art. The sophisticated machinery and techniques involved demand not only advanced theoretical knowledge, however; practical experience is essential. This is the rationale behind Roseworthy College Cellars, used for student training in all courses. The resulting wine is sold to the public—which all gives the marketing students experience.

The practical work starts in the college's vineyards, run by one of Australia's leading viticulturists, college lecturer Peter Dry. Almost every possible wine grape variety is grown for teaching purposes on the 7 hectares, but the principal grapes are cabernet sauvignon, chenin blanc, shiraz, semillon, sauvignon blanc, riesling and cabernet franc.

These provide 22 per cent of the College Winery's 100 tonne crush. The operation is run by Andrew Markides with Clive Hartnell as winemaker. Some 4000 cases are produced for the public, including dry red and white table wines, sparkling wine, fino and amontillado sherries, muscat, vintage and tawny port and pot-still old liqueur brandy. The wines are distributed normally through wholesalers and some 1.6 per cent is exported. Visitors are welcome to tour the extensive grounds of the historic old college on weekdays to see, taste and buy some decent wines. In the process, they help keep the great spirit of this important institution flourishing.

Rovalley Estate, Rowland Flat

Almost in the shadow of the Orlando complex, Rovalley Estate plugs away, as it has for eight decades. It was established in 1919 by Ben Leibich, son of grapegrower Gustav Leibich and grandson of an early Greenock settler and merchant, Louis Leibich. Ben worked the 12 hectares and made the wine until his death in 1941. His three sons, L.A. (Lofty), C.W. (Darkie) and H.K. (Mick) Leibich kept the company going. The next generation was represented by six sons in the business, which at its height had 240 hectares under vine and which was perhaps best known for its pressure-fermented sparkling wines, such as Charmane. Deaths and family feudings in the 1980s led to the sale of the winery to Keith Drage, David Drage and Karl Lambert. Christopher Schmidt tends what is left of the vineyards, 57 hectares at Rowland Flat, and Karl Lambert oversees a substantial crush of 2000 tonnes, making a complete range of commercial and premium table and fortified wines.

The Drage-Lambert management, which took over on 12 April 1989, is undertaking major changes in appearance, facilities, image and marketing direction.

St Hallett Wines, Hallett Valley

St Hallett is a traditional small Barossa family winery that is moving into the 1990s with a new image and new wine styles. Carl Lindner, a partner in Lindner McLean Vineyards and Cellar, traces his family back to their arrival in Australia, in the traditional manner of the Barossa Valley. Former landowner of Buchenwaleden in Silesia, Johann Gottlieb Lindner, settled in the village of Bethany in 1845 with his wife and six children. The youngest, Wilhelm Traugott Lindner, was the father of Carl Richard Lindner, who spent many years as a butcher in the Barossa and who bought land in what became the Hallett Valley in 1912 and planted vines. A small winery was built in 1918, making dry red and dry white. Carl Richard then bought the opposite land from Mr John Jacob, the area's first surveyor.

Carl Richard's son, Carl Wilhelm, better known as Bill, worked for Orlando and took correspondence winemaking lessons from California. He ran the vintage from 1944, from which year the modern company dates. He took on the family business full-time in 1948. When Bill retired his second son Carl, with wife Peggy, took over the operation.

Carl's interest, besides old vehicles, is the vineyards, then totalling 115 hectares; and he had such rising stars as winemaker Robert O'Callaghan on board, winning the Montgomery Trophy at the Adelaide Wine Show in 1980 for the best dry red. But Carl, with a fierce pride in the family traditions, could not see a clear future for St Hallett. In 1988 he took in a partner, Bob 'Lunchtime' McLean, who had achieved great publicity successes with Orlando and Petaluma and was looking for something more personally involving in the Barossa. They then took in a third partner, Stuart Blackwell, a winemaker with wide experience, including working in Africa, who claimed to have had 'a fascination as an adolescent with the magic of fermentation'.

The winery was totally revamped, new equipment installed, the range of wines rationalised, a new label designed by Barossa painter Rod Schubert, new wine styles added and new markets aggressively sought.

Russell Johnson supervises 78 hectares of company vineyards in the Barossa, and another 150 managed by the company, growing principally shiraz, grenache, semillon, sauvignon blanc, chardonnay, cabernet sauvignon and merlot. This gives a crush of 500 tonnes, processed by winemakers Stuart Blackwell and Peter Gambetta. The production, 10 per cent of which is exported to Britain, is 10 000 cases, rising to 30 000 by the mid-1990s.

The five main styles made are semillon, sauvignon blanc, chardonnay, cabernet–merlot, Old Crock tawny port and, the popular masterpiece, Old Block shiraz—a big, rich traditional Barossa red, as grand as ever under its smart new label.

Saltram, Angaston

Saltram, Pinnacle, Mamre Brook, Metala and Mr Pickwick are some of the label names, well known to wine lovers, which represent the old winemaking firm of W. Salter and Son, dating from 1859. It was founded by the adventurous William Salter, who was born in Exter, England, in 1804 and came to South Australia on the 495 tonne *Caroline* to be the local agent of a London merchant, King and Co. His wife died two months after he arrived in the colony and in 1841 he married Mary Nettle.

When the Barossa surveys were thrown open for selection, William Salter purchased a section in the new district. In 1844 he moved his family to the property, a 60 km trip by bullock wagon that took four days. William Salter was a deeply religious man and called his property Mamre Brook, after a verse in Genesis describing some of Abraham's land. His first interest was cattle but prices were low and he turned to sheep, with his younger son Edward helping as shepherd and night watchman. Salter began to prosper and became a person of community standing, treasurer of the district council of Angaston and deacon of the Congregational church at Angaston, which he had been instrumental in founding.

When copper was discovered on his property, the ever-versatile Salter opened the Crinnis copper mine. There was an influx of miners and an extensive plant was erected. When copper prices fell in the late 1860s, the mine was closed and the Cornish miners departed.

William Salter formed a partnership with his son Edward, then aged twenty-two. In 1859 they founded W. Salter and Son and began clearing 4 hectares on the eastern side of the property to plant vines. A shed for making wine was built, and a cellar, which was simply a cave cut into the hill. Details of these activities were faithfully recorded by Edward in his vigneron's journal —an admirable exercise for one with little formal education.

Their first vintage was in 1862 from shiraz grapes and 8200 litres of wine were made. In 1863 a screw press was used for the first time, but it was unsuccessful. Another mill was tried later but foot power proved to be the most satisfactory, and the grapes were crushed in treading boxes until steam power was introduced in 1891. The treaders wore special knee-boots made by the local bootmaker Schulz, who charged twenty-five shillings a pair. From 1863, the Salters fortified their wine with an average of 17

The historic Mamre Brook house at Saltram winery — the original homestead of the Salter family.

per cent absolute alcohol. Grapes from other growers were first bought in 1868 when 16 tonnes of shiraz were purchased. The selling of their wine presented the Salters with many difficulties and William Salter began to travel to promote the product. In 1865 he sold £900 worth in Melbourne.

William Salter died in 1871, aged sixty-seven, and his estate was sworn for probate at £7000. Edward, who had married Emily Oldham of Kapunda, continued to manage the property and planted more vines. By 1873 he had 12 hectares of shiraz and 4 hectares of a grape then called sherry.

The previous year Salter had engaged Alfred Birks, who introduced the wines to New Zealand, and a few years later two more travellers, Anderson and Fleming, were taken on for the South Australian trade. The company was among South Australian exhibitors who won medals at the 1876 Philadelphia International Exhibition. In 1882 an arrangement was made with Thomas Hardy and Sons to buy and find markets for all Salter's wines. This arrangement lasted ten years and established a firm market in London.

The vintage had expanded to about 182 000 litres by 1891; three-quarters of it was dry red for

The old cellars at Saltram.

export. These quantities meant the days of the treading boxes were over and a hydraulic press and a pump driven by a four-horsepower engine were purchased. That year Edward also overcame the heat problem for fermentation, which has bedevilled him from the beginning, by running cold water through copper pipes in the vats.

Edward's sons Charles and Lesley entered the partnership in 1898, each with a quarter share with Charles as manager. Edward retired from the family business in 1902, having also been first chairman of the Nuriootpa District Agricultural Bureau and a member of the South Australia Winegrowers Association. He died in 1913, survived by seven sons.

When Charles Salter went into his own business in 1902, Lesley became manager. He was educated at Roseworthy Agricultural College and held important offices on such bodies as the Federal Viticultural Council. He became friendly with Ronald Martin of Stonyfell, who purchased a one-third share in W. Salter and Son in 1920, when it became a limited liability company, with Ronald Martin as chairman of directors.

When Lesley Salter resigned as managing director in 1937, Saltram Vineyard was managed by H.M. Martin of Stonyfell, and in 1941 it became a wholly owned subsidiary of Martin's company. The Saltram winery worked closely with Stonyfell; winemaking was at the Angaston plant and maturation at the Stonyfell facility at Burnside in the Adelaide foothills.

For sixty-three years Fred Ludlow worked at the Saltram vineyard and winery, an outstanding record of service and one properly honoured by including Ludlow's port among the current range

of fortifieds released. Bryan Dolan, who invented the Metala label, was manager at Saltram for some years before he was transferred to Burnside to become general manager of H.M. Martin and Son.

Winemaking at Saltram was in the hands of Peter Lehmann from 1960 to 1979, after he had trained under Rudi Kronberger at Yalumba and before he left to set up his own label. Lehmann's arrival at Saltram marked a new era in the direction of the company and he lightened the traditional style to make Saltram Mamre Brook and Saltram Metala claret (as Stonyfell Metala was renamed), two of the most sought-after reds in Australia. Given the longevity and richness of the Lehmann wines, the style beforehand must have been extraordinarily big if he lightened it.

Salter's was taken over in 1972 by Dalgety Australia Ltd and Saltram became part of the Dalgety Wine Estates group with Stonyfell, Krondorf/Augustine and Roxton Estate. Saltram was again purchased in 1979, by the Canadian-based Seagram group. The new owners did not start off with a great sensitivity to the way the Barossa worked and Peter Lehmann left rather abruptly, marking a new era for Saltram. But it did mean an infusion of capital, much-needed new equipment and modern marketing strategies. David Armstrong from the Hunter Valley, who soon became a Barossa identity, was a winemaker-manager at Saltram before joining Penfolds.

Saltram, with thirty employees, is managed by David Hongell. Mark Turnbull is winemaker, assisted by David Norman. The company has 20 hectares of vines at Angaston and five at Clare, growing principally shiraz, chardonnay, riesling, cabernet sauvignon and malbec. These provide only 6 per cent of the winery's crush. With the muscle of Seagram, a quarter of the Saltram wines are exported.

A wide range of wines is made, including some sold only at the hospitable and historic cellar door. But the kudos for Saltram comes from its Mamre Brook and Metala table wines; the grand old Mr Pickwick port; and the Pinnacle range, including a minty and mellow shiraz from Eden Valley; spicy and aromatic traminers from the Hunter Valley and a magnificent rich and buttery chardonnay, which at its best comes from the Paxton vineyards in McLaren Vale.

The Seppeltsfield complex in the Barossa Valley.

Seppelt Wines, Seppeltsfield

Seppeltsfield, near Greenock on the western side of the Barossa Valley, is the imposing birthplace of the large company of B. Seppelt and Sons, a complete village in itself and a significant part of the history and the tourism industry of South Australia. It is proof also that the Australian wine industry has a heritage, and one that it can proudly compare with those of other countries. It is from here, for example, that Seppelt regularly releases a 100-year-old port, the only company in the world that can do so every year.

Seppelt, which has red-brick administration headquarters in Adelaide's central business district as part of the South Australian Brewing Holdings group, has extensive operations in South Australia and Victoria, notably at Great Western, and vineyards in several regions; but its soul resides in Seppeltsfield.

The family company, as it was—sometimes with vision and sometimes with extraordinary eccentricities—for nearly a century and a half, was the product of Joseph Seppelt. Joseph

Seppelt was born in Wusterwaltersdorf in Silesia in 1813, son of a soldier who had fought Napoleon in Russia and took eleven years to get home again. Joseph, liberally educated in music and the arts, toured Germany and Italy learning the commercial aspects of tobacco, snuff and liqueur production in order to head the family business. But it declined in the 1840s and he headed for South Australia to try his luck.

On 9 September 1849, with his wife Johanna; two sons, Oscar Benno Pedro and Hugo; a daughter; a group of young men from the family business and thirteen neighbouring families from Wusterwaltersdorf, Seppelt set sail on the *Emmy*, heading for 32 hectares he had bought through a London agent before his departure. Luck was against him; tobacco did not grow well on the property at Golden Grove, which was to become a suburb of Adelaide. The party shifted again, to nearby Klemzig, which was a settlement of Lutherans from Prussia. Again, no luck.

Seppelt kept looking around and in February 1852, the year after his naturalisation, he registered a deal to buy two sections of Nuriootpa and

Joseph Seppelt's original cellar laboratory at Seppeltsfield.

two lots in the township of Tanunda from farmer Hermann Kook. The families, still sticking with Seppelt, settled in Tanunda while the men worked, clearing what was to become Seppeltsfield. The men did not stick, however, when gold fever lured them to Victoria, and Seppelt had bad luck again trying to grow tobacco. He gave it away and turned to cattle and sheep, also planting a small vineyard. In one of those decisions which seem trite in history books but which has enormous ramifications, he encouraged his neighbours to grow grapes and supply them to him so he could make wine. If he couldn't succeed with tobacco and its derivative, snuff, wine seemed pretty close to the liqueurs he had been dealing with back in Europe.

The first wine was made in Frau Seppelt's dairy, which Joseph then converted to a storage cellar. He built the first part of the stone winery in 1867 and established a business rapidly, selling wine to Gawler and other Murray River settlements. He was hit by a sudden bout of delirium tremens in 1868, at the age of fifty-five, and died. He was buried at Greenock and his estate was sworn for probate at £1000.

The eldest son, Oscar Benno Pedro Seppelt, known as Benno—who had been born in lower Silesia in 1845, educated at Tanunda and attended chemistry classes run by C.W.L. Muecke—took over as manager of Seppeltsfield at the age of twenty-one. He married Sophie Schroder on 23 November 1870.

Benno devoted his hard-working life to winemaking and left an enviable record of achievement. He made the Seppelt label a household name, as the saying goes. It was said that his abstemiousness at the table, and his regular habits, kept him youthful. He supervised the building of the famous winery, the first part of it in 1867.

The estate consisted of 225 hectares by 1875 and the stone cellar was doubled in size that year. The holdings and vineyards were gradually extended and a grand new distillery, built largely of Benno's own design, was opened with some pomp in 1877. Extensions continued and by 1878 the capacity of the 1875 building was quadrupled. The abstemious Benno kept at it and completed a vinegar plant in 1882; within three years he had started work on a new winery.

Benno had a flair for invention and his wine-testing laboratory was considered unusual. He also kept pigs, fed on grape skins, and bred merino sheep, winning a silver cup in 1883 for a champion ram. Giving evidence to a select committee on vegetable products in 1887, he said there should be a government-guaranteed company to buy up young wines, mature them and export only the good stuff to ensure Australia's high reputation on the London market.

By the turn of the century Benno was producing 1.8 million litres a year from 600 hectares, and in 1902 the business was registered as a company. While World War I was breaking out, Benno was busy buying the Clydeside vineyard and cellars at Rutherglen in north-eastern Victoria.

This extraordinary man retired in 1916. He had found time to have nine sons and four daughters and, on his retirement, eldest son Oscar, who had spent several years studying winemaking in Europe, took over as chairman of the board of what was now a limited liability company. His father's son, Oscar immediately set out to expand. He bought Chateau Tanunda, 8 km away, after it had suffered prolonged financial difficulties and the effects of a drought. Chateau Tanunda was already well known as a large-scale brandy producer—its name indeed was almost an Australian bar room synonym for brandy—and had been owned by the Adelaide Wine Company, whose winemaker until 1910 was R. George Mann, father of Jack Mann of Houghtons in Western Australia.

Oscar pressed on and two years later bought the Great Western champagne cellars in Victoria. A new winery was set up at Nuriootpa in 1927 to cope with increased production. Another was built beside the railway at Dorrien.

Benno died of broncho-pneumonia in 1931, at the age of eighty-five, just as economic depression was starting to bite. This put the reins on young Oscar a bit and he consolidated. He apparently had too much heart to lay off his workers so he set them to planting the cotton palms that ornament the drive from Seppeltsfield to Marananga towards Dorrien. He made these palms a trademark of all the Seppelt properties.

Seppeltsfield, looking towards Tanunda.

Oscar retired in 1939 after twenty-three busy years as chairman, and was followed by Leo R. Seppelt, who lasted only three years before Waldemar took over. The fourth generation moved in when Waldemar's son, Ian, was put in the chair. He was also in the chair of the Australian Wine Board for nearly twenty years and held many other important posts in the industry. Ian died early, and his cousin Robert took over until Karl became general manager. Karl was the last of the dynasty to control the company, which was floated as a public company in 1970, its shares eagerly eyed by other predatory wine companies. A decade on, the South Australian Brewing Company made an offer shareholders couldn't knock back. The company then expanded by buying Woodley Wines, and in the 1980s rationalised by disposing of Dorrien and Tanunda and all wineries except for Seppeltsfield and Great Western.

Seppelt has a strong team of winemakers, led by Ian Mackenzie and including Tony Royal (white wines), James Godfrey (fortifieds), Nigel Dolan (reds) and Michael Kluczko (champagnes).

Under general manager Warwick Duthy, based in Adelaide, viticulturists Nick Seppelt (maintaining the family involvement) and Michael Toomey are responsible for a couple of thousand hectares of vines in three states: the Barossa, including the great red wine vineyard of Dorrien; Padthaway in the south-east, Partalunga in the Adelaide Hills and Qualco in the Riverland; Great Western and Drumborg in Victoria; and Barooga, source of so much good chardonnay, on the Murray.

This is a strong showing, although they provide only a proportion of Seppelt's crush. The company faces the twenty-first century with some security from the vineyards pioneered by Karl Seppelt. He had the vision in 1960 to pioneer Padthaway (then called Keppoch), a fertile, cool-climate, reliable, broadacre region with conditions similar to those of Coonawarra. He established extremely cool-climate vineyards at Drumborg in southern Victoria, which the accountants hate for their low or even nonexistent yields in really cold years, but which can deliver magnificent fruit for champagne and table wines in good years. And Karl, in 1982, seeing the potential of the Adelaide Hills for cool-climate fruit, bought a 270 hectare property called Partalunga. With an altitude of 500 m and a 675 mm rainfall, it was planted initially with 50 hectares of riesling, chardonnay, sauvignon blanc and cabernet sauvignon varieties in grey sandy loam over schist and sandstone. The first riesling from Partalunga fully justified his faith.

Karl Seppelt, who like his ancestors played a prominent role in the wine industry and commerce, chose when he left Seppelt to set up his own personal wine operation near Partalunga. Future generations should be warned that the blood of Joseph, Benno and Oscar could yet resurface.

The Seppelt company produces every style of wine, except for bag-in-the-box casks; but Seppeltsfield has been specially noted for the production and maturation of fortified wines. With the closure of other wineries, such as Chateau Tanunda, the original home is being expanded to play a greater role in table wines.

The complex already includes winery, cellars, distillery, administration buildings, vinegar plant and a modern quality-control laboratory. The winery and storage buildings are of local bluestone, restored impeccably. At the time it was built, ingenious use was made of gravity, obviating the need for pumping, with the fermentation vats being set in stepped-down rows on the side of a hill below the crusher. Whole cellars are devoted to making sherry and port alone, using solera systems. Another cellar is devoted to making brandy. Many employees live in houses on the estate. For visitors there are gardens, kiosk, barbecue area, oval, tours, museum, gift shop and wine retail store and tastings.

Tarchalice Wine Company, Vine Vale

Christopher M. Schmidt set up a small wine operation on Research Road, Tanunda, in 1984, based on 2 hectares of riesling and shiraz grown by Walter Schmidt. These provide a fifth of their 50 tonne crush, producing full-bodied dry reds and dry and sweet white table wines.

Veritas Winery, Tanunda

Rolf H. Binder emigrated from Hungary in 1950 and five years later bought a winery on Langmeil Road, Tanunda, from C. Vohrer and M. Abel. The large tin shed had previously been a warehouse and loading area for a trucking firm which went out of business in the early 1940s; evidence of the former occupants remains in the wine sales area, where some truck chassis are used as cross supports.

The Binder family worked at expanding the winery and establishing vineyards. Daughter Christa showed wine flair but, in the European tradition, was not 'groomed' to head the family business so went to work for Wolf Blass. Son Rolf G. Binder showed flair too, and he is winemaker. He also runs the family's 30 hectares of vines at Stonewell, growing riesling, semillon, chenin blanc, sauvignon blanc, shiraz, cabernet sauvignon, cabernet franc, merlot and malbec on deep soils with a heavy emphasis on organic fertilisation.

These provide almost all the 125 tonne crush from which 4000 cases are produced of most styles except champagne. Rolf Jr retains his father's famous Bikaver (Bull's Blood) style of red, which is a big seller and not only with Hungarians. He has also introduced some modern styles, emphasising varietal characters, and is producing some quite lovely fresh and smoothly flavoursome reds at budget prices. It is a small and hospitable family winery, with a loyal and ever-growing clientele.

Ward's Gateway Cellar, Lyndoch

Ward's Gateway Cellar is a small winery, established on 13 May 1979, and named because it is the first winery one meets driving into the Barossa from Gawler. Owner-winemaker Ray Ward started working in wineries at the age of fourteen and has done nothing else since, apart from three years in the navy and studying at Roseworthy, where he graduated in 1951. He has worked at Woodley, Yalumba, Renmark Growers and Angle Vale.

Two hectares of vines on the property are reputed to include some of the oldest in the Barossa Valley. Other grapes are purchased locally to crush about 50 tonnes in a remodelled cow barn. A range of varietal wines is made and some ports.

The Willows, Light Pass

Dr Bert Scholz—whose ancestor, a Prussian bonesetter named Johann Gottfried Scholz, set up medical practice at Light Pass in 1845—inherited a 30 hectare vineyard around the family home and hospital. He supplied the grapes from the deep alluvial soil by the North Para River to his mate and second cousin Peter Lehmann, who rated the pinot noir and botrytised semillon from the Willows vineyard as great fruit. With Bert Scholz's death in 1988, a wine company was born in 1989, run by his widow Joan, a former nurse, and two sons, Peter and Michael, both of whom are Roseworthy-trained winemakers.

Peter Scholz, who works at Peter Lehmann Wines, creams off the best 20 per cent of the fruit from the family vineyards and, using the boss's facilities in an amicable arrangement, makes the Willows wines. They include semillon, riesling, a coltish shiraz and a marvellously warm and seductive pinot noir. They are sold mostly at cellar door in the middle of the beautifully set vineyards.

Wilsford Wines, Lyndoch

If there is any confusion between Grant Burge Wines of Rowland Flat and Wilsford of Lyndoch, which trades under the name of Burge Family Winemakers, it could be because they are of the same family. The Wilsford location was settled in 1855 by John Burge, who came from Pewsey in Wiltshire, England, with his nine-year-old son Meshach. They made wine for a time, but sold their equipment and stock to Patrick Auld in Adelaide and carried on with mixed farming, including grapes, until the 1920s when grape prices dropped and winemakers took in fewer grapes.

Percival Burge, of the third generation, began crushing the surplus grapes in 1928—from which year the company is dated—and found ready sales for his sweet wines, which were then popular. Modest expansion followed.

His son Noel Burge was one of the four students to graduate with the first Roseworthy diplomas of oenology in 1938 and, after twelve years with the Berri Cooperative in the Riverland, he returned to join his father. Noel's brother Colin had carried on working in the vineyard and winery and his son, Grant Burge, was to become successful with Krondorf before starting his own winery in 1988, only a few kilometres away.

Noel, Rick and Bronnie Burge revitalised the

image of the old family winery in the late 1980s, shifting from fortifieds to premium table wines. This started with the restructuring of the family vineyards of 15 hectares. These are planted to riesling, semillon, sauvignon blanc, tokay, white frontignac, cabernet sauvignon, cabernet franc, merlot, malbec, shiraz and grenache on well-drained, loamy soils, with minimal irrigation to give moderate yields and high flavour profiles.

They provide almost all of the 98 tonne crush from which the Burge family produce 2500 cases of varietal dry whites and reds, as well as vintage and tawny ports. Their specialty is shiraz with real flavour.

Burge Family Winemakers sell only by mail order and at cellar door—which means that visitors can enjoy the family hospitality.

Wolf Blass Wines International, Nuriootpa

Like Seppelt and Orlando, the Wolf Blass organisation has its administration headquarters in Adelaide; but its muscle remains in its production headquarters in the Barossa Valley, where John Glaetzer oversees an ever-expanding production of bottled table wine, according to the Blass corporate motto of 'quality, character, consistency'.

This is, to an extent, also applicable to the man. The word 'genius' would not have to be used too loosely to apply to Wolf Blass's approach to making and marketing wine in Australia, and he did it with quality, character and consistency.

Wolf Blass was born in 1934 in what became East Germany. His family was divided by war and young Wolfgang had to sneak across borders illegally to visit his family. He had to hustle for everything, and—a short person anyway—he developed a strong emotional survival kit. This forms the basis of his desperate will to succeed in everything he does. Although football and horses were his childhood loves, he followed his mother's family into winemaking and graduated as the youngest holder of the kellermeister diploma from Veitschoechheim Wurzburg. He worked with champagne-makers at Rheims and in the English wine trade and then 'took an adventure' and joined Kaiser Stuhl in the Barossa Valley in January 1961, an appointment

that was the responsibility of general manager Ian Hickinbotham.

'I had tasted Australian wines in England,' Blass once said, 'and thought, I can do something out there—this wine is shocking.' Wolf Blass had discovered the path he would take in his desperate drive to succeed.

There was room in Australia for his craftsmanship, but even more for his understanding of wine's role in life. Blass was appalled at the way women were treated, by men in general and by the wine industry in particular. He saw that women were going to become the dominant consumers and he made red wines with a silken drinkability that would please women as well as men and still develop with age to please the connoisseurs. He wasn't interested in the buzz phrases of the industry; the wine in the mouth of the drinker was what mattered. And in white wines, if the popular taste was for a touch of sweetness in the riesling, or later a touch of oak in the full-bodied whites, that is what he would produce, and produce with quality.

In the 1960s such attitudes were indeed genius, which Wolf Blass exercised in full. He paid top dollar for the best fruit, the best oak and the best facilities; he surrounded himself with successful people; he promoted himself heavily, and therefore the product; and was not afraid to charge a proper price in an era when other wine producers were getting caught in the discounting ratrace. No single wine producer through the 1970s so influenced both the making and drinking of wines—because Wolf Blass understood palates as much as vines, and all that goes between. He has been much imitated by lesser winemakers who imagine all they have to do is buy a bit of wine, blend it up, and shout loudly about themselves to wine writers, and they will be successful; but they are not Wolf Blass, who is a person true to himself.

Blass, after leaving Kaiser Stuhl and working as a consultant, joined Tolley, Scott and Tolley as winemaker, responsible for example for the magnificent TST riesling 1972 and for some fine shiraz reds. During this time he was—quietly, for Wolf Blass—working away on establishing his own label, the first wines for which he made in 1966. In 1969 he bought the Bilyara property, north of Nuriootpa, to be his production headquarters and in 1973 was ready to go it alone.

Machine harvesting at the Wolf Blass vineyard at Sevenhill.

His secret weapon was, and remains, John Glaetzer, his loyal lieutenant and chief winemaker. A Roseworthy graduate of 1969, who also worked at Tolley, Scott and Tolley, he is one of the country's most skilled winemakers. He shares with Wolf Blass a close understanding of grapes and oak in wine. The team around Blass and Glaetzer has always been quite carefully chosen. They all understand that the phenomenal success Wolf Blass wines have had in wine shows is not an end in itself; selling the wine to drinkers is.

The Bilyara centre, expanded rapidly, often presented a brash, even vulgar, face to the public. The company bought grapes from those offering the best quality in any year, especially from Langhorne Creek, which Blass believes in passionately for producing flavoursome red wines. But it also sought some security in having its own vineyards and established a new 49 hectare site in the Polish Valley and Clare.

Continuing success and growth made a $6 million public float seem inevitable. Wolf Blass Wines went public, took over a bottling company, joined for a while with the French Remy Martin group in a marketing venture, bought Quelltaler Estate in Clare, and took a stake in Tim Knappstein Wines in Clare. Wolf Blass himself shifted to an office in Adelaide's central business district and surrounded himself with managers and accountants. But he had already proved himself, through quality, character and consistency.

As the company expands in Australia and internationally, with vineyards development in New Zealand and a trans-Tasman joint venture with Corbans, a bottle of any vintage of Wolf Blass Grey Label cabernet sauvignon, or pretty well any other wine from the Blass stable, will confirm why Wolf Blass, in less than a lifetime, has earned a place of significance in Australian wine history.

Chateau Yaldara.

Chateau Yaldara, Lyndoch

Chateau Yaldara is one of Australia's more unusual winery complexes, situated on the North Para River out of Lyndoch at the southern end of the Barossa Valley. It is invariably on the itinerary of tourist groups, who gape at this fanciful idea of a European chateau.

Hermann Thumm came from a German family which had been involved in winemaking on the Rhine. He gained an oenology diploma and in 1930 went to Persia, where he was involved in several business enterprises including a winemaking firm. In 1941 Persia was occupied by Britain and the Soviet Union: Thumm was transported to Australia where he spent the rest of the war in internment centres. In 1946 he returned to winemaking and after a year with a Barossa company took over the ruins of a nineteenth-century winery and flour mill at Schlenke's Gully. He began to rebuild the shell, which had birds nesting in the ruined walls and waist-high reeds everywhere, along the lines of a European chateau.

The main building, built in the 1960s, is filled with an art collection. Ornamental lakes and a concert hall are included in the complex, which also extends to a highly visible motel.

The Thumm family, with seventy employees, have 20 hectares of vines, planted to shiraz, cabernet sauvignon, riesling and grenache; but these provide only a tiny part of the 5600 tonne crush. Hermann Thumm remains in charge of winemaking, with James Irvine consulting, producing 400 000 cases annually.

Chateau Yaldara is best known for its sparkling wines and champagnes, brandy, non-alcoholic wines, ports and commercial red and white table wines, at quite low prices. As part of a total upgrading, started in the late 1980s, managing director Dieter Thumm is emphasising the Lakewood and Acacia Hill ranges of premium table wines.

ACACIA
♦ HILL ♦

PRODUCT OF
AUSTRALIA

BAROSSA
VALLEY

1989

CHABLIS

750ml

Clare

Clare, about 130 km north of Adelaide, is the most northerly of South Australia's wine-growing areas—it is also one of the most charming. It specialises in growing the classically Australian riesling: a dry table wine aromatically perfumed, high in alcohol, fleshy on the palate and gripping on the aftertaste, and made from the true aristocratic riesling grape (which in Australia has been called Rhine riesling to show its Germanic pedigree). Each of the twenty-one wine producers in Clare, and some others such as Petaluma and Wolf Blass which have vineyards in the area, makes a riesling, and they vary from pleasant to Australia's finest.

The Clare Valley—which extends from the town of Auburn due north to past the town of Clare on a latitude of 33°50′S—is removed from the more popular areas of viticulture and, indeed, is close to the hot northern arid regions of the state where crop growing cannot be sustained. It has altitude, being an extension of the Mount Lofty Ranges, which run north from Kangaroo Island past McLaren Vale, peak in the Adelaide Hills, dip back down past the Barossa, rise again for Clare, then become the Flinders and Gammon ranges before petering out in the desert. The highest point in the Clare region is 615 m near Watervale; major town elevations are Auburn 303 m, Watervale 414 m, Sevenhill 464 m and Clare 398 m.

The Clare Valley is a hilly, wooded oasis in this range, 30 km long and only about 3 km wide. It has a reasonable rainfall, averaging 600 mm, and a heat summation range of 1550°C to 1700°C/days. Summers can be dry, and supplementary drip irrigation is often used. The soils are both ancient and fertile and there is widespread limestone with a considerable amount of slate, sandstone and red clay.

Outside the Valley, to the east of the central township of Sevenhill and towards Mount Rufus, is a subregion called the Polish Valley, so named because it was settled in the nineteenth century by Poles who were Roman Catholics; they thus found religious barriers with the Lutheran Barossa Valley and language barriers with the Catholics of Sevenhill. Its microclimate gives similar conditions to the Clare Valley and it is home to several new and small wine producers,

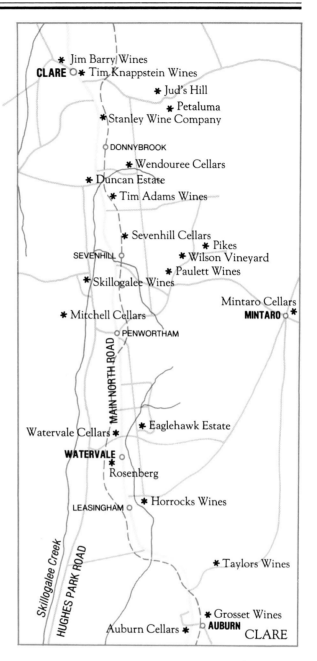

as well as broadacre vineyards established by Barossa companies Penfolds and Wolf Blass.

Pastoralist John Horrocks was the first settler in the Clare Valley and his servant James Green planted vines at Penwortham in 1842, closely followed by George Hawker and Edward Gleeson. In that decade, farming and mining booms in the region were stimulated by the politics of land settlement in South Australia. Clare became a culturally mixed bag. A strong Irish influence showed in such names as Clare, Armagh, Auburn, Inchiquin and Donnybrook. The Jesuits established Sevenhill (so named because Rome was built on seven hills) and gave the

A vineyard in autumn, Clare Valley.

name Tiber to a local creek. Germans gave the name Quelltaler, originally Quellthaler, as a literal translation of Watervale. The nearby town of Mintaro has a Spanish name and Burra is Hindustani in origin. Penwortham is a Lancashire name, even though it was the early home of the parents of the Australian revolutionary Ned Kelly—and they were certainly Irish. What all these influences had in common was an appreciation of the Clare Valley as the garden of the north, and a taste for wine.

By 1903 there were 485 hectares under vine in a radius of 10 km from Clare. Today there are 1655 hectares in the Clare Valley, but the only vineyard surviving from the 1840s is at the Sevenhill College. Clare wineries own about two-thirds of the vineyards; the rest are owned by private growers or outside interests.

Like most wine regions, its fortunes have been somewhat convoluted and it was not until the early 1960s—with the decline of the British export market, the domestic shift in demand from fortifieds to table wines, the move from bulk sales to winery labelling and the beginning of the takeover period—that Clare started to take on a national identity. With a few notable exceptions for stability, such as the Jesuits' Sevenhill, almost every wine producer now in Clare has started in the past quarter of a century or has had an ownership change—this is an indication of the intense interest aroused in the region.

It is a beautiful place to live, and therefore attracts winemakers wanting the independence of their own small operation; and it is a beautiful place to grow grapes, especially riesling, and therefore attracts large companies from elsewhere.

Being somewhat isolated from the mainstreams of the Barossa and McLaren Vale, even though for the tourist the hour-and-three-quarters drive from Adelaide is a small price to pay for visiting the Clare Valley, the winemakers of the region have a great sense of camaraderie. Competition, they say, belongs largely in the marketplace; in the wineries, and socially, there is a high level of exchange of technical information and pitching in physically to help one another. The result of this is that probably no other wine region in Australia can boast such a consistently high standard from all its wine producers.

It is this sense of cohesion that enabled the Clare Valley winemakers to combine and introduce in 1984 the annual Clare Gourmet Weekend, by which local and Adelaide restaurants team up with wineries in the valley, serving specialty dishes to partner specific wines. There is a magic about these weekends in misty autumnal May; the restaurants and wineries make money and promote themselves to the flocking thousands; and the concept has been adopted and adapted by most other wine regions.

Tim Adams Wines, Clare

Tim Adams and his wife, Pam Goldsack, have quickly achieved what must seem like a dream lifestyle, their own winery in the Clare Valley. Tim, who had been making a name for himself as a progressive young winemaker with the big Stanley company, sought his professional satisfaction just outside the town of Clare when, on 8 May 1987, he set up Tim Adams Wines, with cellar door sales and a great view on Warenda Road.

He has a mere half hectare of semillon vines around the winery but is expanding his plantings. In the meantime, he buys in 60 tonnes of grapes from local growers, to produce 3000 cases of riesling, semillon and shiraz. He also has stocks tucked away to release a twelve-year-old tawny port. Ten per cent of the production is exported. At vintage time, Tim Adams crushes an extra 30 tonnes or so on contract for other makers of the region.

Jim Barry Wines, Clare

Jim Barry, an experienced professional, had a long association with winemaking at Clare before he set up his family cellars there in 1968. After graduating with an oenology diploma from Roseworthy Agricultural College in 1947, the year before his brother Brian Barry did, he joined the then Clarevale Wines and eventually became general manager and winemaker. After twenty-two years there, he established the Taylor family vineyards.

During this time, in 1959, Jim and Nancy Barry purchased a property in Clare and the following year planted what he now calls the Original Vineyard at Burston Cottage, named after Edward Burston Gleeson, founder and first mayor of Clare. It is a red-brick cellars and sales area, carved out of the hill with views across the northern end of the Clare Valley.

Jim Barry started making his own wines using other people's facilities and in 1974 he founded his own company.

Even as a kid I used to grow beans and cauliflowers, trying to make a quid...I like the viticultural side of wine. There's terrific variety, with something new every year to keep your interest up. It's better than being a bank clerk: I've got something solid that lasts a lifetime.

This blunt realist of the soil has also got something that will last his sons a lifetime, and they have been progressively taking over the expanding operation.

Mark Barry helps Jim with winemaking and Peter and John Barry tend the company's 80 hectares of vines, in different climates at Clare, Armagh, Watervale and Lodge Hill. Their coup was buying the famous Florita vineyard, on 20

June 1986, from Lindemans. This was the source of the great Watervale rieslings which John Vickery in the Barossa made for the Leo Buring and Lindemans labels.

Riesling is the predominant grape grown by the Barrys, with shiraz, sauvignon blanc, chardonnay, cabernet sauvignon, cabernet franc, merlot and malbec. Eighty per cent of their 800 tonne crush is from their own vineyards.

One notable product is the Sentimental Bloke vintage port, each edition of which bears a different extract from the writings by C.J. Dennis, the poet who was born at Auburn in Clare Valley in 1876.

This is a family company imbued with the earthy spirit of Jim Barry's early big soft reds, while progressing with changing markets. And they're having fun doing it.

Duncan Estate, Clare

Just west of the Clare Caravan Park, on Spring Gully Road, the Duncan family are growing 8 hectares of grenache, shiraz, merlot, cabernet sauvignon, malbec, riesling, sauvignon blanc, traminer, chardonnay and muller thurgau. The microclimate can be frosty, and the cool nights in summer help retain strong varietal character.

Of these grapes, 40 tonnes are sold to other wineries, and Blair Duncan, assisted by John Duncan, keeps 21 tonnes to make a range of table wines, specialising in late-picked styles.

Most of the sales are through cellar door, with some exposure in local and Adelaide restaurants, hotels and motels.

Eaglehawk Estate, Watervale

Wolf Blass of the Barossa has the eagle as his trademark, and when he swooped like the diurnal bird of prey on the historic Quelltaler Wines in 1988, he gave it an aquiline name. In the process, he further upgraded the winery, through winemaker-manager Stephen John of the wine family of that name in the Barossa, and added a new chapter to a long and varied history.

The name Quelltaler was originally spelled 'Quellthaler'. In German 'Quelle' denotes a bubbling spring of pure water and in the idiom of the time 'Thal' meant a vale. Thus the winery name was a German translation of the English town name of Watervale—or Springvale, as the original vineyards were called. They were planted at the base of Mount Horrocks, just east of the town of Watervale, by Francis Treloar in 1865. The first 20 hectares were located, according to records 'where the calcerous soil was kindly suitable, the site well chosen [390 m above sea level] and the vines the finest procurable'.

Treloar sold his property—the vineyard and the grazing land—to Captain Walter Watson Hughes, later Sir Walter and a founder of the University of Adelaide, but stayed on as manager. He established the wine cellars in 1868, engaging Carl A. Sobels as winemaker.

Carl Sobels was born in Quedlinberg, Germany, and migrated to South Australia with his parents in 1847. He married Meta Dohrnwendt at Lobethal in 1867, after living with his winemaker parents at Tanunda. He moved to Springvale in 1869 with his wife and two young children—the beginning of a family that eventually grew to thirteen. He handled the vintages at Springvale and made many extensions to the cellar.

In 1889 a partnership was formed between Carl Sobels and T.G. Hermann Buring to purchase the vineyards and cellars from James McKinnon Richman. One of their descendants has said:

Enterprising, they acquired neighbouring lands; far-sighted, they uprooted acres of unsuitable vines and planted other varieties better suited to produce table wines of the quality for which Quelltaler was becoming noted; prudent, they adapted their cellars, their implements and methods to keep pace with the industry's progress.

The ripping out of unsuitable vines must have taken considerable courage—although, significantly, two of the subsequent major owners of the estate, Remy Martin Australia and Wolf Blass Wines, both restructured the vineyards to bring them into line with contemporary fashions and predictions of future markets.

While Buring and Sobels waited for the earth to be rested, they gathered cuttings from the Adelaide Botanic Garden, of shiraz, riesling, semillon, dolcetto, malbec, cabernet sauvignon and grenache. Their aim was high-quality table wine. Things did not always go smoothly and in 1900 a severe frost wiped out the complete vintage.

The family influence was strong for many years. At a centenary luncheon in 1965, thirty descendants of Carl Sobels were present.

Quelltaler hock and the company's San Carlo claret, Granfiesta sherry and expensive Wyatt Earp port became national names; and in the 1970s winemaker Peter Nichols, an American with an oenology degree from Fresno, introduced new techniques for capturing the delicacy of riesling in a dry white wine. This was at the time when Tim Knappstein was doing similar things at Stanley, paving the way for a new direction for the Clare Valley.

In 1982 Quelltaler was taken over by the Australian arm of the French multinational, Remy Martin, which also had Chateau Remy in Victoria. Australian manager François Henry recognised that a medium-sized winery such as this, if it was to survive in the cut-throat market of the time, had to go either bigger or smaller. He chose the latter and appointed Michel Dietrich as winemaker to produce a small range of excellence, selling off the balance of the grapes as bulk wine to other wineries.

Michel Dietrich, who came from a winemaking family in Alsace, France, had studied winemaking in Burgundy and worked for the Champagne house of Deutz. He came to Australia on a working holiday in 1979 and said, rather privately, that he thought 'a lot of the Australian wines boring'. He saw tremendous personal opportunities, so he leapt at the chance to come back.

He found the Quelltaler soils similar to the limestone-based soils in Alsace and divided the estate into forty-four small paddocks, according to soil types, age of the vines and profile of the land. Each section was managed individually and the grapes picked separately.

From the best of the paddocks, he made some of the most exciting Australian white wines of the 1980s under the Quelltaler Estate label, with Roger Harbord as his assistant winemaker. The wines were too different from the norm, perhaps with too much personality, to win wine show awards; but age revealed just how magnificent they were, and how far ahead of his time Dietrich was in putting flavour and personality into white wines. In 1988 the Wolf Blass organisation, which has been involved with Remy Australia in a joint marketing operation, bought Quelltaler, having earlier established broadacre vineyards nearby in the Polish Valley.

The Quelltaler winery, with its central stone cellar, has a unique atmosphere and the deepest sense of traditional wine heritage in the Clare Valley. Company viticulturist Peter Pawelski tends 140 hectares of surrounding vines, growing riesling, semillon, chardonnay, sauvignon blanc, shiraz, merlot and cabernet franc, mostly on red loam over limestone and slate. These give the distinctive riesling and semillon flavours on which Nichols and Dietrich, and now Stephen John, have been able to capitalise.

The crush is 1500 tonnes and the winery's output is 45 000 cases, rising to 120 000 cases as the vineyards are reorganised, and as Stephen John and his counterparts at the production headquarters in the Barossa sort out who gets what.

The Eaglehawk label, when it was released, met with some resistance, at least among traditionalists who did not see that such a skilfully made range of table wines at affordable prices was another logical step in the long history of the winery. But the Quelltaler name lives on after all, in a newer range of premium wines in the Dietrich tradition, labelled Wolf Blass Quelltaler Vineyards.

Grosset Wines, Auburn

In an old butter factory on Stanley Street, Auburn, Jeffrey and Cate Grosset have a stylish little wine operation, uncompromisingly dedicated to excellence. They offer visitors personalised attention, so long as there are no buses or large groups, no smoking or eating. But they are not often open—for their wines sell out almost as soon as each is released.

Jeffrey Grosset, who looks as though he would be more at home as a bookish antiquarian, was born in Adelaide in 1954 and became interested in wines through seeing the artistic side of some rieslings made by John Vickery at Leo Buring. It was an influence that still shows in Grosset rieslings.

Jeffrey Grosset graduated from Roseworthy College in 1975, and while his family was setting up a vineyard at Auburn (subsequently grubbed out) developed his experience at Seppelt, by touring Europe and at Lindeman's Karadoc.

He made his first wines under his own name at Auburn in 1981, influenced locally by Tim Knappstein and Andrew Mitchell. His skilful control of riesling's delicacy in wines of real fla-

vour and backbone quickly established a small market and assured his status among the local winemakers, some of whom depend on his advice and help.

He and Cate are developing 2 hectares, called the Rockwood Vineyard, of riesling, cabernet sauvignon and cabernet franc, just south of Mount Horrocks. It is the highest elevation in the region, at 565 m, and features advanced canopy management.

In the meantime, with assistant winemaker Peter Leske, the crush is 100 tonnes, 40 per cent of which is from vineyards managed by Jeffrey Grosset—which means no chemicals for pest or disease control. The product is 4500 cases of riesling, chardonnay and cabernet sauvignon blends, representing some of the highest standards of wine in the valley.

Horrocks Wines, Leasingham

The Ackland brothers, Lyall, Trevor and Rodger, a rural family of Orrooroo origins, became grapegrowers of noted excellence in the Clare region since they started planting on a 43 hectare property on the slopes from Leasingham up to Mount Horrocks in 1976. They grow riesling, semillon, chardonnay, cabernet sauvignon, merlot and shiraz.

It was a small step to keeping some of their crop for their own Mount Horrocks label, and their first wine was made in 1982. They also have a cellar door sales and tasting area on Mintaro Road. Jeffrey Grosset is their winemaker, processing 60 tonnes of fruit, which gives 3000 cases of table wines.

The most distinctive is the Mount Horrocks

Cordon Cut, a sweet white dessert wine. When the grapes on selected vines reach a certain maturity and sugar level, the canes are cut, which allows dehydration in the grapes so that there is a more rapid rise in the sweetness without losing acid levels.

Jud's Hill, Clare

There is no winery and no cellar door, only a vineyard. But it produces lovely wines in the hands of its master, Brian Barry. A doyen of the industry, and brother of Jim Barry, Brian Barry graduated from Roseworthy College in 1948. 'It was luck that got me into wine,' he says. 'I was really interested in science. But a man couldn't ask for a better life than the wine industry and I've got a terrific amount of friends who've helped me along the way.'

Brian Barry gained experience as a winemaker at Hamiltons, at Berri Estates and at Stanley in Clare, meanwhile purchasing 33 hectares on Farrell Flat Road, east of the town of Clare.

I found from all the oldtimers that I used to drink with in the front bar of the Bentley's Hotel [in Clare] that this was regarded as one of the best bits of land in the district. So I thought of planting some vines for my retirement and for my son Jud.

He left Stanley rather abruptly and, while embarking on a new career as winemaking consultant, and developing the skills that were to earn him note as a wine show judge, he also concentrated on his Jud's Hill vineyard. He had the great help of Bernie Hanlin, Petaluma's grapegrower. The high-altitude vineyard, of red loam over deep limestone, grows cabernet sauvignon, riesling, merlot, cabernet franc and chardonnay.

Brian Barry uses the facilities of other wineries, including his brother's, to process the 200 tonne of fruit yielded, which gives 8000 cases of cabernet sauvignon, cabernet–merlot, riesling and chablis. They are wines of an attractive silkiness and distinguished flavours.

Tim Knappstein Wines, Clare

Tim Knappstein, with a family background in wine, a personal Teutonic thoroughness and a solid technical grounding, is a driving force in the Clare district. He is regarded by his peers as one of the finest winemakers of the Clare Valley and he has been progressive in tapping new markets from his small winery on Pioneer Avenue, at the northern end of Clare township.

After leaving school in 1962, he joined the Stanley Wine Company, then owned by the Knappstein family. He studied oenology at Roseworthy College, winning the gold medal and graduating in 1965, before returning to Stanley to take over from Peter Weste as winemaker at the age of twenty. In the following years Tim Knappstein created the Leasingham range of table wines which, up to 1976, collected 500 wine show awards, including 120 gold medals and twenty trophies.

During this time he also set up his own operation, then appropriately named Enterprise Wines, and started planting vineyards around his home, off Farrell Flat Road to the east of Clare, in 1972. The intention was 'fun and profit', but after Stanley was taken over by the Australian subsidiary of H.J. Heinz and Company, Tim Knappstein wanted to be a winemaker of a different variety. In partnership with his mother, Olive Knappstein, he took over an attractive 1878 stone building for his winery. Ironically, the building's heritage includes having been a soft-drink factory and a brewery.

State-of-the-art technology was installed and the 1977 vintage was a success, the riesling and the cabernet sauvignon each winning several gold medals. The winery has been progressively extended and upgraded and annual output has reached 38 000 cases. The winery was by then owned by Tim Knappstein and his wife Anne. Wolf Blass Wines has since bought an interest, adding its national and international marketing muscle, so that 5 per cent of production is exported.

The company has no vineyards but 75 per cent of its 450 tonne crush comes from the personal vineyards of Tim and Anne Knappstein, 3 km east of the town, and at Lenswood in the Adelaide Hills.

The Clare vines, at 450 m elevation, grow riesling, sauvignon blanc, chardonnay, gewurztraminer, cabernet sauvignon, cabernet franc and merlot; the Lenswood land—18.2 hectares purchased in July 1981, with 975 mm rainfall and a very cool altitude of 530 m—was planted with riesling, chardonnay, pinot noir and sauvignon blanc.

Tim Knappstein has pioneered in Clare the techniques of top grafting to change varieties in vineyards. He was the national pioneer in the technique of making botrytised wines in the cellar, by harvesting the grapes, placing them on racks and spraying them with botrytis spores under controlled conditions. The result is a beerenauslese or trockenbeerenauslese style of luscious dessert wine. The innovative Tim Knappstein shares with Victorian winemaker John Ellis the distinction of being the first in Australia to use the neologism fumé blanc for a wood-matured sauvignon blanc.

Honest, clean, flavoursome dry riesling, however, and reds which develop complexity and elegance with age, remain the winery's specialties.

Mitchell Cellars, Sevenhill

The husband and wife team of Andrew and Jane Mitchell founded Mitchell Cellars in the beautiful, timbered country off the main highway near Sevenhill in 1975—although so carefully has the modern winery been blended into the 1893 stone cellars that it looks as though it has been that way forever. Andrew, who is rated one of the most accomplished and serious winemakers of the valley, is a graduate of both Flinders University in Adelaide and the Riverina College, studying under Brian Croser; and Jane studied wine marketing at Roseworthy Agricultural College.

Andrew Mitchell, who says, 'I don't want to make anything I don't like', set out for clean-fruited wine, high in acid and elegant on the middle palate, in contrast to the big, high-alcohol, extractive reds for which Clare was then known. His wines stood out from the beginning, with the first full vintage in 1979, and they still do.

Sevenhill Cellars in the Clare Valley.

The Mitchells have 30 hectares of vines, tended by Leon Schramm, at Sevenhill and Watervale. These low-yielding, mature to very old, dryland vineyards give riesling, semillon, chardonnay, shiraz, cabernet sauvignon, merlot and cabernet franc, providing 75 per cent of the winery's crush of 350 tonnes. Neil Pike is Andrew Mitchell's assistant winemaker and the annual output is 15 000 cases.

The best selling lines are the Watervale riesling and the Peppertree Vineyard shiraz, although it may well be the elegant, fruity cabernets that are Andrew Mitchell's best testimonial.

Paulett Wines, Polish Valley

Alison and Neil Paulett bought 47.5 hectares of land at Polish River early in 1982 and within two years had started winemaking; even though the 1983 Ash Wednesday bushfires destroyed most of their vines, making replanting necessary.

Neil Paulett, a 1972 Roseworthy College graduate in oenology, had worked at Penfold's Minchinbury Cellars at Rooty Hill, at Penfolds in the Upper Hunter and at Rosemount Estate; but he had the urge to have his own place. He looked at several areas in New South Wales and Victoria before discovering the Polish Valley.

His vineyard is at 500 m, with good acid clay/loam over slate and sandstone substrata and well drained; a 1200 mm rainfall and a due-easterly aspect which provides shelter from the hot afternoon suns. He has 3 hectares of riesling, shiraz, chardonnay and pinot noir.

PAULETTS

1987
POLISH HILL RIVER
CABERNET MERLOT

PRODUCED BY PAULETT WINES
BOX 50 SEVEN HILL SOUTH AUSTRALIA
PRODUCT OF AUSTRALIA 750ml

The winery crushes 40 tonnes—the Paulett vineyards providing 40 per cent of this—and produces a range of riesling, shiraz, cabernet–merlot, sauvignon blanc and chardonnay. Neil Paulett also works as winemaker at the Stanley Wine Company.

Pikes, Polish Valley

The fish depicted on the labels of the reds and the whites is the fighting pike. The company is owned by the Pike family.

It was established in 1984 with Neil Pike making the wines and Andrew Pike, on weekends off from being viticulturist of the Penfolds group, tending 11 hectares of cabernet sauvignon, riesling, sauvignon blanc, chardonnay and shiraz, on red-brown earth over slate and bluestone subsoils, with an easterly aspect.

These provide about half of the 100 tonnes crushed, which gives this young winery a 6000 case output. The wines, especially the fleshy riesling, have found a ready and well deserved market around Australia, as well as among those who have discovered the warmth of cellar door reception.

Sevenhill Cellars, Sevenhill

The image of cowled monks scurrying silently around cobwebbed cellars is not quite right for Sevenhill Cellars, even though it is owned by the Jesuit Society and run by Jesuit brothers under the name of the Manresa Society Inc. This is the church in action, out in the real world, although the primary job of the cellars remains making sacramental wines for the Roman Catholic and Anglican churches in Australia and abroad. Winemaker Brother John May, who also manages the cellars, is a frequenter of social functions with his fellow winemakers from the Clare Valley; and to destroy the myths, the six cellar employees include two females.

The history of the Order of Clare began with two Jesuit priests who accompanied a party of Silesian settlers to the district in 1845. One of the priests, Aloysius Kranewitter, stayed on to acquire land for the order and in 1852 started planting a vineyard with cuttings from the Hawker estate at Bungaree. In 1863 the Order became automated by graduating from foot power for pressing the grapes to using a winepress.

The cellars were progressively expanded and the vineyards extended to 52 hectares, growing tokay and crouchen (believed to be the first plantings of these varieties in Australia), and riesling, verdelho, frontignac, traminer, pedro, shiraz, cabernet sauvignon, cabernet franc, grenache, touriga, merlot and malbec. The vines are at high altitudes, under a range of microclimates, and most vines are low-yielding, which gives concentrated flavours.

An outstanding figure of modern winemaking at Sevenhill was Brother John Hanlon, who took over when Brother Downey retired in 1951. He was described by Len Evans as having

> a wonderful sense of humour and unique twist of imagination. There was none of the unctuous do-gooding bit for him—he loved man, loved his fellow, understood his foibles and weaknesses, yet could, and did, prick holes in the pompous and eschew the pretentious. He was a great man, a good man and a maker of fine wine.

When he died in 1972 he was succeeded by his assistant Brother John May, who is assisted by Brother John Moten.

Brother John May, with his background as a builder, his Jesuit-honed intelligence and his dedication to serving God, has inherited a proud tradition as the seventh winemaker in more than a century, and the beautiful surroundings of the church of St Aloysius on the edge of the vineyards.

'People will bulldoze history without batting an eyelid', he says, pointing to the open slate fermenters, the diesel-driven crusher, the vaulted underground cellar carved into the solid slate and even a museum of mousetraps, all of which he keenly preserves. Meanwhile, he has built a modern, efficient winery out the back so that it does not conflict with the Sevenhill heritage.

In a dry year, such as 1989, the crush is down to 228 tonnes, all from the Society's own vineyards. As well as sacramental wines, the brothers John make a wide range of dry to medium-sweet whites, dry reds and fortifieds; sold at modest prices, with the College white as the most popular.

The cellars are open to the public. Brother John May says the winery 'makes money for Jesuit education. It is more honest, working with the hands, than begging for charity'.

Skillogalee Wines, Sevenhill

Skillogalee was established in 1970 by Spencer George, with some help from his son, Stephen. But Stephen went off to do his own thing in the Adelaide Hills and Spencer retired. In 1989 the business was bought by Diana and Dave Palmer, who wish to build on the reputation this label had already established for wines of flavour and quality.

They have 20 hectares of vines at Sevenhill, growing riesling, shiraz, cabernet sauvignon and traminer on east-facing slopes at 425–480 m altitude. David Palmer and Darryl Smith tend the vines, and Andrew Mitchell, of nearby Mitchell Cellars, makes the wine, which is an output of up to 5000 cases.

Stanley Wine Company, Clare

The saying in Clare is that when the Stanley Wine Company sneezes, everybody catches a cold. That illustrates how the company dominates the town—socially and in terms of employment—and the region in terms of winemaking. That may be changing as other large companies, such as Penfolds and Wolf Blass, begin to have a greater involvement in the Clare district; and as Stanley itself has scaled back its local operations and become a part of the Hardy Wine Company; but it still remains the biggest wine company of the valley.

The company was founded in 1893, the name derived from the local state electoral district of Stanley, by merchant J.H. Knappstein, medical practitioner Dr Wein Smith, solicitor Magnus Badger and brewer John Christison. The first general manager was Alfred Basedow, then regarded as one of the best winemakers in the country.

Joseph Knappstein gained full control by 1912, and did much to find markets in Britain, which lasted until imperial preferences duties on wine ceased in 1938. He had ten sons and nine of them at some stage or another worked for the company. A trustee company ran Stanley after Joseph's death in 1919, and it was not until 1938 that the family regained the company when Joseph's son Fred W. Knappstein became winemaker, and Otto Knappstein became chairman of directors. Another son, K.H. 'Mick' Knappstein, became manager and chairman from 1962 and continued as a consultant after the family sold the company to H.J. Heinz in 1971.

Stanley has had an impressive array of winemakers in modern times, including Bill Chambers, Peter Weste, Mick Knappstein's nephew Tim Knappstein, Brian Barry from 1976 to 1980, and Chris Proud since then. Chris Proud remained winemaker after Stanley was bought by Hardy, and is assisted by Neil Paulett.

In 1984 Stanley shifted its cask wine production out of Clare by buying Hungerford Hill's facilities at Buronga, on the Murray River in New South Wales. While Buronga continued to buy much fruit from Clare, the loss of an outlet for much Clare fruit seemed dramatic and dangerous; in fact, it was probably the spur for the development in the 1980s of a new approach

Stanley Wine Company.

to quality wine-growing in the region.

The Reynella-based Hardy Wine Company bought Stanley in 1988, gaining the Buronga cask facility and the premium wines on which Stanley was concentrating in Clare. With the purchase soon afterwards of the former Clarevale Cooperative, founded in 1928 and last operating as part of the Penfolds group, the Stanley premises were made to look more inviting for visitors.

The company has 235 hectares of vines at Leasingham, Spring Farm (next to Tim Knappstein's) and White Hutt, growing mainly riesling, chardonnay, cabernet sauvignon, malbec and shiraz. They are on various soils, with yields of about 7.5 tonnes to the hectare, hand-pruned, machine-harvested and about a third are dryland, without supplementary drip irrigation. They provide less than a third of the crush of 4600 tonnes, the rest coming from private growers. Stanley thus handles a third of the grapes grown in Clare, which still makes it a force in the life and wines of the Clare Valley.

Taylors Wines, Auburn

Taylors is second only to Stanley in size in the Clare Valley, and it is a total estate operation, using only grapes from its own vineyards, producing a carefully marketed range of popular premium table wines.

The property, on Mintaro Road in the southern part of the Valley, was purchased in 1969 by the Taylor brothers, John and Bill, two Sydney wine merchants, and their father. The

aim was to set up an estate along Bordeaux lines and the early emphasis was on the two red wines that made the name for Taylors, a straight cabernet sauvignon and a straight shiraz (labelled hermitage). The range has subsequently been extended to white wines, including riesling and chardonnay.

The Taylors invested heavily, and built a long white-arched cellar and sales building, well equipped inside. The wines are distinctively packaged with labels that show the wine record of each wine.

The crusty Morgan Yeatman, a Roseworthy College graduate of 1950 who had worked at Emu, Quelltaler, Seaview and Glenloth, was winemaker. He summarised his attitude:

> I'm looking for soft reds, using only free run juice, with well balanced acid-tannin finishes. I do my damndest to make a wine that's good enough for me to drink. If it's not, then it's not good enough for anybody else to drink. But then, the final judge is the tinkling bell of the till.

The wines were certainly good enough to drink; they scored copious wine show medals; and the till kept tinkling.

He was succeeded by Andrew Tolley, of the Tolley wine family of Adelaide, who was formerly at the Clarevale Cooperative; he furthered Morgan Yeatman's aims, while also concentrating on the development of some stylish chardonnays.

George Finn is in charge of 320 hectares of vineyards all within 2 km of the cellars, growing cabernet sauvignon, chardonnay, shiraz, riesling, crouchen and pinot noir.

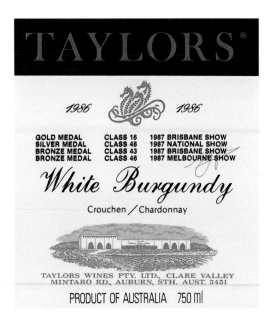

Watervale Cellars, Watervale

Robert and Elizabeth Crabtree say families with children are (usually) welcome to their small family winery in the town of Watervale, for they have pet sheep and other diversions. That leaves the parents free to concentrate on the wines.

Robert Crabtree, a rather eccentric-looking gentleman, founded his small wine operation in 1978 and grows 12 hectares of riesling, shiraz, cabernet sauvignon, pedro and grenache vines at Watervale and Auburn under dryland conditions. He is also a contract grower for another winery.

His own vineyards provide half of his crush of

WATERVALE CELLARS

1987
SHIRAZ
CABERNET SAUVIGNON
68%:32%
CLARE VALLEY

Produced and bottled by Robert Crabtree
Watervale, South Australia

ALC 13.0% BY VOL WINE MADE IN AUSTRALIA 750ML

55 tonnes, from which he produces 3000 cases of table wines and a little muscat. About 12 per cent of production is exported to Britain and the United States.

Wendouree Cellars, Clare

Wendouree might have little more than a cult following, but to its devotees it is one of the greatest of all names in traditional Australian winemaking. Manager-winemaker Tony Brady, although young in years, is aware that he has an old legacy in this quaint winery with its bushland setting on Spring Farm Road, just out of the town of Clare; and he is maintaining the full-bodied red wine style from very old vines.

The tradition was established by Alfred Percy Birks, who set up the vineyards in 1892 as a hobby, one that grew into a trade. By 1913 he was producing 18 000 litres.

The early wines were stored in semi-underground, thatched-roof cellars. New cellars were built in 1914, extended in 1921 and again in 1924. These cellars are still in use.

A.P. Birks, whose name still appears in the official company name, died in 1948 at the age of eighty and was succeeded by his third son, Roland Napier 'Roly' Birks, who had been winemaker since 1917. The company was purchased by the Liberman family in 1974.

Wendouree has 10 hectares, tended by Ian Cerchi, growing mainly shiraz, cabernet sauvignon and malbec. The weighted average of the vines is seventy-five years, and they are not irrigated, which keeps yields low and body and flavour high. Tony Brady maintains the traditional obsession with dry reds in this estate operation, using only Wendouree grapes to crush 48 tonnes and produce 2500 cases. He makes a few dry and sweet whites, almost as a token gesture, and the occasional vintage port; but mostly it is great big gutsy reds which set the traditional heart singing when young, and which can release the gentle profundities of the philosopher when they have meditated in the cellar for several decades.

Wilson Vineyard, Polish Valley

Like many other medical practitioners, Adelaide's Dr John Wilson went into winemaking for several reasons—partly because it seemed an attractive investment; partly because wine had medicinal value; partly because the business represented personal freedoms—but mostly because, despite a Methodist background, he liked the stuff. He set up his wine partnership with wife Patricia in 1974 in the Polish Valley, the subregion for which he has been such a tireless champion.

As he planted the grapes in his spare time while doctoring, he taught himself winemaking 'by the seat of the pants'. He also had a little help from a desperado named Richard 'Rico' Robertson, who at that time had a curious little winery in Clare.

The first wine production was in 1980 off the

A misty morning, Wilson Vineyard.

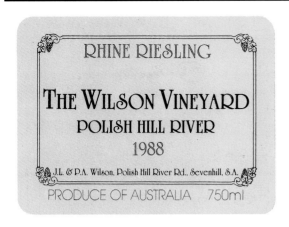

8 hectares of riesling, cabernets, pinot noir, chardonnay and merlot growing on red-brown soil over slate, with an easterly aspect. These vines now provide 85 per cent of the 45 tonne crush, the balance coming from other Polish Valley growers.

John Wilson, who is also known as a train freak and a keen photographer, makes principally dry reds and whites, with some fortifieds maturing; one of his specialisations is sweet late-harvested zinfandel. The quality is constantly improving.

McLaren Vale

As the city of Adelaide grew in the nineteenth century, and houses replaced the vines, it was logical for the vignerons wanting to replant to look south, over O'Halloran Hill. Today, some 150 years later, there is still tension between housing and vines as Adelaide continues to expand; but the McLaren Vale wine region has become beautifully and quite permanently established as vineyard to Adelaide and far beyond.

The Hardy Wine Company and the Penfolds group (through Seaview) are the only really large companies resident in the region; the rest of the forty or so wine producers of McLaren Vale—the number never being certain, so quickly do some come and go—and the many private grape-growers are small, mostly individualistic craftspeople and family operations. This is the essential charm of the area and its wines.

When there is such diversity there can be difficulties in agreeing on anything, even regional nomenclature. Geographically, the region is called the Fleurieu Peninsula, reflecting the role of the French in European exploration of southern Australia; and sometimes the Southern Vales (although this is misleading, since it is the name of one of the wine producers). Marketing enthusiasts have tried to dub it the 'Wine Coast'. Vinously, it properly takes its name from the central township of McLaren Vale, 40 km from Adelaide's central business district and just off the main road to the south coast holiday resort of Victor Harbor. For promotional purposes, the region often embraces wine producers over the South Mount Lofty Ranges towards Lake Alexandrina, in the vicinity of Langhorne Creek.

The suitability of the undulating McLaren Vale area for viticulture, between latitudes 35°30'S and 35°05'S, was recognised soon after the colony of South Australia was proclaimed. John Reynell is usually credited with planting the first vines, in 1838. The climate, with a heat summation of about 1600°C/days, is temperate with reasonably mild summers, cool vintage and freedom from frost due to the moderating influence of the Gulf St Vincent nearby. Rainfall is fairly reliable at 550 mm and drought is rare. Microclimates vary considerably as do soils, ranging from pure sand through sandy loam, limestone and ironstone to rich alluvial soil in the valleys, and heavy red clay on the eastern flats. The area is relatively free of pests.

The wines of Walter Reynell's Reynella and Thomas Hardy's Tintara, and from such winemakers as Dr Alexander Charles Kelly, George Manning, Frederick Wilkinson, William Hammond, A.C. Johnston and Edward Peake found early success; although as the Australian wine industry developed late in the nineteenth century many of them came to be enjoyed anonymously, as parts of blends made up by the big companies. This still happens, if to a lesser degree, as the grapes from McLaren Vale, especially chardonnay, are sought by Barossa and other companies to add full-bodied richness to their blends. Early in the twentieth century, much of the produce of McLaren Vale was exported to Britain, often in bulk. By a coincidence, most early winemakers in McLaren Vale were English, in contrast to the Germanic settlement of the Barossa Valley, and this is celebrated in the region's annual Bushing Festival, which takes Shakespearean images and Elizabethan themes.

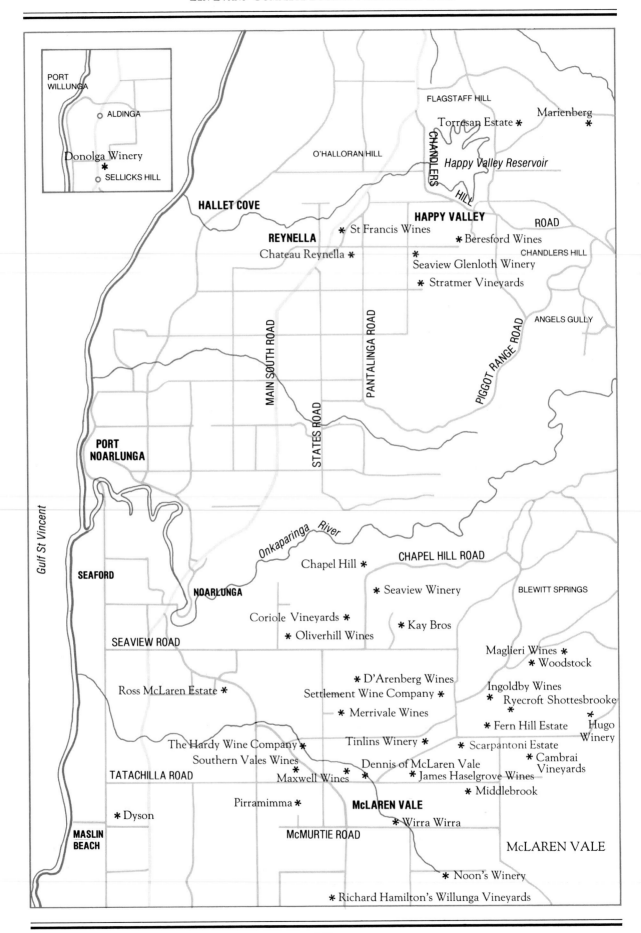

PORT
WILLUNGA

○ ALDINGA

Donolga Winery
✱

○ SELLICKS HILL

FLAGSTAFF HILL

Torresan Estate ✱

Marienberg
✱   ✱

O'HALLORAN HILL

CHANDLERS HILL

Happy Valley Reservoir

HALLET COVE

HAPPY VALLEY   ROAD

REYNELLA

✱ St Francis Wines

✱ Beresford Wines

CHANDLERS HILL

Chateau Reynella ✱

✱
Seaview Glenloth Winery

✱ Stratmer Vineyards

ANGELS GULLY

MAIN SOUTH ROAD

PANTALINGA ROAD

PIGGOT RANGE ROAD

STATES ROAD

PORT
NOARLUNGA

Gulf St Vincent

Onkaparinga   River

CHAPEL HILL ROAD

Chapel Hill ✱

SEAFORD

✱ Seaview Winery

BLEWITT SPRINGS

NOARLUNGA

Coriole Vineyards ✱

✱ Kay Bros

✱ Oliverhill Wines

SEAVIEW ROAD

Maglieri Wines ✱
✱ Woodstock

Ross McLaren Estate ✱

✱ D'Arenberg Wines
Settlement Wine Company ✱

Ingoldby Wines
✱   Ryecroft Shottesbrooke

✱ Merrivale Wines

✱ Fern Hill Estate   Hugo
Winery

The Hardy Wine Company ✱
Southern Vales Wines

Tinlins Winery ✱

✱ Scarpantoni Estate

✱ Cambrai
Vineyards

TATACHILLA ROAD

✱
Maxwell Wines

Dennis of McLaren Vale
✱ James Haselgrove Wines

✱ Middlebrook

Pirramimma ✱

McLAREN VALE

✱ Dyson

MASLIN
BEACH

McMURTIE ROAD

✱ Wirra Wirra

McLAREN VALE

✱ Noon's Winery

✱ Richard Hamilton's Willunga Vineyards

It cannot be pretended that the early wines showed general excellence. They had the English market not only because the big ferruginous quality of the dry reds and fortifieds were supposed to have medicinal qualities for a people lacking sunshine, but also because of preferential treatments for colonial wines. It is probable that they were frequently overripe and jammy, and rubbery with hydrogen sulphide—which was long supposed to give a regional 'cowyard character', but which had almost completely disappeared by the 1980s with improved techniques.

The English market did not survive. In the late 1950s Ben Chaffey started making a more elegant style of cabernet sauvignon at Seaview, and within a few years Eg Dennis and Jim Ingoldby were to form the now-defunct McLaren Vale Wine Company to sell the region's produce through a Sydney wine merchant, H.G. Brown. Thus the basis was laid for McLaren Vale to take its place in the wine boom of the 1960s to 1970s, a decade during which wine consumption doubled in Australia—as did the number of wine producers in McLaren Vale.

Andrew Garrett, McLaren Vale

Entrepreneur Andrew Garrett claims to have the fastest growing wine company in modern history —from 30 tonnes when he set up his own operation in 1983, to 6500 tonnes in 1989.

His headquarters is McLarens on the Lake, which was built as a restaurant, function centre, motel and winery in a gum-studded park on the edge of the McLaren Vale township towards Kangarilla. In 1977 Rod Scroop of the Town House hotel in Adelaide decided to venture into winemaking and put half a million bricks into the complex, then named Hazelmere Estate. The first vintage was 1981, of 50 tonnes, and Iain Riggs left Bleasdale to become the winemaker.

Andrew Garrett, who had been a winemaker with Tolley's Pedare, set up his own label with $3000 which his wife Averil borrowed by taking a mortgage on her city unit. The big step was buying Hazelmere Estate, and in 1987 he opened the cellar door as McLarens on the Lake. In the same year, he bought the Seaview/Romalo cellars at Magill which he planned to use as a champagne-making and tourism facility; but plans were set back by a fire the following year.

Andrew Garrett's chief winemaker is Warren

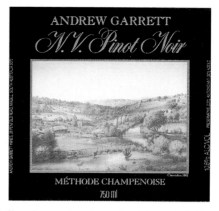

Randall, who trained under Norm Walker at the Magill cellars and became chief champagne-maker for Seppelt Wines at Great Western, which he left in 1989 to return to South Australia. Randall is assisted by Phillip Reschke and Nigel Catt.

Chris Dundon and Julie Cole oversee 235 hectares of company vineyards in McLaren Vale, Padthaway, Clare and at Marlborough in New Zealand. These provide a fifth of the output of 250 000 cases of champagne; dry and sweet whites and reds, the biggest seller of which is Andrew Garrett non-vintage pinot noir champagne.

D'Arenberg Wines, McLaren Vale

In 1912, Francis Ernest Osborn purchased the d'Arenberg vineyard, then naming it Bundarra, which was believed to be an indigenous Australian word meaning 'on a hill'. The property is indeed so situated, with excellent views across the wine region to the Willunga escarpment.

Shiraz and mataro vines had been planted on the property by the Milton family in the 1890s and these were the mainstay of the first vintage, in 1928, of dry reds of the burgundy and claret styles, whites and some port.

The founder's son, d'Arenberg Osborn, born 1926 and named after his mother, Helena née d'Arenberg, joined the firm in 1943; and in 1957 took over completely after the death of his father. D'Arry worked hard to build up the winery and vineyards to total 54 hectares of shiraz, cabernet sauvignon, chardonnay, riesling, grenache, mataro and palomino on undulating terrain of heavy soils to sandy loam, clay and limestone subsoils. Rainfall is 560 mm and these soils provide the colour and body for which d'Arenberg wines are widely known.

View from D'Arenberg vineyards.

The family vineyards provide a fifth of the 1300 tonne crush, the rest being bought from other growers. Winemaker Chester Osborn, who joined the firm in 1980 after oenology training at Roseworthy Agricultural College, maintains his father's traditions of body and colour in d'Arenberg reds, and he also brought a new finesse with such lines as botrytis sweet whites.

Other lines include ports, white burgundy, chardonnay, shiraz, cabernet sauvignon and a fortified white muscat of Alexandria. The company persevered with flagon wines and has a fine name for its red and whites in 2 litre containers and a 4 litre cask, as good-value quaffing wines. The biggest selling line remains the burgundy, which has over the years won several wine show trophies and stands well in the cellar for its rich nobility. About 6 per cent of the 46 000 cases produced is exported.

Beresford Wines, Happy Valley

Hardy's winemaker Rob Dundon and his wife Bronwyn set up their own operation in the old Horndale winery in August 1985. They buy in all their grapes for a crush of 200 tonnes, making sauvignon blanc, chardonnay, pinot noir and a blend of cabernet sauvignon and cabernet franc. Some 30 per cent of Beresford's production goes overseas.

In the same old historic building, Rob Dundon and Tony McEntegart formed a partnership in May 1989 called Bosanquet Estate. Like Beresford, all grapes are bought in for a crush of 750 tonnes. The Bosanquet wines are semillon–chardonnay, fumé blanc, riesling, St Helene cabernet–shiraz and champagne. They are more modestly priced than the Beresford range, and most of the 55 000 cases are exported.

The Horndale building, clinging to a hillside 22 km south of Adelaide like a medieval castle, was started in 1896 by Horn Bros. From 1898, it was under the control of Bernhard Basedow, who purchased the property in 1909. Under Basedow, the company became known for its reds and brandies. The property was then 130 hectares of mainly cabernet sauvignon and shiraz. However, after the Basedow company was sold to Swift and Moore in the late 1940s, the vineyards were sold to Gilbeys Australia Ltd in the 1950s. Horndale then concentrated on brandy for Gilbeys subsidiaries in Australia and

on fortified wines for the British market. Crushing ceased at Horndale in 1971 and it was used by its new owner, the Southern Vales Cooperative, only as a maturation cellar. The walls, 60 cm thick and 7.5 m high, built of stone quarried on the property, provide ideal cool cellaring conditions.

Cambrai Vineyards, McLaren Flat

Graham Stevens, usually to be found unpretentiously wearing a towelling cap, has a reputation in McLaren Vale as the innovator. He has championed many new grape varieties in the region, including zinfandel, muller thurgau, sylvaner, merlot and pinot noir. He has not been shy in trying new blending ideas, either, such as pinot noir and shiraz.

From 1962 to 1969, Graham Stevens worked with d'Arry Osborn at d'Arenberg Wines and as winemaker for Dr Lloyd at Coriole for ten years after that. In 1979 he began planting his own 8.5 hectare vineyard, Cambrai, on Hamilton Road, McLaren Flat. He also has the Mount Wilson vineyards near McLaren Flat.

His wines reflect both his experience and his willingness to push the boundaries of tradition.

Chapel Hill, McLaren Vale

On a hill panoramically overlooking the Seaview winery is a chapel, built by South Australian Chief Justice Sir Samuel Way in 1865 as part of his property, which was then named Seaview Estate.

The chapel was converted to a winery in 1979

and it was bought by the Gerard family in 1987. Winemaker Bevan Wilson, crushing 60 tonnes, produces champagne, riesling, chardonnay, shiraz and cabernet sauvignon table wines, and releases a tawny port.

Coriole Vineyards, McLaren Vale

Coriole, one of McLaren Vale's most famous names of recent history, is a 22 hectare property on Chaffeys Road, opposite the Seaview winery; it became a wine producer almost by accident.

Adelaide general practitioner, Dr Hugh Lloyd, had wanted to grow almonds, which are a major crop in the McLaren Vale region. In 1967 he found abandoned almond groves at Coriole, then rejoicing in the salubrious title of Chateau Bon Sante and possessed of 8 hectares of sixty-year-old vines, old ironstone · buildings and a small but antique winery. The following year, Dr Lloyd had set about becoming a winemaker, re-establishing the vineyards, planting cabernet sauvignon, rebuilding the winery, investing in new equipment, establishing cool-controlled fermentation and, each year, buying new French and American oak hogsheads for maturation. His quest was to make excellent red wines.

For the first vintage, in 1970, Graham Stevens, who was later to found Cambrai, was winemaker, and he helped establish the Coriole name as a quality producer. One of Hugh's sons, Mark, who had a science degree from the University of Adelaide and had gained wine experience in Australia and Europe, took over as winemaker. Mark is obsessed with clean and flavoursome red wines (and also has an interest in art, with which the charming winery has become closely associated). He is assisted by winemaker Stephen Hall.

The 20 hectares of neat vines around the winery, house and colourful gardens are tended by Daryl Marston. They are mostly shiraz and cabernet, some of them original, on red loam over ironstone and limestone, and they give a crush of 200 tonnes. Coriole is almost a total estate operation, buying in less than 10 per cent of its grapes to make dry red and white varietal table wines. A small amount is exported.

Coriole's specialisation remains its clean, warm, rich shiraz, happily combining both earthiness and elegance.

Dennis of McLaren Vale

Daringa, which is the company name behind the Dennis of McLaren Vale label and one of the first landholdings of McLaren Vale, was said to be an Aboriginal word describing the location of a spring of pure water which the white settlers called the Native Well. The winery, on the Kangarilla Road out of the township of McLaren Vale, still boasts among its lawns and trees the first well in the region.

The winery was a joint venture between Ken Maxwell and Egerton Dennis, built in 1971. The Dennis family eventually took full control and Peter Dennis is viticulturist and winemaker.

Eg Dennis was a vigneron, owning a vineyard at McLaren Flat, from the time he returned from war service with the RAAF. With his wartime friend Jim Ingoldby, he founded McLaren Vales Wines in 1965 to market the red wines of the region nationally. The company merged with Ryecroft Vineyards early in 1970 and the group operation, of which Eg Dennis was executive chairman, was sold to the multinational paper group, Reed Consolidated Industries, that same year. Reed Estate Wines was formed by merging J.Y. Tulloch of the Hunter Valley, McLaren Vales Wines and Ryecroft Vineyards. This company was in turn bought by Gilbeys Australia and its name changed to Ryecroft Wines, with Eg Dennis as managing director until his retirement in 1979.

The Dennis family vineyard at McLaren Flat is planted to cabernet sauvignon, shiraz, chardonnay, sauvignon blanc and merlot. Theirs is a total estate operation, with the 12 hectares supplying the 100 tonne crush. In the reds, Peter Dennis seeks intensity of fruit character, colour and some mintiness. The cabernet sauvignon is the star wine of the portfolio, some 5 per cent of which is exported.

Like the Maxwells almost next door, the Dennises make a mead, fermented from South Australian honey, and this is popular with visitors to cellar door.

Donolga Winery, Aldinga

The Girolamo family founded a small operation in 1979, and kept it small, selling their range of varietal table wines and fortifieds only at cellar door, on the Main South Road at Aldinga, and through mail order. Don Girolamo tends the 14 hectares of vineyards at Aldinga, planted principally to cabernet sauvignon, shiraz, sauvignon blanc, chardonnay and riesling. Nick Girolamo is winemaker of the 95 tonnes resulting from this estate operation.

Dyson — VINTAGE 1987

Cabernet Sauvignon

A.G. DYSON — SHERRIFF ROAD, MASLIN BEACH, S.A.

PRODUCE OF AUSTRALIA 750ml

Dyson, Maslin Beach

A.G. Dyson's family business—near Maslin Beach, which is best known in South Australia for being where bathers (legally) bare all—shares with Port Lincoln's Boston Bay Vineyard the distinction of proximity to the sea. The 6 hectares of vines on Sherriff Road, established in 1977, are only 2.5 km from the calming influence of Gulf St Vincent. This, as much as anything, might help explain why Dyson wines tend to be full yet soft.

Dyson grows chardonnay, cabernet sauvignon, pinot noir and sauvignon blanc. From this, in an estate winemaking operation, he makes table wines and a champagne; the cabernet sauvignon is the best known.

Fern Hill Estate, McLaren Flat

Wayne and Pat Thomas are a couple with a no-nonsense taste for good wines; it shows in their own produce. They have half a hectare of vines next to their house and winery on Ingoldby Road, principally of cabernet sauvignon planted in 1977, two years after they set up Fern Hill Estate on land overgrown with bracken fern. The vines, on deep clay soil, are hand-pruned and these provide 6 per cent of the 90 tonne crush.

Wayne Thomas brought to Fern Hill considerable experience, having been a winemaker at

Stonyfell, Saltram and Ryecroft; and a freelance wine consultant in the early 1970s.

The Thomases make a tawny port, riesling, sauvignon blanc, a chardonnay aged in French oak and cabernet sauvignons aged in both French and American oak. The specialisation is a richly flavoured shiraz, aged in American oak puncheons and this is regularly one of the star wines of the region. For a small operation, producing only 3500 cases a year, they are quite widely represented in all states except Western Australia.

Richard Hamilton's Willunga Vineyards, Willunga

If wine production is a hereditary characteristic, Dr Richard Hamilton's interest in viticulture could be explained. He is the great-grandson of Richard Hamilton, who founded the Ewell Vineyards in the earliest days of the colony of South Australia, in about 1837. His father, too, was a vigneron who developed the famous Hamilton Ewell moselle and later founded Leconfield winery in Coonawarra. His interest might also have come from working in the Ewell Winery during his holidays from being a medical student. He is a specialist in plastic surgery, particularly microsurgery of the hand, and proprietor of the winery that bears his name at Willunga.

It is located 45 km south of Adelaide, about 7 km from the Gulf St Vincent, and sheltered by the Willunga Hills, which are a southern extension of the Mount Lofty Ranges. He believes that in Willunga he has a rare combination of soil and climatic conditions, significantly different from those of McLaren Vale proper. The climate is Mediterranean and temperate, with cool sea breezes from the gulf helping slow the ripening process.

Willunga has been a major slate-producing area and the soil on Hamilton's vineyard is slate and gravel over a deep-drained limestone base, which easily enables the vines to reach subsoil moisture. The vines are not irrigated but depend on a 570 mm rainfall, most of which falls in winter.

The Willunga vineyards, established in 1972, include chardonnay, semillon, sauvignon blanc, chenin blanc, cabernet sauvignon and shiraz. There is also a McLaren Vale holding and the viticulturist is Burton W. Hamilton. Hugh Hamilton is the winemaker for this strictly estate operation, crushing 115 tonnes from the company's own vineyards. The specialisations among a range of reds, whites and ports are semillon and chardonnay, and of the 9000 cases produced some 5 per cent is exported.

Richard Hamilton's wines, especially the whites, are characterised by firm flavours, elegance and careful oaking.

The Hardy Wine Company, Reynella

Pioneering McLaren Vale vigneron John Reynell gave work to a twenty-year-old farmer from Gittisham near Honiton, Devon, who arrived in the colony on 14 August 1850, on the sailing ship *British Empire*. The farmer was Thomas Hardy, who was to found what became Australia's largest privately owned wine company.

Hardy stayed for a year in the Reynell vineyards before going to a cattle property at Normanville, south of Adelaide. He was infected with gold fever and made his way to the Victorian diggings. He was soon arrested for not having a digger's licence, spent a night in the lock-up and was fined £1. Hardy did well at the Forest Creek field—not from gold but from a butchering business for which he drove cattle for

Stainless steel Ducellier-Isman tank for fermenting red wine.

the Normanville station to the goldfields. After eighteen months he returned to Adelaide and married his cousin, Joanna Hardy of Somerset, who had been a fellow passenger on the *British Empire*.

In 1853 Hardy invested his new earnings in a property beside the River Torrens, near central Adelaide, which he called Bankside. He worked hard and by 1861 had planted 6.6 hectares with vines, stone fruits and oranges. The first wine vintage at Bankside was 1857 and the wine was matured in a cellar, with a storage capacity of three 450 litre casks, which Hardy had dug out in the evenings after his day's work. By 1859 he had shipped two hogsheads to England in what was possibly the first export of wine in any quantity from the colony.

Hardy went ahead in leaps and bounds. He extended his vineyards to 14 hectares by 1863; a year later his output had doubled and the next year it had quadrupled to 53 000 litres. By then he was buying about half the grapes processed from other growers and blending them to make the sort of wines he wanted, thus laying the basis for the Hardy firm's winemaking practices for the next century.

A milestone in the development of what was to become the Hardy empire was the purchase in 1876 of the Tintara vineyard, about 8 km northeast of McLaren Vale. It had been developed by Dr Alexander Charles Kelly, who has an important place in the history of Australian wine. He wrote two significant books, *The Vine in Australia* (1861) and *Wine Growing in Australia* (1867), and believed in a scientific approach to winemaking. He was also responsible for planting the sauvignon blanc variety. This he did with contour planting—early evidence of ideas on the prevention of soil erosion.

Dr Kelly, a Scot, had practised as a physician in Adelaide before he planted his first vineyard, named Trinity, in about 1842, to make wine for its medicinal value. He then persuaded some prominent Adelaide identities—Sir Samuel Davenport, Sir Thomas Elder, Sir Edward Stirling and R.W. Barr-Smith—to invest in the Tintara Vineyard Company. They purchased a 283 hectare property at McLaren Vale, on which a settler named Manning had planted vines in the 1850s, and the first meeting of shareholders of the new company named the property Tintara. It was hit by the economic depression of the

1860s and was bankrupt by 1873, despite its full cellar of wine. Dr Kelly might have been a good doctor and winemaker but he was not a successful business operator. The only bidder for the bankrupt company was Thomas Hardy, and he recovered the purchase price in the first year from the sale of wine in stock.

Hardy developed the property, clearing more land, planting good varieties and conducting far-sighted experiments in contour cultivation. He expanded the cellar and built accommodation for his employees. In 1878 he bought the unused flour mill in the township of McLaren Vale and converted it to a winery, named the Old Mill cellars. Three years later, Hardy built a substantial bluestone building in Currie Street, Adelaide, for a head office and bottling hall, with champagne production in the basement. The building was the company headquarters until it was sold in 1961, later to be demolished. A further development was the purchase in 1884 of 195 hectares adjoining Tintara. In establishing the new vineyards he was helped by J.G. Kelly, the doctor's son, and Thomas Nottage Hardy, a nephew.

The business grew at such a rate that by 1887 Thomas Hardy took his sons James, Thomas Nathaniel and Robert into partnership, forming the company known as Thomas Hardy & Sons Ltd. James specialised in sales and distribution, T.N. in management and Robert in winemaking. In 1893 an impressive new cellar was built at Mile End, about 2 km west of Adelaide's heart (which was to be sold in 1982, by a nice irony, to become a church college). This gave additional storage capacity of 363 000 litres and an up-to-date laboratory. By 1895 Hardy was the biggest winemaker in the colony, with a vintage of 1.5 million litres.

Winemaker Roger Warren ranked with Maurice O'Shea and Colin Preece as a great blender of traditional Australian wines. He was technical manager until his death in 1960, when he was succeeded by Dick Heath, another prominent name. Heath had graduated from Roseworthy Agricultural College in 1941, and was with the Hardy company until he retired, then as a director, in 1974. He was succeeded by Bryan Dolan, who retired in 1989. Current technical director is Mark Tummel, who had spent his working life with Orlando, and answers to

Guenter Prass—his former boss at Orlando. Under Tummel is an experienced team of winemakers, including Geoff Weaver, Bill Hardy, Tom Newton and David O'Leary.

When Federation abolished duties on wines traded between the states in 1901, the family opened branches in Sydney (where they erected one of the first electric-bulb advertising signs in Australia), in Melbourne and in other centres. A major set-back was a fire in October 1904 which destroyed the Bankside winery.

Thomas Hardy died in January 1912, two days short of his eighty-second birthday. He was an exceptionally able and energetic man, with a full and happy life during which he built up a vast and successful business enterprise. He was active in wider spheres too. As president of the Vignerons' Association he threw his support into the fight against phylloxera; he agitated for the Federation of the nation; and he was president of the Chamber of Manufactures. The people of McLaren Vale honoured Thomas Hardy with a memorial in the town centre, possibly the only such monument in Australia to a winemaker.

Two of Thomas Hardy's sons, James and Thomas Nathaniel, had predeceased him, leaving only Robert and the next generation to carry on the business. The family expanded to buy into the Riverland, at Waikerie, and into the Barossa Valley, at Siegersdorf (now used only as a tasting and sales outlet, although its name lives on in the Hardy company's top-selling riesling). As new steps were taken, old links were broken. Bankside was sold in the early 1920s as the land became more valuable for city growth. By 1926 the original Tintara had outlived its usefulness as a winery and activities there were transferred to the Old Mill cellars in McLaren Vale itself.

By this stage, Tom Mayfield Hardy had gradually taken over control from his uncle Robert, who died in 1927. Tom married Eileen Ponder, who was born in the Barossa Valley in 1923. He built up a reputation as a wine identity but died prematurely in an air crash in 1938. Robert's second son, Kenneth T. Hardy, took over management and became prominent in wine and commercial circles.

Tom M. Hardy's three sons were reared by their widowed mother, Eileen, a remarkable woman who became beloved matriarch of not only the whole family, but of the whole com-

Vineyards, Thomas Hardy & Sons, Keppoch region.

pany. At her seaside home in Adelaide's suburbs, she always had a glass of champagne at 11 am. Among the legends of 'Aunty' Eileen was the story about how she was being quizzed by an immigration official in the United States, or some such place, about her occupation, which had not been recorded in her passport. 'I fixed him with my steeliest stare,' she recalled, 'and said stentoriously, "Drinking, young man, drinking".' She died at age eighty-seven in April 1980 and her image is recalled on the special reds and whites that the company releases as the best of each vintage—the Eileen Hardy range.

The eldest son of Tom and Eileen, Thomas Walter Hardy, gave outstanding service as managing director and chairman but outlived his mother by only seven months. The second son, David, was vineyard director and his brother, Sir James Hardy, who had trained as an accountant, became chairman in 1981, the same year that he was knighted. He is best known as an Olympic and America's Cup yachtsman, but he has also been an international ambassador for the wines of Australia and his company. He has been honoured by the company's release of a champagne called Sir James cuvée brut. Other family members are active in the company, including Bill Hardy, who makes the classic Hardy vintage port and the old show ports.

In 1976 Hardy's acquired the Emu Wine group, the London-based company, which included a winery at Morphett Vale and vineyards and wineries in Western Australia. The Swan Valley-based Houghton group is not exactly a subsidiary; the two have common ownership in the Hardy family. But technical and other links are very close.

One of the company's biggest moves was the purchase, in August 1982, of Walter Reynell & Sons from Rothmans of Pall Mall (having lost to Penfolds a bidding duel over the Kaiser Stuhl winery in the Barossa). Chateau Reynella is the most gracious building of all McLaren Vale wineries, and the oldest continually operating winery in Australia. Hardy's have extensively redecorated the old homestead as the group's headquarters and modernised the winery at a cost of $12 million. In another major development, in 1988, the company bought for $20 million the Clare-based Stanley Wines, which included that company's major cask wine production centre on the Murray River in New South Wales. The Hardy group also distributes the wines of many smaller competitors. The Old Mill cellars at McLaren Vale are principally used for red wines, while whites are handled in the extensive modern additions that have gone on behind the old Chateau Reynella facade.

Viticulturally, the company puts great faith in its 400 hectare holdings at Padthaway, of which 130 hectares are under vine. It also has vineyards around Reynella and at Clare, totalling 670 hectares, under the control of viticulturist Brenton Baker, and the company says the emphasis is on cool-climate and ripe fruit. There are 400 more hectares in Western Australia. These vineyards, and the grapes bought from other growers, give a crush of 50 000 tonnes, making this Australia's largest privately owned wine company.

The Hardy Wine Company used to sell under the Tintara label but put all its products under the Hardy name, covering the spectrum from red and white table wines through champagnes and fortified to brandies.

Although Bob Hagley, long-time winemaker at McLaren Vale, made many fine straight reds, much of the modern company's reputation has been built on blended wines.

Managing director Wayne Jackson has given the modern Hardy Wine Company, with more than 500 employees, a solid, stylish and progressive outlook. To wine-lovers, the Eileen Hardy range is the pinnacle and there are many attractive wines among the Collection range, featuring on their labels paintings by such artists as Arthur Boyd, John Olsen, John Borrace, John Hinge and David Dridan. Through the vehicle of the English-owned Emu Australian Wine Company, purchased in 1976, nearly a quarter of the Hardy wines are exported. This can only grow with the 1990 purchase of two English importers, buying a stake in Chianti producer Ricasoli in Italy, and the takeover of La Baume winery in the Midi in France.

James Haselgrove Wines, McLaren Flat

James Haselgrove, who has a winery also at Coonawarra, founded his own wine operation in 1981 and has 4 hectares of wines in McLaren Vale, as well as 12 hectares in Coonawarra. These grow riesling, traminer, shiraz, merlot and cabernet sauvignon. From them, plus a little more bought in, the family company produces 12 000 cases of dry whites, dry reds, sweet whites, champagne and ports. The most popular is a 'futures' shiraz, by which customers pay in advance for the wine, at a budget price, to be delivered when ready and bottled.

Hugo Winery, McLaren Flat

Colin Hugo grew grapes at Elliott Road, out of McLaren Flat—good grapes with flavour, on a vineyard with a higher elevation than most in the region. His son John Hugo did not know what he would do with himself after finishing school. He worked in the vineyard, got hooked, and ended up taking over in 1970. On seeing the grapes ending up in award-winning wines made by Seppelt and other companies, John decided to make his own wines.

John and wife Liz have bought another vineyard nearby, bringing their total to 15 hectares. They grow chardonnay, riesling, shiraz, cabernet sauvignon, cabernet franc and grenache and produce 7000 cases of dry riesling, late-picked riesling, chardonnay and shiraz; and have stock of tawny port and muscat of Alexandria. This small winery, which makes a particularly distinguished shiraz from carefully tended vines, exports 10 per cent of its produce.

Ingoldby Wines, McLaren Flat

Walter and Kerry Ann Clappis are making very fine wines in a small family winery on Ingoldby Road, McLaren Flat, in the knowledge that they are heirs to an honourable tradition. The name Ingoldby is one instantly associated with McLaren Vale. Jim Ingoldby was one of the major forces for its establishment as a quality wine-growing area. Jim, after studying fine arts, serving overseas in the RAAF and working in an advertising agency, returned to the family's Ryecroft Vineyard in 1950. He learned winemaking there from Aub Chapman, a local identity who has been described as an 'autocratic old man, barely literate, but with a magic touch with wine'. When Aub died in 1957, Jim took over as winemaker and began a new era for Ryecroft.

Jim Ingoldby had great faith in the quality of his dry reds and began bottling under his own label. Up until then, like most other small concerns in the area, wine had been sold in bulk to the big companies. For some years, Ingoldby continued to make sweet wine for export but he concentrated on his good dry reds and sought to establish the identity of the area.

To this end, he formed the McLaren Vale Wine Company with Egerton Dennis and Burr Dodd. It bought wines from local makers and bottled them under the McLaren Vale label, which did much to build the reputation of the area.

Ryecroft was taken over in September 1970 by Reed Consolidated Industries. Jim Ingoldby left Ryecroft five years later and started his own winery on the opposite side of Ingoldby Road, McLaren Flat, where he had purchased 8 hectares of vineyards. He subsequently bought another 6 hectares, growing cabernet sauvignon, shiraz and riesling and making reds of the traditional style.

Being an accomplished water colour artist, Jim Ingoldby built an underground gallery to display his work and that of other Australian artists. Upstairs is a mahogany-panelled tasting room overlooking the vineyards and featuring a large American oak door which Jim made. He was a colourful character, and might be remembered not only for his wines but for his no-nonsense attitudes to wine. 'When Jesus hit the pitcher and turned the water into wine,' he once said, chewing on his cigar, 'he didn't worry about the bloody pH.'

When he retired to his houseboat to paint Murray River scenes, Jim Ingoldby's winery was bought by Walter and Kerry Ann Clappis. They are now growing cabernet sauvignon, shiraz, merlot, semillon, chardonnay and cabernet franc on 20 hectares of vines surrounding the winery. They are planting a new vineyard of 40 hectares between McLaren Vale and Willunga. Paul Buttery is their viticulturist.

The McLaren Flat vineyards are hand-picked and pruned, and no chemical sprays or fertilisers are used. They provide half of Walter Clappis's 250 tonne crush, the rest being bought from other growers in the region.

The specialty is the reds, and this is reflected in the Walter Clappis's successes; he was crowned Bushing King at the 1987 McLaren Vale Bushing Festival for having made the region's best wine of the year. His complex cabernet sauvignons have established a popular reputation.

Kay Bros, McLaren Vale

Kay is a family name long associated with the McLaren Vale district. It goes back to 1890 when the Amery vineyards were established by two brothers, Herbert and Frederick Walter Kay. They built the stone cellars, with their marvellous views over what remained sylvan scenes, on the lines of a model exhibited at the Chamber of Manufactures by Dr J.G. Kelly. The cellars were enlarged in 1927 and again in 1938. The brothers continued in a remarkably long partnership until Frederick died in 1947.

When Herbert died the following year, his son Cuthbert 'Cud' Kay took control. The third generation took over, in the form of Roseworthy College dux of the 1963 graduation class, Colin Kay, as chief executive and winemaker of the small family company. The general manager is Colin Rayment.

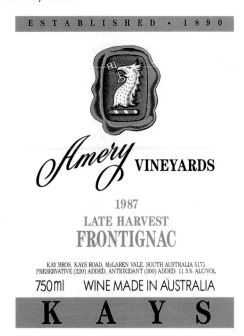

ESTABLISHED · 1890

Amery VINEYARDS

1987
LATE HARVEST
FRONTIGNAC

KAY BROS, KAYS ROAD, McLAREN VALE, SOUTH AUSTRALIA 5171
PRESERVATIVE (220) ADDED, ANTIOXIDANT (300) ADDED. 11.5% ALC/VOL
750ml   WINE MADE IN AUSTRALIA

K A Y S

Cud and Colin Kay in the Kay Bros' Amery vineyard, near McLaren Vale.

The Amery vineyards around the winery, characterised by borders of roses which Cud liked growing as a hobby, total 7 hectares and provide 80 per cent of the winery's crush of 34 tonnes. The soil varies from biscay loam to deep sand, with alluvial soil in the valleys and water-washed quartz on the ridges, with drifts of shallow sand and a little limestone. They have a sympathetic microclimate, with moist cool winters and warm dry summers.

The mix changed with popular tastes and the major varieties became pinot noir, shiraz, sauvignon blanc and gewurztraminer. Colin Kay makes from them a wide range of dry and sweet whites, light-bodied to full-bodied reds, ruby and tawny ports, vintage port and liqueur muscat.

The reds were once noted for being big and solid, and for years many were sold in bulk to P.B. Burgoyne in England, until that company was taken over in 1961 by the Emu Wine Company. Most sales in the 1980s were from the cellar door or by mail order, for the Kay style has a loyal band of devotees. Some is exported to New Zealand. Colin Kay has steered the com-pany's direction to lighter, more elegant styles but the biggest selling line remains the more tra-ditional Kay Bros Block 6 shiraz, made from vines planted in 1892.

Maglieri Wines, McLaren Flat

Steve Maglieri, an immigrant from Italy, estab-lished his own wine firm in 1972 on Gully Road, out of the hamlet of McLaren Flat, originally under the name of Gully Wines. It started as a tin shed which served as office, laboratory, bot-tling and packing line; but Steve Maglieri, with Sandy Watkins and winemaker John Loxton, built up the business to having twelve employees and a fully automated bottling line, separate offices, laboratory and warehouse with a sales and tasting area that is popular for picnics. Families, especially, like visiting Maglieri Wines, for it is one of the few with the sense to have a playground for children.

Steve Maglieri has 76 hectares of vines around the winery, mainly growing shiraz, cabernet sauvignon, riesling and grenache. These, and other growers in the region, provide a crush of

1000 tonnes. The company is expanding its plantings.

A range of table wines, ports and coolers is made and, reflecting Steve Maglieri's origins, he specialises in lambrusco and spumante styles. The big seller is Maglieri lambrusco rosso, a soft and quaffable carbonated light red. He has also produced several gold-medal red wines and, proud of this, he changed the name of Gully Wines to Maglieri Wines in 1979.

Marienberg, Coromandel Valley

Ursula Pridham, from a family of Austrian winemakers, began making wines in Australia as a hobby. In 1966 she and her husband, Geoff Pridham, purchased a property in the Coromandel Valley, 19 km south of Adelaide's central business district and surrounded by suburbs. It became a vineyard of 7 hectares and the family company expanded with the purchase of another property at Bethany, 4 km south-east of McLaren Vale (and not to be confused with the Bethany in the Barossa Valley). This 16 hectare vineyard was planted in 1974, mainly with riesling, cabernet sauvignon and semillon.

Ursula Pridham's first vintage was in 1968 and she attracted attention with an Adelaide Wine Show gold medal for a shiraz and cabernet sauvignon blend from the 1970 vintage. Her range of dry reds, dry and sweet whites and vintage port are characterised by a distinctive, personal style.

Maxwell Wines, McLaren Vale

The winery, one of only a few actually within the boundaries of the town of McLaren Vale, is relatively new, having opened on 17 December 1979. Its founder Ken Maxwell has a long connection with both the area and winemaking there. He was involved in poultry, almonds and grapes in McLaren Vale and started winemaking in 1969, with some success. He and Egerton Dennis set up Daringa in 1973 and built a reputation for solid reds and meads. However, the operation could not support two families so there was an amicable parting and the Maxwells moved up the road to set up their own winery.

The property dates from an original 1839 grant when the town was being established; the winery is red brick, facing towards the road.

Ken Maxwell holds the Dan Murphy trophy in perpetuity, having won it three times, and he and his wife Margaret have twice held the title of Bushing King and Queen, an award given at the annual McLaren Vale Bushing Festival to those whose wine achieves the highest points in the local competition.

Ken and Margie Maxwell established a legend for hospitality as well as for making fine, solid red wines. Control passed to a son, Mark Maxwell, who is a business administration graduate. The winery is still characterised by Ken Maxwell's eccentric contraptions—knocked up from cannibalised washing machines and general junk.

The family vineyards, on Olivers Road, total 8 hectares, growing mainly cabernet sauvignon, shiraz and riesling on brown loam over limestone. These provide half of the winery's crush of

75 tonnes, the balance coming from local grapegrowers.

Maxwell reds are well regarded for their honest flavours. The company also makes dry whites and ports. Its biggest seller, however, remains Ken Maxwell's specialty of mead, a romantically sweet wine made from fermented honey.

Merrivale Wines, McLaren Vale

Originally named South Star Winery, Merrivale Wines began in 1969 when Jack Starr and his wife bought the original 7 hectares, which were planted with shiraz and grenache vines. With the help of son-in-law Michael Bradley, the vineyard was extended to include cabernet sauvignon and riesling and, later, chardonnay.

The winery, on Olivers Road, McLaren Vale, was built in 1973 and the following year Merrivale Wines was incorporated as a public company with the family holding the majority of shares. In 1982 the Barossa-based Krondorf took over the winery; it went into the hands of Mick and Dean Liebich, also from the Barossa. They produce a range of red and white table wines and specialise in club bottlings and commemorative labellings.

Middlebrook, McLaren Vale

Middlebrook Winery Restaurants, on Sand Road out of McLaren Vale, has had a variety of incarnations since its 1947 establishment. It operates as a restaurant, with function rooms, gardens, a lake and vines, under the genial management of Tony Lucas. Its only produce is a honey-cumquat flavoured wine, and Ryecroft uses the Middlebrook label for table wines under licence.

Noon's Winery, McLaren Vale

In 1968 David and Nerida Noon and their five children moved from Adelaide to McLaren Vale to take over an 11 hectare property. It included 5 hectares of established vines, the grapes from which had been sold to local wineries.

By 1971 David Noon was experimenting with making his own wine and it proved successful. He increased production each year and obtained a vigneron's licence in 1976. The crush grew to 48 tonnes, and production is in a new building which includes wood storage for 44 000 litres, together with a separate bottling and cellar door sales area. Grapes from the family vineyard around the winery, principally fifty-five-year-old grenache and shiraz, are supplemented by buying from other growers.

David Noon is assisted in winemaking by Keith Darwin and winery manager Clive Simmons. They make a small range of traditional and maceration styles of dry reds, vintage port, mulled wine and rosé. Sales are only through cellar door and by mail order.

Oliverhill Wines, McLaren Vale

Vincenzo Berlingieri is a scientist-humanist turned winemaker, largely as a result of migrating from Italy. Born in Trieste in 1936, son of a structural engineer and a concert pianist, he completed an engineering degree at Perugia. During this time he had some winemaking experience in the university cellars and this was to stand him in good stead after he had chased a woman to Australia. In 1969 he went up to the Murray River and worked at Lubiana and the Waikerie Cooperative, where in 1970 he made his first vintage port—a style he was to develop a name for.

> I was attracted to winemaking by the romance . . . It offered possibilities for achievement, for flair, creativeness, feeling alive, freedom, a jump back from science to art—and a bit of fun.

Berlingieri worked in several wineries, including Chateau Reynella, before teaming up with a local medico, Dr David Mitchell, to establish the Settlement Wine Company at McLaren Flat in

1976. In the 1980s he found his goal, a place of his own, by buying Oliverhill Wines on Seaview Road, McLaren Vale.

Oliverhill had been established in 1973, at the height of the red wine boom, by biologist Peter Waller, virologist Barbara Magee, general practitioner Don English and wine chemist Bevan Wilson.

Vincenzo Berlingieri, with no vineyards of his own, crushes 53 tonnes of local grapes and makes flavoursome whites; big, gutsy, old-fashioned reds and long-lived ports. His second wife Kiawngo Berlingieri runs a homely restaurant within the ramshackle winery, blending Chinese and Italian culinary styles.

Pirramimma, McLaren Vale

The Pirramimma property, on the Willunga plain just south of the McLaren Vale township, was bought by A.C. Johnston in 1892 when there were only a few grenache vines there. Wine was made in 1900 and rapid progress followed as the vineyards were extended and the winery and cellar improved.

A.C. Johnston's sons, Lex and Digby, took over running the company, and Lex's eldest son, Alex A. Johnston, is currently the manager. Digby's son, Geoffrey D. Johnston, who trained at the Riverina College, is winemaker. Alexander Hammond Johnston is chairman of the company, which in 1935 had been turned from a partnership to a limited liability company, and in 1965 to a proprietary company—A.C. Johnston Pty Ltd—with the Johnston family as shareholders.

The property had 55 hectares under vines and in 1990 this expanded to 150 hectares. Grape varieties are riesling, pedro, palomino, cabernet sauvignon, shiraz, grenache, chardonnay, pinot noir and semillon; growing on varying soils on undulating ground, from sand to heavy biscay overlaying clay subsoil. All have supplementary irrigation.

These provide 85 per cent of the crush, in 1989, of 600 tonnes, making dry whites, dry reds, sweet whites and ports.

Historically, Pirramimma traded in bulk wines to Britain and Canada. Between 1916 and 1946 most of its wines went to W.A. Gilbey Ltd of London, and sales continued to 1966. The com-

pany has moved to concentrate on chardonnay, cabernet sauvignon and maceration reds of high quality, bottled for the local market.

Chateau Reynella, Reynella

The chateau, stylish headquarters of the Hardy Wine Company group, is steeped in the history of wine in Australia. It was John Reynell who planted some of the first vines in the infant colony in the area that was to take its name from his—Reynella, now a southern suburb of Adelaide. This pioneer of the grape was born at Ilfracombe in 1809, of a Devonshire farming family. Reynell arrived in South Australia two years after the founding of the colony and married one of his fellow passengers on the *Surrey*, Mary Lucas, daughter of an admiral. The newlyweds settled on a property which John Reynell had purchased from the South Australian Company before leaving London. It was situated 20 km south of Adelaide and 5 km in from the Gulf St Vincent, on the site of what is now Chateau Reynella.

John Reynell was principally interested in farming sheep, cows, wheat and potatoes; but in 1838 he planted some vine cuttings which, according to his diary, he had brought with him from the Cape of Good Hope.

In 1845 he expanded his vineyard by purchasing some cuttings from John Macarthur in New South Wales. A letter from Macarthur's son, William, which is in the Reynell archives, names prices for riesling, cabernet sauvignon, malbec, gouais, dolcetto, constantia, verdelho, tokay and others—mostly £1 for a thousand. These cuttings were planted on the banks of the Panalatinga Creek, where they were sheltered with almond

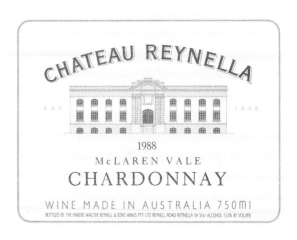

Entrance to Australia's oldest functioning commercial wine cellar, Walter Reynell & Sons.

trees. Reynell at this time was apparently intending to concentrate on winemaking, for also in 1845 he excavated the Cave Cellar, the oldest underground cellar still functioning in Australia, now used not only for wine maturation but also as a museum and function centre, being set in the midst of one of Adelaide's loveliest gardens.

Reynell never had much ready cash, so in 1854 he sold part of his extensive holdings as the site for a town. Blocks were surveyed and sold by auction to form the township of Reynella. The process continues in this area today as the urban sprawl grows.

That year also saw the birth of John and Mary's son, Walter Reynell, who was to build most successfully on the foundations laid by his father. John Reynell died in June 1876 at the age of sixty-seven, and is honoured for his pioneering work in the South Australian wine industry and for his tenacity through many difficult periods.

The Reynells are one of the oldest of many families in which the management of the winemaking business was handed on from generation to generation. Walter Reynell was intelligent and energetic and built up the family fortunes with the creation of the company that became known

as Walter Reynell & Sons Wines Ltd. Walter Reynell was well known in Adelaide business circles when he died in April 1919.

Two world wars were responsible for the deaths of two generations of Reynell heirs. Thus, for some years, the only Reynell blood in the company was its chairman, Ian Thomas, grandson of Walter Reynell's sister, while Colin Haselgrove, well-known winemaker and yachtsman, was managing director.

Reynella joined the takeover boom of the time when Hungerford Hill acquired the company in April 1970. In the next move in the paper shuffling, Rothmans of Pall Mall (Australia) Ltd took control of Reynella in November 1976. Ownership of the company changed again in August 1982, when Thomas Hardy & Sons purchased Reynella and made it the headquarters of the group's expanding operations, with vast modern winemaking facilities and a bottling hall hidden behind the gardens, the original homestead and the imposing chateau facade. The descendants of the original Thomas Hardy had bought the company set up by the man who gave young Hardy his first job in Australia a century and a half earlier.

Not much remains of the Reynella vineyards, but the fruit—growing on red sandy loam with limestone marl subsoil, or heavy gravelly loam with chalky subsoil—is excellent for red wine and ports, especially the vintage ports which are one of Reynella's claims to fame. Hardy has kept the Reynella range going, including the vintage port, although rationalised, with a separate market identity. Some of the most notable wines are the reds, many of them from Coonawarra, and a refreshing rosé which is consistently one of the best in the country.

Ross McLaren Estate, McLaren Vale

In July 1988 Roscon Pty Ltd took over Taranga Estate, imposingly set on the Victor Harbor Road overlooking much of the McLaren Vale region, and renamed it Ross McLaren Estate.

Taranga is said to be an Aboriginal word meaning 'half-way meeting place'. The winery was established in 1974 by Lorenzo Comazzetto, who in the previous year had sold his interest in the Valle d'Oro winery at McLaren Vale to Dalgetys. With a wine-marketing background in Treviso, Italy, this well-known Adelaide businessman wanted to continue in the wine business, so he bought Ross McLaren Estate.

The rich loams over a limestone base proved suitable for early plantings of cabernet sauvignon, shiraz, malbec and riesling varieties, and viticulturist Paul Buttery now tends 40 hectares of vines around the winery and butting onto the main road. Because of the beauty of its position, it would be one of the region's vineyards most photographed by tourists.

Lorenzo Comazzetto died in 1977, having built up the winery, with its shaded verandah supported by large arches in the manner of some Spanish and Italian wineries. John Davoren, a maker of some great reds with Penfolds, became winemaker.

Stephen Bennett is consulting winemaker to Ross McLaren Estate, crushing 130 tonnes. John Russo is marketing and promotions manager and Mrs Phyl Groves is licensee and manager.

Ryecroft Vineyards, McLaren Flat

Ryecroft was put on the map by Jim Ingoldby in the 1960s and has had a chequered career since—but its origins go back more than a century. In 1884 Frederick Wilkinson gave up his job with the Bank of Adelaide and bought the property, then a pig farm. Two years later he planted vines. His first vintage, a burgundy-style wine,

Ryecroft Vineyards.

was in 1895 and he followed it with more plantings. Wilkinson's son, who was to have inherited the company, was killed in World War I and it was purchased by James Ingoldby. The Ingoldbys were closely associated with Ryecroft until 1972 when Jim Ingoldby left to set up his own operation across the road.

Reed Consolidated Industries, the British industrial group which owned Tulloch in the Hunter Valley of New South Wales, bought Ryecroft in September 1970. Four years later, Gilbeys Australia Pty Ltd acquired a majority interest in the holdings and in 1980 it was decided to merge the marketing but not the winemaking of the two vineyards. It was also decided to rename Ryecroft as Wilkinson Estate. That idea did not endure. In October 1980 it changed hands again when it was bought by the Barossa company of Krondorf. It is now a private company owned by Grant Burge (former Krondorf head who now has his own winery in the Barossa), Gordon Grant, Nick Holmes, Paul Buttery and Jim Smith.

Under Gordon Grant's managership, with Nick Holmes as winemaker and Paul Buttery as viticulturist, Ryecroft is a surprisingly large operation for McLaren Vale, with twenty-five employees and a crush of 2500 tonnes. It became renascent as a name for very high-quality wines from the region, specialising in reds and wood-matured whites.

Only 15 per cent of the wines come from the company's own vineyards, 32 hectares of cabernet sauvignon, cabernet franc, merlot, chardonnay and semillon. These are on well-drained, sandy loam soils. About 10 per cent of Ryecroft's 30 000 case production is exported.

Winemaker Nick Holmes also has a personal label, Shottesbrooke, which produces a red of delectable and fashionable complexity and flavour.

St Francis Wines, Old Reynella

St Francis is clearly visible from the main road south through Adelaide's suburbs, which makes it popular with weekend tourists. The owners have capitalised on this by spending much time and money restoring the charming winery building, which is more than a century old and which housed the first licensed distillery in South Australia. It also includes a family restaurant, barbecue facilities, a lake and the new St Francis Village motel.

Karl Lambert, who had spent sixteen years with Penfolds, acquired the property in 1970. High land prices in the area prohibit grapegrowing and St Francis produces wines grown in McLaren Vale, Coonawarra, Eden Valley and Barossa and elsewhere.

The directors are Pompey Donato and David Ward and the wines have been the responsibility of consultants such as Jim Irvine and Rod Dundon. A wide range of table and sparkling wines is released under the St Francis and Governor Phillip labels, totalling 25 000 cases annually. Chardonnay and shiraz (labelled hermitage) are the best sellers. About 5 per cent is exported.

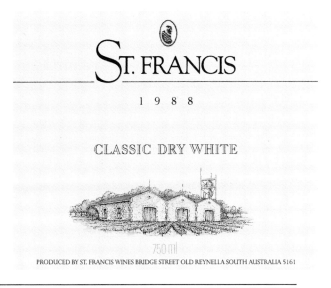

Scarpantoni Estate, McLaren Flat

Domenico Scarpantoni had a family background in winemaking in Libya and Italy. Wine was a natural business for him after migrating to South Australia and he made his first non-commercial red wine in 1958. Scarpantoni gained local experience by working as a cellar hand at Hardy for seven years and then spending six years as viticulturist at Seaview. In 1965 he purchased for the family a vineyard/orchard property in the township of McLaren Flat.

It was restructured to 28 hectares of cabernet sauvignon, shiraz, riesling, chardonnay, merlot, sauvignon blanc, muscat, gamay, pinot noir and semillon, on sand over ironstone, clay and biscay soil. The excellent quality of Scarpantoni wines, especially the reds, is a result of the love and experience Dom puts into these vineyards, which provide 100 per cent of the 5000 cases annual output. Dom Scarpantoni is proud of his vines and minimises chemical treatments.

The Scarpantonis turned their wine hobby into a full business by getting a vigneron's licence in 1979. It remains a small family affair with Dom assisted by his wife, Paula, and daughter Guilia in the business, while sons Michael and Filippo assist with the winemaking, which is constantly being modernised. The family built the Spanish-looking winery themselves.

The range of wines includes cabernet sauvignon, cabernet–merlot, Block 3 shiraz, Block 1 riesling, chardonnay, sauvignon blanc, late-harvest riesling, botrytis riesling, liqueur riesling and vintage port. The modestly priced cabernet is in most years the best testimonial to a dedicated wine family.

Seaview Winery, McLaren Vale

Seven kilometres north of the town of McLaren Vale, in a hollow of the hills separating McLaren Vale and Morphett Vale, is a historic winery, Seaview, which is part of the Penfolds group. Grapes are no longer crushed here—the Seaview wines are made at the old Glenloth winery at Reynella—but the charm of Seaview endures in its use as a maturation facility and cellar door tasting and sales centre.

Its history began with George Pitches Manning, who came from Cambridgeshire in England with his family in 1850. He bought 65 hectares

of virgin scrub, built a home, cleared the land and planted wheat. Optimistically, he named it Hope Farm.

Encouraged by the success of vines at Reynella, George Manning planted a vineyard of 12 hectares and built a winery at Hope Farm, and soon after added a still. He managed to make wine for which there was a ready sale among farmers for a great distance around and he is said to have been very proud of his port, which was liberally fortified with brandy.

George Manning died in 1872, a poor man. His son kept Hope Farm alive until 1892 when he sold out to a young Englishman, Walter H. Craven. Craven changed the name to Hope Vineyards and enlarged and modernised the homestead, cellar and vineyards. After his death and the death of his son, ownership passed to Craven's former manager, G.W. Kay, who ultimately sold it to Ferguson and Chaffey in 1948. Benjamin Chaffey was a Roseworthy College graduate and grandson of one of the pioneering brothers who had established the Murray irrigation settlements. Three years later F.H. 'Friend' Edwards, who had viticultural experience in the Marion district, replaced Ferguson in partnership with Chaffey, and in that year, 1951, renamed the place Seaview.

The Seaview vineyards came under new ownership once more when the British company, Allied Brewers, in association with Castlemaine Tooheys of New South Wales, took over from Edwards and Chaffey in early 1971, and Seaview eventually became part of the Penfolds empire.

There is a panoramic view of the whole property from the roadway on the hill just north of the homestead. Chapel Hill, as it became known, was originally the Seaview Estate, home of Sir

Samuel Way, who was then Chief Justice of South Australia. The chapel (operating as a small winery) was built in 1865 and the property name, Seaview, was adopted by the winery.

Seaview winery is noted for its well-maintained gardens and immaculate appearance. A stainless steel fountain in the form of a trellised vine, the creation of Richard Howard, dominates the foreground. Inside the winery, the story of Seaview from 1950 can be seen beautifully carved in oak, the work of Professor Paul Beadle, previously director of the Adelaide School of Fine Arts. He was also responsible for six famous carvings mounted in the ends of the 4500 litre casks facing the entrance. The six scenes, in jarrah, depict stages in winemaking from vine culture to appreciation.

The Seaview winery is now used as a maturation cellar and a sales and public relations centre. Wine production takes place at the old Glenloth winery at Reynella, and Mike Farmilo is winemaker.

The name Glenloth is not well known; but in 1892 it was on everybody's lips, for that year a five-year-old named Glenloth won the Melbourne Cup at 50:1. Mrs Horn, then planting her small vineyard in the O'Halloran Hill district near the Happy Valley Reservoir behind Reynella, was moved to name it after the horse Glenloth.

The vineyard was bought by Mr and Mrs J.R. Harper Robertson in 1921 and they subsequently built a winery. They made their first wine in 1923 and went on to win many awards for their range of table and dessert wines. In 1942, to cope with the expanding volume of business, a winery and distillery were purchased at Happy Valley, a few kilometres from the vineyard. These were modified and most of the winemaking was transferred there. Glenloth was made into a private limited liability company, with the Harper Robertsons as directors. Their son J.R.W. (Bob) Robertson looked after the winemaking.

The company was taken over in 1966 by Seager Evans and Co of London, and much of the company's wine was sold in bulk in London. In 1971 Glenloth Wines had the distinction of being the first wine industry 'double' of modern times when it was taken over again, this time by the Sydney-based brewer Castlemaine Tooheys. Then, as part of the Penfolds group, it became a major production centre for Seaview wines.

About 30 per cent of Seaview's crush comes from its own vineyards. These, tended by Graham Lewis, are at McLaren Vale for the fuller, richer styles, and at Padthaway in the south-east of the state, for more elegant and distinctive varietal fruit styles. Varieties planted include riesling, chardonnay, sauvignon blanc, cabernet sauvignon and shiraz.

The Seaview brand, under the control of production manager Robin Moody (who also oversees Wynn's Coonawarra Estate), is known throughout Australia especially for riesling and cabernet. Seaview cabernet sauvignon is one of the consistently best commercial red wines in Australia. Seaview brut champagne, one of the nation's biggest sellers in the lower price brackets, is made at Penfolds in the Barossa.

During the 1977 McLaren Vale Bushing Festival, Seaview and its history were honoured by the festival board with the unveiling of a plaque. It stands in front of the exposed subsoil from which George Pitches Manning dug his first cellar in 1850.

Settlement Wine Company, McLaren Vale

The Settlement Wine Company started in February 1977 as the result of a chance meeting between Vincenzo Berlingieri, an ebullient winemaker with experience in the Riverland and McLaren Vale, and David Mitchell, a wine-loving general practitioner in the Reynella area.

The partners chose the name Settlement because they wanted to make wines of a supposed colonial style—big, gutsy and long-lasting —and they started by buying an 1840s cottage on a hillside just out of McLaren Flat. It included a patch of grenache vines.

The first release in 1974 was under the label of the Colonial Wine Company, later changed to avoid confusion with another company of similar name. Until Vincenzo Berlingieri left to set up by himself at Oliverhill, Settlement was developing a reputation for solid red wines and ports.

In February 1987 fire totally destroyed the original winery. Dr David Mitchell, with Janis Gesmanis as winemaker and Peter Dawes as sales manager, set up in the Torresan Wine Estate building in McLaren Vale.

Shottesbrooke

Nick Holmes, winemaker at Ryecroft, makes Shottesbrook wine, a sauvignon blanc and a stylish red blend, in his spare time. They are exclusively from his own vineyard at Myponga. Nick Holmes, who came from East Africa as a child, studied at Roseworthy College and became best known as a winemaker with Krondorf. He raised money to buy his own vineyard by working on construction sites in Germany, oil rigs in the Gulf of Mexico and fishing boats in Alaska; and purchased a 12 hectare property about 20 km from McLaren Vale, at Myponga where the South Mount Lofty Ranges descend to the sea. He grows only cabernet sauvignon, merlot, malbec, shiraz and sauvignon blanc.

Southern Vales Wines, McLaren Vale

The Southern Vales winery, next to the bowling club on the main street of the McLaren Vale township, had its origins in the cellars called The Wattles, built in 1896 to dispose of a surplus of grapes grown in the district. It was Thomas Hardy who talked Cyril Pridmore into starting the emergency pool for grapegrowers and who gave coaching in winemaking and technical assistance. The original cellars are no more, but a stone storage cellar built five years after the first vintage of 1896 is still in use and an inscription on a memorial stone bears the opening date of February 1901. This is considered to be the foundation date of the company that exists today.

In that year Cyril Pridmore bought Sylvan Park from the estate of Thomas Colton and moved from his wooden cottage, The Wattles on Tatachilla Road, into the lovely Colton home. He had 12 hectares under wine grapes and currants, and his malbec returned nearly 5 tonnes to the hectare. In the early days he bought most of his wine grapes from local growers, then about thirty in number.

In about 1910 Penfolds Wines acquired the Pridmore cellars and operated them until 1963, making substantial quantities of wine annually from grapes supplied by the local growers. All wines were transported to Nuriootpa in the Barossa Valley for blending.

Following grape surpluses in the mid–1960s and a government-formed emergency pool to process unwanted grapes in 1964, Southern Vales Cooperative Winery Ltd was formed in February 1965 by 185 grapegrowers in the region. It purchased the Penfolds winery in McLaren Vale, with money from the State Bank of South Australia, which also provided financial assistance to process 2774 tonnes of grapes in the first year. Just before the 1968 vintage, the Cooperative expanded and bought the Horndale winery and distillery at Happy Valley.

In November 1980 a receiver-manager was appointed to handle the affairs of the Cooperative and on 20 May 1982 the assets were sold to Hong Kong businessman George Lau and his son Roland. They settled in the region and built the winery up, intending to supply markets in Asia.

The company, which trades under both the Southern Vales and Tatachilla labels, was then owned by local grapegrowers and winemakers. From its crush of 4500 tonnes it produces 10 000 cases annually. Winemakers Roland Walquist and Jane Paull follow such predecessors as Grant Burge and Ian Wilson, making full-bodied dry whites, soft dry reds and ports, with semillon a specialty. This historic and substantial winery is undergoing a resurgence under new ownership.

Stratmer Vineyards, Reynella

Geoff Merrill, a voluble and hirsute character, attracts much personal attention. He is also an astute wine judge and a serious winemaker, whose products deserve to attract much attention. He makes wines under the Geoff Merrill name and the Mount Hurtle label with his Stratmer Vineyards company, operating from a converted historic farmhouse on the corner of Byards and Pimpala Roads, Reynella.

Geoffrey Lewis Merrill, who was born in Port Augusta in 1954, trained in winemaking at Seppelt and in South Africa before he joined Chateau Reynella on 4 November 1975, where he was to become chief winemaker. Merrill's discipline is the main reason for the renaissance of the Chateau Reynella as a name for quality in the late 1970s. In 1980 he put out his first wine under his own name, made privately in his own time, and this led to going solo, with Goe di Fabio as his assistant winemaker in an 1897 property refurbished in 1987 and opened for cellar door tastings and sales, with a stylish function area, barbecue facilities and conservatory.

He has 22 hectares of vines at Coonawarra and Reynella, growing cabernet sauvignon, chardonnay and merlot, planted with close spacing and high fruit exposure trellising. As these come into bearing, his 300 tonne crush is made up of fruit bought from other growers, mostly in the McLaren Vale region.

Geoff Merrill specialises in dry table wines, red and white, producing 24 000 cases a year, a quarter of which is exported. His Coonawarra-McLaren Vale red blends are quite seductive, with fresh flavours, clean structures and long buttery-acid finishes.

Tinlins Winery, McLaren Vale

The traditional spirit of McLaren Vale is evident with Tinlins, a small, family company, little known outside the region and selling almost all of its produce only from the winery. It was set up in 1975 on Kangarilla Road, McLaren Vale, by J. Tinlin and W.D. Tinlin. They have 80 hectares of established vines, growing cabernet sauvignon, shiraz, grenache, riesling, sauvignon blanc and pedro, giving a 390 tonnes crush and producing mainly claret, moselle and tawny port styles at budget prices. They also make vermouth, ginger wine, marsala, sherries, apricot wine, coffee nectar and spumante.

Torresan Estate, Flagstaff Hill

Gino Torresan, founder of the Happy Valley Winery which produces under the Torresan Estate and Cambourne Wines labels, was born in the northern Italian province of Treviso. He grew up amid vineyards and his father, Agostino Torresan, was an accomplished winemaker. In 1939 Gino migrated to Australia and tried mining and dairy farming. In 1958 he purchased a vineyard at Happy Valley on which he established his own winery. Its tasting room is now shaded by a 300-year-old gum tree.

The vineyards were more than 100-years-old, having been planted by Mrs Horn, a founder of the famous Horndale winery. A program of trellising was commenced, with the shiraz and cabernet sauvignon vines 2 m high in the Italian style. Gino's son John Torresan tends the 12 hectares of vines, now the only ones in this suburban region, and also 5 hectares at McLaren Vale, growing mainly cabernet sauvignon, shiraz, riesling grenache and pedro.

The winery was built in two stages, having started crushing in 1965. The original building was built into the side of the hill and had two storeys, the lower being maturation cellars, and the upper the vintage areas. In 1969 a new section was built to house crusher, press, stainless steel fermentation and storage tanks and 45 000 litres capacity of American oak puncheons and casks.

Michael Torresan and Tim Mortimer are the winemakers for the 500 tonne crush, some 80 per cent of which is bought in from other growers. They make a premium range of table wines and a mid-range white label series of dry reds, dry whites and ports, and are best known for their white label shiraz.

Wirra Wirra, McLaren Vale

It is said that 'Wirra Wirra' was an Aboriginal name for 'between the gums'. This might well refer to the wine company's setting, surrounded as it is by tall eucalypt trees. One of its owners, Greg Trott, might say it refers also to the feeling of the wine in the mouth. Ambiguities abound in the strange eccentricities of Mr Trott. But this is nothing new at Wirra Wirra.

It was established by Robert Strangeways Wigley, whose middle name was not inappropriate. Born in 1864, he studied law and architecture and played cricket for South Australia. Tales of his pranks as a young man include feats of horsemanship inside the Adelaide Town Hall and towing a pie cart down King William Street, to the consternation of its patrons and owner. In 1893 his family sent him off to rusticate in McLaren Vale and there he began building cellars, using the plans of a split-level design that his

friend Alex Johnston had used at Pirramimma down the road. Thus the company dates from 1894. Bob Wigley died in 1924, having contributed much to the life of the district and made many good wines, most of which were sold in England through Burgoynes of London. In 1936 the original 97 hectares were sold by his family, and the cellars, with only 3 hectares, fell into disuse.

In December 1969 the winery, by then virtually derelict, and the surrounding land were bought from Vern Sparrow (son of Wigley's foreman, Jack Sparrow) by cousins Greg and Roger Trott, and re-established. Greg Trott, who had spent five years with the Southern Vales Cooperative, has a vineyard across the road from the winery and runs the operation full-time. Roger, an accountant, has a property at McLaren Flat. In a gesture worthy of the wonderful Wigley, the Trotts spent a frantic five weeks gathering equipment. Then, armed with an ancient wooden Bagshaw crusher, a pump and an old French press, they made their first wines in the open air amidst the ruins.

The next five years were spent rebuilding the cellars. Ironstone and slate were quarried, and bricks taken from old demolished cottages. The huge oregon beams and flooring are from a historic Adelaide Methodist church. The winery is one of the prettiest and most hospitable of the region, with log fires in winter, a church bell on a tower to ring, a trousered engine and Greg Trott's wry charm. Out the back are very serious modern winemaking facilities, run by Trott and assistant winemaker Ben Riggs.

Roger Trott has the Moray Park Vineyard at McLaren Flat, an excellent microclimate close to the southern end of the Adelaide Hills. These, plus Greg Trott's Bethay Vineyards, total 63 hectares, growing riesling, sauvignon blanc, semillon, chardonnay, cabernet sauvignon, cabernet franc, merlot, shiraz and grenache.

These vines provide about 40 per cent of the 440 tonne crush, other grapes coming from David Paxton's Hillstowe vineyard, one of the finest private vineyards in the McLaren Vale region; from other local growers; and from Clare, the Adelaide Hills and Coonawarra. The range produced is dry and late-picked rieslings, sauvignon blanc, a semillon–sauvignon blanc blend, chardonnay, a pinot noir–chardonnay champagne called The Cousins, tawny port, vintage port and several reds—the most famous of which is the Wirra Wirra Church Block dry red. An association with Brian Croser of Petaluma gave Wirra Wirra a leap forward in wine quality in the 1980s and it has become one of the highly respected names in McLaren Vale.

Woodstock, McLaren Flat

J. Scott Collett, whose Woodstock at McLaren Flat has been convincingly to the fore in the quality standards of McLaren Vale wines since its establishment in 1974, has wine in his blood. His father is Doug Collett, who had a long and distinguished career in Australian wine.

Following war service as a fighter pilot, Doug Collett obtained an honours diploma in oenology from Roseworthy College, having studied with Roger Shipton, Brian Barry, Bryan Dolan, John Stanford, Ray Kidd, Phil Tummel and other later prominent names, under such teachers as Alan Hickinbotham. He took over from Ben Chaffey at Emu in 1949 and the following year went to Berri Estates in the Riverland to take over from winemaker Noel Burge. Within six months he had taken over from Alex Kelly as technical manager and stayed there until 1967. A six-month scholarship to Montpellier in France in 1960 gave him a background in table wines and he introduced many new techniques to Berri, including air-bag presses and refrigeration—laying the technical basis for Australia's white wine boom. In 1967 Doug Collett set up his own consulting service to the industry, BICE Ltd, and helped build up and advise many small-to-medium cellars, including Tulloch, Coolawin, d'Arenberg, Angle Vale, Elysium, Krondorf, Anakie, Hungerford Hill and the Wine Society. He also contributed greatly to the industry with his involvement in the Australian Wine and Brandy Corporation and the Wine Research Institute.

Doug Collett now lives in semi-retirement, tending his own tiny patch of 'hobby' vines at Waikerie, but in the 1970s he was particularly active establishing Woodstock. The original Woodstock vineyards were bought in 1972 and reconstituted to cabernet sauvignon. A modern cellar was built in 1974 and the company dates from this year.

A Collett son, Scott, graduated from

Roseworthy College with an oenology diploma in 1978, worked as senior winemaker at San Bernadino in Griffith, and spent six months in the Napa Valley in California before returning to take over the business.

The company has 25 hectares at McLaren Flat, growing cabernet sauvignon, shiraz, chardonnay, semillon and grenache on sand over clay soils. These provide 60 per cent of the 350 tonne crush.

Woodstock, on Douglas Gully Road, has picnic and barbecue facilities, a function centre called the Woodstock Coterie, which does Sunday lunches, and a native animal reserve across the road. It is popular with visitors. The products, including cabernet sauvignon, shiraz, riesling, chardonnay, semillon, sauvignon blanc, tawny port, vintage port and botrytis sweet white, are also popular with wine lovers. The cabernet is a particularly fine wine, richly flavoured and elegantly constructed, with a long cellaring life.

Langhorne Creek

The area known as Langhorne Creek is usually considered a part of McLaren Vale, promotionally and statistically; but it has distinctly different viticultural conditions, being on the western side of the South Mount Lofty Ranges, down on the flatlands towards the Murray River and Lake Alexandrina. There is only one operating winery in the region, Bleasdale, but a couple of dozen private growers, with more than 200 hectares under vines along with mixed farming, provide top-quality fruit to major wineries elsewhere. To the south-west, towards the sea, are two wine producers, Temple Bruer and Currency Creek, which can for convenience be considered under the Langhorne Creek heading as their vineyards have similar climatic conditions.

Langhorne Creek, 70 km south-east of Adelaide at latitude 35'S, is named after Alfred Langhorne, who brought a mob of cattle overland from New South Wales in 1841 and settled in this area, between the town of Strathalbyn and Lake Alexandrina. A unique feature of the area is the rich and fertile alluvial loam on the river flats. The soil is enriched with silt by the annual flooding of the Bremer River, coming down from Callington and Mount Barker. The

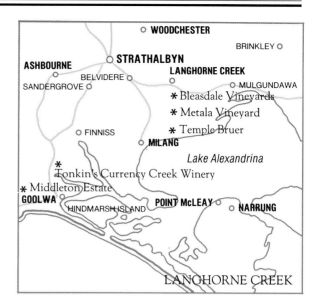

rainfall is low, only about 350 mm a year, but the vines get a thorough soaking in the winter floods. A system of floodgates forces the water over the banks and into the vineyards. They have supplementary irrigation in summer. These features add up to wines with distinctive and individual character.

The grapes, especially cabernet sauvignon, which develops a magnificent richness of flavour, are keenly sought by Barossa wineries such as Seppelt and Penfolds. The distinctive style of Wolf Blass reds owes much to a consistent use of premium Langhorne Creek cabernet. One prominent grower, with a 28 hectare vineyard, is Angus Borrett, who married a daughter of Frank Potts Jr.

The most famous vineyard is the historic Metala, named by Arthur Formby when he planted 12 hectares of cabernet and shiraz there in 1890. In the early twentieth century, Ronald H. Martin, of Stonyfell at Burnside, took over the vineyard and cellars at Metala and considerably extended them; but the winemaking operations and storage were moved to Stonyfell (now itself no longer a winery but a function centre in the Adelaide foothills).

The Metala vineyards, with 8 hectares of cabernet and 10 hectares of shiraz, some of them the original century-old vines, are owned by Mavis Butler. The grapes are processed at the Saltram winery near Angaston, which has proudly inherited from Stonyfell and revitalised the Metala wine label, invented by Bryan Dolan in the early 1960s.

Bleasdale vineyards at Langhorne Creek.

Bleasdale Vineyards, Langhorne Creek

Frank Potts of Bleasdale was the pioneer vigneron of Langhorne Creek proper and, with the closure of Bremer Wines, the Potts family are again the only winemakers.

Frank Potts was born in 1815 in England and came to Australia at the age of twenty-one. He was impressed by the fertile soils and huge red gums of Langhorne Creek and settled there. In 1850 he bought 126 hectares on a Crown grant and named the property after the Reverend J.I. Bleasdale, who was then an influential figure in the Australian wine world. The resourceful, inventive and hard-working Potts built a hut for his large family of six sons and four daughters. His wife died in childbirth and he later married Anne Flood and had two more sons.

In the early 1860s Frank Potts planted 12 hectares on either bank of the Bremer with shiraz and verdelho. He dug a water channel along both banks of the river and constructed a water pumping mill of his own design. By using the weir, the entire vineyards can be flooded. Ever resourceful, he made his own bricks for the cel-

lars from clay on the property. He made twin presses, wine pumps and casks—all from huge slabs of the massive red gums growing around the district. He also built a still.

Frank Potts appointed his third son, Frank Jr to take over responsibility for the operation as soon as he was old enough. Sons Fred, Henry and Edward planted their own vineyards. Edward also established his own winery, Kookaburra Cellars, which was absorbed into the Bleasdale cellars when Edward died in 1919.

Later in life, Frank Potts Sr confined his activities to boatbuilding and constructed everything from paddle steamers for the Murray River to racing yachts. He died in 1890, after a very active life and was surely one of the most amazing men in the history of Australian wine.

In 1904, Frank Jr purchased the Bridge Hotel in the township of Langhorne Creek and 36 adjoining hectares were cleared and planted. He died in 1917 leaving a widow, six sons and four daughters. Frank Jr's wife, Alice, carried on with the enterprise and made progress even through the 1930s depression. Strong women have always played a major role in the history of Bleasdale

Bleasdale winery.

These vineyards provide 60 per cent of the 990 tonne crush, from which Michael Potts makes a wide range of wines. The dry white verdelho is worth seeking for its solid flavours, and the madeira is an enriching experience; however, the finest wine of Bleasdale, as of the region in general, remains the cabernet sauvignon.

Middleton Estate, Middleton

Greg Marky and John Lewis in 1980 established a company called Marklew Wines and a wine operation called Middleton Estate, on Flagstaff Hill Road, 3 km inland from Middleton beach near Victor Harbor. On gently undulating alluvial country, Greg Marky has 10 hectares of semillon, riesling, cabernet sauvignon, shiraz and merlot. In an estate operation, winemaker and winery manager Nigel M. Catt uses only these grapes for the range of whites and reds and a champagne. The crush is 25 tonnes but this is being expanded to 300 tonnes as the vineyards, on a 47 hectare property, expand.

Middleton wines are available at cellar door and in certain restaurants. The biggest seller is the shiraz.

Temple Bruer

On the Angas River delta near Langhorne Creek, David and Barbara Bruer grow 8 hectares of red grape varieties, the planting of which started in 1973. An architect's son, David Bruer, who studied chemistry at Flinders University in Adelaide, had an interest in agriculture and thought of setting up a grapevine nursery. But he got involved with the Adelaide Amateur Brewers and Home Winemakers Club and instead found himself lecturing in chemistry at Roseworthy Agricultural College.

He established his vineyard, which like the Langhorne Creek vineyards uses flood irrigation, with such techniques as training the vines in Geneva double curtains, bunch reduction at flowering time, no herbicides, hand-pruning and hand-picking. He made the first wines in 1981 and started to develop techniques to match his excellent viticulture. Assisted by David Haeusler, he crushes 120 tonnes from his own vineyard and about 30 tonnes of white grapes from neighbours and other areas.

Temple Bruer, which has cellar door facilities

(as, indeed, in most wine pioneering, although they are rarely given adequate recognition by a paternally blinkered society). On her death in 1935, the estate was divided among her children. Arthur B. Potts inherited the winery and the original 40 hectares, which he converted to a company in 1948.

Until the mid–1960s mainly fortified wines were produced, but the range has now expanded to cover red and white table wines and sparkling wines as well as fortifieds.

Bleasdale, which has a National Trust classification and many historic and recreational attractions for visitors, now has twenty employees, directed by Ann Scutchings and Michael Potts. The family company's vineyards total 40 hectares of cabernet sauvignon, shiraz, malbec, merlot, verdelho, riesling and grenache on the alluvial flood plains. The vines are kept reasonably cool in summer by the tempering effect of the nearby Lake Alexandrina. In some years the floods have come early, even before all the grapes are harvested. Bleasdale must be the only wine company in the world which has had to harvest grapes by rowboat, as photographs in their gallery attest.

in nearby Langhorne Creek, releases Eden Valley riesling, Auburn chablis, botrytis riesling, dry rosé, sparkling burgundy, hermitage–malbec and cabernet–merlot. The red blends are finely flavoured wines.

Tonkin's Currency Creek Winery, Currency Creek

On 19 July 1969 Wally and Rosemary Tonkin set up a wine operation at Currency Creek near Goolwa, where the Murray River enters the Southern Ocean, and near the site of the first white explorations and settlements in South Australia. It was originally called Santa Rosa, but as the Spanish-looking building expanded with an excellent rural restaurant and peacocks and other exotica strutting around, and as the wines gained some note, Wally Tonkin chose to stress his name and that of the location.

Wally Tonkin, from a farming background at nearby Strathalbyn, likes growing things. Chief among his loves on the estate are grapes, and he has 18.5 hectares under vine: chardonnay, semillon, sauvignon blanc, riesling, pinot noir, cabernet sauvignon and shiraz. The soils are sandy loam slopes running to black peat by the nearby Black Swamp. The location's unique microclimate, almost a Bordeaux homoclime, tempered in summer by Lake Alexandrina, grows some of the best sauvignon blanc and semillon in the state. The fine-flavoured wines are made by Wally's son, Phillip Tonkin, with Brian Croser of Petaluma as a consultant.

It is a total estate operation using only the company's own grapes to crush 200 tonnes and produce 5000 cases of varietals, plus champagnes and fortified wines. The premium wines sell out each year, the firmly herbaceous sauvignon blanc usually being the first to go.

Coonawarra

There is a magic to the name Coonawarra for winelovers in Australia, and for many in other countries. No other area of the nation has so established itself as so consistently producing such splendid dry red wines. There is also a magic to the place, although it is not so readily apparent to the casual visitor.

Coonawarra, which is midway between

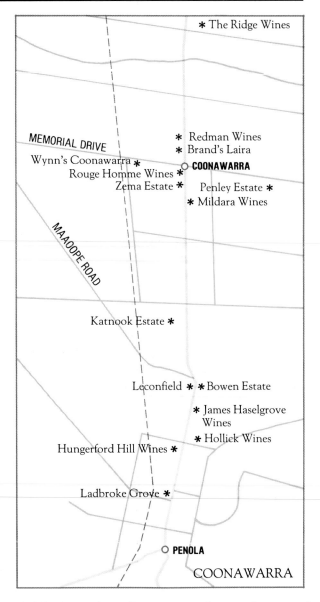

Adelaide and Melbourne in the south-east of South Australia, and off the main highways at that, is not exactly a tourist mecca. Those who do flash through, perhaps to fill up the car boot with a new wine release from one of the small, lesser known winemakers, and perhaps to stay overnight at one of the comfortable motels, may see little more than the verdant and vigorous vines across the marrow-chilling, cold plains. But there is a strange beauty to this flat country, with its leaden skies by day and sometimes the aurora australis blazing across the night sky, or eerie and inexplicable lights across what remain of the swamps. Some of the romance of the region has been communicated by such poets as John Shaw Neilson; some of the mysticism seems also to be communicated in the red wines it grows.

Soil, climate and the way the vines are handled by the vignerons also play a part in this wine which, for quality, matches that of the fat lamb, cheeses, vegetables, pine forests, fallow deer and lobsters harvested in the south-eastern green triangle of South Australia.

The principal viticultural section of Coonawarra is fertile red soil, varying from 200 m to 1.5 km wide. This is the dirt the locals call 'terra rossa', a strip 15 km long of richly nutritious red loam, friable and porous and to a depth of 30 cm at the most. The subsoil is calcareous and chalky, consisting of modular travertine limestone and clay to a depth of 1.5 m. On either side of the terra rossa is the heavy black rendzina, almost claylike in texture and more difficult to work than the red—although much more useful now that the region has been drained. Tiny shells are found here—remnants of times when the land was covered by the Southern Ocean which, now only 60 km away and 60 m lower, continues to exert a maternal influence on the area. The subsoil is similar to that of the terra rossa.

Underneath both sorts of soil is a high and pure table of water which plays a critical role in viticulture. The roots of the sturdy *Vitis vinifera* quickly penetrate the hard limestone shell, difficult as it seems, and draw on this water, resulting in vines of great vigour. For some winemakers, the vigour and the yields are too much, and they slash back the foliage in summer to keep the crops and quality manageable. The theory, which seems almost like a political philosophy, is that vines that get it too easy put everything into short-term indulgences of leaf growth and not enough into firm grape flavour.

Such conditions underground also need the right climate for ripening the grapes in summer, and Coonawarra has that. It is situated at 37°17'S, which is as far south from the equator as any vineyards, save some in Victoria and Tasmania. This means that after the wet winters—and this region has wet winters—there is a long mild summer, with a seven-month growing season.

The number of hours of sunshine is a significant factor in the quality of table wine. Ideally, there should be no more than the adequate amount of sun to ripen the grape over a relatively long period so that the full flavour and sugars can develop while the acidity is retained. In warmer climates the sugars come on too fast for the acids, and in really cold climates the grapes simply do not ripen. In traditional Australian fortified wines and commercial table wines, the acid balance is not so important, because the acid can be adjusted in the winemaking process; however, in table wines with aspirations to subtle elegance and longevity, the natural balance is important.

One measure of the product of temperature and days of sunshine is heat summation. Coonawarra has a heat summation of 1285°C/days, which is the same as Bordeaux in France.

Such a climate can also present problems for grapegrowers. When the summers are too cloudy or cold, ripening in Coonawarra can be difficult. With harvest late in the season, extending into April and sometimes even June for some wine styles, autumnal rains can bring on the risk of fungal diseases, although there is an increasing ability to control these. One of them, Botrytis cinerea, is actually desirable as an integral part of late-harvested white grapes for dessert wines.

Winter and spring frosts can be a hazard in Coonawarra and the overhead sprinklers on many Coonawarra vineyards are not there for summer irrigation, as virtually none is required —but in the worst frosts, the sprinklers spray fine droplets of water into the air, which freeze and protect the naked plants from frosts.

Being at the mercy of all these climatic factors, Coonawarra does have its marginal years, those when the quality is less than others; but the wines in good years are among the finest in the world, with dark purple colours when young, developing with maturity a glowing richness of red colour. They are strong and rich of flavour, but without the big-bodied blowziness of warmer climate wines. Tannic grip and high acidity give them the balance to age with complexity and refinement.

The inventor of Penfold's Grange Hermitage, Max Schubert, has declared shiraz to be the king of the grape varieties grown in Coonawarra; but most winemakers put their money on cabernet sauvignon, perhaps because in the 1970s this started becoming a more fashionable name on the Australian wine market. Some of the best wines, however, have been blends of the two varieties, such as Lindeman's Limestone Ridge. Winemakers are also discovering merlot, malbec and cabernet franc as blending varieties for greater palate complexity. Pinot noir and various white varieties have been tried in Coonawarra with varying degrees of success.

Since the 1970s there has been a new push for improved viticultural techniques in Coonawarra, led by such big-company viticulturists as Ian Hollick, Vic Patrick and Colin Kidd; this has been accompanied by a realisation among winemakers that Coonawarra is a name to be fostered and guarded jealously.

As much as half the fruit grown in Coonawarra is bought, either as grapes or as finished wine, by outside companies. The large ones, such as Orlando and Chateau Reynella, use it with integrity, proudly proclaiming on the labels that the wine is from Coonawarra; some companies, however, use Coonawarra material to bolster their own and often inferior produce. The level of integrity of those producers resident in Coonawarra is, like those of Clare, remarkably high.

The reign of Coonawarra as a great wine region is surprisingly brief, dating really from the 1950s. But it was established as a viticultural area in 1890 by John Riddoch who formed the Coonawarra Fruit Colony, including the growing of wine grapes.

The visionary Riddoch was born in Banffshire, Scotland, in 1826 and went to Victoria in 1852, with his parents and four brothers, in search of gold. In 1861 John Riddoch with his wife and children bought a 13 750 hectare property called Yallum near Penola in South Australia and ran 50 000 sheep with cattle, horses and deer. He was encouraged by a Scottish shepherd and gardener, William Wilson, who had come from the gold rush to find that in the Penola area fruit trees and vines grew as if by magic. Wilson, therefore, is often considered the pioneer, although it took Riddoch to translate this to a grander scale.

As a prominent local identity, Riddoch served in State Parliament and became close friends with the poet Adam Lindsay Gordon. After retiring from Parliament, he took a portion of his estate, which had grown by this time to 250 sq. km, and surveyed 800 hectares to be the Coonawarra Fruit Colony, in blocks of 4 to 12 hectares. Settlers were charged £25 a hectare and given ten years to pay at 5 per cent interest. As

an encouragement, Riddoch planted 100 hectares of his own land with vines and fruit trees. While the experiment was still in the flush of enthusiasm, John Riddoch, half medieval feudal baron, half modern property developer, died at Yallum on 15 July 1901, at the age of seventy-three.

Riddoch is honoured today, but his colony failed after only fifteen years, through faulty economics, bad judgments about allotment sizes, inadequate preparation for the severe weather and human error. Not even the appointment of Roseworthy gold medallist Ewen Ferguson McBain as winemaker, and the building of an imposing triple-fronted stone cellar—variously known as Chateau Comaum, and Wynn's Coonawarra Estate—produced the great wines that were expected. Some leaseholders simply walked off, bitter and angry, as their grapes went to distillation; 140 hectares stood uncertainly silent. Further factors working against Coonawarra were that marketing wine from such an obscure and physically remote region, notwithstanding the addition of a railway line, was extremely difficult; and, like the Adelaide Hills, the region was capable of producing only fine table wines when the market wanted heavy fortifieds.

Through the 1920s, 1930s and 1940s, some of the blockers battled on—names such as Webber, Arnz, Sharam, Alexander, Hoffman, Darwent, Alders, Pounsett, Snelling, Treikelman, Skinner, Richardson and Childs. Some of those names are still there. But one person saved Coonawarra— Bill Redman.

Redman's tenacity, and the help of some external supporters, enabled the region to survive for the next half a century of failure. Then came the renaissance, which can almost be traced in decades: the promotion in the 1940s of the region by Tony Nelson of Woodley Wines; the purchases in the 1950s by David Wynn of Chateau Comaum; the growth in the 1960s of public interest in table wines and the move into Coonawarra of big money; the boom in the 1970s of technologically sophisticated winemakers; and the new viticultural technologies of the 1980s—the world had discovered Coonawarra.

If Coonawarra as a great wine name is a relatively recent development, the broadacre viticultural region of Padthaway, 64 km to the north, is even newer. Sheep safely grazed amid the beautiful tall gums of this area, south of the village of Padthaway towards Keppoch, until Karl Seppelt, who also pioneered vineyards development at Drumborg, planted a broadacre vineyard here in 1964. Lindemans, Wynns, Hardy, Tolley's Pedare and private growers followed, all with large vineyards to supply wineries elsewhere, for the Padthaway region has no wine-production facilities.

The original theory was that cool-climate viticulture on fertile soils with reliable weather would provide reasonable-quality grapes anonymously for commercial table wines and champagnes, with low production costs through economies of scale. Fortunately for wine drinkers, Padthaway turned out to grow some fine fruit indeed, especially the white varieties. Lindemans was to the fore in recognising this and produced many 100 per cent Padthaway varietal wines, labelled as such.

Some Coonawarra vignerons, jealously guarding the name of their region, get touchy about Padthaway and are quick to point out that it has differences. It does, the chief one being that it does not have the history or even the intrinsic romance of the land further south; but it has many more similarities with Coonawarra, including soils over porous limestone over high water tables and cool and humid climates. Indeed, throughout the south-east of South Australia there are thousands and thousands more hectares of similar land, even with occasional patches of terra rossa. If global pollution further exacerbates the atmosphere's so-called Greenhouse Effect, warming southern Australia noticeably, it can be expected that the twenty-first century will see considerable viticultural expansion in this area.

Official statistics put Padthaway and Coonawarra together as having 3200 hectares under vine, which is 13.9 per cent of South Australia's vineyards, and constantly expanding. The yield is 20 000 tonnes of wine grapes. Such quantitative figures do no justice to the qualitative role of Coonawarra, and increasingly of Padthaway.

Bowen Estate

Doug and Joy Bowen are uncluttered people, keen of intelligence, big of heart and dedicated to their wine estate; it shows in their wines, the reds of which are quickly snapped up for the cellars of the cognoscenti with each release.

Doug Bowen has a rural background, brought

Bowen Estate winery.

PRODUCE OF   AUSTRALIA

BOWEN ESTATE

COONAWARRA

CABERNET SAUVIGNON MERLOT

1987

ESTATE GROWN AND PRODUCED BY
D. F. & M. J. BOWEN   COONAWARRA   SOUTH AUSTRALIA
PRESERVATIVE (220) ADDED

750 ml   12.7% Alc./Vol.

Doug Bowen, while making some of the finest reds in Coonawarra, all from his own vineyard, is also a source of inspiration and help to others in the region. That generosity of spirit seems also to be reflected in his cleanly and richly flavoursome wines.

Brand's Laira

As a baker, Eric Brand was familiar with yeasts and fermentation, which is fundamental to the grape's leap to immortality in winemaking. That may have disposed him to the business. So too did marrying Nancy, daughter of Bill Redman, during World War II. In 1950 they bought an orchard block which had been part of the original Coonawarra Fruit Colony, established by John Riddoch. It was planted with peaches and apricots, and with grapes which Eric Brand sold to the Redmans for wine.

The 28 hectare property includes the original vineyards of Captain Stentiford, who had retired there from the sea in 1986, and named it Laira after a sailing ship which traded around Australian and New Zealand ports in the 1890s. The name Laira was adopted as a brand name for the wine the Brands were to make and a depiction of the ship marked the label.

In 1965 Lindemans bought Rouge Homme from the Redmans and Eric Brand decided to make his own wine. He began humbly with an antique basket press, a must pump and four concrete fermenters he built himself. The first bottling under the Laira label was in 1966, with the help of sons Bill and Jim. Over the years the

up in Mildura after his father, a Melbourne pharmaceutical chemist, moved to the River for health reasons. Doug Bowen went to an agricultural college but at intercollegiate sports meetings encountered such blokes as Phil Laffer and Phil Waldeck, who told him about the 'plonkies' course' (as oenology at Roseworthy Agricultural College was sometimes called). Bowen was fascinated by the mechanics of winemaking. 'I had picked and pruned around Mildura,' he recalled, 'and could never understand how those rotten sweaty sultanas could be turned into a decent bottle of booze. (I now know they can't!)'

He went to Roseworthy College and graduated in 1971. He worked for Chateau Tahbilk, Hungerford Hill, on the Murray, and in Mildara's vineyards at Coonawarra—the region to which he had felt drawn since making a special study of it at college. In 1972 he and Joy bought the property that became Bowen Estate and started planting 23 hectares of cabernet sauvignon, shiraz, merlot, riesling and chardonnay. The grapes are grown with the minimum of sprays and are picked by hand.

Bowen was a winemaker with the great John Vickery at Lindemans in Coonawarra from 1975 to 1977, when he left to open his own property to the public. The original tasting room was a shack at the back of the ramshackle house and almost all the winemaking was done in the open air. He later built an impressive cellar building of local Mount Gambier sandstone and the first vintage in that was 1982.

Eric Brand and his sons, Jim and Bill, in the Laira winery.

business expanded and annual production grew to more than 140 000 litres.

The original winery, adjacent to the new Redmans winery, became offices and a charming tasting room; out the back is a new and well-equipped winery.

The vineyard consists of 16 hectares, planted to shiraz, cabernet sauvignon, malbec, grenache, merlot and white varieties. These give a range of table wines and the occasional sparkling burgundy; but it is the reds that uphold the Brand's tradition. The periodic releases of Original Vineyard shiraz, from 1896 vines, show a big smooth red with a terrific concentration of flavour.

Both sons, Bill and Jim, studied at the Riverina College of Advanced Education and have been able to maintain the dry solidity of Eric Brand's style while modernising the wines.

Nancy Brand inherited from the Coonawarra Fruit Colony a magnificent stand of walnut trees growing down the drive from the main road to the winery, and from these she makes pickled walnuts. The menfolk might have won gold medals with their wines but she has won not a few local pickles competitions with her walnuts, which are sold at cellar door and marvellously complement the wines.

James Haselgrove Wines

James Haselgrove has 12 hectares of vines in the southern part of Coonawarra, as well as four at McLaren Vale. The Coonawarra operation features a luncheon restaurant, serving the wide range of wines under his labels, which total

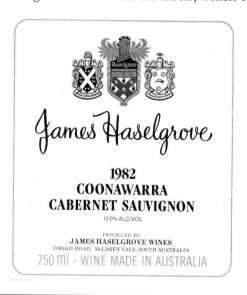

12 000 cases. Among the interesting wines from the Julianne vineyards at Coonawarra are a wood-matured riesling and a floral gewurztraminer.

Hollick Wines

As a prominent victiculturist, Ian Hollick might be expected to know something about grapes. He was vineyards manager for Mildara Wines in Coonawarra from 1979 to 1983, in the footsteps of his uncle Bob Hollick. He put that knowledge to his own service as well with a vineyard he started planting in 1975, called the Neilson Estate, at the southern end of the Coonawarra strip, and on the northern edges of the town of Penola. The grapes were sold to other wineries.

Ian Hollick and his wife, Wendy, went into their own winemaking business in 1983, with cellar door tasting and sales in the hut where poet John Shaw Neilson was born in 1872.

The purchase of a nearby block in 1987, replanted and named the Wilgha vineyard, give a total of 24 hectares of immaculately tended cabernet sauvignon, shiraz, merlot, cabernet franc, pinot noir and riesling, using a blend of traditional and modern techniques according to the variety and wine style required. Hollick produces only dry table wines, a cabernet sauvignon blend, shiraz, pinot noir, chardonnay and riesling; but there are also a bottle-fermented champagne and a botrytis riesling when conditions permit.

Winemaking was helped along by Doug Bowen. But when a red won a trophy at a Melbourne Wine Show, Hollick hired a full-time winemaker, Pat Tocaciu, a 1975 oenology graduate from Roseworthy College and wine show judge, who came from Tollana and Penfolds in Nuriootpa but who was born at Mount Gambier.

Hollick reds quickly established a name for impeccable quality and the pinot noir is one of the real wines from that variety in the region.

Hungerford Hill Wines

A significant producer in the Hunter Valley region of New South Wales, Hungerford Hill acted in 1971 to secure its access to precious Coonawarra fruit by purchasing a 162 hectare property from Doug Balnaves. The first vine was planted by Bill Redman on 24 July 1971.

Doug Balnaves, who has lived in the area all his life, was retained as vineyard manager and he supervises 63 hectares, all mechanically pruned, most on terra rossa, and mainly of cabernet sauvignon, cabernet franc, merlot, pinot noir, chardonnay and riesling.

Most of the winemaking from the 270 tonne crush is done in the Hunter Valley, and the winemaker is Adrian Sheridan. The best of the Coonawarra material comes out under the Hungerford Hill Coonawarra Collection label.

In 1980 the company opened a cellar door tasting and sales outlet in Coonawarra, with a pretty picnic area, playground and lakes, managed by Kirsty Bailey.

Katnook Estate

Katnook is said to be an indigenous word meaning 'fat land' and this could describe the fertile character of the Coonawarra district of which Katnook is one of the major names, if not well known. The proprietor is a major Coonawarra grapegrower but only a small part of the fruit handled is selected for its own Katnook label.

The property was one of the earliest leases granted in the region, issued in 1851 to Messrs Solomon, Josiah and Thomas Austin. The lease, known as Cupman and Penola, included what were to become Yallum homestead and the Coonawarra railway station. John Riddoch purchased his land from this property on 10 June 1863. Riddoch set up an office at Katnook House in 1890 to manage the affairs of his Coonawarra Fruit Colony and this building still stands. It is depicted on Katnook labels.

Young vines in the Hungerford Hill vineyards.

When Riddoch's scheme collapsed, the Crown took over Yallum Estate in March 1906, when it was subdivided again. Katnook station was then 350 hectares.

Current vineyard plantings started in 1968 when the Melbourne-based pastoral company, Rentiers Pty Ltd, controlled by financiers David and Peter Yunghanns, moved into the area with the Coonawarra Machinery Company. It has 400 hectares under vine. Leon Oborn supervises the growing of, principally, riesling, chardonnay, cabernet sauvignon, shiraz and pinot noir, with the aim of producing long-living table wines with soft tannins and full flavours.

Katnook Estate started making red wine in limited quantities in 1977 and subsequently expanded the crush and the processing facilities. The winery is in the original Katnook woolshed, where John Riddoch made his second vintage at Coonawarra before building his own cellars. Katnook harvests all varieties by mechanical harvesters, working in shifts through the night and delivering the grapes to the winery within an hour of picking.

The first full commercial vintage, bearing the distinctive Katnook label, was 1980. The company creams off the best of the fruit it handles to produce 30 000 cases annually of Katnook chardonnay, cabernet sauvignon, riesling, pinot noir and chardonnay brut champagne. It also releases the more affordable Riddoch range of riesling, cabernet sauvignon, shiraz, chardonnay and fumé blanc (some of which are grown at the company's vineyards at Iraak on the Murray River in Victoria, and which must be the only example of fruit coming into the south-east from elsewhere).

The general manager is Ray Stehbens, a self-taught engineer from a cane-growing family in Queensland. He moved to Coonawarra with his family in 1968, running the Coonawarra Machinery Company, and when he was commissioned to start the winery for the company he went off to do some studying at the Riverina College at Wagga Wagga, as he says, 'so I'd know what I was talking about'.

His son, Wayne Stehbens, assisted by John Weeks, is winemaker. He started the oenology course at the Riverina College but, like his father, preferred practical experience. That paid off when a Melbourne Wine Show trophy was

awarded to his Riddoch cabernet sauvignon 1986, made from Coonawarra fruit.

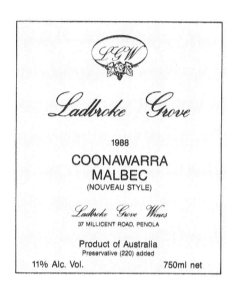

Ladbroke Grove

Peter and Carol McDonald set up Ladbroke Grove on 1 January 1982, with 2 hectares of vineyard in the middle of Coonawarra, growing cabernet sauvignon and shiraz. This provides most of their crush of 10 tonnes, from which 1000 cases of cabernet sauvignon, shiraz, riesling and malbec are produced.

The wines are processed at the former power house and cold store on the Millicent Road, and the tasting and sales area is in the main street of Penola in the former Penola Hotel (now the Bushman's Restaurant, behind which is the Coonawarra Motor Lodge), in which the McDonalds are partners. The name Ladbroke Grove was taken from the Tube station near which Peter and Carol McDonald lived in London.

Leconfield, Coonawarra

Everybody, except those who knew him, thought Sydney Holmes Hamilton had retired when he left Hamilton's Ewell Vineyards in 1955, to safely potter about in his vineyards at Happy Valley. But, in 1974, at the age of seventy-six, he set up a winery in Coonawarra, determined to make an Australian cabernet sauvignon of Bordeaux style. In less than a decade he'd pretty well got there.

He brought a wealth of experience to it, of course, as patriarch of one of the wine industry's

LECONFIELD

COONAWARRA
1986
CABERNET MERLOT

CHATEAU BOTTLED AT LECONFIELD, COONAWARRA
750ml PRODUCE OF AUSTRALIA 12·5% ALC/VOL
PRESERVATIVE (220) ADDED

Coonawarra is Australia's finest wine growing district. The Leconfield vineyard has a reputation for producing fine wine year after
year, maintaining a consistent high quality whilst asserting its
unique character over different vintages. This first blend of two
classic grape varieties demonstrates these qualities which makes
Leconfield red wine arguably some of the finest in Australia.

famous families and as a winemaker who had made significant contributions to the development of Australian wine this century.

The Hamilton family was among the first in South Australia to grow grapes for commercial wines. Richard Hamilton, who started it all, was born on 13 February 1792 in Scotland, almost two centuries before the Hamilton name was to reach Coonawarra. On 7 June 1837 he bought a land order, signed by Robert Torrens and Rowland Hill, which gave him the right to take up land in South Australia. With obvious alacrity he departed for Port Adelaide, arriving in October 1837 with his wife Anne and their large family. They took up the designated block in the Marion district near Glenelg and named it Ewell after their former home in Surrey.

Richard Hamilton cleared the land and planted 2 hectares with vine cuttings he had brought from Cape Town, in either late 1837 or 1838. The vineyard, which was 3 km from the sea, grew to 63 hectares and by 1840 it is said 5500 litres of wine was being made at Ewell.

The Hamiltons, like many Australian wine-makers, developed a family tradition of sons following their fathers in the business. Henry Hamilton followed Richard, who died at the age of sixty, and was responsible for considerable new plantings in 1860. Henry's son, Frank, was eventually followed by his grandson, Eric, whose son Robert became chairman of Hamilton's . . . until the dynastic control ended when the

Victorian-based Mildara group bought the company. The Ewell vineyards were eventually snuffed out by the asphalt of a bus depot.

However, the Hamiltons had spread their net wider than Ewell (and the echoes keep ringing throughout the story of South Australian wine, not just in Coonawarra). The Hamiltons had acquired a winery at Springton in 1938, which had been built by William Rayner in 1890 on land that belonged to Oscar Benno Seppelt. This Adelaide Hills winery went to Mildara, but a branch of the Hamilton family bought it back again. Other properties bought and then sold included the Wood Wood vineyards in Victoria and the Old Mill Bond Store in the Adelaide Hills, which became Petaluma's Bridgewater Mill.

Meanwhile, back at Ewell, Frank Hamilton's wife, Violet, gave birth to Sydney in 1898. The lad spent several years as a merchant seaman before returning to the winery. After a taste of a champagne, which his brother Eric brought back from France, Syd conceived the idea of making a light, semi-sparkling white wine, despite disbelief in the wine trade. This was the start of the famous Ewell moselle, a style which its creator claimed changed considerably since its inception in the early 1930s, becoming a still, light, sweetish white and one of the biggest sellers in Australia.

Hamilton visited vineyards in France in 1936 and in the Champagne region found out about temperature control. He introduced it to Australia in 1937, a technique that helped revolutionise antipodean winemaking. Not content to retire on these laurels, he investigated the eastern states and Tasmania for a site on which to grow his dream red wine, and settled on Coonawarra. He won the approval of Bill Redman for the selection of his piece of land, a derelict 27 hectare farming property.

Syd Hamilton, after planting and building up Leconfield for six years, sold it to his nephew, Dr Richard Hamilton, who already owned a vineyard and winery at Willunga in the McLaren Vale region, specialising in white wines. He pursued his uncle's philosophy and his 1982 cabernet won a trophy at the Sydney Wine show. The integrity of Leconfield was demonstrated when, the following year, the entire red wine production was dumped, as Doug Bowen across the road also did, because of fungal infection in the vineyards. For so many different reasons, in different regions, 1983 was a terrible vintage for South Australian winemakers.

The winery, run by Hugh Hamilton, has 55 hectares of vineyards on terra rossa, growing cabernet sauvignon, merlot, cabernet franc, shiraz, riesling and chardonnay. There is also a small plot further south, next to Ian Hollick's, planted to pinot noir and chardonnay for a champagne released under the Richard Hamilton label. Richard Hamilton and John Innes make the wine in a total estate operation, producing 8000 cases of dry reds and whites, with sweet whites when conditions are favourable. Leconfield cabernet sauvignon has consistently been a neatly structured and enjoyable red.

Mildara Wines

In the 1950s, when the Australian wine industry was discovering Coonawarra, the Victorian-based group, Mildara Wines (founded in 1888), was one of the first major companies to follow Wynns in securing a presence on the terra rossa. The company started buying wine for Redmans in 1953, at higher prices than had previously been paid; and in 1955 bought 12.5 hectares of orchard for £3000, which was planted to vines and supervised by the Redman family. As riesling, semillon and palomino had not been used for wine in Coonawarra before, a few hectares of each were planted experimentally, in addition to the traditional cabernet sauvignon and shiraz. Expansion started in 1960 with the purchase of 16 hectares of old shiraz vines, and Ray Edwards was appointed vineyards manager, establishing a tradition for Mildara of viticultural excellence.

Further additions were made to the Mildara holdings and they came to total 400 hectares, with viticulturist Brendon Provis continuing the traditions of Ray Edwards, Bob Hollick and Ian Hollick. Principal varieties are cabernet sauvignon, shiraz, merlot, cabernet franc, malbec, chardonnay, riesling and sauvignon blanc. The Mildara vineyards have poplars growing around them like huge hedges; they look pretty and act as efficient windbreaks.

The Mildara emphasis on the vines is reflected in the appointment as manager at Coonawarra of Vic Patrick, who achieved prominence as vineyards manager for Wynns, up the road.

Mildara wines, Coonawarra winery.

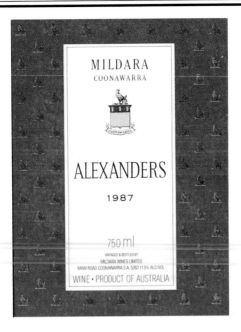

Patrick was a graduate of both Roseworthy College and the College of Viticulture and Oenology at the University of Surrey in Britain, and was with Wynns from 1973 to 1987. He also has his own vineyard which, appropriate to his Irish name, he calls the Blarney Block.

Up to and including the 1962 vintage, the grapes grown by Mildara were vintaged at the Redman's Rouge Homme cellars and provided the wines used in the first Mildara cabernet–shiraz blends. Indeed, that is why winemaker H.R. Haselgrove up at Merbein wanted Coonawarra fruit in the first place, to elevate the Bin 23 blends. But the Mildara tonnage was becoming too much for the Redmans to handle and a Mildara cellar became essential. This was built and processed the 1963 cabernet, the first 'pure' Mildara Coonawarra red. Many in the company had misgivings, but it proved to be one of the company's great vintages and the line became an Australian classic.

The Coonawarra winery went through some bad patches. The product survived them because of the intrinsic quality of the fruit, and the white label cabernet sauvignon has been a consistently flavoured red of delicious quality. Gavin Hogg as winemaker at Coonawarra, handling a crush of 3000 tonnes, maintains the white label tradition, and the interesting white varietals; he has also helped Mildara achieve a greater complexity in its herbaceous style of red wines with two new lines developed in the 1980s, Alexanders and Jamiesons Run.

Alexanders is a blend of cabernet sauvignon, merlot, cabernet franc and malbec, made with techniques Gavin Hogg learnt while on study trips to Bordeaux. The varieties are fermented separately with a yeast strain from Bordeaux and the juice pumped over bundles of vine canes to help extract colour and complexity from the skins. After fermentation, the cap of skins is allowed to sink and macerate with the wine. Further complexity is added with maturation in hogsheads of Troncaise, Vogues, Alliers and Nevers oak. The result, launched from the 1986 vintage, is a magnificent wine, rich in fruit flavours, powerfully structured yet finishing dry and elegant, and capable of great cellar life. The Jamiesons Run is a somewhat similar line, blended of cabernet, merlot, malbec and shiraz—at a considerably cheaper price—and it achieved great popularity.

Penley Estate

Kym Tolley, of the Tolley wine family and also the great-great-great-grandson of Dr Christopher Penfold (hence Pen-ley), started planting a vineyard 2 km from central Coonawarra on 12 July 1989. Tolley, who graduated with a wine-marketing diploma from Roseworthy College in 1976, most recently worked with Penfolds at Nuriootpa before going solo.

Stage one of Penley Estate was planting 47 hectares of the 166 hectare property with cabernet sauvignon, pinot noir, shiraz and chardonnay, and the release of the first shiraz–cabernet, with fruit sourced from Coonawarra, the Barossa and McLaren Vale. Stage two was planned for 1990—the planting of 40 hectares and the building of a cellar. The aim is to settle on a chardonnay, three reds and a champagne.

Redman Wines

The Redman name has been synonymous with Coonawarra. The pioneer Redman, William Leonard, had an enormous influence on the development of the wines of the area and was to Coonawarra what Maurice O'Shea was to the Hunter Valley and Colin Preece to Great Western.

Bill Redman arrived in Coonawarra in 1901, the year of the death of the founder of the infant

Redmans' Redbank winery.

Coonawarra Fruit Colony, John Riddoch. He was fourteen at the time, sixth in a family of seven boys and three girls. His Mancunian father, John Redman, was a railway ganger at Stewart's Range near Naracoorte, where the family ran the post office. Bill had left school in the fourth grade and gone to work for a skin buyer in Naracoorte for five shillings a week before going to Coonawarra with his sixteen-year-old brother Albert ('Dick'), looking for work. They were employed in Riddoch's winery, Dick picking grapes and Bill working in the cellars, being paid £1 for a six-day week. At the end of the grape-picking season he was given a permanent job.

He learnt to make wine under the guidance of Ewen Ferguson McBain, a Roseworthy College graduate and a good teacher. Bill stayed at Coonawarra through a bad period to become head cellarman at the age of nineteen. After a short spell away doing farm work at Pinnaroo, he returned and stayed.

By then, Bill's father was working a dairy at Coonawarra with two other sons. When 16 hectares of Riddoch's vineyards came up for sale, the family bought the property on generous terms: £150 deposit and the balance of £750 over ten years at 4 per cent interest. Bill went into partnership with father and brother Robert in 1908.

The Redmans did well out of their first vintage, which went to make Riddoch brandy. This was the only time Redman grapes were not used for wine. Bill Redman got the backing of Douglas A. Tolley in 1909 to make wine for export to Britain. Tolley sent the hogsheads to Coonawarra and agreed to pay a shilling a gallon. The Redmans had no winemaking equipment and began with a crusher bought from the teetotal Alexander family, on the condition that none of the wine made from it could be sold in the area. They had little other equipment and simply improvised, using Tolley's hogsheads, with the tops removed, for fermentation.

In 1920 Tolley refused to buy any more Redman wine because its high quality affected the sale of Tolley's other wines—clients in Britain wanted only the Coonawarra wines. Bill Redman then arranged with Colonel David Fulton of Woodley Wines to take his wine, provided it could be matured in oak casks in Coonawarra for two years first. Colonel Fulton advised Redman to lighten the style with earlier picking, more of a claret, and thus the forerunners of modern Coonawarra reds were made.

Grapegrowing at Coonawarra was never a proposition that ran smoothly and from 1908 to 1946 Bill Redman made the only Coonawarra wines sold. The Redmans survived the crises of the area and kept on making wine, even though in December 1913 Bill married a niece of the poet John Shaw Neilson, Lilian Neilson, who was a notoriously strict Presbyterian.

In late 1945 the managing director of Milne and Co, which was then making brandy in Coonawarra, approached Bill Redman and said Coonawarra could not support two wineries. He made an offer to buy Redman's property. It was refused. So Milne sold the old Riddoch cellars

Redbank winery at Coonawarra.

and a company called Chateau Comaum Pty Ltd was formed to buy it, with Bill Redman as manager. This is the chateau that was to become famous under the Wynns name, featuring on all labels of Wynn's Coonawarra Estate wines.

When Bill's sons, Owen and Leonard, returned from service in World War II, they joined their father and jointly ran the cellars. Bill and Owen took the 10 hectares of vineyards and 100 hectares of open country and formed their own company, W.L. and O.D. Redman. In 1947 the Redmans entered their claret in the Adelaide Wine Show and won first prize, the first recognition of wine under their own name. In 1950 the company was renamed W.O. and D. Redman, when Len left the company and Don, just out of the RAAF, joined.

The Redmans continued to sell their wine to Woodley and for several years they competed in wine shows against themselves—the Redmans label against the Woodley label, although the Redmans had made both wines.

In 1952 David Wynn on behalf of his father, Samuel Wynn, bought the Riddoch cellars for S. Wynn and Co. In the same year, Bill Redman retired to become a kind of elder statesman of Coonawarra.

The Redmans continued making wines and in 1954 put their product on the market under the label Rouge Homme, a less than literate translation of their name, plucked from a French–English dictionary, so the legend goes. The Redmans were still selling some wine in bulk, as well as managing Mildara's new vineyards and winning wine show awards. By 1965 the fame of Coonawarra had been established and the big companies moved in. Rouge Homme then owned 160 hectares of terra rossa, with 30 hectares of vines in full bearing, and sold them to Lindemans. Within days of the sale to Lindemans, Owen Redman was back in business, buying 16 hectares from Arthur Hoffman, a descendant of one of the original colonists.

The Redmans–Lindemans sale was often painted as a classic conflict between the canny country yokel and the cityslicker accountants, with arguments about who won. Time showed that each won. Lindemans had the money and muscle to make a great national brand of Rouge Homme, and Redmans had the tenacity to keep their family traditions going. Bill Redman stayed on in Coonawarra, living with his daughter Nancy and son-in-law Eric Brand until he died at the age of ninety-two. Arthur Hoffman became a valued institution with Redmans Wines, as the company, which dates itself from 1966, was to become named. From 1966 to 1968 Owen made his wine in Brand's cellars, although his output was only 9000 litres a year. He took a trip around the world, tasting wines, and opened his attractive new Redbank Winery on 15 March 1969, next to Brands.

Don Redman took a wine retailing business in Adelaide for a while and Owen and Edna Redman went to live in Adelaide, commuting by Mercedes Benz for the vintage as the company passed to the control of sons Bruce, Duncan and Malcolm.

Bruce Redman graduated in oenology from Roseworthy College in 1975 and gained experience in McLaren Vale and the Barossa. In 1979 he went overseas for two years and worked in Bordeaux for a vintage. Duncan moved to London as a chartered accountant. Malcolm completed an apprenticeship in fitting and turning, specialising in the construction of wine equipment and plant maintenance.

Malcolm and Bruce Redman have 32 hectares

of cabernet and shiraz growing, yielding 340 tonnes in a total estate operation, with which they produce about 18 000 cases of dry red wine—nothing else. Wholesome, flavoursome, enjoyable and popular wine it is too.

It was once said that Bill Redman 'dreamt of Coonawarra becoming a kind of Medoc of the southern hemisphere, but he never really expected it to happen'. The expectation was wrong; the dream was right.

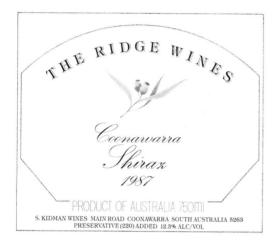

The Ridge Wines

Twenty kilometres north of Penola, as far north as the definition of Coonawarra properly stretches, Susie Kidman's grazing property named Limestone Ridge (being no relation to the Lindemans vineyard and wine of that name) was partly converted to wine production on 18 December 1984, with the establishment of The Ridge Wines.

The bottle sales area is a converted stables built in the 1850s, and the place, set amid tall gums as a relief to the vinous monoculture that prevails in the main part of Coonawarra, exudes a rural charm.

Sue and her husband, Sid Kidman, a descendant of the cattle baron Sir Sidney Kidman, have 2 hectares under vine, growing cabernet sauvignon, shiraz and riesling. From this, Ken gets 16 tonnes of grapes to make 1100 cases of three varietal wines with promise.

Rouge Homme Wines

Lindeman Holdings—which until its 1990 sale to the Penfolds group was the large Sydney-based wine arm of the Philip Morris tobacco corporation—like most other large Australian wine companies, could not remain immune when Coonawarra's fame and unique qualities started to become widely known in the 1950s. Following Wynns and Mildara, it took a stake in the region by buying the famous Redman vineyards and the trading name Rouge Homme in 1965. From these, and from its new plantings, it has made the Rouge Homme brand name truly famous. It has also made some magnificent wines from its Coonawarra vineyards under the Lindemans label, vying with Mildara and Wynns as the great Coonawarra red wine producer of major size.

The responsibility for this commitment by the Lindeman company to a place in the future lies with Ray Kidd, who was general manager in Sydney. After war service, and coming from a grapegrowing background, Kidd graduated from Roseworthy Agricultural College, as gold-medal dux in 1949, along with Tony Herbert, Doug Collett, Bryan Dolan and Ray Shipton. He brought to Lindemans formidable cellar skills and a sense of direction. The styles of wine produced throughout the company for three decades were largely a product of his personal tastes and personal vision. Not only Ray, but also Colin Kidd played an important role in developing the vineyards.

Colin Kidd joined the company in 1968 and became Lindeman's national vineyards manager, staying in Coonawarra as a measure of the importance of this region to the company.

The first new vineyard planted by Lindemans was Limestone Ridge, in 1966 and 1967. It is twenty hectares of shiraz and four of cabernet

Pruning, Rouge Homme vineyards.

sauvignon, and was the first vineyard in Australia with its own microclimate control system. One of its functions, during frost conditions, is to spray tiny water particles which freeze and protect the delicate shoots of the vine. This is the vineyard which produces the black-labelled Lindeman's Limestone Ridge cabernet–shiraz, one of the most magnificent richly flavoured, firmly structured red wines of Australia.

The St George Vineyard, which produces an individual-vineyard cabernet sauvignon of fine fruit and elegance, dates from the beginning of the century, when it was established by Surgeon Major-General Hinton St George, who built a home and planted vines on the property. These were grubbed out in the 1930s and the house became derelict. Lindemans believed it to be the best piece of land in the district and bought it in 1967, the following year planting it with cabernet sauvignon cuttings taken from the Rouge Homme vines, which in turn had come from the Riddoch nursery. Great care is devoted to this vineyard. Between 1972 and 1978, each vine in the 12 hectare property was monitored and the weakest replaced. The red soil between the vines

is kept bare to minimise interference with the feeding roots.

St Cedd's Vineyard, named after a local church, is 24 hectares, planted in 1972 with traminer, chardonnay, cabernet sauvignon, malbec, cabernet franc, merlot and pinot meunier.

The Nursery Vineyard, named after the vine nursery established by Henry Richardson on the site in 1892, is 35 hectares on the eastern side of the terra rossa strip. It was planted in 1969 and 1970 with cuttings from the Florita vineyards in the Clare Valley. Riesling was the dominant variety, with shiraz, cabernet sauvignon and muscadelle (tokay). As a comment perhaps on the role of red and white varieties in Coonawarra, the vineyards were replanted and grafted so that cabernet, shiraz, merlot, cabernet franc and malbec were the major varieties. The name was changed to the Pyrus Vineyard, since pears were among the fruit grown on the block in its days as part of the Coonawarra Fruit Colony. In 1985 Lindemans started making a red wine solely from this vineyard, labelling it Pyrus. The wine is a blend of cabernet sauvignon, merlot, cabernet franc and malbec and it is matured in new Nevers and Limousin oak puncheons and hogsheads before bottling. Pyrus has set new standards of complexity, richness and harmony in red wines for Lindemans, and it ranks with Mildara Alexanders and Wynn's John Riddoch as one of the most attractive red wines of Coonawarra.

With these four vineyards, and the Rouge Homme vineyards, which produce a range of high quality and popular reds and whites, Lindemans has about 200 hectares in Coonawarra—although the company does like to maintain separate identities in the marketplace for Lindemans and Rouge Homme. It also keeps its operations separate from others in the Penfolds group. The modern winery, opposite Skinners General Store in the centre of Coonawarra, also processes the fruit from the company's 580 hectares at Padthaway.

Lindemans, more than most large wine companies perhaps, believes in corporate art rather than individual art; when it comes to winemaking, many palates, usually led by Philip John who is based at the Karadoc winery, are involved in the decision-making and the blends. But the fine viticultural work of Colin Kidd found its counterpart when John Vickery, from the corporation's Leo Buring winery in the Barossa Valley, was in charge of the vintages at Coonawarra from 1975 to 1981. His skills in handling the magnificent fruit, and his attention to detail, firmly established Lindemans as a great red wine producer of Coonawarra. The reds are characterised by processing with an abhorrence of oxidation, by an emphasis on fruit quality almost to the point of portiness, by low-wood character and usually by the encouragement of early malolactic fermentation. Vickery was succeeded as winery manager by Greg Clayfield, from a local farming family and with an intuitive understanding of the area and its seasons. He was Vickery's understudy in 1980 and when the sorcerer's apprentice took over, the wine show trophies kept rolling in.

Wynn's Coonawarra Estate

As part of the Penfolds group of wine companies, Wynn's Coonawarra Estate handles the 90 hectares of Coonawarra vineyards established by Penfolds in 1961 as well as its own extensive holdings. It thus has 600 hectares under vine, under viticulturist David Murdoch, making Wynns the largest grower of the area. It also had one of the most substantial presences in the marketplace and, if indirectly, the longest history.

The cellars, which owe their survival to being bought by the Wynn family in the early 1950s—thus paving the way for the discovery of Coonawarra by other major wine companies—were built by John Riddoch for his abortive Coonawarra Fruit Colony. Through the early part of the twentieth century the vineyards around them produced fruit thought fit only for distillation, and the Barossa Company Chateau Tanunda bought them in 1919, planting more vines to make brandy. The enterprise was unsuccessful and by 1921 it had been bought by Milnes of Adelaide, which also thought the grapes fit only for brandy.

Woodley Wines, under the direction of first David Fulton, then Tony Nelson, had bought and championed the wines of Bill Redman, and in 1946 sought to secure a greater stake in Coonawarra grapes by buying the former Riddoch property. Woodley restored the cellars to production and renamed it Chateau Comaum,

WYNNS
COONAWARRA ESTATE*
CHARDONNAY
VINTAGE 1988
COONAWARRA ESTATE PTY. LTD.
WINE PRODUCT OF AUSTRALIA 750 mL

with an arrangement that Bill Redman and his sons would manage the vineyards and make the wine. The new enterprise had an inauspicious beginning with an attack of downy mildew. Not even Tony Nelson could succeed, and by 1951 it was decided to sell the place to grazing interests—which meant the vines would be uprooted and the cellars used as a woolshed.

Melbourne wine merchant Samuel Wynn had been buying wines quietly from Redmans for a few years, and he was particularly impressed with some of the wines from the 1930s and with how well they had aged. Samuel Wynn was appalled at the idea of allowing vineyards of such quality to become defunct and he tried to interest a number of large companies in forming a consortium to run the vineyards as a non-profit venture, but this idea was not warmly received. So he decided to buy Chateau Comaum and its 90 hectares, which his son David Wynn did on 2 October 1951. He had the inestimable help of Bill Redman's nephew Jock Redman as vineyard manager, and of a promising young winemaker, Ian Hickinbotham, who had graduated from Roseworthy College in 1950 and worked with the Wynns on the Modbury Estate project. Ian Hickinbotham was the second son of Alan Hickinbotham, the great educator at Roseworthy College, and made important contributions to Australian wine industry with his research into malolactic fermentation. After Wynns, Ian Hickinbotham worked at several wineries, most notably Kaiser Stuhl, and in a long and distinguished career sired Stephen Hickinbotham, one of the most brilliant winemakers of modern times in Australia, until his death in an air crash on 2 September 1986.

In 1952 Ian Hickinbotham produced the first Wynn's Coonawarra Estate claret.

The background to the extraordinary Wynn family, which endures in Adam Wynn at Mountadam in the Adelaide Hills, was with Shlomo Weintraub, who was born in Russian-occupied Poland in 1892 of a family that made wine from raisins for Jewish religious ceremonies. At the age of twenty-one, with his new bride Chava, he fled military service and on 12 November 1913 they arrived in Melbourne. One of his first actions in the new country was to change his name from Weintraub (meaning 'wine grape') to Wynn; and he became known as Samuel Wynn—Zionist, humanist and winemaker.

By 1918 he had bought a Bourke Street wine shop and two years later became proprietor of the Café Denat. Wine wholesaling followed, and successfully, being based on the principle of sound wine at low cost. Wynn found out how to make vermouth in 1925 and developed the brand Boronia. In the same year he became involved in winemaking at Magill in Adelaide and was responsible for exporting wine to Britain.

Samuel Wynn had three sons: two were doctors and the third, David Wynn, became managing director of S. Wynn and Co Pty Ltd, Samuel being the governing director. At the beginning of the 1950s, Wynns had begun marketing wines in glass half-gallon flagons to promote the everyday use of wine, and this was a forerunner of the Australian wine boom. Wynns was also one of the first companies to produce wine in 4 litre bag-in-the-box casks.

To ensure a supply of suitable grapes for flagons, the Modbury Estate was developed in the Adelaide foothills (subsequently to become housing), and the company, headquartered in Melbourne, established operations at Yenda. In 1970 Wynns became a public company listed on the Melbourne Stock Exchange. In February 1972 it was bought for $7.5 million to become part of the brewing concern, Castlemaine Tooheys, and eventually, in 1985, part of Adelaide Steamship's Penfolds group.

Samuel Wynn, combining natural talents with the opportunities of a developing country, had many successes; none greater, perhaps, than the move to Coonawarra. The national marketing of Wynn's Coonawarra Estate, and the reception by a nation starting to discover the pleasures of quality wine, attracted Mildara, Lindemans and others to develop Coonawarra further.

After the Wynns departed, the estate—like many other wineries of the time subject to the essentially unproductive takeover boom—was buffeted by the demands for returns on shareholders' funds. This was a bleak time for the winery, and investments in quality suffered. Wynns remained popular with its Coonawarra Estate hermitage especially, a bargain-priced red for many years; but it was not until the arrival of winemaker John Wade in 1978, a Riverina College graduate who had worked in the Hunter Valley, that some of the magic started to be regained. This was also the time when the viticultural work of Vic Patrick, who subsequently went to Mildara, started to bear fruit. A further stimulus to quality came with the Penfolds takeover and the production management of Robin Moody, and the winery management of Peter Douglas.

There have been many friendly arguments among winemakers in the cellar about which parcel of wine goes to Penfolds (for such wines as the Penfolds Bin 707 1986, which won the prestige Adelaide trophy as the best red in the 1989 Adelaide Wine Show), and which to the Wynns range. But Peter Douglas as winemaker, assisted by Peter Bissell, does enjoy a fair degree of autonomy from the group's production headquarters in Nuriootpa, and Penfolds considers Wynn's Coonawarra Estate—like Lindemans—an important institution with a great integrity of style to be maintained.

The wine range expanded to include riesling, chardonnay, shiraz (labelled as hermitage), cabernet–hermitage, pinot noir and cabernet sauvignon. From 1982, in good years, the company releases a John Riddoch cabernet sauvignon as its flagship, an intensely rich wine, powerfully oaked for longevity and a fitting partner to the best of Mildara and Lindemans.

Wynn's Coonawarra Estate wines are distinguished by their labels, featuring a woodcut of the triple-fronted cellars, built by John Riddoch. Fittingly, it is one of the best known premium wine labels in Australia.

Zema Estate

For refreshment of the spirit it is hard to beat the Zema family, who set up their own winery right in the middle of Coonawarra in 1982 and make wholesome, unpretentious plummy/berry Coonawarra reds in the traditional style. Demetrio Zema was a painter whose father and grandfather had made wine in Reggio Calabria, Italy. He and wife, Francesca, with sons Matt and Nick, have 8 hectares of vines next to Rouge Homme, growing mostly shiraz and cabernet sauvignon, hand-pruned, hand-picked, with no irrigation. The 70 tonne crush is handled by Matt Zema, under Ken Ward, a Riverite who has been known to drink water—occasionally. Ward is one of the widely experienced old hands of the business, who graduated from Roseworthy College in 1943.

As well as the wines, the winery also sells Francesca Zema's pickles, which are excellent.

Port Lincoln

Boston Bay Wines

The French explorer Nicholas Baudin found at the foot of South Australia's Eyre Peninsula what he thought to be the best place on the continent for a European settlement. He named it Port Champagny. He might have been right, for this place, which the indigenous Nauo people called Kallinyula, has a larger deep-water harbour even than Sydney. He might have been right about the name, too. The town of Port Lincoln which grew there on the shores of Boston Bay Harbour, a fishing industry centre and tourism paradise, was the scene of some grapegrowing in the nineteenth century, although with unrecorded results. But until the twentieth century, wine-growing regions had to be close to their markets, as McLaren Vale and the Barossa developed close by Adelaide. In the late twentieth century, Graham and Mary Ford planted the Boston Bay vineyards just north of Port Lincoln, and found rapid success.

Ford, an abalone diver and self-confessed adventurer, was persuaded by Richard Robertson, who had dabbled in winemaking in Clare, that the climate by the bay was a cross between McLaren Vale and Bordeaux and that grapes would flourish. In 1984 the two of them started planting 7603 vines on a former oats paddock, just across the highway from the azure water, 50 m away. Graham Ford passed the abalone diving business on to his sons, and he and his wife Mary became vignerons—tending the vines, building a cellar with playground and deer park for tourists, and promoting the wines initially in Adelaide, a mere 670 km by road away (but 250 km by air).

The soil is fast-draining over limestone, with an easterly aspect, and rainfall is 575 mm,

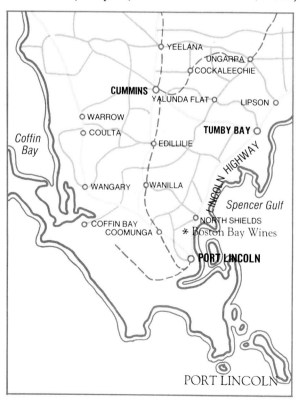

necessitating supplementary irrigation. The warmth of summer is tempered by the harbour breezes and the only viticultural problems appear to be the pretty but hungry Port Lincoln parrots and the salt spray. Four hectares of riesling, cabernet sauvignon and merlot are grown and the wine is processed by Doug Lehmann at Basedows in the Barossa. Graham Ford quite correctly describes the wine as 'a bloody good drop'.

The early success of the fleshy Boston Bay riesling, the first wine released, accelerated the plans of another local group, led by Dr Ian Fletcher, to develop its nearby Dallacolline Estate vineyard as a commercial wine operation.

It can confidently be predicted that Port Lincoln will not be a threat to Coonawarra; but, as with people who have tried grapegrowing on Kangaroo Island off the South Australian coast, it joyously broadens the possibilities in the Wine State.

Northern Territory: Alice Springs

Chateau Hornsby

Denis Hornsby set up a vineyard in the desert of the Northern Territory in 1979. Once, before that, he used to be sane, a pharmacy student in Melbourne, born at Deniliquin in New South Wales. Then he visited Alice Springs on his honeymoon with his wife, Miranda, and was bitten by the Centralian bug. He returned to run a pharmacy but, being an interested wine drinker, he determined to plant a couple of hectares of vines. After abandoning the first site, he purchased a 120 hectare block 11 km south-east of Alice Springs, on which a citrus orchard had been attempted, and planted 2.5 hectares with cabernet sauvignon, shiraz, riesling, semillon and chardonnay.

The land is gently undulating, deep, coarse red sand—redder than anything Coonawarra knows. It hardly ever rains. Drip irrigation is used, but it takes a lot of water, so porous is the soil, stretching the two bores to capacity. Kangaroos, birds and wirly-wirly winds are constant enemies of the grapes. The temperature on a summer's day might hit 44°C. And there is the constant temptation just to sit and look at the

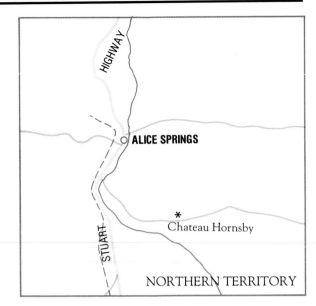

searing blue of the sky and the stunning red of the nearby Macdonnell Ranges, and open a cold can of beer. Still, such is the power of wine that Hornsby perseveres.

In 1977, with Roseworthy Agricultural College lecturer Gordon Cook as winemaker, the self-taught Hornsby, with a battered viticulture textbook his constant companion in the bull-dusted ute, produced his first wine. The best said about it was 'tolerable'.

The wines improved, the vineyards expanded and Miranda Hornsby opened a bush restaurant, with Centralian entertainments and access for tourists from Alice Springs by camel. It was an instant tourism success, but Denis

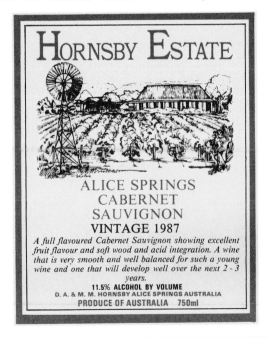

Hornsby remained serious about making wine, experimenting with double-pruning to force the ripening period into the cooler winters.

He has also learnt to ride with the climate. When a Chateau Hornsby label says 'early-picked', it is not a dig at late-picked wines, but means picked as early as December. This can be confusing when it comes to nominating the year of vintage. One wine was labelled as 'The first wine in the world'—picking the grapes, which is always a matter of friends and partying in the cool of night, started at a minute past midnight on the first day of January.

The 1500 cases produced annually by Chateau Hornsby are sold locally only. However, the rest of the world should know that with determination, effort, flair and wit—and perhaps a healthy touch of insanity—anything is possible, even growing wine in the desert in the middle of Australia.

Riverland

It is a sobering thought that in arid climates every drop of juice in the grape, and hence the wine made from it, has been drawn up through the trunk from the soil; in the case of wines from South Australia's Riverland that means basically from the Murray River. This vast area, producing more than half the state's wines, extending from Cadell at the west and upstream through Qualco, Waikerie, Kingston-on-Murray, Moorook, Glossop, Loxton and Berri to Renmark, is so arid that it is almost totally dependent on water from the massive Murray, Australia's largest river and doubtless the world's slowest flowing. A lazy old thing and a source of great romance, the Murray takes its time to flow 5000 km, fed by the melting snows of Kosciusko and the Great Dividing Range in New South Wales, down across the plains where it marks the

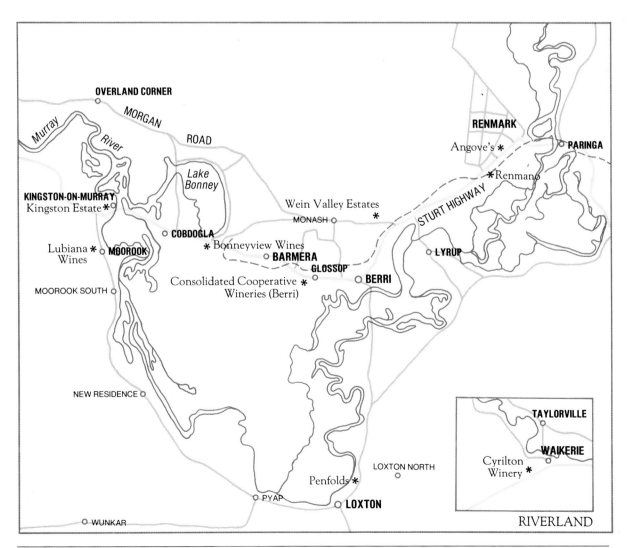

border between New South Wales and Victoria, across the flatlands of South Australia, into the treacherous Lake Alexandrina and, with one final exhausted gulp, across the sandbars of Goolwa into the Southern Ocean. With its tributaries, such as the Murrumbidgee and the Darling Rivers, it drains 107 million hectares, one seventh of the continent.

Beautiful yes, but with its annual flooding and the dispersal of so much water across the plains, it was seen last century as a waste for agriculture, fit only for the paddle steamers which carried the wool clips down to the sea when the river ran high and took back supplies to the pastoral stations. Under an agreement among the Federation-minded governments of New South Wales, Victoria and South Australia, a plan was evolved to erect a series of locks which retain the floodwaters and maintain the river at a high level throughout the year. The first ten locks were built between Blanchetown and Mildura (1600 km from the river mouth). The damming effects allowed widespread irrigation of the surrounding fertile plains and a complex system of dams, locks, pumping stations and irrigation channels developed.

While South Australia's Riverland contains 2.5 per cent of the state's population, it accounts for about 11 per cent of the gross value of rural production, all because of the development of irrigation in this sunny Mediterranean climate. The region produces 85 per cent of the state's stone fruit, 17 per cent of berries, 9 per cent of pome fruit, 95 per cent of citrus, 16 per cent of vegetables, 98 per cent of dried vine fruit, 94 per cent of table grapes and—of course—62 per cent of South Australia's wine grapes. Truly, a province of plenty.

Despite the extent of the region, viticultural conditions are basically similar throughout. The vineyards have generally been established on level or gently sloping land which is easily irrigated. The soils are mostly alluvial sandy loams of low humus content, overlying limestone subsoils. Along the Murray they can vary from fairly heavy clay to limestone and red sand but the area around Renmark consists of pure sand and this is characteristic of the area where the grapes are grown. Climatically, this holidaymaker's paradise is hot and dry, with summer temperatures above 30°C and annual rainfall of less than 250 mm. These are good conditions for growing crops under irrigation, and that is why, when the irrigation is not overdone, Riverland wines can be like bottled sunshine.

The vineyards vary considerably in size. Typically they consist of individually owned areas of about 10 hectares, although some are as small as two hectares—which explains why there are 2400 growers in the Riverland. Some survive only because of the lifestyle not because of intrinsic commercial viability. The big companies have enormous areas under vines, some with hundreds of hectares at a time. Angove's Nanya vineyard, for example, is 450 hectares. On the plains, shelter belts of eucalypts and almonds are common as wind protection around the vineyards, which alternate with the deep evergreen foliage of citrus groves, the colours under the stark sun enhanced by frequent outbursts of brilliant yellow sunflowers gone wild.

If the town of Berri has become the commercial and governmental administrative centre of the Riverland, Renmark remains the old social queen. The site for the town, on the west bank of the Murray, 360 km from Adelaide, was chosen by George Chaffey in 1887. It was he who named the town Renmark, the name said to have been given by local Aboriginal people to the area, meaning 'red mud'. Renmark is well designed, with broad avenues and parklands along the river front to speak of an era past when a grand future was seen for this pioneering centre. There is only one hotel, and that is owned by the community.

The town is the centre of Australia's first irrigation area, which is run by the primary producers themselves through the Renmark Irrigation Trust.

The areas administered by the trust include more than 4800 hectares of orchards and vineyards. The trust was responsible for repairing and concreting the water channels which were already in a state of near uselessness when it took them over, laying the basis for the full development of irrigation and locking this century. In 1937 the trust began a massive draining project to combat the problems caused by overwatering. In the 1980s, there grew some realisation among politicians—especially in Adelaide, which relies on the Murray for most of its water supply—that heavy irrigation was one of the major factors slowly killing the Murray with salinity and other pollutions. A million tonnes of salt a year passes through the Murray mouth into the ocean, suggesting a huge ecological problem.

The base of the Murray is an old seabed and there is a natural movement of salty groundwater towards the river; this was exacerbated over the last century by excessive vegetation clearance and heavy irrigation. The problem for governments—Commonwealth and the three relevant states—has been to save the Murray as one of Australia's pressing environmental problems without destroying agriculture. The politicians kept making promises but at least in 1985 they did establish the multi-government Murray Darling Basin Commission. One of its major functions is changing agricultural techniques and in the long term this could have quite a significant effect on the Riverland as a wine producer—most probably by reducing its volume while at the same time increasing the quality of the grapes produced. This would be in line with trends in Australian wine consumption which in the 1980s started moving from quality, discovered by drinkers in the wine boom of the 1960s, to quality. In the 1980s, many Riverland growers and winemakers discovered that the future lies not in the regional traditions of heavily-irrigated bulk wines but in the more concentrated flavours of premium wines. But to return to the history.

The Berri irrigation area was proclaimed in 1910 and Loxton is the newest, being established by the Commonwealth and state governments after World War II in a scheme to settle returned soldiers on the land, as had been done elsewhere after the first World War.

In the early days, the most popular grape variety planted was muscat gordo blanco, of which large areas were put in for drying as raisins. The purple zante currant was also widely grown. In later years, a new variety, the seedless sultana, was introduced and soon outstripped the gordo in favour with the buying public. This resulted in a huge glut of unsaleable gordos, threatening the livelihood of many growers. In order to get some return from their crops, the growers at Renmark formed a cooperative distillery, each putting up a part of the capital. This proved successful and cooperatives became an important feature of Riverland winemaking. However, they had first to overcome many problems.

Initially, only fortified spirit was made, for sale to established wine companies. There was a limited demand for this commodity, however, and the distillers began to use the spirit in making their own sweet white wines. Finding a market for this product was not easy, as the public did not take readily to its unusual flavour. This was overcome with the development of a market in Britain and the use of the wine in wine cocktails. Sales increased and the whole output of the cooperative wineries was readily absorbed. But fashions changed and the cooperatives found some difficult times until flagon wine drinking became popular in the 1960s, followed by the bag-in-the-box casks.

The cooperatives were run by the grower-shareholders themselves. In order to operate efficiently the management, charged essentially with quitting the grapes for the best return, instructed the growers when to deliver their grapes, after the growers had kept estimates of their crops. Thus the wineries were kept running smoothly at full capacity. The system of cooperation operation worked well on the whole, resulting in fair returns to the growers and general prosperity for the irrigation settlements.

The full range of wine styles is made in the Riverland, from the full spectrum of grapes. Gordo and sultana remain dominant, partly because they are so versatile and give growers flexibility to cope with any sudden changes in the market. These white varieties make simple, friendly wines for casks and even basic sparkling wines and cheap bottled wines, and they can be used for drying or as table grapes. Of the 173 000 tonnes of grapes grown in the Riverland, some 24 000 tonnes go to these other purposes. After the 39 000 tonnes of sultanas and 32 000 tonnes of gordo harvested, other prominent varieties include doradillo, grenache and palomino, used for the brandies and ports at which many Riverland wineries excel.

The 1980s, however, saw a realisation that modern temperature-controlled winemaking technologies and improved viticulture, even under irrigation in a hot climate, could produce wines of better quality. The 1987 figures for premium varietals grown in Riverland were: 31 per cent of all chenin blanc grown in Australia, 27 per cent of all sauvignon blanc, 23 per cent of all shiraz, 11 per cent of all chardonnay, 10 per cent of all pinot noir and 8 per cent of all riesling.

Although the Riverland has, in Berri Estates, probably the largest single winery in Australia, and in Angove's a substantial brand operation, very little of the wine grown in the region comes out under known Riverland labels. Much of it finds it way into the anonymous mass-market wines of, especially, Hunter Valley and Barossa companies. Because of this, the Riverland winemakers—whether tiny individualists often of Mediterranean origins making their sunny wines or big companies such as Berri/Renmano with their advanced technologies and sophisticated marketing—have become quite jealous of the quality of the wines that bear their names. A result of this, in turn, is that the Australian wine snob fashion of the 1970s, the deriding of any Riverland wines, has given way to a realisation that although the styles are invariably quite different from those of the cooler climate regions, the Riverland produces many wines of warmth and charm and, because of the broadacre economies of scale, at good value.

Angove's, Renmark

Thomas Carlyon Angove pioneered winemaking from Murray-irrigated grapes. (At least he was the first officially, for it is difficult to imagine that the early growers on the settlements did not have a taste for the homemade). He was the eldest son of Dr W.T. Angove, who began making wine at Tea Tree Gully in Adelaide in the 1880s, thus founding the firm that bears his name. T.C. Angove, who in 1910 graduated with an oenology degree, married Margaret Kelly, granddaughter of Dr A.C. Kelly, well-known McLaren Vale winemaker and author.

T.C. Angove established a distillery and processing house at Renmark, but a year earlier there had been a gordo glut and about 400 tonnes went to Angove's Tea Tree Gully distillery to be made into brandy spirit. After this experience T.C. Angove set up at Renmark to produce spirit for use at Tea Tree Gully. In 1913 the Riverland operation expanded with the establishment of a winery at Lyrup to the southwest of Renmark. Expansion continued at Renmark with brandy and fortified spirit; Lyrup was the centre for vermouth and sweet dessert wines; and dry table wines were made at Tea Tree Gully. In the 1920s overseas markets were

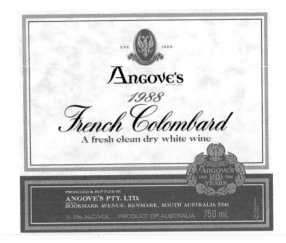

found and in 1929 a subsidiary was formed to handle business in Britain. The same decade saw Ron Haselgrove join Angove's and also winemaker John Guinand. World War II caused the export market to collapse.

In 1947 another Thomas Carlyon Angove, known as Tom, became the third generation to head the company, five years before his father died. Tom Angove, a prominent identity in the wine industry, was of mechanical bent and many of his 'inventions' still feature in the neat and extensive winery complex. The next generation became involved in 1971 when John Carlyon Angove joined the company with a science degree and postgraduate work in commerce. He made Angove's one of the largest privately owned wine companies in Australia, with 150 employees and with 7.5 per cent of its produce going to export.

The company has extensive vineyards of 450 hectares, tended by Mark Crowe. The Nanya vineyard, to the east of Renmark, is largely planted with premium varieties and numerous small experimental parcels, and is thought to be the largest single vineyard in Australia. Principal varieties are riesling, sauvignon blanc, chardonnay, colombard, shiraz, chenin blanc, cabernet sauvignon and pinot noir. About two thirds of the company's crush, handled by winemakers Frank Newman and Ian Marchant, comes from its own vineyards; the rest is bought from local growers.

Angove's is best known for its brandy; the St Agnes brand is its biggest seller. Connoisseurs says the considerably more expensive St Agnes Very Old brandy is Australia's finest. Good quality Armagnacs from France have been compared with it. The company is also known for Stone's Green Ginger Wine, which has something of a cult following ranging from newspaper editors to bikies, and for the respectable quality of Marko vermouth. Much of its effort in the 1980s has gone into a range of varietal table wines, clean and fresh and modestly priced.

Bonneyview Wines, Barmera

'A very small company,' says partner Robert Minns defiantly, 'and the aim is to stay that way. I'd hate to "have to" get a bit bigger.' He and fellow winemaker Noel Sibley, having founded Bonneyview in 1976, instead are concentrating on producing a distinctive style.

It shows on Barmera's main road, across from Lake Bonney, in Bonnyview's charming cellar door sales area, with colonial style architecture and pottery gallery. It is rather more hospitable in appearance than many Riverland wineries, those built in days when wine tourism had not yet become important to regional economies and to wine promotion and sales.

Next to the winery is the Bonneyview heart, a mere 2 hectares of vineyard, which supplies more than half the company's wine. Unlike local trellising systems, Robert Minns's vines are trellised high to promote coolness and a corresponding lengthening of the ripening period. Also unusually, plantings are close spaced. Varieties planted are cabernet sauvignon, shiraz, merlot, malbec, petit verdot, black frontignan, chardonnay, white frontignan, sauvignon blanc, currant and touriga. These produce dry reds, dry whites and sweet fortifieds, distinctively flavoursome wines at modest prices.

Consolidated Cooperative Wineries

One of Australia's largest wine producers, Consolidated Cooperative Wineries (CCW) sells a million cases of wine under its own labels annually in Australia. Yet CCW is not a household word. It is better known as its constituents, two cooperatives at Renmark and Berri which merged on 1 July 1982. Chief executive John Pendrigh believes the rationalisation of production, administration and marketing benefits the 1000-plus shareholders of those two constituents, which retain their separate identities —

Berri and Renmano. CCW also runs the former Angle Vale cooperative winery (which is discussed in the Adelaide chapter) and the company exports to 26 countries, the largest market being Sweden.

The Berri Cooperative Winery and Distillery had its beginnings in 1918. That year a distillation plant was established to make fortifying spirit from the surplus dried fruit left after packing operations were complete. Four years later, a new company was formed to take over the distillery and increase its capacity to deal with the large tonnage of grapes produced by repatriated soldiers. H.R. Curren of Berri was active in gaining support for the formation of the cooperative and W. Gillard was first chairman. From its first vintage in 1922, when 100 tonnes of grapes were crushed, the cooperative grew at a steady rate.

In 1958, in a decision of major importance, a separate winery was established at a cost of £100 000. The winery was designed to make table wines for which there was then a reemerging demand. Growth continued and Berri became the largest single winery/distillery not only in the Riverland but in Australia (challenged perhaps by Lindemans Karadoc complex in north-west Victoria). In 1982 it crushed its millionth tonne and since then it handled some 45 000 tonnes a year.

Much of the new face of Berri can be traced to the influence of Doug Collett, a Roseworthy graduate of 1949 who came to replace Noel Burge as winemaker in 1950 but within six months had replaced Alex Kelly as technical manager. In 1960 Collett won a scholarship to study in France and, in those days before Australia had become the world leader in wine technology, came back with new ideas for air bag presses and cold fermentation. Thus, Berri which made base wines for Lindemans Ben Ean moselle and Orlando's Barossa Pearl, played a significant part in paving the way for Australia's white wine revolution.

It was also a grand time to be alive on the River, when Collett had with him such winemakers as Brian Barry (1952–76), Graham 'Orgie' Williams (1951–52 and 1959–73) and Ian Mackenzie (1959, 1964–67) who was later to become chief winemaker for Seppelt at Great Western. The laboratory was not used only sterile analysis of wines, but often rang to Doug

Collett's regular toast: 'To your astonishingly good health in the face of insurmountable odds.' Collett left to become a winery consultant in 1967 and founded Woodstock in McLaren Vale.

As a true cooperative, the winery was supported solely by 500 grower-members whose vineyards are located within an 11 kilometre radius of the winery. The wide range of products includes table wines, fortified wines (from a magnificent reservoir of age), Passionwine, brandy and five-litre casks, as well as selling much in bulk. The company is not too proud to emphasise the energy it puts into quality in its Berri Estates five-litre casks, for more than half the wine sold in Australia is in casks.

Berri's stablemate in CCW is Renmano, another of the big cooperatives that dominated the South Australian Riverland. It was established in 1916 when 130 local grapegrowers registered the first cooperative winery in Australia. They bought a distillery which operated on the present site, just out of Renmark, from 1914.

At first the function of the growers' distillery was to make use of grapes not suited to the dried-fruit market. In the first year of operation the new cooperative handled 1000 tonnes, all of which was processed into spirit. This trend continued for twenty years. Then the group started to produce fortified wines, which the market called for at the time.

After World War II, as more ex-service personnel took up soldier-settlement properties around Renmark, they planted such wine grape varieties as palomino, pedro, mataro, crouchen and shiraz. Existing shareholders also replanted with these varieties, which enabled Renmano to enter the table wine market. As the table market expanded in Australia, shareholders planted classical varieties such as cabernet sauvignon, malbec and riesling.

Since 1970 the product mix changed substantially to table wines. Before then most of the production was sold in bulk to other wineries but the swing was to emphasising marketing under its own label.

In 1979 Renmano introduced a new packaging and labelling style. The average crush is now about 20 000 tonnes a year, the storage capacity 19 million litres and the number of grower-shareholders has increased to about 500.

The winery advises growers of new grape varieties and improved viticultural techniques such as trellising for mechanical pruning and harvesting. Most of the grapes handled by the winery are mechanically harvested, covering some 30 varieties ranging from the ubiquitous gordo and sultana to such premium varieties as cabernet sauvignon, shiraz and pinot noir.

In common with other Riverland wineries, vintage starts in the middle of February and continues to late April. From early January, the laboratory staff are taking statistical samples of shareholders' grapes so the winemakers can determine the time when the acid-sugar balance is optimum for harvesting.

When the grapes have been crushed at the winery, the extracted juice is refrigerated then clarified by filtration before cold fermentation in controlled-refrigeration stainless-steel tanks. After fermentation the wine is stabilised and filtered before being bottled or put into wood casks for maturation. Ageing of wine and brandy is carried out in small wood casks, imported from France, the United States and Germany.

Even under the centralised management of CCW, Renmano, with David Hayman as winemaker, retains its own marketplace identity. It makes a full range of budget to premium table wines, fortified wines and brandy and is best known for its better-class commercial wines in two-litre wine casks. But it is staking its reputation on its premium table wines under the Chairman's Selection range. It quickly found acceptability with the cabernet sauvignon in this range as one of the better quality, modestly priced reds on the market; but Renmano's faith in the Chairman's Selection range was fully vindicated when the chardonnay 1988 started sweeping the wine show circuit and, to the confusion of those who had not noticed the decade's improvements in Riverland wines, took off the Australian Wine of the Year award. As with the winning of a 1972 Melbourne Wine Show trophy by a young red made by Brian Barry at Berri, it was a reminder of the power of the Murray.

Cyrilton Winery, Waikerie

The charming stone cellars of Cyrilton echo an historic involvement by the Hardy Wine Company, headquartered in McLaren Vale, which was an early discoverer of the possibilities of wine grapes in the irrigation area of the Riverland. The company's first venture in the Waikerie area was the erection of a small winery on the banks of the Murray River for use in the 1915 vintage. The first year's intake was 80 tonnes of grapes. Four years later, the winery was sold to a group of returned soldier-growers and became the Waikerie Cooperative Distillery.

Also in 1915 Robert Hardy, with Samuel Sage, purchased irrigable but virgin land at Waikerie. It was cleared and planted under Samuel Sage's supervision and was named the Cyrilton vineyards after Cyril Hardy, brother of Thomas. The Hardy company was later to buy full interest in the property.

A further step in 1916 was a contract with Fred Metters for the purchase of grapes from his property at Murray View, 16 kilometres downstream from Waikerie, with the condition that the company build a new winery there. John Stoward, a great-nephew of the founder of the Hardy firm and an engineer and winemaker who had built the previous Waikerie winery, built a winery at Murray View. The 1300 or 1400 hogsheads of wine from the first vintage were shipped in steamer-towing barges downstream to Morgan, then taken by rail to Mile End in Adelaide, which was then the Hardy headquarters.

When this winery was sold, John Stoward built another at Cyrilton in time for the 1921 vintage. It expanded to play an important part in Hardy's fortified and commercial wines and brandies. At its peak, the company had 40 hectares under vine at Waikerie.

The stone cellar door building, one of the most attractive in the Riverland, passed through various hands after Hardy withdrew in the 1980s, and in 1990 its future was still uncertain.

Kingston Estate Wines, Kingston-on-Murray

The name is only starting to become known to the public, but the Kingston Estates Wines family partnership, which was founded in 1979, crushes 12 000 tonnes. Of this, 80 per cent is bought from growers in the region; the balance is from the company's 15 hectares of vineyards at Kingston-on-Murray (the full name of which is used to avoid confusion with the resort town of Kingston in the southeast of South Australia).

Winemaker Bill Moularadellis grows chardonnay, sauvignon blanc, colombard, shiraz, cabernet sauvignon and merlot and supplies buyers-own-brands and other wineries.

He has, however, started putting his winemaking skills to the Kingston Estate name and is entering the domestic market with impressive late-picked botrytis sweet whites, rich chardonnays and mellow reds produced by carbonic maceration.

Lubiana Wines, Moorook

Steve and Monique Lubiana have in their family winery at Moorook a specialist champagne cellars, making for their own label and for others and with plans for expanding with vineyards in Tasmania. However, their background is a classic Riverland story.

Steve's grandfather, Andrea Lubiana, came from a family in Trieste which has been making wine for three generations. He lost everything in World War II and emigrated from Italy to Australia. After several years of selling wine he decided to try making his own for the ever-increasing market among Melbourne's Italian community. In 1959 he bought the remains of a former distillery, founded in 1919, on the hilly slopes of Moorook near Berri in the Riverland. Using primitive equipment and the help of neighbours he got through his first crush of 40 tonnes.

Business was good and Mario Lubiana joined his father in 1960. All wine produced for the next three years found ready markets in the eastern states and the whole Lubiana family moved to live at Moorook. The winery was virtually rebuilt with extensions completed in 1973. In 1975 the Lubianas had a record crush, producing a million litres of wine. They also developed their own premium-variety vineyards.

Lubiana has produced a vast array of wine styles, and the cabernet sauvignon remains a specialty, but in the 1980s Steve Lubiana saw the potential for premium champagnes and started to specialise.

Penfolds, Loxton

Australia's largest wine group, Penfolds, bought into the Riverland in 1987, taking over the Loxton Cellars which had been founded in 1948 as the Loxton Cooperative Winery and Distillery.

The Loxton Irrigation Area was established to settle ex-service personnel as primary producers. An area of about 2400 hectares was developed and the cooperative was established to process the grapes, which it started to do in 1952.

Growth was steady and most of the output was bulk wines, chiefly used by wine companies elsewhere for casks and flagons. It also produced fortified wines, brandy, grape juice concentrates and de-alcoholised wines for sale to other winemakers for blending or relabelling. There was a tiny production under its own label for cellar door sales. It is the only winery in the Riverland which can actually be visited from the river.

The winery was, and still is, a technological leader in the region and crushes about 22 500 tonnes. One of its specialisations is spinning-cone concentration machinery for capturing the delicate grape and wine aromas which can be lost in the fermentation process. These can then be blended back into the wines later.

Penfolds winemakers Stuart Auld and Jon Ketley supervise the crush, and Kevin Pfeiffer is winery manager. It is here, in the 20 hectares of company vineyards tended by Don Schultz, that many new varieties have been tested for Riverland plantings, including taminga, colombard and ruby cabernet.

Wein Valley Estates, Monash Wein

Valley Estates, near the unique adult playground of Monash, has a unique operational structure: it is a private company, founded on 1 March 1985, with none of its own vineyards, and it

keeps 160 local grower-suppliers closely involved through all aspects of wine production through to bottling. Company management, under Chris Gregoriou, believes this operational philosophy has led to a high level of pride in the company's product. It also involves a diverse range of cultures in the winemaking—supervised by winemaker Otto Konig—and as a result the company claims to be able to produce wines to suit all palates.

Wein Valley Estates handles almost every variety of grape known in the Riverland and from its crush of 7350 tonnes produces a quarter of a million of cases of table wines, fortifieds and liqueurs, of both Australian and European styles. Its biggest selling lines are moselle, port, riesling and Greek-style retsina, a dry white flavoured with pine resin. For a young company, Wein Valley Estates has a wide distribution network, including Australia's eastern states and Japan.

WESTERN AUSTRALIA

John Hanley

The history of the wine industry in Western Australia goes back to the founding of the colony in June 1829. The first recorded planting of vines was by Charles McFaull in 1829 near the present-day suburb of Hamilton Hill. This venture floundered owing to inadequate soils and the lack of water.

Shortly after, Thomas Waters, a trained botanist, brought vine cuttings, along with a wide portfolio of other specimens, from South Africa and proceeded to successfully cultivate these on his land grant at South Guildford. Records indicate that wine was made in 1834 and that commercial quantities were being produced in 1842, when he bartered part of his vintage for other goods. Diary notes kept by Waters suggest that he practised some rudimentary but effective cultivation and disease control techniques on his property, known as the Olive Farm. He published his personal experiences and successful husbandry techniques in a treatise which became the handbook for pioneering farmers.

The original Olive Farm cellars, complete with the pioneer's hand-hewn well intact, are still operational under the stewardship of the Yurisich family. Three generations have maintained and preserved this unique piece of history—the oldest operational cellars in Australia. Certainly the composition of the varieties in the vineyard and the winery technology are different to what Waters would recognise. However, at the foot of the property (surrounded on both sides by urban and commercial development and fronting the major east-west highway) the Swan River still peacefully flows towards the city and the port of Fremantle, very much in the way it must have done back in the 1830s.

The Houghton development in the Swan Valley was the largest of the early initiatives. Again, records of wine production date back to 1859 when the property was owned by the colonial surgeon Dr John Ferguson. Houghton in later years became the focal point for winemaking in the west.

The tentacles of the vine followed other pioneers to the Avon Valley north-east of Perth, to Bunbury and Busselton in the south-west and to regional developments north of Albany.

The rich, well-watered soils of the Swan Valley, within easy reach of the fledgling capital, maintained its pre-eminence as the major centre for vines and winemaking. So important was this industry that the government seconded New South Wales specialist viticulturist Adrian d'Espeissis to oversee the orderly development and management of the state's vineyards. D'Espeissis was an enthusiastic professional who had gained first-hand experience in European vineyards. This enthusiasm flowed over into his field exercises, which involved participants in pruning and vineyard cultivation competitions. He was largely responsible for importing and cataloguing important new grape types to expand the options of growers. His own publication *The handbook of Horticulture and Viticulture of Western Australia* is still very topical and is included in the libraries of most serious grapegrowers and winemakers.

This century has seen many new initiatives and developments, firstly by Italian and Yugoslav migrants in the Swan Valley and on the Wanneroo coastal plain, and more recently in the southern parts of the state. Dr John Gladstone's erudite paper 'The Climate and Soils of South Western Australia in Relation to Vine Growing', published in 1965, provided the catalyst for the development of what has become widely known as the Margaret River and Mount Barker wine regions. Government viticulturist Bill Jamieson planted a trial vineyard of riesling and cabernet sauvignon on the Pearse property, Forest Hill, west of Mount Barker, in 1966, and in 1967 Perth physician Tom Cullity established his Vasse Felix vineyard at Margaret River, with similar varieties. The polarisation of these two areas is now well documented and other subregions, such as Frankland River, the Porongurups and Manjimup–Pemberton, have quickly been identified as equally exciting.

Swan Valley

The Swan Valley has been the focal point for winemaking in Western Australia for 150 vintages. A true valley nestled between the Darling Range and the coastal plain, it is within an easy thirty-minute drive from the city. Many visitors to the West take advantage of the river ferries that make daily runs from central Perth to the larger wineries situated adjacent to the upper reaches of the Swan River.

The climate is typically Mediterranean, with hot summers and cool wet winters. Perhaps the best time to visit and see the Valley at its best is during spring. The weather is mild, the wildflowers are in full bloom and the vines are flush with new growth. One should avoid the vintage months, which normally fall between January and March, as winemakers are usually working around the clock and have few spare moments to discuss their wines. February can be extremely hot with 40°C temperatures not uncommon for most of the month. Some relief is experienced from the 'Fremantle Doctor', a frequent on-shore breeze that tends to waft in around mid-afternoon—bringing some mitigation for the grape pickers, who often experience temperatures beneath the vines of up to 50°C.

The soils, as one would expect, are deep rich alluvial sandy loams. So fertile are the soils alongside the river that many vignerons supplement their income with other cash crops such as melons, vegetables and citrus orchards. Abundant ground water is withing easy reach of the surface to augment the natural rainfall. Deeper artesian bores provide supplies to those with broader acre enterprises. Pockets of lighter, less fertile soil lie east of the Great Northern Highway. These grey sandy tracts, while unsuitable for viticulture, have proven to be ideal hobby farm locations or horse studs.

Attractive prices and a buoyant export market into South-East Asia has seen a resurgence in the table grape and dried fruit industries. Experimentation by the State Department of Agriculture has led to the development of many options in the production and storage of premium fruit. It is now possible through proper handling and the judicious use of controlled atmospheric techniques to hold table grapes from one vintage virtually through until the next.

Swan Valley winemakers fall broadly into three categories. At one extreme are the ethnic cottage industry producers, descendants of the Yugoslav or Italian settlers, who produce beverage wine to cater for the bulk market. Sadly, many of these operations have disappeared over the last two decades as the younger generations have elected to pursue other careers, or capitalise on the increasing property values. The next strata is shared by those who have had the foresight to replant with premium table wine varieties, upgrade winery facilities and embrace the best elements of twentieth-century technology. Usually they have purchased additional land to bring a little economy of scale to their operations. Typically, however, the average holding would still only be in the vicinity of 10–15 hectares. Many specialist grapegrowers in the Bindoon or Chittering Valleys provide an important supply bridge to these medium-sized wineries. The third group consists of the two larger wineries in the valley, Houghton and Sandalford, who crush better than half of the state's total wine grape production. However, on a national basis, they are considered relatively small fry alongside the likes of Penfolds, Lindemans or Orlando.

The natural elements of soil and climate dictate the destiny and style of Swan Valley wines. They are usually generous in weight and bouquet, full-flavoured and relatively high in alcohol. Sophisticated winemaking techniques have all but eliminated many of the old sulphide problems of the past. The introduction of temperature-controlled fermentation has ensured that most of the fresh, delicate fruit characters are retained. Early picking, selected yeast strains

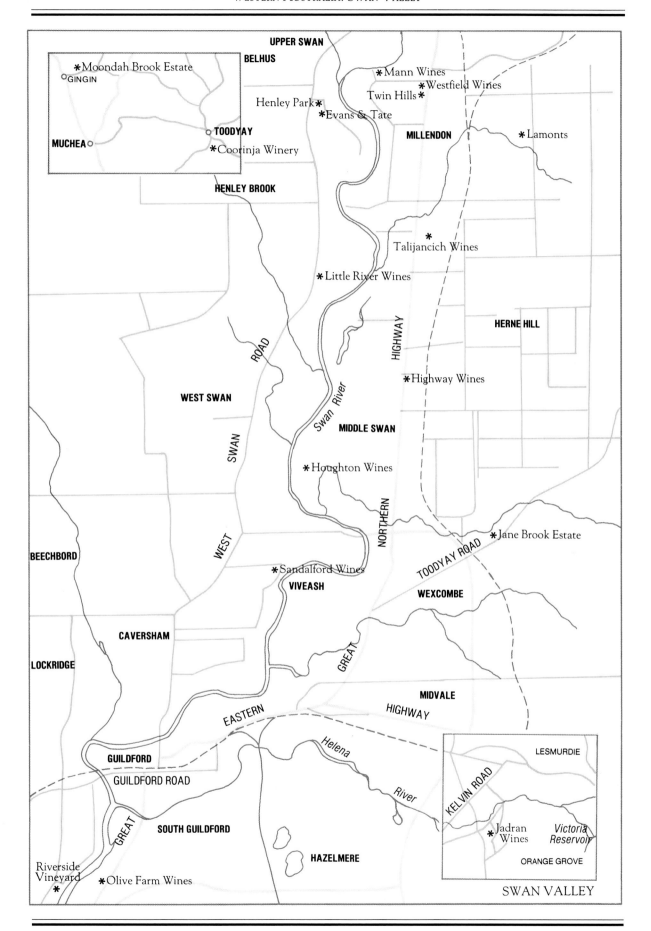

UPPER SWAN

BELHUS

*Moondah Brook Estate
○ GINGIN

Henley Park *

* Mann Wines
* Westfield Wines
Twin Hills *
* Evans & Tate

MILLENDON

* Lamonts

○ **TOODYAY**

* Coorinja Winery

MUCHEA ○

HENLEY BROOK

* Talijancich Wines

* Little River Wines

HERNE HILL

WEST SWAN

ROAD

SWAN

Swan River

HIGHWAY

* Highway Wines

MIDDLE SWAN

* Houghton Wines

WEST

NORTHERN

* Jane Brook Estate

BEECHBORD

TOODYAY ROAD

* Sandalford Wines

VIVEASH

WEXCOMBE

CAVERSHAM

LOCKRIDGE

GREAT

MIDVALE

EASTERN

HIGHWAY

Helena

GUILDFORD

GUILDFORD ROAD

River

LESMURDIE

KELVIN ROAD

GREAT

SOUTH GUILDFORD

* Jadran
Wines

*Victoria
Reservoir*

HAZELMERE

ORANGE GROVE

Riverside
Vineyard
*

* Olive Farm Wines

SWAN VALLEY

and gentle presses ensure that the modern Swan styles are light years ahead of what was generally available in the 1960s.

The doyen of the Swan winemakers, the legendary Jack Mann of Houghton, and his colleague Charles Kelly at Valencia, were for many years the only professionally trained winemakers in the valley. Today, it is not uncommon to find either a Roseworthy, Wagga Wagga (Riverina College) or European graduate overseeing the operations at even the smallest operation.

Coorinja Winery

Coorinja is the oldest non-metropolitan winery in Western Australia. Situated 80 km north-east of Perth, near the historic town of Toodyay, it still clings to the last vestiges of nineteenth-century respectability. The solid-stone winery, built in the 1870s (not unlike those at Rutherglen of a similar era), provides a cool resting place for travellers in what is otherwise a wheat and sheep region. The Wood family acquired the property in 1919. Winemaker Hector Wood and his family follow traditional practices. Vintage is relatively short, commencing in February and usually out of the way by the end of March. Vineyards on the property are very low yielding and more than likely uneconomic—they do, however, produce fruit of intense flavour. Varieties planted include muscat, shiraz, malbec, grenache and semillon. Production is centred on fortified styles. The tawny port styles are particularly sought after. A range of full-flavoured table wines is usually available for tasting and purchase. The grounds, complete with running creek, provide an ideal location for a family picnic.

Evans & Tate

Evans & Tate established its first vineyard in 1971, on a farming property at Bakers Hill, approximately 60 km north-east of Perth. They named the property Cote de Boulanger. Planted to cabernet sauvignon, it provided the backbone for the classic Gnangara red wines up until 1982, when economics dictated that the vines be pulled. Sadly, few bottles of the intense berry-flavoured cabernet remain—I have a few of each vintage which, although curiosity pieces, will be interesting to review in a decade or two.

In 1972 John Tate and former partner, John Evans, purchased the well-known Swan Valley property Gnangara. This unique location, on a bend of the Upper Swan at Henley Brook, has some of the very best alluvial loams in the valley. The varieties planted include shiraz and cabernet. Extensive replanting has taken place and the old cellars have been refurbished.

Interest in cool-climate viticulture in the Margaret River district led to the partners' selection of prime land at Metricup in 1975. They named the property Redbrook and wines produced from the 25 hectare vineyard are labelled to indicate their Margaret River origin. Typifying their interest in red wine, more than 8 hectares of this new site was committed to cabernet sauvignon. Other varieties selected included merlot, cabernet franc and hermitage. White varieties are centred on chardonnay, semillon and sauvignon blanc.

The Redbrook wines have been outstanding, especially the chardonnay and semillon. Great things are anticipated from the merlot if the first few vintages are indicative. The produce of Evans & Tate now enjoys international recognition with exports to England, Malaysia, New Zealand, Belgium, the US and Switzerland.

The benchmark wine from this prestige cellar is the Gnangara Shiraz—probably the most awarded of Western Australian red table wines. Other top labels include the Redbrook cabernet and the Redbrook merlot. Whites that should be included in any cellar are the Margaret River chardonnay, and the complex herbaceous semillon from the same vineyard.

Henley Park

Situated in Swan Street, Henley Brook, the property was developed by the Yujnovich family in 1935. The vineyard and winery for many years had the enviable reputation of being the most immaculately husbanded in the West. Mark Yujnovich, also a dedicated winemaker, produced an extensive range of wines. His vintage ports, fortified with selected aged brandy, were benchmarks in the West Australian industry. Those with a keen eye and palate for this style religiously beat an annual path to the winery on the release of the new wines. The property was sold to Claus Petersen in 1987. Vincent Desplat, a young Frenchman with a long family history of winemaking, has taken over the duties in the winery and produces a small range of fresh, flavour-packed wines that sell extremely well. His light reds, in the Beaujolais mould, are particularly worth trying. The top white table styles include chardonnay, chenin blanch and semillon.

Highway Wines

Highway Wines, on Great Northern Highway at Herne Hill, has long been run by the Bakranich family. They have approximately 11 hectares under vine—mostly shiraz and grenache, with some semillon and tokay. Most of the wine sold is to a regular clientele at cellar door.

Houghton Wines

The Houghton label (with its famous Blue Stripe) is synonymous with Western Australian wine. The Houghton property, 22 km north-east of the city, was originally known as Swan Location II, a grant of 3240 acres made by King William IV to one Henry Revett Bland on 10 January 1835. The property was purchased by a syndicate of British servicemen stationed in India named Lowis, Yule and Houghton. Yule became the resident manager, but the property took its name from the senior ranking officer, Lieutenant Colonel Richmond Houghton, although he never actually came to Australia.

In 1859 the colonial surgeon Dr John Ferguson purchased Houghton, which had, by this time, been reduced to some 300 hectares by subdivision. It would seem that Dr Ferguson, in common with a number of other famous Australian doctors of the era, believed in the health-giving properties and qualities of wine, and it was this belief that led to the purchase of the established vineyard. (Although much of the early history of the vineyard is poorly documented, current research suggests the first vines were actually planted between 1830 and 1836.)

It was the energy and enterprise of Dr Ferguson's son Charles, who spent fifty years living and working on the property, which was to ensure Houghton's place as the finest vineyard in the state. Under his stewardship a substantial homestead was built (recently extensively renovated and now used as the corporate offices), and part of the original dwelling was incorporated within the cellars. Legend tells us that it was in this section of the cellars that Western Australia's only bushranger, Moondyne Joe, was captured while helping himself to a cask in 1869.

During these years, another part of the original property, which had also been sold off shortly after assignment, and known in the intervening years as Strelley, was purchased by Charles Ferguson and combined with the vineyard under the name of Houghton. The Houghton property stayed with the Ferguson family until 1950, when it was sold to the Emu Wine Company of South Australia. It came under the control of the South Australian winemaking family Thomas Hardy & Sons in 1976 when Hardy's acquired the stock of the London-based parent company of Emu Wines. Under the guidance of Hardy's, the Houghton property has undergone major redevelopment in the technical and winemaking areas.

A strong feature of the winery was the long association of the Mann family as winemakers. In 1910 R. George Mann left the original Chateau Tanunda and joined Houghton. R. George's son Jack joined his father in 1922 and took over as winemaker in 1930, eventually retiring in 1972 having been associated with fifty vintages. Jack Mann was an outstanding character with strong convictions and complete dedication to his three loves of Christianity, cricket and chablis. His most famous wine was, of course, the unique Houghton White Burgundy—first made by him in 1937. It became a benchmark style in Australia and remains a testimony to this great Australian; it is still one of the country's best selling and most sought-after wines. Jack and his wife, Angela, lived out retirement on the property until his death in 1989, in his eighty-fourth year.

The current senior winemaker, responsible for the 4000 tonne vintage, is Peter Dawson. Peter was born and educated in Victoria and studied microbiology and biochemistry at La Trobe University. He joined Houghton in 1978 and subsequently completed a second degree through the Riverina College of Advanced Education, graduating with a Bachelor of Applied Science.

At Houghton today there are 50 hectares of vines, a further 90 hectares at Moondah Brook (60 km north of the Swan Valley near Gingin), and 90 hectares at Frankland River (300 km south of Perth). Sixteen different varieties are

Houghton vineyard at sunset.

cultivated with Rhine riesling, chenin blanc, cabernet sauvignon, verdelho and chardonnay being the major components. In 1989 the group announced a major new joint-venture initiative, which proposes to establish a new 80 hectare vineyard 5 km from the southern township of Pemberton. The first fruit is expected to be harvested during the 1992 vintage.

Approximately 8 per cent of Houghton production is exported. A major export development program resulted in large exports of premium wine to the UK, Scandinavia, Canada and the US.

It would be almost irreverent not to recommend the white burgundy. The style took on new dimensions under the gifted hand of Jon Reynolds (winemaker between 1977 and 1984). He increased the percentage of chardonnay in the blend and the judicious use of new French oak. The Reynolds' wines developed superbly and won numerous show awards.

Peter Dawson has followed the Reynolds' dictum, further bolstering the complexity of this line. Sadly, too greater percentage of the annual crush is consumed immediately the wine is released. Age gently brings the components of fruit and oak together and softens the natural acids, providing an altogether new experience for lovers of the famous Blue Stripe. For the impatient cellarer, Houghton regularly releases stocks of aged white burgundy that have been held back for maturation and showing. These are not to be missed.

Other premium-reserve wines are released under the Gold Reserve label. Recent outstanding lines have been the Reserve Chardonnay, Chenin Blanc and Frankland Rhine Riesling. The Gold Reserve Verdelho is probably the best of this sought-after variety in Western Australia. The exquisite cabernet rosé, again championed by Jon Reynolds, has been the outstanding wine of its type in Australia for almost a decade—a rosé to be enjoyed in the spring and summer of its release, perhaps with a block or two of ice and/or a dash of soda.

The red table wines to follow include an increasing portfolio of labels indicating fruit from the new southern regions. The Houghton Frankland Shiraz and Margaret River Cabernet are wines for cellaring.

Later picked, sweeter wines such as the Autumn Harvest Semillon and the variously labelled auslese or beerenauslese rieslings are delightful dessert styles.

Occasional reseases of fortified wines are marketed mainly through the cellar sales area. The prestige Centenary Port is a classic tawny style that exudes the generous soils and sunshine of the Swan Valley.

Jadran Wines

Jadran is located on Reservoir Road, Orange Grove, an outer Perth suburb, to the south-east of the city. Established in the late 1920s by the Radojkovich family, it is now under the control of elder son Steve, who oversees the vineyards, winemaking and cellar door sales operations. Like most of the smaller vineyards that developed through European migration, Jadran has an excellent collection of rare grape varieties that can be traced back to the early selections from the Cape (South Africa) and the European field trips of the early Government viticulturists. Steve Radojkovich is not only delighted to talk to anyone interested in the history, but will probably produce a unique bottle of an exotic variety such as Sercial. Steve has won many awards with his table and fortified wine styles—culminating in 1975 with a special trophy for being the most successful, smaller West Australian winery exhibiting at the Perth Wine Show. The current releases are well made and extremely good value. Most of the annual vintage is sold direct from the cellar.

Jane Brook Estate

Formerly Vignacourt Wine Cellars, David and Beverley Atkinson purchased this established vineyard and winery in 1972, looking for an alternative lifestyle away from the pressures of the corporate world. Vignacourt was already well known and even though David had limited wine knowledge and less winemaking experience, he quickly threw himself into the rigours of his new challenge. The vineyards were upgraded, the winery refurbished and an almost multinational merchandising program mapped out. Jane Brook (named after the creek flowing through the property) came to fruition in 1984 with a name change and new livery. David and Beverley are tireless workers for the Swan Valley fraternity and many promotional campaigns and initiatives

Jane Brook Estate Wines.

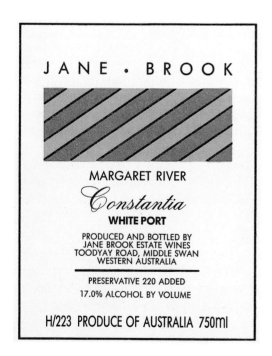

have spring from the fertile minds of this delightful couple.

Principal varieties grown at Jane Brook include shiraz, cabernet, verdelho and chenin blanc. David also sees an increasing role for chardonnay and sauvignon blanc in his varietal portfolio. A winery that is considered a must when visiting the Swan. David and Beverley are great hosts and their swag of show medals attest the quality of the wines made.

If you are a fortified wine fan, Jane Brook has much to offer. David's cabernet sauvignon vintage port and liqueur sweet whites are probably the best of their type in Western Australia. Complementing these one can find perfectly acceptable chenin blanc, chardonnay and sauvignon blanc styles. The premium dry reds made at the cellar exhibit the warm richness of the climate, some attractive new oak flavours and a pleasing balance.

Lamonts

Neil and Corin Lamont's delightful estate along Bisdee Road, Millendon, sits comfortably in a micro-environment of its own at the top end of the Swan Valley. Daughter Kate, along with sister Fiona and local friends, run a well-patronised restaurant adjacent to the winery. A great place to stop, reflect and soothe the mind and body. Picture windows take in the ordered rows of vines and an irregular stand of native eucalypts beyond.

The winery has only been functional since 1978. Much of the winemaking has been a combined effort between Neil, Corin and Corin's father, the legendary Jack Mann. Consequently, a great deal of the Mann ethos and traditional techniques have been imparted. This is reflected in the styles of wines made and the varieties utilised. Unfortunately, the annual vintage is very restricted and the principal source of the Lamont label is the cellar door (and, of course, the daughters' restaurant).

To supplement the fruit from the home vineyard, Neil buys in approximately half of his needs from other specialist growers in the Swan Valley and the adjacent Bindoon Valley. Navera (a unique Jack Mann cultivar), verdelho and chenin blanc are used widely in the dry white wines, while cabernet and hermitage are the mainstay of the reds. Sadly, the influence of Jack Mann will not be around for the 1990 vintage but I feel sure his love of 'flavour, balance and refinement' will long be part of Neil and Corin Lamont's wines.

The Navera dry white, a light crisp style with an excellent long flavour profile, is a must for those masked tastings. The Lamont White Burgundy is the old Houghton style revisited, made from a blend of verdelho, semillon and chenin blanc. (Chardonnay will increasingly become a component.) It is fermented using natural yeasts, which have the effect of revealing the rich, unadulterated fruit flavours, unlike the bready yeast characters so reminiscent of cold, artificial ferments. The palate is long and indicative of fully sun-ripened fruit. Neil also markets an almost French-style sweet white table wine made from the Navera variety. In the sauternes mould it is intensely flavoured, albeit elegant and highly refined. Perhaps the treasure among the limited range is the Pedro and Navera fortified blend. Gathered from eighty-year-old vines late in summer, the fruit has an average sugar reading of 30° baumé (the highest I have heard of in Western Australia). The Lamont's winery is very much a piece of living Swan Valley history.

Little River Wines

Situated on West Swan Road at West Swan, Little River Wines (formerly Glenalwyn Wines) was established by George Pasalich in 1933 and subsequently developed by his son Len, who in turn sold to the Murfitt family in 1986. Premium varieties have been planted in recent years and extensive renovations made to the winery. The winery specialises in table wine styles which include riesling, frontignan and a chenin. Recent vintages of 100 tonnes have been reported, significant for a small Swan Valley winery. The talented Rob Bowen is the consultant winemaker.

Mann Wines

Maintaining the family tradition, Dorham Mann has established a small, specialised sparkling wine cellar at his home in Memorial Drive, Baskerville. Employing the skills gained through a lifetime of practical and professional application, Dorham astutely crafts locally grown cabernet sauvignon fruit into a highly sophisticated, bottle-fermented, pink champagne style that completely belies its Swan Valley heritage. The artistry has been carried further into the very tastefully designed label and dressing of the bottle. Highly recommended.

Moondah Brook Estate

Moondah Brook Estate is situated in the rich foothills of the Darling Range at Gingin, some 60 km north of the Swan Valley. Planting commenced in 1968 and now totals 90 hectares. Varieties include chenin blanc, tokay, verdelho, riesling, chardonnay, cabernet sauvignon, shiraz and malbec. The first vintage from Moondah Brook was 1972, with the release of a varietal chenin blanc. Subsequently, the property has become a valuable source of fruit to cater for the ever increasing demand for the famous Houghton White Burgundy. Trophy-winning verdelhos, chardonnays and chenin blancs all attest to the wisdom of selecting this property, which has become a valued extension of the Swan Valley estate.

Houghton has maintained the practice of distinctly labelling the Moondah Brook range of table wines. Classics include the Chenin Blanc, Verdelho, and Cabernet Sauvignon.

Olive Farm Wines

Olive Farm, as detailed in the introduction, dates back to the early settlement of Western Australia when Thomas Waters first named his property in early 1830. Waters, who was born in England and trained professionally as a botanist, was working in South Africa when Captain James Stirling set off to establish the colony of Western Australia in 1829. Waters decided to join the colonists and arrived on the *Caroline* in September of that year. He brought with him rooted vine cuttings packed in barrels and numerous other seeds and plants from South Africa and England. These were planted out on his 20 hectare grant at South Guildford. (A prize grant with a wide frontage to the Swan River.)

While working in South Africa, Waters had learnt the rudiments of winemaking. He put this experience to practical application in 1834 when he crushed what is generally acknowledged as the state's first vintage. What became of this auspicious first crush is not known; however, later records of the property indicate he regularly bartered his produce for the necessities of the day—at an agreed base price of two shillings a gallon. In addition to his duties at Olive Farm, Waters performed a great deal of honorary horticultural work in and around the settlements of Perth and Guildford. He produced an almanac on crop growing, cultivation and the control of native pests. Other local achievements included the identification and cataloguing of indigenous toxic weeds and shrubs. For this work, Waters was granted an additional 40 hectares of land adjoining Olive Farm.

Sadly, Waters was tragically drowned on 28 February 1869. His eldest son William, who took over the property, lacked his father's dedication and the farm soon became overrun. In 1920 the 60 hectares were sold to William Padbury, who subdivided the property into twenty-two blocks. The homestead block was purchased by a John Woodward in 1923, who retained it until 1933 when he sold to Ivan Yurisich. By this time the vines were gone and Ivan, who had toiled in the goldfields for twenty years, set his sights on recreating the history that was. He cleared the land with a horse-drawn, single-furrow plough and replanted the vineyard with cuttings from the Houghton property, given to him by the new winemaker Jack Mann.

The old Waters cellar was extensively renovated and a small winery rebuilt. His first vintage produced a modest 900 litres of dry red table wine. Ivan's son Vincent took over the major workload in 1963 and he in turn has been succeeded by his son Ian, a Roseworthy College oenology graduate and regular wine show judge in Perth. In the early years of the 1980s it was not uncommon to see the three generations actively involved at the crusher or wine press.

History still runs deep at the Olive Farm—regrettably, the grove of old olive trees has been cleared from the property frontage to permit road widening, but one may still view the original work of Waters in the old cellar. Obviously the surroundings are very much of the twentieth century, with Ian operating one of the most technically sophisticated small wineries in the state. The surrounding vineyard is planted mainly to cabernet sauvignon, shiraz, chardonnay, semillon and chenin blanc. Additional grapes are sourced from Bindoon, and Ian has a 30 hectare property under development on the Belhus Estate at Upper Swan, where he has planted chenin blanc, chardonnay, verdelho, cabernet sauvignon, cabernet franc, merlot and pinot noir.

The wines of Olive Farm have always followed consumer trends. Vincent Yurisich established an enviable reputation for the Olive Farm Rosé, semillon and sauternes style. In the 1970s he was regularly adjudged the state's leading winemaker at the Royal Agricultural Society Perth Wine Show. He also put his creative talent towards the production of a miniscule quantity of bottle-fermented sparkling wine, using the madeline variety as a base. Most of this was snapped up by cellar devotees when released around Easter time each year. Ian's table wines also reflect contemporary preferences, with the accent switching to the lightly oaked chardonnay, semillon, chenin blanc and a very good chablis style. A brace of dry reds and, of course, the sparkling range complete the cellar list.

The Olive Farm chardonnay is skilfully made in the classic mould (barrel fermentation, lees ageing and slow maturation in imported oak). The oak itself is stored in a large cool room to maintain a reasonable temperature and inhibit rapid extraction. The current-release sparkling wine, produced from chardonnay, has an attractive fruit and yeast bouquet, elegant mousse and a small persistent bead. Altogether extremely well crafted. The top red table wine release is the cabernet sauvignon–shiraz–merlot blend. A combination of richly intense fruit flavours and a judicious sprinkling of oak.

Riverside Vineyard

This tiny 2 hectare vineyard has an attractive frontage to the Swan River at Bassendean. Situated directly opposite the Olive Farm property, it enjoys all the benefits of being located in a built-up residential area, yet exudes the peace and tranquillity of a far more relaxed rural environment. Under the ownership and direction of Laurie and Moira Nicoletto, the winery has produced many attractive table and fortified wines. The smooth, full-bodied shiraz has won much critical acclaim in the show ring and enjoys a strong personal following. A small range of fortifieds, including a very attractive vintage port style, can also be purchased at cellar door.

Sandalford Wines

The history of Sandalford has roots that go back to the establishment of the Swan River colony in 1829. Founder, John Septimus Roe, was one of the original settlers who arrived with Captain Stirling. He became the state's first Surveyor General in 1829 and in 1840 was granted the property. He named it after an historic estate in Berkshire, England. For almost a century the family maintained Sandalford, principally to produce table grapes and currants. After World War II, Roe's great-grandsons, John and David, began to develop the commercial aspects of the winery, which up until this time was a small, interesting sideline rather than a retail operation. Following David's untimely death in 1969, John reorganised the business, and Sandalford became a company with John Roe and a Perth-based merchant bank the principal shareholders. In 1972 the company purchased a major property at Metricup (Margaret River) and developed a 140 hectare vineyard. In 1973 the Government Extension Oenologist, Dorham Mann, joined the group as chief winemaker.

The winery and base is still maintained in the Swan Valley, at Caversham. Its range of Caversham Estate wines are produced from fruit grown on the home property. Sandalford is the second biggest Western Australian winery (after Houghton), with approximately two thirds of its grape needs now coming from the Margaret River vineyard.

In 1979 the British Inchcape Group acquired all the shares in Sandalford not held by John Roe and his family. Another division of Inchcape, Taylor Ferguson, assumed distribution responsibility for Sandalford Wines. Since 1987, Frenchman Christian Morlaes has been senior winemaker, following the retirement of Dorham Mann. With typical resolve and the influx of much-needed capital, Morlaes is quietly turning the ship around. Recent wines have been more than acceptable and the only major problem the Group has yet to come to grips with is the low yields at Margaret River and the late spring gales that devastate the young growth—resulting in up to a 50 per cent crop loss of selected varieties.

The Sandalford Matilde cabernet rosé has always been a favoured wine for West Australians during summer. Made in the lighter Mateus style, it is fresh, tangy and flavourful. Recent releases of Margaret River Estate verdelho have also been highly prized. Verdelho has shown great potential since its debut in Margeret River in the last decade. It has the dual capacity to drink well when young but can become increasingly complex given patient bottle maturation. Other lines to emerge under Morlaes include the Margaret River riesling and cabernet sauvignon. The top fortified style in the Sandalford cellar is the incredibly concentrated Sandalera. Again, like the other high-sugar styles of the Swan Valley, it attains an almost fruit essence quality about it with small portions sufficient to experience the most richly flavoured dessert wine.

Talijancich Wines

Formerly Peters Quality Wines, Talijancich Wines is located on Hyem Road, Millendon. The combined efforts of father and son team Peter and James Talijancich have been largely responsible for producing many extremely fine fortified muscat styles in recent vintages. However, it is the older vintages, some dating back to the early 1960s, that have caught the attention of local show judges. Intensely concentrated, they embody an almost essence-like quality, reminiscent of liquid raisins. In the prestigious annual Sheraton Perth Western Australian Wine Awards they have probably scored more praise from the visiting national judges than any other single entry. Sadly, quantities are limited and they retail for a price that reflects twenty-five years' maturation. However, what they do represent is the Swan Valley, its heritage and a style that can only be duplicated in exceptional vintage years. The Talijancichs also produce a small quantity of acceptable table wine from the family vineyard fruit and that supplied by contract growers.

Twin Hills

Located on Great Northern Highway, Baskerville, towards the top end of the Swan Valley, Twin Hills has been the family winery of the Kraljevich family since 1947. Mark and Eddy Kraljevich have successfully taken over the property from their father. They concentrate on a range of table and fortified wines made from grapes grown on the superb alluvial loams common to the Baskerville area. The whites, chenin blanc and verdelho in particular, are most appealing.

Westfield Wines

The Kosovich name has been synonymous with the Swan Valley and Western Australia since 1922, when the current winemaker's father established his modest vineyard and cellar at Baskerville. Looking at the property today, he obviously had a great deal of foresight. John Kosovich, his wife, Mary and their children share a comfortable home set back from the highway, a superb vineyard that is spoken of in reverence as the best on the Swan, and a winery that lacks nothing in technology or love. John Kosovich is reluctant to speak of his successes. Indeed it's hard to engage him in any conversation if you are new on the scene. However, behind this laconic facade lurks a razor-sharp mind, a wit of great proportion and the accumulated knowledge of some forty vintages.

If one was seeking advice on wine-growing, pest control or winery practice, you could not go past asking John for his contribution. Acknowledged as a master viticulturist, Kosovich has reworked his father's vineyard, gently correcting and rearranging the vineyard composition. Completely unafraid of the summer's sweltering heat, he has elected to plant premium varieties such as riesling, verdelho and chardonnay for his whites; cabernet sauvignon and shiraz for his reds.

A tiny merlot planting has recently come on stream, offering the devoted customer base a further exotic alternative. A true French semillon completes the range in the table wine line-up. To re-create an interest in high-quality, full-flavoured fortified styles, Kosovich has painstakingly set up his own modified solera system to produce a contemporary liqueur muscat and hermitage base. The work is a labour of love as such a project inevitably takes at least one generation to come to fruition. If the seed wines are anything to go on, the ultimate blends should be quite outstanding. Mark your diaries for ten years hence!

The Kosovich touch can be seen throughout the entire range of wines. The white table varietals are perfectly balanced, have long flavour profiles and a delicacy that is totally out of character for the Swan Valley. On several occasions I have tabled the 1986 Westfield Chardonnay in the presence of some very august company. Time and time again the wine (served masked) has been ascribed to the various quality regions of northern Burgundy. The same tasters have been completely perplexed by the perennial quality of the verdelho and semillon wines.

The temptation to buy additional land or fruit from the cooler regions of the southern part of the state has crossed the Kosovich mind more than once. However, his allegiance to his heritage has held sway. The cellar reds, skilfully crafted with a selection of high-quality oak, rate with the best. Again, complexity and balance are the principal players. All this is achieved and made possible by careful clonal selection, the best vineyard husbandry and pure skill in the winery. Westfield is very much a hands-on winery—and very few hands besides those of John and Mary Kosovich intrude into the artistry. The annual crush is well below 100 tonnes. If the modern-day bean counter was to run his slide rule over the family's return on investment he would weep. The Kosovich rationale and lifestyle is one of admirable old-fashioned values. The cellar door prices signal this, for they rank as the best, on a pure quality basis, in Western Australia. Most of the production is sold at the cellar or via a small national mail order list. A tiny percentage has crept into specialist stores and Perth restaurants.

Another of Kosovich's innate talents is his ability as a judge of wine. He has represented his peer group on the Perth judging panel for the last decade and has one of the most objective palates I have encountered on the Australian circuit.

As a hobby, the dedicated oenophile has experimented with early-picked cabernet sauvignon as a base for sparkling wine. Early days yet, but the indicators are there that this may become a much larger diversification, perhaps even commercial—but then is there anything commercial about the Westfield enterprise?

One could confidently recommend most of the small range made by John Kosovich. Indeed, as I have observed in the habits of regular visitors to the cellars, a mixed carton tends to be the order of the day. However, to be specific, the mainstream lines are without question the wonderfully elegant chardonnay and the seductively smooth cabernet sauvignon. Unfortunately, quantities are limited so the wise tend to place standing orders or at least register their names on a mailing list. Not far behind the flagships are the verdelho, with its telltale honeysuckle character and varietally typical merlot. The generic white burgundy blend is representative of the contemporary version that made the wines of the West famous. For lovers of the fresh, richly flavoured port style, Kosovich's Westfield cabernet vintage port is a must.

South-West Coastal Plain

The nomenclature for this region, spreading from the northern metropolitan suburb of Wanneroo to the outskirts of Busselton, 240 km to the south, is rather a misnomer. I would have seen it more correctly delineated simply as the West Coastal Plain. The fact that one third of it happents to be in the south-west is immaterial. The region has little parallel with either of its neighbours, be it the Swan Valley in the north, or the Margaret River district to the south.

The common characteristics that encompass the entire strip, are the magnificent stands of native eucalypts (known as tuarts), the rich grey sands, the underlying limestone formations and an abundance of salt-free water trapped below. (Capel Vale, which sits beside the meandering Capel River in the south, has, by location a high percentage of alluvial loams deposited by the water system over many centuries.) The grey tuart sands form a buffer between the coast (sometimes within view) and the more fertile hinterland. They range in places from less than a kilometre wide to around four at best.

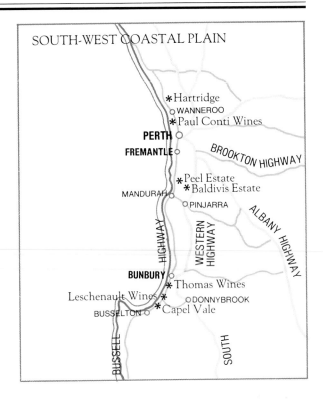

Being within close proximity to the coast, the region receives plenty of rain, has little or no frost problems (excepting Gelorup), and is well within the influence of the moderating summer sea breezes. Perhaps one of the most underrated positive benefits the location boasts is the protection offered by the tall tuarts. These tend to lessen the impact of the salt-laden, northwesterly winds that hit the west coast at the critical bud burst and flowering periods in the vineyards. (Margaret River hasn't been as fortunate and crop losses of up to 40 per cent have been reported.)

Vineyards have been established on the coastal strip since the latter half of the nineteenth century. To the south, the pioneers in the Bunbury region had thriving vineyards exporting wines to the United Kingdom, while in the Wanneroo district, Italian market gardeners had wineries supplying the needs of Perth and the goldfields in the 1920s. At its height, the Luisini Vineyard (south of Wanneroo) ranked with the biggest in Australia. Fluctuating fortunes and an encroaching urban sprawl saw many of the vineyard areas subdivided in the 1950s and 1960s. Today what is left is protected by owners committed to tradition.

The wines throughout the region have a common quality that makes them readily identifiable to the trained palate. Invariably, the weight of the wine is less than in adjacent regions, tending more to medium-light body; and the natural berry flavours are more precise and intense. Perhaps the shiraz variety is the best indicator of these qualities among the red table wines, and white frontignac, championed by Paul Conti, in the whites. Interesting experimentation with newer exotics, such as sauvignon blanc and chardonnay, could mean some exciting prospects for the future.

Baldivis Estate

Tucked away a little further inland than the majority of coastal developments, the Baldivis Estate vineyard and winery is part of a wider diversification involving the production of avocado pears, limes and table grapes. Perth entrepreneur, Peter Kailis, developed the property in 1982 with an eye to the export markets in South-East Asia. Son-in-law and property manager, John Galatis, has worked tirelessly to see the property through to fruition. Wine-wise, the initial crush in 1987 received little publicity due to the minimal quantities involved. The 1988 and 1989 vintages have produced commercial quantities under the guidance of a specialist consultant. These will be available in the market place, initially in Western Australia and Victoria. Negotiations are in hand to appoint distributors in Sydney and Brisbane.

The 8 hectares of wine grapes focus mainly on the premium varieties, chardonnay, sauvignon blanc, cabernet sauvignon and merlot. Wines released have all shown positive fruit flavours and balance. Weight has been a problem but given vine maturity and additional finessing in the handling of the crop, one expects this to be but a momentary concern.

The Baldivis Estate Chardonnay offers a great deal. It has bell-clear fruit flavours and an elegant balance. John Galatis has shown great skill in sensitively applying only minimal French oak to match the medium-weight fruit. A tight style that deserves a year or two to show its best. Turning to the Estate red wine, the astute Galatis has wisely elected to produce a light easy-drinking style from his early crops of cabernet and merlot. Blended to perfection, they make an ideal luncheon red where fruit and flavour length predominate over extractive characters.

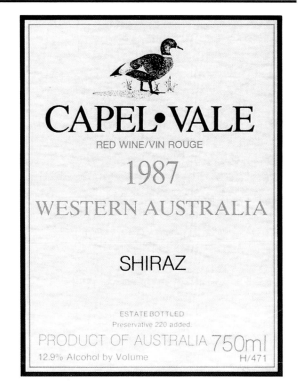

Capel Vale

Located on the southern banks of the Capel River, a kilometre or two to the south of the township of Capel, this vineyard and winery shot to national prominence within ten years of its establishment. The high profile accorded to the wines emanating from this spartan, no-fuss, high-tech winery is largely due to the dedication of the owners, Peter and Elizabeth Pratten, together with the skill of winemaker Alan Johnson.

The Prattens came to Bunbury in the early 1970s and soon realised the potential of the Capel district for winemaking. They established their vineyard on an attractive block sitting above the lower reaches of the local river. The picturesque property, complete with billabongs and flocks of wild ducks (hence the label logo) is within earshot of the Geographe Bay coastline and enjoys an almost perfect viticultural climate. They chose to plant the conventional varietal vineyard of that era, concentrating on cabernet sauvignon, shiraz, riesling and traminer.

Peter, a professional radiologist, built his simple but highly functional winery in 1979 and had the foresight to engage industry consultants Brian Croser and Tony Jordan to advise him for the early vintages. The extremely talented and energetic Pratten successfully introduced many innovations to winemaking at Capel Vale and his questioning approach to convention has seen his wines scoop many awards Australia-wide.

Equally enthusiastic, the Roseworthy-trained Johnson has worked alongside Pratten, crafting and fine-tuning the wines for the discriminating market place. Perhaps the most outstanding achievement of the partnership was the early realisation that the Capel Vale vineyard alone could not produce wines of optimum quality. The lateral-thinking Prattens carefully examined the deficiencies in their early wines and sought out grape suppliers in other regions to supplement the Capel styles. The whites were bolstered by higher acid, more aromatic fruit from Mount Barker, and the reds' peppery shiraz from Mount Barker, and a modicum of peppermint-enhanced cabernet sauvignon from Margaret River. Intuitively (to Peter Pratten anyway), a complex exercise was carried out in conjunction to match the natural fruit qualities of the final blends with the best oak available. (It's a great shame that all new winemakers don't undertake such searching experimentation to link up the best type of oak for the style, flavour and weight of their own wines.)

The time, research and effort, not forgetting the sizeable investment, has all paid off for the venturers. Today the Capel Vale label is in the vanguard of contemporary Australian wine. It has been the recipient of numerous trophies, medals and accolades. Consumer acceptance has grown to the point where the Prattens have had to expand their vineyard interests at Capel and, latterly, Mount Barker.

The Capel Vale Riesling ranks with the best in Australia. The 1986 was even ascribed by show judges as the best. Recent vintages, including the elegant limey 1989, have been equally as good. It is perhaps with this line that the individual skills of Pratten and Johnson tend to focus best of all. The wine is always impeccably balanced and carries all the hallmarks of an outstanding light-bodied table wine. The Mount Barker fruit component in the blend heightens the bouquet with an attractive citrus overtone and provides the positive acid finish to the wine. The home vineyard portion provides the necessary mid-palate flavour and depth. Altogether a wine of regular reliability that can only be influenced by seasonal variation.

The Capel Vale vineyard chardonnay comes from specially sourced clones that have been proven bearers of varietally indicative fruit. Vintage techniques that are secret and sometimes highly esoteric, together with a liberal choice of high-quality French oak, all combine to ensure that this wine is made to standards that invariably produce results both show judges and consumers are looking for. In tandem, these two wines, together with the highly sought-after semillon–sauvignon blanc and the little parcels of riesling–traminer made in the past, have all contributed to the reliability of the Capel Vale label, and the acknowledged industry belief that Pratten and his team are the most consistent small winery in Western Australia when it comes to white wine production.

The Capel Vale reds carry a dual promise; they are immensely approachable when youthful, yet one can also have full confidence in their potential to mature well. The cellar shiraz style has perhaps the best coastal-plain character. It comes with an almost cherry-like bouquet (liberally spiced by the Mount Barker fruit), and a tight fruity palate, rounded out with positive, albeit integrated oak characters. It is not an astringent wine, nor does it lack grip and style; it is a wine that has a strong following amongst the connoisseurs of the variety, and for that reason Peter Pratten has wisely maintained its presence in his line-up. A regular winner of trade tastings and show awards since the first vintage back in 1980.

The Capel Vale cabernet is something of an enigma since it promises much when youthful, tightens up with adolescence and only blossoms forth in all its glory when it deigns appropriate. Impressively made, the wine is a great favourite of many oenophiles, myself included. It is a well-crafted amalgam of variously picked fruit to provide acids, tannins and flavours in the most exacting composition. The meshing of Capel/ Margaret River/Mount Barker fruit is tightly framed by elegant smoky French oak to give one the overall sensation of up-front fruit, depth of flavour and an oak saddle—all very reminiscent of a Bordeaux red rather than a West Australian. As mentioned earlier, a superb experience when young but also an opportunity that should not be denied, given five to eight years careful maturation.

Like many other innovative winemakers, Peter Pratten has turned his attention in recent times to the manufacture of a high-quality sparkling wine. Given his dedication and the ability to attract the right source of fruit for his base wines, I can confidently predict great things to come in this area. Two indicator wines he and the enthusiastic Johnson have made to date show the nuances of benchmark examples, and with minor finessing could be in the forefront of the Western Australian push into this elusive but rewarding niche.

Hartridge

Hartridge was developed in the early 1970s by Jim Yates, a chemical engineer at the Swan Brewery. He wisely chose to plant a small, manageable vineyard specialising in chenin blanc and cabernet sauvignon—varieties which have proven quite outstanding on the light coastal soils. He achieved his greatest success with the 1978 cabernet sauvignon, which won the trophy at the Perth Wine Show for the best Western Australian dry red table wine.

Poor health led Yates to sell his 4 hectare vineyard and winery to Perry and Faye Sandow in 1981. (Yates maintained contact via a consulting brief.) Perry Sandow, well known in Perth television circles for his expertise as a freelance photographer and lighting engineer, sought the professional support of local winemaker David Cooper to help with his initial vintages. Sandow has now taken over most of the vineyard and winery duties, maintaining the two styles championed by Yates and Cooper. Quantities are small, with most being sold at cellar door. Limited volumes have been marketed through specialist stores in Sydney and Melbourne.

The chenin blanc is a workmanlike dry table style displaying attractive varietal flavour and crisp natural acid. The Hartridge cabernet sauvignon is a tightly structured style showing positive berry flavour and elegant oak.

Leschenault Wines

Well-known Bunbury couple, Betty and Barry Killerby, pioneered their 16 hectare vineyard in 1973. Located adjacent to Lakes Road, Gelorup, between Bunbury and Capel (200 km south of Perth), Leschenault Wines is very much typical of the grey tuart sand country encountered along the coastal strip. The surrounding stands of tuart and other native eucalypts abound with native birds and fauna—this has been a constant source of concern for the Killerbys, especially prior to vintage when marauding parrots can devastate 50 per cent of their crop in a matter of days.

Leschenault takes its name from Port Leschenault, the early name for Bunbury. (Leschenault was the name of the botanist on the French vessel under the command of Baudin, which explored the nearby coastline in 1803.)

Barry Killerby, a long-time Bunbury medical practitioner, with a close affinity for the land, decided to emulate the steps taken by other local medicos in the district, such as Pratten, Cullen and Pannell. He set about clearing and planting his property to cabernet sauvignon, shiraz, pinot noir, traminer, semillon and chardonnay. He trickle-irrigated the entire 16 hectares from an abundant underground water source and quickly learnt to cope with the natural predators and the disadvantages of being the only vineyard in the area. The first vintage in 1977 was made in the winery constructed by the good doctor.

His effervescent wife stepped into the breach as marketing manager. Within several vintages, largely due to the energy of the Killerbys and their daughter Anna, the Leschenault name spread to the east coast of Australia where markets and wholesalers were established.

The winery, with increasing tonnages coming in successive years, was extensively expanded and technology-improved to cater for a wider diversity of styles. The Killerbys also saw the benefits to be had by having an outside consultant on contract and appointed Robert Bowen to oversee critical sectors of their operation. This inspired move, together with the fruit from maturing vines, rewarded the hardworking couple handsomely when Leschenault took the trophy as the most successful small West Australian exhibitor at the 1989 Perth Wine Show.

Progressively, Barry Killerby has learnt to manage his new environment; recent wines have shown increased sophistication and a better, more intense fruit quality. Vine husbandry, improved and more extensive oak storage and the influence of Bowen, have all contributed in part to the overall result. One can but predict some outstanding wines from this small, isolated winery in the next few vintages.

The 1989 Leschenault chardonnay blitzed all but Murray Tyrrell's impressive Vat 47 at the Perth Wine Show. The Killerby wine received 18.80 points out of a possible 20 in the young chardonnay class, won a gold medal and capped it off with the trophy for the best Western Australian chardonnay. The wine displayed very subtle, intense fruit with length and balance. The winemaker skilfully married these natural flavours with some excellent wood. Admirable current drinking with the promise of more, given the patience of two to three years' bottle maturation. The companion wine, so to speak, that caused much excitement from the 1989 vintage, was the semillon. A top wine, again showing tight fruit, superb balance and some highly polished winemaking techniques. Over the years I have always been impressed with the Leschenault reds. They are most indicative of the vineyard, having tight berry-like structures, and long flavour profiles. The shiraz, in particular, has been a favourite; however, I have always thought it may have benefited from some additional complexing, be it oak related or the addition of another variety.

Paul Conti Wines

Established by Carmelo Conti in 1925, the vineyard and winery on Wanneroo Road, Wanneroo (a northern metropolitan suburb of Perth), has been a district landmark for several generations of wine enthusiasts, as well as providing an essential necessity of life to the local southern European community. Today, Carmelo's son Paul is at the helm of both vineyard and winery, with his own son Jason taking more than a passing interest in the annual ritual.

Conti has the distinct advantage of being able to source fruit from three vineyards under his control—one to the rear of the winery; a larger more productive unit to the east of Wanneroo at Marginiup; and a newer development planted to chardonnay at Yanchep. The sum total of hectares is less than twenty—very much the size of the majority of local West Australian plantings under owner-winemaker control.

Growing up in an industry of changing consumer demands that has seen preferences swing from fortified wines to red table styles, then onto the delicate white wines, Paul Conti has coped with change extremely well. Given that his formal training was gained at his father's side in the vineyard and winery, Conti, like his colleague John Kosovich at Westfield, has developed obviously inherent talents that have won national recognition for him and his wife, Anne. Their efforts in producing delicate fruity styles devoid of the oxidation and sulphur-related problems so common in small wineries in hot climatic zones is to be commended.

Conti was one of the first West Australian winemakers to recognise the contribution played by high-quality grapes in the final analysis of premium wine production. In conjunction with the Department of Agriculture, he initiated and carried out extensive vineyard and vine research to improve production and vigour in the tuart sands of his Wanneroo properties. The manageable size of his holdings ensured complete control from pruning through to spraying and ultimately picking. As older industry identities are quick to point out, 'great wines are always made in the vineyard'—Conti therefore had a head start over most.

Conti's skills also became apparent in his small but efficient winery following a heavy investment program. He quickly and competently changed the style of his two premium wines—the dry red shiraz and the white frontignac—to reflect changes seen in the marketplace. Stainless steel, temperature-controlled fermentation tanks replaced his father's concrete vats; imported yeast strains selected for their ability to enhance bouquet and flavour were used in lieu of the wild natural yeasts; and new imported French and American hogsheads made an initial appearance. These long-range plans paid early dividends, with Conti becoming the most successful exhibitor among the smaller wineries at the Perth Wine Show on several occasions. His flagship wines became household names and order exceeded supply.

From 1976 until 1983 Conti entered into a joint-venture agreement with Betty and Tony Pearse of Mount Barker to process the fruit from Forest Hill vineyard. This association provided mutual benefits under a new Conti–Forest Hill label. Difficulties were continually experienced, however, in getting the grapes to the winery in optimum condition because of distance (some eight hours by truck). Because of this, in 1984 the Pearses elected to establish their own Forest Hill label and contracted local Mount Barker winery Plantagenet to process their fruit.

Conti's foresight and astute marketing ability was again characterised by his wisdom in planting one of the first major vineyards to chardonnay, north of the cooler regions. He also recognised the special attributes of the high-acid colombard variety, and for some time successfully produced an award-winning style.

Today his program of vineyard management and winery reinvestment continues. Production is still miniscule but both Conti and his wife can share a great deal of pride in what they have done and in their contribution to the Western Australian industry.

Conti has wisely chosen to produce varietal table wine that is in complete harmony with the local environment and soils. The wine most commonly associated with Paul Conti is what is affectionately known as the 'Conti Fronti'. A delicate, light-bodied white table wine with a touch of residual sugar. The late-picked sugar character cleverly masks the usual attendant hardness of the white frontignac. Quite the best of its type in Australia. The best selling dry white table wines are the chenin blanc and chardonnay. The chenin is a well-made crisp style with good varietal aroma and flavour. In some years, dependent upon the season, it may carry the barest touch of sugar. The Conti chardonnay, grown in the new Yanchep vineyard, is more in the lighter aromatic limey mould than the buttery battledress versions so often seen from warmer districts. Wood plays an important role in the make-up of the wine and I believe Paul is not yet satisfied that he has aligned the right oak with his particular fruit.

The shiraz produced on the estate—labelled Marginiup Hermitage—is a soft, full-flavoured style, again reflecting the climate and soils. It sees a short period in oak, which is designed primarily to complement rather than contrast the flavours.

Peel Estate

The Peel Estate vineyard takes its name from the larger grant of some 1 million acres made to Thomas Peel in 1834. It was developed by Will Nairn and his UK partners, from what was principally a 400 hectare grazing property, which supported stud Brangus cattle and Suffolk sheep. Inspired by his father and grandfather, both keen

wine men, and the State Viticulturist, Bill Jamieson, Will set out his initial plantings, mainly shiraz, in 1974. Much of his early encouragement came from the respected Wanneroo winemaker, Paul Conti. Both shared comparable properties, both had a particular liking for the shiraz variety and, of course, individual commitment to the land. Needless to say, Conti took all the grapes from the property until the completion of the Peel Estate winery in 1980. Constructed from specially prepared bricks, under the supervision of a talented young architect, it fits aesthetically between a copse of magnificent tuarts and the vineyard. It is a no-nonsense winery, functionally designed to accommodate each phase of the process, with a mezzanine floor fitted to permit visitors a panoramic view of the total operation.

The initial hectares of shiraz have now been joined by 4 hectares of chenin blanc, 2 hectares of chardonnay and 2 hectares each of cabernet sauvignon and sauvignon blanc. Trials of verdelho, zinfandel and semillon have also been planted. Will Nairn, who also judges at the Perth Royal Show, has quickly learnt the winemaking craft. In the short space of ten vintages he has won major trophies for both the Peel Estate shiraz and cabernet sauvignon. The chenin blanc style has achieved somewhat of a cult following. It can be procured either as a dry varietal with a touch of new oak or, alternatively, in a late-picked style. Early vintages of chardonnay have been quite outstanding. Will has experimented within fairly wide parameters to establish the definitive style. One has great confidence in the future direction of the label given the quality of the indicator wines. Will Nairn has also learnt to source the particular types of oak most suitable for the weight and intensity of his wines—another confidence booster for the future. Peel Estate is both an attractive destination to visit, less than an hour's drive south of the city, and a focal point for typical coastal region wines.

All wines are usually available for tasting, depending on availability. (Again, another boutique producer crushing less than 50 tonnes.) The classic wood-matured chenin blanc with its crisp fruit flavour and subtle French-oak background, is a celler must. Ideally, this should be bracketed with the chardonnay for comparative purposes prior to tasting either of the two premium reds—shiraz or cabernet sauvignon. Both reflect the tight berry-like flavours so typical of the coastal soils. Neither is a weighty, extracted style but each can be confidently cellared for up to five years.

Thomas Wines

Well-known Bunbury pharmacist Gil Thomas caught the wine bug in the early 1970s after helping Bill Pannell complete the early vintages at Moss Wood. The enthusiastic Thomas quickly took up the advice of another colleague and in 1976 planted out the family's pony paddock on his Gelorup property to pinot noir and chardonnay. Situated behind his new homestead (5 km south of Bunbury), the grey tuart sands of the new vineyard took many applications of fertiliser, humus and water before showing any marked impression on the newly planted canes. Indeed Gil was overheard to say at a Bunbury Bacchus Club function in his honour that each bottle from his first crop in 1983 had been costed at $200 each, given the investment committed to that point. Needless to say, the proud father recouped but a fraction of that and philosophically hoped for a more benign road ahead.

The Thomas pinot style has good varietal definition and character. Thomas has experimented with several differing sources of French oak to achieve optimum harmony. Most vintages have figured prominently in Perth Wine Show results, winning medals alongside the acknowledged national pinot noir experts. One pleasing feature of the venture is that as both vineyard and winemaker mature, the results reflect more typical Burgundian styles. Quantities are still tiny given that the 2 hectare block only produces on average 5 tonnes per vintage. A note to Gil Thomas, care of the Bunbury post office will, however, put you in touch.

The talented Thomas also processes selected batches of cabernet sauvignon from the south-west region. Depending on fruit availability, this may be sourced from nearby Donnybrook or from the boom area of Margaret River. Invariably, these wines are well crafted and, as a consequence, highly sought after. (Thomas has twice won the top red wine trophy at the Perth Wine Show for champion dry red table wine.) Most wine is sold at cellar door or through specialist retailers in Perth.

The Thomas pinot noir, made in the Vosne style rather than the Chamertin, is characteristically fruity when young; however, it develops Burgundian 'spicy' qualities with age. The texture is typically light and silky. The wines are seldom released in chronological vintage order, Thomas preferring to hold back individual vintages until he is satisfied that the wine has matured sufficiently.

Lower Great Southern Region

Geographically, this region encompasses that area between the Frankland and Kalgan Rivers and the towns of Cranbrook and Albany—an area 60 km square bisected by the Albany Highway. The focal points are the regional port of Albany on the southern coast and Mount Barker in the hinterland. Albany, the oldest settlement in Western Australia, enjoys the benefits of an extremely temperate climate, a magnificent harbour and some of the most scenic coastline in the state. It is the holiday destination for many city folk who don't mind the five-hour trek given the undulating terrain, the superb scenery and the rich grazing country adjacent to the major highway.

Spring is an ideal time to visit the region as the renowned wildflowers can be seen in their totality and the cool crisp weather enjoyed at its bracing best. Local tourist bureaus, a strong feature in the West, are extremely helpful and provide the necessary expertise in guiding visitors to the many remote points of beauty.

The region basically has it all. The Stirling Range, containing some of the state's tallest peaks (which are easily accessible), stands as an ancient sentinel to the east—here snow is known to fall in late October and November. The long coastline to the south provides opportunities for surfing, sailing and fishing. The renowned hardwood timbers jarrah and karri grow prolifically throughout the area and many of the nation's finest wool and cattle studs have developed here since settlement in the late 1820s.

Perhaps the only negative feature of the region is the vast distances between the wineries. A trip around the key vineyard areas involves a journey of some 400 km and the best part of two to three days to do it justice. The climate is most suitable

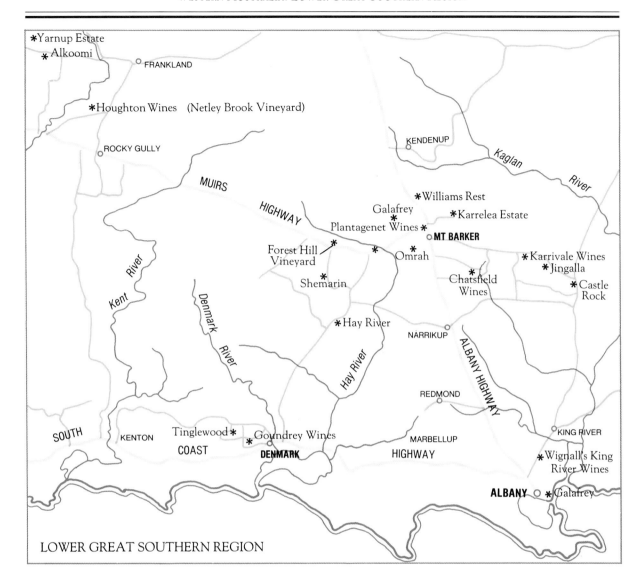

*Yarnup Estate
  *Alkoomi   o FRANKLAND

      *Houghton Wines   (Netley Brook Vineyard)

                                                    KENDENUP
      ROCKY GULLY   o   Kaglan
         o   River
             MUIRS
                                                      *Williams Rest
                 HIGHWAY   Galafrey   *Karrelea Estate
                            Plantagenet Wines *   *
             Forest Hill *   *   o MT BARKER
             Vineyard   * Omrah   *Karrivale Wines
                          *   Chatsfield   *Jingalla
         River   Shemarin   Wines   *Castle
                                                        *   Rock
    Kent   Denmark
                                  *Hay River
                            River   NARRIKUP   ALBANY HIGHWAY
                                   Hay River   o
                                                  REDMOND
                                                     o
    SOUTH   KENTON   Tinglewood * Goundrey Wines   KING RIVER
                              COAST   *   MARBELLUP   o
                         DENMARK   HIGHWAY   *Wignall's King
                                                                         River Wines

                                                        ALBANY o *Galafrey

LOWER GREAT SOUTHERN REGION

for premium wine production. Overall the heat degree temperature summation is a mere 1400°C at Mount Barker, making it one of the coolest areas in Western Australia between spring and autumn. Rainfall is normally around 1200 mm per annum. Summer temperatures are moderated by frequent cloud cover and chilly nights.

Frost is a constant danger in lower pockets of land and few will forget the disastrous 'black frost' of 1981 which cut a wide swathe through the Frankland River vineyards, devastating up to 80 per cent of the new growth on the Alkoomi property. Other constant fears are the increasing salinity of the rivers and soils; the ever-present ravenous bird population, which comes to the fore during the ripening season; and the changing weather pattern, said to be caused by that new phenomenon the so-called Greenhouse Effect. This is highlighted in longer summers

when both vines and water reserves are under stress. As a consequence, most vineyards are trickle-irrigated to enhance fruit quality. Grape yields are barely economic, but this is compensated for by the additional fruit intensity so often seen in the riesling, shiraz and malbec wines of the Lower Great Southern.

The genesis that led to the development of the region was the 1955 report of Californian Professor Harold Olmo, who reported favourably on the viticultural possibilities of the cooler southwest (Margaret River) and Great Southern (Mount Barker) regions. Sir Charles Court, in 1965, then Minister for Industrial Development, commissioned the Department of Agriculture to act on the Olmo report and the equally favourable findings of Dr John Gladstones, who reported on the climate and soils of the southern areas of Western Australia. Bill Jamieson, the principal State Viticulturist, was given the task of developing a small 5 acre vineyard on the Forest Hill property of Tony and Betty Pearse, some 20 km to the west of Mount Barker. Quite astutely, he chose the riesling and cabernet sauvignon varieties for the trial, with the first vintage occurring in 1972. Much has been written and spoken of this pioneering venture by Jamieson, which entailed a personal contribution far beyond the requirement of his public office. He worked tirelessly to bring the experiment to a successful conclusion. Who can ever forget the magnificent 1975 riesling that became the most awarded dry white table wine ever made in Western Australia? Jamieson was helped throughout his ten-year project by Dorham Mann, who was largely responsible for the oenological side of the trial. Fittingly, the conclusions reached vindicated the work of Olmo and Gladstones and a new wine region was born. Jamieson and the Government of Western Australia relinquished the lease on Forest Hill in 1976, with the vineyard reverting back to the ownership of the Pearse family. For his contribution to Western Australian viticulture, over nearly fifty years with the Department of Agriculture, Bill Jamieson was awared an MBE by the Queen. He retired in 1979.

Alkoomi

In 1971 Frankland River farmers, Merv and Judy Lange saw the opportunities offered by diversifying into grapegrowing and planted a small vineyard on their prized 1200 hectare property Alkoomi, an hour's drive north-west of Mount Barker.

The Langes soon developed that incurable disease that has been known to afflict many people approaching viticulture for the first time. The interest soon became totally consuming, the area under vines expanded and plans for a winery were drawn up. The Langes' enterprise came to fruition in 1976 with the arrival of the first vintage. Wisely, they contracted this and the following two vintages to local winemakers.

In 1979 the winery, constructed of local stone and hardwood, was completed and the Langes crushed the first fruit at Frankland under the watchful eyes of consultant oenologist Michael Peterkin. As quantities increased it became necessary to employ a full-time specialist winemaker. John Wade (ex-Wynn's Coonawarra) was appointed. Subsequently, Kim Hart has taken over the production role leaving the vineyard and marketing management to the very capable Langes.

The Alkoomi vineyard has 22 hectares under vines with further plantings planned in 1990. Principal varieties include cabernet, riesling, shiraz and the fabled malbec. Recent additions include semillon, sauvignon blanc and merlot.

The wines of Alkoomi, although subject to some horrific seasonal difficulties (frosts in 1981 and 1982, droughts regularly thereafter and hungry local bird life), have been outstanding. They all carry a depth of varietal intensity unseen elsewhere in Australia. The acids and flavour lengths are positive and the more esoteric fruit components beautifully balanced. Indeed, one could say a winemaker's dream! I have always been impressed with the honesty of these wines and the particular, careful manner in which they are handled. One can well expect great things from this isolated little winery that has been virtually carved out of the harsh rural Australian landscape. The arrival is definitely worth the journey—the wines speak silently for themselves. Alkoomi wines are distributed nationally.

Show judges and consumers would tend to concur that the Alkoomi cabernet ranks with the best in Australia. Its limited production alone precludes it from being more widely known. Intensely coloured and flavoured (the 1977 is drinking well presently), it takes some time to shake off the robes of innocence and complex to maturity. Being only medium-bodied it has little need for heavy oaking. Lange has experimented extensively with several oaks from central France to ensure the best amalgam of complementary flavours. The total package has become highly sophisticated in recent vintage with the addition of a small percentage of merlot. The 1985 release being quite superb.

The Alkoomi cabernet is a frequent winner of major awards at the Perth, Mount Barker and Sheraton Perth West Australian Wine Competitions. The winery's malbec, adjudged by some influential critics as the best of its variety in Australia, is equally as impressive as the cabernet. Quantities are extremely limited, but if one can search out a bottle of a top year (1983, for example) a treat is in store. Shiraz, sometimes labelled hermitage, has been impressive in outstanding years (1986) and the early vintages of merlot have shown Pomerol-like qualities. (Sadly, this varietal is destined to become a component in the cabernet sauvignon.)

The Alkoomi riesling has the local acid/fruit structure that appeals to the dedicated oenophiles. It is a great shame that most of the vineyard whites are consumed within twelve months of release, as history would show that the riesling is enhanced with three to five years bottle development. The natural lemony flavours mellow with the acid and develop long flavour profiles not unlike the varietals from South Australia's Eden Valley. Recent releases of semillon and sauvignon blanc have shown regional affinity.

Blackwood Crest

Although they are located a little north of the Great Southern district, Max and Roslyn Fairbrass consider the wines from their Blackwood Crest Estate to have more than a close affinity with this region.

Located near Boyup Brook on one of the State's best merino holdings, the 4 hectare vineyard, since its establishment in 1977, has become the focal point for local tourism. Varieties planted include riesling, semillon, sauvignon blanc, cabernet and shiraz. Annual production runs at 15 tonnes, with all wines being made and matured on the property.

Successive vintages since 1981 have highlighted riesling and shiraz as the more varietally indicative cultivars. The light, elegant riesling has found a ready market in the local community, while the percentage of the peppery shiraz committed to a vintage-port style has excited fortified wine lovers from further afield. Max has indicated that early trials of semillon and sauvignon blanc have been particularly exciting; these could well become the major cellar lines.

The careful vineyard husbandry and cellar practices have resulted in several Blackwood Crest wines coming to the fore in recent local Shows. The port style, fortified with special aged spirit, has been a consistent winner. Further vineyard expansion is planned for the spring of 1990.

The limited production to date has precluded distribution beyond selected Perth stores and restaurants. However, a note to the Fairbrass family, care of the Boyup Brook Post Office, will ensure a place on the growing mailing list.

Castle Rock

Angelo and Wendy Diletti, have selected a sloping site high up in the Porongurup range, east of Albany, as their vinous Xanadu. The location is exposed to a wider range of climatic variations to that experienced in Mount Barker, a short thirty-minute drive to the north. The vineyard is distinctly cooler due to the 300 m altitude and enjoys an extended ripening period. The wines are therefore noticeably different from other regional styles, and given further vintages may well prove to be from the choice location of the district. The opportunity to purpose-plant pinot noir and chardonnay for sparkling wine production must appeal to the Dilettis and two pioneering vignerons nearby. The potential is unlimited given the acid and flavour levels seen from early crops.

Riesling and cabernet sauvignon form the staple varieties. Both have shown outstanding promise. The 1986 Castle Rock riesling is an extremely fine wine ranking with the 1986 Capel Vale as the top white wines of that vintage. It is less giving than other Mount Barker wines yet has that crystal-clear varietal flavour that is a delight to approach when young and offers a great deal more given patient cellaring. Possibly the style to watch closely in the future.

The cabernet is a slow developer and less impressive first up. To be fair, the vines are young and a mere three vintages have had the opportunity to express their worth. I feel the fruit has outstanding potential but is very much in need of a lateral-thinking winemaker who can craft the fruit with the due complexity it deserves, right from the vineyard to bottling. The choice of oak will need to be thought through wisely, as the juice has lighter, more perfumed fruit than the richly intense flavours of Mount Barker. All wines to date have been made at Alkoomi, an arrangement that well suits the Dilettis, who both have senior positions in Albany and a young family.

Top years of the riesling, like 1986, have few peers in the district. Forest Hill approaches the mark; however, it is very much a case of comparing an outstanding Eden Valley style (Castle Rock) to the fine wines of Clare (Forest Hill)—in the end it comes down to a subjective judgment as to preferences.

Chatsfield Wines

The Chatsfield vineyard (previously known as Watermans) is located on Watermans Road, 10 km south of Mount Barker. The initial plantings were made by Ron Waterman, a professional agricultural consultant, in 1976. A great supporter of supplementary watering during the vines' growing and ripening seasons, Ron raised the ire of many local growers when he installed the region's first vineyard trickle-irrigation system. The results were positive; the Waterman rieslings of the early 1980s had a distinctly longer, more intense mid-palate flavour profile—an attribute that caught the eye of both the discerning consumer and the show judges. As is the norm in Australian agriculture, others in the area then rushed to imitate the Waterman initiative. Most winemakers now recognise the value of such a back-up system and budget for the installation as a mandatory practice.

The major emphasis of the early plantings focused on riesling and traminer. The wines have been made in turn by Plantagenet, Capel Vale and more lately by Michael Goundrey. Vine plantings have increased to around 9 hectares with the addition of chardonnay, shiraz and cabernet franc. The property has recently been purchased by Dr Ken Lynch, another medical enthusiast who has been caught up in the pleasurable pursuits of wine.

The attractive spice-enhanced traminer, the elegant riesling or the lighter-bodied shiraz are all recommended. All display attractive fruit aromas and clean crisp flavours. Late-picked white styles are made as seasonal conditions permit.

Forest Hill Vineyard

Forest Hill, a top Mount Barker orchard and stud sheep property, was the site chosen by State Viticulturist Bill Jamieson for his experimental vineyard in 1965. During the vintage years (halcyon days even!) 1972 to 1975, the vineyard produced outstanding crops of high-quality riesling and cabernet sauvignon which ultimately became wines of a quality hitherto unseen in the

West. The last vintage (1975), off nine-year-old vines, eclipsed all expectations, with the riesling winning some ten gold medals and nine trophies at national shows.

From 1976 until 1983 the Pearses entrusted Paul Conti with the vintaging of the Forest Hill fruit. During that period the grapes were trucked to the Conti Wanneroo winery in the cool hours of the night and processed immediately on arrival. Somehow the journey failed to preserve all the magical qualities seen in the 1973 and 1975 vintages and the resultant wines, albeit of medal-winning quality, never reached the previous heights.

The Pearses then looked to local champion Robert Bowen to process their fruit at Mount Barker's Plantagenet winery. Curiously, the old qualities returned immediately with the 1984 riesling being adjudged the top West Australian white wine at both the Perth and Mount Barker shows. Bowen was also successful with the cabernets from the property and added a light port style to the Forest Hill range.

During the intervening years, Betty and Tony Pearse, along with son Bruce, extended plantings to 20 hectares and added a new range of varieties at Forest Hill. Traminer, chardonnay and sauvignon blanc gave the owners the necessary depth to the white table styles on offer. Of these, the delicate traminer and the citrus melon-like chardonnay impressed most. It is unfortunate that the market isn't currently attuned to traminer, because the Forest Hill version is perhaps the best of the variety I have seen nationally. Obviously the cool climate and the long ripening period is conducive to bringing out the inherent positive qualities of the grape—very much akin to the German and Alsation styles. Fashions change and we may well see a resurgence of interest.

Due to a change in personal circumstances the property was offered for sale in 1989. Perth entrepreneur, Robert Holmes à Court negotiated the purchase, and future wines will be made at Vasse Felix. Bruce Pearse has been appointed manager of the Forest Hill property. The Australian wine industry owes a great deal to the visionary Pearse family. It was their personal commitment to the new project which largely turned around a depressed orchard and grazing-related community to the important and nationally focused winemaking region it is today.

Unquestionably, the riesling from the Forest Hill vineyard stands head and shoulders above the balance of the lines offered. The pristine colour, elegant intense varietal flavour and clean acid finish are benchmark qualities apparent in all releases to date. Vintage variation may impact on one or all of these components but the quality remains constant. The riesling has the ability to take some age well, providing a further extension and dimension. One can only suggest you find an acceptable vintage, purchase a case and follow the progress of maturation over a three-year span.

Recent chardonnay and traminer releases have been extremely attractive. Both share the same tight palate structure and fresh acid finish as the riesling. A slight exposure to French oak has complemented the citrus chardonnay characters beautifully. The Forest Hill cabernet, like other counterparts in the region, displays vibrant purple colours, rich intense fruit and a soft but positive tannin tail. Age adds a necessary complexity.

Galafrey

The Galafrey venture is headed up by Ian and Linda Tyrer, who came to the Mount Barker region in 1975 from Melbourne. Coming from the high-tech world of computers and electronics, they were attracted by the solitude and opportunites for creative expression in the district. Vine-growing and winemaking appealed and their 12 hectare vineyard—planted to riesling, chardonnay, muller thurgau, cabernet sauvignon, cabernet franc, pinot noir and merlot—was set out slightly west of the township. Early vintages were made under contract until the hardworking couple (who have studied oenology by correspondence) established their own base, an old Albany woolstore. Ian and Linda have converted the historic building into an attractive residence, model winery and sales outlet. The wines made to date reflect the rich gravelly loams of the vineyard and the due care and attention the Tyrers devote to their products. Production is small by industry standards with vintage yet to exceed 40 tonnes. Ian is an innovative thinker and caters well for the heavy tourist trade as well as the connoisseur. A recent addition to the cellar range includes a very delicate riesling-based sparkling wine.

As the principal varieties of the vineyard are riesling and cabernet, the major label emphasis has always reflected this specialisation. The riesling displays the delicate fruit flavours of the Mount Barker area and the cabernet the usual rich, full-fruit characters. Both the 1988 vintage riesling and the 1985 cabernet were prize winners at the Mount Barker Show.

Goundrey Wines

Michael and Alison Goundrey typify the very essence of the Australian spirit of endeavour. In 1971 Michael, a part-time grazier and contractor, and his young schoolteacher wife, decided to diversify into grapegrowing, following the successful cultivation of vines on the Forest Hill property. They initially planted a small vineyard on the Sheldon Park property near the historic St Werburgh's Estate, 5 km or so to the west of Mount Barker.

Well before the onset of the first commercial crop in 1975, the Goundreys realised the vineyard was a little beyond a part-time undertaking, so Michael's grazing cum contracting commitments were wound back. He entrusted the 1975 fruit to Plantagenet and set off to learn the art of winemaking in Perth. Ted Grassi, respected Swan vigneron, was only too happy to put the enthusiast through the rigours of the trade.

He was so impressed with Goundrey's enormous capacity for work and thirst for knowledge that he asked him back for the 1976 vintage as well. With this practical experience under his belt, Michael headed back to Mount Barker in time for his own first vintage, which he carried out in what had previously been the family garage. Two, perhaps three, Humes concrete well liners served as fermentation vats, while several lonely hogsheads resting in the background awaited the first Sheldon Park cabernet sauvignon.

The conditions were basic but the enthusiasm of the young couple ensured that the vintage was one to remember. I have a clear recollection of trying the fermenting juice and being extremely impressed. I was even more delighted ten years later when tasting my only bottle of the vintage in the company of a group of show judges, half of whom picked the masked bottle as a leading Bordeaux.

As volumes increased, the family garage was doubled. In 1979 the vintage outgrew the garage and the couple were able to purchase an old butter factory in Denmark. This gave them the capacity and the badly needed exposure to the growing tourist market.

In between vintages, Michael purchased additional land in Denmark, planting 13 hectares of vines: riesling, cabernet sauvignon, chardonnay and sauvignon blanc. He named this new vineyard Windy Hill.

The couple then consolidated, sold the Mount Barker vineyard and relocated the family to this aesthetically beautiful coastal town, 50 km south of Mount Barker. This commitment was a quantum leap forward both in financial and volume terms. However, the zeal of the Goundreys was unswerving even in the face of a great deal of personal privation.

The success of vintages 1979 and 1981 placed the Goundrey name firmly before the West Australian public. A series of outstanding vintages followed and the Goundrey label moved to national prominence; culminating with the 1985 cabernet being selected as one of Australia's top wines in a major Sydney exhibition, as well as scooping the major prize at the Sheraton Perth West Australian Wine Awards.

During 1988 the Goundrey family joined forces with Denbarker grazier Tony Riggall and purchased the historic Langton property to the west of Mount Barker. Plans were prepared for a new rammed-earth winery and a vineyard, which will eventually encompass 150 hectares. Already some 65 hectares have been committed to vine

and the first vintage at Langton in 1989 saw 300 tonnes of local fruit processed. In a further negotiation, the partnership contracted to buy the Chateau Barker vineyard from the Cooper family, renaming it Williams Rest. Having transcended state and national boundaries, the international market may well be in the sights of the group, especially as developing vineyards mature and the marketing plans unfold.

Goundrey Wines are progressing in terms of positioning their products and establishing a desirable merchandising profile. Given the ground covered since 1971 it is possible that we will see the name Goundrey ranked with that of Mondavi and Rothschild in the early part of the next century—in recognition of a similar unselfish contribution and professional vision.

The Goundrey cabernet sauvignons have always been inspiring wines. As the craftsmanship and skills of the Goundrey team have been honed with experience, the wines have become tighter in structure and steadily more sophisticated. New oak, from various sources, plays an important role in the winery's endeavour to determine the optimum style. Blending of varieties has been a further extension of experimentation, pitched at reaching the most complete and harmonious composition. The correlation with the better cabernet sauvignons of France is deliberate.

The supporting role, albeit on the same stage, is played by the Goundrey shiraz—a top wine which regularly displays attractive, ripe, peppery aromas with an elegant balance of sweet integrated oak.

The Goundrey riesling is a consistent label that can be relied on for positive fruit characters, flavour length and crisp natural acids.

Hay River

The Hay River vineyard is located on the Mount Barker–Denmark Road, almost equidistant between the two towns. The 6.5 hectares of vines were planted in 1974 totally to cabernet sauvignon. It has a textbook location; protected, gently east-facing slopes, with well-drained deep gravelly loam soils. The initial husbandry was entrusted to David McNamara by the syndicate of Perth businessmen, headed by Robert Ruse and Darryl Smalley, who have leased the vineyard. Subsequently, specialist vineyard consultant Ron Waterman managed the property on behalf of the group. It is now under the watchful eye and direction of Michael Goundrey. The initial vintage was made by Jane Paull in temporary facilities on site. Ensuing vintages were made at Plantagenet by Robert Bowen, until a new management agreement was concluded with Michael Goundrey, who oversees both vineyard and winemaking.

The hallmark of the Hay River cabernet is the bright, attractive berry character that emanates from the pristine fruit—indeed, the quality of the fruit is a direct reflection of the superb vineyard and its management. The elegant fruit lends itself to a much more light-bodied style than the mainstream of Mount Barker cabernets. The most outstanding wine produced to date is the recently released 1987 cabernet, which won a gold medal and three trophies at the 1989 Perth Wine Show. Among these accolades was the award for the Best West Australian Dry Red. The cabernet is highly recommended, especially the 1987 vintage, if you can track it down!

Houghton Netley Brook Vineyard

This Frankland River vineyard is some 300 km south of Perth, near the small township of the same name. The vineyard, which is leased by Houghton, is part of a 7000 hectare grazing property developed by the Roche family of Adelaide. The first vines were planted in the spring of 1968 and now cover some 90 hectares. Since the first vintage in 1972, largely made by Sandalford, the property has become home for the steely aromatic riesling and pungent peppery light-bodied shiraz styles. In 1981, following the deferral of a decision to build a winery on the site, Houghton entered into a five-year lease of the vineyard—subsequently renewed. Principal varieties cultivated include riesling, cabernet sauvignon, shiraz, malbec, chardonnay and semillon.

Between 1977 and 1984, under the winemaker Jon Reynolds, the Houghton Netley Brook wines achieved outstanding results in the marketplace, with the Frankland River riesling all but becoming the generic restaurant wine in Western Australia. This particular style, developed by Reynolds, captures the freshness and flavour that is so typically Frankland. Excellent drinking when released in the year of vintage, it has also demonstrated a capacity to age well. The celebrated and much-awarded 1983 release has variously been judged the top wine in several national shows, after some six years' bottle maturation. The strong affinity riesling has for the Great Southern is no better demonstrated than in the Houghton late-harvest styles. The Beerenauslese of 1984 has long been the benchmark sweet wine in the West. It combines the luscious qualities of fresh, late-picked fruit with an almost citrus-like, late-acid palate.

The 1982 Houghton Frankland shiraz typifies the distinctive qualities shiraz exudes in this isolated outpost of Australian viticulture. It has a crushed black pepper spicy character on the bouquet, and a combined berry-flavoured palate, not unlike the best wines of Côte Rotie in the Rhône region of France. These special fruit qualities have been enhanced over two decades by the resident manager Ted Holland, who has devoted his extensive field experience to the enrichment of the vineyards. Much of the Houghton success can be traced back to his well-manicured vines and high-quality fruit.

Houghton Frankland River wines are distributed nationally through the Hardy/Houghton chain. Special releases are available at the Houghton cellars.

A successful search for the older Houghton Frankland rieslings and late-picked styles will highlight the qualities espoused above. One should take care when serving these particular recommendations as many of the subtle qualities are inhibited with chilling—thirty minutes in the bottom of the refrigerator is more than adequate. Any representative collection of Australian wine should carry a modicum of the Houghton Frankland shiraz, if only to compare and contrast with the wide diversity of similar varietals grown throughout Australia. However, many informed oenophiles consider the label epitomises the essence of this much-maligned variety.

Howard Park Wines

The private label of John and Wendy Wade. Since his arrival in the Mount Barker district in 1986, Wade has established an enviable reputation for the production of outstanding dry red table wines. After completing an early stint at Alkoomi and Goundrey Wines, an offer to join Plantagenet was taken up, following the resignation of Rob Bowen. In each instance, his principals have favourably viewed his request to process small parcels of high-quality grapes on his own account. His releases have been eagerly snapped up, given both the reputation of the man and the excellent press that preceded the marketing thrust.

Quite obviously the Howard Park cabernet sauvignons are the wines that have created the most interest. Superbly crafted fruit, sourced from the premium vineyards of the district, is judiciously married to hand-selected French oak then matured to optimum balance. In the true Wade fashion, extraction plays a major role in the final composition. These are truly wines for the longer term rather than for immediate consumption.

The Howard Park rieslings are by no means secondary wines to the cabernet releases. Wade, in his own right, has elected to produce an individual style with a great deal of concentrated flavour, as opposed to the lighter, more ethereal wines one has come to expect from the region. Beautifully balanced, they can be enjoyed on release or held over for the complexities that develop with patient cellaring.

The Howard Park wines are truly handcrafted, made professionally and elegantly packaged. Availability through the trade is nigh impossible. One can but suggest a letter of enquiry to the Wades, care of their home address Little River Road, Denmark, Western Australia.

Jingalla

This tiny 8 hectare vineyard is established on the tourist route in the scenic Porongurup ranges, 20 km east of Mount Barker. Developed by brothers-in-law Geoff Clarke and Barry Coad, together with their respective wives in 1979, it now boasts riesling, semillon, verdelho, shiraz and cabernet as the feature varieties.

The first vintage in 1983 was an immediate success—this was made for the partners by Michael Goundrey at his Denmark complex. Such was the relationship that the arrangement has continued successfully. The wines have been deliberately fashioned in the fresh, fruit style with minimal extraction to permit early release and enjoyment. The lighter style dry reds have been extremely well received by consumers.

The verdelho variety has been a tactical vic-

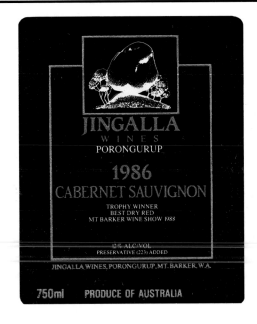

tory for Jingalla. Very little has been planted in the region so the novelty value alone ensures the partners an almost guaranteed turnover and cash flow. The wine receives a touch of oak and is bottled while still quite fresh.

The cellar door sales area and vineyard is located adjacent to a major district tourist spot, which provides a captive audience for the Jingalla products. A small percentage of various vintages have found their way to specialist cellars in Melbourne; however, the bulk of each release is sold within a 50 km radius of the cellars.

The various light dry red styles and the verdelho are well worth trying.

Karrelea Estate

This small vineyard to the north of the Mount Barker township is husbanded very much in a chemical-free regime. Local farmers and proprietors John and Jan Pickles oversee the management and fruit production, with Plantagenet responsible for the winemaking on a contract basis.

I have been more than impressed with the early wines from the Estate—the 1987 and 1989 riesling in particular. The cabernet-based reds have also displayed elegant soft flavours and a structure which tends towards early drinking rather than long-term maturation. Unfortunately, yields are low due to the ravages of the local bird population. Obivously they too have a preference for gold-medal grapes! Limited availability in specialist Perth stores.

Karrivale Wines

Karrivale is the new label for the McCready family vineyard, located high up in the Porongurup Ranges, to the east of Mount Barker. Established in 1979 with 2 hectares of riesling, the vines have flourished to the point that principal Campbell McCready has been encouraged to commit an additional 5 hectares to vines, approximately a half to shiraz and the balance to chardonnay. The elevation and the exposure of the vineyard to summer and early autumn sunshine has contributed to the quality of the early riesling vintages, these being made under contract at Plantagenet and released under the Narang label. Like the neighbouring Castle Rock and Jingalla vineyards, Karrivale enjoys a unique micro-climate and an unparalleled view across a broad plain to the rugged Stirling Range beyond.

It is perhaps a little early to predict vineyard styles, however; the Karrivale riesling has a somewhat fuller flavour than its neighbours—more akin to the standard Forest Hill benchmark. McCready is also excited about the regular post-vintage patterns of cloud cover and humidity levels that may be positive contributors to a botrytis infection at some future time. I share his enthusiasm, as the only other wine successfully made under similar conditions, the 1982 Plantagenet riesling from memory, was an outstanding example.

The Karrivale (Narang) wines are distributed through selected merchants in Sydney, Melbourne and Perth.

Omrah

Omrah was the first of the new major vineyards in the Mount Barker area. Established as an investment trust by Perth epicurean Stewart van Raalte, the property encompasses some 88 hectares of vines—mainly chardonnay, cabernet and sauvignon blanc. Day-to-day operations are under the watchful eye of vineyard consultant Ron Waterman. All units in the trust, together with long-term contracts for the purchase of grapes, were taken up and executed before planting commenced. First vintage is in 1990.

Plantagenet Wines

The Plantagenet winery in the Mount Barker township is perhaps the best known of all the Lower Great Southern labels. The partners behind the name include local identity Tony Smith, who has been the guiding hand since the inception in the late 1960s, the Meredith–Hardy family in England, and Perth chartered accountant Rob Devenish.

The company's two vineyards to the south-west of Mount Barker are known as Bouverie and Wyjup. Premium varieties planted include cabernet sauvignon, shiraz, malbec, pinot noir, riesling, chardonnay and traminer. Total area of vines is approximately 25 hectares. The partners also draw fruit from the Devenish family vineyard at Bindoon (60 km to the north of Perth).

In 1974 Tony Smith was able to negotiate the purchase of an old disused apple packing shed in the centre of Mount Barker. After refurbishment, including the purchase of basic wine-making equipment, the premises were ready for the first vintage, under the guidance of David McNamara in the autumn of 1975.

McNamara, who had previously worked at Houghton following the retirement of Jack Mann, quickly came to grips with the vagaries of his new challenge and produced some cracker-jack cabernets—the 1976 and 1977 stand out particularly. The 1977 is still opening magnificently and even winning show awards in museum classes. McNamara left in 1978 to pursue his own vineyard interests. He was succeeded by Robert Bowen, who had trained under Brian Croser at Riverina College. Bowen's impact was immediate and the district took on a new light in the eyes of the critics. Plantagenet has also made wine under contract for six other local vineyards, so the influence of the Bowen touch became apparent over a wide range of labels.

As the venture prospered, the partners reinvested most of their revenue in improving the winery and cask storage. This early decision in planning for the longer run gave the winemaker a competitive edge and saw Plantagenet scoop the pool of show awards throughout the early 1980s. The most consistent varietal has been the riesling. As is documented in other areas, it found a natural home in the district and flourished both in the vineyard and winery. Hardly a vintage has gone by without the Plantagenet riesling scoring some major award. The style has remained consistent with the

Plantagenet Ruby Port.

Croser ethos—fruit and balance being totally paramount.

Not to be outdone, the red varieties fought back to prominence, especially in the 1982 and 1983 vintages. Initially labelled hermitage, the Plantagenet shiraz of these vintages set new dimensions for the variety, previously only seen in the best Rhône wines of France. The attractive vibrant colours seen in earlier trials of Forest Hill cabernets was apparent, but the bouquet rocketed out of the glass heavily redolent of quality cracked black pepper. The palate was long and silky smooth. Bowen was astute enough to program the oak maturation to underscore the fruit flavours, merely adding a further flavour dimension. The 1983 vintage was outstanding as a youngster and records indicate that in its formative days it would have matched any red table style produced in that era. Its maturation will be interesting to observe.

The Plantagenet cabernets, while not as immediately appealing as those produced over at Margaret River, are made for the longer term. Occasionally, when vintage conditions are perfect, it does show early—the 1985 was a case in point. Recent releases made under the guidance of the new winemaker, John Wade, have been made in a similiar mould, perhaps a touch more extractive. They deserve a good five years in the bottle prior to appraisal.

Rob Bowen also tested the market by releasing a series of port styles, ruby and vintage character. Most were sold under the Plantagenet Kings label. They were spotlessly clean and fresh but perhaps a touch too fruity for the classic specification. Plantagenet's top releases are marketed under the Kings Reserve label. Invariably in small parcels, they are difficult to procure, but a letter to the winery may put you on the list for up-and-coming releases.

The total winery crush is yet to exceed 300 tonnes—50 per cent in its own right, the balance for neighbouring growers. The contribution of Tony Smith, Rob Bowen and Plantagenet cannot be emphasised enough. It is largely due to their personal efforts that Mount Barker is where it is today, right in the front ranks of Australia's table wine producing regions.

Among the myriad of new releases, the riesling is perhaps the most anticipated. Coming from a zero base less than 15 years ago, it has become one of the best selling and most sought-after wines in the state. It can be approached with total confidence when six months old and hence has a strong following in the restaurant industry. Again, like counterparts at Alkoomi, Goundry and Forest Hill, it has the ability to age well, bringing out further complexities in the bouquet and palate.

Both the Plantagenet shiraz and cabernet sauvignon rate well in preferences as to the top cellar red. French oak and the vast experience of new winemaker John Wade will come more into play, and the positioning of these two wines in the future will be worth watching. Plantagenet wines are marketed nationally.

Shemarin

This is the private label of Robert and Denise Bowen. In 1980 Bowen purchased land some 20 km from Mount Barker to establish his own interest in the district he had come to cherish since arriving at Plantagenet as winemaker in 1978. The Bowens have planted sauvignon blanc and chardonnay to date. Initial releases under the label have resulted from the purchase of outside fruit. I have been impressed by several zinfandels under the label and a recently released sauvignon blanc. Since resigning from Plantagenet in 1988 to freelance as an industry consultant, Bowen has undertaken further development on his property, so the label may take on a higher profile in the marketplace.

Denise Bowen, a talented graphic artist, is responsible for the outstanding label and packaging of the Shemarin releases.

Tinglewood

This miniscule property behind the Denmark township is a tribute to the tenacity of the Wood family, who have virtually carved their vineyard out of the virgin forest. This entailed the felling of huge local hardwoods, the removal of the resultant stumps and the back-destroying task of breaking and excavating some fifty truckloads of

granite rock. Bob Wood then set about planting and trellising the 1.5 hectares—main varieties include riesling, cabernet and shiraz. All wines made to date have been processed by Michael Goundrey in the Denmark winery. Quantities, naturally are extremely limited.

Wignall's King River Wines

Wignall's is Western Australia's most southerly producing vineyard. Located on Chester Pass Road (Highway One), a comfortable ten-minute drive from the coastal township of Albany, the vineyard of 9 hectares has thrived since being planted in 1982. Bill Wignall, a retired veterinary surgeon, has a lifestyle which would be the envy of most. He and his equally industrious wife, Pat, combine the running of a model vineyard with the management of one of the state's most outstanding Charolais studs. Having come into viticulture with a strong science background, Bill was adequately equipped to delineate the most suitable area on his small farm for vines. He promptly determined the various deficiencies in structure and chemical composition before even the most basic soil preparation. Suffice to say, it ranks today with the best managed vineyards in the state. Almost intuitively the Wignalls elected to plant chardonnay and pinot noir as the mainstay varieties (later adding cabernet sauvignon, sauvignon blanc and semillon). From the outset the choice proved propitious, with early vintages in 1985 and 1986 winning gold awards.

The Wignall wines are made under contract by Plantagenet, an arrangement that will continue indefinitely. The family run a busy sales outlet from their King River property, with limited stock always available in Sydney, Melbourne and Brisbane.

One certainly cannot go past the cellar specialties of chardonnay and pinot noir. By virtue of the southerly location the wines tend to be tightly structured, with indicative varietal and Burgundian character.

Yarnup Estate

The Yarnup vineyard was established by graziers Jeremy and June Roberts in 1980 as an additional cash crop on their extensive 750 hectare property west of Frankland. Varieties planted include riesling, semillon, cabernet and pinot noir. Recent crops have been sold locally. The Roberts have

Vineyards, South-west region of Western Australia.

no plans afoot to build their own winery, preferring to concentrate on other intensive farming interests. Jeremy has been a keen member of the Mount Barker and Frankland Wine Producers Association, and a driving force behind the very well-executed Mount Barker Wine Show.

The South-West

Geographically, the region encompasses all that area between the Port City of Bunbury, some 200 km south of the state capital, through the shires of Capel and Busselton, to the remote coastal resort of Augusta. In wine terms, it embraces the enlarged headland that falls between the Capes of Naturaliste and Leeuwin and is generically referred to as the Margaret River district. It is a rare and precious piece of Australian grandeur, a strange dichotomy of rugged coastline, wide fertile plains and stately forests of native hardwood.

The Dutch visited in the seventeenth century, mapped the coastline, then retreated, having neglected to explore beyond the coastal sand dunes. The French were more inquisitive. They regularly visited the region between the eighteenth and nineteenth centuries, but in the final analysis concurred with the Dutch opinion that the south land had little to offer commercially or strategically. Their brief presence remains indelibly engraved on the regional map, having named Geographe Bay, Capes Clairault, Mentelle, Freycinet and other prominent features.

British settlement at Augusta and Margaret River was, however, more permanent. Coming from middle-class farming stock, they appreciated the unique opportunities the land offered. Wide tracts between the two major capes were cleared and the state's southern beef and dairy industry was born. Viticulture was part and parcel of these early agricultural initiatives. Vineyards were established at Augusta, Yallingup and Busselton. Shipping records indicate wine was exported to the UK from Busselton in the 1890s.

The depression of the 1930s and a fall-off in export opportunities saw the region decline economically until the mid 1960s, when Perth physician Tom Cullity led the new wave of vinous pioneers back to Margaret River.

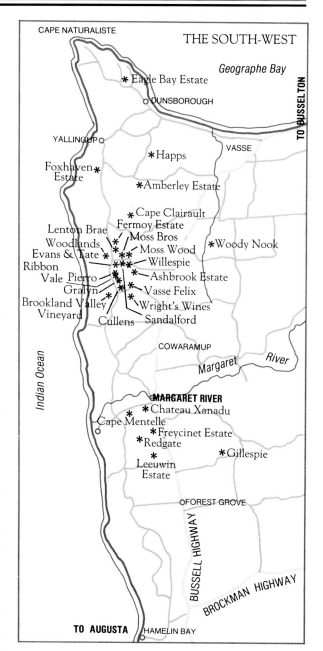

In less than twenty-five years the wines of south-western Australia have established an enviable reputation worldwide. International recognition has come in the form of export orders to some twenty countries, medals and trophies in European competitions and the august columns of respected British Masters of Wine. The wine industry and the tourism that comes with it has put life and soul back into the Margaret River district.

Amberley Estate

This exciting project on Thornton Road, Yallingup, under the management of Albert and

Bridget Haak, is the first major development in the area since Leeuwin Estate. Forty hectares of vines were planted between 1986 and 1989, on south-facing slopes opposite Rivendell Gardens.

A spacious state-of-the-art winery is currently under construction. This will be fitted out and readied to receive the Estate's first vintage in 1990. The Haaks and their new winemaker, Eddie Price, expect an initial crush of some 170 tonnes. Flagship wines will be a cabernet sauvignon–merlot–cabernet franc blend and a semillon–sauvignon blanc. Naturally all wines will be 100 per cent Estate grown, made and bottled.

Ashbrook Estate

Ashbrook, the Devitt family property, is situated in the heartland of the vineyard belt off Harmans South Road, Willyabrup. The rustic mud-brick winery is approached via a long private driveway through lush pastures, tall timber and a sizeable herd of prime beef. In spring, the wildflowers that grow on the rich gravelly loam soils of Ashbrook are a visual treat. Brothers Tony and Brian Devitt commenced development of the property in 1976, planting the proven varieties cabernet, cabernet franc, merlot, semillon, chardonnay and verdelho. Sauvignon blanc has been added to the vineyard, which now covers some 12 hectares. The wines of Ashbrook come with an impressive pedigree. For a start, they are made by a talented team with unparalleled qualifications in Western Australia. Tony, the state's principal viticulturist, a qualified agricultural scientist trained under Bill Jamieson at the Department of Agriculture before completing his Roseworthy degree, then took over the reins from his boss in 1979. The Ashbrook venture is very much a case of putting into practise on weekends what he preaches during the week. Vintage, which usually occurs during early March, accounts for most of his annual leave. Brother Brian, a highly qualified educationalist, now coordinates and manages the property from the Margaret River end. The functionally designed winery is a model high-tech unit equipped to cope with any contingency that might eventuate during vintage or bottling. The best available oak is sourced from world suppliers. It has also been the practice of the partners to hold the red wines for additional

maturation following packaging. White table wines released include the aforementioned varietals, plus two extremely well-made rieslings (made from fruit purchased in the district). Ashbrook wines are marketed nationally.

The rieslings, one sweet, the other dry, are among the best produced in Margaret River; full-flavoured, rich, long palates and good balancing acid. The sauvignon blanc is state-of-the-art—grassy, herbaceous and very intense. A stylish wine perfect with seafood. The Ashbrook chardonnay is almost Burgundian in structure and flavour—superb oak background, a classic. Cabernet sauvignon has been performing well in the vineyards of Willyabrup and the Ashbrook wine confirms the affinity.

Elegantly styled in the light- to medium-bodied mould it has an attractive berry-fruit bouquet overlaid with some very fine oak. The intensely flavoured palate is long and the finish firm without being overly extractive.

Brookland Valley Vineyard

This commercially designed vineyard owned by Malcolm and Dee Jones was a first for Margaret River. Professional consultants were appointed from the outset to supervise and manage the latest in technology and husbandry. This included the close planting of vines, vertical trellising, irrigation and the application of organic practices. The objective is to have vines in balance so as to consistently produce premium fruit (and ultimately wine). Premium varieties planted in 1984 include cabernet sauvignon, cabernet franc, merlot, chardonnay and sauvignon blanc.

The first vintage in 1989 was contracted to Cape Mentelle with the initial release of wine in January 1990.

Cape Clairault

The Clairault winery on Henry Road, Willyabrup, is readily identifiable in that the facade has a distinctive Dutch influence reminiscent of the fine South African Cape architecture. The connection, one soon discovers, is that partner Ani Lewis has strong roots in that country and has adopted the gabled roofline in memory of her homeland. Husband Ian, an Australian, is a geologist of some note. Looking for an alternative lifestyle, they purchased their 66 hectare farm in 1977 and following the success of the nearby Cullity and Cullen initiatives, decided viticulture was the answer to their prayers.

There are now 7.5 hectares under cabernet, riesling, semillon and sauvignon blanc. The Clairault vineyard, slightly north of the mainstream Metricup properties, enjoys a distinct microclimate, having greater elevation and marginally higher sun hours and day degrees. The resultant wines do tend to have greater depth of flavour without any apparent diminution of freshness or acid. The laconic and self-effacing Lewis, who has all but sacrificed his gold-prospecting role to become a full-time winemaker, taught himself oenology with some pretty spectacular early results. Each of his cabernets since the 1982 vintage has won at least one major award. The 1982 achieved national recognition by winning the prestigious *Canberra Times* Trophy, awarded for the best dry red table wine in premium classes at the 1984 National Wine Show. Since this early flush of success, Ian has continued to keep his wines in line with consumer preferences. The most recent release of cabernet is noticeably tighter and has been exposed to a wider selection of new oak—a positive step that has not gone unnoticed.

The main white wine produced at the tiny 50 tonne winery is the celebrated sauvignon blanc. Since the first vintage in 1987, this light, aromatic wine, with its distinctive grassy character, has become a best seller with demand far outstripping supply. Show highlights include trophies in two major exhibitions and a 'best of show' award at the 1988 Sheraton Perth competition. Ian Lewis indicates that the secret of his wines' success comes from the fact that he simply allows the fruit to maximise flavour levels before picking and vintage, exercising only minimal influence in the production and bottling phases. Nature, according to Ian, is largely responsible for the impressive line-up!

Cape Clairault cabernet sauvignon is a wine highly appreciated by the cognoscenti in the West. A little is available in the Adelaide, Melbourne and Sydney markets. Consistency is a high priority in Ian Lewis's winemaking philosophy, so the sensible thing would be to place a standing order for each release—if the quantity is too great, you may want to substitute several bottles of the aromatic sauvignon blanc in lieu.

Cape Mentelle

If Vasse Felix is the best known Margaret River winery in New York, Cape Mentelle could claim that honour in the United Kingdom, and for that matter the Commonwealth of Australia, to boot. The rationale behind such a bold claim revolves around the simple fact that the winery is run by a visionary with an international perspective.

David Hohnen, a major shareholder in the project, is also the senior winemaker, marketing manager and dynamo, who has largely contributed to the high profile and success of this small, isolated winery that rocketed to prominence in August 1983 after winning the Jimmy Watson trophy at the Melbourne Show. In achieving this accolade, his 1982 cabernet sauvignon beat some of the best one-year-old reds ever produced in Australia.

By winning the 1983 award, Hohnen created a little vinous history—he became the first West Australian to achieve this honour, and what's more, his product was one of only two non-South-Australian wines that, until that time, had received the award. Proving that it wasn't a shot in the dark, Hohnen entered his 1983 cabernet the following year and repeated the performance. Quite correctly these back-to-back awards confirmed Cape Mentelle's status as one of Australia's leading producers of premium red table wine.

Hohnen is by nature a serious contemplative person who would prefer nothing better than to preserve his anonymity and get on with his great love of crafting fine wine. Alas, the pressures of the modern-day small winery preclude such luxuries.

Cape Mentelle came into being in 1977, when David Hohnen released his first wines. This only came to pass after a circuitous route involving Hohnen working for a short time in the South Australian industry, studying oenology in California and managing a Victorian vineyard. This experience was to stand him in fine stead as we saw in his first releases—individual creations unlike the mainstream hitherto produced in Margaret River. One can only speculate about the contribution of his two close friends Dominic and Bernard Portet, both winemakers with a wealth of French traditional winemaking experience, who must have played leading roles in the stylistic influence of the early Cape Mentelle cabernets.

From 1977 through until 1982 the reds all carried substantial grape tannin and new French oak characters—very much components of the top Bordeaux clarets that the Portet brothers knew so well from their days at Château Lafite. Hohnen also travelled regularly and widely to review the wines and techniques of those he respected.

Never content to rest on his laurels, he is a great, if reluctant, promoter of his wines and region. His annual 'Great Cabernet Tasting', which features twenty (usually including at least two first-growth Bordeauxs) of the world's best cabernet-based wines, is an event not to be missed. Here, quite unabashed, he pitches his own red against a selection of the same vintage, chosen by an independent party. The Cape Mentelle winery invariably comes out among the top three in this professionally run blind tasting—a further exercise by Hohnen to confirm his global outlook and direction.

All Cape Mentelle reds—there are three made: cabernet, shiraz and zinfandel—are fermented in stainless steel then transferrred to large oak vats for settling and follow-up malolactic fermentation. They are then transferred to new French oak hogsheads for a twelve-month rest. Worldwide distribution follows bottling and further cellar maturation.

To display their versatility, Hohnen and his assistant winemaker John Durham, also produce two outstanding cellar whites; a chardonnay and a semillon–sauvignon blanc–chenin blend. Both carry the Hohnen trademarks of flavour and oak, and both have shown a distinct propensity to carry a little age well. One might say these are the red drinker's white wines!

Having a professional team around him has permitted Hohnen to expand the Cape Mentelle vineyard to 18 hectares of his favourite varieties. Additional fruit is purchased from his brother-in-law (chardonnay), and a long-term contract grower (grenache).

Both the cabernet and shiraz have a strong following, each redolent of the variety at its best—tinged with a modest cool-climate, herbaceous influence and elegantly married to attractive new smoky oak.

The semillon blend is an old favourite which, depending upon seasonal conditions, is made to put away for further maturation. (The excellent 1982 vintage drank well after seven years in the bottle.) Three years cellaring permits all the flavour components to amalgamate into a very complex fruity wine that is in many ways strikingly similar to the dry white table wines of Bordeaux.

Chateau Xanadu

The recent wines from Xanadu have all but reached the heights espoused by Coleridge in his classic poem *Kubla Khan*, particularly the chardonnay and semillon made by ex-wine maker John Smith.

Xanadu is one of the newer wineries to the south of the township, sharing a common boundary with Cape Mentelle. Vines were first planted in 1977 and now include cabernet sauvignon, cabernet franc, chardonnay, semillon and sauvignon blanc. The early vintages were made by Theo Radke. John Smith came on the scene in the mid-1980s and, largely due to his influence, Xanadu quickly grew in profile, gaining most successful awards at the Perth Wine Show and trophies at the Sheraton Perth West Australian Wine Awards.

The downside to the excellent fruit produced at Xanadu is the extremely low yields. The local soils are very hard and less fertile than those to the north of Margaret River. Being within earshot of the coast and exposed to the prevailing westerlies hasn't been a positive factor either. However, property owners Drs Lagan and Sheridan philosophically accept the consequences, given the exceptional wines that have been made to date. I would rank the 1987 chardonnay with the top half-dozen made in Margaret River to date. The richly herbaceous 1988 semillon, with the slightest hint of French oak, is also a gem to be treasured. Smith has been coming to grips with his red wines and again the 1987 and 1988 vintages have shown the intrinsic qualities expected of cabernet in all its glory. One hogshead of cabernet franc made in 1988 was strongly reminiscent of a great Pomerol. Xanadu wines, although limited in quantity, are distributed nationally.

John Smith regrettably left the winery just prior to the 1989 vintage. His place has been taken by Connor Lagan, the Roseworthy-trained son of the proprietors. Quite obviously he fills a big pair of boots left by Smith, but he is an enthusiastic, intelligent young man and the changeover shouldn't greatly disrupt the flow of these excellent wines.

The chardonnay wines of 1987 and 1988 vintages reflect the marriage of very fine oak and the quintessence of the hallowed variety. On a par, but certainly a horse of a different colour, is the Xanadu semillon of 1988. A very finely made wine with flavour and good, crisp mid-palate acid. Smith's deft use of new oak is very much a strong feature of both the chardonnay and semillon styles. Watch for the release of the 1988 cabernet.

Cullens

Di Cullen is very much, albeit reluctantly, the matriarch of the Margaret River wine industry. A great promoter of all the region's wines, she has seen the area grow from inception to the point where wine world dignitaries beat a path to her cellar door seeking advice and direction. Di, together with husband Kevin, are long-time residents of Willyabrup. Prior to going into viticulture in 1971, they owned several farms on either side of Caves Road (the main north–south route), one of which happened to be adjacent to Tom Cullity's Vasse Felix vineyard. Having a lifetime interest in table wine, they sought Tom's advice and in no time had a sizeable vineyard of their own planted to cabernet and riesling.

Nearly two decades down the track, the Cullens have expanded the vineyard to 28 hectares and the varietal mix to eight major cultivars. They are in the comforting position of having two daughters to support them in cellar sales and winemaking. Di Cullen is an extremely capable individual and has largely run the winery and vineyard, while husband Kevin, the senior medical officer in nearby Busselton, has devoted his life to community medicine.

The Cullen's property is markedly different to that of the majority in the area, the soils being the major difference. Cullens have planted on a pocket of granitic sands, while others sought the comfort of the more benign gravelly loams. The results of this fascinating experiment came to fruition in 1975 when comparisons could be made between their first vintage and the wines of

MARGARET RIVER
WESTERN AUSTRALIA

Vines were first planted in the Margaret River region of Western Australia in 1966. The maritime climate of the area with its cool wet winters and temperate dry summers provides ideal conditions for grape growing. After only 20 years Margaret River is recognised both internationally and within Australia as a producer of world class wines.

Due to the extremely dry growing season of the 1988 vintage, the grape quality of the Chardonnay was exceptional. These grapes were harvested on two separate occasions, to give acid balance and fullness of flavour. The wine was entirely barrel fermented. This was followed by seven months on the lees in Allier and Nevers barriques.

Recommended bottle ageing 2-5 years.
VIN BLANC   WHITE WINE
CONTAINS SULPHITES

CULLENS

MARGARET RIVER
Chardonnay
1988

PRODUCED & BOTTLED BY CULLENS WINES AUSTRALIA
WHITE TABLE WINE ALCOHOL 13.5% BY VOLUME 750ML
PRODUCT OF AUSTRALIA/PRODUIT d'AUSTRALIE

Vasse Felix. While exhibiting similar telltale purple colours in the distinctive peppermint overtones of the region, the Cullen's wine appeared leaner and more tightly structured than the cabernets from Vasse Felix. It became apparent that they would be wines for cellaring rather than early consumption. Strangely, the natural attributes of each winery's rieslings were reversed when comparative masked tasting results were tabulated. Fifteen vintages on the initial differences appear to remain; Vasse Felix has fuller, fleshier reds and Cullen's whites have greater fruit depth and intensity. This is but one of a thousand permutations that have exercised the minds of growers in the area. Without wanting to labour the point that macro-differences are apparent in micro-situations too greatly, I have often used the Haut Medoc analogy when describing the fruit flavours of cabernet in the general area of Margaret River, though curiously these have shown to be reversed in order once again. The flavour profile of the northern vineyards is akin to the cabernets of Margaux, while the more austere southerly grown fruit (Leeuwin, Freycinet and Gillespie) has a greater commonality with the Paulliac commune. Again, it's the factors and interaction of a minute variance in climate and different soil types.

Di Cullen feels that the winemaking skills of the area have now reached a satisfactory plateau of sophistication. The new challenges will come in developing better vineyard practices and vine management systems. Already she is experimenting with organic fertilisers, new trellising techniques and the wider spacing of vines. The object of the exercise is to transfer some of the natural vine vigour into greater grape flavour concen-

Cullens Willyabrup winery.

Wine tasting.

tration. Having the luxury of her Roseworthy-trained daughter, Vanya, running the winery, has given Di the time and space to carry out a range of esoteric trials aimed at improving the Cullen products.

In 1989 the major thrust has revolved around chardonnay, with ripening and flavour characteristics being closely monitored. Burgundian techniques and oak trials are also under close scrutiny. A further realisation that the Cullens have come to in evaluating options into the next century is that riesling is a lesser variety in the district than first thought.

The love affair with Burgundy goes beyond chardonnay. Di and Vanya Cullen are both fascinated with pinot noir and its idiosyncratic nature. Recent wines reflect a marathon effort to craft and coax the inherent characters of the variety. If the tank samples tasted follow through to the bottle, we shall all be in for a treat—I did observe distinct similarities to the wonderful silky wines of Nuits!

The Cullen cabernet blend ranks with the better wines of Western Australia. Given that the oldest vines are now eighteen years of age and are producing consistent, if not predictable, flavours. Di's major aim is to pursue and harness the complexities of this prestige varietal. Sweet berry flavours and a fine new oak frame are becoming the trademarks of the Cullen cabernet–merlot—the cellar's flagship red table wine.

Oak also plays a feature role in the Cullen sauvignon blanc. The wine is made more in the fumé fashion than the lighter herbaceous style. The toasty oak fills out the ripe gooseberry-like characters admirably.

The future direction for Cullens is one of fine-tuning its already classy range. The wines, given the low yields and the high costs associated with production, are extremely well priced—especially when comparing wines of similar quality in the international marketplace. The Western Australian industry is very fortunate to have the Cullens so vitally involved in such a positive manner.

One cannot go past the chardonnay and sauvignon blanc for quality and value. Both encapsulate the true varietal flavour of the grape and have been melded with some fine oak from central France. These are wines that deserve two or three years cellaring to allow the components to properly integrate. The Cullen pinot noir is being made to international specifications. It has style, flavour and true Burgundian character.

Consistently the Cullen cabernet sauvignon has impressed when seen in district line-ups. Recent releases show the benefit of Vanya's technical experience, and one can only speculate about whether her very fine 1989 wine will reach the same levels of excellence that her mother's 1982 achieved—what a pleasing conundrum.

Eagle Bay Estate

Eagle Bay is the most northerly of the Margaret River vineyards, situated high on the Naturaliste peninsula with panoramic ocean views. Perth barrister, Jim Mazza, established the vineyard in 1982. There are now 10 hectares planted to chardonnay, semillon, riesling, sauvignon blanc, merlot and shiraz. Limited wine has been made since 1987. I can recall, however, being impressed with both a medium-bodied dry white style, displaying attractive varietal character, and a light elegant red entered in the recent Sheraton Perth West Australian Wine Awards.

Fermoy Estate

Fermoy Estate is located on the northern side of Metricup Road, Willyabrup, adjacent to Moss Wood, and opposite the Tate vineyard, Redbrook. (In very good company one might say.) The property takes its name from the town of Fermoy in County Cork, which was founded by an ancestor of one of the present proprietors. Vines were first planted at Fermoy in 1985. Varietals now represented on the 11 hectare vineyard include cabernet, pinot noir, merlot, chardonnay, semillon and sauvignon blanc. A striking feature of the plantings is the abundance of vigour brought about by the excellent soils that have influenced the magnificent Moss Wood wines since 1973. To counter the natural vigour, an elaborate trellising system has been developed, based on the work of Professor Carbonneau of Bordeaux.

Winemaker Michael Kelly made his first vintage in 1988 and immediately walked away with the valuable trophy for the best light-bodied red at the 1989 Sheraton judging—the winery's first showing. The award wine, a stunning cabernet sauvignon with deep vibrant crimson colours and an aromatic berry bouquet, was quite reminiscent of a young Margaux commune wine. Kelly had skilfully matched these outstanding characters with a sensitive exposure to new oak, altogether an outstanding wine.

Shortly afterwards, I was privileged to try the follow-up wine out of cask at the winery in company with English Master of Wine, Sarah Morphew. As attractive and impressive as the 1988 vintage was, the 1989, even at six months of age was already showing signs of greatness. All the elements that won gold for the prior vintage were present in the youngster, but concentrated to an almost essence-like level. Given that the astute Kelly can guide this gem safely through its formative stages, it should at least rank with the 1982 Cape Mentelle cabernet as the most important red wine made in the region.

Fermoy have released two further wines, a 1989 semillon and a 1989 sauvignon blanc. Both are clean and well made; however, they tend to lack the depth and intensity of the young reds. In fairness to the proprietors and the winemakers, the vines are still extremely young.

As quantities of wine will always be limited, the mailing list is the best avenue to ensure you are advised of new releases. Definitely move mountains to procure a bottle or two of the superb 1989 cabernet sauvignon! Merlot may be considered as a varietal release at a future date.

Foxhaven Estate

This northern 3 hectare vineyard is located near the junction of Caves Road and Canal Rocks Road, Yallingup. David and Libby Hunt first planted vines in the early 1980s as a recreational pursuit on their weekend property. However, the recreation aspect diminished in 1985 when vintage approached and the serious business of winemaking took over. David, a director of a major real estate company in the city, regularly commutes from Perth to drive away the ravaging silver-eyes at vintage and to manage the property.

To date, several very good rieslings have been made—the 1986 vintage with a touch of residual sugar was by far the best seller. One example, the 1987, indicated that elusive Rhiengau quality seen in the 1972 Vasse Felix wine.

A small quantity of cabernet sauvignon has been made from each of the 1986, 1987 and 1988 vintages. David has elected to mature these in new American oak hogsheads. The Hunts plan to double the vineyard over the next five years, adding semillon and sauvignon blanc.

Quantities are in short supply but a letter to the Hunts' private address (43 Falls Road, Lesmurdie, 6076) may prove fruitful. The riesling is made in the crisp, traditional style of the premium areas, such as Clare and Eden Valley.

Freycinet Estate

Tucked away off Gnarawary Road, south of Margaret River, stands the new winery of Peter and Jennifer Gherardi. The model vineyard reflects the fact that Peter is the government consultant responsible for the southern vineyards of Western Australia. Like his chief, Tony Devitt (Ashbrook), it seemed only right that he should put into practise the principles espoused in his day-to-day role as a viticulture and oenology adviser. He left no stone unturned in the choice of varieties, the design and layout of the vineyard and the symmetry of the winery.

Planting began in 1979 and has progressed to 12 hectares of selected semillon, sauvignon blanc, chenin and cabernet. Not only has Gherardi been particular about his choice of clones, but also the positioning of each variety on the property. Suffice to say, the careful planning has paid dividends.

The Gherardi wines were made under contract until the completion of the Freycinet winery in 1987. Quite obviously the owners' involvement in the total operation and maturing vineyard has seen a turn-around in the flagship products.

The wide parameters of the three white varieties have been exhaustively trialled in the winery and oak compatibility experiments evaluated to ensure that best possible marriage of flavours. Recent offerings at cellar door include a straight varietal semillon, sauvignon blanc and chenin. The outstanding 1986 cabernet is nearly depleted, but I am assured that the 1987 will be a worthy successor.

I have always admired the flavour and varietal intensity of the Freycinet sauvignon blanc. Gherardi has been only one of a few winemakers astute enough to achieve this without retaining any trace of residual bitterness. A pefect summer drink. Peter has deliberately kept his red table wines in the light- to medium-bodied range. All have clean, crisp berry flavours and balancing new oak. The cabernet sauvignon style is tightly structured, has attractive middle-palate flavour and gentle tannin. Well recommended.

Gillespie

Perhaps the most remote of all Margaret River vineyards is the Gillespie family vineyard and winery. Sited in a natural valley east of Witchcliffe, it is approached along Davis Road. So isolated is the vineyard that the family have had to contend variously with ravaging indigenous fauna such as kangaroos, emus and rabbits. Birds have enjoyed the sweet fruits of the cabernet, semillon and riesling varieties planted beneath the enormous stands of hardwood that ring the ordered rows of green vines. Grape damage can amount to 60 per cent of total crop in warm years, when the gum blossom fails to show its red carpet across the treetops.

The wines made by Alastair Gillespie · are workmanlike and a reflection of his dedication. The cabernet is almost Bordeaux in that it is tightly structured and moderately tannic. I very much enjoyed the 1982 style when young and fortuitously saw the potential in the wine for ageing. In recent years, it has softened to an intense mulberry-flavoured wine with attractive balancing oak and a long elegant palate. As mentioned elsewhere, the fruit intensity of the southern-most vineyards is quite different to that of the Willyabrup area. Maturation is essential to see these wines at their best.

The Gillespie enterprise is now approaching fourteen years of age and with the hindsight of some ten vintages the wines are developing greater complexity. Well worth viewing. Distribution is mainly at cellar door. Limited stocks are sent to Sydney, Perth and Melbourne merchants.

One should review both the cabernet and the semillon to personally understand the real differences that microclimates, soils and the winemaker's influence can make.

Gralyn

Graham and Merilyn Hutton, long-time Margaret River identities and farmers, added vines to their highly diverse agricultural interests in 1975. Their attractive property, with a wide frontage to the main Caves Road, is eminently suitable for viticulture, having rich, well-drained, gravelly soils and abundant water.

Graham takes particular pride in his vineyard and his husbandry is second to none. Major plantings include the mandatory cabernet, shiraz and riesling. A unique winery was constructed in 1978 for the first vintage. It takes the form of a huge concrete tank, sunk partially below ground level, with soil banked on most sides for insulation—it is effective and innovative. A new restaurant has added further to the quiet ambience of the property.

The Huttons have displayed a keen marketing flair with their range of wines on offer. These include red and white table wines through to a comprehensive range of port styles. Distribution is mainly from the winery.

One of only a few wineries in the area to seriously broach fortified wine production. The port range is worthy of serious contemplation.

Happs

The quality wines that emanate from this northern Margaret River vineyard are the produce of a difficult environment tamed by a fervent artistic winemaker with the sole goal of producing the highest quality wines. Erl Happ, a gifted former schoolmaster, first dabbled in winemaking in the early 1970s, having planted a few vines on a block adjoining his Busselton home and ceramic studio. Spurred on by the efforts of his local colleague Bill Pannell, he decided to look beyond the domestic vineyard and searched for suitable land among the established vineyards at Metricup and Willyabrup. Curiously, he found his Xanadu atop the Naturaliste Ridge near Dunsborough. A magnificent holding with panoramic views of the distant ranges and Geographe Bay. (The difficulties came later in the form of equinoctial storms and ancient soils that were abundantly fertile.)

The resourceful Happ and his equally talented wife, Ros, built their own rambling home, pottery and winery between 1977 and 1981. Constructed of adobe bricks (sourced from local clay) the overall scope is one of space and integration. The pottery and residence surround a central courtyard and a magnificent garden. Natural timber, recycled hardwood and stained glass add character and a sense of antiquity to the development.

The vineyard (first planted in 1978) consists of cabernet, shiraz, merlot, verdelho and chardonnay. On the advice of a friend, he also pioneered the district with a few hectares of three Portuguese varieties: Touriga, Tinta Coa and Souzao.

The idyllic winery, again with much of the necessary equipment (including a stainless steel crusher) being hand-made by Erl, saw its first vintage in 1981. Vine maturity, experience and the harmony of a better range of oak have all contributed to an increasing sophistication in the Happ wines. The early cabernets, which lacked depth and complexity, have been supplanted by vibrant crisp wines showing elegance, flavour length and judicious oak inference. The flagship red for my money is the winery's merlot. In a top year it has nuances of Pomerol, albeit in a less structured manner. A delightfully soft wine with the capacity to age and complex. Oak has been used sensitively to complement flavours rather than contrast.

Erl's early white styles have also caught the attention of the connoisseurs—the light chablis-like chardonnay, in particular. Happ's answer to the Australian light red enigma is the light pastel-shaded Fuschia. A slightly sweet, scented wine made from shiraz. Extremely popular with cellar patrons. A series of port styles, made to vintage specifications, have been regular show winners. Obviously the progress of the Portuguese varieties will be closely watched as tonnages account for greater proportions of the blend. Certainly a strong feature of recent releases has been the quality of the fortifying spirit.

Having achieved the desired levels of quality control in the winery, Happ turned his attention to improving his vineyard. The lush soils had to be modified, the destructive birdlife controlled and vine vigour arrested. As would be expected of a lateral thinker, Happ came up with a series of individual solutions that seem to have at least met the objects of his research. Trellising has been changed to the high open-lyre system and a large part of the vineyard has been completely enclosed. One hopes that Erl Happ may, in later years, produce a small technical manual on his approach to overcoming adversity in the small vineyard and winery. I'm sure it will encourage the brave, but, equally, it will dispel the roman-

tics who fancy being weekend vignerons. More power to the Happ family, they have achieved much for themselves, as well as their colleagues, at Margaret River. Never tell Erl or Ros Happ it cannot be done!

Evolution of flavours would tend to indicate merlot and chardonnay as the varieties with greatest potential. An odd couple indeed but two labels to watch for in the future. Happ's wines are distributed nationally.

Leeuwin Estate

Leeuwin Estate exudes affluence and self-assurance yet it appears at odds with the environment. This strange dichotomy can be traced back to the architecture of the main building and ambience of the landscaped gardens. The Californian-inspired design and the trickling water tinkling through the green fernery is strangely out of character with the noble karri trees that fringe nearby Boodjidup Brook, and the brown summer landscape that is Australia. Come what may, West Australians are indeed fortunate to have Leeuwin Estate, its wines and Denis Horgan, the inspiration behind the most technically equipped, professionally run operation in the state. The professionalism starts with the people: John Brocksopp, vineyard manager; Bob Cartwright, senior winemaker; Stephen Reagan, executive chef; and the general manager Bob Reynolds. This management team would have few peers in Australia; they also have an excellent support crew that continues to reinforce the confidence of the patron.

Leeuwin came into being by accident. Denis Horgan had acquired the property in a business takeover and sought the advice of the State Department of Agriculture as to its optimum use. Vines had proven to be successful in the district and Horgan was attracted to the idea of such a development on his property.

A vineyard nursery was established in 1974 and Stan Heritage, one of the most respected viticulturists in Australia, was appointed to oversee the major development. During 1975 and 1976 some 90 hectares of vines were planted. The choice of varieties was very much inspired by Bill Jamieson; cabernet, malbec, chardonnay, pinot noir, traminer and shiraz. Robert Mondavi, the Californian winemaker, advised in the initial phases (his son Tim assisted Bob Cartwright with

Leeuwin Estate winery.

LEEUWIN ESTATE

1987

Margaret River

Rhine Riesling

750ml

PRODUCE OF WESTERN AUSTRALIA

ALCOHOL 12% BY VOLUME

PRESERVATIVE (220) ADDED   ANTIOXIDANT (300) ADDED

the 1977 Tyrrell and 1982 Petaluma as the top wines of that era. Perhaps while the 1980 and 1981 have tended to soften, the magnificent 1982 should still be a great dinner wine on New Year's Eve in the year 2000. For some reason, recent releases, although very good, have failed to live up to the big three vintages (1980, 1981 and 1982)—a phenomenon I have observed and seen repeated throughout the district with the ageing of riesling and chardonnay vines. The inherent essence-like quality of the varietal disappears from the middle palate and the brilliant green/gold condition takes on a more subtle limpid sheen.

The Estate's other whites, riesling and, to a lesser degree, traminer, maintain a growing presence in the marketplace. These naturally tend to be much lighter in weight and extraction than the chardonnay, and exhibit the softer more ethereal qualities in the German tradition. The riesling is best drunk on release; however, a year or two bottle age can heighten and intensify the spicy characters of the traminer. Bob Cartwright has also managed, given the long autumn weather patterns of Margaret River, to make several top, late-harvest rieslings.

That other misfit of the Australian industry, sauvignon blanc, has found what would appear to be a totally accommodating domain on the gentle slopes at Leeuwin. Within the space of a mere three vintages, the local wine established new parameters for the variety in Australia. Cartwright displayed admirable empathy with his grapes when he elected to make a light dry white floral style, rather than opt for the big herbaceous version of the heavily oaked styles so popular in the USA. The soft delicate bouquet has an appealing floral aroma not unlike petunias. The palate is shot full of long elegant fruity flavours that conclude with a pleasant acid finish. A new and commendable direction for this variety.

early vintages), hence the link with the American mission-style building.

The loose gravelly soils on Leeuwin ensured that the conventionally planted cuttings got away to a flying start; but they have proven to be difficult hosts in mature years—especially as the management have elected not to irrigate. As a consequence, yields are slight (among the lowest in Margaret River), and costs of production abnormally high per tonne. This is best seen with the pinot noir and chardonnay production, which in dry seasons can be as low as 2–3 tonnes per hectare.

In 1982 the 3 hectares of shiraz were grafted over to sauvignon blanc. Economically it proved to be a wise decision, but with the passing of the Leeuwin Hermitage label one of the district's top red styles was lost forever. (Well, we hope not!)

The winery's first vintage came in during the autumn of 1978. Bob Cartwright was appointed winemaker, a position he still retains albeit now with a wider role involving promotion and tasting visits to other parts of the world.

By 1980 quantities were becoming a little more commercial, and the label became a national entity—especially with the release of the superb 1980 chardonnay, for this was a wine that surpassed previously known levels of flavour and quality. Follow-up wines in 1981 and 1982 maintained the high standard. The 1982 ranked with

The Leeuwin reds have caused much discussion around the dinner tables of oenophiles. Quality is never questioned, but price is. Invariably, price is a benchmark the Australian consumer looks at closely and questions. Perhaps in ignorance, perhaps in wisdom, he finds it hard to part with 10 per cent of his take-home salary for a single bottle of Leeuwin pinot noir. As indicated earlier, the price is a factor directly related to the miniscule production, the high cost of new French oak casks and the holding costs at the winery. In the end, however, it is an experience that one should have at least once. If you haven't had that opportunity I suggest you await the release of the 1989 vintage. This vintage, more than ever, is made in true Burgundian fashion and encapsulates the broad oriental spice characters of the pinot variety at its best. Of the older vintages, the light silky 1983 wine appeared to have won most votes from those who understand the idiosyncratic nature of the beast.

The cabernet sauvignons from the 1979 vintage onwards are an object lesson in style, quality and understanding. Early wines, particularly the 1979, were high in tannin and made with an over-abundance of new oak. I can well remember discussing the wine with John Brocksopp, the then newly appointed vineyard manager at the Mount Barker Show. I suggested that the wine was unbalanced and needed ten years to integrate and show its best. Thankfully that advice was taken, the wine softened and was recently released at a premium price. (James Halliday, the noted wine critic, described it as one of Australia's best!)

Cabernet can be fickle at Margaret River and follow seasonal variations. The outstanding recent vintages 1982 and 1985 have produced grapes and ultimately wine of exceptional quality. The vintages of Leeuwin cabernet from these years were highly acclaimed. Intervening years have been up to the usual high standards set by Horgan, but not outstanding.

The Leeuwin orchestral concerts, which started in 1983, when Horgan hosted the London Philharmonic, have deservedly received international publicity. Another string to the Estate's bow is the very fine restaurant that offers a wide choice of locally grown produce under the direction of Stephen Reagan. Here one may partake of prime beef, freshwater crustacea, or a fillet of fish caught a kilometre or two away that very morning. Dinner at twilight shouldn't be missed as the setting sun sends its final light through the tall karri trees, picking them out as the aged sentinels of this historic property. At night, floodlights bring another perspective to the Australian bushland.

Leeuwin Estate wines can now be purchased through specialist outlets in most capital cities.

Choosing a Leeuwin Estate wine is very much a personal decision and by no means an easy one given the range available. For informal occasions the riesling and sauvignon blanc would be appropriate. When celebrating, the chardonnay of a top year is mandatory. Depending on the occasion one could opt for the Estate's exceptional pinot noir or cabernet.

Lenton Brae

Near to the Moss Wood property on Caves Road at Metricup, Lenton Brae is the 10 hectare vineyard and retreat of prominent Perth businessman Bruce Tomlinson. Planted to mainly chardonnay, sauvignon blanc and cabernet sauvignon in 1983, Lenton Brae has produced only two vintages to date. Bill Jamieson, a colleague of Tomlinson, has provided a degree of professional consultancy in the formative phases of the operation.

Early wines show clean, intense fruit flavours and the attractive herbaceous characters so reminiscent of the quality Margaret River products.

Moss Bros

Jeff Moss, ex-vineyard manager at Houghton, was loath to let his lifetime love of viticulture slip by when he retired from Houghton's; so, in the Australian tradition, he resolved to maintain the best of both worlds and lifestyles, by purchasing a small farming block on Caves Road at Metricup. Along with sons David and Peter, he planted 8 hectares of vines in 1985. Hedging their bets and looking at all possibilities, they included cabernet, merlot and cabernet franc as the mainstream red varieties; with semillon, sauvignon blanc and chardonnay wisely heading up the choice for white table styles. In a further show of family spirit, a daughter has since headed off to learn winemaking at Roseworthy Agricultural College.

The first commercial crop of fruit came with the 1989 vintage. Jeff elected to contract this out to a local freelance winemaking team, Mike and Jan Davies. Results came somewhat more immediately than anticipated with the semillon–sauvignon blanc winning a medal in open company at the Perth Wine Show. A record Jeff hopes to maintain with subsequent vintages!

A small winery may be on the drawing board within two to three years. In the meantime, they have built adequate cellaring space and are preparing their initial products for the market-place. Specialist stores in Perth and Melbourne are currently being targeted. Cellar sales will follow in the near future.

Moss Wood

The magic that is Moss Wood goes back a mere two decades to when Busselton doctor Bill Pannell and his wife, Sandra, planted the second vineyard in Margaret River. After an exhaustive search for land with the correct soils and right aspect, they chose a fertile plot on the corner of Metricup Road and Caves Road, several kilometres north of the pioneering Vasse Felix vineyard.

In 1969 they planted cabernet sauvignon on the best slope of the block and later followed up with plantings of semillon, pinot noir and chardonnay. The property has long been regarded as among the most fertile in the region. Crop tonnages, except in times of frost or bird invasion, have never been a great concern. Newer plantings, however, are on lighter soils but appropriately these have been dedicated to chardonnay and pinot noir—varieties that need to work hard for flavour maximisation.

The first vintage in 1973 was eagerly awaited by oenophiles and potential vineyard developers. Certainly, comparisons were being made with the early vintages of Vasse Felix but that's where the matter rested. Each of the good doctors were following regimes to the beat of different drums. In the final analysis the Vasse wine was lighter in weight, higher in berry flavour and less overtly complex. From the outset the Moss Wood cabernets had more flesh, a distinctive peppermint fruit character and a very rich, long complex palate. Following vintages, particularly the 1974 and 1976, were outstandingly good. The 1975, a particular favourite of Pannell's, had almost Bordeaux qualities about it. Only the 1978 failed to live up to expectations, in fact the winemaker decided not to release this vintage.

In 1980 a small quantity of cabernet was set aside for an additional year's maturation. This was released as the 1980 Reserve. The extra year in oak further complexed the middle palate, filling it out with rich smoky characters not unlike the full rich wines of the Haut Medoc. The wines of the 1980s have followed the tradition of the

1970s, with their rich ripe fruit, excellent French oak and elegant structure. If anything, the new owners, Keith and Clare Mugford, have added a further dimension of finesse to the palate with subtle changes to the production cycle.

Before handing over the reins to Keith Mugford, Bill Pannell made several outstanding pinot noirs from maturing vines on his lighter soils. The 1981, which subsequently developed Corton-like characters, is without the shadow of a doubt the most outstanding wine of the variety yet made in Australia. Many times it has been served masked at important tastings where it has been described, much to the later chagrin of the speakers, as one of the top Burgundies. The Mugford style is a lot leaner, more in the traditional Australian manner. However, he has experimented widely with new oak and various shippers of oak to Australia in an effort to find the most ideal portion for his wine.

The whites of Moss Wood have lived in the great shadow cast by the cabernets and, to a lesser degree, the pinots. Semillon was Pannell's initial white choice, following a traditional Bordeaux approach given the success of the cabernet. Chardonnay was a later arrival. The early semillons were fruity, crisp and attractive early drinking. Pannell also experimented with wood maturation. This added a further dimension to the natural fruit flavours that fortunately lacked the heavy, herbaceous characters already starting to show through in several neighbouring estates' wines. The golden chardonnay vintages were eagerly snapped up and are still very much in demand. The cellar mailing list is still the best method of procuring Moss Wood wines. Distri-

bution of the small quantities of these scarce, high-quality wines is extremely limited. Keith and Clare Mugford try valiantly to maintain an even-handed approach to representation in specialist stockists throughout Australia.

I cannot recall any single bottle of Moss Wood wine that I haven't enjoyed. Undoubtedly the cabernets have been the most exciting line, but interspersed has been the odd silky pinot noir with that elusive wild-strawberry bouquet. Recent releases of chardonnay have been highly sophisticated.

Pierro

Michael Peterkin is an urbane, pragmatic person who desires above everything else to make high-quality wine. A recent review of his new releases would indicate that this dedicated professional has achieved that and more in his brief association with the West Australian industry.

Following graduation from Roseworthy College, Michael came to live at Willyabrup while working in a busy medical practice in Busselton. In 1980 he purchased an undulating property on Caves Road, just south of the Willyabrup Brook bridge. It is one of the most picturesque properties in the heartland of the vineyard area. To the credit of Peterkin he has approached his development in a sensitive fashion, in an effort to preserve as much of the natural bushland as possible. A small dam has been built to carefully blend in with the aesthetic surroundings of the vineyard and rammed-earth winery.

Michael adopted French techniques when planning his vineyard. This involved the close planting of vines—between 4 and 5000 per hectare as opposed to the conventional 2000. Special trellising and machinery had to be developed to cope with this regime, which was unique to Margaret River. From the outset he elected to specialise in pinot and chardonnay and it is these two varieties which dominate the 6 hectare vineyard. Other cultivars planted include cabernet, semillon and sauvignon blanc.

With the vineyard now maturing Peterkin has turned his attention to the sophistication and finessing of his wines. This has involved a myriad of trials, involving yeast strains, differing types of oak and fermentation techniques. Burning the midnight oil has paid off—especially with pinot

and chardonnay. The quietly spoken Peterkin recounted that he had been down the long road of high-tech winemaking without achieving the level of satisfaction he had hoped for. Forsaking convention, he has reverted to many centuries-old practices that have produced better flavours and more traditional wine styles.

Peterkin is one of only a few to have come close to mastering the vagaries of pinot noir in Australia. Using French techniques, he has made two amazingly good wines that have strong resemblances to the better growths of Beaune. Not too far removed and for which he is perhaps better known, is the Pierro chardonnay. A classic wine style that has won many awards during the brief period Peterkin has been crafting it—with the skill and aplomb a Puligny grower would be proud of.

Appropriately the 1989 vintage is shaping up to be his best yet. A word of warning, however, if you are a fan of the big buttery styles with a hint of residual sugar, these wines are not for you. The Pierro styles are totally reliant on fruit quality and the special complex flavours that come from fermentation and oak. By their very structure they have the predisposition to mature well in the bottle.

The wines are distributed nationally, although only in limited quantities. The point should be made that Pierro is a very small operation relative to the South Australian or Victorian specialist wineries. Production, is limited and most releases are promptly snapped up. A letter to the winery should get you onto the mailing list—an early plea for an allocation of the 1988 pinot noir and the 1989 chardonnay is strongly advised.

The other delightful line that Peterkin is justifiably proud of is his Trois Cuvée. A light, dry wine blended from semillon, sauvignon blanc and chardonnay.

Redgate

Founded in 1977, Redgate is yet a further example of why the Margaret River region has caught the attention of the wine world. After a mere handful of vintages under his belt, successful Perth engineer-turned-winemaker Bill Ullinger beat some of the best Australian winemakers in winning the Montgomery Trophy at the 1984 Adelaide Wine Show. Bill and son Paul play down the award and are reluctant to talk of the many prizes that have come their way. The wines speak for themselves, however, and the rewards are highly justified. Father and son are great contributors to the promotion of the region and there are not many grower committees or working parties that Bill hasn't been actively involved in.

Redgate, located off Boodjidup Road, south of the Margaret River township, was formerly an old cattle-grazing property and is within earshot of the coastal beach of the same name. Leeuwin Estate and Freycinet are close by. The Ullingers have 18 hectares planted principally to semillon, riesling, sauvignon blanc, chenin blanc and, naturally enough, cabernet. The winery sits atop a high point on the property, affording excellent views of the estate and beyond. The Redgate range of wines has broad appeal. The extensive list includes an attractive sauvignon blanc, a very good medium-dry white (late-picked style), and a bracket of reds. Distribution is mainly at the winery although it is possible to source a limited range through specialist suppliers.

The lightly herbaceous sauvignon blanc and the elegant cabernet-based reds have commanded recent positive comment and are recommended.

Ribbon Vale Estate

The 'Ribbon' in Ribbon Vale refers to the shape of John James's vineyard. Very much in the same way as the neighbourhood shops are strung out on the curbside in suburban Sydney, Ribbon Vale is a long, narrow, winding strip of land (less than 200 m wide and 1.5 km long) between two extensive farming properties. Bought in 1977 and planted to semillon, sauvignon blanc, chardonnay, cabernet sauvignon and merlot, the property has outstanding panoramic views from the elevated points, especially from where the new winery is situated. This new complex, which overlooks Caves Road and the valleys beyond, is divided into an extensive processing area with a more commodious barrel and storage area beyond. The design capacity envisages an ultimate crush of 100 tonnes, although going on past experience John may have to review this as his own tonnages increase and the demands of tourism and the domestic market take hold.

From 1982 until 1989, when the new building was completed, the Ribbon Vale wines were made either under contract or with the aid of friends at their own local wineries. The 1989 vintage was the first complete processing on home turf. John has entrusted the delicate process to husband-and-wife team Mike and Jan Davies, Roseworthy graduates who similarly contract the winemaking at Cape Clairault.

In recent years the Ribbon Vale whites have attracted a great deal of positive comment, especially the semillon and sauvignon blanc. The semillon is usually pale straw in colour with highlights of green on the edges, the bouquet fresh and fruity with a slight herbaceous lift. The palate is lighter and more delicate than the traditional styles. Altogether a most attractive wine. Some releases have the further dimension of new oak flavours. The sauvignon blanc is also an individual style being full-flavoured and redolent of exotic tropical fruits. The estate red wine is normally a blend of the varieties cabernet and merlot. (The most recent release has 60 per cent merlot.) It is an intense wine with a full rich middle palate and firm tannin finish.

Invariably, the Ribbon Vale semillon comes up trumps as a luncheon wine selection. Most consumers are delighted by its lightness, delicacy and refined flavour profile.

Vasse Felix

I can recall my opening remarks at an address given to a charity group when I said, 'If not for Dr Tom Cullity and Vasse Felix there may not have been a Margaret River wine industry'. Dr Cullity, a Perth physician, took up the challenge in 1967 and, with armfuls of vine cuttings given to him by colleague Jack Mann, established the first vineyard in the Margaret River region. The attractive property on Harmans Road South has since become a mecca for world wine lovers. Indeed, merchants from around the globe come regularly to plead with management for a greater allocation of the fine wine.

Twenty years ago Tom Cullity relied on agriculture scientist Dr John Gladstone's advice that the area was suitable for viticulture. In true pioneering spirit he planted the premium varieties of cabernet, malbec, shiraz, riesling and traminer. Each weekend he would make the 500 km round-trip from the city to check the vineyard's progress. The locals were highly sceptical about the venture but were impressed by his resolve and the capital being injected into the economy. Murray Neaves, a semi-retired builder, and his wife were appointed managers and the property gradually began to take shape. An experimental vintage in 1971 provided the dedicated band with valuable experience for the commercial quantities that were to follow.

The 1972 vintage arrived concurrent with a plague of silver-eyes that couldn't believe their luck. The fruit that was saved was treated with kid gloves. Fermentation was carried out in semi-enclosed stainless steel tanks set into concrete pipes. Cullity set up his own cooling system by pumping water into the pipes, creating a moat effect between the pipe and the steel tanks. The resultant wines were nothing short of stunning. I can remember tasting the riesling a month after fermentation ceased and was amazed at its almost Rhiengau quality. Needless to say it swept all before it at the Perth Wine Show, winning the gold award.

The cabernet sauvignon was even more remarkable. It had a vibrant purple robe that shone luminously through the glass, and a bouquet that was unique and individual. One cannot ever forget that delicious fragrance of crushed mulberries and wild strawberries that pervaded the room when a bottle was uncorked. It was these two wines that created an almost

overnight rush for land as sceptics became devoted brethren and fell over each other to become part of the new industry.

In 1973 David Gregg, an English dairy technologist, and his wife, Anne joined Cullity and the venture became more commercially oriented. Subsequent vintages attracted more column space around Australia than any other wines. Demand for the Vasse Felix wines far exceeded supply—at one stage they were being rationed out at two bottles per client. As volumes increased the winery expanded, with much of the equipment being made on site by the resourceful Gregg, who mastered any situation that developed or that required rugged initiative.

A retrospective tasting conducted with Cullity and Gregg to mark the tenth vintage of Vasse Felix was most enlightening. One could track the development of the vineyard, the maturing of the varieties and the increasing sophistication of the winemaking team.

Long before people realised the importance of good oak, Cullity and Gregg were shipping in French casks. To satisfy their stringent quality control they eventually went to the trouble of purchasing sawn oak to carry out seasoning trials. Oak and the particular attention the Vasse Felix team gave to it was largely responsible for the fine tannin backbone and structure of the cabernet. The other important element was the prudent addition of malbec to the cuvée. Cullity and Gregg also imported quantities of the best Bordeaux reds and used this regularly as benchmarks for their own wines. In summary, it could be said that the vision of this team, with the foresight to go beyond tradition and embrace international parameters, contributed largely to their own success and became an important catalyst for the region itself.

Having seen the fruits of his labour come to fruition, Cullity sold to his faithful steward. In turn, David and Anne Gregg sold to Perth entrepreneur Robert Holmes à Court in 1987. The Greggs remain as managers.

Recent innovations include the launch of the region's first sparkling wine. A tastefully packaged salmon pink wine made in the strict non-vintage brut style. Premium varieties, including a high percentage of pinot noir, have been sourced from regional growers over several seasons for the release.

Gregg also produces one of the state's top light dry reds, marketing it under the Clairet nomenclature. It is a fresh fruity style showing elegant smoky characters and a fresh acid palate.

Everyone who visits Margaret River should have Vasse Felix on their itinerary and, if possible, should purchase a bottle of cabernet sauvignon. It's living history and a very good wine to boot. The attractive stone cellar and tasting facility is professionally managed and the now-extended range (fruit being purchased locally to broaden the range and supplement the riesling and cabernet which is always in short supply) is usually available for tasting. Take time to linger and enjoy a light luncheon over a bottle of sparkling wine. Recent extensions provide a comfortable environment, complete with panoramic views across the vines that have made history possible.

Willespie

Willespie on Harmans Road, Metricup, was established by Kevin and Marion Squance in 1976. Subsequently, the partners have planted 15 hectares of the elevated holding to verdelho, riesling, semillon, merlot and cabernet. Early vintages were made under contract by David Hohnen at Cape Mentelle. From the outset the verdelho fruit produced an elegant floral dry white style that had wide consumer appeal. So successful has the variety been for the Squances that they have recently decided to expand the plantings to 4 hectares. The sad truth with the Margaret River verdelho is that it is so immediately attractive that few bottles are ever kept back for bottle maturation. Consequently consumers miss out on the wonderful wild honeysuckle characters that develop with an additional three years ageing.

The Willespie winery is a magnificent two-storey affair. Extensive use has been made of local stone and hardwood. From the upper balcony, visitors can enjoy a wide panorama of the vineyards, bushlands and rolling hills beyond. In 1988 the Squances appointed Mike and Jan Davies as contract winemakers. More recently John Smith (ex-Xanadu) has joined the team. The young Roseworthy-trained couple have fitted in extremely well and have shown a strong affinity for the district and the local fruit—particularly the white varieties.

Willespie's first major show success came in 1989 at the Sheraton Perth West Australian Wine Awards, when they were awarded first prize and the trophy for their 1987 cabernet sauvignon, in the dry red, full-bodied class. The judges described the wine as a complex example with length and flavour.

Riesling grown on the property produces a soft, floral wine of indicative varietal flavour. The Willespie semillon (which has a minor percentage fermented in new barrels) has a soft grassy character about it and the merest flavour of oak, which tends to tighten up the back palate. Very attractive and once again skilfully made.

Willespie wines are distributed nationally. One cannot bypass the Willespie verdelho for it consistently ranks with the Ashbrook Estate example as the top wine of its type in the district. Who can argue with the learned judges and not mention the 1987 cabernet sauvignon!

Woodlands

This tiny 5 hectare vineyard, established by David and Heather Watson in 1974, has an enviable reputation for producing cabernet sauvignons of outstanding merit. The property on Caves Road (diagonally opposite Moss Wood) hasn't the rich gravelly loam soil structure found throughout Metricup. Consequently, the vines have to fight harder and longer for nutrients. A southerly aspect, and bushland on two sides of the vineyard, tends to inhibit available sun hours. As a result, the Woodlands wines are lighter in weight and body, they have more subtle fruit aromas and tend not to have a great need for extended oak maturation. (One regular taster of the region's wines has often described Woodlands as the Margaux of Margaret River because of the violets he sees in the bouquet.)

The wines of the early 1980s were outstanding. Seasonal conditions had some impact on the 1983 and 1984, resulting in more light-bodied styles; however, more recent examples have been extremely sound.

The Watsons also market, albeit in tiny quantities, a pinot noir of light Burgundian structure. Distributed mainly through a regular mailing list. Small quantities are regularly sent to Sydney. When basically only one wine is produced at a winery it has to be good. David

Watson works extremely hard to make sure this happens on a regular basis. We therefore recommend the Woodlands cabernet—particularly if you are lucky enough to find a hidden trove of 1981 or 1982.

Woody Nook

Woody Nook is located on Metricup Road, Metricup. Run by Jeff, Wynne and Neil Gallagher, this family-owned vineyard, established in 1982, has 5 hectares under vine. Principal plantings include cabernet sauvignon, merlot, semillon, sauvignon blanc and chenin blanc.

Small quantities of a fresh dry white style (sauvignon–semillon blend) and a light dry red cabernet blend are available at the cellar cum restaurant on the property.

Wright's Wines

Wright's, opposite Vasse Felix on Harmans South Road, Cowaramup, has been accredited as the most consistent producer of high-quality shiraz in the Margaret River district. While John Tate and David Hohnen might challenge that broad statement, most would agree that Henry Wright's elegant wine, with that telltale aroma of crushed black pepper, is more than acceptable.

Henry and his wife Maureen came to Margaret River from Kenya. They settled on a mixed farm in Cowaramup but later elected to pursue grapegrowing and winemaking. In 1974 they planted 12 hectares to premium varieties on a new property and quickly learnt the trials and tribulations associated with intensive agriculture.

A large practical winery was built behind several large peppermint trees adjacent to a gently flowing creek on the south-east corner of their property. The soft lines of the building have a comfortable old-world character that fits the environment admirably. The overall atmosphere is one of peace and tranquillity.

The Wrights have cultivated a steady cellar door trade and built up a substantial mail order list. Wines available include several dry white tables styles, the shiraz mentioned above and a very attractive cabernet sauvignon. They also market a white port made from riesling. Depending upon seasonal influences the shiraz or hermitage, as it is labelled, can be outstanding.

The Perth Hills

Vignerons went into the ranges behind the coastal plain to escape the heat of the Swan Valley as far back as the 1860s. They planted

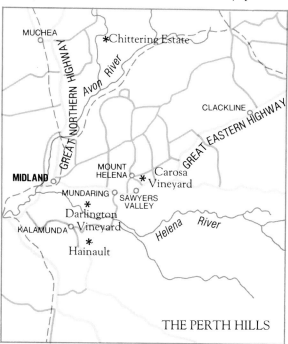

THE PERTH HILLS

extensive vineyards, many of which were physically carved out of the hillsides along the eastern rail line. From all accounts they achieved their principal aim of producing more delicate wines, by taking advantage of the undulating terrain and altitude. The rich ironstone soils and the cooling influence of the low overnight temperatures gave the pioneers a competitive edge over those on the Swan.

Today, much for the same reasons and the close proximity of the metropolitan market, many new initiatives have seen the hills come alive once more with row upon row of green vines. The commercial vineyards producing retail quantities of table wine include Hainault, Carosa, Darlington and the exciting Chittering Estate to the north of Perth.

Carosa Vineyard

Carosa is located in the leafy hills township of Mount Helena. Jim Elson planted cabernet, chardonnay, merlot, pinot noir and riesling in the mid-1980s. The first vintage was in 1987. To date, quantities have been extremely limited. One of the better new releases from this winery is the 1989 Carosa chardonnay.

Chittering Estate

A partnership between the South African Schapera family and Perth's fishing industry leaders, the Kailis Chittering Estate, while perhaps not a designated Hills Vineyard in the true sense, is located in one of Australia's most picturesque settings, at the northern end of the Swan Valley. While the mean local temperatures can be relatively high, Chittering is conditioned by its elevation of 330 m. The rich soils and the abundant water in the district have contributed to the viability of many orchards and vineyards for the best part of the twentieth century. Classic varieties have been planted extensively, with some 40 hectares now committed to vines.

Winemaker Steven Schapera studied at U.C. Davis and with Louis Martini in California's Napa Valley. A devoted Francophile, he aims to employ many classic French techniques in his state-of-the-art winery.

Recent releases have impressed with their well-merchandised packaging. The vineyard's chardonnay was the pick of the most recent vintage. A lighter style, less extracted and with bell-clear chardonnay fruit flavours. Oak is dominant at this stage; however, I believe the fruit will assert itself in the months ahead to blend beautifully with the smoky oak characters.

Darlington Vineyard

The Darlington Vineyard nestles in the Perth Hills' most beautiful village with views across a wide, natural valley. Balt and Francesca Van Der Meer purchased and developed the beautiful 15 hectare block in 1983. Following in the footsteps

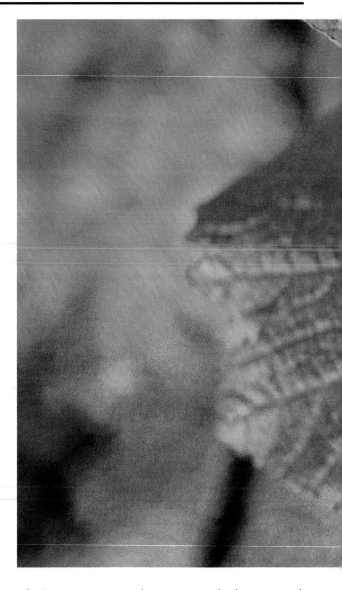

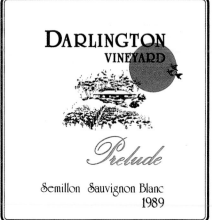

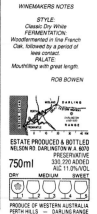

WINEMAKERS NOTES

STYLE:
Classic Dry White
FERMENTATION:
Woodfermented in fine French Oak, followed by a period of lees contact.
PALATE:
Mouthfilling with great length.

ROB BOWEN

ESTATE PRODUCED & BOTTLED
NELSON RD. DARLINGTON W.A. 6070
PRESERVATIVE
750ml   330,220 ADDED
ALC. 11.0%/VOL

DRY   MEDIUM   SWEET

PRODUCE OF WESTERN AUSTRALIA
PERTH HILLS — DARLING RANGE

of the vignerons who pioneered the original Darlington Vineyard in the 1880s, they have physically launched themselves into preparing and planting the steep gravelly loam slopes. Balt has also designed and built a solid attractive winery that commands an excellent view over the estate.

The partners recently appointed a consultant winemaker and adviser—a positive move given the excellent results achieved with the 1989 vintage. I was particularly impressed with the chardonnay, cabernet and the shiraz. A strong feature has been the balancing of the rich, intense fruit flavours with very good seasoned French oak. Certainly a label to watch.

Limited availability throughout Australia, but a letter to the Van Der Meers (Lot 39 Nelson Road, Darlington) will put you in touch.

Pinot noir grapes in the Lefroy Brook vineyard, Pemberton.

Hainault

Located on Walnut Road, Hainault is one of the 'older' vineyards—having been founded in 1979. Peter Fimmel has worked tirelessly to establish both the identity of his own enterprise and the Society of Hills' Growers.

Wines available include an attractive dry-style gewurztraminer, semillon, chardonnay, cabernet sauvignon and an elegant pinot noir. Peter was particularly thrilled to have his 1986 chardonnay chosen by the *Age* newspaper in Melbourne as an outstanding example. The cabernet is a fairly solid, intense wine. It contains a small addition of merlot to soften and broaden the middle palate.

Hainault wines are distributed in Perth, Sydney and Melbourne.

TASMANIA

Ian Mackay

The wine industry in Tasmania is now being accorded a serious place in the overall picture of Australian wine. It has taken some time for such recognition to take place. Grapes were grown and wine was made in Tasmania, or Van Diemen's Land as it was then, long before there was commercial production in either Victoria or South Australia. In our smallest state production remains tiny but distinctive and of the very highest quality. There are encouraging signs that bigger and better things are in store.

The first commercial plantings in Tasmania were begun in the 1820s by Bartholomew Broughton at his Prospect Farm in what is now the Hobart suburb of New Town. Broughton appears to have been a remarkable man. He was a convict who became a Treasury clerk, and eventually won a pardon and made enough money to buy a substantial property. Some sources suggest he planted his first vines in 1823, but *The Times* of London reported in 1824 that 'grapes, in particular, had succeeded beyond expectation'. Were they Mr Broughton's grapes they were talking about? It is doubtful that his vineyard would have cropped so encouragingly in its first year; however, we do know he was producing wine by 1827 when the *Colonial Times* recorded a local judge's declaration that Mr Broughton's wine was as superior to Mr Blaxland's 'as fine Port to Blackstrap'.

Broughton died in 1828 at the tender age of thirty-two, and Prospect Farm was bought by Captain Charles Swanston. Swanston, described as 'a commercial adventurer', planted more vines, producing 7300 litres of wine in 1848. It was, apparently, pretty good stuff. The Hobart *Town Courier* of 1 November 1848 said of his wine: 'The claret will be found superior to any

imported, and promises to exceed in flavour the First Growth of France'.

Swanston died in 1850, however, and his vineyard fell into neglect. The picture, from a wine lover's view, was equally depressing elsewhere in the colony. Dr Mathias Gaunt was making wine from his own grapes grown at Windemere, East Tamar, in the 1840s, at about the same time that William Effingham Lawrence was tending 1.5 hectares at the junction of the South Esk and Tamar Rivers in Launceston. In 1866 there were no fewer than eight Tasmanian vignerons represented at the Intercolonial Exhibition in Melbourne, but within a few years all signs of winemaking in Tasmania had disappeared.

There was a recovery staged in 1884 with the arrival in the colony of Italian silk merchant Diego Bernacchi. He formed the Maria Island Company and had 16 hectares under vine by 1886. He had grand plans of producing 440 000 litres of wine by 1894, but his venture on a rocky outpost off the east coast of Tasmania foundered for want of financial support. Nevertheless, the Tasmanian Government appeared encouraged by his efforts and in 1893 debated a Bill to regulate the sale of locally made wine.

It didn't succeed either, and by the time of Federation in 1901 Tasmania was the only state with no commercial wine production. Many reasons have been given for the decline. The main one was probably climatic. At the time, the Australian appetite was for fortified wine, which required warmer conditions than were normal south of Bass Strait. It has also been said that because pesticides and fungicides were not available the vineyards of Tasmania succumbed to unaccustomed pests.

It was not until 1956 that another Tasmanian wine recovery began. It appeared in the form of Jean Miguet, a fifth-generation winemaker from Provence in southern France, who came to Tasmania as an engineer working on the Trevallyn dam and power station, which was part of Tasmania's pioneering hydro-electric scheme. He arrived in 1955, and bought some land at Lalla, 20 km north of Launceston, where he planted a hectare of vines including pinot noir, chardonnay, Rhine riesling, cabernet sauvignon and grenache. This introduction of European culture was not appreciated by either the local inhabitants or the authorities. Miguet and his wife were vilified as agents of the devil for providing the means of making the demon drink. At one stage their vines and trees were sprayed with 'Agent Orange', the defoliant 2,4-D. A final blow came when the Tasmanian Government refused to grant him a licence to sell his wine. He contrac-

ted leukaemia in 1975 and died the following year in Provence.

The second of a new generation of wine pioneers was Claudio Alcorso, another European immigrant, who in 1957 planted half a hectare of vines on his Moorilla Estate on the Derwent River just north of Hobart. Both the CSIRO and the University of Tasmania took an interest in events as they unfolded at Moorilla, which was in many ways a test-bed for the expanding industry we know today.

Dr Andrew Pirie and his brother, David, certainly took a scientific approach in seeking out a site for their vineyard at Pipers Brook, near Launceston, in 1975. The following year work was started on an adjoining block on Heemskerk—now the state's largest vineyard—by Graham Wiltshire, widely regarded as a father figure in Tasmanian wine. It was probably the quality of Heemskerk which drew the attention

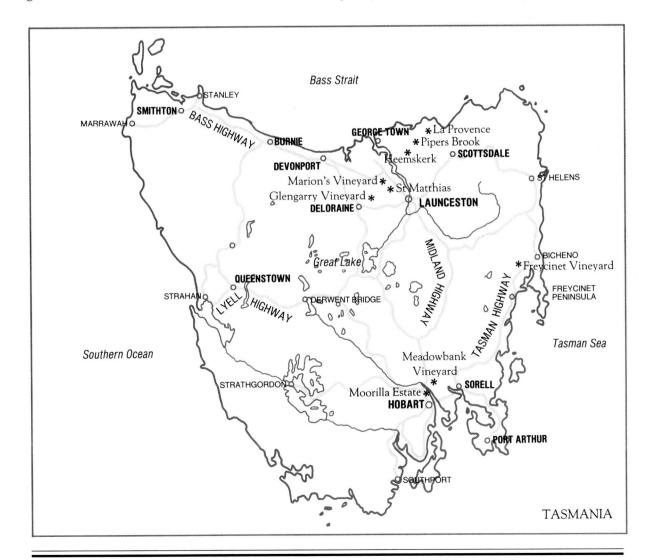

TASMANIA

An aerial view of Moorilla Estate winery, Tasmania's first modern-day commercial vineyard, situated on a peninsula on the River Derwent, 10 km north of Hobart.

of mainland Australia to the style and potential of Tasmania, although progress in terms of volume and market penetration has been painfully slow at times.

Nobody doubts the quality. Andrew Pirie has pointed out that Tasmania is 41°–42° from the Equator, while Bordeaux is 45° north. The sun is hotter in Hobart than in Burgundy, however, which means grapes ripen more regularly. Tasmania has other natural advantages over wine-producing areas elsewhere in Australia. Land is cheap by mainland standards and labour tends to be more freely available. On the other hand, hillside planting is generally required to avoid frost and maximise exposure to the sun, and wind and birds are constant problems.

Dr Pirie tentatively divides the island into four climatic categories:

- **Huon Valley/Bream Creek:** Mean maximum January temperature (MMJT) less than 21°C. Restrained fruit character. Marginal region, with a problem of ripening reds, particularly cabernet sauvignon, in some years.
- **Pipers Brook/Berriedale/Lilydale:** MMJT 21°–23°C. Especially suitable for early varieties. Cabernet not fully ripe in some years. Delicate wines. Well suited to chardonnay.
- **Tamar Valley:** MMJT 23°C. Suitable for mid-season varieties. Cabernet sauvignon and merlot with good colour and tannin, and good pinot noir where not over-cropped. Lower incidence of herbaceousness in cabernet sauvignon.
- **Campania/Richmond:** MMJT over 23°C. Good colour in all reds. Stronger flavours.

The experience of the past ten years or so has shown that pinot noir and chardonnay have perhaps the greatest potential. The involvement of the Champagne house, Louis Roederer, in a joint venture to make sparkling wine at Heemskerk is sufficient testament to this. Other red varieties tend to be much more lightly structured and with softer tannins than elsewhere in Australia, but there are some fine Rhine rieslings and traminer also appears to have potential.

The Vineyards Association of Tasmania was formed and in 1986, with the help of the Tasmanian Government, its members introduced an appellation control system which is by far the most demanding in Australia. Legislation empowers the Licensing Board of Tasmania to monitor production, bottling and labelling, and guarantees to domestic and overseas consumers that the bottle of wine they buy is actually what it claims to be.

Accredited wines have to be free of winemaking faults, and growers wishing to label wine as 100 per cent Tasmanian are required to register before vintage each year with the Commissioner for Licensing. Production audits conducted by the Department of Agriculture then ensure that only Tasmanian grapes are made into wine bearing the appellation certificate.

By the beginning of 1990 there were fewer than 100 hectares of commercially producing vines planted in Tasmania, a minuscule amount by mainland standards. There were signs of mainland interest and other expansion, however. In 1987 Dominique Portet, of Victoria's Taltarni Vineyards, planted 13 hectares of champagne grapes—pinot noir, pinot meunier and chardonnay—on a lovely property at Clover Hill, overlooking Bass Strait, about 10 km from Pipers River.

Dominique Portet's theory is that the Tasmanian wine will add fruit intensity and acid to the sparkling wine he makes at Taltarni. The arrangement is that Andrew Pirie will crush the fruit at Pipers Brook and then the must will be taken to Victoria to be fermented.

Another sparkling wine venture is the St Patricks Vineyard at Bellingham, also in the Pipers River area. In a deal with Yalumba and therefore indirectly with the Champagne house Deutz, Leigh and Janet Gawith have planted 3 hectares of pinot noir and chardonnay. The Gawiths already had 3 hectares of pinot noir, cabernet sauvignon, cabernet franc, merlot, petit verdot and sauvignon blanc; but in the Yalumba joint venture they are contracted to supply a minimum of 30 tonnes and a maximum of 50 tonnes of pinot and chardonnay for five years. They hope to double the yield 8 to 10 tonnes per hectare usually expected of pinot noir in Tasmania by adopting new growing methods. These include the use of the Te Kauwhata trellis system from New Zealand, which, with close planting, reduces leaf growth and encourages optimum grape bearing on each vine.

Delamere Vineyard, established by Richard and Dallas Richardson in 1983, is situated between Pipers Brook and Bellingham, north of

Heemskerk. They have 2 hectares of pinot noir, with 7500 close-planted vines on each; and the first wine, made by Andrew Pirie, was produced in 1986. Since then production has improved steadily, and new plantings at Delamere include chardonnay, sauvignon blanc and semillon.

Other developments in the area include Idelwilde, a 97 hectare property at Pipers River bought by a Swiss group headed by Bernard Rochaix. So far, 3 hectares of cabernet sauvignon, cabernet franc, merlot and sauvignon blanc have been planted under the supervision of Alf Edgecombe, previously from the Swan River in Western Australia. There was a small crop from the close-planted vines in 1989, and plantings in the future will include chardonnay and pinot noir.

The Tamar Valley is where Graham Wiltshire expects a lot of future development to take place. An indication of this is the success of Don Buchanan's Loira Vineyard, where 6 hectares of chardonnay, pinot noir, cabernet sauvignon, cabernet franc, merlot and sauvignon blanc have been planted since 1985. Don, a Roseworthy graduate who worked for Lindeman at Karadoc and consulted for Kaiser Stuhl and Krondorf, is one of the Apple Isle's few graduate oenologists. He hopes eventually to have his own winery but in the meantime is using a local apple cool store to make small parcels of wine with equipment brought from the mainland to assist him in his consultancy business. Among his neighbours in West Tamar is Ralph Power, whose half-hectare vineyard produces small amounts of cabernet sauvignon, pinot noir, Rhine riesling and chardonnay.

Certainly the climate is an important factor in what happens to vines in Tasmania; and the slightly more northerly, maritime conditions in the Tamar Valley are a contrast to those at Glaziers Bay, south of Hobart, where Eric and Gette Phillips planted 8 hectares of pinot noir in 1982 on part of their commercial flower-growing property. Their Elsewhere Vineyard could well be the most southerly vineyard in the world—it is about 43° south, but the vines spread out across a north-facing hillside which Eric believes is 2°–3°C warmer on average than Hobart itself. Getting the fruit ripe is a problem, however, and the Phillips had to be careful to avoid frost areas when planting their vines. Their first wine was

released in 1988 and since then production has increased steadily.

Bruce and Jane Gilham's d'Entrecasteaux Vineyard and Winterwood Winery is a 2 hectare property at Gardners Bay, 65 km south of Hobart and inland from Port Cygnet and the mouth of the Huon River. Their first wines were released in 1989. They were the result of a skimpy first vintage, which meant some blending went on, but results were surprisingly good. There was a Beaujolais-style carbonic maceration wine made from pinot noir and cabernet sauvignon; a fumé blanc made basically from chardonnay; and an unfortified dessert wine made from muscat de saumur, a rather odd variety which Bruce found in the now defunct Tasmanian Government Viticultural Research Station. It apparently comes from the Saumur region of the Loire Valley and, although Bruce describes it as 'a beast of a thing', it has a sweet, muscat character which he finds beguiling. He's a fairly beguiling character who describes himself as an 'uppity peasant'. He worked for Tim Knappstein in the Clare Valley of South Australia and later for Stanley Wines and then the South Australian Brewing Company. When he and Jane bought Winterwood he started the oenology course at Riverina College in Wagga Wagga.

In 1990 the Gilhams began extending their vineyard along terraces cut into a hectare of land overlooking the original vineyard. Bruce had worked in Germany for a while and was impressed by the way growers there were able to ripen grapes through sun exposure and radiation from the stony, gravelly terraces. He believes he can achieve the same effect.

George Park experiences similar conditions on his property at Campania, 40 km north of Hobart; so much so that he calls it Stoney Vineyard. In 1973 he planted 0.4 hectares of cabernet sauvignon, cabernet franc, pinot noir, Rhine riesling, traminer and sylvaner on black-grey loam studded with limestone. The climate there is surprisingly warm and his wines display good ripe fruit character. He makes them himself in his own small winery and his reds, pinot noir and a blend of cabernets, are filled with intense berry fruit flavours and soft fruit tannins, which suggest plenty of ageing potential.

Freycinet Vineyard

The east coast wine-growing region of Tasmania is centred around Bichenot, a picturesque little fishing village where the quality of the local crayfish is legendary. In fact owner Geoff Bull was an abalone diver who opted out of the underwater game and bought this lovely property overlooking Great Oyster Bay in 1980. He was only the second owner of the land since European settlement.

He and his wife Suzanna planted 2 hectares of grapes, cabernet sauvignon, pinot noir, chardonnay, Rhine riesling, sauvignon blanc and muller thurgau; and they picked their first crop of 2.5 tonnes in 1985. They had to replant trees they had removed earlier to provide some shelter from wind off the sea; but the vines have done well, the muller thurgau in particular bearing generously. Cabernet and sauvignon blanc have been less successful, with the pinot and chardonnay somewhere in between.

Both of the reds have produced fine wines, however, with deep crimson colours and beautiful berry characters in bouquet and palate, in what can only be described as typical Tasmanian style. The chardonnay has been fermented in oak and it is a subtle, reserved wine with plenty of character and good ageing potential. Most of the wine is sold at cellar door and through local hotels.

Glengarry Vineyard

Gavin Scott's 2.7 hectare Glengarry Vineyard is at Exeter in the Tamar Valley near Launceston. He got his start in viticulture as a partner in a consortium which took over La Provence Vineyard, established by Frenchman Jean Miguet at Lalla in 1956. The partnership sold La Provence to Stuart Bryce in 1980, by which time Gavin and Anne Scott had bought the land for Glengarry.

In 1980 they planted cabernet sauvignon and pinot noir; merlot, cabernet franc and more pinot was planted in 1981 and 1982; and chardonnay came a couple of years after that. The vineyard is a former apple orchard on typical West Tamar grey sandy loam, which is much poorer soil, generally, than the rich red loam typical of the Pipers River region further east. Nevertheless, this helps control the vigour of the

vines, and when basal leaves fall—usually towards the end of February, the driest month—the fruit goes on to ripen very well. Similar conditions exist in another vineyard at nearby Legana which Gavin leases with his friend Steve Hyde.

The cabernet sauvignon from Glengarry and Legana are quite different, however; the first is strong and firm with intense blackberry character; and the other is greener and more herbaceous, but with rich berry flavour and soft tannins. The Glengarry pinot noir is also a very promising wine, rivalling the Pipers Brook, according to some critics, in depth of flavour and balance. Most of the wine is sold at cellar door, and visitors are welcome.

Heemskerk

The Heemskerk vineyard is situated at Pipers Brook, north-east of Launceston. It is named after the flagship in which Abel Tasman discovered Tasmania in 1642. It had its beginnings in 1966, when Launceston engineer Graham Wiltshire and his friend Michael Curtis planted a small vineyard at Legana on the Tamar River.

They grew small amounts of cabernet sauvignon and Rhine riesling. In 1973 the wines they made were spotted by Bill Fesq of the well-known Sydney wine and spirit merchants Fesq & Co., and Colin Haselgrove, one of the great figures in Australian winemaking, who had then recently retired as managing director of Walter Reynell & Sons, the South Australian company which produced Reynella wines. They were so impressed that in 1975 they set up a consortium to establish Heemskerk. This comprised Graham Wiltshire, Barry Larter of Launceston, and the Fesq and Haselgrove families.

After a long search land was bought adjacent to what was then the new Pipers Brook vineyard being planted by Dr Andrew Pirie, and 20 hectares were planted to chardonnay, pinot noir, cabernet sauvignon and Rhine riesling. The first wines were made in 1980 at the small winery at Legana, where the vineyard comprised a further 1 hectare of cabernet sauvignon.

The cabernet sauvignon from Heemskerk very quickly established itself as an outstanding wine and, although there were some problems with ripening in cooler years, the potential for the consortium looked bright. By 1983 it was clear to

Graham Wiltshire that northern Tasmania's climate was remarkably similar to that of the great Champagne region of France, and he came to the conclusion that there was no reason why it could not produce premium-quality sparkling wine. In 1984 he and Mark Fesq, who was also enthused by the idea, convinced Jean-Claud Rouzard, the President of Champagne Louis Roederer, to visit Heemskerk and see the potential of the place for himself.

What he saw and tasted were enough to immediately commit him to a shareholding and today the company is owned equally by the Wiltshire, Fesq and Roederer groups. Since 1985 a further 12 hectares of chardonnay and pinot noir have been planted at Heemskerk; and in 1988 a new vineyard was established on the banks of the Tamar River, fifteen minutes from Launceston. The site, known as the Rebecca Vineyard, was chosen after a careful search for a microclimate which would complement that of Heemskerk itself.

In 1986 trials began on various trellis designs and vine training and pruning methods, and now the original section of Heemskerk vineyard is gradually being converted to the open lyre trellis advocated by Alain Carbonneau of Bordeaux. All new plantings use the system, which allows maximum exposure to light and sun. The first batch of grapes specifically for sparkling wine production was pressed in 1987, and in November of that year Jean-Claud Rouzard spent two days at Heemskerk blending and re-blending samples before a final base wine was selected for secondary fermentation in the bottle.

Base wines from 1987, 1988 and 1989 were still undergoing ageing on yeast lees by the time the fourth wine was made in 1990. Graham Wiltshire and his assistant Ruth Marquis spend a great deal of time travelling to Roederer in Reims and to California, where Roederer Estate is established in the Anderson Valley in the northern part of the state. The first Roederer Estate wines were released to great acclaim in the United States, and great anticipation surrounds the release of the first Heemskerk offerings.

In the meantime, production of Heemskerk's very fine table wine continues, and these are now concentrated on cabernet sauvignon, chardonnay and Rhine riesling. Graham Wiltshire, a seminal figure in the growth of the industry in Tasmania, also continues to make wine on a consultancy basis for a number of his neighbours. On top of all his other duties, he works hard as president of the Vineyards Association of Tasmania.

La Provence

In the introduction to this section we mentioned the part played by the French engineer Jean Miguet in the renaissance of the Tasmanian wine industry. Miguet, a fifth-generation winemaker from Provence, bought land at Lalla, on Brown Mountain in the picturesque north-west of the state. Here he established the first vineyard since the decline of Tasmanian viticulture half a century before.

Miguet wanted to bring the delights, or at least some of them, of his native Provence to this faraway corner of the world. However, his best efforts were spurned by locals, who drank beer and spirits but for some reason feared a Frenchman's wine, and by the Tasmanian Government, which refused to grant him a licence to sell his products. Tragically, he contracted leukaemia in his adopted land and returned to France in 1975, dying a year later in Provence.

His vineyard was sold in 1975 to a consortium of three Launceston men who were interested in wine; among them was Gavin Scott, who later established his own property, Glengarry Vineyards, in West Tamar. In 1980 La Provence was bought by RAAF Wing Commander Stuart Bryce and his wife Kay. The property was managed by Graham Wiltshire of Heemskerk until Stuart retired and moved to Tasmania in 1984.

The Bryces immediately bought a neighbouring property away to the east, and expanded plantings from Miguet's original 0.8 hectares to 3.2 hectares. They replaced old grenache vines and grafted over cabernet sauvignon, which had proved difficult to set and ripen, to chardonnay. The vineyard now produces only chardonnay and pinot noir—the two great Burgundy varieties—both of which are made into straight varietals. While all this was going on, Stuart completed the wine science degree course at Riverina College in Wagga Wagga; and now, although Graham Wiltshire continues to make the La Provence wines, Stuart has an increasingly hands-on role.

La Provence has an elevation of some 200 m

Grapes, Tasmania.

above sea level but fortunately is in a wind shadow, which protects it from boisterous southerlies. The soil is heavy clay and, although some young vines have suffered from wet feet, Stuart believes conditions are ideal for chardonnay and pinot noir. So far he has been extremely pleased with the wines offered for sale since 1986. He picks his grapes a full ten days after picking begins at Pipers Brook, a mere 20 km away, which makes it the latest picked vineyard in Tasmania.

The chardonnay is fermented in new French oak and consistently produces a fine golden wine with a long elegant finish very much in the Burgundian style. The pinot also shares the richness of Burgundy and since 1989 it has been labelled Miguet pinot noir, in honour of the vineyard's founder. Parts of the vineyard are still very young, but eventually the Bryces will be crushing 20 tonnes each year for a total production of some 2000 cases.

Marion's Vineyard

Marion's Vineyard, established in 1980 by Mark and Marion Semmens, is a beautiful property on the Foreshore Road overlooking the Tamar River at Deviot, near Launceston. It was originally known as Tamar Vineyards, but Marion's tireless efforts in helping create the ambience of the place makes the name change entirely appropriate. Originally 5.5 hectares of pinot noir, cabernet sauvignon and chardonnay, with a little muller thurgau, were planted in the doleritic and ironstone soils on the southern side of the river valley; and a further 6 hectares were added in 1987.

The early wines were mainly experimental, testing the waters as it were; and pinot noir has since emerged as the variety most suited to conditions there. The first pinot wine was made in 1984 and, like many first wines, it had surprising depth and richness with well-flavoured plummy fruit and firm tannins. The 1985 was softer and more supple, the fruit more like cherries than plums, and since then the cellar style has developed nicely.

Cabernet sauvignon has also come along well, with very good berry flavours and some elegant herbaceousness, and the chardonnay is also showing great promise. The first, made in 1986 and released the following year, had plenty of

peach and melon flavour and a firm acid backbone which suggested it would age beautifully.

Marion's Vineyard is a splendid place to visit while exploring the Tamar Valley, and there are all kinds of facilities, including a swimming pool and volleyball court. A natural grass amphitheatre above the winery has become a venue for concerts and jazz festivals.

Meadowbank Vineyard

Meadowbank is the name of a 4000 hectare grazing property at Glenora in the Derwent Valley of Tasmania, 75 km north-west of Hobart. When the Ellis family bought it in 1976 they found it included a 2 hectare patch of two-year-old vines, mainly cabernet sauvignon and Rhine riesling. Gerald and Sue Ellis set about extending the vineyard, planting several more hectares to chardonnay and merlot. The original vines were on 3.7 m rows, the new ones close planted 1.3 m apart in 1.6 m rows.

What is so extraordinary about Meadowbank wine is that up to 1985 it was made in Victoria. Gerald Ellis sought winemaking advice from the redoubtable Ian Hickinbotham and his late son Stephen, who at the time were operating the Anakie vineyard and winery near Geelong. In what began as an experiment in 1980, riesling grapes were picked and immediately chilled in refrigerated sea-containers, which were then shipped across Bass Strait for vinification. The wines were labelled both Meadowbank and Hickinbotham and attracted quite a lot of attention, although volume was obviously low.

At the time, the Hickinbothams were very keen on the idea of working with cool-climate fruit and this was certainly an opportunity to do that. Both their riesling and cabernet had distinctive cool herbaceous character, although there was not much fruit flavour development once the wines were bottled. Nevertheless, the Ellis effort has continued at Meadowbank with wines after 1975 made by Andrew Pirie at Pipers Brook. A winery was built at Glenora in 1990 and winemaking duties were taken over by Andrew Hood.

Moorilla Estate

Among the European immigrants who set about resurrecting the Tasmanian wine industry in the 1950s was Claudio Alcorso, an Italian silk and

The Moorilla Estate is located on the River Derwent. The total area in picture is now under vine.
Moorilla's total annual crush is 150 tonnes.

textiles manufacturer who settled in Hobart and began planting grapes on the banks of the Derwent River in 1957. A few experimental rows eventually grew into Moorilla Estate, a beautiful riverside property at Berriedale now run by Claudio's son, Julian.

In establishing which grapes grew best in that very southerly part of the world they worked closely with such organisations as the CSIRO and wine research institutes in Australia and overseas. One of their close friends and advisers was Dr Bob Menary, a senior lecturer in horticulture at the University of Tasmania. As well as working on Moorilla Estate, together they established a new vineyard at Bream Creek on the east coast of Tasmania south-west of Bicheno.

Over the years there have been plantings of Rhine riesling, cabernet sauvignon, shiraz, gewurztraminer and pinot noir; and it is this last variety which has shown most promise. There are now some 2.4 hectares at Berriedale, which Julian Alcorso hopes will eventually all be pinot; and his newer plantings there are on a lyre trellising system, which reduces the leaf canopy and exposes the fruit for better ripeness.

This has already shown up in the quality of both fruit and finished wine, with higher sugar levels and better acid projecting the character of pinot noir in a much more satisfying way. At Bream Creek, which was begun in 1974, results have been mixed. The vineyard is exposed to cold sea breezes, which cause problems with flowering and fruit set, and ripeness is a touch-and-go affair. There have been some good cabernets, however; and pinot noir, chardonnay and riesling of sufficient standard to appear under the Moorilla label.

By 1990 Moorilla was set to become the most productive winery in the state. Out of a total Tasmanian crush of 675 tonnes, it processed 150 tonnes of its own fruit; and shortly before vintage Julian Alcorso announced a $500 000 visitor and wine-tasting centre offering year-round supplies of Tasmanian wine, meat, cheese, seafood and other delicacies. Plans are to continue the Mediterranean theme of Moorilla Estate's lovely Berriedale establishment, which Julian believes can become a major tourist attraction.

Claudio Alcorso retains his ties with Moorilla, most noticeably through the wine labels which are printed on fabric. He remains a well-known patron of the arts in Hobart and has worked hard for the preservation of historic sections of the city, particularly Battery Point.

Pipers Brook

Pipers Brook is perhaps the archetypal Tasmanian vineyard and winery. It was established in the Pipers River valley north-east of Launceston in 1974 by the Pirie brothers, Andrew and David. Dr Andrew Pirie is one of the more remarkable figures in Australian winemaking—one who made a very deliberate decision to follow his art in the cool, European-like climate of Tasmania.

He studied agricultural science at Sydney University, where he became Australia's first PhD in vine physiology. In 1971 he went to Europe to seek winemaking experience, and did so by working with such distinguished companies as Avery's in Bristol, Hugel in Alsace, Remoissenet in Burgundy and Sichel in Bordeaux. He then spent twelve months as wine projects officer at Riverina College in Wagga Wagga, New South Wales. The idea of finding the best place in Australia, by European standards, to grow grapes and produce wine was always in his mind. An uncompromising search for ideal soil and weather conditions eventually led him to Pipers Brook, where he and his brother planted 10 hectares of chardonnay, Rhine riesling, gewurztraminer, cabernet sauvignon and pinot noir.

The European style was followed to the letter in the vineyard: the vines were planted 1.1 m apart in rows 1.8 m apart, in what was one of the first close-planted estates in Australia. Rows were hedge trimmed to enhance fruit quality. The first Pipers Brook red to be released was the 1981 cabernet sauvignon, a lovely wine which had been matured in new French oak barriques. While still in wood, it won a gold medal in the Royal Hobart Show, the first of many subsequently awarded to Pipers Brook. The 1982 cabernet was even better, with richer fruit, softer tannins, and a distinctly Medoc-like character. Later vintages have shown seasonal variation; some wines have been greener and more herbaceous than others, but a distinct, and distinctive, cabernet cellar style has emerged.

Rhine riesling has also varied from year to year but elegance and good acid structure have always been its hallmarks. Chardonnay has been more consistent but still shows some interesting variation. The same could be said for pinot noir, which, as elsewhere in Tasmania, is emerging as a very Burgundian style of wine.

Everything about Pipers Brook is admirable, from the cultured look of the vineyard to the dedicated winery practices and the quality of its finished wines and their utterly elegant labelling. Its products are in great demand and short supply, making them some of the most sought-after wines in the country, and deservedly so.

A typical Tasmanian vineyard.

St Matthias

In the 1960s the Tasmanian Department of Agriculture set up an experimental vineyard at Rowella, in the Tamar Valley west of Launceston. Small patches of literally dozens of varieties were planted in an attempt to find out what, viticulturally speaking, the Apple Isle could grow best. Cuttings were supplied to growers all over the state and in 1982 the government decided it had played its part in getting the wine industry back on its feet.

In that year the Rowella vineyard was bought by Laurie and Adelle Wing, who called it St Matthias after the delightful church on the other side of the Tamar River which now appears on their labels. They began a replanting program in 1983, and now have 4 hectares of Rhine riesling, chardonnay, pinot noir, cabernet sauvignon and merlot planted 1.3 m apart in rows 2.5 m apart. Their first vintage, in 1987, produced 20 tonnes of grapes, and it has increased slowly but surely since then.

Their wines are made by Graham Wiltshire at Heemskerk and they all show good fruit character, something for which the beautiful Tamar Valley is becoming increasingly well known. The pinot noir, in particular, has deep soft black cherry flavours and soft tannins, and could well prove to be the pick of the bunch. It is another indication that pinot could emerge as Tasmania's most successful variety, red or white.

QUEENSLAND

Len Evans

Ballandean Estate

This is the wine name of Sundown Valley Vineyards, which used to be Angelo's Winery at Ballandean.

Angelo Puglisi, third-generation wine man, is a tremendous enthusiast and at the forefront of Queensland wine. Australian wine, rather, for he was one of those who insisted on the deletion of 'Queensland winemaker' classes from the Brisbane Show. 'We have to compete nationally, we have to stand on our own feet.' All very commendable.

Ballandean Estate is planted to shiraz (4 hectares), cabernet sauvignon (4), some merlot and malbec; and chardonnay (2 hectares), semillon (2), Rhine riesling (1) and some sylvaner and chenin blanc. Some fruit is also bought in. Altogether 16 hectares of vineyard and between 120 and 140 tonnes of fruit are crushed, making 20 000 cases of wine.

Angelo's wines have won several gold medals in Open Classes at Brisbane, particularly for reds. The emphasis is on straight varietals in 750 ml bottles, which are sold either at cellar door or through national distributors Tucker Caon.

Bassett's Romavilla Winery

The town of Roma, now famous for its oil and natural gas, is the centre of a small segment of the Queensland wine industry. It is located about 512 km west of Brisbane, 300 m above sea level, and in the dry belt west of the Great Dividing Range. The long summers in Roma are hot indeed, and often dry, though the average rainfall is 560 mm.

It was in this unlikely environment that

Samuel S. Bassett, a Cornishman who had spent some time in the Hunter Valley, established a vineyard in 1863. He began by clearing the scrub in an area along the Bungil Creek—which only runs after heavy rain—and had vine cuttings sent out by bullock wagon from Toowoomba. Most of the cuttings withered and died on the journey, but Bassett planted the few survivors on the sandy loam creek banks and built up his winery, until eventually he had 180 hectares planted to grapevines.

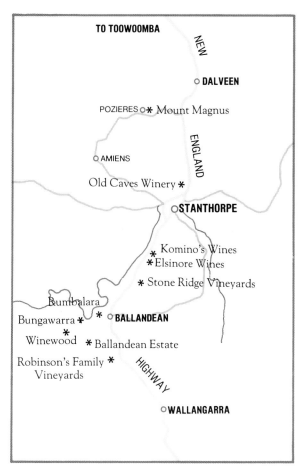

429

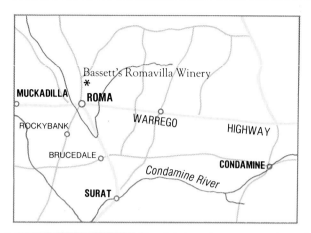

Varieties grown were (and are) riesling, solverino, syrian, portugal, red muscat, white muscat, black muscat, black cluster, red hermitage and mataro. Samuel Bassett travelled throughout Queensland selling his wines and won numerous prizes for them at the Brisbane Exhibition.

The present cellar was built in 1878 and has a large storage capacity. In the early 1900s great vats were fitted with cooling coils as a means of reducing heat during fermentation. The water for the coils was pumped from a 15 m well by a Ryder & Ericson hot-air pumping engine. Romavilla claims to be one of the first wineries in Australia to use cooling during fermentation.

In 1898 Mr Bassett sent his son William down south to learn winemaking from Leo Buring. William's brother Frank became vineyard manager, and his three other brothers all travelled for the winery. William Bassett continued to work at Romavilla.

The winery was taken over in 1975 by David and Bill Wall (brothers of Peter Wall, of Yalumba fame) and their sister, Mrs Brian Sproule. Early in 1976 David became the sole owner of Romavilla. The area under vine has declined to 15 hectares, of Rhine riesling, chenin blanc, crouchen, syrian, muscat and shiraz. David is encouraging local growers to increase production, and purchases grapes from them.

The grapes are grown on various types of soils, from alluvial flats to sandy loam. There is no irrigation. The vintage is mainly in January and February but extends to March.

David Wall is marketing a new range of wines and has modernised winemaking methods. As the area is so well suited climatically to the production of fortified wine, he intends to continue

his production in this area; however, with the must cooling and temperature-control equipment that he has installed in the winery, he plans also to produce high-quality table wine.

The galvanised-iron winery has underground cellars with a storage capacity of 545 000 litres. The crushing machinery can process 40 tonnes of grapes per day and a hydraulic press is also used. The majority of their wines are fortified, with a dry and sweet table wine also being made.

Incidentally, one interesting claim to fame of the Romavilla winery (which has nothing to do with wine) is that Billy Hughes, one-time Prime Minister of Australia, worked in the vineyards there before World War I. Is this the only time an Australian leader has laboured in a vineyard?

The injection of David Wall's enthusiasm and technical knowhow should go a long way to restoring the fame of the Romavilla name.

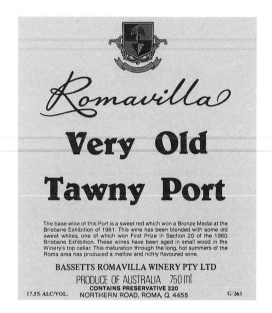

Bungawarra Vineyard and Winery

Bungawarra vineyard is close to the township of Ballandean, about 20 km south of Stanthorpe. It was established in the 1920s by Angelo Barbagello, who produced wines from table grapes mainly for Italian communities all over New South Wales and Queensland. He made his wines in an enormous concrete vat and sent them off to his customers, usually by rail, in 365 litre casks.

Alan Dorr and Philip Christensen bought the property in the late 1970s, making the first wine from a 7 tonne crush in 1979—and it won a gold

Romavilla winery near Roma.

at the Redland Bay Show.

The property covers almost 20 hectares on the northern slope of a granite outcrop ridge, over 700 m above sea level. The area is typical of high country, with heavy frosts in winter and cool nights through most of the year. The soil, which is well drained, is mostly light, coarse-grained, decomposed granite. About half the property is suitable for viticulture.

When Alan and Philip took over Bungawarra, there were about 5 hectares of vines, some nearly as old as the vineyard itself. Of this, only the muscat remains. Many of the older and less productive vines were pulled up, and new plantings of traminer, pinot chardonnay, pinot noir, malbec and cabernet sauvignon were made. A continuing program of further plantings and provision of trickle irrigation is being implemented. There are now 11.5 hectares in all, producing about 55 tonnes, which makes a total production of about 4000 cases.

The emphasis today is on dry reds and whites and dessert muscat. Bungawarra has done particularly well in the Courier-Mail/Sheraton Hotel awards, which do a great deal to foster Queensland wines. The winning wines are featured on the Sheraton wine list.

Philip Christensen (who now owns the company outright, having bought out the other shareholding in 1986) has won classes in fortified wine, dessert wine, and dry white and red; establishing him as one of the forces for quality wine in Queensland today.

Elsinore Wines

Owned by Peter Love, who was once with the Wine Information Bureau, Elsinore Wines is at Glen Aplin, near Stanthorpe, and is planted to semillon, chardonnay, shiraz and cabernet sauvignon.

Both table and fortified wines are made, and sales are mainly at cellar door. Picnic and barbecue areas are available and coaches and groups are welcome.

Felsberg Vineyards Winery

A small operation owned by an executive brewer (Mr Otto Haag, the general manager of Castlemaine Perkins), who, in this case, is 'not in a hurry'.

He bought the property, 850 m above sea level, in Townsends Road, Glen Aplin, which is in the Granite Belt, in 1983 and began planting. So far there are between 5 and 6 hectares of vineyard and Otto's laconic comments reveal something of the trials and tribulations of the would-be wine producer.

We've got chardonnay, that seems to be very good, we've made some, have great hopes; traminer, excellent stuff but who wants it; Rhine riesling, don't know about that; merlot, doesn't seem to do much so far; cabernet sauvignon, well, that's funny stuff, all over the place, don't know how that will turn out; pinot noir, we've got an acre, makes pale, anaemic stuff, not much good, probably pull it out; and shiraz, very good, lovely fruit makes good wine.

Otto stresses that he works at other things and does not need a crust—and is trying very hard to do everything right. Eventually, they intend to make 3000–4000 cases, but only 'if it's the proper stuff'.

They've built a stone-walled winery and, as more and more fruit becomes available, they will, to put it simply, find out just what they can do. As one who knows just how difficult it is to get it right, I wish them great success.

Foster's Wines, Atherton Tablelands

This must be getting close to being the most northerly vineyard operation in Australia. It is at Kalunga, near Herberton, on the tablelands inland from Cairns. Christopher Foster is the winemaker-manager. His father started planting grapes there in 1956, and now they have 25 hectares of vineyard, of which 10 hectares are in wine grapes. However, they do crush both muscat and isabella; in fact, a light, fruity, slightly sweet red from the latter variety is their most popular wine. They sell bulk, flagon and bottle, and cellar door sales are pre-eminent with a growing tourist trade.

Of the wine grapes, there are 2 hectares of shiraz, some mataro; 1.5 hectares of villard blanc, Rhine riesling, chardonnay and semillon. The

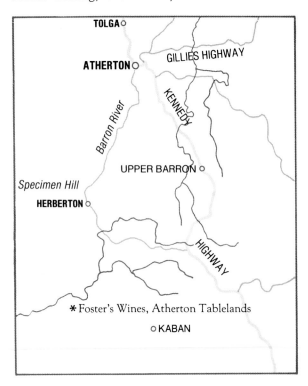

Foster's Wines, Atherton Tablelands

crush varies between 20 and 40 tonnes, generally producing the equivalent of 2000 cases plus.

There is no relationship with the other beverage company of the same name.

Komino's Wines

Between Ballandean and Stanthorpe, about 8 km south of Stanthorpe.

This small family operation is shared by Stephen and Penelope Comino, who were encouraged by Murray Tyrrell to become involved in wine, and their son Tony, who now runs the vineyard and winery.

They planted 6 hectares in 1976, 1.5 hectares of shiraz, 1 hectare of chardonnay and including semillon, Rhine riesling, chenin blanc and cabernet sauvignon. Another 4 hectares are being developed. The crush is about 50 tonnes and altogether about 4000 cases is produced, mostly dry varietals which are sold at cellar door and by mail order.

The difference between the name of the winery and that of the family is that they wanted to soften the Greek name. Having no 'C' in Greek language, when they arrived in Australia they adopted one.

Mount Magnus

Mount Magnus, formerly the old Baltimore Cellars at Pozieres, some 25 km from Stanthorpe, is now owned by Brisbane businessman John Matthews. Andrew Braithweight is the winemaker and Paddy Kassulke runs the winery sales.

They have 12 hectares of chardonnay, shiraz, cabernet sauvignon and emerald ruby and crush about 60 tonnes, as well as purchasing some material.

A wide variety of wine is available from chardonnay to marsala, mostly for the passing and tourist trade. Coaches are encouraged and catered for, and there are barbecues, farm animals and picnic grounds.

Old Caves Winery

The Old Caves Winery is situated on the New England Highway, 2 km north of Stanthorpe. The proprietor and winemaker is David Zanatta. He built the winery on the property in 1979 and 1980 and has no vineyard, preferring to buy from local contract growers.

The crush is between 40 and 50 tonnes,

making 3000–4000 cases, all of which is bottled. The main grapes crushed are shiraz, chardonnay and cabernet sauvignon in that order. The most popular wines are a chardonnay and a dry white which is a chardonnay and semillon blend; a light fruity red from shiraz; a fuller red from cabernet sauvignon and shiraz; and tawny port.

Over half the sales are made at cellar door. The rest is by mail order though David does make a feature of private bottling, selling bottled wine under the supplied label of the customer.

J & N Ricca

The vineyard now owned by Joe and Nina Ricca was purchased in the early 1960s by Joe's parents, Mr and Mrs S. Ricca. Joe and Nina bought it in the early 1970s and have updated the facilities.

It is situated in the heart of the grapegrowing area known as Sundown Valley, near Ballandean. It may well have been one of the first vineyards there, as indicated by the crushing pit on the property, which was installed on 20 February 1935 and used for crushing grapes with the feet. In 1949 there was a new building constructed near the old one. The last building erected was completed in May 1981 and is equipped with more modern facilities for crushing grapes and storing wine.

The vineyard consists of 18 hectares of table and wine grapes. Wine varieties include shiraz, cabernet sauvignon, Rhine riesling and semillon.

The Riccas mainly produce dry red and white wines which are sold to the public in bulk. They do not sell to other wineries for bottling and do not bottle their own wine.

Robinson's Family Vineyards

The Robinson's family winery lies to the south of the Ballandean township, in Queensland, near the border with New South Wales.

John and Heather Robinson began planting vines there in 1969–70 after searching the southern Queensland area for suitable land. Soils are well-drained, decomposed gravel, and the temperature and cool climate are ideal for quality grapegrowing. The average January temperature is 20°C.

John Robinson has lived in France near the vineyards of Beaujolais and Burgundy, and in 1975 he and his wife made a study tour of the French and German vineyards. Heather Robinson's family founded Saltrams Wines in the Barossa Valley, so they are both deeply interested in wine. John was also a wine science student at Riverina College under Brian Croser, and I can remember him doing a vintage with Max Lake in the Hunter.

The varieties planted by the family are chardonnay, traminer, semillon and sauvignon blanc for the whites; and the cabernet sauvignon, pinot noir, shiraz, merlot and malbec for the reds. Some shiraz is bought from local vineyards.

The modern winery/tasting room complex contains refrigeration and cold fermentation facilities. Red wines are matured in French and American new casks, while the chardonnays receive French oak treatment. Current production is up to 6000 cases, distributed on the eastern seaboard, with a little going to export. There are also cellar door sales.

In 1989 Rod McPherson and Phillipa Hanblepon, both trained at Roseworthy, became joint winemakers.

Rumbalara Vineyards

Rumbalara is the previously named Granite Belt Vignerons, run by pioneer Bob Gray and his wife, Una. The vineyard and winery are at Fletcher.

Rumbalara (an Aboriginal word meaning 'the end of the rainbow') was first planted to grapes in 1928, and small quantities of wine were made by the then owners John (Giovanni) Verri and his father. Most of the grapes grown were, however, destined for the table grape market.

Classic European wine grape varieties were planted during the 1970s and full production now varies between 30 and 70 tonnes. Generally, about 4000 cases of wine are made.

Rumbalara is situated at an elevation of 760 m above sea level, making it one of the highest altitude vineyards in Australia. The consequent cool climate results in growing and fermentation conditions that enhance the varietal character of the grapes.

A wide range of grape varieties has been planted, partly because of the experimental nature of wine-growing in a new commercial area. Major white varieties planted are semillon, and Rhine riesling, with smaller quantities of sylvaner. The major plantings of red grapes are cabernet sauvignon, pinot noir, shiraz and black muscat; with smaller quantities of mataro, malbec and cabernet franc. Grape plantings total 12 hectares. An English country-style cider is produced from local apples.

All wine is made in the winery, which is situated at Rumbalara, by Bob Gray and his son Chris. Bob, whose previous profession was that of civil engineer, is the first Queensland graduate from the wine science degree course at Riverina College.

The policy is to produce only quality wines, and all wines are bottled at the winery. No bulk wines are sold. As well as wines for the table, dessert wines are produced—these were the first fortified styles made in the Granite Belt district. The wines are marketed under Rumbalara labels.

Stone Ridge Vineyards

A small, quality-oriented company run by Jim Lawrie, an ex-Brisbane businessman, with help from his accountant wife, Ann Kennedy. Jim represents the growing band of Queensland city people who are moving to the Stanthorpe area and planting grapes, regarding it as a district of great promise.

Jim and Ann first bought the property, near

Glen Aplin, about 12 km south of Stanthorpe, in 1981. The small winery was built in 1985, and grapes were purchased locally, mostly shiraz, while their own 2 hectare vineyard was growing. In their vineyard they have planted shiraz, chardonnay, marsanne, rousanne, viognier and muscat. The crush is 12–15 tonnes and approximately 1000 cases are produced, selling at cellar door and by mail order. Jim is particularly proud of his 1987 shiraz.

Jim and Ann do not live on the property but in the old stationmaster's house at Glen Aplin. They are pleased with their move and sure that the area has great potential.

Winewood

A small family operation in Ballandean run by Ian Davis, who is a schoolteacher, and wife, Jeanette Davis, a town planner. Started in 1985, the ambition is to grow slowly without much debt, and to develop through their own resources.

There are 4.5 hectares of vines, mostly semillon and shiraz, though there's also marsanne, chardonnay, cabernet sauvignon, cabernet franc, merlot and malbec.

At present over 15 tonnes are processed. The aim is to develop 1000 vine sections into potential 500 gallon batches, be they straight varietals or blends. Over 1000 cases are made and this will grow slowly in the future. The reds are intentionally full-bodied with the exception of a light-bodied dry red made by the carbonic maceration method.

All sales are cellar door. The Davis's are wine enthusiasts extending their hobby to the limit by becoming producers.

FROM VINEYARD TO TABLE

Anders Ousback

Many people incorrectly consider that any collection of bottles is a cellar, but it is merely a collection or store of wine. The experienced storeman or collector has a wine for every occasion: a fresh crisp white, and something more developed; the youthful red and a more mature one; a bottle of champagne for a christening, and a sweet sherry for a favourite Aunt. Once you become interested in mature reds and developed whites and discerning in your choice and price of wines, it is time to start a cellar.

A wine cellar should really be below ground level and contain 'bins' of maturing wine and incorporate the wine store. However, if the 'bins' are above ground level, the expression 'cellar' is still accepted.

Determining Your Cellar Requirements

Let us assume that in a week you drink three bottles of white and four of red wine. One bottle of red and white is inexpensive, pleasant and ideal for quaffing; purchased in dozen lots when quantity is at a minimum. The second white is a crisp young aromatic such as a Rhine riesling or traminer; this can be picked up from time to time in half-dozen lots. The final white is a developed wine such as a Hunter Semillon or Eden Valley Rhine Riesling requiring perhaps four years' (cellar) maturation. To enjoy the luxury of drinking one four-year-old white per week you will need to have on hand eighteen dozen wine of this type—between one and four years old.

The second and third bottles of red can vary from five to seven years in age. These wines will have spent two years in wood and bottle before

being released by the various wine firms. To drink two a week, you will need just on thirty-seven dozen red of this group, with new wines constantly replacing the mature wines as they are consumed.

The final red may be a wine of, say, eight years' cellar age; made up of the ends of bins you used to drink with five to seven years age on them; and a few special wines purchased and put aside until they reach maturity. Add to your list another four-and-a-half-dozen bottles.

So, finally, you have a stock of just on sixty-two dozen drinking and maturing wines that has taken you a total of eight years to attain, and on the basis of purchasing the wines when first available, you have waited three years before you get your first glass of developed wine.

Obviously one just doesn't start a cellar by going out one day, purchasing sixty-two dozen bottles of wine and sitting back waiting for the wine to reach maturity. The cellar develops from the store. Every now and then you drink a youthful red that you enjoy. Suitably impressed, you buy a dozen. Perhaps a small winemaker, whose wines you enjoy, makes a good vintage available, and knowing the demand for his wine you purchase a dozen while you can—and so the cellar begins.

Storing Wine

My suggested cellar of sixty-two dozen is based on one bottle of wine being drunk each night; and assumes that a certain percentage of the wine is youthful and the balance mature. This will vary greatly from person to person but everyone must make reasonable allowance for the storing of both youthful and maturing wine.

Hydraulic wine press at G. Gramp & Sons, Orlando winery, South Australia.

Modern homes have little provision for a suitable storage area for the maturation of wine. Not all wines need be contained within the one area for everyday drinking wines are often more easily stored in the kitchen or sideboard for easy access. Despite insufficient space for maturing wines rarely does the true wine enthusiast stop purchasing wine because of lack of space. Somehow there is always room for one more bottle.

The storage area (cellar) must be cool with a constant temperature: 10°C to 13°C (about 50°–55°F) is ideal. Wine can tolerate temperatures up to 24°C (75°F) but this, and temperature fluctuation, causes rapid maturation. This must be avoided for the slower a wine can mature, the greater will be the complexity and subtlety of the developed flavours. Avoid light also as this can cause wine colour to fade.

Some humidity is desirable but excess humidity can damage labels and the general appearance of the bottle. Too dry an atmosphere may enable cork weevils to breed which could damage the wine. Good ventilation prevents mould or stale air and removes any strong odours near the cellar. These odours could eventually permeate the cork and taint the wine.

The cellar should be free from vibrations and movements which, over a long period of time, can adversely affect the quality of the wine.

With the exception of tawny port, sherry, madeira and muscat, wine to be stored for any length of time must be kept on its side so that the cork remains moist. This stops excessive amounts of air entering the wine, causing it to become 'oxidised'.

Wine purchased in any quantity should be stored in a 'bin' or container, in which bottles of the same wine are kept. This gives easy access to the wine and enables one to know at a glance how much of that wine remains.

Whatever their construction, wood, metal, agricultural pipes, plastic foam, etc, the bins should be of uniform shape to facilitate easy stacking; strong enough, so that they can be built onto (should space permit it), and large enough to hold 6, 12, 24 bottles, that is, the multiples in which you purchase your wine. Cost should also be considered. The initial cost for a few bins may not be high, but multiply this by the number of bins you intend to have and you will soon find that it equals the price of another couple of dozen bottles. In a large cellar the bins are numbered, corresponding to those kept in the Cellar Book which is described later in this section.

What to Cellar

When buying for cellar maturation, buy wine that will become better with age (that is, build up flavours that we recognise as being synonymous with quality in an old wine). What is the point in cellaring a wine unless it can improve? A wine may have fresh grapiness, but there is no point in keeping it a few years just to soften the acid and tannin if the fruit becomes stale.

To be able to determine if a wine is suitable for cellaring when young is probably the hardest thing to do in wine. It requires years of experience in constant tasting; examination and retasting. A young wine, particularly a red, is often firm, hard, dumb, and showing excess of tannin and acid. But is there the right amount of acid and tannin? Will the wine lose that hardness? Will the fruit develop?

Never presume that just because you like a wine, it is suitable for cellaring. Wine merchants (not the local bottle shop), food and wine magazines, articles, experienced friends and your own knowledge and understanding will all help.

Ageing and Maturation

Ageing and maturation are perhaps the most mystical and misunderstood aspects of wine. Quite a few opinions are available, the majority backed by extensive scientific research and experimentation, but for each opinion there is an exception that prohibits any rules being made.

Chemically, ageing is a continuous state of decomposition which occurs very rapidly during the initial stages of winemaking, through destalking, crushing, pressing, alcoholic fermentation and possible malolactic fermentation. From this point onwards the rate of decomposition slows down, though the speed varies within the individual wine styles.

Total acidity decreases and alcohol, sugar, acids and other components are transformed into innumerable complex compounds such as esters, aldehydes and acetals. The precipitation of salts is also important. All wine ages up until the point when it is drunk. Maturation is more positive, and is the ageing of the wine to increase its quality, consequently not all wine can be said to mature.

Generally speaking, white and rosé wines lack the tannins and pigments (maturation constituents) of red wines and, as a result, have somewhat less capacity to mature after bottling. These constituents as well as acid, sugar and alcohol, although themselves changing their structure and producing flavours with age, tend to act as preservatives enabling grape flavours to 'develop' resulting in those that we recognise as being synonymous with quality in a mature wine.

Wine can mature in two ways: firstly, in the cask, and secondly, in the bottle. In the first group are the styles such as tawny port, sherry, madeira and fortified wines in general, whose excellence comes from a process of oxidation resulting in the formation of aldehydes (notably acetaldehyde) and other compounds as well as those derived from the cask, giving the wine an aged character. Once bottled these wines have no capacity to mature.

In the second group, quality is related to specific odourants and flavours supplied by the grape variety, the absence of air, and good reducing conditions. The length of time required to produce a maximum of desirable flavours varies considerably within the table wine styles. A few months in the case of some white wines, to fifty or sixty years in that of a vintage port.

Cask ageing/maturation is the time wines of the second group spend in wood prior to bottling and is important in hastening the clarification and stability and also imparting wood flavour to the wine. Wine in cask is also susceptible to air (oxygen) entering via the pores in the wood and between the staves. This initial contact with air is strongly related to quality of the bottled wine, particularly red wines, where the casks themselves vary in the amount of air they allow to come in contact with the wine resulting in 'cask characters' quite unrelated to the wood flavours picked up.

In Bordeaux, volatility is a positive quality factor in a great claret. In the Hunter Valley, initial exposure to air, while the wine is in cask, highlights wine flavours by oxidation. Tyrrell, for example, retains his best wines for maturation in cask numbers such as 9, 11 and 84, and even if the same wine went into all three casks, each for the same length of time, three different wines would emerge for bottling. When a wine is bottled, sulphur is used as a sterilising agent to prohibit oxidation.

Although bottle ageing is not completely understood, it has been determined that the finest wine flavours will be formed in the absence of air. This statement is supported by the fact that wine ages as well in hermetically sealed tubes as it does in corked bottles. The importance of air entering the wine via the cork is much overrated as long as the cork is sound and prohibits wine weeping from the bottle, in which case, air will take the place of the displaced wine. What is generally overlooked is that 8–10 ml of air are present in the average bottle of wine which can play a role in the changes that occur. Care is always taken at time of bottling so that oxidative changes are at a minimum and reducing conditions can be set up.

Over-Ageing

Any wine, regardless of its style, should be drunk at its best, that is, when there is a maximum of desirable flavours. As mentioned in the preceding section, the length of time varies considerably depending upon the style of the wine. With age

Tisdall's Mount Helen vineyard.

the acid riesling loses its freshness, the fruit becomes stale and the finish coarse. The red wine from a good vintage, however, may require many years to reach the quality level, during which time it will soften, the basic elements of wood and fruit will marry and flavours will be built up. The complication (fascination) that arises with maturing wine is when to pull the cork, which can be largely open to debate in regard to a specific wine.

The understanding of old wines (those past their best) is complicated by their scarcity and the consequent lack of exposure one gets to them. Within this old wine syndrome, whites possibly suffer the most. Much the best part of old sauternes are the flavours produced by oxidation even though the sugar content decreases with age. Madeirisation rears its flavoursome head in many types, and old dry white champagne styles can, and often are, drunk as delicate old white wines when they have lost their sparkle.

When one is fortunate enough to taste these very old wines, don't denigrate them simply for being old and not drinking at their best, for age itself is not a fault. Judge a thirty-year-old Hunter as a thirty-year-old Hunter and a fifteen-year-old Eden Valley Riesling as a fifteen-year-old Eden Valley Riesling. Considering the class and keeping an open mind are the essentials.

On Crusts and Deposits

During the process of maturation (especially decomposition) it is not uncommon for wines to form a deposit in the bottle. This deposit can range from fine crystals in a white wine, to large sheet formations adhering to the sides of a vintage port bottle.

The fine deposits present in some white wines are a crystallisation of the excessive amounts of tartaric acid (the predominant acid in wine) that precipitates to form tartaric crystals (notably calcium tartrate and potassium bi-tartrate).

Normally this excess is removed before the wine is bottled by chilling it to a near freezing point, and holding the wine at this temperature for five to seven days. This process is known as stabilisation. Occasionally one can see this deposit in white wines made before the availability of suitable refrigeration equipment. At any rate, their presence is neither harmful to the consumer, nor derogatory to the quality of the wine.

The crust in a red wine is not only natural, but is desirable. It is a process by which a wine gets rid of its excesses. The crust in a mature vintage port is greater than that of a mature red because of the larger amounts of tannin and colouring (organic) matter present in the former, and also the fact that fortified wines cannot tolerate, in solution, as much iron and copper as can red wines.

The actual state of the crust—that is, fine, coarse, granular, sheet, etc, depends not only upon the style of the wine, as previously mentioned, but also the way in which the wine has been cellared. Movement and overly high temperatures will inhibit crust formation thus limiting the precipitation of any excesses a wine may have.

Where to Buy Your Wine

Having reached a stage where you have space to mature some wine, and a desire to fill those empty bins, where are you going to get your wine? The answer to this is not as simple as it may first appear. As soon as you become a little discriminating, you will find that not every wine and spirit shop stocks the particular wine you want. So get in touch with the particular company who will be able to tell you of a local outlet for their wines.

If 'only available from the vineyard—no local agency' answers your query then find out the address of the vineyard (it's usually on the bottle) and write to them. As a rule these small makers are most helpful. Ask to be put on a mailing list and you will receive regular information about their wines.

There is an increasing number of wine lovers making annual pilgrimages to various vineyards and winemaking areas in order to purchase new vintages. Much can be learned from these trips, both in seeing the vineyards, and tasting the wines available for purchase. Often the vigneron himself is available, and only too pleased to answer questions and advise on the purchase of his wines. Direct vineyard buying has the advantage of obtaining wine at prices considerably less than in urban centres. Don't be deterred by some reactions to your request for a particular wine.

'On quota.' Most of the time a problem of scarcity creating its own demand. To get some, you have to either pay above the suggested retail price, or purchase a quantity of lesser wines.

'The wine has been unavailable for a couple of months.' In this case arm yourself with a wallet and go on a wine hunt, from bottle shop to bottle shop. These hunts can be rewarding in that you may stumble across something a little older or even a previously wanted wine. No good huntsman ever returns to the table empty-handed.

'Never heard of it.' A common cry, so try elsewhere. If the cry becomes too common, make sure that you're asking for the correct wine.

Wine Auctions

Merchants in Sydney, Melbourne and Adelaide are conducting wine auctions with some regularity. These are serious auctions in the sense that they are free from the hysteria of charity auctions and their 'tax-deductible' high prices. A great feature of the Barossa Valley Vintage and Rutherglen Festivals are the auctions that are attached to them. These auctions bring to light a great number of rare and old wines that, apart from the satisfaction that it gives the wine lover just to know of their existence, also enables him to fill a number of gaps he may have in his cellar. The tasting held prior to some of these auctions represents a rare opportunity to taste many famed but rarely seen wines. Even if you don't purchase anything, there is always the satisfaction of being with other wine enthusiasts and seeing the prices that the market is bearing for older wines. It is unusual for a collector to walk away disheartened with prices realised for wines that he may have in his own cellar.

Wine Labels

Unlike the large wine-producing countries of Europe the relative youth of the Australian wine industry has not given rise to the heavily policed 'appellation contrôlée' systems. We have certain legislation such as the Pure Foods Act and Consumer Affairs but these control what is in the bottle rather than the way it gets there.

Some vignerons in the Hunter Valley, Mudgee and Victoria, for example, have banded together to produce an in-house system aimed at guaranteeing the purity and quality of their wines. These may be taken as an example of the commitment of the vignerons involved but not necessarily an assurance of quality. The Hunter 'benchmark' and 'classic' classifications are quality assessed but since the entry for judging is optional it does not follow that a wine that is without such a certificate is not of quality.

How to Buy Wine

With the exception of the 'wine hunt' and auctions, where one may come across an old bottle, nearly all the wines purchased will be young—generally one to three years. The older a wine is, the greater the risk of it being faulty. That, however, does not mean that all young wine is sound.

The following notes may be useful when purchasing and unsure of condition. Rules such as never buying wine that has been stored standing upright, or has been exposed to extremes of temperature, should go without saying.

The cork should always be flush with the top of the bottle. If the cork is protruding from the neck it indicates either that the wine has been exposed to high temperatures—causing the wine to expand and thus forcing the cork out; or that the cork has been put in incorrectly in the first place (often the case with small vineyards still using hand-corking machines). Ensure in both young and old wines that there are no signs of the cork 'weeping'. In an old wine 'weeping', or wine slowly seeping from the cork, can indicate that the cork has lost its elasticity and has started to contract. If this is the case check the ullage, or the air space in the bottle. If excessive, the two almost guarantee an unsound wine. In the case of some young wines, however, it is not uncommon to find that excessive moisture has built up under the capsule. This is due to capsuling taking place immediately after corking, without giving the cork time to rest. When a cork is put into the bottle the solution in which it has been soaked to sterilise it and make it sufficiently elastic to fit into the bottle is displaced with some of the wine in the bottle. The solution then seeps out of the cork and accumulates under the capsule. This natural displacement, however, is not to be confused with 'weeping'.

Heavy ullage also is quite natural in the case of very old wines, and is not really a problem so long as the cork is firm. These wines, however, must be treated with caution.

Colour should always be considered. Golden or brown shades in a white wine are strong indications of over-ageing. No matter what their age, reds should always have a red colour about them. Shades of brown are acceptable; indeed, in old reds they are expected; but it is rare for a red wine to have lost its colour and still be drinkable.

From Cellar to Table
Decanting

Since the crust in a mature wine is an 'excess', it is logical that to best appreciate a wine and to take advantage of this natural process of 'excess elimination', it is necessary to remove the crust from the wine before drinking. This is done by carefully pouring the wine from the bottle into another vessel, so that one is left with the pure wine, free from the crust. This is known as decanting.

As age is no rule to the amount of crust a wine has or should have, decanting for the removal of the crust may not be necessary for wines ten, even fifteen years old; but, when it is necessary, care should be taken.

The wine to be decanted can either be stood upright for some hours, depending on the size and structure of the crust, before opening, so that the deposit in course suspension may slide down the side of the bottle and accumulate on the base; or, the bottle to be opened can be removed directly from the bin. In the case of this latter method, it is advisable to decant as close as possible to the bin where the wine is kept, as moving the bottle from cellar to dining room could disturb the crust. For the same reason it is necessary to have a wine basket or cradle to keep the wine free from movement when drawing the cork.

With a sharp knife, or similar instrument, cut the capsule around the neck of the bottle. Move the blade around the neck—not the neck over the blade. Lift off the top of the capsule and, with a clean cloth, wipe any deposit that may have accumulated on top of the cork. Carefully insert the corkscrew and draw the cork. Rewipe the neck of the bottle.

Many people prefer to rinse the decanter with

a small amount of the wine before the actual process of decanting begins. This will remove any foreign odours or deposits that may be present in the decanter. To rinse a decanter from a bottle that has been standing upright is not advisable, unless the bottle, once moved from the vertical, can be kept in that position while rinsing.

If using a basket it will now be necessary to remove the bottle, ensuring that it remains as close to the horizontal as possible.

Over a light (a candle is most suitable), pour the wine, slowly at first until sufficient air has made its way into the bottle to stop the gurgling sound that will cause a current, into the rinsed decanter. The light, best under the shoulders of the bottle, will allow you to see when the crust is approaching the neck. At this point stop pouring to reveal the clear wine in the decanter.

When purchasing a decanter make sure that the decanter will hold the contents of a wine bottle. Many decanters, particularly those that form part of a suite, are made to be artistically pleasing first, and practical second. It is not uncommon to find decanters holding no more than 20 fl oz, which in the case of the average 26 fl oz bottle has obvious consequences.

A good way to 'clean up' a wine that has not had sufficient time to rest is to pass it through the paper cone of a coffee filter. Test the brand of filter paper first to ensure there is no flavour collected during the filtering. Even if the wine has rested, this is a very practical way to get the last ounce or two out of a good bottle that would normally be discarded with the sediment.

Decanting Funnels

To aid the passage of the wine from bottle to decanter, a 'decanting funnel' is most useful, particularly for those new to this skill. These funnels are hard to come by, but a great asset if you own one. They vary from the traditional conical-shaped funnel, in that the narrow end turns at an angle directing the course of the wine to the side of the decanter, instead of splashing onto the wine below. This more gentle handling of the wine causes less aeration, or breathing.

Apart from the bend at the narrow end, the true decanting funnel has a sieve in the form of a piece of fine metal mesh, normally attached to the base of a cup that fits snugly into the top of the funnel. This sieve is particularly useful in the

case of old vintage ports as it stops any large flakes that may have become liberated from the body of the crust from entering the decanter.

Do not limit the use of the decanter to crusted wines only. Why serve wine at the table in the bottle from the cellar? Remember, a decanter is a practical ornament, a bottle is only a temporary home for the wine.

The Cellar Book

No matter how large or small your collection of wines may be, a 'Cellar Book' is a practical necessity. One can gain much pleasure from owning a cellar, by recording the when and where of a wine's origin, its price and so on.

The provision of a space in the Cellar Book for one's tasting notes, such as in the example below, will enable you not only to follow the development of various wines, but more particularly the changes in tastes and the palate of the author.

Although not essential, a section for 'Occasion' provides space for useful commentaries that may be related to the drinking of the wine, necessary in avoiding repetition of serving the same wine or food to your guests. Also, by making a note of the food, you will have a record of which wines go well with what foods. With time, the Cellar Book develops into a fascinating record of the wines that have passed through your cellar, and, therefore, over your palate.

As a subsidiary to the Cellar Book, the enthusiast will have a tasting book for recording his own impressions and the opinions of others on wines outside his own cellar. Constant thought in describing a wine's flavour will enable you to become, firstly, more exacting in your appraisal of a wine; and, secondly, more fluent in relating your tasting experiences to others.

Very often you will hear or read of a wine that takes your interest, or of the success of a particular vintage. If unavailable either for tasting or cellaring, keep a list of these wines (for convenience in the back of either the Cellar or Tasting Books), so that at a later date you will not forget about the wine.

Within either of these volumes it is a good idea to make a list of the various times of the year that the large and small wine companies make their wines available for purchase. As a result of the

NAME: LINDEMANS WHITE BURGUNDY BIN 3870. VINTAGE: 1970

DESCRIPTION: SEMILLON FROM BEN EAN VINEYARDS

ORIGIN: PURCHASED FROM SYDNEY CELLARS 3/8/71 PRICE $2.20.

DATE	QTY	BAL	OCCASION	TASTING NOTES
3/8/71		12		
9/8/71	1	11	FIRST TASTING	GOOD HUNTER FLAVOUR CLEAN ACID
				FINISH. NEEDS MORE TIME.
21/9/71	2	9	DINNER PARTY WITH	AS ABOVE - SEEMS TO HAVE
			SMITH & JONESES	FILLED OUT A BIT. ALL THOUGHT
			GRILLED WHITING-TOO	IT BEST WINE OF THE EVENING
			OILY FOR THIS WINE!	

continual demand for, and scarcity of, fine wines, far too often one only gets to hear about them when they are no longer available.

If you cannot be bothered with a Tasting Book, a popular practice is to fasten the labels from the wines consumed into a book; relevant notes being recorded on that page. I have even heard of people who keep the corks from the wines they drink, writing on them the date the wine was drunk and their opinions—brevity and a clear hand being vital requirements.

Home Bottling

Home bottling is becoming increasingly popular, particularly amongst people with whom wine has a strong acceptance. The bottling (as well, no doubt, as the use to which the balance of the wine is used) is as good an excuse for a party as any. Half-a-dozen friends, some empty bottles, wine, corks, and a length of plastic hose are really all that's necessary to produce one's own 'Private Bin'.

Many wine firms sell their produce to the public in either wood, stainless steel, plastic or enamel-lined drums for bottling. One should never expect to get a great vintage wine from these companies, since a 'great' wine is too valuable to appear under any label save that of the company that produces it. Also there is the possibility that the wine may not be bottled correctly and with time, 'goes off'. The first cry from the owner will be that he has been sold poor wine—

not that he could be at fault for not bottling correctly. What one can expect, at best, is a very good drinking wine, sometimes capable of undergoing maturation in bottle, and most important of all, it will be at a reasonable price.

If the wine for bottling is in cask allow it to rest for at least a week so that any matter in suspension will settle. Apart from the necessity to bottle with greater care, the only other disadvantage of sediment is that a few bottles towards the end of the cask will have to be discarded.

Bottles

If the wine is of quality and has the constituents for maturation, one is advised to buy new bottles, in case any off-flavours develop, possibly years after bottling, due to unclean bottles. There is very little against using second-hand bottles, so long as they are known to have contained nothing else but wine—if in doubt, discard. The mistake that many make is in supposing that a quick rinse is all that is necessary. Thorough washing is essential to remove any harmful germs or bacteria that may contaminate the wine, and also to remove any chemicals that may result in chemical spoilage.

Firstly, the bottles should be thoroughly washed by scrubbing with a bottle brush or a powerful hose. The bottles should then be soaked in a complex detergent, providing that it is odourless, or for best results, use 1 or 2 g of sodium metabisulphate (available from any chemist). The solution is then heated to a temperature of 50°C. The bottles must again be rinsed free of all washing products, and stood base up to allow them to drain properly.

Bottling

Rarely will any home bottler come in contact with any bottling machine more sophisticated than a length of plastic hose pipe for siphoning the wine from cask to bottle.

If the wine is in wood, open the cask by banging with a hammer around the 'bung'. In this way the bung will slowly rise because of the vibrations set up by the hammer. Never drill a hole into the cask—you will forfeit the deposit paid on the cask as well as expend a lot of effort in repairing the 'stave'.

Attach the end of the hose that comes into contact with the wine to a length of wood (a broom handle is most suitable) with a few bands of wire, ensuring that the end is about an inch and a half from the end of the piece of wood. In this way the hose will be kept close to the bottom of the cask, yet sufficiently above it so that no sediment will be drawn off. A tap can be fixed to the other end of the hose to minimise waste.

The Cork

Unlike the bottles, it is essential that the corks are new. Prepare them by first rinsing in cold water to remove any dust. The corks must then be heated to give them the elasticity required to fit into the bottle. This can be done by soaking in warm or boiling water, though this may dissolve some of the elements responsible for a cork's elasticity. More preferable is to steam the corks in a colander over boiling water for 5 to 10 minutes.

Before the wine is bottled it is advisable, as a final precaution, to rinse the bottle with a little of the wine to follow. Pass the rinse from bottle to bottle, changing it every couple of dozen or so.

Corkers

For the backyard bottling set-up, nothing more elaborate than a manual hammer or beer action corker is required.

Capsules

Though unnecessary, the addition of a capsule is a final touch that removes the wine from a back-

yard effect. Aluminium capsules are available in a variety of colours and only require a crimping ring to mould the capsule in place. Plastic caps are fixed by heat (a little hot water) whereby they shrink into place providing an easy effective seal. It is preferable, though not always practical, to capsule a few weeks after bottling. The resting time will allow the cork to displace any wine and adjust to the bottle.

The composition of the capsule varies, plastic, aluminium foil, sealing wax and lead being the most popular materials employed. Nowadays the capsule is mainly used to aid the presentation of the bottle, although it can be effective in stopping cork weevils from burrowing into the cork and spoiling the wine. Sealing wax is perhaps the most effective in reducing the displacement of wine with air. Lead, by far the most desirable, is considered a possible source of lead poisoning. For this reason, a plastic disc or cap is inserted above the cork, under the capsule to avoid possible lead contamination by contact with the wine.

Labels

It only remains for the bottle to be labelled. Again, though not essential, it is a finishing touch. Inevitably a friend with some artistic ability will produce a label suitable for the wine and the occasion. The variations on 'Fred's Rough Red' are endless. No special glue is required to keep the label in place but a labelling stand, simply constructed from a few pieces of wood, is advisable to keep the bottle in place to ensure the label is put on straight.

On Opening the Bottle

Unlike many popular beverages, opening a bottle of wine isn't just a matter of lifting a crown seal. Before you can get to the cork it is necessary to cut the capsule, the neater the better, in aiding presentation.

Corks

Air is kept from any quality wine by a cork, of which there are four groups:
1 *The flange cork:* This type appears on the majority of fortified wines and consists of a length of cork about 30 mm in length, on top of which is a plastic top or flange preventing

the cork falling into the bottle. Since fortified wines, unlike table wines, are not drunk at one sitting, the flange cork is convenient for resealing the bottle until it is empty.

2 *The standard cylindrical wine cork*, used for table wines and the odd fortified. These vary in length from 25 mm to 50 mm or more. These corks should be of one piece, although cheaper and lesser quality corks can often be found comprising two longitudinal pieces.

3 *The layer cork*, used almost exclusively for sparkling wines. Here discs of cork of various thicknesses and qualities are cemented together, the highest quality cork being at the end which comes in contact with the wine. The advantage of using this type for sparkling wine is that the hardest cork, generally that which is the lowest quality, will be at the opening of the bottle. Should too porous or soft a cork be used, it will be ineffective in keeping the gas in the bottle.

4 *The composite cork*—again used almost exclusively for sparkling wines. The cork is 'composed' of many small pieces of cork, mainly remnants that are cemented together and moulded to the required shape.

Still Wines

Having cut the capsule on a still wine, any deposits that may have accumulated due to age should be wiped from the top of the cork lest they fall into the wine when the cork is drawn. Insert the corkscrew, preferably at an angle, with even and constant pressure, and draw out the cork in the manner dictated by the type of screw being used. Opinions vary as to the best type of corkscrew. The single-shank corkscrew with its steel spiral I find the best, since it burrows into the cork whereas the actual 'screw' type cuts the cork, often causing it to break. Whatever the type of screw being used, the tip should be sharp otherwise the cork will crumble.

Often in both young and old wines, the cork breaks. This is due to the screw not being inserted correctly (as mentioned previously), the age of the cork or mainly because of the vacuum created when the cork is drawn from the bottle. Particularly in old corks it is advisable to turn the corkscrew till its end protrudes from the base of the cork in the bottle. This will allow air to enter the wine, prohibiting a vacuum forming.

Regrettably, with some wine bottles, the sides of the neck are not parallel and flare out to the shoulder, making the cork easier to push into the bottle. The cork is also more difficult to remove since it is conical in shape and acts like a wedge when being removed. Extra care is needed with this type of bottle.

Sparkling Wines

Always handle a sparkling wine like an old red wine with sediment. Allow it to rest in the refrigerator or ice bucket; and if chilling a few cases for a party allow a good twenty-four hours for the wine to rest.

Peel the foil, and remove the wire cage securing the cork from the top of the bottle. Take a cloth or similar to get a good grip on the cork. If necessary, a special pair of nippers can be used. Slowly turn the cork one way and the bottle in the opposite direction, gently pulling on the cork till it rises from the bottle. There should never be a 'pop' only ever a 'sigh'. To avoid losing any froth, hold the bottle slightly inclined thus giving the wine a larger surface area when the wine is opened for the excess gas to escape. Return the bottle to the vertical and wipe the top of any dirt or deposits common on sparkling wines which have undergone a second fermentation in the bottle.

Glass Temperature

The temperature of the glass receiving the wines is of importance mainly when serving sparkling wines. The warmer the glass the faster a wine will lose its sparkle. Apart from over-chilling the wine to compensate for this, pour a little of the sparkling wine into one of the glasses, rotate it in the glass, and pass it on like-wise to the other glasses. This will lower the temperature of the glass and also remove any impurities that may be present from which the bubbles stream. On no account should ice cubes be placed in a glass to chill it for inevitably moisture will be left in the glass and this can affect the flavour of the wine to follow.

Breathing

Breathing refers to drawing the cork on a bottle of wine some time prior to it being drunk. This removes certain scents and odours and allows other flavour components to develop.

The correct breathing of wine is one of the

most neglected facets of wine appreciation, and isn't just a matter of drawing the cork of a young red or decanting a vintage port some time prior to drinking.

What happens is that a current of air passing over the wine allows off-flavours that may have been collected during vinification, or have built up as a result of maturation, to evaporate. Many of these off-flavours are more volatile (that is, evaporate quicker) than the actual flavour components of the grape produced by fermentation. Breathing, therefore, not only improves the drinking qualities of a wine by the removal of off-flavours, but also by allowing the more complex and subtle grape flavours to appear.

Breathing Times

The higher the molecular weight of a wine, the longer the breathing time required. Young red wines and vintage ports with their high levels of tannins, acids and sugars, require more breathing than old red, rosé and white wines (lower in molecular weight). Vintage port is the only exception to fortified wine styles requiring breathing to develop flavours, although sherry, madeira, and so on, may have off-flavours due to bottling in which case a certain amount of breathing is necessary.

Temperature is important as the higher the temperature, the greater will be the speed at which odiferous substances leave the wine. This does not mean that one should warm wine to hasten its breathing, since these volatiles leave a wine at different stages, depending on their rate of volatility. An increase in temperature will cause evaporation of some aldehydes and esters (flavour components) and alcohol that would normally remain.

Just as one should never heat a wine with the intention of hastening its breathing, so too, should one never re-decant or shake a wine in order to aerate it further. If, when the wine is poured, it is found to require further breathing, allow it to develop ('bloom') in the glass. It is always better to under-breathe a wine and have to wait for it, than it is to over-breathe and be unable to bring the wine back.

Off-flavours in Wine

During vinification the grape juice comes in contact with a variety of containers and substances capable of passing on flavours to the wine. Some of these flavours are desirable, others, though undesirable, necessary, and the balance totally undesirable. Some of these may leave a wine on breathing; others, due to their low concentration and nature, will be taken over by stronger characters as the wine develops/matures. The balance, however, will become an integral part of the wine, removing it from any claims to greatness.

Recognising off-flavours requires skill and continuous exposure. Unless these flavours are pointed out by someone familiar to their characters, the taster may, although recognising their presence, confuse them as a positive quality factor in wine.

As mentioned, any receptacle with which wine comes in contact is capable of tainting it. Those in the list below appear with some regularity. Although the majority are self-explanatory, their causes and characters appear in the glossary.

Cork
Filter pads
Chemical (sterilisation agents and insecticides)
Yeast
Rubber hose pipe
Earthy (soil contamination)
Concrete
Metallic (metal contamination)
Dirty wood
Mould
Sulphur
Burnt sugar

Serving Temperatures

Temperatures play a very important role in our appreciation of wine. Too cold a red and it appears dumb and ageless; to warm a white, and it tastes flat and flabby. The reasons for this variation are quite simple. White wines have a lower molecular weight than do red wines, and as such require a lower temperature to allow the volatile flavours to vaporise. The importance of volatiles in relation to taste has already been discussed. Temperature governs the amount of volatiles a wine makes available for olfaction.

There are no cast iron rules as to the temperature at which wines should be served, for just as in the selection of wine, the kind that is most pleasant to him that drinks it, is the best. Personally, I prefer Hunters slightly warmer than Coonawarras. The views as to the exact temperature of sparkling wines vary considerably, and no doubt each opinion has validity.

The context in which the wine is being served is very important. A rich Hunter White Burgundy served at the beginning of a meal needs to be considerably cooler than the same wine drunk with a soft cheese at the end of a light luncheon.

Good-quality red wines should be served at room temperature, approximately 18.3°C. What lesser quality wines lack in their flavour they compensate for by being refreshing, consequently their temperature should be cooler, say 15.5°C.

To bring a red wine up to room temperature, stand it in the room in which it is to be drunk a few hours before serving. This procedure is termed *chambre* and relies, of course, upon the fact that the cellar is cooler than the dining room, and that the latter is at 18.3°C. Above this temperature the alcohol in red wines, any wines for that matter, begins to evaporate, adding its own smell to that of the wine. Don't expect much from the room temperature red if it is 43.3°C in the shade, and heaven stop the zealous host standing his reds in front of a radiator to increase the temperature. If a red is too cold, hold the bowl of the glass in the palm of the

hands. No artificial way is sufficiently gentle.

Generally, white wines and rosés should be served between 4.4–10°C, sparkling wines more specifically at 7.2°C, although I have never seen a thermometer thrust into a glass and a wine being declared too hot or too cold. A small amount of trial and error influenced by personal preference is the best advice one can give.

As for ice buckets versus refrigerators in the chilling of whites, I know of no reason, nor have tasted any difference, between wines chilled either way, although each has its own advantages. The ice bucket fails to chill the neck of the bottle, quite important in the case of sparkling wines where the difference in temperature causes considerable loss of gas. On the other hand, I know of no refrigerator as portable as an ice bucket.

With the exception of the driest sherry styles that are often chilled to advantage when served as an aperitif, all other fortified wines such as madeira, port and muscat, remain at room temperature.

From Table to Palate

Wine Tasting

The term 'wine tasting' may seem to be something of a tautology, for, after all, it is rare that one is incapable of detecting flavour when drinking wine. The term, though, is more specific in meaning and refers to the conscious examination of all facets of a wine for the assessment of quality. By all means drink wine to make the meal merry, to quench the thirst and raise the spirits—for that is the purpose of most wine. When, however, you are presented with a wine of quality, treat it with the respect it deserves and allow yourself to extract the maximum pleasure, by tasting.

How to Taste

Apart from the practice of 'listening' to the crackle of champagne and 'feeling' the viscosity of certain fortified wines, when tasting one brings into play three senses—sight, smell and taste (their approximate importance being in the ratio of 3:7:10 respectively, according to judging systems).

	°C	°F	
	21.0	70	
Red wines and fortified dessert wines	18.3	65	Room temperature
	15.5	60	
	12.7	55	
Rosé and white wines			Cool
Fortified aperitif wines	10.0	50	
			Cold
Sparkling wines	7.2	45	
			Cracking
	4.4	40	cold

Sight The first step in tasting a wine is to examine the colour and condition; far too often this first step is neglected, or not given the necessary consideration.

It should be remembered that there are two constituents of colour: hue and density of hue. 'Hue' is the actual shade—red, yellow, brown, etc—whereas 'density' is the concentration in which that hue manifests itself.

In order to appreciate the nuances of colour, tilt the glass (to achieve a range of depths) over a source of light; or preferably a negative background, such as a piece of white paper. Examine closely that area just past the meniscus and into the wine, for it is here that the final subtleties of colour are best detected.

Characteristics of a Wine Detectable by Sight

Style: Whether the wine is still or sparkling; red, white or rosé. Strength can be related to density of hue (body).

Condition: Cloudiness can indicate an undesirable presence of protein or bacteria, with the result that the wine is unsound or decomposed. Sediment can indicate age or method of winemaking (that is, degree of fining, stabilisation). Shades of brown in both red and white styles can indicate a wine past its peak, madeirised or oxidised.

Age: Some red wines change from purple/garnet in colour to orange/red, brick-red or brown-red; whites from pale green/yellow to golden-yellow.

Grape Variety: The purple of cabernet sauvignon, the red of shiraz, the green of rhine riesling, the yellow of semillon, etc.

Region: The dense red/purple of Clare; the brick-red of the Hunter, and so on.

Alcohol (and *Glycerine*) *Content*: Determined by the 'tears' a wine forms on the inside of the glass (legs).

Oxidation: Indicated by the presence of brownness.

Viscosity: The more viscous a wine, the slower it will move in the glass.

Nose Nosing a wine refers to the detecting of flavours by smell. To best appreciate this facet of a wine, rotate the glass, allowing the wine to rise up the sides and release its smell. The wine is easier to smell by employing this practice, for it follows that volatile flavour components are leaving the wine. Do not, therefore, swill the wine for too long a time—a few turns are sufficient.

The first smell will tell you the most. Re-smelling will enable the taster to detect further nuances. Nosing a wine before introducing it to the palate can get to the stage where no new flavours can be perceived; and the level of perception is diminishing, since the olfactory sense has become familiar with those flavours given off by the wine. Don't dwell any longer than is necessary. If further examination is required, the sense of smell can be momentarily refreshed by exhaling in short blasts via the nose.

Characteristics Detectable by Smelling

Age: The freshness of the aroma or the extent to which the bouquet has developed.

Grape Variety: The 'blackberry' scent of cabernet sauvignon, the 'sweet' smell of grenache, etc.

Area: The higher the quality of the wine the stronger will be the regional character. The famed 'mint' of Coonawarra; the 'cow sheds' of McLaren Vale; the 'fruit salad' of Northern Victoria, and so on.

Voluminous: Related to volatility. The bigness of a wine's 'nose'.

Quality: The absence of faults and the presence of desirable scents; their number and degree of complexity.

Sound: A wine without fault is said to be sound. This does not, however, imply that the wine is of quality.

Faults: A variety of faults are readily detectable on the nose:

Firstly: Those collected during vinification:
* chemicals and insecticides used for sterilisation and inhibiting bacterial growths;
* substances with which a wine has come in contact that have imparted their own flavour, for example, rubber hose pipes, concrete fermenting tanks;
* flavours resulting from poor winemaking; excesses of oak, acid, sugar, tannins, greenness (malic acid) resulting in poorly balanced wines.

Secondly: Flavours that have developed as a result of bottle ageing:

- primarily aldehydes produced by the oxidation of alcohol;
- oxidation of delicate-flavoured components.

Palate Though a misnomer, palate refers to the detection of flavour whilst the wine is in the mouth.

Taste results from chemicals in solution stimulating nerve endings (taste buds) on the lips, palate, and primarily the tongue. Sweetness is detected at the tip of the tongue; sourness (acid) at the sides; salt behind the tip and bitterness at the back.

It is important to remember that with the exception of the four primaries, most tastes are in actual fact smelled. What happens is that volatiles are detected in the upper nasal cavity, while the wine is in the mouth.

When tasting a wine's palate, take a good quantity of wine into the mouth, to ensure that all areas of the tongue come in contact with the wine. The polite sip allows saliva to reduce the effectiveness of a wine. Drawing air through pursed lips will enable more volatile flavours to penetrate the upper nasal cavity.

When tasting a large number of wines, particularly fortified wines, don't swallow—spit. This practice is never considered undignified—it is expected.

Characteristics Detected by the Palate

Primaries: Sweet, salt, sour, bitter. Often these tend to act against one another. For example, certain sugars reduce the taste of malic and tararic acid, the more bitter a wine, the less sugar will be apparent and so on. Degrees of perception vary between individuals—one man's sweet can be another man's sour.

Grape Variety: Determined by structure as well as flavour. Cabernet sauvignon has a firm finish; Australian Rhine rieslings tend to lack flavour on the middle of the tongue ('head and shoulders').

Style: Burgundy style falls off the back of the tongue, whereas the claret style does not. The Hock style has a delicate acid finish; the White Burgundy style is softer and richer.

Condition: Whether the wine is sound and free from fault.

Picking grapes in the sun.

Area: Relative degree of flavours, acids, tannins, peculiar to certain winemaking areas.

Age: Amounts of acid and tannin; the degree of development.

Faults: See 'Nose'. The majority of faults appear on both the nose and palate; excesses of primaries, lack of balance.

Body: The apparent viscosity.

Quality: Related to the absence of fault. Balance, finish, suppleness, etc.

Alcohol Content: Spirit detectable at the back of the palate.

Order of Tasting

The best order of tasting is firstly to examine the colour, then nose and finally palate. It is strongly advised that this order be adhered to since it is a regular sequence of appreciation that will allow the taster to examine the widest range of wine characters, and therefore derive the greatest satisfaction from the wine he drinks. Unaided by the nose and palate, a taster can form a series of opinions on colour alone, which can be later confirmed or rejected by further tasting. To drink a wine before smelling it familiarises the olfactory sense with the majority of flavours normally derived from nosing, and will consequently lessen the perception to the balance of scents and odours.

Comparative Tasting

Just as one should taste in an order that will allow a wine to show a maximum of characters, so too should a group of wines be tasted without allowing one wine to dominate another.

Few people are able to completely remove themselves from the atmosphere that surrounds them when tasting. How often the wine drunk amongst friends at the end of an enjoyable meal appears lacking when tasted in sobriety. Similarly, many of the nuances of a great wine drunk alone are lost. It is perfectly possible to judge a fine wine on its own but its real qualities will be thrown into perspective if tasted alongside another wine, even if it is dissimilar in style.

Order of Serving

Whereas a dry wine stimulates the palate, a sweet wine satisfies it. An acid wine will taste excessively sour if tasted after a sweet wine. The same thing occurs when a light wine is drunk after a full-bodied wine, the former will appear thin and lacking in character. So too, with a delicate wine and a fully flavoured wine. As a general rule for tasting, serve dry before sweet, light before full, young before old.

Apart from tasting in an order that allows flavours to appear in their true perspective, our level of appreciation is also affected by comparative quality. Taste a great wine before a lesser one and the latter will show poorly, whereas if tasted with wines of its own class, it will not appear as inferior. Both style and class must always be considered when tasting.

Note Taking and Judging Systems

Unless you possess a god-gifted memory capable of recalling the characters and names of all the wines you drink, you should take notes when tasting. With time, you can build up a vinous vocabulary allowing you to become more exacting when describing wine flavours. The vocabulary also enables you to converse more fluently (no pun) with fellow tasters.

Although not for the beginner, judging wines by awarding points is excellent for evaluating the merits of individual wines tasted in a group. The following example is based on the French Brunet System and is employed in Australian Show Judging.

ORIGIN	TASTED AT	DATE ....
TASTER	CLASS	

Vat No. or Identification	Gallons	Colour and Cond.	Nose	Palate	Total Points	Ranking	Remarks and Recommended Treatment
		3	7	10	20	Personal Group	
....							....
....							....
....							....
....							....
....							....
....							....

Wine Judging

Some judging systems:

1 Out of 200 points:

colour	10
limpidity	10
bouquet	40
alcohol	10
suppleness	20
body	30
finesse	20
flavour persist.	10
general balance	50

2 Out of 30 points:

Sight:	colour	1–5
	limpidity	1–5
Smell:	bouquet	1–5
	persistence	1–5
Taste:	body	1–4
	suppleness	1–3
	mouth aroma	1–3

3 System using a series of numbers:

colour	
bouquet	
equilibrium	all out of ten
freshness	and optimum score = 10
finesse	
body	
character	all 1 to 10
acidity	opt. 5–6
hardness	excess 6–10
state of devel.	lack 5–1

e.g. a good young wine: 67778 67564

Wine Preferences

I'll never forget the comment made by a friend when I presented him with a glass of my great Australian Sauternes. He considered the colour, examined the bouquet, pondered over the palate, and spat out the wine, declaring: 'Brilliant! I could imagine no better Sauternes. Such flavour, so complex and so perfectly balanced.'

'Then why did you spit it out?' I enquired.

'Oh, I hate sweet whites,' he replied.

The experienced taster judges a wine without being affected by personal likes and dislikes. Far too often a wine is denigrated because of the taster's dislike for the style, mostly a case of lack of understanding and familiarity. Remember: just because you like it doesn't mean it's good. By all means have preferences and specialise in these, but keep an open mind, and approach all wines trying not to be swayed by the comments of fellow tasters, and your own lack of experience.

Successful Tastings

A successful tasting depends not only upon the quality of the wine served, but is strongly related to the amount of appreciation that can be gained by the tasters. The following points should be considered by those organising a tasting to ensure this appreciation.

One of the greatest failings of many tastings is the presence of odours or smells in the room where the tasting is to be held. Strong cheeses, floral decoration, a poorly aired room, all contribute to reducing the performance of the taster.

Smoking when tasting is not only considered ill-mannered, but lessens the perception of the smoker as well as that of his fellow tasters. Colognes, strong perfumes and make-up (particularly lipstick) should never be worn for the same reasons as smoking is undesirable.

Ensure that a sufficient number of clean tasting glasses are available. Often when serving a large range of wines, or when there are quite a few tasters, one may not have the quantity of glasses required. This can be remedied in two ways. Firstly, the 'community' glass method where one or two glasses are placed in front of each wine available for tasting, and are shared by all those attending. Apart from being somewhat unhygienic, the glasses will readily pick up many scents (particularly perfumes and colognes) from the previous taster. Secondly, and more desirable, every taster is given a glass for each group of wines served—that is, one glass for reds, one for whites, and so on. Before starting on a new wine a small amount of it is put into the glass and 'rinsed' to remove any previous wine. The main disadvantage of insufficient glasses is that it prohibits comparative tasting.

There must be sufficient light and a white background to best appreciate the colour of the wine.

Make sure that the wines available for tasting are at the correct temperature.

The importance of serving wines in their correct sequence has been mentioned previously. To make sure the taster will have no difficulty in following the order, mark the wines numerically either on the labels or on tags to avoid confusion.

With any tasting involving a large number of wines, palate cleansers should be provided for the tasters. Each taster will no doubt have a cleanser that appeals to him more than others, so a variety may be needed. The most common are mild cheese, dry biscuits, and olives. Cheese has a tendency to coat the palate thus reducing the effectiveness of the taster. Olives, though popular, are really too strongly flavoured. Dry biscuits (water crackers and the like) should be salt free and not served with butter. By far the best palate cleanser is cold soda water. It is neutral in flavour, refreshing and revives the palate.

Have a supply of pads or tasting sheets and writing implements. Felt-tip and fountain pens are not as practical as pencils and biros.

When organising a serious tasting, bring together interested people. It is so off-putting to the enthusiast to be surrounded by hard drinkers scarcely thinking about what they are drinking. Try to have one experienced person or professional at the tasting. Apart from being the best way for a newcomer to learn, the presence of an expert will eliminate many differences of opinion that arise through the uncertainty of the inexperienced.

Don't embarrass your guests by exposing them to too large a number of wines, or to a style with which they are not familiar. Although the latter may be interesting, unless the taster has some background knowledge, the range will appear little more than confusing.

Just as various wines should be drunk in certain classes, so too should various tasters only drink certain wines. How it hurts to see one's last bottle of a great wine slide down the gullets of the disinterested or the uninitiated.

Blind Tastings

'Blind tastings', or tasting a wine not knowing under what label it appears, is perhaps the most honest way to evaluate quality, for what an impressionable lot we are. No matter how knowledgeable or experienced the taster may be, his opinion of the wine can only be affected by his awareness of the label.

Through blind tastings the palate of many an expert has crumbled and often that of the amateur has risen to illustrious heights. But just how valid is blind tasting?

An 'expert' can be wrong. The reason for his inaccuracy can simply be that he isn't the expert he or others make him out to be. On the other hand, he could have been given a glass from a poor bottle; the wine may not have been authentic to label. Perhaps through his expertise he may have been confused by many subtleties unrecognisable to one not so experienced. It must be remembered that we taste wines to assess their quality—not to pick them as being such and such, nor to praise one palate and denigrate another.

When and How to Taste Blind

Nothing is more agitating than being expected to taste wines blind when you are either incapable or not in the mood. Before the exercise begins, ensure that everyone wants to taste blind. Don't produce a 'masked bottle' at the end of a long tasting, when the palate is tired and beyond its best, and allow sufficient time for the tasters to give their answers.

Try not to give the tasters any idea of what the wine is. For this reason decanting is the best solution. A glimpse at the bottle shape, the colour of the capsule, even seeing the cork, will limit the options a taster may allow himself, and the majority of times he'll come up with the wrong answer.

It is advisable to ask a series of questions, or options, as opposed to the one 'What is it?' For example: 'What is the dominant grape variety of this wine? From which winemaking area does the wine come? What is the vintage, it it pre- or post-1985?' In this way an initial mistake can be corrected, allowing the taster to progress with less uncertainty. Try not to drag out the questions and ask only those which can be related to the actual flavours of the wine.

Bottle Variations

It is significant to mention at this point the important role bottle variation plays in tasting. The saying, 'there are no great wines, only great bottles', although coined when winemaking lacked its present sophistications, is still valid. Bottle variation isn't really so surprising when one considers the different conditions to which a wine can be exposed.

At any wine tasting, particularly at shows, two or more bottles of every entry or sample are always on hand. One for tasting and the second to be called for should the first have an outstanding fault or off-flavour. Except for the trained eye that can distinguish the subtleties in the variation of colour, the only positive way to determine any differences is by tasting.

The biggest single factor contributing to variation is the cellar. Since no two cellars can experience the same temperature, light, movement and such, so it follows that bottles drawn from such cellars will vary according to the cellar differences. A wine that was purchased young, and kept in the one cellar all its life, will be better than the same wine that has changed hands many times and will have therefore had more exposure.

The cask from which the wine was drawn is relevant. Large wine companies with their scientific bottling and blending facilities are more capable of producing variation-free wines than small makers. Though this is not to say that they do. The first bottle drawn from the cask can differ from that bottled last, particularly when filtering is done on the bottling line. A new set of filter pads can strongly taint the initial wines passed through them, giving the wine a strong asbestos flavour.

After bottling, differences often exist in the levels or ullage of the wine. As a result, one bottle will have more air (especially oxygen) to act upon it. Corks differ in their lengths, condition and porosity. One cork will allow more wine to seep from the bottle than a second. Another may contain bacteria, which through inadequate sterilisation will manifest itself, giving the wine a 'corked' character.

The more full-bodied and higher in alcohol a wine is, the less susceptible to variation it will be through its resistance to bacteria and odours. Fortified wines have nowhere near the variation of table wines. A fresh acid riesling has less resistance than a Sauterne, and so on.

In this highly mechanised world, wine, the man-made product of the vine, continually defies standardisation. Perhaps this is the true mystique. Having realised the differences to which a wine can be exposed, don't now cry out 'bottle variation' whenever disappointed by a wine.

Travelling Wines

Often when you visit a wine-growing region, you can come across a particular wine that takes your fancy. Suitably impressed you buy a quantity of the wine and take it with you, or have it delivered. A few weeks later, the wine arrives at your home, you pull the cork and taste it to find that it is nothing like the wine tasted at the vineyard. The first reason for this difference can be the wine isn't the same, either by a confusion in the ordering of the wine, or through the lack of integrity of the winemaker. The second possibility is, at the winery, amongst the casks, the grapes, and after quite a few glasses of wine, with the senses mellowed and the heart light, one was apt to become over enthusiastic about the wine, with the result that when it is received in sobriety, it only has a measure of its previous character.

Another reason is that the wine was tasted in cask, possibly before clarification and fining. Bentonite, a fining agent, can account for considerable loss of flavour in a new wine, though with age the wine will have its former flavour restored. Filtering, bottling and sterilisation agents all take their toll of a young wine, resulting in it being termed 'bruised' or 'knocked'. Some winemakers consider the pumping of a wine so harmful as to have their wineries designed employing gravity in the movement of the wine, considering this to be the most gentle method of handling.

The last hypothesis, travel, is perhaps the

soundest reason for the variation in the wine, particularly if it has not been given sufficient time to rest, and is not just peculiar to newly bottled or young wines. Indeed, the effects of movement over a considerable length of time and fluctuations in temperature, will have a greater consequence in an old wine than in a young wine. The effect of transport, movement and temperature fluctuation, is such that in the past the rolling motion of ship transport was used on wines in cask as a means of ageing.

Wine in the Bottle

The ullage in a bottle of wine is responsible for much of the loss of quality resulting from travel, for here the air space tends to percolate through the wine as well as causing currents in the bottle. Certain elements of wine—the colour, and tannins in particular, are not really dissolved but are in a state of colloidal suspension. Nothing is more fragile, chemically speaking, than these suspensions. They can be broken by fluctuations in temperature, by oxidation, movement, even prolonged high and low frequency sound waves. Ullage is important, and any wine for long transport should have as small an air space as possible. The fragility and changeability of the bouquet is notorious, breathing being a good example of just how instable it is. It is not surprising that transport can change its chemical balance and modify this even more.

Most owners of private cellars allow their wines to rest after transport before attempting to taste them, but usually they are not left long enough. Several weeks to several months are necessary for a wine to recover its full bouquet and taste.

Not all wines will suffer from travelling. I know of many examples of wines that contradict any rules on travel. Max Lake has written extensively on the 'travelability' of Hunter wines (*Hunter Winemakers* Ch. 13, pp. 118–125).

To minimise the effects of movement and temperature fluctuation wine should be transported upright so that the air space, as mentioned, will not percolate through the wine. If the wine is old, with considerable ullage and sediment, it is advisable to decant it into a smaller bottle such as a German riesling bottle which only holds 24 fl. oz. In this way the wine can be decanted free of sediment and, when the cork is replaced, will be free of ullage. This is only advisable if the wine is going to be drunk no more than a few days after decanting, since the quality of the rebottling cannot be guaranteed.

Ullaged Bottles

Every wine deteriorates once the cork has been drawn, though the rate of deterioration depends on the style of wine. It is essential to drink sparkling wines as close as possible to being opened, for once flat they have lost their most appealing character.

Often a bottle of table wine is not drunk in the one sitting, and is held over till the next day when it is finished. Re-corking the wine immediately after pouring helps minimise the amount of volatiles that will evaporate, otherwise by the second day it will appear flat and lifeless. White wines will carry over better, and should be stored in the refrigerator. Much the same practice applies to flagon wines, but particularly in the case of reds, it is advisable to decant the flagon into three bottles, recorking each. Depending upon the care that is taken when bottling, the wine is capable of lasting a few weeks.

Fortified wines, because of their higher amounts of alcohol, can be opened considerably longer than table wines before there is a marked change in their character. But after a few weeks, or particularly towards the end of the bottle, they will lose flavour and become stale. As a general rule the more full-bodied the fortified, the longer it can be opened—Fino sherry, for example, should be finished before an old liqueur port.

Glassware

The varieties and patterns of glassware are innumerable. The great vineyards of Australia, unlike their European counterparts, have not influenced a design to equal their magnificence, so there is no unique Australian glassware, such as the Romer of Germany, or the classic Claret and Burgundy glasses.

The best glassware for drinking wine is made from the purest lead crystal, which, because of its brilliance, enables the colour to be best appreciated. Coloured glassware (unless one possesses an extraordinary understanding of colour blending), is for the crystal cabinet and not for the table.

Decorated, engraved or cut glass is tolerable up to a certain point. Other drinking vessels are available crafted in silver, pewter, wood and a variety of other materials. Although they may reflect the great skill of the silversmith or pewter craftsperson, they do not allow a wine to show its colour, have no advantage over crystal (save durability) and are little more than affectations.

The shape is most important and in any style the lip should be narrower than the bowl, enabling the wine to be swilled in the glass so as to condense the bouquet for olfaction. The most suitable glass for still wine styles is that with a total capacity of 6–8 oz of wine. A stem to elevate the bowl from the base is essential, particularly in the case of white wines where the temperature of the wine will be affected by that of the hand. One glass of 5 oz capacity, two-fifths full, is perfect for the enjoyment of fortified wines, brandies and liqueurs. As for the bird-bath in which champagne and sparkling wines so often appear, I appeal to manufacturers to cease their production and governments to ban their use, for there is no surer way to rid a wine of its finest quality, its sparkle, which is often the product of years of work.

Care of Glassware and Decanters

All the work in decanting a fine wine will be wasted if the decanter and glasses are not free of smells which result from incorrect cleaning and storing. Glass and crystal, although appearing so, are not smooth substances but have microscopic pores capable of being filled with cleaning fluids or housing substances that can communicate a foreign taste to the wine.

To clean either decanter or glassware, avoid using perfumed detergents. Pure soap flakes and a little warm water is all that is necessary. After washing they should then be rinsed thoroughly in cold water and a final time in warm water so that they will dry without streaks. Glassware should be inverted on a tea cloth and left to drain. This is not as easy with a decanter because of the weight of their base and small top. Before putting either wine receptacle away, polish them with a lint-free tea cloth, good linen being the best.

If the decanter is encrusted with the colouring matter of red wines, a little chlorine bleach will remove it. Use vinegar to remove a lime deposit that may be caused by hard water. Take care to thoroughly rinse the decanter, lest traces of these agents remain.

Store glassware in as negative an atmosphere as possible. Many new building materials can transmit very strong smells to the air, which will be absorbed by the glass. Wooden cupboards, due to their lack of airing, readily build up an unfavourable musty smell. Never store glasses upside down as they will become tainted. Decanters should never be stored with their stoppers in, as no air is able to circulate. Whenever taking glasses from their storage place, smell them first to ensure their neutrality—it may be necessary to rewash them.

Wine and Food

Good wine and good food are one of the simplest of modern pleasures. Far too often though the business is complicated by rules and regulations that end up dazzling rather than illuminating. The best rule is quite simply, 'drink what you like with what you like'. If you are interested in wine, there is a very natural extension to an interest in food and then further to the compatibility of the two. Personally, I drink tea with Chinese food, beer with curries and saki when eating Japanese food—wine somehow never really works and this is probably to do with those cuisines being based on tea rather than on wine.

The fundamental rules of dry before sweet, light before full, young before old, are equally applicable to drinking wines with food, as they are when tasting. Just as one aims at a balance of colours, flavours and textures within the menu, the wines served should be treated similarly. There is little point in serving one developed white burgundy after another, no matter how well they complement the food. Serving a fresh riesling style before the white burgundy will both enhance the second wine as well as offer variety to the palate.

Champagne and high-quality champagne styles have a reputation of being able to be served throughout any meal. If only one wine is being served, champagne will combine better with a variety of dishes than any other wine style. Rarely though, is it the one wine served, the progression being from Brut, through to sec and demi-sec styles, which in themselves offer considerable variety.

Shaking tables used in the preparation of champagne.

The more delicate or subtle a wine, the more delicate the food that should go with it. For this reason you will often find a great old red being drunk with nothing more than a soft cheese and unsalted cracker biscuits. A fine tawny port lends itself perfectly to freshly cracked nuts, though this instance is more a result of menu compilation than the requirements of the wines.

Cooking with Wine

Wine is a wonderful medium with which to cook since it can take the place of any liquid when cooking a dish, as well as lending an extra dimension to the dish because of the flavour it adds. Regrettably, low-quality wine is far too often used when cooking, 'the anything handy will do' attitude. No matter how competent the cook, his culinary results will be disappointing unless he uses the best ingredients.

Often faulty wine (corked) is used when cooking—a valid practice up to a point. An oxidised red can enhance the flavour of a stew but can also give it an off-flavour. Any wine found to be so affected should be brought to the boil first and allowed to cool. In this way, the presence of the off-flavour is less noticeable. (During the cooking of wine the alcohol evaporates and is therefore quite suitable for children.)

GRAPE VARIETIES

Graham Gregory

The inherent characteristics of the grape, more than any other factor, predetermine the style and quality of a wine. While climate influences the levels of sugar, acid, pigments, tannin and the intensity of fruit flavours in grapes, the relative winemaking quality of different varieties is remarkably consistent from region to region.

Almost all commercial grapes grown in Australia are varieties of the species *Vitis vinifera*, commonly referred to as the European or Old World grape, which had its origin in both Europe and Western Asia. The reliance on *V. vinifera* in Australia contrasts to the situation in some other viticultural nations of importance, notably France, where roughly 20 per cent of its vineyards consist of hybrids of *V. vinifera* and native American grapes. This is a legacy of the devastation which ensued during the late 1880s following introduction from America of the root insect pest, phylloxera and the fungal diseases, downy mildew and powdery mildew. Use of American species either as rootstocks or for hybridisation provided the means of resistance to these disorders.

About 24 000 varieties of *V. vinifera* have been named. However, it is likely that only around 5000 are genuinely different varieties, and only a small proportion of these are grown commercially. In France, the official statistics list 216 varieties planted to the extent of 10 hectares or more, of which 179 are *V. vinifera* and thirty-seven are hybrids. The number of commercial varieties in Australia is much smaller, around seventy with an area of 10 hectares or more. This is partly a reflection of the strict quarantine prohibition which applied to the importation of grapevines for a long period before the early 1960s because of the dangers of introducing exotic pests and disease. However, following the development of sophisticated methods to identify the presence of disease, particularly virus diseases, a large number of introductions have been safely made and this is now having an effect in broadening the composition of Australia's vineyards.

Even so, most of the so-called 'new varieties' that are coming on to the oenological scene in Australia are not recent introductions. Indeed, varieties such as chardonnay, sauvignon blanc and pinot noir, which make up this category, have been grown here for a long time, but only in small quantities. That this is the case is a testimony to the early pioneers of the wine industry—those who chose the vines that came in with the First Fleet in 1788; Captain John Macarthur who brought in an assortment from France in 1817; and the former school teacher, James Busby, who in 1832 imported a mammoth collection of 600 varieties.

The question is frequently asked why it took so long to exploit varieties that had such a long-established reputation for high quality overseas. There are several reasons.

Firstly, there was only limited interest in table wines in Australia up to the early 1960s. So much so, that it was not until 1968 that sales of table wines exceeded fortified dessert and aperitif wines. Now the ratio is nearly 7:1 in favour of table wines. With the absence then of the more recent consumer interest in table wines, there was little commercial incentive to explore the potential of the generally lower-yielding, premium-quality grapes.

Secondly, in the successful endeavours which have been made to lift the standards of Australian table wines, initially most effort was

Grapes in the Moorilla Estate vineyard.

directed towards improving methods of vinification. It was not until problems in the winery were largely overcome that attention was focussed on the vineyard, particularly in respect to the grapes being grown.

Finally, although the identity of most varieties was well established, with some grapes no-one was too sure about what they actually had. This is not surprising; with 24 000 or so to work through, the identification of grapes is by no means an easy task. It is axiomatic that until the true identity of a variety has been established and its quality potential thereby recognised, there is no incentive to attempt realisation of its virtues. In no case did this apply more than with chardonnay, the production of which has increased from virtually nothing in 1977 to 21 000 tonnes in 1988, and a predicted 47 000 tonnes by 1992. It is indeed incredible that such a famous grape could be overlooked for so long. There is no doubt that its increased popularity in Australia is directly related to the resolution of its birthright in the late 1960s, at which time commercial interest in the variety also began to emerge.

The description of varieties which are given in this chapter attempt to outline the significance of each in Australia and elsewhere. It should be noted that in contrast to the internationally accepted practice, capitals are not used to commence varietal names in this text.

The area given for each variety represents the total Australian plantings in 1987–88 and were compiled by the Australian Bureau of Statistics.

Red Wine Varieties

Aleatico
Area: *not recorded separately*
Aleatico has achieved greatest fame in the Apulia (Puglia) region in the south-east corner of Italy. Here it is used to make the distinctive Aleatico di Puglia; a dark, sweet, dessert wine which has a muscat character and a relatively high-alcohol strength (14–15 per cent). After picking, the grapes are allowed to partially dry before crushing and fermentation. Further north, it is also used for a similar dessert wine, namely Aleatico di Portoferraio from the island of Elba, just off the Tuscany coastline.

It formed a part of the plantings made by Dr Thomas Fiaschi on his Augustine vineyard at Mudgee and is still grown in that district in small commercial quantities.

Alicante Bouschet
Synonym: *Alicante Henri Bouschet*
Area: *not recorded separately*
Alicante bouschet is not grown commercially in Australia. In France however, it is a significant variety with over 20 000 hectares grown there, mostly in the southern departments bordering the Mediterranean.

It is a teinturier variety meaning that the pulp, and juice, are coloured. In consequence, the wines of alicante bouschet are intensely coloured and are only suitable for blending. In France, it is also extensively used for the making of grape juice.

Barbera
Area: *15 hectares*
Despite being one of the world's most widely planted grape varieties, barbera is only a minor commercial variety in Australia with the largest plantings in the MIA (New South Wales) and Riverland (South Australia). It is the most important grape of Italy, production being centred in the Piemonte where it accounts for about 50 per cent of the planted area. It is a heavy producer and is used for vin ordinaire, mostly marketed under its varietal name. The Piemonte barbera wines usually have intense colour, and a rather astringent flavour, the tannin and acid content being high.

Barbera is also planted extensively in Argentina and since 1970 has become prominent in California, in the face of commentary that its acid and tannin content there are excessive. It is particularly suited to mechanical harvesting.

Unless fashions in wine consumption change, the potential usefulness of barbera in Australia will be restricted to blending.

Bastardo
Synonyms: *trousseau, incorrectly called touriga (MIA, Barooga and North-east Victoria) and cabernet gros (South Australia)*
Area: *31 hectares*
Bastardo is classified as one of the best-quality varieties of the many black grapes grown in the classic port wine region of the Douro Valley in

Portugal. Here the varieties are graded into five categories, ranging from very good (muito boas) to bad (mas). Another which is rated muito boas is touriga, which in Australia is now considered to be invariably incorrectly named and is, in fact, bastardo.

The so-called cabernet gros of South Australia was also identified as bastardo by the noted French ampelographist, Paul Truel, during his visit to Australia in early 1976. Here, interest in the variety—which was minimal—may be rekindled now that its correct identity as a high-quality port grape is known.

Although the area of bastardo in Australia is small, it has established a reputation for producing excellent port-style wines. However, cropping has been erratic due to susceptibility to rain damage.

In Portugal, the true touriga is grown more widely than bastardo and there are two strains, T. Francesa and T. Nacional, which are morphologically identical except for seed shape, the former having long beaked seeds as distinct from the squat seeds of the latter. T. Francesa yields considerably larger crops than T. Nacional.

Blue Imperial
See cinsaut.

Bonvedro
Synonyms: *incorrectly called carignan in Australia, and probably Miguel d'Arco at Barooga*
Area: *67 hectares*
Bonvedro is a Portuguese variety also grown in north-east Spain under the name of cuatendra.

In Australia, plantings of bonvedro are mostly located in South Australia, particularly in the Barossa Valley. It is not popular with growers because of its greater susceptibility to disease, drought and frost than alternative varieties. However, in the absence of these problems, it is vigorous and productive. From a quality viewpoint, its wines are low in colour and tannin and suitable only for commercial-grade wines or blending.

Cabernet Franc
Synonym: *breton (Loire Valley of France)*
Area: *195 hectares*
Cabernet franc is mostly found in Australia as odd vines in blocks of cabernet sauvignon. How-

ever, there have been recent plantings of cabernet franc in various regions including Coonawarra–Padthaway, Clare, the Barossa in South Australia and in southern Victoria. It is better suited to cool climates than cabernet sauvignon as bud burst and ripening are earlier.

In France, cabernet franc ranks similarly to cabernet sauvignon on an area-planted basis. Primarily one of the principal red grapes of Bordeaux, it is also grown extensively in the Loire Valley where it is blended with cabernet sauvignon for the appellation wines of Cabernet d'Anjou and Cabernet de Saumur. Cabernet franc is also widely grown in Italy, particularly in the north.

The wines of cabernet franc are of high quality with a distinct varietal character and are softer than those of cabernet sauvignon. It is vigorous and more productive than cabernet sauvignon but does not attain the yields of the high-cropping merlot, to which it bears a strong resemblance.

Cabernet Gros
See bastardo.

Cabernet Sauvignon
Area: *3622 hectares*
Cabernet sauvignon is regarded as the world's premium-quality grape for dry red table wines, the use to which its production is almost entirely applied. Small quantities are used for rosé and vintage port.

In France, the area of cabernet sauvignon has doubled since the late 1960s. The plantings there are mostly concentrated in the department of Gironde (Bordeaux) where it is the major variety of the best wines of the Medoc. It is regarded as the best-quality grape of the five red varieties whose wines are permitted, by law, to carry a Bordeaux appellation. The others are merlot, malbec, cabernet franc and petit verdot–merlot being the most extensively grown, with an area more than twice that of cabernet sauvignon. The Bordeaux reds are mostly made from blends of several of these five varieties. There are also limited plantings in the Anjou region of the Loire Valley, where it is blended with cabernet franc to produce the better of two types of rosé made there, namely Rosé de Cabernet, the other being Rosé d'Anjou. It is also grown extensively in

Chile, Bulgaria, the USA (California) and South Africa.

Cabernet wines possess a strong fruit flavour and bouquet which has been likened by some to the smell of freshly crushed gum leaves. Being high in acid and tannin, the wines mature slowly but retain their quality and freshness for many years. In Australia, its wines have attained eminence as straight varietals but it is still commonly blended with shiraz to good effect.

A little more than two-thirds of Australia's cabernet is grown in South Australia, where it is represented in all major districts. The Coonawarra–Padthaway cabernets are, rightly, the most highly regarded. They are of outstanding quality, possessing a rich purple colour and strong fruit flavour which (for want of a better analogy) is often described as 'minty'. Another feature of these wines is their clean, crisp finish to the palate which is derived from a combination of relatively high levels of acid and tannin. Some of the Coonawarra cabernets bear a remarkable resemblance to the reds of Bordeaux, which is not surprising in view of the similarity in climate of the two regions, and the common component of this fine wine grape.

The cabernet wines of Clare, the Barossa, Adelaide and the Southern Vales areas tend to be more full-bodied and slightly softer on the finish. Although their fruit flavour is usually less intense than those of Coonawarra, many cabernet wines of top quality originate in these districts. Cabernet has become a significant variety in the Hunter Valley even though shiraz continues to be preferred by most vignerons there.

Cabernet has been grown commercially in the irrigation districts for only about twenty years, but it has proved to be one of the best-quality red varieties presently available for these areas. Its inherent capacity to produce flavoursome wines of high colour and tannin balances the combined influence of high temperatures and ample soil moisture which normally results in red wines that are lacking in these components. However, hot conditions may result in musts with a high pH.

It is a vigorous variety with a straggly growth habit, carrying medium crops of small-to-medium-sized loose bunches. In appearance the cabernet vine can be identified by its strongly lobed and shiny leaves. Because of its loose bunches, cabernet is resistant to rain damage and its small tough berries are readily mechanically harvested.

High-performance clones of cabernet which have been either selected here or imported from overseas are now available, and this has further encouraged wider acceptance amongst Australian grapegrowers.

Carignan

Synonym: *carignane (California)*
Area: *not recorded separately*

Quantitatively, carignan is the most important variety in France, where it occupies more than 16 per cent of the wine grape area. It is grown entirely in the southern departments bordering on the Mediterranean.

In California, plantings of carignane (as it is spelt there) exceed that of all red wine grapes and all specialist wine varieties; it is used for bulk red table wines, and its area has expanded in recent times. It is also prominent in several areas of Spain.

In Australia, the variety that carries the name of 'carignan' is, in fact, bonvedro.

Cinsaut

Synonyms: *oeillade, blue imperial*
Area: *62 hectares*

Cinsaut in Australia has declined in importance with most remaining plantings located in the Barossa Valley, Rutherglen, Corowa and in the Murrumbidgee Irrigation Areas.

Cinsaut is an important variety of the Midi and Provence regions in the south of France, where it is grown in association with grenache and carignan. Of no importance in California, it is nonetheless the principal red wine variety of South Africa where it was previously called 'hermitage'.

Cinsaut is productive, mid-season in maturity, and of average vigour. The berries, though not too large, are fleshy and more agreeable to eat than most other wine grapes.

It is used for both table wines and port which are of standard quality with no obvious varietal character. Some winemakers in Australia have produced good dry red blends of cinsaut with shiraz and even cabernet.

Dolcetto

Area: *not recorded separately*

Although not grown in Australia, dolcetto is one of the principal grapes of the Piemonte region of Italy. Its wines are rather plain in flavour and light in body but possess excellent colour, being rich and bright.

Durif

Synonym: *incorrectly called petite sirah in California*

Area: *not recorded separately*

As the late Alan Antcliff of CSIRO pointed out, the small commercial plantings of durif in north-eastern Victoria are mixed with a closely related variety, peloursin. Here it was originally used for ports, but now mostly for table wines which have high tannin and intense colour that require long ageing.

The so-called petite sirah of California is durif of which there are nearly 3000 hectares. It is highly regarded there for table wines, especially in the cooler regions and has become popular for planting in recent years. There are only a few hundred hectares in France, where its wines are regarded as 'ordinary'.

Esparte

See mataro.

Frontignac

Synonyms: *muscat de Frontignan, frontignan, brown muscat (Australia); moscato bianco, moscato d'Asti, moscato di Canelli (Italy); muscat d'Alsace, muscat à petits grains blanc, rosé and rouge (France); muscat blanc (California)*

Area: *not recorded separately*

The name frontignac is recommended for use in Australia which is acceptable nomenclature to the Office International de la Vigne et du Vin, whereas frontignan is not.

There are several clones of frontignac which possess different berry colours ranging from white to black. The red (or brown) clone is most widely grown in Australia, but the others are also present and often intermixed in the one vineyard. This has led to confusion regarding the correct nomenclature of the variety. At Rutherglen–Corowa, it is generally believed that brown muscat and frontignac are distinct types, the former being darker in colour and producing wines of more intense muscat flavour, but morphologically identical in other respects. However, the noted French ampelographist Paul Truel has identified all as being the different coloured clones of frontignac.

About half of the plantings here are in South Australia, mostly in the Barossa Valley. It is also an important grape in north-eastern Victoria, Corowa and the Murrumbidgee Irrigation Area.

Frontignac is responsible for the best of the muscat dessert wines made in Australia. The rich, luscious character of these wines is unique and probably unmatched by any from elsewhere in the world. The frontignac muscats of Rutherglen and adjoining districts have acquired the greatest fame, but wines of equal quality are made in the Barossa and the MIA.

The variety is also used for dry white table wines. These possess the distinct fruity flavour of the muscat grape but are often rather austere, particularly on the finish to the palate, and to cover this a little residual sugar is usually retained.

In the Appellation d'Origine Contrôlée (AOC) region of Muscat de Frontignan in the south of France, only the white clone of frontignac is grown commercially. It is used for one of the few sweet fortified wines (*vins doux naturels*) made in that country. The red and white clones are grown to a limited extent for table wines in Alsace under the name Muscat d'Alsace. In Italy, as moscato bianco, it is widespread and is used for the popular Asti spumante sparkling wines.

The vine has moderate vigour and produces reasonably good crops of compact, cylindrical bunches, the berries of which are inclined to shrivel before harvest.

Gamay

Synonym: *gamay beaujolais*

Area: *not recorded separately*

Gamay has potential in Australia for making light, fresh, fruity-flavoured dry reds of a style that should readily find a place in the market—the true luncheon red, soft on the gums, easy on the stomach, and with a bouquet and taste of all things bright and beautiful.

Its exploitation here has been thwarted by difficulties encountered in introducing correctly named disease-free clones. (It is a long, technically boring story.) However, authentic clones brought in from Europe in the late 1960s were at last released for commercial trial in the early 1980s.

In France, there are large areas of gamay, grown mostly in the Beaujolais sub-district of Burgundy. All wines entitled to the appellation of Beaujolais must be made from gamay. It is also grown in the Loire and Rhône Valleys, northern Italy and Switzerland; in the latter it is usually blended with pinot noir, the resultant wines being labelled either 'Goron' or the higher-quality 'Dole'.

A few commercial plantings of gamay have been made recently in Australia and their performance will be eagerly watched.

Grand Noir

Synonym: *grand noir de la Galmette*
Area: *not recorded separately*
Grand noir is grown commercially to a limited extent in the Corowa–Rutherglen region where it is mostly used for port.

It continues to be a significant grape in France, but its area there is declining. Its cultivation is concentrated in the southern-most departments but extends north to Charente and Charente–Maritime.

Grand noir, like alicante bouschet, is another of the relatively few teinturier varieties with coloured juice.

Grenache

Synonym: *garnacha (Spain)*
Area: *2255 hectares*
Although Australia's third most important red grape, grenache has fallen from favour, with plantings declining from 6301 hectares in 1976 to the present area quoted above. Of the total, 1956 hectares are located in South Australia.

In New South Wales and Victoria, there is very little grenache grown outside the irrigation areas. Likewise in South Australia the majority of plantings are in the Riverland, but there is still a substantial area in the Barossa Valley and the Southern Vales. Quality-wise, it certainly performs best in fairly dry situations where its inherent deficiencies are less pronounced.

Grenache is grown extensively in other parts of the world. It is the second most important red grape to carignan in France where it is located almost entirely in the southern parts of the Rhône Valley and in the Midi (Languedoc) region bordering the Mediterranean. Although it is mostly used there for *vins ordinaires de consommation courante*, grenache is also an important component of the higher-quality Appellation d'Origine Contrôlée (AOC) wines of Chateauneuf-du-Pape and Tavel, where it constitutes 80 per cent of the red grape plantings. The distinctive rosés of Tavel originated from the natural tendency of the grenache there to produce wines that are light in style. In addition, the sweet fortified aperitif wine of Banyuls, which lies on the Mediterranean coast bordering Spain, is made from grenache.

In Spain, where it is known as garnacha, it is the most important red wine grape accounting for about 15 per cent of the planted area. Outside Europe, the largest areas are found in California and Australia.

Grenache wines mature at an early age, and because of this it is favoured by Australian winemakers for commercial-grade dry reds and ports. It is also commonly used for rosés, for which it is well suited. Grenache dry reds are pleasant when young, having a light, fresh style and a grapy palate. However, when compared with the better-quality varieties, its wines lack colour, tannin and character, particularly when grown in the hot, irrigation districts where deficiencies of this kind tend to be accentuated.

The variety is readily identified by its erect growth habit and shiny, entire leaves which are hairless on both the upper and the lower surfaces. It is a heavy producer of medium-sized, tight bunches which are predisposed to breakdown when wet weather is experienced near vintage.

Hermitage

See shiraz.

Jacquez

Synonyms: *lenoir, black Spanish, cigar box grape, blue French grape*
Area: *not recorded separately*
Apart from rubired, jacquez is the only commercial variety grown in Australia that is a hybrid of *V. vinifera* and other *Vitis* species. It is a natural hybrid of unknown origin. In the MIA, where there are small commercial plantings, it is

incorrectly called Uva di Troia (or Troya) which is, in fact, a genuine vinifera species.

In the south of France it is not only used for wine but as a rootstock with moderate resistance to phylloxera. Possibly it is the same variety as the jacquez of South Africa, which is the most popular rootstock there.

Its wines possess intense colour but they are only suited for blending purposes because of a very high pH and blackcurrant-type flavour.

Malaga, Black

The small plantings of this dessert, table variety are all located in Western Australia. It appears to be of only minor importance elsewhere in the world and is of no significance for production of wine. (See Waltham cross.)

Malbec

Synonym: *cot (France)*
Area: *212 hectares*

Three-quarters of the malbec grown in Australia is located in South Australia where it is represented in all districts.

Malbec is notorious for its irregular cropping characteristics because of the frequent failure of its berries to set normally. However, this problem has been partly overcome by use of improved clones.

Malbec grapes.

Despite agronomic faults, malbec is one of the specified Bordeaux varieties where, of the reds, it ranks fourth in importance to merlot, cabernet franc and cabernet sauvignon. It is also the principal red grape in Argentina where, in contrast to other regions, it apparently crops well. These differences in performance could well be due to genetic variations between clones of the variety, coupled with differing levels of virus infection.

The limited quantities of malbec wines made in Australia are of good quality, rich in colour and in tannin—a description that could be applied equally as well to the French wines of this variety. Here, it is mostly seen in blends with cabernet sauvignon and/or shiraz. It is a moderately vigorous grape with a spreading growth habit. Its fruit matures early in the season and is easily harvested by machine.

Mataro

Synonyms: *mouvédre (France), balzac (Corowa), esparte (Great Western), monastrell or morastell (incorrect)*
Area: *666 hectares*
On an area basis, mataro ranks fifth as a red

Mataro grapes.

wine variety in Australia but its significance is declining rapidly. Of the total, 515 hectares are located in South Australia where it assumes greatest importance in the Riverland and Barossa regions.

Although widely distributed throughout the world, mataro is not an important grape other than in Spain where there are substantial plantings. There are only small areas in France and in California (where it is regarded as a grape without merit).

Some winemakers have used it to good effect in blends with shiraz, but the overall performance of mataro in Australia rates it as only average in quality. The wines are of neutral flavour and usually possess a rather hard finish. It is used for both table wines and ports.

Its principal attribute is its late bud burst and capacity to recover after frost. It can therefore be used for frosty situations.

Merlot

Area: *316 hectares*
Merlot is the principal red grape of Bordeaux where 85 per cent of France's plantings of this variety are located. It is also grown extensively in northern Italy.

Used mostly in blends with cabernet sauvignon and cabernet franc, merlot is a standard varietal component of some of the finest Bordeaux appellations. It makes wines of good fruit character but they are comparatively low in acid and contain less tannin than those of cabernet. For this reason, they are softer when young, and drinkable at a much earlier age.

In Australia, commercial merlot wines only began to emerge in the early 1980s, yet already there are clear indications of its potential for quality Australian wines.

Merlot is a vigorous grape and a good producer, with a reputation for yielding more than others in the 'cabernet family'. On the other hand, its cropping tends to be more irregular.

Meunier

Synonyms: *miller's burgundy (Australia), pinot meunier*
Area: *23 hectares*
In France, the centre of production is the Champagne region where it comprises 44 per cent of

the planted area. It makes good champagne base wines, but not in the same quality class of those from chardonnay and pinot noir.

Commercial plantings in Australia are mostly located in southern Victoria and are often mixed with pinot noir to which it appears to be a simple sport with tetraploid dermal tissue. Meunier has a late bud burst and is therefore less susceptible to frost damage than pinot noir. It makes attractive, light dry red wines.

The distinctive feature of the variety is its very white and hairy shoot tips, giving rise to the name of miller's burgundy.

Mondeuse

Synonym: *refosco (Italy, California, Argentina)*
Area: *13 hectares*
Commercial plantings of mondeuse in Australia are confined to north-eastern Victoria. It is now used entirely for table wine but is said to be particularly suitable for ports.

It is grown in many parts of the world but is nonetheless a comparatively minor variety. In France, it is the principal variety in the vineyards of Savoie and Ain.

Muscat Hamburg

Synonyms: *black muscat, muscat de Hambourg (France), muscato di Amburgo (Italy)*
Area: *666 hectares*
A specialist table variety of high quality, muscat Hamburg assumes most commercial significance in Queensland, followed by New South Wales and Victoria. The fruit has a strong muscat flavour and was recognised as having the best eating qualities of all fresh grapes grown in Australia. However, it is now being superseded by seedless varieties. The best fruit is produced in non-irrigated districts such as those near Sydney, at Mudgee in the New South Wales central tablelands and Stanthorpe in Queensland. Not a particularly good shipping variety, it is mostly grown fairly close to the principal market outlets.

Muscat Hamburg is also a very popular table grape in France with most plantings located in the department of Vaucluse in the Rhône Valley. It is not important in California.

Although popular with some amateur 'backyard' winemakers, its wines are of indifferent quality possessing a mild muscat flavour but lacking body.

Nebbiolo

Area: *not recorded separately*
Although not a commercial variety in Australia, nebbiolo is the quality grape of the Piemonte (Piedmont) region of Italy. Its wines tend to be named after the place of origin in contrast to the others of Piemonte which retain the varietal name. Nebbiolo produces Barolo which is usually regarded as the best, requiring long ageing, and Barbaresco which is close in quality to Barolo but not aged as long. Other wines of nebbiolo produced in small districts of northern Piemonte include Gattinara, Carema, Lessona and Ghemme.

Nebbiolo wines have good colour and a rather high tannin content, but are by no means as 'inky' as those of barbera.

Petit Verdot

Area: *not recorded separately*
All Bordeaux red wines must be made only from five specified varieties either on their own or in blends with the others. Petit verdot is one of the five and the least important, representing less than one per cent of the combined area of the others. The variety is not grown commercially in Australia.

Pinot Noir

Area: *785 hectares*
Pinot noir is one of the earliest maturing red wine varieties and for this reason it can be grown successfully in the cold grapegrowing regions of Switzerland, Germany and northern France. However, because it has an early bud burst it is susceptible to spring frost damage which demands careful site selection for good air drainage to avoid damage.

France has the world's largest plantings of pinor noir. All the renowned red wines of the Côte d'Or portion of Burgundy that are entitled to the appellation of 'Bourgogne' or higher Burgundy classifications, must be made from pinot noir. It is also one of the three principal varieties for the white sparkling wines of champagne where it ranks second in importance to meunier, another black-skinned grape. Normally, blends of pinot noir and chardonnay base wines make the best champagne; it is said that 'pinot provides the strength and fabric to the wines—while chardonnay their delicacy and elegance'. It is an important grape of Beaujolais, another sub-region of Burgundy, where it is planted on the calcareous soils. (Gamay, to which pinot noir is closely related, is grown on the granite soils of Beaujolais.)

Pinot noir and gamay are also the two red grapes of Switzerland, where in the Valais they are usually blended to produce the wines labelled 'Goron' and the higher-quality 'Dole'. The very best wines of the Valais, however, are made solely from pinot noir and are labelled 'Dole-Pinot Noir'. It is an important grape in the cooler parts of California and is grown commercially further to the north in Oregon.

Pinor noir has been grown in Australia for a long time but as recently as the mid-1970s the total area here was less than 50 hectares. Since then, interest in variety has increased both for dry reds and champagne-base wines. Significant new plantings have been made, particularly in South Australia which now has 392 hectares, followed by New South Wales (197 hectares), and Victoria (155 hectares).

Originally, the most famous Australian pinot noir wines were made in the Hunter Valley. This is somewhat surprising, because the variety usually develops insufficient colour when grown in such warm regions. For this reason it has been mostly blended with shiraz, although amongst the straight pinots that continue to be made in the Hunter are some magnificent wines. Nonetheless, its performance overseas indicates that pinot noir is more suited to cooler districts such as the south-east of South Australia, where indeed the largest plantings in that state are located. Wherever it is grown, it is apparent that experience and skill is needed to retain the distinctive floral characters, sometimes described as 'violets', in its wines. Whereas Australian vignerons soon mastered the secrets of producing chardonnays that are equal to and mostly better than world class, pinot noir has presented a more formidable challenge.

Pinot noir is an extremely variable variety with many clones, of which twenty or more have been either selected in or imported to Australia. The clones are not only morphologically different in respect to leaf shape, growth habit, berry and bunch characteristics, but some seem to be better adapted to particular regions than others.

More work needs to be done here to unravel the full mystery of this variety.

Pinot noir possesses moderate vigour but generally is a low yielder. However, its yield disadvantage is mitigated to a large degree by use of selected, high-performance, virus-free clones.

Rubired

Area: *44 hectares*

The variety was bred by Professor Harold P. Olmo of the University of California and released in 1958. It was intended as a port-wine type and, having red juice, it produces wines of intense colour even when grown in hot irrigation districts. This has prompted its use as colouring material for table wines.

It is a hybrid of tinta cao and alicante ganzin. The latter contains some *Vitis rupestris* in its breeding, which has imparted to rubired some resistance to fungal diseases and bunch breakdown.

Most of Australia's small area of rubired is located in the Sunraysia and mid-Murray districts of New South Wales and Victoria.

Ruby Cabernet

Area: *94 hectares*

Ruby cabernet is another variety bred by Professor Harold Olmo, being released in 1948. It is a hybrid of carignan and cabernet sauvignon. The aim was to obtain a grape that would produce quality reds in hot irrigation districts. To a large degree this seems to have been achieved, although it is generally accepted that the excellent aroma of its wines is not fully carried through to the flavour. It is a distinctly heavier cropper than cabernet sauvignon and, like its parent, is readily harvested mechanically.

It has become a significant variety in California with a planted area similar to that of cabernet sauvignon. Despite susceptibility to fungal diseases, ruby cabernet has shown considerable promise in Australia where most plantings are located in the Riverland of South Australia.

Rutherglen Brown Muscat

See frontignac.

Sangiovese

Area: *not recorded separately*

Sangiovese is the principal variety used for the

making of the Chianti wines of Tuscany in Italy. Traditionally, Chianti is made of a mixture of several grapes—namely sangiovese (50–60 per cent), canaiolo nero (15 per cent), trebbiano and malvasia bianca (25–35 per cent) and colorino (small varying amounts).

Sangiovese is a vigorous and productive grape which tends to produce neutral wines on its own. Commercial plantings are negligible in Australia.

Shiraz

Synonyms: *syrah (France), hermitage*
Area: *4904 hectares*

Shiraz is Australia's principal variety for the production of fortified and non-fortified red wines. This is in contrast to the situation in other wine-growing countries where the variety is comparatively unimportant.

In France, it represents less than 2 per cent of all red wine grapes. Nonetheless, the red wines of the small but famous region of Hermitage in the Rhône Valley are made totally from shiraz. It is also grown elsewhere in the Rhône Valley, notably at Châteauneuf-du-Pape, near Avignon; there it is one of the several specified red varieties, and although grenache predominates, shiraz is accepted as a better-quality type. Indeed, it is well regarded generally in France, where recently the area has been greatly increased, especially in the south, for the purpose of adding character to wines based mainly on carignan and grenache.

The petite sirah of California is not shiraz as was once thought but is, in fact, durif. Similarly, the principal red variety of South Africa called 'hermitage' is truly cinsaut; shiraz accounts for less than 1 per cent of the plantings there. A little shiraz is grown in Argentina and Italy.

In Australia, the area of shiraz is more than any other true wine variety, red or white. It is grown in virtually all districts, being used for both table wines and ports. During the 1960s and 1970s, the area of shiraz in Australia increased considerably with production reaching 75 000 tonnes in 1977. However, in the ensuing ten years, many plantings were removed, especially in the Barossa and Hunter, and production declined by more than 33 per cent to 49 000 tonnes in 1987. To a large degree this reflected the shift in demand from dry reds to dry whites which occurred over this period.

Shiraz wines are of good colour, contain moderate amounts of acid and tannin and possess a positive though mild fruit flavour. As with all varieties, the intensity of its colour, acid and tannin increases as the temperature of the region in which it is grown decreases. This accounts for the difference between the Hunter Valley and South Australian shiraz dry reds, the former being lighter and softer in style, due to less tannin and acid, than the more assertive and full-bodied wines of the cooler Barossa Valley, Clare and Coonawarra districts. Shiraz is often blended to good effect with virtually all other red varieties.

With the exception of a few hectares of pinot noir, shiraz was the only red grape grown in the Hunter Valley until 1963. In this district its wines, while being soft on the palate, develop an earthy flavour which is rather unique.

The shiraz wines of Rutherglen and other parts of north-eastern Victoria are usually more full-bodied and fruitier than those from either South Australia or the Hunter. At least a part of this can be attributed to the tendency in these districts to pick the grapes at a rather more advanced stage of maturity than elsewhere.

Shiraz is a good growers' grape. It is vigorous and produces good crops of medium-sized bunches which are mid-season in maturity. The bunches stand up to wet weather near harvest better than most varieties, but the berries tend to wilt when ripe and become more difficult to mechanically harvest. It is easily distinguished in the vineyards by the whitish tips to the young shoots, in the spring and early summer, and by its trailing growth habit.

Tarrango

Area: *not recorded separately*

Bred in Australia by a CSIRO team at Merbein, led by the late Alan Antcliff, it was released for trial in 1975. It was designed for the making of inexpensive red table wines that are ready for drinking soon after vintage. It is vigorous and the vine yields well.

Tarrango wines have an attractive bright red cherry colour and a pleasant flavour. They have low pH and a good titratable acidity.

Tinta Amarella

Synonym: *known in Australia as Portugal in the past*

Area: *11 hectares*

Tinta amarella is widely grown for port wine production in the Douro Valley of Portugal where of the five quality classifications for grape varieties, it is ranked in the second-best category, namely boas (good).

All plantings here are located in South Australia, mainly the Barossa, where it is said to have no special attributes and is usually blended with other varieties to make port wine.

Touriga

See bastardo.

Troia

See jacquez.

Zinfandel

Area: *not recorded separately*

In California, zinfandel is second only to carignan in importance as a red wine grape. It is a vigorous good cropping variety, but the bunches are tight and extremely susceptible to rain damage and bunch rots near maturity. These deficiencies will severely limit its exploitation in Australia, where there are no districts with a sufficiently dry harvest period to approach that of the San Joaquin Valley of California.

It makes good-quality dry reds with a distinct, almost raspberry character when young.

White Wine Varieties

Albillo

See chenin blanc.

Alvarelhao

Area: *not recorded separately*

Alvarelhao is grown in the Douro Valley of Portugal where it is used for the making of white port wines, for which it is officially classified as being of mediocre quality. I am not aware of commercial plantings in Australia.

Aucerot

Area: *not recorded separately*

Aucerot is an Australian name, there being no variety elsewhere in the world which carries this nomenclature. Paul Truel, the French ampelographer, has expressed the opinion that its derivation may come from the little known and unimportant arcat or arcet variety.

Aucerot has been grown for many years in very small quantities in the Hunter Valley, specifically at Mount Pleasant, Pokolbin and Fordwich near Broke. It makes good-quality dry whites although the variety is now invariably blended with others.

Biancone

Synonym: *incorrectly called white grenache in Australia*

Area: *61 hectares*

The true identity of this high-yielding grape was resolved by Paul Truel as the Corsican variety, biancone. The true grenache blanc of France does not appear to be represented in Australia.

Virtually all Australian plantings are located in South Australia, mainly in the Riverland. Apart from its high yield, it has no great merit even though odd winemakers claim it is useful for dry whites.

Blanquette

See clairette.

Chardonnay

Area: *2978 hectares*

Chardonnay has been grown in Australia for a long time but until the early 1970s there was only a mere handful of vines. That such a famous grape could be overlooked for so long may seem surprising but, to a large degree, the answer lies in the uncertainty that existed as to its true identity, being previously confused with white pinot—to which, in fact, it bears no resemblance. The issue was resolved in the mid-1960s and commercial interest in the variety soon followed. It is somewhat ironic that chardonnay is one of the easiest varieties to identify in that it has the distinguishing characteristic of a 'naked' petiolar sinus meaning that the first branch of the main veins from the petiole form the leaf margin at the top of the sinus. Other varieties have a leafy edge to these veins.

Of the white varieties, chardonnay ranks fourth in importance in France, being grown extensively in the north of the country with about half its area in Bourgogne and most of the

Chardonnay grapes.

balance in Champagne. In the former region, it is responsible for the Appellation d'Origine wines of Bourgogne, taking in Montrachet, Meursault, Chablis and Pouilly-Fuissé. It is also the white variety of Champagne, where it is normally blended with pinot noir to make the finest wines, except in very good years when the Blanc-de-Blancs, made solely from chardonnay, may be superior. In all, there are more than 13 000 hectares of chardonnay in France. It is also the premium white table wine grape of California, where its area doubled between 1975 and 1985 to 10 000 hectares.

The first person in Australia to make a straight commercial chardonnay wine of a quality that made people stand up and take notice, was the Hunter Valley vigneron Murray Tyrrell. This was in 1971 and his first to receive small oak maturation, and with it considerable acclaim, was the Tyrrells Vat 47 of 1973. It has since enjoyed unprecedented popularity amongst both consumers and winemakers, being the most highly sought-after wine grape throughout the 1980s. It has been commanding the highest prices of all varieties and during the 1989 vintage pay-ments between $1500 and $2000 per tonne were more the rule than the exception.

Significant new plantings are continuing to be made and the non-bearing area of young vines in 1987–88 represented 21 per cent of the total. It is reliably predicted that by the 1992 vintage, its production will reach 47 100 tonnes compared with 20 637 tonnes in 1988. If this eventuates, it will rank as the third most important wine grape behind Rhine riesling and shiraz, but excluding the multi-purpose sultana and muscat gordo blanco varieties.

Chardonnay is a good growers' grape and has performed well in all climatic regions of Australia, from the cool southern areas to the hot inland irrigation districts. It yields well, is easily harvested by machine and has few problems apart from an early bud burst which makes it susceptible to spring frost damage. Because of the latter, careful site selection for good air drainage is a must.

From a winemaking viewpoint it is an excellent grape, largely owing to its ability to retain relatively high acid levels even at an advanced stage of maturity. Its wines have a distinct varietal character which has been variously described as resembling peaches, apricots, quinces and even figs; but none of these descriptions do them justice. Most winemakers in Australia are following the Burgundian tradition of fermenting in small, new, oak casks for the top chardonnay wines which are usually left on gross lees for several months before racking. Where this is not done, they are almost invariably matured in small oak for a period after fermentation. The combination of chardonnay grape flavours with those extracted from the oak provides the depth and complexity to its wines which consumers find so appealing. The manner in which oak is used affects the style of chardonnay wines with rich and toasty characters resulting from long exposure to oak, and more elegant, fruitier wines from lesser oak contact.

Chasselas

Synonyms: *sweetwater, gutedel (Germany and Alsace); chasselas doré (California); fendant (Switzerland)*
Area: *12 hectares*
As well as being used for wine, it is sometimes

Chasselas grapes.

sold as an early maturing table grape, under the name of sweetwater.

Chasselas is grown in Switzerland, Alsace and Germany as a wine variety but even more widely throughout Europe as a table grape. It is the principal wine grape of Switzerland, where it is also known under the name of fendant.

In Alsace it represents about 20 per cent of the total plantings and is used there for wines of only standard quality.

The European chasselas wines are by no means in the premium-quality class but they are pleasant, well balanced and have a mild, fruity flavour. Some Australian winemakers regard it as well suited for champagne.

Chenin Blanc

Synonyms: *steen or stein (South Africa); pineau de la Loire (occasionally in France and California)*
Area: *517 hectares*

About 60 per cent of Australia's chenin blanc is grown in the Barossa and Riverland regions of South Australia where, until the 1970s, it was incorrectly called albillo (or sherry). Western Australia accounts for 20 per cent of plantings

and here it was also incorrectly called semillon prior to 1970. The remaining plantings are mostly located in Victoria. Variability within chenin blanc has been acknowledged and attributed to a heterogeneous genetic make-up.

In France, it is one of the principal grapes of the Loire Valley, being used in part for the Appellation D'Origine Contrôlée wines of Anjou and Touraine, and commonly for the sparkling wines known as mousseux. It has also become an important variety in California and is well represented in Argentina and Chile, being incorrectly named pinot blanco in Chile.

It is grown extensively for dry white wines and sherry in South Africa where steen is now officially recognised as chenin blanc. It occupies about one-third of the vineyard area there.

A common feature of the wines of chenin blanc, albillo and steen is that all are rather high in acid. This supports the synonymity of the three and makes it a useful variety for well-balanced table wines in hot regions.

Chenin blanc is fairly vigorous and produces good crops of compact, medium-sized bunches. It is rather susceptible to fungus diseases which will limit its utilisation to areas of low summer rainfall.

Chenin blanc grapes.

Clairette grapes.

Clairette

Synonym: *blanquette*
Area: *28 hectares*

Clairette is known as blanquette in Australia, where all commercial plantings are recorded to be located in New South Wales, mostly in the Hunter Valley.

In France, it is grown extensively in the south, where practically all the white table wines are blends of this variety and ugni blanc (trebbiano). It is regarded highly as a base wine for vermouth and is the grape of the Appellation d'Origine Contrôlée districts of Clairette de Bellegarde and Clairette du Lanquedoc and, in association with muscat, is responsible for the sparkling wines of Clairette de Die. It is also grown commercially to a small extent in South Africa.

In France, as in South Africa, clairette makes wines with a distinctive though rather assertive fruity aroma and bouquet. They have a reputation for their tendency to oxidise. Its winemaking performance in Australia is similar, although occasionally some fine elegant wines were seen which carried the blanquette label. It is often used to advantage for blending with varieties like semillon and trebbiano.

The foliage of the clairette vine is very similar in appearance to that of doradillo with which it is sometimes confused. However, its berries are oval in shape whereas those of doradillo are round. It is a vigorous variety, producing good crops of moderately large, loose and late-maturing bunches. Some vines have a marked tendency towards poor berry setting, which is caused by virus infection.

Clare Riesling

See crouchen.

Colombard

Area: *612 hectares*

Colombard is a comparatively recent introduction from California where its area has more than trebled over the last fifteen years, mainly in the hot Central Valley. It is still well represented in France although its area there has declined substantially in recent times. It is used in France for white table wines of the quality classification of *vin de consommation courante* and for distillation. For the latter purpose it produces brandy of high quality; however, it is grown only to a relatively small extent in the Cognac region. By and large, plantings are confined to the south-western departments, especially Gironde where it is regarded as an accessory white wine grape. It is also a useful white wine grape in South Africa.

The main feature of the variety is its high acid content in hot and cold regions alike. This is its most-favoured attribute both in California and Australia, being mostly used for blending to produce good-quality table wines. It also has a moderately positive varietal flavour.

It is significant that over 80 per cent of the plantings in Australia are located in the Murrumbidgee Irrigation Areas, Sunraysia, and the Riverland, where faith in the variety is evidenced by the fact that production is expected to more than double by 1992. Colombard is a vigorous high-yielding variety that is very susceptible to oidium but moderately resistant to downy mildew and bunch rot.

Conacazo

Synonyms: *known as false pedro (South Australia) and common palomino (Sunraysia) before being correctly identified*
Area: *not recorded separately*

Conacazo is a minor Spanish variety which is no longer authorised for planting there. It produces neutral wine and has been mainly used in Australia for fortified and distillation wines.

Crouchen

Synonym: *Clare riesling*
Area: *569 hectares*

Much confusion previously surrounded the true identity of Clare riesling which is very similar to semillon both in morphological characteristics and winemaking qualities. However, following up leads from other viticulturists, Alan Antcliff of the CSIRO first identified Clare riesling as a variety known as crouchen in France where it has all but disappeared. His opinion was confirmed by the French ampelographer Paul Truel during his visit to Australia in 1976.

It seems to be grown only in Australia and South Africa where it was originally known as riesling.

Here, 84 per cent of the plantings are in South Australia where it is well represented in the Barossa and Riverland districts. It is used exclusively for dry white table wines which resemble those of semillon, though they are somewhat more delicate in style. However, it has lost favour with winemakers and its area has nearly halved since 1980. Additional comments are given under semillon.

Doradillo

Area: *1025 hectares*
Doradillo is probably Australia's most prolific wine grape and, as such, is traditionally the nation's principal distillation variety. It produces wines of neutral flavour, which are therefore well suited for the distillation of fortifying and brandy spirit. Some winemakers also regard it highly as a base wine for premium-quality dry sherry, and the results achieved justify its use for this purpose. The declining demand for brandy and fortified wine has resulted in a 50 per cent reduction in its area over the last ten years.

Most plantings are located in the inland irrigation districts where it commonly yields crops of 37 tonnes or more per hectare.

The noted, early viticulturist, François de Castella, considered doradillo to be synonymous with the Spanish variety Jaen. However, it is not clear whether this is the case. Certainly, apart from the possibility of Spain, the variety does not appear to be grown to any extent in other parts of the world.

Doradillo grapes.

The vine is only moderately vigorous and rather more sensitive than most to poor drainage. Doradillo may be distinguished in the vineyard by its dark-green lobed leaves, which carry a heavy white felt on the undersurface. Its extremely heavy crops of large, conical bunches are late in maturing.

Emerald Riesling

Area: *37 hectares*
Emerald riesling is a comparatively new variety bred in California by Professor Olmo. It is vigorous and productive, making wines of high acidity and low pH. However, the flavour of its wines has been questioned, many maintaining that there is no particular varietal character and that overall it has no advantages over colombard.

Virtually all Australian plantings are in South Australia.

Farana

Synonyms: *mayorquin (France), planta pedralba (Spain), damaschino (Sicily), formerly known as false trebbiano (Australia)*
Area: *not recorded separately*
Of Mediterranean origin, farana is the name used for this variety in Algeria.

A little is grown in the Barossa where it produces high yields and is used for both table and fortified wines.

Fumé Blanc
See sauvignon blanc.

Furmint
Unless grown under a synonym, furmint is not represented in Australia. It is responsible for the finest white table wines of Hungary, including the luscious Tokay of the Hegyalja district.

Gewurztraminer
See traminer.

Gordo
See muscat gordo blanco.

Grenache, White
See biancone.

Irvine's White
See ondenc.

Listan

See palomino.

Malvasia Bianca

Area: *not recorded separately*

Malvasia is an Italian grape which, together with trebbiano—another white variety—makes up between 25 and 35 per cent of Chianti wines —the balance, of course, being red grapes.

It has no commercial significance in Australia.

Marsanne

Synonym: *ermitage (Switzerland)*
Area: *41 hectares*

Almost all Australia's plantings of marsanne are in the north-east of Victoria, where it is used for white table wines.

Marsanne is grown in the Rhône Valley of France, but is only a minor variety; and to a limited extent in the Valais of Switzerland, under the name of ermitage. It is a robust grape which produces reasonably good crops, but its wines generally lack varietal character and tend to age rapidly.

Montils

Synonym: *chalosse*

For many years montils has formed, to a minor degree, a part of the varietal mix in the Mount Pleasant vineyard in the Hunter Valley where it has been used in blends with other grapes for white table wines. It is of no significance elsewhere in Australia.

There are small plantings in France, mostly in the department of Charente.

Muller-Thurgau

Synonym: *riesling sylvaner*
Area: *14 hectares*

Reputedly a cross between riesling and sylvaner, and now suspected of being a seedling of riesling, Muller-thurgau has become the leading wine grape of Germany. Although grown elsewhere in Europe, it is unimportant in France, there being only a small area in Alsace. It has become a significant grape in New Zealand, where it represents 50 per cent of the crush and its wines are amongst the best dry whites made there.

Its wines do not possess the character of riesling but are nonetheless fruity and pleasant and well regarded in Germany.

It is well suited to cold regions, being the earliest maturing of all white wine varieties. It also recovers well after frosts because the secondary buds are fruitful. It is vigorous and productive but very susceptible to fungal diseases.

Muscadelle

Synonym: *sauvignon vert (incorrectly in California)*
Area: *396 hectares*

Muscadelle was formerly known as tokay in Australia and it was widely assumed that it originated from the Tokaj–Hegyalja district of Hungary and was possibly Harslevelii, one of the two varieties grown there. However, in 1976 the French ampelographer, Paul Truel, identified it as muscadelle, one of the three Bordeaux white wine grapes.

It is traditionally used in Australia for the production of fortified sweet white dessert wines for which it is unsurpassed by other varieties. These honey-flavoured wines are not widely seen commercially but are equally as luscious and distinctive as the frontignac dessert wines, without the pungent muscat flavour of the latter. More recently it has been used for dry white table wines which possess a rich, full flavour.

Eighty per cent of plantings are in South Australia, notably the Barossa Valley, with most of the balance in Victoria where it is highly regarded at Rutherglen.

In France, it is mostly grown in Bordeaux where it is used in small amounts in association with sauvignon blanc to add 'perfume' to the wines of semillon grown in Sauternes, Barsac and Graves. It is also grown to a limited extent in California under the incorrect name of sauvignon vert.

Muscadelle matures early and is moderately productive of rather large, loose bunches that can attain a high sugar content.

Muscat of Alexandria

See muscat gordo blanco.

Muscat Gordo Blanco

Synonyms: *muscatel, muscat of Alexandria, hanepoot (South Africa)*
Area: *4041 hectares*

Muscat gordo blanco, or simply gordo as it is mostly called here, is Australia's principal wine variety. It is a multi-purpose grape dried for

Muscat gordo blanco.

raisins, sold as a fresh table grape and crushed for wine and unfermented grape juice. In 1987–88, 63 650 tonnes of gordo were used for wine compared with the next most important variety sultana with 53 327 tonnes, and then shiraz with 48 069 tonnes. In the same year, 71 147 tonnes of gordo were dried.

It has a strong muscat flavour and in warm areas the grapes can become very sweet when the acid levels are low. By virtue of its flavour, it is mostly used for blending with wines of more neutral varieties, notably sultana, to make bulk dry white table wines. It is also the principal component of Australian 'cream' sherry to which it imparts its muscat flavour.

Plantings of gordo in Australia are concentrated in the inland irrigation districts of the Riverland, Sunraysia and Murrumbidgee Irrigation Areas.

The vine lacks vigour, but when planted comparatively close together the yields per hectare are quite high. Its bunches are medium-sized, loose and of mid-season maturity. Poor berry setting can be a problem especially for table grapes and it is susceptible to erinose (vine leaf blister mite) and nematodes.

In California, it is occasionally dried, but mostly used for dry and sweet wines. A similar situation applies in South Africa where it is called hanepoot. It is grown in several regions of Spain, being an important component of the sweet Malaga wines. A little is grown in Jerez where, after partial drying, it is used to make sweetening material for Spanish sherries.

Ondenc

Synonyms: *Irvine's white (Victoria), sercial (incorrectly in South Australia)*
Area: *28 hectares*

The correct identity of Irvine's white, grown in the Great Western district of Victoria, was a puzzle for a long time. The name was a local one, having been given for (or by) Hans Irvine, one-time owner of the Great Western Champagne Cellars. However, Paul Truel found that Irvine's white was identical to the South Australian sercial and the correct name of both was ondenc.

Ondenc is grown in France in the departments of Gers (Armagnac) and Gironde (Bordeaux), where it is used for brandy and white table wine. Interestingly enough, until a few years ago it was incorrectly called folle blanche in Armagnac.

Hans Irvine acquired Joseph Best's property at Great Western in 1888 and brought a team of French experts there to develop champagne production. Much of the credit for the finesse and elegance of the early Great Western champagnes was attributed to Irvine's white from which they were made. The small plantings that now remain in Australia are almost equally divided between Victoria and South Australia.

The true sercial is one of the four main grape varieties of the Madeira Islands, a Portuguese territory in the Atlantic Ocean. The famous fortified aperitif/dessert wines of this region carry the name of the variety from which they are made, sercial producing the best of the dry madeiras.

Palomino

Synonyms: *paulo (at Langhorne Creek, South Australia), listan (France), white French (South Africa)*
Area: *Palomino and pedro ximenez—1385 hectares*

For some reason or another, unbeknown to me, the vital statistics of palomino are combined with pedro ximenez. A premium dry sherry grape, 85 per cent of plantings are in South Australia, particularly the Barossa and the Riverland. There are also some plantings in the Murrumbidgee Irrigation Areas, and in the Sunraysia district.

Ondenc grapes.

Overall, the area has halved during the 1980s in keeping with the decline in demand for fortified wine.

Palomino constitutes almost 90 per cent of all grapes grown in the Jerez region of Spain which, under the appellation laws, is responsible for all that country's sherry production. The other varieties of Jerez are mainly pedro ximenez (about 10 per cent of plantings) and a little muscatel (muscat gordo blanco), both of which are used only for sweetening material, being partially dried in the sun on esparto grass mats before crushing.

Palomino is grown commercially in California under the incorrect name of 'golden chasselas'. It also comprises more than 20 per cent of the plantings in South Africa, where it is known as white French.

It is a vigorous, highly productive variety carrying large, loose bunches. The distinguishing features of palomino are its dark-green, deeply lobed leaves which are heavily felted on the undersurfaces. It may be mistaken for doradillo, but matures much earlier and has more red colouration on the leaf stalks and shoot tips.

Palomino is not a suitable grape for table wines.

Palomino grapes.

Pedro Ximenes

Area: *see palomino.*

Pedro ximenes (also spelt ximenez) is a vigorous-growing variety and in good seasons produces extremely heavy crops of large, easily harvested bunches. Yields of 50 tonnes per hectare have been recorded in irrigated districts. However, its berries are highly susceptible to splitting following the incidence of rain when the fruit is approaching maturity. Because of this serious disadvantage, it has been replaced by palomino as the top dry sherry grape in Australia. Nonetheless, the clean, neutral-flavoured wines of pedro ximenes continue to be highly regarded for flor sherry, particularly the delicate fino styles.

The variety has distinctive, shiny, five-lobed leaves which are hairless on both upper and lower surfaces.

Pinot Blanc

Area: *not recorded separately*

The confusion which has surrounded the distinction between pinot blanc and chardonnay in Australia is not surprising as to some extent a similar situation has existed in Europe. In fact the two are quite different, pinot blanc being a colour variant of pinot noir and readily distinguishable from chardonnay by virtue of the naked petiolar sinus of the latter. All commercial plantings in Australia which were previously called white pinot were, in fact, chardonnay.

Alsace is the only region of France where pinot blanc assumes commercial significance. Here the variety is said to produce a rather neutral-flavoured wine of high acid which is excessive in some seasons. For this reason it is normally blended with auxerrois blanc, a low-acid grape which imparts to the resultant wine a full fruit flavour; the blends are invariably labelled 'pinot blanc'.

Pinot blanc is grown to about the same extent in Germany as in Alsace and there are some plantings in northern Italy.

Pinot Chardonnay

See chardonnay.

Pinot Gris

Synonyms: *rulander (Germany), tokay d'Alsace, malvoise (Loire)*
Area: *not recorded separately*

Pedro ximenez grapes.

Pinot gris is not of commercial significance in Australia but interest is occasionally expressed in the variety.

It is another colour variant of pinot noir, having much less red pigment in the skin. It is one of the premium-quality varieties of Alsace and more importantly the Sudbaden region of Germany, particularly the Kaiserstuhl district which is on the other side of the Rhine River to Alsace. It is also grown in northern Italy and can be found in central and south-eastern Europe.

In Europe, it makes impressive deep golden wines that possess a rich fruit flavour. However, it has a low acid content and this could limit its usefulness in Australia.

Rhine Riesling

Synonyms: *riesling (Germany and France and the preferred international name), white riesling (California)*
Area: *3703 hectares*

Whereas Australian winemakers look mostly to chardonnay and semillon for white burgundy style table wines, Rhine riesling is rightly regarded as the premium grape for the fruitier and crisper hock styles. The majority of plantings are located in South Australia (2874 hectares) mainly in the Barossa, Coonawarra–Padthaway and Clare districts.

Rhine riesling, as the name implies, is the premium variety of Germany where it accounts for about a quarter of the total area of wine grapes, ranking second to muller-thurgau. Rhine riesling, nonetheless, assumes pride of place in the quality Rheingau and Mosel regions where its area represents about 70 and 95 per cent of the totals, respectively.

Although traminer is the variety that comes first to mind when thinking of Alsace, the Alsatians regard riesling as their premium wine type and are jealous of its high quality and dryness in relation to the German rieslings, which are often slightly sweet.

Riesling is also grown widely elsewhere in the world including Italy, Switzerland, Austria, Chile, California and South Africa where, in all cases, it is rated amongst the best of the white table wine varieties.

The cool South Australian districts are responsible for the best local riesling wines. Here

the prominent, fruity aroma and flavour of its wines are well balanced by a fresh crispness to their finish, brought about by comparatively high levels of acidity. They are fine, elegant wines when young, but develop an 'oily' consistency and complexity with bottle age that many favour.

A distinguishing feature of Rhine riesling is its red shoots in the spring. It has round, three-lobed leaves which are rough and often puckered on the upper surface. Other distinctive features of the variety are its small, tight cylindrical bunches, short bunch stalks and spotted berries. It is comparatively early in maturity.

Riesling has reasonable vigour but is only moderately productive. The release of a big range of selected clones that have been imported from Europe has helped to correct this disadvantage.

Sauvignon Blanc

Synonyms: *surin (in parts of the Loire), fumé blanc*
Area: *730 hectares*

The popularity of sauvignon blanc in Australia has increased considerably throughout the 1980s and with 20 per cent of plantings being young, non-bearing vines, a continuing expansion in production can be anticipated. Over half the area is in South Australia with the balance more or less evenly divided between Victoria and New South Wales, apart from 50 hectares in Western Australia.

In France, about half of the plantings are located in or near the Bordeaux region. There it is blended with semillon and muscadelle to produce the famous wines of Sauternes, Barsac and Graves. It is also grown extensively in the Loire Valley, where it is responsible for the wines of Pouilly Fumé, Sancerre, Quincy and Reuilly.

In California, it is grown in both cool and warm areas and is highly regarded for its distinctive wines. It is considered to be one of the best quality varieties for the hot San Joaquin Valley.

Sauvignon blanc produces soft wines of pronounced varietal flavour, similar to that of English gooseberries. Recent research in Australia has shown that the intensity of its flavour is closely related to the concentration in the grapes of the compound methoxypyrazine, which increases as the temperature of the region where it is grown decreases. This explains why New

Zealand sauvignon blanc wines possess such a powerful varietal character.

It is a vigorous variety and a good yielder of small compact bunches.

Semillon

Synonyms: *Hunter River riesling (now unacceptable), greengrape (South Africa)*

Area: *2573 hectares*

On an area-planted basis, semillon now ranks third to riesling as a specialist white table wine variety, being surpassed by chardonnay over the last few years. Although represented in most districts, two-thirds are located in New South Wales, being especially prominent in the Murrumbidgee Irrigation Areas and the Hunter Valley. There are also substantial plantings in the Barossa.

It is the second most important white variety in France, mostly planted in the Bordeaux region, where its area surpasses that of all other varieties. In association with sauvignon blanc and muscadelle, it is responsible for the luscious sweet wines of Sauternes and Barsac and the drier whites of Graves. Although the proportion of these varieties is not specified, the wines usually consist of about 85 per cent semillon, 10 to 15 per cent sauvignon blanc, and the balance muscadelle. Traditionally, infection of the fruit with *Botrytis cinera* ('noble rot') is necessary to produce the best of the Bordeaux sweet wines.

It is the leading white variety of Chile and there are large areas in Argentina and also South Africa, where under the name of greengrape it constitutes about 10 per cent of the plantings.

The reputation of Hunter Valley white table wines was established on the semillon variety which now represents 40 per cent of the white grapes grown there, having lost ground to chardonnay (33 per cent), in recent years. Mature Hunter semillons possess a distinctive and readily distinguished regional wine style. The unique flavour of these wines is such that persons unaccustomed to them often need time to acquire a true appreciation of their worth. They contain only moderate amounts of acid, except when the grapes are picked immature, and are consequently soft on the palate. The mild fruit flavour of the grape is supplemented by characters that develop after bottling, providing

a rich complex wine. Because of their softness, Hunter semillons are ready to drink at an early age, but this belies their capacity for comparatively long storage. For best value they should not be consumed before five years, providing the wines are well made. Ten years or more is by no means excessive maturation for a good Hunter semillon.

The variety has also proved extremely valuable for white table wine in the hot inland irrigation districts, which accounts for its popularity in the Murrumbidgee Irrigation Areas.

The most distinguishing features of semillon are the bronze tips and reddish-brown streaks on the actively growing shoot tips in the spring, contrasting with the grass-green tips of crouchen (Clare riesling) with which it is similar in other characteristics. The leaves are mostly five-lobed, sometimes three-lobed, and their upper surface has a distinctive rough texture.

It possesses moderate vigour, is mid-season in maturity and highly productive of medium-sized compact bunches, which have a tendency to break down following wet weather near vintage. It is a difficult variety to harvest by machine and is very susceptible to rootknot nematode.

Sercial

See ondenc.

Sultana

Synonym: *Thompson seedless (California)*

Area: *16 209 hectares*

Sultana is the most commercially important grape variety in Australia and in the world. As with muscat gordo blanco, it is a multi-purpose grape being dried, sold as fresh fruit (very popular with consumers by virtue of its seedlessness), and crushed primarily for table wine but also for distillation. In 1987–88, the quantity of sultana used for wine in Australia was 53 327 tonnes, ranking second only to gordo which it has surpassed on a number of occasions in the past. The total fresh weight production of sultana in 1987–88 was 343 260 tonnes of which 265 603 were dried and 24 330 consigned to local and overseas fresh-fruit markets.

For beverage wines, it has the attribute of comparatively high acid levels; and while it tends to be neutral in flavour, this is not a serious disadvantage for the high-volume sales market for dry white and sparkling wines. Thus there is justification for its nickname of 'Murray Valley pinot'. To provide additional 'fruit' to its wines, it is usually blended with gordo. The variety has distinct advantages to the winemaker for distillation. It is productive and, in contrast to other distillation grapes, matures early. This enables fortifying spirit to be distilled from wine made early in the vintage, thereby avoiding the need to hold large stocks from one year until the next.

With the increasing availability of other white varieties, it is reasonable to assume that its importance as a wine grape will decline. But winemakers have learnt to use it to advantage, and because of the large area planted, big quantities of sultana are bound to be vintaged for a long time.

Nearly all of Australia's plantings are grown in the dry Murray Valley irrigation districts of Sunraysia in Victoria and New South Wales, and the Riverland of South Australia. Successful cultivation is possible only in dry climates due to its susceptibility to downy mildew, oidium, anthracnose (black spot), berry splitting and bunch rot.

Sweetwater

See chasselas.

Sylvaner

Synonym: *silvaner (Germany)*
Area: *131 hectares*
Sylvaner is widely grown throughout Central and Eastern Europe. Until recently it was the leading grape of Germany but has lost this position and now ranks third to muller–thurgau and riesling.

There are numerous small plantings in Australia but the variety has not taken on to any extent because of the indifferent quality of its wines here.

It is a vigorous and productive grape, although in Europe it is generally thought to yield a little less than chasselas and muller–thurgau.

Sylvaner is capable of producing distinctive wines but they are often neutral in flavour and may be rather astringent on the finish. They are well suited for blending with those of more strongly flavoured varieties.

Taminga

Area: *39 hectares*
Taminga is a new Australian variety bred by a CSIRO team at Merbein led by Alan Antcliff. Its parentage is (farana x sultana) x traminer.

Released in the early 1980s, commercial plantings are confined to the Riverland and Sunraysia regions. It is a high-yielding variety of aromatic white grapes, suited to hot climates.

Tokay

See muscadelle.

Traminer

Synonym: *gewurztraminer*
Area: *650 hectares*
Of all white varieties, traminer produces table wines with the most obvious varietal flavour and bouquet. They possess a pronounced spicy, aromatic character that resembles the flavour of litchi fruit. In Australia, it is commonly blended with other varieties and marketed as traminer–riesling.

Most of Australia's traminer is now located in South Australia (312 hectares) where it is represented in most districts. In New South Wales there are 266 hectares, of which more than half is grown in the Hunter Valley, the most of all Australian regions.

Probably the best-known traminer wines are made in Alsace. Because of the wide range of different-flavoured grapes grown there, Alsace is one of the few regions of France where the wines are given a varietal, as distinct from regional, nomenclature. Gewurztraminer and traminer are one and the same variety, the prefix 'gewürz' being the German word for 'spice'. Normally in Alsace the two names are used to denote the strength of character in the particular wine, 'gewurztraminer' being applied to those with the strongest flavour. However, some makers label all the wines gewurztraminer except when the merchant specifically requests traminer.

There is marked clonal variation within the variety in respect to strength of flavour and berry colour, which ranges from a deep pink to white. Only pink clones are being planted now in Alsace as there are no known white clones that produce anything but relatively neutral-flavoured wines. Most pink clones are strongly aromatic, although some of these lack adequate flavour intensity. Also, the pink clones are invariably more vigorous and productive.

Under the name of savignin, traminer is grown in other parts of France to Alsace, notably in the Côtes-du-Jura to the east of Burgundy where it is responsible for the curious *vins jaunes* or yellow wines. These are subject to a flor yeast treatment during the course of their preparation.

Good clones of traminer are moderately vigorous and yield comparatively good crops of small, early-maturing bunches. The variation in berry colour that exists in Europe also applies in Australian plantings.

Trebbiano

Synonyms: *ugni blanc (south of France), St Emilion (Cognac) and the now unacceptable names of white shiraz and white hermitage which were used in Australia in the past*

Area: *1414 hectares*

Most trebbiano is located in New South Wales (913 hectares), followed by South Australia (415 hectares). The majority of the New South Wales plantings are in the Murrumbidgee Irrigation Areas and those of South Australia in the Riverland districts.

The name trebbiano comes from Italy, where it is the leading white wine grape. It is not commonly known that trebbiano, in combination with malvasia bianca, traditionally makes up 25 per cent of the varieties used for the production of the red wines of Chianti; the other varieties are all red grapes, namely sangiovese, canaiolo nero and colorino. The two white varieties are no doubt responsible for lightness in character of this classic regional wine style. Trebbiano is grown elsewhere in Italy and contributes to many of the better-quality dry whites of that country.

Under the name of St Emilion, it is best known throughout the world as the grape of Cognac. In this region, which extends over the departments of Charente and Charente-Maritime, to the north of Bordeaux, around 40 000 hectares of the variety are grown. Emphasising its value as a distillation grape, there are also significant plantings in the Armagnac region in the department of Gers. It is known as ugni blanc in the Provence region of the south of France, where it is frequently blended with clairette for dry white table wines. As with Italy, it is also the most important white wine grape in France with a total area of about 130 000 hectares there.

The versatility of trebbiano overseas is reflected in its use for all classes of white beverage and distillation wine in Australia. It produces rather austere table wines of neutral flavour, but blends well with more fruity types.

Trebbiano is a vigorous, highly productive variety of mid-season maturity, though significantly later than semillon. It is distinguished in the vineyard by its thick large leaves, and long cylindrical bunches which are often forked at their tip. Although its berries resist rain damage, it juices badly when machine-harvested. It is also susceptible to rootknot nematode.

Ugni blanc

See trebbiano.

Verdelho

Synonym: *gouveio (Portugal)*

Area: *111 hectares*

About half the verdelho grown in Australia is located in Western Australia and most of the remainder in the Hunter Valley of New South Wales.

Classically, verdelho is a top-quality white port variety of the Douro Valley of Portugal where it is generally known under the name of gouveio. It is also responsible for one of the four

Verdelho grapes.

types of fortified aperitif/dessert wines of the Madeira Islands.

In Australia, verdelho has proven attributes for blending with the white table wines of semillon and trebbiano, adding richness and fullness to their flavour. Of recent times, there has been renewed interest in verdelho as a straight varietal which is becoming popular with consumers. Occasionally it is used for the production of very attractive fortified wines that are mostly marketed under the name of madeira.

Bud burst, flowering and ripening are early and it is very susceptible to oidium (powdery mildew).

Waltham cross

Synonyms: *rosaki (Middle East), regina (Italy), dattier (France and California)*
Area: *1188 hectares*

Waltham cross is another multi-purpose grape with the utilisation of its production almost equally divided between drying (for raisins), fresh fruit and winemaking. Nearly three-quarters of the planted area is in Sunraysia and the balance in the Riverland. It is sometimes wrongly called malaga or white malaga in South Australia.

It is grown widely throughout the world, including the south of France (where its full title is dattier de beyrouth), the Middle East, South Africa, California and Italy, where it is the principal table variety.

White Frontignan (Frontignac)

See frontignac.

WINE GRAPE PRODUCTION IN AUSTRALIA		
Variety	Average 1985–86 to 1987–88 tonnes	Projected 1991–92 tonnes
Cabernet sauvignon	25 681	30 000
Chardonnay	19 186	47 100
Chenin blanc	5 910	10 200
Colombard	10 590	24 400
Crouchen	9 298	7 000
Doradillo	27 067	22 500
Grenache	32 756	28 500
Mataro	9 990	9 100
Muscadelle	4 095	4 400
Muscat blanc	5 365	5 900
Muscat gordo blanco*	83 858	88 600
Muscat hamburgh	1 584	1 400
Palomino	26 315	20 600
Pinot noir	3 343	7 100
Rhine riesling	41 110	52 000
Sauvignon blanc	4 038	7 100
Semillon	37 928	40 000
Shiraz	51 453	49 300
Sultana*	337 198	345 400
Traminer	7 308	10 500
Trebbiano	26 884	28 600
Verdelho	667	1 000
Waltham cross*	15 219	13 500
Total	786 862	854 500

* Multi-purpose grapes — quantity used for winemaking (average 1985–86 to 1987–88):
Muscat Gordo Blanco   72 070
Sultana   48 311
Waltham cross   3 647

Excludes Tasmania and Queensland

Source: Australian Bureau of Agricultural & Resource Economics—Supply Projections for Wine Grapes, May 1989.

GLOSSARY

acetaldehyde (CH$_3$CHO) An aldehyde produced by the reduction or oxidation of ethyl alcohol. This compound constitutes much of the flavour of sherry.

acetic When a wine has an excess of flavours produced by bacteria having converted ethyl alcohol into acetic acid, it is said to be acetic.

acetic acid (CH$_3$COOH) The principal volatile acid, and the acid of vinegar. Tolerated quantities in wine 0.5–1.2 grams per litre.

acetic bacteria The organisms in wine which, under suitable conditions, convert ethyl alcohol into acetic acid.

acid (i) Notable presence of acid in a wine style, particularly when young. (ii) Unbalanced because of an excess of acid.

acidity Usually expressing the total acid content of a wine.

aerobic Needing air to live; thus will not become marred by the presence of acetic acid unless air is allowed access.

aftertaste The character that sometimes lingers in the throat and back nasal passages after a wine has been drunk. Can be both pleasant or unpleasant giving an indication of quality and condition.

aggressive (i) A very young wine, particularly red, high in acid and/or tannin. (ii) An excess of a wine component dominating all others (e.g. aggressive oak). Not pleasant.

agrafe—agraffe clip 'U'-shaped clip involved in the making of champagne and champagne-style wines for securing the tirage cork during second fermentation.

agreeable A wine without fault, but lacking greatness; nondescript.

alcohol Usually indicating the ethyl alcohol resulting from fermentation.

alcoholic High in alcohol.

aldehydes Volatile fluids produced by the oxidation of alcohol. These form a large group of compounds, intermediate between acids and alcohols.

alkaline Opposite of acid.

altar wine Wine used for sacramental purposes. As such it must be pure and natural without any additives.

amontillado Spanish. A wood-matured fino sherry.

amoroso (i) A very old wood-matured sweet sherry, older than amontillado, younger than oloroso. (ii) Sweetened oloroso sherry.

ampelography The science of classifying vine varieties.

aperitif French term for appetiser. Taken before meals to stimulate the palate.

appellation d'origine System of guaranteeing the authenticity of a French wine to its region, by the French government. The strong ruling of the Institut National des Appellations d'Origine are valid only within France itself.

appellation d'origine contrôlée Literally 'controlled place of origin'. A term appearing on French wine labels, guaranteeing not only the authenticity of the place from where the wine came, but also that the wine is indicative of the quality standards of that area.

Armagnac A brandy made in the Armagnac region in the south-west of France.

aroma The scent of a grape variety in a young wine. With age, aroma decreases.

aromatic (i) Strong in varietal, odiferous substances. (ii) Characteristic of the variety.

arrest fermentation The addition of spirit to fermenting must to kill yeasts before complete conversion of grape sugar to alcohol has taken place. The resulting wines are sweet.

ascorbic acid (C$_6$H$_8$O$_6$) Vitamin C. Used as a wine antioxidant.

assertive Possessing one particularly striking quality which appears immediately, such as taste or smell resulting from the grape, soil etc.

Asti Town in the north of Italy whose vineyards are famous for producing a sweet sparkling wine (spumante).

astringent (i) Tannins derived from grape pips and wood. (ii) An excess of tannins in a wine; the quality of causing the mouth to pucker.

attractive Pleasant to drink.

auslese German term referring to the individual selection of bunches of white grapes due to their degree of ripeness. The resulting wines are comparatively sweet.

austere Strong in character, though showing no excesses.

baked Hot, almost sweaty smell which comes from overripening of grapes.

balance Wine characters and flavours in a complete harmony. No dominance of any one character.

barriquant An old French expression for a small wine cask.

barrique A french cask or hogshead, particularly the Barrique Bordelaise, holding approximately 225 litres of wine.

baumé Measurement of grape sugar. One degree baumé (1°), is equal to 1.8 per cent of sugar.

Beaujolais A wine-producing region of southern Burgundy, France. The majority of red wines produced there are noted for their appealing quality of being suitable to drink when very young—within their first year.

beerenauslese German. Referring to the selection of individual overripe grapes for the production of very sweet white wines that rank amongst the greatest wines in the world.

beeswing A fine sheet crust appearing in an old bottle of port wine.

bentonite A colloidal clay used in the fining of red wines for the removal of unstable protein.

bentonite slugging (i) A red wine overfined with bentonite. (ii) A young red wine recently fined with bentonite, not showing the amount of grape fruit expected. The wine may appear dumb, flat.

bianco Italian term for white wine. Indicates a semi-sweet style of Vermouth.

big Indicating a wine full of flavour and high in alcohol and tannin.

bilginess Off-flavours and odours derived from slime bacteria in water-logged casks.

bin A container, space or area in which bottles of the one wine are kept for maturation.

bin—private Traditionally a personal reserve of wine for the consumption of the winemaker or heads of a wine company; not available to the public. The term has now lost all meaning, save to distinguish one class of wine from another within those produced by one company.

binning Cellar term for the storing of wine in bottles for maturation.

bite Indicating a considerable degree of acid and tannin. Generally a good element in a young wine that mellows with age.

bitter Wine fault detectable at the back of the palate. Usually an aftertaste.

blackcurrants Referring to fruit-smell. Detectable mainly in cabernet sauvignon grapes.

blanc French term for white wine.

bland Characterless but not necessarily unpleasant.

blended wine (i) The mixing of two or more wines to maintain a standard or increase quality. (ii) Lack of integrity on the part of many winemakers, accounting for the high output of premium wine-producing areas.

bodega (i) Spanish equivalent of the French 'château'. (ii) A large Spanish ground-level cellar.

body The degree of bigness or weight of a wine in the mouth.

Bordeaux One of the most celebrated wine-producing regions of the world. It is situated in the south-west of France, and produces red, white and rosé wines.

botrytis (Botrytis cinerea) (i) A parasitic fungus or mould that attacks grapes in certain climatic conditions, causing evaporation of moisture and condensation of sugar. When controlled, the fungus is responsible for producing the greatest sweet white wines of the world. (ii) A flavour imparted by the above-mentioned mould.

bottle age To an experienced taster, bottle age is easily recognisable in the bouquet. Bottle age gives a vital indication of a wine's maturity and development in the bottle.

Generally a red wine with bottle age becomes soft and mellow; a white wine mellows and develops a honeyed quality.

bottle sickness Off-flavours that may be present in a wine after bottling.

bottle stink (i) Presence of odours obtained during bottling that leave a wine upon breathing. (ii) Hydrogen sulphate (H_2S).

bouquet Scents produced by maturation.

breathing Allowing a wine to come in contact with air by drawing the cork prior to serving. Normally carried out with red wines to allow the development of the bouquet.

breed Impeccable flavour of a wine from a great vineyard or area.

bright Perfectly clear.

Brix degrees Degrees indicating the approximate sugar content of wine; converts to 1° of proof spirit per degree Brix through fermentation.

broad Throughout bouquet, taste and aftertaste, the wine has a certain spread-out style.

brut Term originally used to describe entirely unsweetened champagne. It now denotes the driest champagnes and champagne-style wines, which generally contain some degree of liqueuring.

bung The stopper in a wine cask.

Burgundy (i) One of the most famous wine-producing areas in the world, located in eastern France. (ii) Outside France, the name of a style of wine considered similar to that of Burgundy.

buttery Description of smell and taste.

cabernet (i) The name of grape varieties responsible for many of the finest wines in the world (e.g. cabernet sauvignon, cabernet franc, cabernet gris). (ii) An abbreviation for cabernet sauvignon (Australia).

cabinet wine German wine term (Kabinett) applied to high-quality wines. Originally the special reserve of the vineyard owner.

cake Pressed grape skins and pips after removal from the fermenting tank after fermentation.

carbonated wines (i) Unfortified wines made sparkling by the direct injection of carbon dioxide gas. (ii) Lowest wine on the theoretical quality list of sparkling wine.

carbon dioxide (CO_2) The gas released during fermentation, and that present in sparkling wine styles.

cask A wooden barrel usually bound with iron hoops, used for storing wine. No set volume.

casse The presence of clouding or precipitation in a wine, resulting in off-flavours.

cave French term for cellar.

cellar (i) Area attached to a winery where wine is made, stored and/or bottled. (ii) Area for storing wine (domestic).

cépage French term for grape variety (e.g. the cépage cabernet).

cedarwood A characteristic of bouquet found in many clarets.

Chablis (i) Outstanding white wine-producing area of northern Burgundy in France. (ii) Outside France, the name of a style of wine considered similar to the wines of Chablis.

chambrer French. To place a wine in a room so that the wine takes on the temperature of the room. Usually done with red wines and normally there is an increase in the temperature of the wine.

Champagne (i) Name of a wine-producing area of north-eastern France, famed principally for its production of finest quality white sparkling wines. (ii) Outside France, the name applied to many sparkling white wines sold domestically.

chaptalisation The addition of sugar to the must in order to build up alcohol after fermentation.

character A wine possessing a combination of distinctive and unmistakable qualities.

characteristics Indicating the distinctive style and character of a particular grape, district, vintage.

Charmat, Eugene French scientist responsible for developing an inexpensive process for the making of sparkling wine.

Charmat process Basically, the making of white wines in bulk in sealed tanks to retain CO_2 gas given off during fermentation. The sparkling wines produced by this method are rated above carbonated wines but much below those produced by the *méthode champenoise*.

chateau bottling In France, particularly the Bordeaux region, a guarantee suggesting that the wine is untampered with and authentic, because it has been bottled at the chateau where it was made.

Chianti Wine-producing region of central Italy.

citric acid ($C_6H_8O_7$) Used in winemaking to increase total acidity.

claret (i) English term for the wines of Bordeaux. (ii) General term for red wines supposedly bearing a resemblance to the wines of Bordeaux.

classic Of the highest quality.

clean No outside wine flavours present.

climat Term used in Burgundy, France, equivalent to the 'cru' of Bordeaux.

cloudy Matter in suspension, obscuring the colour.

cloying An oversweetness in relation to the degree of acid in a wine.

coarse Unclean finish; lacking in finesse.

Cognac Grapegrowing region of western France, famed for the high-quality brandies it produces.

collage Fining process to which wine must be subjected before bottling.

colour extraction The gaining of colour by fermenting must with the skins.

common Nondescript; ordinary.

commune In France, a wine-producing township or parish.

complete A wine in which all flavours and components are harmonious and balanced.

complex Many faceted smell and taste: usually the sign of development in a fine wine.

concentrated must High baumé grape juice racked straight off the skins, boiled down, or concentrated. Useful as a sweetening material.

condition The clarity and soundness of a wine.

continuous press A horizontal grape press, somewhat like a conventional meat mincer. The grapes are fed in one end, the liquid is pressed out, and they are ejected as a hard, almost dry core. No wine of any real quality is made in this fashion.

controlled fermentation Fermentation so regulated, generally through refrigeration, to slow down or speed up the process as required. Used widely for making clean, crisp white wines in Australia.

cooked A heavy or baked character indicating the use of heat—either natural or assisted—to speed up the development of fortified wines in particular.

cooper Craftsman who makes wine casks.

cooperage General term for the manufacture or repair of wine casks.

corked Wine tainted by an off-flavour derived from a faulty cork.

côte French term for a vineyard slope.

cracked Odours and flavours produced in a wine by chemical decomposition.

cream sherry (i) Very sweet sherry, normally achieved by the addition of concentrate. (ii) A trade name for sweet sherry, often one containing some muscat variety.

crisp A fresh, firm wine with positive acidity; an attractive quality in white wines.

cru French term denoting a vineyard of high quality.

crusher Machine used for the extraction of juice from grapes prior to fermentation.

crust Mostly organic matter precipitated in a young wine.

cuve French term for a wine vat.

cuvée French term for the contents of a cuve, both in the cask and in the bottle.

decant *Domestic* (i) The pouring of a wine from the bottle to another vessel to aid presentation. (ii) The careful pouring of a wine from the bottle to another vessel for the removal of crust or deposits that may be present. *Cellar* (i) The pouring of wines from one bottle to another to hasten maturation by exposure to air (oxygen). (ii) The pouring of wines of the same type into a larger bottle.

deep An aroma revealing many different qualities.

delicate Of good quality. Though light in flavour, without fault. (Normally whites.)

demijohn Large wine receptacle of 5–45 litres capacity.

demi-sec French term for 'half-dry' wines. Normally used for sparkling wines to indicate that a wine is semi-sweet.

depth A wine with many interlocking flavours—rich and subtle.

dessert wine Wine suitable to be drunk with or after dessert (e.g. sauternes, port, champagne, madeira).

developed Showing maturation.

distillation The art of obtaining spirit by vaporisation.

distinguished Obvious and outstanding character and breed.

domaine French term for a wine estate.

domestic Wine term for an everyday drinking wine.

dosage French term for sugar solution added to sparkling wines before bottling; the expedition liqueur.

downy mildew A vine fungus.

dry Showing no sugar: without sweetness.

dull Uninteresting, insipid.

dumb Grape fruit showing no development.

earthy (i) Bouquet and flavour reminiscent of certain soil types. (ii) Contamination with soil due to poor winemaking, or by the by-products of soil fungi.

elegant Of high quality, with finesse.

essence Strong, complex varietal character.

estate Corresponding to the French 'château' (e.g. Wynn's Coonawarra Estate).

esters Organic compounds corresponding to the salts of inorganic chemistry. They have a sweet, fruity smell.

estery Strong scents derived from bottle maturation relating to esters.

ethyl alcohol (C$_2$H$_5$OH) The alcohol produced by fermentation.

expedition cork This is the cork used for the production of champagne and champagne-style wines after disgorging.

expedition liqueur The liqueur added to champagne and champagne-style wine to replace the wine lost from disgorging.

extra sec French for extra dry. Normally used on sparkling wines to denote lack of sweetness.

extract Soluble solids adding to a wine's body and substance.

fading (i) An old wine past its peak, losing its flavour and character. (ii) A wine left standing in the glass, having lost flavour and bouquet by breathing.

fat (i) A big soft wine, usually high in glycerine. (ii) Wine fault; overdeveloped flavour at the back of the palate.

fermentation Usually indicating the change from must to wine; i.e. alcoholic fermentation in which yeast converts sugar into alcohol and by-products.

fermentation tank Vessel in which fermentation takes place.

ferruginous (i) Tasting of iron. (ii) Iron flavours derived from soil type.

filter pad (i) Asbestos sheet used for filtration. (ii) Off-flavour derived from asbestos gained from filtration.

filtration The removal of solids from a wine before bottling.

fine (i) Delicate, distinguished. (ii) Of high quality.

fine champagne (syn. Grand Champagne). The finest cognacs (not the sparkling wine—champagne) blended from the subdistricts of Grande and Petite Champagne in Cognac.

finesse Term denoting high quality and breed.

fining Method of clarifying young wines before bottling.

finish (i) The flavour remaining at the back of the palate after a wine has been swallowed. (ii) The end of the wine in the mouth.

fino The driest sherry style.

firm Finish at the back of the palate; an aftertaste related to tannin.

flabby (i) When a wine finishes (back of the palate) with an overdeveloped fruit flavour. (ii) A broad soft middle palate with no depth or body.

flagon A 2 litre bottle of wine. Outside Australia the expression refers to a vessel for serving wine; it has a narrow neck, a handle and a spout.

flat (i) Sparkling wine that has lost its gas. (ii) Loss of freshness, character and/or flavour.

fleshy Fresh, youthful, full-bodied varietal flavour.

flinty Indicates a trace of gun-flint in the bouquet and flavour of certain white wine grapes grown on certain soils, e.g. chablis.

flor A unique yeast which grows on the surface of certain wines, mainly sherry, which imparts its own particular flavour.

flor fino (i) A fino sherry upon which the flor yeast has been allowed to grow. (ii) A very delicate form of sherry.

flowery The pleasant aromatic quality normally present in white wines.

fortified Wines to which spirit has been added.

foxy Sweetness scent and flavour of wines produced from *Vitis labrusca*.

fragrance An attractive, crisp, slightly scented smell found in many young wines, especially many fine white wines.

frappé French term for serving temperature—'chilled'.

free-run Wine that runs freely from the grape skins after fermentation. Often it is bottled separately from the 'pressings' that follow.

fresh (i) An appealing quality of a young wine showing no off-flavours; high in acid. (ii) An unexpected character that may be present in an old wine.

fruity Fleshy quality of a young wine with strong varietal character.

fuder German term for a wine cask holding 1000 litres.

full (i) Wine at optimum maturity. (ii) High degree of body.

fût French term for a particular wine barrel.

gelatine A fining agent.

generous Full of flavour; strong in character.

glucose (C$_6$H$_{12}$O$_6$) Grape sugar.

glycerol (CH$_2$OH.CHOH.CH$_2$OH) A by-product of fermentation. Sweet, viscous.

goût de terroir French tasting term used in reference to flavours present in some wines (notably red) imparted by the soil.

Grand Champagne (syn. fine champagne). An expression appearing on a Cognac label, denoting the finest district of Cognac and therefore the finest brandies.

grand cru French term for an exceptional vineyard or site.

grand cru classé A classification of the best wines of the Bordeaux region of France.

grape The fruit of the vine.

grapy Showing fresh varietal character.

Graves (i) A subregion of Bordeaux, France, noted for its red and white wines. (ii) The name applies to white wines considered similar to those of Graves in France. Two general styles can be found: dry graves and sweet graves.

green (i) Presence of malic acid. (ii) Not yet ready for drinking.

gunflint A wine flavour from chalky subsoils; found in white wines. True French chablis is often referred to by this term.

guyot A method of training vines.

hard (i) Strong tannin in a young wine, lacking a soft finish. (ii) Tannin detectable at the back of the palate, derived from poor-quality oak.

harsh Presence of an undesirable character, attributed to wood tannin.

head and shoulders An expression used to describe wines (usually white) that have fine varietal aromatic characters on the nose and beginning of the palate, but which lack body and intensity of flavour on the middle palate.

Hermitage (i) Important area of the Rhône Valley in France, producing both red and white wines. (ii) Syn. shiraz, a red grape planted extensively in Australian vineyards.

hock (i) British name for wines from the Rheingau region of Germany. It is derived from the Rheingau town of Hochheim. (ii) General term for wines of the Rhine type, particularly those made from riesling.

hogshead A cask of varying capacity (usually 300 litres), used for storing wine.

hollow A wine with a foretaste and finish but failing on the middle palate.

honeyed A characteristic fragrance of certain mature wines, indicating bottle age, e.g. sauternes.

hybrid Cross between an American and a European vine variety by cross-pollination as opposed to grafting.

hydraulic press A vertical press used for pressing the skins and seeds after fermentation.

imperial A large wine bottle of the capacity of eight normal 750 mL bottles, used in the Bordeaux district of France.

incrustation The formation of a crust in wines, specifically vintage port.

jammy Off-flavours resulting from heavy pressing of hot-picked fruit. Found mainly in red wines.

Jeres de la Frontera Town in Spain which is the centre of the 'true' sherry trade.

jeroboam A large wine bottle. When used in reference to champagne, the capacity is four standard bottles; in Bordeaux, five.

keg Small wine cask, usually of less than 45 litres capacity.

labrusca (Vitis labrusca) A species of grapevine found in northern America.

lactic acid Acid resulting from malolactic fermentation.

late picked Grapes left on the vine longer than usual to increase sugar level and lower acidity. Process used in the production of sweet white styles and fortified wines.

LBV (Late Bottled Vintage) A term adopted from overseas usage to denote a young port style, made in the vintage port manner but which is bottled with a little more wood age and meant for immediate drinking.

lees Deposits (residue) in cask or bottle.

legs The viscosity from alcohol (and a little glycerine) as seen on the inside of a glass of wine.

liebfraumilch (i) By German law, a term applied to certain wines of Rheinhessen. (ii) General term implying a hock style of wine to which sugar has been added.

light Lacking body, pale in colour; but well balanced.

limpidity The state of clarity and cleanness of a wine.

lively Refers to a fresh, young wine or an old wine with youthful characteristics.

long Great wine; staying power of flavours on the palate after the wine has been swallowed.

luscious A wine with soft, sweet, fruity and ripe qualities in balance.

maché French term used to describe a tired wine, i.e. one lacking in flavour due to travelling; 'bottle sickness'.

Madeira (i) Island off the coast of Spain famous for its fortified dessert wines. (ii) General term for wines resem-

bling those produced on the above-mentioned island.

maderisation The oxidation of alcohol to acetaldehyde.

maderised An oxidised white wine showing the presence of acetaldehyde. The flavour is reminiscent of madeira wine.

maitre de chai French term, literally 'master of the cellar', i.e. the head cellarman.

malic acid (COOH.CH$_2$.CH[OH].COOH) The acid of fresh grapes, particularly when unripe.

malolactic fermentation The decomposition of malic acid by bacteria to lactic acid and carbon dioxide.

marc (i) The residue of grape skins and seeds after the juice has been extracted. (ii) A brandy spirit made from distilling the marc.

Marsala (i) Town in north-west Sicily, producing the principal fortified dessert wine of Italy. (ii) General term for wines resembling those produced at the above-mentioned town.

matty A strange phrase I use meaning coarse and thick-grained on the back of the tongue.

mawkish Flat, flabby, slightly bilgey.

meaty A rich, heavy wine.

mellow A characteristic normally associated with maturity and age where the wine has acquired a particularly attractive softness.

mercaptan An organic chemical formed in wine as a derivative of hydrogen sulphide. The latter is produced by yeast and combines with other natural ingredients of wine to produce a range of smelly compounds which have odours reminiscent of onion, garlic, burnt rubber, skunk, stale cabbage and asparagus.

metallic (i) Exhibiting a flavour of a metal. (ii) Contamination by metals with which a wine may have come in contact.

méthode champenoise A French term often used to describe traditional champagne-making; i.e. second fermentation taking place in the bottle.

methuselah, methusalem Giant bottle with the capacity of eight bottles, used for champagne and champagne-style wines.

mildew An abbreviation for downy mildew.

mis en bouteille au château French. Literally, 'put into the bottle at the château'.

mis en bouteille au domaine French. Literally 'put into the bottle at the domaine'; the Burgundian equivalent of chateau-bottled.

mistelle The fortification of high baumé grapes to retain natural sugar and grape juice. Used as a sweetening agent for vermouth.

moelleux French term for soft, sweet, fruity wines, particularly sauternes.

Mosel (i) The famous German river, an area noted for its premium-quality white wines. (ii) Generally (outside Germany), a sweet white wine style. The sweetness can either be gained by late picking or adding sugar after fermentation.

Moselle (i) The river in France. (ii) An Australian fruity wine style, generally containing some sweetness.

mouldy Off-flavours, derived from bacterial infection of grapes or cask, which have been retained by a wine.

mousseux French sparkling wines made outside the Champagne region.

mousy A flat yet acetic smell and taste which is a sign of bacteriological disease.

mouth-filling Quality of the wine, the flavour of which excites all our olfactory receptors.

mulled wine Wine to which sweetening and spices have been added. This wine is served hot.

muscat A sweet grape; many different varieties.

mushroomy A smell of mushrooms often associated with sparkling wines.

musky Spicy.

must The mixture of grape juice, skins and seeds before fermentation. During this process it is termed as fermenting must.

musty Having a smell of old cupboards.

nebuchadnezzar An oversized champagne bottle holding the equivalent of twenty normal bottles.

negative Lacking character, without flavour or scent.

neutral Without definitive flavours or characters.

noble Of high breed.

noble rot see **botrytis**.

nomenclature The way in which a wine is named; e.g. hock, riesling, cabernet.

nondescript Lacking character, ordinary.

nose The scents and odours of a wine.

nuance Having aspects comparable to specific smells, e.g. blackcurrants, almonds.

nutty Characteristic pungent flavour of sherry.

oak chips Off-cuts of oak used to give a wine an 'oak' flavour and scent. The flavour at the back of the palate will be notably bitter.

oak essence Oak extracts used to give a wine an oak flavour and scent.

oak shavings As for oak chips, except the wood takes the form of shavings and oak dust.

obvious (i) Strong in character; lacking complexity. (ii) Of highest quality.

odour Off-smells present in a wine.

oenology The science of wine.

oidium (Oidium tuckeri) A vine mildew commonly known as powdery mildew.

oily Oils derived from grape pips or stalks present in wine. Result of poor winemaking.

olfactory The sense of smell.

oloroso An old wood-matured fino sherry.

Oporto Centre of the Portuguese 'port' trade. Port gets its name from the abbreviation of the name of this town.

organoleptic An analytical test, by use of the senses, of food and wine.

ouillage The topping up of casks that have become ullaged due to evaporation.

over the hill Wine past its best, overmatured.

overtones Secondary flavours and scents individually detectable.

oxidase Enzyme introducing oxidation.

oxidation Chemical decomposition of a wine because of the presence of oxygen.

oxidised The dominance of flavours produced by oxidation.

palate The area inside the mouth consisting of a number of taste-sensitive areas which combine to give an overall flavour impression; the character of wine in the mouth.

pasteurisation Sterilisation by heat at less than 100°C.

peardrops Associated with acetone characters in wine.

penetrating A powerful wine, high in alcohol and volatile esters.

peppery A raw harsh quality caused by immature and unsettled components which have not had time to marry, but a characteristic often found in young red wines and young ports of peppery overtones.

perfumed Powerful scents produced by maturation.

pétillant French for moderately carbonated wine.

Petite Champagne (syn. fine champagne) A subregion of the Cognac district of France, noted for its high-quality brandies.

phylloxera (Phylloxera vastatrix) The 'vine louse', a root-eating insect (on non-resistant rootstocks) which eventually kills the vine.

pinot Family of grapevines responsible for some of the greatest wines of the world.

pipe A large cask of tapered ends used primarily for Portuguese port wines. Contents, 520 litres.

piquant An agreeably fresh, tart taste due to acidity.

port (i) Portuguese fortified wine. There are two main styles: vintage port and tawny port. (ii) General style of fortified wines imitating those of Portugal.

porty Red wine showing flavours and character similar to port wine.

pot still The old and simplest form of still, employed for making the finest brandies.

pourriture noble (syn. noble). (*See also* **noble rot**.)

powdery mildew (syn. oidium). (*See also* **oidium**.)

powerful Used to describe a big red wine.

precipitation White crystals of excessive amounts of calcium tartrate or potassium bitartrate that may 'precipitate' in unstabilised white wines and some red wines.

pressings Wine gained from pressing the skins and pips after fermentation. It is higher in tannin and acid than the wine fermented from the must, but lacks the flavour and character of the latter. Often the pressings are put back into wine to build up deficiencies of tannin and/or acid.

pricked Wine smelling of ethyl acetate nearing volatility.

puncheon A large wine cask of varying capacity.

pungent Very aromatic, often 'earthy'.

punt Indentation (for strength) at the base of champagne bottles and various European wine bottles. Originally the punt was formed when bottles were hand-blown, to give them a flat base.

pupitre French. A hinged rack for holding sparkling wines by the neck prior to dégorgement.

quinta Portuguese term for vineyard.

race French quality term describing distinction and breeding in a wine.

racking The drawing of clear wine off its lees.

rancio (i) An oxidised flavour found in old sweet whites. (ii) The developed wood character of an old dessert wine.

refreshing Pleasant acidity.

rehoboam Large champagne bottle, equivalent to six normal bottles.

residual sugar Sugar remaining after fermentation has been completed.

resinous Resulting from the addition of resin.

rich Obvious, i.e. rich in flavour, rich in fruit.

riesling (i) Syn. Rhine riesling. (ii) Crisp, acid white wine style.

rioja Most important table wine-producing area of Spain.

robust Rich, full; strong in alcohol.

rootstock The type of vine root on to which the grapevine is grafted. Selection of the rootstock is dependent upon its performance in relation to the topography.

rosado Spanish term for rosé.

rosata Italian term for rosé.

rosé A very light red wine.

rouge A French term for red wine.

rough An unpleasant red wine, usually so because of an excess of tannin.

round Well-balanced and mature.

rubbery A disagreeable quality, most likely a consequence of the presence of mercaptan. Frequently found in old white wines.

ruby port Blended port wine, generally speaking a young sweet wine in its early stages, i.e. the colour has not become 'tawny' through age.

sappy A term used to describe a quality of inherent life that will develop a fine young wine.

Sauternes (i) French subregion of Bordeaux, famed for its sweet white wines. (ii) Sweet white wines, imitations of the above-mentioned region. Far too often they are nothing more than sweetened whites.

scented A wine having a very high-toned, obvious aroma that can be associated with a flower, fruit, etc.

sec French for 'dry'. Normally used in reference to champagne.

secco Italian term for dry wine.

sediment Deposits appearing in wines (mainly red) due to ageing.

sekt German white wine.

sensuous Rich, soft texture and flavour.

sherry English term for the fortified wines of Jerez in Spain. Australia has had considerable success at imitating the various styles of sherry.

Shiraz (i) A city in south-west Iran near the Persian Gulf, which gave its name to the best known Persian wines. (ii) One of Australia's foremost red wine grapes.

show awards There are two systems of judging wines used in Australia, the conventional (long used in this country) and the international. The same points system is used for both, the difference being that in the international system the wines are judged one at a time, whereas in our conventional system the total number of wines in a class is lined up at the same time. The latter is still by far the major system used.

Points are awarded out of a total of twenty: 3 points maximum for colour and condition, 7 points maximum for nose, and 10 points maximum for palate. The 'nose' includes both aroma and bouquet; and the 'palate' includes body, depth, flavour, balance, finish. To win a gold medal a wine must score 18½ points or more; a silver, 17–18 points; a bronze, 15½–16½ points. Therefore a wine can lose only 1½ points to win a gold medal, a typical gold score being 3/3, 6½/7, 9/10. Generally speaking, to win a bronze a wine must be free from fault, having good fruit character and be true to the style of the class. To compete for the higher ranks it must have more style, finesse, depth of flavour, complexity, etc.

The major wine shows are judged by three panels of three, with any number of associate judges (in Adelaide there are also nine associates). A chairman of judges organises the judging and settles disputes or style discussions. All judges and associates act on an honorary basis, some giving a great deal of their time so that both the industry and wine-lovers may benefit.

There are an increasing number of regional shows being initiated and developed, which, as well as some long-established ones, must encourage small makers. There are also small makers' classes at major shows. However, it is often forgotten that the idea behind the large-quantity classes (those for which up to several thousand dozen bottles must be available of the wine entered) is to enable the wine-buying public to have a reasonable chance of obtaining some of the winning wine when it becomes available.

simple Obvious, straightforward and not complex.

smooth A soft, silky wine with no rough edges.

soft A term applied normally to red wines with a pleasing finish that is not hard or aggressive. Often a product of maturation.

solera Method of producing certain fortified wines, particularly sherry, by rotation of casks.

sound Without fault.

sour Wine spoiled by sourness on back of palate.

sparkling A wine made effervescent by the inducement of carbon dioxide.

spätlese German term for the late picking of white grapes to increase their sugar level and therefore reduce water content.

spicy Herbaceous aroma and flavour characteristic of certain grape varieties, e.g. traminer.

spirity The obvious presence of alcohol.

spritzig German; presence of carbon dioxide gas.

spumante Italian term for sweet sparkling wine.

stabilisation The chilling of a white wine to near freezing point to precipitate tartaric crystals.

stalky Oily character derived from grape stalks. Mainly red wines; indicative of poor winemaking.

stewed A rather sweaty nose, i.e. stewed plums.

still (i) Non-sparkling wine styles. (ii) Sparkling wine that has lost its gas.

strong A big, full wine, high in alcohol content.

stuck fermentation Natural fermentation not completed because of the killing-off of active yeasts due to an excessive rise in temperature.

sturdy A wine of considerable size and quality.

subtle Characteristics are not immediately obvious or detectable, often through being delicate or refined.

sugary A wine high in sugar content, such as a sauternes and/or one with a sweet aroma.

sulphur dioxide (So$_2$) Agent used for sterilisation and as an antioxidant.

sulphurous Wine showing the presence of sulphur.

supple Amiable, mouth-filling, very pleasant drinking.

sweet The obvious presence of residual sugar in a wine.

syrupy Usually used in reference to a rich sauternes, thick and sweet.

tang—tangy A rich, sharp, zestful wine.

tannin Natural ingredient of wine derived mainly from grape pips and stalks.

tart Possessing agreeable acidity (malic) to a marked degree.

tartaric acid (COOH.[CO.OH]$_2$.COOH) The principal acid of wine.

tartrates Potassium and calcium salts of tartaric acid, which often crystallise.

tastevin French term for a small silver wine cup used for tasting wine, principally in Burgundy.

tawny (i) The colour of an old red wine. (ii) Style of port matured in the cask.

thin Unbalanced; fruit too light to match tannin and acid.

three star A quality grading of the brandies of Cognac and Armagnac.

threshold The point at which a given taste or smell can be recognised. This level varies from substance to substance, person to person.

tirage cork This is the cork used in the making of champagne and champagne-style wines, when the wine is first bottled.

tirage liqueur Sugar solution added to the base wine in the production of champagne and champagne-style wine. During the second fermentation in the bottle, it will be converted to alcohol and carbon dioxide gas, the latter giving the required pressure after bottle fermentation.

tonneau French. (i) A large wine barrel. (ii) Standard wine measure in Bordeaux of approximately 900 litres.

trockenbeernauslese German term for the very late picking of white wine grapes. The wines are extremely sweet, rivalled only by sauternes as the greatest dessert wines.

ullage The air space present in a bottle of wine, between the cork and surface of the wine; also the air space in the top of a cask of wine.

unbalanced Not balanced. (*See also* **balance**.)

unripe Wine made from grapes picked before they have reached a total sugar/acid balance.

vanillan A wine with a richly developed fruit flavour similar to that of vanilla.

varietal Character of wine derived from the grape.

vat A container in which wine is fermented.

velvety Soft in texture, mellow.

vermouth Basic white wine to which many flavour components are added. Not considered a wine style.

vigneron French term for winemaker.

vignoble French term for vineyard.

vigorous (i) Healthy vines. (ii) A youthful wine requiring maturation.

vin French term for wine.

vinegar Often suggests bacteriological infection, the smell of ethylacetate being present; unpleasant to drink.

vinegary The character of volatile acidity, usually of ethylacetate.

vinicide A dinner table term for a great wine drunk before its time.

vinification The art and science of making wine.

vinosity A tasting term related to the alcoholic strength, and particularly to the grape character.

vinous Reminiscent of wine.

vintage The gathering of the grapes.

vintage port The richest and 'fullest' bodied of the port styles. It is bottled traditionally after spending up to two years in oak casks, after which it matures for many years, like a red wine.

vintage wines Wines made in a specific year, indicated on the label.

viscous Wine showing the presence of glycerol.

viticulture The art and science of winemaking.

Vitis vinifera The species of vine responsible for most of the world's quality wine.

volatile Wine spoiled by acetic acid.

volatile acid (syn. acetic acid). (*See also* **acetic acid**.)

volatile acids Fatty acids of which the main one is acetic acid. Others include carbonic acid, butyric acid (C$_3$H$_7$COOH), propionic acid (C$_2$H$_5$COOH) and formic acid (HCOOH).

volatility The degree of evaporation of esters as detected by the olfactory sense.

VSO Grade of Cognac; Very Special, Old.

VSOP Very Superior Old Pale. Used for both Cognac and Armagnac brandies. The term is being used so loosely for brandies not from Cognac, that one critic suggested it means Very Suitable On Puddings.

VVSOP Grade of cognac; Very, Very Special Old Pale.

watery Low in alcohol, lacking.

weep Wine leaving the bottle because the cork has lost its elasticity.

wein German term for wine.

weingut Wine estate.

well-made Without fault.

white port Popular sherry-style wine; made in Portugal and imitated elsewhere.

wine The fermented juice of the grape.

woody (i) The presence of oak in a young wine. (ii) An offensive excess of oak present in a wine.

xérés French for sherry. Originally the name given by the ancient Romans to the sherry city of Jerez.

XO Grade of cognac. Generally the oldest available on the general market.

yeasts Single-cell organisms responsible for the fermentation of sugar into ethyl alcohol.

young An immature wine.

youthful (i) A young wine. (ii) An unexpected character that may be present in an old wine.

zestful A wine of good fruit and crisp acidity, i.e. lively, fresh.

zing As above, usually associated with young Rhine riesling.

INDEX

Page references for illustrations are printed in italic.